Arnaud Bernard

The Gospels

Distributed into Meditations for Every Day in the Year

Arnaud Bernard

The Gospels
Distributed into Meditations for Every Day in the Year

ISBN/EAN: 9783741176289

Manufactured in Europe, USA, Canada, Australia, Japa

Cover: Foto ©Andreas Hilbeck / pixelio.de

Manufactured and distributed by brebook publishing software (www.brebook.com)

Arnaud Bernard

The Gospels

THE GOSPELS

DISTRIBUTED INTO MEDITATIONS FOR
EVERY DAY OF THE YEAR

AND ARRANGED

ACCORDING TO THE HARMONY OF
THE FOUR EVANGELISTS

BY

L'ABBÉ DUQUESNE

TRANSLATED FROM THE FRENCH AND ADAPTED
TO THE USE OF THE ENGLISH CHURCH.

VOLUME II.

SOLD BY
JAMES PARKER & CO., OXFORD,
AND 377, STRAND, LONDON;
AND RIVINGTONS,
LONDON, OXFORD, AND CAMBRIDGE.
1881.

PRINTED BY THE DEVONPORT SOCIETY OF THE HOLY TRINITY,
HOLY ROOD, OXFORD. 1881.

THE GOSPELS

DISTRIBUTED INTO MEDITATIONS FOR EVERY DAY IN THE YEAR.

Meditation LXXX.

SERMON IN THE PLAIN.

Observe here, 1. four blessings bestowed upon men by Jesus Christ; 2. four blessings announced to men by Jesus Christ; 3. four curses uttered against men by Jesus Christ. S. Luke vi. 17—26.

FIRST POINT.

Blessings bestowed upon men by Jesus Christ.

The first blessing is that He came down to us. *And He came down with them and stood in the plain.* After that Jesus had made upon the mountain the choice of His Apostles, He came down with them and His other disciples, and remained in the plain for the instruction and consolation of the multitude who awaited Him. In how many ways has not Jesus come down to be with us! He came down from the bosom of God into the womb of the blessed Virgin, in order to make Himself man like us, and to bring Himself within our reach, that He might be seen and loved of us; He came down from His throne in heaven, to lead a homely life in the midst of us, and to put Himself within our reach to imitate Him; He came down from the sublimity of His contemplation, in order to adopt a simple and familiar language with us, and to put Himself within our reach, so as to be understood by us. All that Jesus did was only a continual condescension towards us, which has made Him always sacrifice His glory to our needs, or rather has made Him always glory in procuring our welfare. Shall we forget that He still comes down daily from heaven upon our altars in order to offer Himself up for us, that He remains continually with us, and from the altar comes down into our hearts, in order to become united to us, and to be one with us?

2. The second blessing, is that He has called us to Him. *And the company of His disciples and a great multitude of people out of all Judea and Jerusalem, and from the sea coast of Tyre and Sidon which came to hear Him.* This prodigious multitude of persons who were waiting for Jesus in the plain had not come there without being drawn by His grace. Is it not thus that this God of goodness has called us from the ends of the earth into the knowledge of His Gospel? Is it not thus that from the immense distance to which we have been cast by our sins and our unfaithfulnesses, He calls us still daily to Him in order to teach us His doctrines, to deliver us from the devil, and to heal our souls of their sicknesses? Let us then go to Him, let us no longer resist His invitations, but let us join ourselves to that multitude of faithful souls who follow Him with courage, and serve Him with fervour.

3. The third blessing which Jesus Christ bestows on men, is that He listens to, and grants our prayers. *A great multitude of people out of all Judea and Jerusalem and from the sea coast of Tyre and Sidon which came to hear Him and to be healed of their diseases, and they that were vexed with unclean spirits: and they were healed.* As soon as Jesus had come down, He was surrounded by a multitude of sick people, of maimed, and of those who were possessed by evil spirits, who implored His help, and all the sick were healed, and all the evil spirits driven away. Shall we never have trust in a God so powerful and so good, always ready to listen to our prayers, and Who desires more than we ourselves to grant them, to heal us, to purify, and sanctify us?

4. The fourth blessing, which Jesus Christ bestows upon men, is to suffer us to touch Him that we may

draw our strength from Him. *And the whole multitude sought to touch Him: for there went virtue out of Him and healed them all.* This multitude, impatient to be healed, did not wait till Jesus should lay His hands upon them, or till He should make His voice to be heard. Each one was eager and used every effort in order to reach Him and to touch Him, without observing either decorum or moderation in so doing. Nevertheless does our Lord drive away this importunate crowd? Does He command His Apostles and His disciples to send them away? No, He suffers them to give vent to their impetuosity, He only sees their faith, and only thinks of rewarding it, and the life-giving virtue which came forth from Him, and to which neither malicious spirits, nor sicknesses, nor infirmities could resist, healed them all. O goodness! O infinite love! O Jesus! art Thou not still the same to us? We touch Thee in receiving Thy sacraments; it is from Thee that comes forth that virtue which they possess in order to heal our sicknesses, to strengthen us, to nourish us, and enable us to persevere unto the end. Why have I not the same eagerness in partaking of the Blessed Sacrament of Thy Body and Blood; wherefore do I make no effort in order to receive It worthily, to receive It with that faith which penetrates to Thee, which touches Thee, and draws forth miracles from Thee?

SECOND POINT.

Of the four blessings announced to men by Jesus Christ.

1. The first blessing is for those who are poor. The works of corporal mercy having been accomplished, the people remained in silence in order to listen to Jesus. *And He lifted up His eyes on His disciples, and said, Blessed be ye poor: for your's is the kingdom of God.* You who are poor, that is to say, you who have left all for Me, you who are destitute of all the hopes of earth, you who have no riches, and who do not murmur that you have them not, who neither desire nor strive to gain

them, you are *blessed*, because *your's is the kingdom of heaven;* because, free from earthly cares, you receive the Gospel of the kingdom, you taste its truths, you possess its divine treasures; because your heart being purified from the stain of riches, God dwells there, and establishes there His reign by His love; because, your heart being raised above the false treasures of the earth, God rewards your courage and your nobleness of heart by the possession of the heavenly kingdom which you will enjoy one day, and which you already possess by a solid and assured hope. Ah! let us suffer willingly some moments of poverty, when a kingdom awaits us, the possession of which, if we will it, cannot fail us. How easy it is to gain this blessing! Poverty is so common a lot, why should we then only accept that which is painful in this condition, without gaining for ourselves from it what there is that is profitable to us? Wherefore, by the uselessness of our murmurs, of our desires, and our efforts, should we increase yet more its sufferings, and deprive ourselves of its true happiness?

2. The second blessing is for those who hunger. *Blessed are ye that hunger now: for ye shall be filled.* We suffer hunger, when we are reduced to the want of the necessaries of life, and this is one of the greatest trials to which any one can be subjected. Must it then be that so many unhappy beings should not know the blessing attached to their sufferings? We suffer hunger, when we are in want, if not absolutely of the necessaries of life, at least of those things, of which the privation makes life hard and painful. We suffer hunger when through a spirit of repentance and of self-denial, we fast, we practise abstinence, we deprive ourselves of all that might satisfy our tastes and inclinations. All those who suffer this hunger are blessed, because they are filled in this world with the bread of angels, and the sweetnesses of grace, and in the next world, with God Himself, and the delights of eternity.

3. The third blessing is for those who weep. *Blessed are ye that weep now: for ye shall laugh.* There are

tears of resignation which the disgraces and troubles of
this life draw forth from us, but which are only shed in
God's Presence and on His Bosom, at the foot of the
cross of Jesus, whilst joining them to those which the
divine Saviour has shed for us. There are tears of repentance which the sight of our sins draw forth from us.
When the heart is contrite, if tears do not actually flow
down from our eyes, at least the tears of the heart shed
over us a sense of mourning. There are tears of devotion, which meditation on the benefits which we have
received from God, on the mysteries of Jesus Christ, and
the sufferings of the Passion of Jesus cause to flow.
Happy they who weep in this manner with resignation,
in a spirit of repentance and love, because they will rejoice,
because the day will come to them, when not only will
their tears be dried up, but all their soul will be inun-
dated with a perfect and eternal joy.

4. The fourth blessing is for those who are persecuted,
hated, rejected, scorned, and outraged for the cause of
Christ. *Blessed are ye, when men shall hate you, and
when they shall separate you from their company, and
shall reproach you, and cast out your name as evil,
for the Son of Man's sake. Rejoice ye in that day,
and leap for joy; for behold your reward is great in
heaven: for in the like manner did their fathers unto the
prophets.* Although there is no one who may not have
his share in this beatitude, it has a more special reference
to those who belong to the ministry. It is specially
for them to know its blessedness, and to meditate on
the reward which awaits them in heaven: and we must
make a distinction between those who are hated and
persecuted by evil-doers, or unbelievers, for the truth's
sake, and those who consider themselves persecuted,
because they are kept within bounds by their lawful
superiors, or by the authority of the Church. It is our
duty not to join with evil-doers in increasing the persecution of the labourers of the Gospel: not to take
offence at their sufferings, or to despise them on account of the opprobrium which they endure, but, on

the contrary, to esteem them happy, and to respect them so much the more, and to remember that it is thus that the prophets and apostles of old have been treated. Let us examine what share we have in these beatitudes, and let us labour to gain for ourselves as large a share in them as we can.

THIRD POINT.

Of the four curses pronounced by Jesus Christ.

1. The first is against the rich. *But woe unto you that are rich, for ye have received your consolation.* What is then the crime of the rich? Our Saviour does not say; Woe unto you, because your riches have been unjustly acquired, because you have made use of your wealth for purposes of sin, of oppression, or of leading others into sin: the heathen have known such morality; but He says; *Woe unto you, for ye have received your consolation.* The world sees no harm in it; but this fatal consolation makes people, in most cases, insensible to the things of God; the rich have no love for Him: indifferent to heaven, of which they have no hope, wearied with religion, its dogmas, its maxims, its exercises, in which they have no faith; hardened to the misery and desolation in which their neighbour lives, they have no charity towards him. What will their punishment be? Not only will they no longer have any thing to expect from the liberality of God, having set all their happiness in their riches, and finding their consolation in them, but they will fall into an extreme poverty, into a total indigence, into the absolute and eternal privation of the Sovereign good, and of the God of all consolation. How then can we avoid a like fate? If, far from placing our consolation in our riches, we only look upon them with fear, only make use of them with reservation, and employ the greatest part of them in works of piety, zeal, and charity.

2. The second curse is against those who are filled. *Woe unto you that are full! for ye shall hunger.* What is then their crime? Our Lord does not speak here of those who allow themselves in excesses of in-

temperance in eating and drinking; even the heathen themselves had a horror of them. He speaks of those whose life is entirely sensual, and is passed in the delights of good living, and who refuse nothing to their appetites. Their crime is the same with the rich, an entire insensibility towards God, a total indifference towards heaven and salvation, an insurmountable distaste to the exercises of religion and repentance, and a pitiless harshness towards their neighbour. Their special torment will be to endure bodily and spiritual hunger and thirst, the one caused by the heat of the flames in which they will burn, and the other by being deprived of God, the Sovereign Good, Who is alone capable of filling them.

3. The third curse is against those who are merry and joyous. *Woe to you that laugh now! for ye shall mourn and weep.* What is their crime? Our Lord does not speak here of those who give themselves up to unseemly joys, or to shameful pleasures, which even the heathen have condemned; He speaks of those who are only occupied with their own pleasures, and who only think of procuring for themselves every kind of comfort and convenience, on whose path every thing smiles and prospers, and whose life is only a chain of amusements and diversions. Their crime is the same as that of the preceding, and their punishment will be the same. They pervert the order which God has established for this present life, and the future life: they make a time of enjoyment, of rest, of joy, and of pleasures of this life, which is so short, and which God has made a time of trial, of repentance, of tears, and of sufferings, and they will only find in the next life which will be eternal, tears, despair, and torments both of body and soul.

4. The fourth curse is against those who are applauded, spoken well of, and loved by men. *Woe unto you when all men shall speak well of you! for so did their fathers to the false prophets.* Although this curse is directed against all those who encourage themselves in their sins by the approbation of the world, yet it has more special reference to those who are employed in the instruction

and guidance of souls: it is for them to set at nought the approbation of men, and to examine well from whom it comes and whence it arises. The false prophets were always applauded, because they adopted the line of the nation where they lived, because they flattered it in its errors, because they only spoke things which were agreeable to their hearers, and never uttered any thing which could trouble their conscience, or run counter to their pleasures. Let us examine what share we may have in these anathemas, and let us labour to escape as far as we possibly can from their consequences.

Prayer. Ah! Lord! I understand Thy meaning: the true happiness of the Christian consists in despising wealth, in living in sorrow and in tears, in being hated and persecuted. It is to this contempt, to these trials that Thou dost award an abundant recompense, which will have no bounds but Thy munificence, the treasures of which are inexhaustible. May my life then be intermingled with the passing bitterness of repentance and of affliction, that I may one day escape the eternal bitterness of Thy divine vengeance. If Thou dost find me worthy, O Jesus, to follow Thee in poverty, and if such is my lot, let me be content, may I cherish my lot, that Thy blessing may rest upon me: if Thou dost place me in a state of prosperity and abundance, may I be humble, charitable, and mortified, that I may have no share in the woes which Thou dost pronounce. Amen.

Meditation LXXXI.

CONTINUATION OF THE SERMON IN THE PLAIN.

OF CHARITY TOWARDS OUR NEIGHBOUR.

Jesus Christ teaches us here, 1. the rules and the perfection of Christian charity; 2. the insufficiency of worldly charity; 3. the motives of Christian charity. S. Luke vi. 27—38.

FIRST POINT.

The rules and the perfection of Christian charity.

Jesus, in speaking to His disciples, had uttered His

blessings and His curses. His blessings were for them, and those who should follow their example: His anathemas on the other hand, were pronounced against those whose life should be opposed to their's. He then turned Himself towards the people, and said: *But I say unto you which hear.* Grant me grace, O divine Saviour, to be of the number of those who hearken to Thee, to understand the beauty and the perfection of Thy law, and to meditate on the rules of conduct which Thou art about to lay down for me.

1. First rule, respecting our inward feelings. To enmity, to hatred, oppose the contrary feelings, love, and acts of kindness. *Love your enemies, do good to them which hate you.* Let us sound our hearts by this rule. In vain would we seek to persuade ourselves that we love those whom we look upon as our enemies, if when occasion offers, we do not render them all the services that lie in our power. But if on the contrary, we injure them, we thwart them, or rejoice in their disgrace, can we believe that we love them, and that we are fulfilling the law of charity?

2. Second rule, respecting our words. To injurious words, to slanders, to calumnies, to imprecations, oppose blessings, praises, prayers. *Bless them that curse you, and pray for them which despitefully use you.* Let us examine our words by this rule. How many satirical remarks, how many criticisms, railleries, murmurings escape us every day against those whom we think to have spoken evil of us! how many cutting replies do we not make, which we look upon as proofs of feeling or of courage, of which we boast, and in which we pride ourselves, and for which Jesus Christ condemns us!

3. Third rule, respecting our actions. To violence, oppose a perfect patience, to fraud, a generous and beneficent liberality. Whether violence is exercised upon your good name, or your possessions, show a gentleness, a charity which is invincible. *And unto him that smiteth thee on the one cheek, offer also the other, and him that taketh away thy cloke, forbid not to take thy*

coat also. It is allowable, doubtless, to employ the means of justice, in order to obtain reparation for injuries done to our good name, or for the restitution of our property; but we ought never to have recourse to them at the expense of charity, and there are occasions where charity forbids us to have recourse to justice. *Give to every man that asketh of thee: and of him that taketh away thy goods, ask them not again.* That is to say, give, lend, render a service to whoever asks you, whether he be known or unknown, a friend or an enemy, without examining too minutely whether he is or is not in need. Charity is generous, beneficent, and liberal. If any one takes what belongs to you without asking you, and carries it away with him, do not ask him for it back again. The occasions of practising this rule, and on which we cannot exact the restitution of our poverty without transgressing the law of charity, are more frequent than we think for; but its fulfilment is but little known, little relished, and very rare.

4. Lastly, the general rule of charity. *As ye would that men should do to you, do ye also to them likewise.* As ye would that men should act towards you, so act towards them. This rule, well meditated upon, well applied, well observed, will decide all questions, will appease all the murmurings of the heart, will hinder all the indiscretions of the tongue, will banish all injustice of action. Put yourself in the place of others, and put others in your place. Think that you have found yourself placed in the situation in which others are; others being situated as you are, what would you require of them then? do the same yourself now.

SECOND POINT.

The insufficiency of worldly charity.

1. In love. *For if ye love them which love you, what thank have ye? for sinners also love those that love them.* Worldly people love those who love them. Are not these the limits to which we carry our charity?

We pride ourselves on having a good heart, and attaching ourselves to those who shew us affection, and being faithful in our friendships; but in all this what sacrifice do we make to Almighty God, what reward have we any right to expect from Him, and what thanks can we hope for? None. Even sinners, heathen, idolaters, love those who love them.

2. In its benefits. *And if ye do good to them which do good to you, what thank have ye? for sinners even do the same.* Worldly people do good to those who do good to them, and say good of those who say the same of them, of those who are in their interests, who belong to their party. If our charity is confined to that, it is in no way a Christian charity. We only do what sinners do. Our pretended charity is of no merit in the sight of God, and will receive no reward from Him.

3. In its services. *And if ye lend to them of whom ye hope to receive, what thank have ye? for sinners also lend to sinners, to receive as much again.* Worldly people lend, give, render services to those from whom they have received them. We defend ourselves with warmth against the imputation of ingratitude, and we are right; we do not forget the services which have been rendered us, and we are always ready, when occasion offers, to render the like; but we exact also that our services should likewise be rendered to ourselves, and all this is just. But if we only give, lend, and do services to others with such self-interested views, we are very far removed from Christian charity, and we ought not to hope to receive the reward of them.

THIRD POINT.

Motives of Christian charity.

1. The greatness of the reward. *But love ye your enemies; and do good, and lend, hoping for nothing again: and your reward shall be great.* Let us bear in mind that we have in heaven, a liberal Rewarder and a tender Father: let us bethink ourselves that in giving

up now and for ever these vile and temporal interests, which are the only mainspring of the greater part of our actions, that in giving, doing good, and lending without hoping for any return, and without seeking for any advantage from so doing, we shall find our true interests in a far more noble and real manner; our Lord Himself assures us that our reward will be great in heaven; is not that promise capable of touching us and acting on our hearts?

2. The glory of being the children of God in following the example He has set us. *And ye shall be the children of the Highest; for He is kind unto the unthankful, and to the evil. Be ye therefore merciful, as your Father also is merciful.* We complain of the ingratitude and of the malice of mankind; but their malice, and their ingratitude, are they not infinitely greater towards God? See nevertheless what goodness, what liberality, what longsuffering He manifests towards them. Can we regard it as an act of weakness or of meanness to imitate our God, to make ourselves like unto Him, and to act so to be numbered amongst His children? Is it befitting further that we should complain of the ingratitude and malice of others? What are we ourselves towards God? Is it not we ourselves, who are these ungrateful and wicked men whom He loads with His benefits, and on whom He pours down the abundance of His mercies? All that He requires of us, is that we should show Him some return for them, by being merciful and doing good to others, as He has done to us. If we refuse to obey a law so gentle, we shall be no longer His children, but monsters of ingratitude who deserve only hell.

3. The blessedness of being treated by God as we shall have treated our neighbour. You fear with reason the judgement, which, when you leave this world, you will have to undergo at the tribunal of the sovereign Judge; but our Saviour has put within your reach a means of rendering that Judgement favourable to you: *Judge not,* He says, *and ye shall not be judged,* that is

to say, banish from your minds and from your hearts all those inward and secret judgements, those judgements which you pronounce so boldly, and which you give out as truths which have been proved: those judgements which are all to the disadvantage of your neighbour. Those judgements test the intentions, the ideas, the designs, and all that there is in man that is the most impenetrable. Reform then all those judgements, or rather do not pass any judgements on others, and you will have nothing to fear from that of God. You fear to be condemned at the tribunal of the sovereign and divine Majesty; do you desire to avoid the condemnation which you fear, *condemn not, and ye shall not be condemned.* Interpret in good part all that your neighbour does; and if you cannot do that, forget, or ignore all that he does that is evil, do not think and do not speak of it, and God will not condemn you. You fear that your sins will not be forgiven to you. Here is the means to assure yourself of their forgiveness as much as it is possible for you to do; forgive others yourselves, *forgive, and ye shall be forgiven.* Never recall the past faults of your brethren, never talk over them either amongst yourselves, or with others, and you will be forgiven yourselves. You hope for everything from God, both what you need for your body as well as your soul, for time and for eternity. Do you desire to draw down upon yourselves His blessings? And who would not desire to possess them? Here is the means by which you may obtain them. *Give, and it shall be given unto you; good measure, pressed down, and shaken together, and running over, shall men give into your bosom. For with the same measure that ye mete withal, it shall be measured to you again.*

Prayer. This fulness of blessings, this measure of happiness which Thou wilt bestow one day, and which is none other than Thyself, O my God! Thou wilt only grant it in return for the charity, for the love which I shall have towards my brethren. I have resolved: friend or enemy, I will treat my neighbour as

Thou dost command me, as Thou dost deal with me, with longsuffering and patience. My love towards those who do me good, shall not only be those natural feelings of gratitude, that self-interested intercourse of mutual duties, in which Christian doctrine has no part, and which in no way differs from that of unbelievers; but I will love my enemies, I will love my brethren, because Thou dost love them, O my God, and as Thou dost love them. Amen,

Meditation LXXXII.

CONCLUSION OF THE SERMON IN THE PLAIN.

By six comparisons or similitudes. S. Luke vi. 39—49.

FIRST POINT.

Of the two first comparisons.

1. First comparison. Of the blind man who leads another blind man. *And He spake a parable unto them; Can the blind lead the blind? shall they not both fall into the ditch?* This is a warning for all those who have the direction or guidance of others. Ministers of God, those whom you have to guide are blind, beware that ye are not blind likewise yourselves. If you do not know the ways of God, the precepts of the Gospel, the rules of faith, you will lose yourselves with those of whom you have the guidance. This is also a warning to those who ought to be led. It is for them to take care not to allow themselves to be guided by those that are blind themselves. Let them first of all take care to pray the Lord to give them a faithful guide. And in the choice which they make of one, let them beware of judging by certain talents which often flatter their vanity more than conduce to their edification, and

let them feel sure that he draws his knowledge from pure sources. Let them also see if he is exact and enlightened in his dealings with them; lest they run the risk of falling into hell together with their guide.

2. Second comparison. Of the master and of the disciple. *The disciple is not above his master; but every one that is perfect shall be as his master.* These words set before us first of all, the misery of those who are formed and led by blinded or corrupt guides, and they are a continuation of the first comparison. If the masters are evil, we cannot expect but they should form evil disciples. Parents and friends, fathers and mothers, masters and mistresses, and you, whoever you may be, who without knowledge and without right principles, are the guides of others, and instruct and advise them, when your disciples, your children, your friends, your pupils shall be like you, they will believe themselves perfect and thoroughly enlightened, whilst at each step they will stray, they will dash against hidden rocks, and will have a grievous fall. These words represent to us also the blessing of those who have taken Jesus Christ for their Master, who are guided by the precepts of the Gospel and the rules of faith. We have the happiness to be of this number; let us then remember this precept of our divine Master, *The disciple is not above his Master;* let us remember it when we are humiliated, despised, or are called upon to suffer injuries, calumnies, torments or even death. Jesus Christ has suffered all that, and it is in the resemblance that we shall have to Him that our perfection consists.

SECOND POINT.

Of the two following comparisons.

1. Third comparison. Of the beam and the mote in the eye. *And why beholdest thou the mote that is in thy brother's eye, but perceivest not the beam that is in thine own eye? Either how canst thou say to thy brother, Brother, let me pull out the mote that is in*

thine eye, when thou thyself beholdest not the beam that is in thine own eye? Thou hypocrite, cast out first the beam out of thine own eye, and then shalt thou see clearly to pull out the mote that is in thy brother's eye. A heretic perceives faults and abuses in the Church, but he does not see the crime of his own separation from her; he does not see that in the sect to which he belongs, impiety and blasphemy are raised into dogmas, which he believes as so many articles of faith. A layman sees in the clergy, self-interested motives and dissipation, and he does not behold in himself injustice, licentiousness, impiety and irreligion. A worldly person sees in those who live a life of devotion, an affectation of sensibility, and caprice, and he does not see in himself anger, revenge, and conduct which gives rise to scandal. How many failings do we not see in others, whilst we have in ourselves those which are far greater! A pharasaical zeal which is as common as it is despicable, which makes us clear sighted and exacting towards others, whilst we never think of examining ourselves, and never dream of reforming our conduct. Hypocrites that we are, let us turn our thoughts within, let us make our pretended zeal of some use by employing it first of all upon ourselves. Let us begin by correcting ourselves before we take upon ourselves to correct others; let us begin by taking out the beam out of our own eyes, before we seek to take out the mote out of our brother's eye.

2. Fourth comparison. Of the good and bad tree. *For a good tree bringeth not forth corrupt fruit; neither doth a corrupt tree bring forth good fruit. For every tree is known by its own fruit; for of thorns men do not gather figs nor of a bramble-bush gather they grapes.* By this precept, let us learn to justify our neighbour, and to condemn ourselves, to see nothing in others but that which may edify us, or at least nothing at which we take offence, and to see nothing within ourselves, but that which grieves us. Do not let us believe the evil which is told us of our brethren, when we only

see them produce, on the one hand, fruits of sweetness, which are meant by figs, that is to say, deeds of patience, modesty, submission, and edification, and on the other hand, fruits of strength, which are pourtrayed by grapes, that is to say, deeds of zeal, firmness, and constancy. But for ourselves, let us examine what trees we are in the garden of the Saviour. What fruits do we bring forth? Perhaps we are only like barren trees, which produce no fruit; perhaps we are like the bramble and the thorns, which no one can approach without being torn or pricked by them. Our crabbed temper, our brusque manner, our haughty tone, our offensive words, are they not brambles? Ought not our criticisms, our satirical words, our murmurs, our slanders, our unguarded discourses which are offensive to modesty, or are directed against religion, and many other such like faults which we can discover in ourselves, make us fear lest we should be in the field of the Lord, like those thorns which He will be obliged to pull up and throw into the fire?

THIRD POINT.

Of the two last comparisons.

1. Fifth comparison. Of the good and evil treasure which is hidden in the heart. *A good man out of the good treasure of his heart bringeth forth that which is good; and an evil man out of the evil treasure of his heart bringeth forth that which is evil: for out of the abundance of the heart his mouth speaketh.* All men carry about with them in their hearts a treasure, that is to say, a store which they cherish with ardour, which they increase daily, and which they hide with care. 1. Observe the nature of this treasure. In the good, it is a precious treasure of virtue, of the love of God, of religion, piety, charity, good works, pure intentions, and pious desires: in the wicked, it is an abominable treasure of vices and corruption, of falsehood and injustice, of inordinate love of creatures and of one's self. Let us examine our hearts, and see what is the treasure which we are

storing up there. 2. Consider what will be the revelation of this treasure. Every one here below keeps the treasure of his heart hidden. Humility hides it in the good, and hypocrisy in the wicked ; but, in the great day of judgement, hypocrisy will be unmasked, and humility will have no place. How glorious this day will be for the good, and how overwhelming for the wicked! To the treasure of the good, God will, on His part, add a treasure of glory and of eternal felicity ; to the treasure of the wicked will be added a treasure of anger, and eternal punishment. Let us then renounce the treasure of iniquity, and let us acquire the treasure of virtue. 3. Examine what we draw from this treasure. We can only draw forth from our treasury what is therein. That which comes forth from the heart, are our works: we act according as we are influenced by it. Thus, let us see of what nature our works are, whether they are good or evil, and we shall know of what nature is the treasure of our heart, whether it is good or evil. Let us judge especially by our words, for *the mouth speaks out of the abundance of the heart.* Now, what is the chief subject of our conversation with others or amongst ourselves ? If it is of God, of Christ, of the mysteries of our faith, of the hope of a Christian, then our treasure is good : but it is evil, if our conversation is only directed towards the faults of others, if we only moralise in order to find an opportunity for criticism, if our words offend either against religion or purity ; and if our discourses turn only upon trifles, frivolous amusements, and idle subjects, then it is at least vain and useless. 4. Consider what ought to be the increase of this treasure. The more we draw from any treasure, the more does it diminish. The contrary happens in the treasure of our hearts ; the more we draw from it, the more we increase it; the more we are occupied with vain and frivolous amusements, the more the heart becomes vain and frivolous ; the more sins we commit, the more we love sin, and the more we desire to commit ; the more good deeds, on the contrary, which we do, the more do we desire to do; the more we speak of God, the more shall we delight in speaking of Him. Alas! how much time do we lose in filling continually the treasure house of our heart with contemptible nothingnesses, whilst we might fill it with precious things, with immortal riches, which would crown us with glory, and procure for us perfect and eternal happiness!

2. Sixth comparison. Of the house built upon a solid foundation, or without any foundation. *And why call ye Me Lord, Lord, and do not the things I say? whosoever cometh to Me, and heareth My sayings, and doeth them, I will shew you to whom he is like: He is like a man which built an house, and digged deep and laid the foundation on a rock; and when the flood arose, the stream beat vehemently upon that house, and could not shake it; for it was founded upon a rock. But he that heareth, and doeth not, is like a man that without a foundation built an house upon the earth: against which the stream did beat vehemently, and immediately it fell; and the ruin of that house was great.* In vain do we call upon the name of the Lord, if we do not practise His doctrines; in vain do we call ourselves Christians, if we do not live as Christians. He who, believing in Christ, practises His commandments, is like unto him that builds on the rock. Temptations, persecutions, even death, nothing can destroy the building; it is founded on eternity. On the contrary, he who, believing in Christ, does not obey His law, is like unto him that builds on the ground and without foundation: that building, which was only solid in appearance, and without any real strength, will soon crumble away, and only serve to set forth the folly of him who raised it. Was it worth while to spend so much on constructing a building which should fall into ruins? Alas! am I not myself that senseless person?

Prayer. Ah Lord, the building of my salvation ought to be an eternal building; I will then establish it upon the rock, that is to say, on the practice of Christian virtues. Not content with hearkening to Thee, O divine

Jesus, with admiring Thy doctrine, with accepting the truths which it teaches, my heart and my actions shall be conformable to my faith, that I may be able to present myself with confidence one day before Thy dreadful Judgment seat. Amen.

Meditation LXXXIII.

JESUS RETURNS TO CAPERNAUM, AND ANSWERS THE BLASPHEMIES OF THE SCRIBES.

Jesus offers here the most perfect model of the patience, of the firmness, and of the severity of true zeal. S. Mark iii. 20—30. S. Luke vii. 1.

FIRST POINT.

The patience of true zeal.

1. *The patience of the zeal of Jesus with the importunity of the people.* *Now when He had ended all His sayings in the audience of the people, He entered into Capernaum, and they* (He and His disciples) *went into an house. And the multitude cometh together again, so that they could not so much as eat bread.* Our Lord had passed the night in prayer; since the morning, He had made choice of His apostles, He had then employed Himself in healing the sick, those who were possessed with evil spirits, and in instructing the people. His instructions being ended, He had need of rest and food; He sent the multitude away, and went back with His twelve apostles to Capernaum. A fresh concourse of people besieged the house where He entered, He again yielded to their entreaties, so that neither He nor His apostles could take any food. Thus the occupations of Jesus Christ often encroached upon His rest and His meals; there was only the time of prayer upon which they never broke in. Should not then a pastor, who

ought to give even his life for his sheep, let his flock feel that they have a claim upon his time? Must he not prefer the affairs which concern the soul, the conscience and the salvation of his neighbour, to his own comforts, which concern only the health of his body and the present life?

2. The patience of the zeal of Jesus with the false judgments of men. *And when His friends heard of it, they went out to lay hold on Him; for they said, He is beside Himself.* The relations of Jesus do not appear, for the most part, to have taken much interest in that which concerned Him; they did not follow Him at all, and it is probable that they were not witnesses of the miracles which He worked; if they knew anything of them, they had only learnt it by vague and confused reports, and judging by that superficial knowledge, they came to the conclusion that devotion and fanaticism had obscured the mind of our Blessed Saviour, and that He and those who followed Him were under a delusion. As for them, like wise men, they believed that it was their duty to put a stop to the scandal; and whether this idea came to them of themselves, or whether it was suggested to them by the Pharisees, they came to Capernaum, not in order to hear, nor in order to examine into the matter, but to possess themselves of the person of Jesus, as of that of a madman, who was a dishonour to His family, and who might draw down upon Him the hatred and the persecution of powerful enemies whom He was making at Jerusalem by the freedom of His remonstrances. We do not know what attempts they made, nor what hindered them from carrying out so strange a design; but we only know that they did not carry it into execution. Thus we hear sometimes in the world, the relations of those who wish to devote themselves to God, or to adopt a regular system of life, adopt the same language with regard to them, and strive, by the same motives, to turn them away from their pious intentions; thus also we see amongst Christians, those who are so only in name, who having only

a superficial knowledge of religion, treat every thing as error, fanaticism, or delusion; men who know nothing save by hear-say, who only judge of things by the unbelievers whose society they frequent; men who are as blind and senseless, as they believe themselves to be wise, enlightened, and in a condition to set others to rights.

3. The patience of the zeal of Jesus with the calumnies of the wicked. *And the scribes which came down from Jerusalem said, He hath Beelzebub, and by the prince of the devils casteth He out devils.* The scribes were more instructed than the relations of Jesus, they repaired with an eager curiosity every where, where they knew that Jesus was. There were some who came from Jerusalem in order to hear Him speak, and to behold His works; but as they had adopted their own opinions, they did not come to learn, to be edified, or to verify the facts; they only came in order to censure, to criticise, to pour ridicule on our Saviour, and to decry His teaching. Thus are Thy labours misjudged, O my Saviour; thus do they charge Thee with the most atrocious calumnies, offer Thee the most deadly affronts: thus do they think of treating Thee as a madman, or as a magician, at the very time when Thou didst spend Thyself with Thy labours for our salvation, and that of Thine enemies themselves; thus dost Thou teach Thy ministers to advance the work of God, notwithstanding the difficulties and oppositions which they may meet with.

SECOND POINT.

The firmness of true zeal.

1. The firmness of the zeal of Jesus in order to preserve the people from being misled. *And He called them unto Him, and said unto them in parables, How can Satan cast out Satan? And if a kingdom be divided against itself, that kingdom cannot stand. And if a house be divided against itself, that house cannot stand. And if Satan rise up against himself, and be divided, he cannot stand, but hath an end.* Jesus had

made no complaint either of the indiscretion of the people, or of the atrocious calumny of His relations; but He would not suffer the discourses of the scribes, because they tended to mislead the people, and to lead them away from the faith. Let us be patient, let us be dumb under insults which are only personal; but do not let us suffer that any one should give utterance in our presence, to discourses which are likely to mislead those who hear them; our silence on these occasions would contribute to mislead them and would make us sharers in the sin.

2. The firmness of the zeal of Jesus in confounding those who were leading them astray. The reasoning which our Lord employed was simple, within the comprehension of those to whom it was addressed, and of invincible power. Jesus made use of it on other occasions, and the scribes have never been able to reply to it. If we are obliged to be present in any society where religion is attacked, it is our duty to make ourselves acquainted with the answers which we ought to give to unbelievers, in order to put a stop to their presumption, and to confound them if we cannot convert them. They are only bold when no one contradicts them; their attacks are only strong in the sound of their words, and their apparent confidence; but a single word will serve to disconcert them, to reduce them to silence, and sometimes to put them to flight.

3. The firmness of the zeal of Jesus in establishing the truth. *No man can enter into a strong man's house and spoil his goods, except he will first bind the strong man, and then he will spoil his house.* Our Lord declares to us here that which He has done for us against the enemy of our salvation; He has bound him, He has taken away from him the power to hurt us, so that he can no longer exercise any empire over us except through our own fault. The devil is now like a chained lion which can only frighten us by his roarings, but which can only wound those who have the fool-hardiness to approach to him. Our Lord, after having chained the evil spirit, has spoiled

his house by taking from him the souls and bodies of which he had possession, by overturning the altars which had been erected to him, by destroying his worship, and bringing to nought idolatry. Let us thank Him for so great a benefit, and let us keep at as great a distance as we can from a furious enemy, who has neither lost the desire nor the hope of ruining us eternally.

THIRD POINT.

The severity of true zeal.

1. *The severity of true zeal does not lead the sinner to despair.* *Verily I say unto you, All sins shall be forgiven unto the sons of men, and blasphemies wherewith soever they shall baspheme.* Take then courage, sinners, whoever you may be; it is Jesus Christ Himself Who assures you, that all your sins, however great they may be, shall be forgiven to you, if you will have recourse to His merits, and to the means of grace which He has given to you whereby to obtain His pardon. It is He Himself Who gives you this assurance, at the very time when He is being outraged by wicked men, and that He is about to pronounce against hardened sinners the severest judgment that His lips ever uttered. Hasten then to have recourse to His mercy, and do not make His goodness a pretext for impenitence, which will lead you as it has done many others, to eternal condemnation. Timid souls, whom the remembrance of your past sins throws sometimes into perplexity and discouragement, reassure yourselves from these words of your Saviour.

2. *The severity of true zeal does not flatter the sinner.* *But he that shall blaspheme against the Holy Ghost hath never forgiveness, but is in danger of eternal damnation.* The blasphemy against the Holy Ghost, properly so called and completed, is final impenitence, death in mortal sin, whether the sinner have refused to be converted at his death, or whether an unexpected death have not left him the time. The blasphemy against

the Holy Ghost, begun and most often followed by final impenitence, is the sin of the scribes, who attributed to the power of the devil, the miracles which Jesus performed by the virtue of the Holy Spirit. It is moreover the sin of unbelievers and deists, who seek to destroy Christianity. It is also the sin of those who will not recognize the work of the Holy Spirit in the Church of Jesus Christ, and lastly, of everyone who lives in a state of mortal sin, at the risk of being surprised in it at any moment and of dying in it. Ah! let us not be such enemies to ourselves as to give no thought to those words *ever ; eternal damnation.* Let us remember that these words were spoken by Jesus Christ, Who in uttering them, has revealed to us the impenetrable depths of His Divine justice, and has sought thereby to lead us to a prompt and salutary repentance.

3. The truth of true zeal does not asperse the sinner. Jesus spoke to them thus, *Because they said, He hath an unclean spirit.* Jesus did not speak in this manner save in order to refute the blasphemy of the scribes, and to hinder them from misleading others, and He did so without speaking of them by name, or addressing His words to them, seeking rather to gain them over than to confound them. It was their obstinacy alone, and the necessity of preventing greater scandals, and of instructing future generations, which led Him hereafter to unmask these hypocrites; besides which He never called them save by the general terms of scribes and Pharisees; which did not prevent the possibility of there being some among them, as there were in reality, who sincerely sought the kingdom of God, and clung closely to our Saviour. Let us adore this goodness of the Saviour, and let us make Him our Pattern; after the example of Jesus Christ, let our greatest severity be always tempered by gentleness.

Prayer. Yea, Lord, gentleness and moderation shall always be my portion, whether in despising calumny, or in refuting it. I will rise up against impiety; but I will spare, yea, I will even seek to gain, if I can, the sinner. Grant me, O my God, this precious gift of Thy mercy, which pardons even the blasphemer who dares to outrage Thee. Grant that I may not fall into the hands of Thy justice, when it can no longer pardon; grant that I may not abuse any longer by my delays, Thy long-suffering, which pardons all to the truly contrite sinner. Inspire me with the feelings of true repentance. Lead captive the devil, that conqueror of my soul; take away from him my heart, where he has taken up his abode; subdue in it the sinful passions and desires, which he has implanted there, and which he continues to inflame, so that, triumphing here below by Thy grace over Thine enemies and mine, I may be a partaker in the triumph of Thy glory in eternity. Amen.

Meditation LXXXIV.

HEALING OF THE SERVANT OF A CENTURION CONSIDERED AGAIN.

Consider here, 1. what intercession with Jesus can effect; 2. what progress in holiness we must make in order to please Jesus; 3. what is the goodness of this God-Saviour towards us. S. Luke vii. 2—10.

FIRST POINT.

Of intercession with Jesus.

1. We must do so with discrimination. *A certain centurion's servant, who was dear unto him, was sick, and ready to die. And when he heard of Jesus, he sent unto Him the elders of the Jews, beseeching Him that He would come and heal his servant.* The centurion chose those who were of most account in the town to intercede in his favour with Jesus, and to persuade Him to come to his house to heal his sick servant. Let us also recommend ourselves to the prayers of righteous men who are on earth; they are friends of Jesus, and their power is great.

2. We must accompany this intercession with good works. The elders of the Jews at Capernaum having come *to Jesus, they besought Him instantly, saying, That he was worthy for whom He should do this; for he loveth our nation and hath built us a synagogue. Then Jesus went with them.* Jesus yielded to the prayer of these Jews, and accepted the grounds upon which they founded their request. But what does our Saviour, our great Intercessor, Who ever liveth to make intercession for us, behold in us? By what do we plead with Him on our behalf, or on behalf of those we love? Does He behold our fasts, our almsgiving, our devotional exercises, the worship of our hearts which we render unto Him? If, on the contrary, our life is a dishonour to our Christian profession, instead of our acts of worship being intercessors with Him, let us be convinced that we shall only find in them accusers, who will require our condemnation at the hands of God.

3. We must make use of this intercession in a spirit of humility. *And when He was now not far from the house, the centurion sent friends to Him, saying unto Him, Lord, trouble not Thyself; for I am not worthy that Thou shouldest enter under my roof; Wherefore neither thought I myself worthy to come unto Thee; but say in a word, and my servant shall be healed.* The centurion only employed the mediation of the elders of Capernaum, because he thought himself unworthy to present himself before Him. It is in the same spirit of humility that we should draw nigh unto Jesus. We do not doubt His goodness and His power; but we know our own unworthiness. But our Saviour, far from rejecting the prayer of the centurion, yields to the request which the centurion makes, and praises his faith.

SECOND POINT.

Of progress in virtue in order to become pleasing to Jesus.

1. In order to advance in holiness, we must profit by

the intentions of Providence towards us. This officer, who here entreats for help from Jesus was a Gentile; he had been born and brought up in the midst of idolatry. Providence places him in the only country in the world where the true God is worshipped, in the very centre of the ministry of the Son of God, and soon he recognizes the God Who is worshipped there, and loves the people who pay to Him solemn worship; he does more, he favours this people by his authority and his bounty. Hardly has he heard speak of Jesus, and of the wonders which He works, than he believes in Him. An upright heart who loves God, finds no difficulty in believing in Jesus Christ, His Son.

2. In order to advance in holiness, we must profit by afflictions. Some trial was needed by the centurion, in order to make his virtue shine forth. One of his servants falls ill, he is reduced to the last extremity; this centurion enkindles his faith, and implores the help of Jesus with as much humility as trust. Sincere humility, founded, on the one side, on the knowledge of his own weakness, and on the other, on that of the greatness and Almighty power of Jesus! Pride has driven us away from God, afflictions ought to bring us near to Him.

3. In order to advance in holiness, we must profit by the special favours which God bestows. *For*, says the centurion, *I also am a man set under authority, having under me soldiers; and I say unto one, Go, and he goeth; and to another, Come, and he cometh; and to my servant, Do this, and he doeth it. When Jesus heard these things, He marvelled at him, and turned him about, and said unto the people that followed him, I say unto you, I have not found so great faith, no not in Israel.* If this centurion is not the same as the one of whom S. Matthew speaks, as least we may say, that he had the same feelings with him; and makes use of the same expressions; and obtains of the Saviour the same praise for his faith, and the same answer to his prayer. *And they that were sent, returning to the house, found the servant whole that had been sick.* The

friends of the centurion, having arrived at the house, found him whom they had left in a dying state, restored to life and health. Judge what were the love, gratitude, and fervour of so good a master, and of a servant who had deserved to be so dear to his master, after this favour shown to him. Does not this faith of the centurion, which puts to shame the want of faith of the Israelites, condemn us? What progress have we made in holiness during our life? Providence has placed us in situations the most favourable for our salvation: how have we profited by them? Good examples have been set before us and have offered themselves to us for our imitation: with what emulation have they inspired us? Favours have been poured down upon us, we have been surrounded by tokens of a singular protection, by which we have been delivered and saved from numberless perils and dangers: by what added fervour have we testified our gratitude? Alas! let us not abuse all these blessings, and let us not go back daily in the ways of virtue instead of advancing in them!

THIRD POINT.
Of the goodness of Jesus.

This goodness shines forth in His acts, in His words, and in His works.

1. Goodness of Jesus in His actions. As soon as He is asked to come, He sets off without delay; and is He stopped when He is at the point of arriving, He stops. What condescension! And yet for whom was this all done? For the servant of a Roman centurion, a Gentile. He could have healed him without going to him; He might have answered to those who entreated Him, as He did to that nobleman who prayed Him for his son; Go thy way; you will find him healed. But no, for fear that some scorn might appear in this reply, He sets off at once. In the sight of God, all are equal, Jew and Gentile, master and servant, son and servant; their souls are equally precious to Him, and He has died equally for all; it is faith alone, it is holiness alone which

will distinguish them one day in His eyes. Do we look upon different conditions of mankind with the same judgement and the same consideration?

2. Goodness of Jesus in His words. Jesus cannot behold that which is virtuous and good without praising it; and the day will come when He will reward it. What praise do we deserve at the hands of Jesus? Can He praise our faith, our love, our zeal, our fervour, our good works, our desire to please Him, our earnestness in serving Him? Now, if He cannot praise any thing in us now, how can He reward us one day? Alas! very far from applying myself to gain praises from Jesus Christ, have I not lived till now, so to draw down upon myself His displeasure, and one day, His reproaches, and His punishments? Jesus puts the faith of the centurion above that of the Israelites, not in order to mortify the latter, but in order to stir them up to a holy emulation. Alas! do we not see every day those who are newly converted from sin, and who have turned from sin to repentance, who put us to shame by their fervour, although we have made a profession for a long time of living regular, orderly lives? Jesus sets before us these examples in order to confound our faint-heartedness, and to re-animate our fervour; shall we then continue to resist His goodness, and shall it never conquer the malignity of our nature?

3. The goodness of Jesus in His works. Jesus praises the faith of the centurion, but without speaking of his request, without declaring whether He would grant it or no, without saying anything with regard either to the sickness or to the healing of the servant, and without making known to the by-standers what He would do. But the miracle was already wrought. Jesus returned to His own home, and the deputies to the centurion, whose servant they found healed. Can Jesus refuse anything to a humble prayer animated by faith? Shall we never know our Saviour, so as to love Him only, and put our whole confidence in Him?

Prayer. Ah Lord, the servant of the centurion was

less dear to him than my soul is to me. It is languishing, this soul of mine, it is in the most imminent danger eternal death. In this terrible state, I am more unworthy, than that Roman officer to approach unto Thee, O my Saviour, and to obtain healing from Thee. But as the faith of this centurion rendered him worthy to receive Thee in his heart by Thy grace, even when he acknowledged himself unworthy to receive Thee in his house, so let the lively feeling of my unworthiness, with which I am more than ever penetrated at this moment, obtain for me from Thy infinite goodness, deliverance from my troubles, from my weaknesses, from my lukewarmness in this life, and in the next world, the reward of Thy own gifts in me. Amen.

Meditation LXXXV.

INSTRUCTION GIVEN BY JESUS TO HIS APOSTLES ON THEIR FIRST MISSION.

1. Jesus sends forth His apostles; 2. He instructs them as to the virtues which they must practise; 3. He teaches them what is the conduct which they are to follow. S. Matt. x. 5–15. S. Mark vi. 7—11. S. Luke ix. 1—5.

FIRST POINT.

Of the sending forth of the Apostles.
1. Who sends them? It is Jesus Christ. *These twelve Jesus sent forth.* All the twelve received their commission direct from our Saviour. It is He, Who still sends forth, by the hands of His appointed ministers, the pastors, and the clergy who preach His words; let us receive them from His Hand, and let us profit by their instructions. But if we are ourselves the messengers of Jesus Christ, let us set out with diligence, with submission, with joy, and with full trust that He Who sends us, will support by His grace the choice which He has made of us.

2. How does Jesus Christ send forth the apostles? Two and two. *And He called unto Him the twelve, and began to send them forth by two and two.* Wherefore this conduct? They were to bear witness to the truth wherever He should send them; now the testimony of one man did not suffice according to the law. By which means, Jesus Christ willed perhaps to mark the union which ought to exist amongst His ministers, amongst His true disciples. Besides which an associate in our labours serves as a help, consolation, and counsel to us in the difficult functions of the ministry: as a preservative, support and defence, in temptations, against our own weakness, and in all our actions, as a witness and a guarantee against false suspicions, calumnies, and slanders. And by this means, Jesus secured to His apostles these resources in the perplexities of their ministry.

3. What was the place to which Jesus sent His apostles? He ordains the place, not according to their views, tastes, or inclinations, but according to the designs of His infinite wisdom. *And commanded them, saying, Go not into the way of the Gentiles, and into any city of the Samaritans enter ye not: but go rather to the lost sheep of the house of Israel.* The time was not yet come when the Gospel was to be preached to the Gentiles; it was needful that it should first be preached to the Jews, who ought to be more disposed to receive it. The will of God is manifested to us by a concourse of events of which Providence disposes, by the inward voice of God which directs those who will be attentive to it. The less we follow our own will, the more sure we are of following that of God, and of finding success in our efforts.

4. For what end does Jesus send forth His apostles? *And, as ye go, preach, saying, The kingdom of heaven is at hand.* That is to say, the reign of the Messiah, the reign of grace, the reign of love and of holiness is at hand. It has come to us, we live under that happy reign, which is to lead us to the kingdom of God, to

heaven: this kingdom is not far from us; let us hasten then to wash away our sins by repentance, to render ourselves worthy of our eternal bliss by good works, and to place ourselves in the state in which we should wish to die. Let us preach this kingdom ourselves, and let us make it unceasingly the subject of our reflections and of our conversations.

5. With what authority does Christ send forth His apostles? *Heal the sick,* He says to them, *cleanse the lepers, raise the dead, cast out devils.* He sends them forth with the power to work the same miracles as He did: miracles, not of display and vainglory, but of doing good and of charity, such as those should be which announced a saviour, a deliverer. To heal the sick, to cast out devils, to raise the dead; with such proof of their ministry, could any one doubt that they were setting forth the truth?

SECOND POINT.

Of the virtues which the apostles were to practise.

1. Disinterestedness. *Freely ye have received, freely give.* Remarkable words, and of great extent, since they exclude not only the possessions of fortune, but besides, the more chosen gifts of glory, favour, and esteem. He who seeks after these gifts in the exercise of his ministry, who receives them, rejoices at them, and clings to them when they are offered to him, has not *freely given.*

2. Abnegation. *Provide neither gold, nor silver, nor brass in your purses; nor scrip for your journey, neither two coats, nor shoes, nor yet staves.* What a command! In the journies which you are about to undertake, you are not to carry any purse at your sides in which you have gold and silver, nor carry any scrip for your journey in which you have provisions, nor any arms, nor staves wherewith to attack or to defend yourselves, and do not take with you any coats, or shoes,

to change, if you should require them. Clothed and shod in a simple manner, with *a staff only* in your hand whereon you may lean for support. It was in this state of poverty and destitution that the apostles were to present themselves in order to preach the Gospel to those who did not know it. Although in preaching to Christians, we are not obliged to follow out to the letter the severity of this precept, it is nevertheless certain that the more we approach to it, the more likely are to we to win over souls to God.

3. Trust in God. *For the workman is worthy of his meat.* Those who are sent by God need not fear, even in the midst of barbarous nations, that food should fail them. But they must be *workmen* who are assiduous and diligent in their work, according to their calling and their talents. If they do nothing, and live in a shameful idleness: or if they work only in order to make attacks perhaps on the Church herself, and to fight against her: or if they are only occupied in things which do dishonour to her, of what are they worthy, save of the punishment which is reserved to them? Again, those who work must appropriate their hire only to provide for their support and their needs, and the necessities of their families, not for their elevation, their luxury and needless expenditures, their pleasures, nor to gratify their avarice, and love of money, but they should devote all that remains to them, after having provided for the necessaries of life, to the needs of the poor, and the service of the Church.

THIRD POINT.

Of the conduct which the apostles ought to follow.

1. The choice of a house. *And into whatsoever city or town ye shall enter, inquire who in it is worthy: and there abide till ye go thence.* As soon as you arrive in a place, you shall enquire whether there be there any God-fearing man, any virtuous Israelite, of

known uprightness, and good reputation, with whom you may dwell. Not alone the clergy, but every one who values his own salvation, cannot be too careful in choosing as their place of residence, one whither they themselves and their good name will be equally secure.

2. Conduct of the apostles on their entrance into the house which they have chosen. *And into whatsoever house ye enter, first say, Peace be to this house. And if the son of peace be there your peace shall rest upon it; if not it shall turn to you again.* At the first step which you take into the house which shall be pointed out to you, salute with friendship those that dwell in it, wish them the peace and blessing of God, by saying to them, *Peace be to this house.* If this house deserves the blessing which you wish it, if it is worthy to receive you, and does receive you, your wishes will be fulfilled on it, God will hear your requests, and will fill it with blessings. If, on the contrary, this house is not worthy to receive, and refuses to lodge you, do not think that your wishes are useless, your blessings will return upon your own head, you will reap the fruits of your charity, your peace will *turn to you again*, so that you may carry it to another house which shall be more worthy than the first. The greeting of true Christians, and specially of the apostles, is not like that of the world, the language of pure ceremony, which often has no meaning and is often wanting in sincerity; it is on the contrary, a fervent prayer offered to God, and a wish full of charity towards a neighbour. An efficacious wish, if the neighbour is worthy of it, and if he is not worthy, a wish, the charity of which will always meet its reward. How many opportunities have we not of exercising charity at so small a cost! Wherefore should we lose them then for want of attention, and of a recollected spirit? When God's ministers visit the sick, they enter the house with the same words of greeting. Happy the house, happy the sick person who is worthy to receive this peace, so needful at these moments when the fear of death generally brings with it so much trouble and disquietude.

3. Conduct of the apostles during their sojourn in the house which they were inhabiting. *And whatsoever house ye enter into, there abide, and thence depart.* Our Lord expressly commands them, after having chosen a house and having been received there, not to go out of it in order to take another, but to remain there until the day of their departure. How full of wisdom and goodness is this command! In changing their abode, they might give rise to evil reports, or to suspicions disadvantageous to the place, and might themselves be seeking only their own convenience and comfort in so doing, only in order to gratify their own self-love. How much care is needful, how much we ought to inconvenience ourselves, in order to prevent the least scandal.

4. Conduct of the apostles when they leave a house or a city which shall have refused to receive them. *And whosoever will not receive you, when ye go out of that city, shake off the very dust from your feet, for a testimony against them. I say unto you, that it shall be more tolerable in that day for Sodom, than for that city.* The apostles were directed, on withdrawing from these cities or houses, to shake off the dust from their feet as a witness against the ungrateful men who should have refused to listen to them, that grace and the Gospel have departed from them. These unhappy men will rejoice at it, they will glory in it, they will mock at a ceremony of which they do not choose to understand the mystery, it will become the object of their scorn and of their contempt; but at the day of judgement their lot will be more terrible than that of the inhabitants of Sodom and Gomorrha. How many nations, kingdoms, and towns have thus set themeslves against the preaching of the Gospel, and will continue to do so! How many besides, after having received it, have corrupted it by innovations and errors which have made them despise first of all the voice and the threatenings of the Church, and then shortly afterwards break through the bonds of apostolic unity! How many souls have rejected in private the unwelcome light of the Gospel, in order to

follow their own inclinations, and to yield themselves up to their own passions with more freedom.

Prayer. Alas! Lord, am I not of that number? How do I receive Thy holy Word, O my God? How do I regard those who preach it to me? If I refuse to hear them, or if I will not practise any thing of that which they make known to me; if I do not profit by what I read, by that which Thou Thyself dost inspire into my mind, O my Saviour, what will be at the last day my punishment and my despair? What! shall I turn then against myself Thy benefits, and shall I make of the instruments of my salvation so many instruments of my ruin? No Lord, I will seek to profit by all the means of salvation which Thou didst lavish upon me, all the moments of grace with which Thou dost provide me, and I will no longer close my heart to that peace which Thou dost offer to me. Amen.

Meditation LXXXVI.

FIRST CONTINUATION OF THE INSTRUCTIONS GIVEN BY JESUS CHRIST TO HIS APOSTLES.

OF THE PERSECUTION WHICH THEY MUST EXPECT.

Examine, 1. the nature of this persecution; 2. the manner in which to bear up under it; 3. the motives for enduring it. S. Matt. x. 10—27.

FIRST POINT.

Of the nature of this persecution.

1. It will be unjust and unreasonable. *Behold, I send you forth as sheep in the midst of wolves.* That is to say, feeble, unarmed and without defence, I send you into the midst of those who will censure My teaching, who are enemies to the morality which I inculcate, and persecutors of My religion. Their persecution of

you will have no other cause but their own ill-will, and their natural antipathy to holiness, and their avidity for those possessions of which they will despoil you, or which they believe to belong to you.

2. Their persecution will be ignominious and slanderous. *They will deliver you up to the councils, and they will scourge you in their synagogues.* The senate and the tribunals will assemble in order to ruin you. Their plots against you will have all the apparatus of all the formalities of justice which are employed against real culprits, who are convicted of being disturbers of the peace, blasphemers, injurious men and rebels, and after having made you pass for such in the judicial assemblies, and in the authorised synagogues, they will condemn you to suffer the most degrading punishments.

3. Their persecution will be public and cruel. *And ye shall be brought before governors and kings for My sake, for a testimony against them and the Gentiles.* In despair at not being able to close your mouths, and not having the right to dispose of your lives, they will drag you before temporal powers, in hatred of Me and of My doctrines, in order that they may obtain the sentence of death against you. Jews and Gentiles, all will join together in order to exterminate you: your death will gratify their rage and their fury; but in dying, you will preach My Gospel publicly, and your death will be a witness which will prove to them that the kingdom of God is come.

4. Their persecution will be particular and in their own families. *The brother shall deliver up the brother to death, and the father the child; and the children shall rise up against their parents, and cause them to be put to death.* The most sacred bonds shall be no protection against persecution. The brother will not listen to the voice of blood, nor the father, to the feelings of his heart, nor the mother to the cry of nature; they will only follow their own angry passions; the brother will himself give up his brother to death; and the father will lead his son to it; children will rise up

against their fathers, and will sacrifice them with their own hands. Authorised it appears, by that zeal which the law commands the Jews to bear towards apostates, they will look upon you as such, and they will never cease their persecutions of you until they have seen you expire in a painful death.

5. Their persecution will be general and universal. *And ye shall be hated of all men for My Name's sake.* Compassion is to be found in men's minds for even the most infamous criminals, when they are led out to suffer the sentence of punishment; but you will not find any: the exasperation against you will be general, you shall be despised, insulted, hated and detested by every one. In virtue of your office as My apostles and ministers, you shall be an object of hatred to these untractable Jews who are your brethren according to the flesh, and whom you labour to make your children according to the Gospel. You will not draw down upon yourselves this fury, and this execration by any personal acts on your parts; but it will be Me, Whom they will hate in you, and because you will have always on your lips My Name, Which they have in abhorrence, they will not be able to endure you. Such then, O divine Jesus, is that which Thou dost foretell, and that Thou dost promise to Thine apostles and Thy disciples. Will it be possible that the world will adopt such inhuman feelings on their behalf, and that it will pursue them with so much animosity? Alas! Thy prediction, Lord, has been verified to the letter. This persecution which Thou hast announced, has lasted three hundred years, and it has been renewed several times since. Will it be possible that in the midst of so cruel and so obstinate an outburst, Thy religion should be held up, should triumph, should be extended, and should be perpetuated? Yes, my God, and this is what we behold with our own eyes. But with what weapons dost Thou then arm Thy disciples against so many enemies? What sort of defence are they to employ in order not to sink under the weight of so many and such violent attacks? They will have no other weapons

against these ravenous wolves, save gentleness, patience, and charity. And this is that which sets the seal to the marvels of Thy Almighty power, and which proves that the establishment of the Christian religion can only have been the work of Thy right hand.

SECOND POINT.

Of the manner in which to bear up under persecution.

Our Lord gives to His apostles no other means of bearing up under persecution than the practice of the most perfect virtues. What are these virtues?

1. An unchangeable gentleness. *I send you forth*, He says to them, *as sheep in the midst of wolves.* There are no enemies more cruel than those whom religion will raise up against you; but I will notwithstanding that you employ against them no other weapons, that you cherish no other mind, or dispositions than those which are set forth by the sheep. Its character is gentleness: it is incapable of anger or of resistance.

2. A perfect simplicity. *Be ye therefore harmless as doves.* A simplicity which excludes all double dealing, all lying, all guile. Let all your words and all your conduct breathe naught save simplicity and candour. How many hearts have not this sincerity and this openness drawn to Christianity! On the contrary, the unbeliever and the heretic are false in all their proceedings: their secret underhand practices whereby they seek to strengthen their party are full of deceits and of impostures, and the exposition of their doctrines is filled with equivocal statements and with disguises. Double dealing is in their hearts, lying on their lips, and perjury in their oaths; they deny the evidence of facts, they falsify others, they cavil at an expression, and calumniate their adversaries, and seek only to impose on them, to take them by surprise, and to deceive them.

3. A reasonable wisdom. *Be ye wise as serpents.* This wisdom consists in keeping ourselves always on our guard, in not rashly exposing ourselves, without reason,

in watching, praying, and being prepared for whatever may befall us. It consists in not stirring up nor adding to persecution by acts of imprudence, on our part, by an unseasonable zeal, which is ill ordered; it consists in preserving our faith and our innocency at the expense of our body, and our life, as the serpent, when attacked, will guard his head at the expense of the rest of his body, with which he covers it: it consists in escaping from danger on certain occasions, and in facing it on others. *When they persecute you in this city,* if it is a persecution which is directed only against yourself, if your presence, far from being of use, only serves to irritate the fury of your enemies, and to increase the disturbance, *flee ye into another,* without being held back by the claims of flesh and blood, by the friendships which you may have contracted there, by the delights or enjoyments the place may afford you. Your presence will be of more service elsewhere; for, in the dealings of Providence, the unbelief of the one brings about the salvation of others. But if you are a minister of Christ, if you have a flock committed to your charge, and it is they who are the objects of this persecution, then remain to support and encourage them, and sacrifice yourself for them. *Beware of men,* their persecution is dangerous to you, but their flattery is far more dangerous. As for the rest, places of refuge will not be wanting unto you; *for verily I say unto you, ye shall not have gone over the cities of Israel, till the Son of Man be come.* Our Lord speaks here, doubtless, of the terrible vengeance which the unfaithfulness of the Jews was about to draw down upon them in the destruction of their nation by the arms of the Romans; but He also sets forth to us here the severity of His last judgment against those whom His Gospel has not sanctified, and placed in safety from the darts of His anger.

4. A filial confidence in God. *When they deliver you up, take no thought how or what ye shall speak: for it shall be given you in that same hour what ye shall speak. For it is not ye that speak, but the Spirit*

of your Father which speaketh in you. In virtue of this confidence, and through the effects which this promise has produced, slaves, unlettered men, tender virgins and young children, have been seen to confound the tyrants, by the wisdom of their answers, and to reduce them to silence.

5. An unshaken constancy. *He that endureth to the end shall be saved.* It will not suffice to have begun well, nor even to have done much: we have done nothing, if we do not persevere to the end: without this final perseverance, there is no crown, no reward, no salvation to be hoped for.

6. An intrepid courage. *Fear them not therefore: for there is nothing covered, that shall not be revealed: and hid, that shall not be known.* This precept is true in the ordinary dealings of life; sooner or later, every thing is brought to light. Never therefore do any thing of which you would be ashamed, if it were made known. Fear not the calumnies of the wicked, their plots will be discovered, and you will be justified. This precept is a truth which is yet more universal with regard to the last judgement. It is there in truth that every thing will be disclosed, and revealed. Think of this in all that you think, in all that you do, and in all that you suffer. Our Lord applies this general precept here to His doctrine. *What I tell you in darkness, that speak ye in light: and what ye hear in the ear, that preach ye upon the house-tops.* Inaccessible to fear, ye are to show forth in broad day-light, and to publish on the roofs of the houses, what I have taught you in My private conversations with you, so to say, in darkness and in your ear. The preaching of true religion ought to be public and forcible, courageous and fearless: it ought to be maintained before the tribunal of judges, at the foot of the thrones of kings, and on the scaffolds: it ought to make itself heard by Jews and Gentiles, Greeks and barbarians, to the ends of the world, to the consummation of time, till the Son of man, the Author of that holy religion, comes Himself to judge the world, to reward His servants, and to punish their persecutors.

THIRD POINT.

Of the motives for enduring persecution.

1. The cause for which we suffer. *Ye shall be brought before governors and kings for My sake. Ye shall be hated of all men for My Name's sake.* We may suffer all the afflictions of this life for God, because they come to us from His Providence, to which we ought to submit with resignation, and this motive is capable of alleviating the greatest sufferings: but when the immediate cause of our sufferings is our devotion to His service, and the open profession which we make of our religion and our attachment to His Chuich, it is then that we truly suffer for Christ, and for the glory of His Name. Now, what happiness, what glory, what sweetness to suffer for Christ! And such was the triumph of the apostles: after having suffered stripes and many indignities, they went forth from the councils, filled with joy and rejoicing that they had been counted worthy to suffer for the name of Jesus.

2. The effects of these sufferings. *For a testimony against them and the Gentiles.* The first effect of these sufferings, is the salvation of our neighbour. The wisdom of God has known how to bring good out of evil. How many Gentiles, even how many executioners has not the blood of the martyrs converted? The persecutions which the Church has suffered bear witness to us even to the present time, and are for us a proof of the truth of our religion. The second effect of sufferings, is our own salvation. *He that shall endure unto the end shall be saved.* At this price, is there any thing difficult to us? What are all the sufferings of this life? Persecutions, torments, insults, disgrace, sicknesses, penances, mortifications; what are all these in comparison with our salvation? All these are as nothing, and salvation is an infinite glory and bliss; all these are but for a moment, and salvation is an eternal and perfect happiness. Courage then, my soul: yet but a mo-

ment, and we shall enter the haven, and immortal glory will be our reward.

3. *The example of Jesus Christ.* *The disciple is not above his master, nor the servant above his lord. It is enough for the disciple that he be as his master, and the servant as his lord. If they have called the master of the house Beelzebub, how much more shall they call them of his household?* The example which ought to animate and support us under our sufferings, which ought to make us look upon them not only as light, but also as sweet and glorious, is that of Jesus Christ. He is our Master, we are His disciples: He is our Lord, we are His servants; if He, the Master of the house has been called Beelzebub, and treated as one possessed with a devil, why should we be troubled at any names which may be given us, and at what injury can we take offence?

Prayer. Alas! Lord, Thou dost not yet speak to Thy disciples, save of the blasphemies which men have dared to utter against Thee; with what courage will they feel themselves animated, when they shall have seen the fury and the rage of Thine executioners attack Thy sacred body; when they shall have seen Thee covered with Thy blood, exhausted by tortures, laden with reproaches, and expiring on a cross? Who can at this remembrance, not desire to suffer, not glory in being like to Thee? Ah, it is indeed needful that the disciple should be as his master! And what is that which I suffer in comparison of that which Thou hast done for me. Alas! if piety, if devotion, if the practice of good works, if religion brings down upon me some words of scorn, some mortifications, some slight contempt, instead of rejoicing at it, and strengthening myself so much the more in that which is good, am I not all at once disturbed, disconcerted, and ready to perjure myself? Am I a Christian? Am I Thy disciple, O Jesus? Ah divine Saviour, fill me with Thy strength and Thy adorable wisdom: animate me with Thine own spirit, and grant that I may suffer for Thee. Amen.

Meditation LXXXVII.

SECOND CONTINUATION OF THE INSTRUCTIONS GIVEN BY CHRIST TO HIS APOSTLES.

OF THREE DUTIES WHICH HAVE RELATION TO GOD.

These duties are, 1. the fear of God; 2. trust in God; 3. the profession of faith in Christ. S. Matt. x. 28—36.

FIRST POINT.

Of the fear of God.

1. *It is just. Fear not them which kill the body, but are not able to kill the soul : but rather fear Him Which is able to destroy both soul and body in hell.* Fear is a sort of homage which we render to the person whom we fear. The fear of God, which is the beginning and the foundation of wisdom and of perfection, is a homage which we render to His divine knowledge, by which He knows all our actions, to His holiness, which hates sin, to His justice, which condemns it, and to His power, which punishes it. We have not the fear of God when we offend Him, when, with deliberate purpose, we do that which may displease Him, and when we omit doing that which we know we ought to do in order to please Him, when we present ourselves before Him without reverence, and pray to Him without attention. Can I say that I have the fear of God, I who sin so boldly, in so many ways, and on so many occasions?

2. *This fear rises above all human fear.* There is no one more intrepid than he who fears God alone. What has he to fear from men? Their power can only extend over his body, and that only for a short time; the body may fall under their blows, the soul flies away and escapes from their anger: but God is the Master of the body and of the soul, and He has an eternity in which

to take vengeance. Alas! how often have I not feared men rather than God! I have not been threatened with torments and death, and yet I have feared to be seen, or to be remarked: I have feared a word of scorn or of contempt, I have feared words which might be spoken of me in my absence, and of which I should have been ignorant; I have not then yet the beginning of wisdom, the fear of the Lord.

SECOND POINT.
Of trust in God.

This trust in the Lord is founded on His infinite Providence, and on His infinite bounty.

1. On His infinite Providence. *Are not two sparrows sold for a farthing? and one of them shall not fall on the ground without your Father.* Here is a truth on which we do not sufficiently reflect, and which, well meditated upon, would be a source of peace and tranquillity to us. No, in all nature, in the physical and in the moral world, nothing can take place without His knowledge, without the command and permission of the Creator. The least events, like the greatest, are subject to His Providence. As He would not be God, if any of these events could escape His knowledge, so in the same way, He would not be God, if any one of them could take place without His commands and His will. Should not such a truth, which is supported by the authority of Jesus, make us feel a deep repose in the Lord, notwithstanding the vain efforts of the world, to take it from us? The simpler the comparison is which the Saviour makes use of, the more sinful is our mistrust, and the greater ought to be our confusion.

2. Trust in God founded on His infinite goodness. *But the very hairs of your head are all numbered. Fear ye not therefore; ye are of more value than many sparrows.* God ordains the lot of a sparrow: but man, whom God has created in His image, and in His likeness, whom He has destined to share His glory, His

bliss, and His eternity; man, of whom He is not only the Creator, but also the Father, and whom Jesus Christ has redeemed by His Blood: can man not be the object of His tenderness, and of the cares of His Paternal Providence? Do not fear any thing then; all the hairs of your head are counted, and not one will fall without the permission of your heavenly Father. Do not fear then, the malice of men, unforeseen accidents, the loss of fortune, the sufferings of illnesses, nor even death itself; let us rest with calmness in the bosom of the providence of a God, Who is our Father, let us receive from His Hand all that He permits to happen to us, and let us be assured that He will proportion His succours to our trials, and His rewards to our faithfulness.

THIRD POINT.

Of the profession of faith in Christ.

Jesus Christ teaches us, 1. what will be the effect of our profession of faith in Christ in the next world; 2. what will be the effect of it even in this world.

1. What will be the effect of it in the next world? *Whosoever therefore shall confess Me before men, him will I confess also before My Father, Which is in heaven. But whosoever shall deny Me before men, him will I also deny before My Father which is in heaven.* To confess Jesus, is to declare ourselves boldly for Him, to make an open profession that we are of the number of His disciples, and to believe the truths which He has revealed to us; it is to practise faithfully His doctrines, to follow His precepts, and to perform all our religious duties without any human respect; it is to uphold the cause of Christ against those who attack it, to defend His faith, His doctrines, His servants, to combat, as far as lies in our power, the calumnies which are spread abroad against His holy religion, and to oppose ourselves to the persecutions which men desire to raise up against it. To fail in these obligations, is to deny Christ, and to be ashamed of Him. Let us examine ourselves on all

these points, and let us consider the consequences of them. Those who, before men, shall have declared themselves for Christ, will have the approval of Christ; He will declare Himself on their side in heaven, He will acknowledge them as His disciples, as His friends, as His brethren, as His fellow-heirs; on the contrary, Jesus Christ will disavow those who have not dared to declare themselves for Him; He will disown them, He will reject them as not being His, as having no claim to His inheritance, since they have not been willing to take part in His shame. What happiness for the one! what woe for the others! And before whom will Jesus make this distinction? Before His Father Which is in heaven. Alas! where will human beings then be? where will be then their power? where will be their threats and their promises? After that Jesus shall have thus declared Himself for the one, and shall have thus disowned the others, what will follow? It is that the first, having Jesus for their Mediator, will be admitted by their heavenly Father into the kingdom of heaven, in order there to reign for ever: and the others, disowned, rejected, condemned by the Son, without support, and without resources, will fall into the abyss of hell, there to burn in hell-fire for all eternity with the evil spirits.

2. What will be the effect of our profession of faith even in this world? It will be a continued and everlasting war between the flesh and the mind, between the slaves of the world, and the worshippers of Christ, a war which it is needful to be forewarned of, in order that we may keep ourselves ready, that we may be exercised in it, that we may fight in it, and not be surprised if it is cruel, long, and obstinate. *Think not*, says Jesus, *that I am come to send peace on earth; I came not to send peace, but a sword. For I am come to set a man at variance against his father, and the daughter against her mother, and the daughter in law against her mother in law. And a man's foes shall be they of his own household.* Jesus Christ is the God of peace; He brought peace down to men, and it only depends upon mankind

whether they will enjoy it. A heavenly peace, by which, if they will accept it, they are reconciled with God, Who forgives their sins; they are reconciled with themselves by enjoying the repose of a good conscience; they are reconciled with other men, to whom they wish only good. But as there are those amongst mankind who do not desire this peace, of which they would, if they could, even deprive the disciples of Jesus Christ, it is against them, and to these latter, that Jesus Christ has come to bring a sword; a spiritual sword, with which we must arm ourselves from our childhood, which we must courageously use through our whole lives, and never part with till our death; a sword, which ought to divide, and cleave asunder the ties of nature, cut asunder all the bonds which would hold us back in sin, or in error, or which are opposed to the will of God, and our salvation. The world does not know this sword; everything is good to it, so long as it is not disturbed in the enjoyment of earthly possessions. Heresy does not know this sword: all sects are united, when at that price they can enjoy earthly peace; or if heresy takes the sword in order to maintain itself, it is the material and destructive sword which Jesus Christ has proscribed, and not the spiritual sword which He has brought on the earth. Lastly, the cowardly and faint-hearted man does not know this sword, or does not make use of it; he allows himself to be gained over by marks of affection, to be drawn aside by good nature, to be corrupted through weakness, and he does not understand that his most dangerous enemies, those whom he ought to distrust the most, and sometimes even to separate himself from, when they are an evident obstacle to his salvation and his perfection, are those with whom he is most closely connected, and with whom he lives.

Prayer. Make me hate, O my God, every thing which would separate me from Thee; make me love every thing which comes from Thine Hand. May I fear nothing but to fear too much men who are so powerless, and not to fear Thee, Lord, enough, Thou Who alone canst either save me or cause me to perish, and

Who wilt of a surety save me, if I cling only to Thee. O weak men and powerless like myself! what have I to fear or to hope for from you? I despise equally your good and evil fortunes, your favour and your anger, and I declare myself boldly for Jesus Christ, my Saviour and my Master. Ah! Lord, grant that I may be penetrated only with the salutary fear of Thee; may I know and dread but one evil, that of offending Thee; but one true unhappiness, that of losing Thee; may I be constantly Thy true disciple here below, that so Thou mayest present me hereafter to Thy Father, as the inheritor with Thee of Thy Glory in Heaven. Amen.

Meditation LXXXVIII.

CONCLUSION OF THE INSTRUCTIONS GIVEN BY JESUS CHRIST TO HIS APOSTLES.

OF THE LOVE OF JESUS CHRIST.

Our Lord gives here four qualities of the love which He requires from us: He wills that this love should be predominant, crucifying, quickening, and zealous. S. Matt. x. 37—42.

FIRST POINT.

A predominant love.

A love which wills to be preferred before every other love, and to which we must sacrifice all else. *He that loveth father or mother more than Me is not worthy of Me; and he that loveth son or daughter more than Me is not worthy of Me.* It is the same with every other affection. Let us examine here our hearts conformably with this rule. We love a person more than Jesus Christ, when we are not willing to separate ourselves from them out of love for Jesus Christ; if, in order to please that person, we break the law of Jesus Christ; if the love of that person weakens, is at variance with, or counterbalances the love of Jesus Christ, distracts us, turns us away, or gives us a distaste of the love of Jesus Christ. Such an one *is not worthy of Me*, says our Saviour. No, Jesus asks for a noble, generous love, which raises us above all which He has created, and He merits it, because He is Himself infinitely great, and above every thing, because, although He is infinitely great, He loves us more than any one, be they who they may, can love us, because He has done more for us than any one else could do for us, because He has the power and the will to make us happy, and that He alone can procure for us solid, infinite, and eternal happiness. Such an one *is not worthy of Me*, says our Lord, that is to say, he is not worthy to have Jesus Christ as his Mediator and Saviour, but only as his Judge and Avenger.

SECOND POINT.

A crucifying love.

A love which only offers crosses to us, and for which we must suffer every thing. *He that taketh not up his cross, and followeth after Me, is not worthy of Me.* To take up our cross, is to accept heartily all the troubles of this life, from whatever source they come to us, whether from our condition and our station, whether from the course of nature, such as the seasons of the year, or diseases; whether from unforeseen accidents, which are always under the directing Hand of Providence; or from the hand of men, from their malice or infirmities; it is to suffer all this without complaint, without murmurings, without impatience: it is to add to all that, voluntary crosses, such as privations, penances, or mortifications. Now who can do all that, save out of love? To follow Jesus Christ, is to suffer for Him and like Him, with the same virtues, and for the same end as He did, and by uniting our crosses to His, whence ours draw all their value. He who does not do so, *is not worthy of Me*, says our Saviour. No, Jesus Christ seeks for noble souls, and generous hearts, and such is the trial to which He puts them. We must be very cowardly not to be willing to suffer any thing under the eyes of our King, when we see that King Himself face all dangers, undergo every hardship, and expose Himself to every suffering, and bear all. Ah! what shall we call such cowardice, that we dare not follow Him, and will not neither share His dangers nor His fatigues? Such an one *is not worthy of Me*, says Christ; He is not worthy to have Me for his Leader and his King, to be numbered amongst My soldiers, to take part in My victories and to triumph with Me in heaven, where I shall only admit noble and generous souls; he will only merit the opprobrium which follows cowards, and the punishment which deserters and traitors bring upon themselves.

THIRD POINT.

A quickening love.

A love which asks of us our life in order to preserve it to us. *He that findeth his life shall lose it; and he that loseth his life for My sake shall find it.* To find our life in the meaning which Jesus Christ gives to it, is to seek the safety of our own person at the expense of our faith and innocence; it is to follow our passions at the expense of the law of God; it is to procure for ourselves pleasures and amusements at the expense of our duties; it is to prefer our own will to that of God, and our liberty to the call of God; it is to seek ourselves in every thing, to do every thing with reference to ourselves, to our own self-love, our vanity, our own convenience, and to rest in ourselves as in our own sovereign happiness. How blind and unhappy is he who embraces so fatal a course! this life which he loves so passionately, and to which he is so attached, he loses it for all eternity, where he will be in one continual death, in an absolute privation of every happiness, in fearful torments. Let us weigh well this truth; let it disturb our pleasures, and give us a distaste for them, and bring us back to the paths of wisdom.

To lose one's life in the meaning which Jesus Christ applies to it, is to die rather than lose our faith or our innocence; it is to renounce our passions, our vicious inclinations, in order to keep within the limits of an exact observance of the law of God; it is to die to the pleasures of sense, to the frivolous amusements of the world, in order to confine ourselves to the practice of our duties; it is to bury our lives in retirement, in prayer, in penitence; it is to refer everything to God, to work only for Him, and His glory, and to forget one's self entirely. How happy and wise is he who embraces so profitable a course of life! This life which he appears to neglect and of which he seems to make no account, this life which he does not enjoy, which he exhausts in fatigues, which he loses, which he spends, in one word, which he sacrifices, he will find it again in eternity, where he will have the fruition of God in a perfect life and in ineffable delights. Ah! let us unceasingly recall this truth, that it may animate, support, and fortify us. Alas! if this self-seeking were in its nature only a venial sin, would it not always be a transgression against the love we owe to our God, and consequently be so much loss to our own souls throughout eternity? Lord, how much grace do I not thus lose each day!

FOURTH POINT.

A zealous love.

A love which Jesus Christ requires even from those who are not destined to the sacred ministry of His Church. *He that receiveth you receiveth Me, and he that receiveth Me, receiveth Him that sent Me. He that receiveth a prophet in the name of a prophet shall receive a prophet's reward; and he that receiveth a righteous man in the name of a righteous man shall receive a righteous man's reward. And whosoever shall give to drink unto one of these little ones a cup of cold water only in the name of a disciple, verily I say unto you, he shall in no wise lose his reward.* Zeal is not so entirely a qualification belonging to the ministry, that no one else can have a share in it, and in its rewards. He who receives an apostle into his house receives Jesus Christ Who has sent him, and God Himself Who has sent Jesus Christ. With what joy, with what fervour, with what attention ought we not to receive the ministers of the Gospel! He who receives them, not out of any human motive, but as the ministers of Jesus Christ, shall have himself the reward of a minister of the Gospel. He who receives a righteous man, not on account of his relationship, or because he is a fellow citizen, or a friend, but because he is righteous, and a friend of God, shall receive himself the reward due to a righteous man. Should not such liberal promises move those who are rich to employ their wealth zealously in works for the relief and encouragement of those who labour for the salvation of souls? It is this pious zeal which has given to the Church these revenues, whereby she supports so many of her ministers, which has founded so many establishments for the instruction of the young, and the relief of the poor, which has provided funds for missions, schools, and hospitals. Happy they who are now animated by the same zeal! But every one has it not in their power to shew forth their zeal by large gifts. Love will shew itself in the smallest things, and it will give a value to the smallest services which it renders. God sees the heart, and the love by which it is enkindled. A glass of water given to a disciple of Jesus Christ, because he is His disciple, will have its reward. Who would have believed it? but this divine Saviour assures us Himself that it is so. How sweet it is to serve so liberal, so beneficent a Master. It is not so when we serve the world; how many services are there not which are passed over or ignored; and amongst those which are known, how few meet with any reward, and what a reward it is!

Prayer. It appertains only to so good a Master as Thou art, O my Saviour, thus to reward the smallest services. With how many means dost Thou not supply me, whereby I may in some way have a share in the honour of serving Thee, and of receiving a recompense from Thee! I will avail myself of them, by doing all that lies in my power, to help on the work of Thy ministers, to forward their labours, and to carry out their undertakings; a thousand times blessed, if by that means, I can prove my love to Thee. But this is too little for my heart; to bear my cross, to take it up from choice, of my own free will, or at least to accept it willingly, to follow Thee, O my Saviour! that is to say, to unite my sorrows to Thine, and to take pleasure in walking constantly in Thy footsteps, such are the resolutions which I form at this moment: sustain them by Thy grace. O my heart, how unworthy wouldest thou be, how base and despicable, if thou couldest refuse to yield to these tokens of the love which thy Creator requires from thee! What hast thou to love, if thou dost not love Jesus? Amen.

Meditation LXXXIX.

SENDING FORTH OF THE TWELVE APOSTLES.

1. What was to be the place where they should take up their abode; 2. what was to be the subject of their discourses; 3. what were to be their actions. S. Matt. xi. 1. S. Mark vi. 12, 13. S. Luke ix. 6.

FIRST POINT.

What was to be the place of their abode.

1. It was not to be their native country. *And it came to pass, when Jesus had made an end of commanding His twelve disciples, He departed thence, to teach and to preach in their cities.* Jesus, in joining to Himself twelve Apostles, had no intention thereby to exonerate Himself from a share in their labours, and to procure for Himself rest from work, but only to hasten on the Work of God. After having finished His discourses and His instructions to them on the duties of the

ministry, the engagements they had entered on, its fatigues and dangers, its fruits and successes, its privileges and rewards, He commanded His apostles to set out, and to go forth and put them in practise in all the cities of Galilee which He had pointed out to them, and He departed Himself in order to preach and teach in the cities of the country where He then was. It is not in a person's native place that he reaps most fruit from his labours: private interests, jealousies, family feuds, considerations which one's family may exact, even the alleviations and comforts they provide for him, the influences of those who have known one from childhood, all these often prove great hindrances to the work of the ministry.

2. It was not either in large cities that they were to seek for the place of their labours. *And they departed and went through the towns, preaching the Gospel, and healing every where.* The towns and villages were the first scene of action. It was there that the apostles, after having left Jesus Christ, and having divided themselves into six bands, distributed themselves to publish the Gospel, and to exercise the power of miracles which Jesus Christ had communicated to them. The dwellers in the country are the most cherished objects of true zeal, because, on the one hand, they are most deprived of instruction, and on the other hand, they are more open to the influences of the Gospel. One rarely meets with great crimes in the country, and men's passions are less easily excited than in large towns; the occupations of those who live there are of a more innocent and peaceful nature, and they often need only to have a holy life set before them in order to follow it. How many opportunities of doing good in country homes are there not for him who is possessed with true zeal!

SECOND POINT.

Of their discourses.

The apostles, following the example of Jesus Christ and S. John Baptist, exhorted the people to repentance;

they announced the coming of the kingdom of God, and the terrible scourge of divine wrath which would follow the unbelieving Jews. *And they went out, and preached that men should repent.* Such is the Gospel which is still preached: to pretend to seek for salvation without repentance is to contradict what Jesus Christ, His forerunner, His apostles and His Church have set forth. Let us then examine with the greatest care,

1. What our own repentance is, that is, how we receive the troubles and afflictions of this life, which are, as it were, an act of penitence laid upon us of necessity: how we practise the fasts and days of abstinence enjoined by the Church, which are acts of penitence laid upon us by precept: how we mortify our senses, our inclinations, our fleshly lusts: what use we make of prayers and watchings, and acts of self-mortification, which are acts of voluntary and external penitence: how we detest our sins, how we weep for them, and avoid the occasion of falling into them, which forms our inward penitence: with what earnestness, sincerity, grief, and desire to amend our lives, we confess our sins, and seek for their forgiveness, which are outward acts of repentance.

2. How we preach repentance to others, that is to say how we instruct those who are dependent on us, in the necessity of repentance, how we make use of every occasion to inspire those with whom we have any intercourse with a true desire of repentance, and conversion to God. One word of a master or of a friend spoken in season will prove often more efficacious to the salvation and conversion of a soul than the most eloquent discourses. How many opportunities we lose of exercising a ministry, which, though not high sounding, is none the less conducive to the glory of God, and useful to our neighbour and ourselves!

THIRD POINT.

Of their actions.

And they cast out many devils, and anointed with

oil many that were sick, and healed them. It was not of themselves and without a motive that the apostles preached repentance, and anointed the sick. Our Lord, in sending them forth to preach and to heal the sick, was laying the foundation of His Gospel. Two considerations offer themselves here to our minds.

1. In time of sickness. Observe that this anointing possessed, under the hands of the apostles, the miraculous virtue of healing the sick. S. James alludes to it. " Is any sick among you, let him call for the elders of the Church, and let them pray over him anointing him with oil in the Name of the Lord ; and the prayer of faith shall raise the sick : and the Lord shall raise him up, and if he have committed sins, they shall be forgiven him." Let us, in time of sickness, suffer willingly what God wills to lay upon us ; He will give us the graces needful to suffer with resignation, and will make our sufferings the means of purifying our souls. In the same spirit of faith, let us seek to procure for all sick persons, whom we see, our relations or friends, or those in our house, all the spiritual helps they need ; let us animate their courage to withstand the natural fear of death, and let us call to their minds the promises of Jesus Christ.

2. In time of health. Let us seek while yet in health to prepare ourselves for sickness, let us think whilst we are still strong and well, what sickness is. In what state will our bodies be then ? How will then all the objects which have pleased them, tempted them, drawn them into evil then affect them ? What would we then give to have used our senses aright, which God gave us only in order to help us to serve Him ? Let us then make of them now a holy use ; let us begin by asking God for forgiveness for all the sins which we have committed through them, then let us put far from them all that can lead them into sin, let us close them against all that might corrupt them, let us put on them the bridle of the law of God ; and bring them lastly into captivity in the chains of His divine commandments, if we desire to enjoy peace during this present life, and solid comfort and hope in the hour of death.

Prayer. Suffer me not, Lord, to close my ears to so many calls to repentance; and since a Christian life must needs be a life of continual penitence, grant that my life may be penitent, that so it may be holy, and lead me to an eternity of bliss. Amen.

Meditation XC.

JESUS RAISES TO LIFE THE SON OF A WIDOW OF NAIN.

1. The meeting of Jesus; 2. what Jesus does to raise the dead to life; 3. what the dead man does when raised; 4. the admiration of the people. S. Luke vii. 11—17.

FIRST POINT.

The meeting of Jesus.

And it came to pass the day after, that He went into a city called Nain; and many of His disciples went with Him, and much people. Now when He came nigh to the gate of the city, behold, there was a dead man carried out, the only son of his mother, and she was a widow; and much people of the city was with her.

1. A meeting worthy of admiration. A meeting of life and death, of consolation and desolation. On the one hand, Jesus, accompanied by His disciples, and followed by an innumerable crowd of people, advances towards one of the gates of the city of Nain. On the other hand, a funeral procession comes forth with pomp out of this same gate, in order to go and bury without the city walls, according to the custom of the country, a dead person, who had evidently been much thought of, to judge by the numerous assemblage who accompany him. This meeting was not the result of unforeseen chance, but of the admirable providence of God, Who wills thus to shew forth the glory of His Son, and make known to us the powerful and gracious Saviour Whom He has given to us.

2. *A meeting full of instruction.* It is a young man who is being borne forth to be laid in the ground, an only son who has died in the flower of his age, taken away from the world, its pleasures, honours, possessions, from all his hopes and expectations, accompanied by a crowd of relations, friends, fellow citizens, all in mourning, sorrow, and tears; such is the world in its true point of view, and such as we must regard it in order to be able to judge impartially of it. O deceptive world! in vain dost thou boast thy pleasures, dost thou display thy luxury, and thy riches, dost thou make all resound with the noise of thy senseless joys, and thy superb feasts; in spite of thyself, thou art constrained to change thy adornments, and to present to us these mournful scenes which lay bare thy decay, thy feebleness, and thy nothingness. Young persons, do not let yourselves be deceived by it, whatever promises the world may make you, it cannot assure you life; and if that is taken away from you, all that it can then do for you, is to conduct you in pomp to the place of your burial, where your name, your memory, your plans and your hopes will alike be buried with you. Ah! rather cling to the Conqueror of death, follow Jesus Who alone can deliver you from the grave, and make you pass from a peaceful life filled with true and solid consolations, to a blessed and eternal life.

3. *A meeting most touching in its character. And when the Lord saw her, He had compassion on her.* The mother of this young man was following the dead body of her son; her grief was extreme, her cries and tears melted all hearts. She had already lost her husband, and in losing this only son, she lost that which was dearest to her in the world, she lost her consolation, her support, her delight, and that which formed her entire happiness. Jesus sees her in this state of grief, and He was moved with compassion. This divine Saviour, Who never beheld any one in grief without being touched by it, could He be otherwise at the situation of this desolate mother? Is He not the God of the widow, the Consolation of those who are in sorrow? Let us then have

recourse to Him in our afflictions. Ah! if He has comforted this afflicted mother, who did not know Him, and who looked for no help from Him, will He be insensible to our tears, when we claim His succour, and when we ask it of Him with fervour?

4. A meeting full of blessing. Jesus advanced towards this desolate mother, *and said unto her, Weep not.* Who then can make use of such language? who can say in so sad a situation, *Weep not?* Ah, it is Thou alone, O Jesus, Who couldest speak in this manner, since it is Thou alone Who couldest dry up the source of our tears, or make them flow with calmness. Happy moment when Jesus says to a soul, *Weep not,* or rather weep only for Me, and your tears shall be your consolation. Ah! if we had recourse to Jesus in all our sorrows, He would make us hear in the depths of our hearts these comforting words, *Weep not,* cease to weep, I will repair all your losses, or rather turn them to your advantage; weep only for your sins, and shed no tears save those of repentance and the love of God.

SECOND POINT,

That which Jesus did in order to raise the dead man.

And He came and touched the bier: and they that bare Him stood still. And He said, young man, I say unto thee, Arise.

1. Jesus drew near. It is thus that He acts in order to bring about the conversion of a sinner dead to grace, who is carried away by his passions, which are on the point of precipitating him into hell. He draws near to him by the remorse which He excites in his heart, by the inward grace which solicits him to return to life, by the light which breaks in on his soul, sometimes from a sermon which he hears, sometimes from a book he reads, and sometimes at a moment when he looks for it least. Happy moment to him who knows how to profit by it! How often has not Jesus thus drawn near to each one of us! Let us then shew forth our gratitude to Him.

2. Jesus touched the bier, and those who bare it stood still. The expectation of the spectators doubtless was great, and we may believe that the heart of the mother was deeply agitated. Such is the expectation of saints in Heaven, such the agitation of heart which that tender mother, the Church, experiences, when God in His exceeding mercy, touches the bier of a sinner who seemed to be hopelessly lost, when God stretches out His Hand over that which was the occasion and the cause of his sin; when He cuts short the course of dissipation and of license through the opening of a mission, of a retreat, or of the solemnities of Lent; or by some other means by which the sinner is awakened; when He strikes the sinful flesh by some accident, illness, or infirmity; when He effaces the features of that beauty by which he was captivated; when He suffers that his good reputation which covered his shameful intrigues should be injured by slanderous reports, and sometimes destroyed by signal infamy which reveals the hidden iniquity: when He overturns those plans of acquiring fortune, either by unforeseen accidents, or by acts of injustice or treachery. This helpful Hand, these salutary blows which, by checking the impetuosity of his passions, give the sinner time to commune with himself, and furnish him with the most powerful motives to return to God.

3. He commands. *Young man, I say unto thee, arise.* Sinners dead to grace, do not close the ears of your heart to the voice of your Saviour; arise, come forth out of that state of death, and come back to life. Young persons, it is to you specially that this command is addressed; learn then the means whereby you may escape death. It is during your youth that it is blessed and happy to give yourselves to God, to dedicate yourselves to His service, and to make the path of holiness, your own. How many good deeds are there not to be done, how many sins to be avoided! Do not wait for a more advanced age; perhaps you will never see it, perhaps the voice of God will then only make itself heard but feebly, perhaps you will no longer listen to it. That

JESUS RAISES TO LIFE THE SON OF A WIDOW.   63

which is at least certain is, that then you will find far greater difficulties in the way of your conversion than in your youth, and such perhaps as you will not have the courage to surmount; but even if you should succeed in overcoming them, what regret will you not experience that you have thus wasted in a life of sin the best years of your life! Pray Jesus to draw near to you, to touch you, and to command you.

THIRD POINT.

What the dead man did when brought back to life.

And he that was dead sat up, and began to speak. And He delivered him to his mother.

1. Hardly had the dead man heard the Voice Which called him, than he sat up. What must have been his surprise, when he found himself on a bier, surrounded by a crowd of people, who were carrying him to the grave! Such ought to be the first acts of the sinner, when he has heard the voice which recalls him to life; he ought to raise his head out of the abyss into which he was plunged, and consider the terrible position in which he is. Alas! can he behold without a shudder the danger of his situation, the life he is leading, the paths he is following, and the frightful precipice to which it leads? Ah! the grave is nothing in comparison to hell.

2. *He began to speak.* Would this young man, when brought back to life desire to return to his bier, to fall asleep again in the sleep of death, and be led to the grave? No, doubtless, and it was to escape such a risk that he began to speak. Ah! wherefore then, after having begun to raise ourselves out of the state of faintheartedness and sin of which we can foresee the fatal results, why should we stifle these salutary thoughts which urge upon us to raise ourselves out of it? why plunge once more into forgetfulness of God, into that tumult of the world, and let ourselves be carried away by all these evil inclinations which lead us to hell? Why

do we not hasten to speak and to come forth from so sad a condition! He spoke, but what did he say? that is not related; but it is possible that he told the bearers and those engaged in the funeral rites, to leave him, and announced his restoration to life. Such ought to be the language of a sinner, who, penetrated with the horror of his condition, sighs after the moment of deliverance. He ought to speak in order to dismiss, and to remove from him all that has brought him into the death of sin, to confess his past sins, and his present resolutions; he ought to speak, in order to edify others by the modesty, and circumspection of his discourses, and manifest thus the truth of his resurrection.

3. He walked. Those who were carrying forth the dead body, having heard the voice of him that was raised from the dead, laid forthwith the bier down on the ground. The young man then got up on his feet, and Jesus, taking him by his hand, led him and restored him to his mother. Oh inconsolable mother, with what transports of joy didst not thou receive back thy beloved son, the object of thy tenderness! Ah! did ye not both throw yourselves at the feet of your Saviour, and did not your tears, excited by a joy as lively as it was sudden, bear witness to Him of your love and your gratitude? O sweet moments, when a converted sinner, led back as it were, by the hand of Jesus, is given back restored to life to the Church, his mother, who had mourned over his death, and is re-admitted to the participation of her divine mysteries? How often has one not seen cheeks wet with those precious tears of repentance which a tender devotion has caused to be shed!

FOURTH POINT.

Admiration of the people.

This admiration appears in their fears, in their praises, in their conversations.

1. In their fears. *And there came a fear on all.* At the sight of so many wonders, a religious awe seized all

hearts and kept all the spectators in a profound silence. Let us seek to be penetrated with the same feelings, and let us prostrate ourselves in reverence before the Majesty of God; let us adore in silence these striking wonders of the power of our Redeemer.

2. In their praises. *And they glorified God, saying, That a great prophet is risen up among us: and That God hath visited His people.* Admiration could not long remain dumb: it burst forth suddenly in thanksgivings, and by a general acclamation, each one praised and blessed God that He had condescended to visit His people of Israel, that He had sent in their days the great prophet, the Messiah promised to their fathers. Let us join our praises and our thanksgivings to those of this people, let us detest the infidelity of these Jews and of these wilful unbelievers, who will not acknowledge Jesus Christ by these divine marks. Would that our praises could make amends for their contempt! Would that their indifference might redouble our love and gratitude, and that their unfaithfulness might increase the fervour and zeal of our faith! Would lastly that our fervour might edify them to their conversion!

3. In their conversations. *And this rumour of Him went forth throughout all Judea, and throughout all the region round about.* All Judea and all the neighbouring country resounded with the noise of this miracle, and of the other wonders which were related on this occasion. They were spoken of every where, and men could not cease to speak of them. And we, what is the subject of our conversation with others and amongst ourselves? Ah! how much better known and loved would Jesus Christ be, if He were more often the subject of our conversations, and the object of our thoughts!

Prayer. It is not only by my words, by my feelings, but by my actions that I desire to glorify Thee and to make Thee known, O blessed Jesus. Grant to the prayers of Thy Church, Thy Spouse and my tender Mother, the real and perfect conversion of my heart, so often the victim and prey of death and sin; grant that, truly raised from the death of sin, I may live by Thy grace alone until through that grace I enter into Thy glory. Amen.

Meditation XCI.

S. JOHN BAPTIST SENDS TWO OF HIS DISCIPLES TO JESUS.

The sacred text here sets before us for our meditation, 1. the embassy sent to Jesus by S. John; 2. the answers given by Jesus to the messengers of S. John; and 3rdly, the warning given by Jesus to them. S. Matt. xi. 2—6. S. Luke viii. 18—29.

FIRST POINT.

The embassy sent to Jesus by S. John.

1. The occasion on which this embassy was sent. *And the disciples of John shewed him of all these things. Now when John had heard in the prison the works of Christ* . . . The report which the disciples of S. John Baptist brought to him, of the wonders which Jesus wrought, of the doctrines which He taught, and the great reputation which He was gaining for Himself, was the occasion of this embassy. S. John was at that time kept in prison by Herod king of Galilee: we shall see presently for what reason. It was a sensible consolation to him in his chains, to learn the various miracles which Jesus worked, and the striking wonders which He performed in the sight of the inhabitants of Palestine. It is an act of charity to visit prisoners, and those who from infirmity or sickness, are deprived of their freedom; it is an act of charity to bring to such the comfort with which religion inspires us.

2. The reason of this embassy. *And John, calling unto him two of his disciples sent them to Jesus.* The disciples of the saintly forerunner, although brought up in the school of the most enlightened men, were still somewhat imperfect and very uneducated. They had

moreover so high an idea of their master, and were so much attached to him, that notwithstanding the teaching they had received from him, they could not persuade themselves that Jesus was the Messiah they looked for, and it was with difficulty that they could restrain themselves from looking on Him as a rival. In this idea, they could not witness without some feeling of jealousy, His reputation grow, and the number of His disciples increase. In order to effect a radical cure of their prejudices, S. John made use of the account which they themselves had just given to him of the works of Jesus. He called two of his disciples, and sent them to Jesus, in order that they might, of themselves, become convinced of the truth. It is thus, that S. John, although in prison, still found means to exercise his ministry, and to labour for his master's glory; it is thus that he profited by every opportunity to make Christ known, and that he knew how to correct with gentleness the defects of his disciples, and to make that at which they had taken offence serve to their edification. If we had the same zeal for the glory of God, and the salvation of our neighbour, how many opportunities should we not find whereby we might advance both the one and the other!

3. The subject of this embassy. It was to enquire of Jesus whether He were the Messiah whom they looked for. *He sent two of his disciples, and said unto Him, Art Thou He that should come, or look we for another?* An important question which the synagogue had put to S. John, and which S. John in his turn, desired his disciples to put to Jesus. Let us put it to ourselves? Is Jesus He Who should come to save the world? Is He *He that should come* to judge it, or do we *look for another?* To judge by our want of love towards Him, our want of faith in His words, our want of hope in His promises, our want of obedience to His laws, our want of conformity to His examples, would not any one have a right to ask of us whether we are looking for another, another who should favour our inclinations, our ambition, our avarice, our self-love; another who should re-

ward riches, greatnesses, pleasures, and every vice? Now, if we believe that Jesus Christ, Who has come, is our Saviour and our Judge, if it is true that we look for none other to save us and to judge us, how then is it that we do not love Him, and how is it that we do not serve Him with our whole heart?

SECOND POINT.

Answer of Jesus Christ to the messengers sent by S. John Baptist.

Jesus, in His answer, gives the proofs of His divine mission, which are miracles, prophecies, and the union of miracles and prophecies.

1. Miracles. *When the men were come unto Him, they said, John Baptist hath sent us unto Thee, saying, Art Thou He that should come? or look we for another? And in the same hour He cured many of their infirmities and plagues, and of evil spirits; and unto many that were blind, He gave sight.* These deputies, having come to Jesus, found Him, as was His wont, surrounded by the multitude whom He was instructing, and the sick whom He was healing. This divine Saviour received the messages of John in the midst of this numerous assemblage, whose confidence and prayers announced His divine power, far more than the splendour which shines around the throne of kings could have done. He listened calmly to that which the messengers had been commanded to say to Him: and at first, instead of replying to them, He caused to draw near the infirm, the sick, the blind, the lame, and the possessed who followed Him; He healed them and delivered them all, and worked in their presence such prodigies of power and goodness as characterize the true Messiah, and a Saviour-God. Such was the first response of Jesus to the deputies; an answer by act, and truly worthy of a God; such ought to be our's to questions of unbelief. Jesus Christ is asked if He is the Messiah, and His answer is to work miracles; let us shew like Christians,

let us shew by our works to the unbeliever what we are.

2. Prophecies. *Then Jesus, answering, said unto them, Go your way, and tell John what things ye have seen and heard; how that the blind see, the lame walk, the lepers are cleansed, the deaf hear, the dead are raised, and to the poor the gospel is preached,* that is to say, to the poor in spirit, to the humble in heart, to those who have a contrite heart, who are in affliction, and who repent of their sins. The intention of Christ, in speaking to the messengers of that which they had seen, was to recall to their minds the prophecy of Isaiah, where these things were foretold of the Messiah. The accomplishment of prophecy is one of the strongest proofs, as is also that of miracles, since both could alone come from Him, Who is the absolute Master of all time and of events. The prophecy of Isaiah had reference to Christ; but had it not also Christianity in view? Christ fulfilled it, and His ministers are also continually fulfilling it. Why then does it not find its fulfilment in each one of us in particular? Why do we make divine truths and the graces which have been foretold useless by our unfaithfulness?

3. The union of miracles and prophecies. Each of these proofs taken separately, would suffice to convince any reasonable mind; but from their union there results a strong proof to which there can be no resistance. However little attention is paid to the past, the converted world is an invincible proof of the truth of the miracles of Christ. The Jewish people, dispersed throughout the world by a Providence which is in itself a miracle, proves invincibly the truth of the prophetic books. The Jews themselves have these books in their hands, and the miracles foretold in these books are those which Jesus Christ has wrought. What can one desire more in order to feel the most perfect and immoveable conviction? Let unbelievers gather together, as much as they will, wonders which are spread abroad in heathen histories: wonders which are for the most part absurd, ridiculous, and unseemly: wonders written long after their

pretended occurrence, and without any eye-witnesses being produced to attest their verity: wonders which no one has cared to examine or to contradict; wonders which lead to nothing and prove nothing, and which are not adduced in support of the religion of those who are said to have worked them: shall one dare to compare them with the miracles of Jesus Christ, foretold so many centuries before they were worked, with miracles which have changed the face of the universe? No, Lord, Thy ways are far above the ways of men: neither men nor devils can feign anything which can approach to the magnificence of Thy works.

THIRD POINT.

The warning given by Jesus to the messengers of S. John Baptist.

And blessed, our Saviour adds in conclusion, *is he, whosoever shall not be offended in Me.*

1. Examine the occasion of this offence. Who could, Oh Jesus, Divine Pattern of all perfection, find in Thee whereat to be offended? Nevertheless Thou hast been a stumbling block to the Jews, and Thou art so still to many Christians? And what is the reason of it? It is, in the first place, the sublimity of Thy mysteries, and the incomprehensibiltiy of Thy ways. The proud man, who does not know himself, would desire to understand Thee, to penetrate the secret of Thy counsels, and to know the reasons of Thy conduct. It is, in the second place, the holiness and purity of Thy doctrine. The voluptuary believes its practice to be either impossible, or at least too difficult for him to subject himself to it. It is, in the third place, Thy seeming feebleness, as Man, and that of Thy mystic Body, which is the Church. The Jew who expected a Saviour, Who should deliver him, not from the yoke of his sins, but from the yoke of the Romans, seeing in Thee only poverty, gentleness, humility, was *offended in* Thee. And how much more

so, when he saw Thee expire on the Cross? Even so in Thy Church, the greatest mysteries are worked, the most signal graces are communicated through the Sacraments, under the most simple symbols of water, bread, and wine, and the words of the priest. The administration of that Church is committed into the hands of feeble men, who are subject in themselves to error and to passions. And how many have been offended even till they have separated from her and fallen into schism? To govern such unteachable spirits, it would need men of another race, or Angels from Heaven; and yet not even then, would they cease to be disquieted, since the promises of Jesus Christ Himself do not re-assure them. Let us examine whether we are entirely free ourselves from having any share in these offences.

2. Consider the misery of those who are *offended in Jesus*. This offence which they take fills their minds with thick darkness, so that they are unable to perceive the evidence of the proofs of religion. The most striking miracles, the most perfect fulfilment of prophecy, the most well-attested facts make no impression on them; their mind is only occupied in seeking for forced interpretations, and sophisms, to which they cling with obstinacy, however devoid of probability, however absurd, or ridiculous they may be. If unbelievers think that religion is an error, it is not an error which they are content to regard with feelings of compassion towards those who profess it; they hate this religion, and those who follow it, they persecute it by open force, they calumniate it without shame, and only breathe forth murder, blood, and carnage against it. Jesus was the first victim of this fury: after Him, His apostles, His disciples, and the martyrs of the first centuries, down to this day, and till the end of the world, all those who make a profession of living a godly life will suffer persecution. Lastly this offence fills their conscience with troubles and disquietude. Those who have forsaken Christ, His law and His Church, may seek indeed to shut their eyes to the light, it penetrates in spite of

them, and the little which reaches them suffices to trouble them. What doubts, what thoughts, what remorse come to disquiet their conscience, and to torment them! Is it indeed true, say they amongst themselves, is it indeed true that the secret crimes with which I defile my conscience are nothing, that God has created me only for this life, that the Christian religion is but a fable, that the Church is in error, and that I can without crime despise her decisions? Ah, my God, who can resist Thee, and yet be at peace! Woe be to him who is offended at Thee, and who does not adore all that is in Thee, and all that comes from Thee!

3. Let us meditate on the happiness of those who are not *offended in* Jesus Christ. Their mind is enlightened by the purest light of truth: not only do they feel the triumphant force of the proofs of religion, but in that which causes offence to others, and which repels them, they find that which is to them the confirmation of their faith. They see in the obscurity which surrounds the mysteries of the Christian faith, an incomprehensiblity worthy of God, and which extends over all His works, and even over those of nature. They see in the purity of gospel teaching, a holiness worthy of God, which elevates them, ennobles them, consoles, and quickens them, and renders every thing easy to them. They see in the humiliations of Jesus Christ, the power and the wisdom of God, and in the weakness of the Church, a Providence worthy of admiration, the continual assistance of the Holy Spirit, and the sensible effect of the great promises which Jesus has made to her of His Indwelling Presence, unto the end of the world. Their hearts are filled with the tenderest charity, their zeal has no bitterness in it: they leave to Christian princes, the charge of restraining, according to their wise judgment, the wicked and the rebellious. As for them, they desire only their conversion and their instruction. Their conscience enjoys the profoundest calm. Unshaken in their faith, assured that they are walking in the right way, they fear only their own weakness, and, secure in

the help of Him Who strengthens them, they have a foretaste of the eternal blessings which are promised to them.

Prayer. O truly blessed, he who is not offended in Thee, O Jesus, Who adores Thee, loves Thee, and follows Thy blessed example! such are my resolutions: vouchsafe to confirm them. Yea, my Saviour, it is Thee Whom I will henceforth to follow and to serve, it is in Thee alone that I will place all my hope and all my love. Enlighten more and more my mind with Thy pure light, make me to walk with a firm and constant step in the practice of Thy holy commandments, open my heart to Thy divine Word, and make it teachable to the inspirations of Thy Divine Spirit; give me that quickening spirit, that is, that spirit of detachment, gentleness, humility, and penitence, which can make me taste and practise the divine maxims of Thy holy Gospel. Amen.

Meditation XCII.

DISCOURSE OF JESUS CHRIST RESPECTING S. JOHN BAPTIST AFTER THE DEPARTURE OF HIS MESSENGERS.

Jesus, in this discourse, 1. utters the praises of S. John Baptist; 2. He then speaks of the kingdom of heaven, preached by S. John Baptist; 3. He speaks against the conduct which the chiefs of the Jewish nation had adopted towards Himself and S. John Baptist. S. Matt. xi. 1—9. S. Luke vii. 24—35.

FIRST POINT.

The praise of S. John Baptist.

1. Jesus praises the firmness of his courage. *And when the messengers of John were departed, He began to speak unto the people concerning John, What went ye out into the wilderness for to see? A reed shaken with the wind?* S. John Baptist, who had withdrawn

from his childhood into the desert, had remained there until God called him to the public ministry of preaching, that is to say, until the age of thirty years. His public life was as austere as was his private life. In giving scope to his zeal, he had changed nothing in his manner of life, in his feelings, nor in his outward appearance. At the court, he was such as he had been in the desert. Neither the favours, nor the threats of the monarch had been able to shake his courage. Although at that moment in prison, he was as much devoted to the duties of his mission, as when he had enjoyed his entire freedom. Alas! how different am I, oh my God, it is I who am like that reed, which bends to every wind. I know my duty, and in order to fulfil it, I form the best resolutions; it seems to me, in the fervour of my resolutions, that I am a cedar that cannot be shaken; but at the least temptation, or the slightest occasion in which distaste or human respect are in question, all my resolutions vanish away. More feeble than a reed, a breath makes me bend, throws me down to the ground, and I know myself no longer.

2. Jesus praises the austerity of the life of S. John Baptist. *But what went ye out for to see? A man clothed in soft raiment? Behold, they which are gorgeously apparelled, and live delicately, are in kings' courts.* Luxury in dress, sumptuous appointments, the delicacies of the table are to be found amongst the rich and powerful of the world; those who enjoy a moderate fortune approach as nearly to them as they can, often far beyond their means; those, who have renounced this soft and self-indulgent life, return to it often in a manner very contrary to that which which is edifying. But it was not thus with S. John Baptist. What raiment! what food! what a man! and how fit he was to preach repentance! But how do I practise it? I am not in the palace of kings; if I were, I should not be exempt from the obligation I am under to repent, and yet, in the station in which I am, yet do I give no proofs of repentance; I am unwilling to forego anything, or to give up

any indulgence, and if I have not every thing I desire, it is no merit on my part, since it is not without murmuring that I dispense with it.

3. *Jesus praises the greatness of the ministry of S. John.* But *what went ye out for to see? A prophet? Yea, I say unto you, and much more than a prophet, This is he, of whom it is written, Behold I send My messenger before Thy face, which shall prepare Thy way before thee. For I say unto you, Among those that are born of women, there is not a greater prophet than John the Baptist.* S. John was a prophet, because he announced the Messiah; but he was more than a prophet, in that not only did he set forth that the Messiah would come, but in that he showed Him as present; because he made Him known as the Saviour and Judge of men; because he prepared His way by preaching repentance, and because lastly, he was himself the subject of prophecy, being that messenger of whom the prophet Malachi spoke, who was to be sent to prepare the ways of the Lord; thus Jesus Christ sets forth, that of all those who were born before John the Baptist, there was no prophet, there was no man who was greater than he, none whose calling was so eminent, or who had acquitted himself of his mission with more dignity and fidelity. Oh happy S. John, to merit to be thus praised by Christ! but woe be to us, who seek only the praises of men! Jesus praises that which is worthy of praise, but men often praise that which is worthy only of blame; Jesus praises S. John Baptist in adversity and in prison, men only praise those who are in prosperity; Jesus does not praise S. John either in his own presence, or in that of his friends and disciples, and men only praise us to our faces, or before our friends, and often, when we are absent, only speak of us in order to blame us, to criticise or to censure us? Is it not thus that we praise others?

SECOND POINT.

Of the kingdom of heaven, preached by S. John Baptist.

1. *Its excellence. But he that is least in the king-*

dom of God is greater than he. S. John Baptist, in his office of forerunner, was above all other prophets, because he foretold the kingdom of God as being at hand, and as beginning already to be established. This kingdom of heaven is the Church of the Messiah, the Church of Jesus Christ; the Church which comes from heaven, and which will return to heaven, a Church which is heavenly in its Author, in its mysteries, in its worship, in its sacraments, in its precepts, in its doctrines. Now, if the employment of S. John Baptist, which consisted in preaching the approach of this celestial kingdom, and in preparing men's minds for its coming was so great, how much greater is the dignity not only of those who, in this heavenly kingdom, are destined to hold the first places in it, to govern it, to establish it and to ordain her ministers, but even of those who hold the lower offices in her, who instruct and form Christians, who set forth the mysteries of God and of His Christ, to whom are committed the ministry of reconciliation, the distribution of the treasures of heavenly grace, on whom is bestowed the office of communicating the graces of the Sacraments, wherewith to nourish themselves and true believers, and lastly, of perpetuating the kingdom of heaven until the end of the world! oh priests, oh Christians! how great is our dignity, how august our happiness! But if, through the dignity of our position, we are raised above S. John Baptist, what efforts should we not make in order to approach to his virtues? What ought to be our life, our purity, our union with God, our insensibility to things of earth, our earnestness about the things of heaven!

2. The sufferings which the heavenly kingdom promises. *And from the days of John the Baptist until now the kingdom of heaven suffereth violence, and the violent take it by force.* S. John Baptist began to preach the kingdom of heaven, and forthwith this divine kingdom, hardly announced, hardly begun, has been a prey to violence. Its enemies, listening only to their jealous fury, have sought to ruin it, to scatter it, to anni-

hilate it from its first commencement. S. John had only begun his preaching, when the Pharisees persecuted him, and obliged him to withdraw. This saintly forerunner is now in prison, whence he will only come out to suffer a violent death; such is the lot of the Church of Jesus Christ; persecuted from its very birth, it will be so to the end. But it is the kingdom of God, the kingdom of heaven, and men can do nothing against God, nor earth against heaven, and this Church will continue till the end of the world. The fury of tyrants will multiply the number of Christians, and the violence of the tortures will add to the crown of the martyrs. But this lot which the Church will continually experience is also that of each one of its members, who will not enter into the glory of heaven, unless they have done violence to themselves, to their natural inclinations, to their evil propensities, and to their passions.

3. The economy of the kingdom of God. *For all the prophets and the law prophesied until John. And if ye will receive it, this is Elias, which was for to come, He that hath ears to hear, let him hear.* Let us not weary of admiring the works of God in the religion which He has given unto men; its foundation has been always the same, but the form of it has been different according to the different dispensation revealed by God to men. The entire development of the adorable mysteries which it contains, and of the ineffable benefits which it bestows, has been reserved to the time of the Advent of the Messiah, and of the establishment of that Church, of which Jesus Christ is the Head, and which is called the reign of God, the kingdom of heaven, which S. John Baptist was the first to preach, and of which he beheld the first foundation. Until the time of S. John Baptist, in all the times which preceded him, the tradition of the patriarchs, the law of Moses, and the preaching of the prophets have only been prophecies of the future establishment of this divine reign. The Jewish people were indeed the people of God, the synagogue-church of God; but that was not the reign

of God, the kingdom of heaven; it was only the shadow, the figure, and the promise of it. Jesus Christ is the *Sun of Righteousness*, as the last of the prophets calls Him, Who has arisen *with healing in His wings;* that is to say, Who has spread light, dispersed the shadows, fulfilled the types, and accomplished the promises. S. John Baptist was the middle point between the prophets and Jesus Christ. He has been the aurora which has announced the rising of that divine Sun. In order to make us understand what was the office of S. John, our Lord tells us that he is Elias, that same prophet whom God had promised *before the coming of the day of the Lord.* Such is the economy of the kingdom of God, or of the Christian religion; the last of the prophets announced the coming of S. John Baptist; S. John has set forth Jesus, and declared that He was the Messiah; Jesus has established the kingdom of God, and destroyed the reign of the devil; He has called His Apostles, and filled them with the Holy Ghost; the Apostles have laid their hands on their successors, and have conferred on them the like blessings, and thus on till our times, so that we can trace the ministry of our Church up to the times of the Apostles, and to Jesus Christ, and from Jesus Christ through S. John Baptist to the prophets and the law, and then through tradition, from the patriarchs up to the first man, to whom the first promises were made. What other religion than the Christian religion presents thus without interruption a prophetic and historical chain which includes all times? It is not a system of apparent resemblance, it is an executed plan, of which the monuments exist over the surface of the earth, and in the hands of those who cannot be suspected of any connivance. The Jews have the same prophetic books as Christians; schismatics and heretics have the same history of the Gospel as members of the Church. Oh divine and holy religion! it is those only who wilfully shut their eyes in order not to see, and close their ears so as not to hear, who can still refuse to acknowledge thee. What happiness to be born in this holy Church, to live and die in her!

THIRD POINT.

Of the conduct of the chiefs of the Jewish nation with regard to S. John Baptist and to Jesus.

1. Conduct compared with that of the people, and opposed to it. *And all the people that heard Him, and the publicans justified God, being baptized with the baptism of John. But the Pharisees and lawyers rejected the counsel of God against themselves, being not baptized of him.* When S. John began to preach and to baptize, all the people and even the publicans hastened to respond to the designs of God, and to embrace the repentance needful in order to receive the Messiah: but the great, the learned, the Pharisees, who made profession of the most exact observance of the law, the scribes, who made a profession of interpreting and explaining that same law, and of understanding it more perfectly, would not, for the most part, humble themselves to receive the baptism of John. They only sent to ask him if he were the Messiah, and when he answered that he was not, they contented themselves with remaining as they had been, in expectation of the Messiah's coming. They despised thus the designs of mercy which God had for them, and having refused through pride to enter into the dispositions of Providence, after having despised the precursor, they came at length to put to death the Messiah. All is great, all is important in the designs of God. He who despises the first means of salvation offered to him, in order to await others still greater, often misuses them all. Those who think themselves saints, wise and learned, lose themselves often through their pride, their false lights, and their false wisdom.

2. Conduct compared to that of children and like unto it. *Whereunto,* adds Jesus, *shall I liken the men of this generation? and to what are they like? They are like unto children sitting in the market place, and calling one to another, and saying, We have piped unto you, and ye have not danced: we have*

mourned unto you, and ye have not wept. For John the Baptist came neither eating bread nor drinking wine; and ye say, He hath a devil. The Son of man is come eating and drinking and ye say, Behold, a gluttonous man, and a wine-bibber, a friend of publicans and sinners! That is to say, to whom shall I compare this generation of unbelieving men whom nothing can move? whom do they resemble? They are like those naughty children, whom another troop of children reproach in the public places, with their bad temper, scorn and indifference to the invitations which are given to them; and such is the natural portrait of those of whom I speak; they are so well satisfied with their own artificial and critical spirit, that, under whatever form wisdom offers itself to them, they find some excuses whereby to dispense themselves from following it. And, in truth, the chiefs of the Jews, resting with ostentation on their holiness and their knowledge, being also as little moved by the austere life of S. John, as by the ordinary and holy life of Jesus Christ, blasphemed both equally. According to them, S. John was a wild and fierce man possessed by the devil, and Jesus was a man who loved to eat and drink, and was a friend of sinners. Such are still the discourses of the world, which, instead of profiting by the different kinds of virtues of which the Church offers to it the example, blasphemes against all which it will not imitate. According to it, if any one retires from the world in order to serve God, it is weakness of mind, disappointment, or spite which lead them to do so. Ah, say they, cannot one be saved in the world? If any one living in the world seeks to lead a regular and Christian life, then he is made a mock of, and is shunned. O perverse world! thou dost revile every thing, thou dost reject every thing by which thou mightest be saved! Alas! do we not too often follow the world, in its judgments and in its scorn?

3. Conduct compared to that of the children of wisdom, and contrary to it. *But wisdom is justified of all her children.* The world thinks itself wise and treats

as fools those who, in despite of its maxims, attach themselves to the maxims of Jesus Christ; but those believers whom it despises are the children of wisdom, and their conduct justifies the ways and the works of the wisdom of God; for whilst the falsely wise of this world misuse all in order to offend God, and to lose Him, and to remove themselves far off from Him, these children of Incarnate Wisdom make use of every thing in order to cling more closely to Him, to serve Him, and to save their own souls. In whatever situation God places them, in abundance or in indigence, in prosperity or in adversity, in health or in sickness, in tumult or in solitude, they are faithful to God, and everything contributes to their sanctification. And thereby is the wisdom of God justified in the measures which it employs for the salvation of man. Worldlings will not acknowledge it now; but they will acknowledge it at the last day, when they will be forced to own their follies, and to confess, but too late, that they have deceived themselves.

Prayer. Of which number am I, O my God? and how have I justified until now Thy Wisdom in all which it has done for my salvation? Bring my heart back to the right way by making it more humble, and then all Thy ways will appear right unto me, and I shall no longer regard ought but Thee, and that which comes to me from Thee. Be my strength and my support, O Jesus; sustain me, that I may not be like a weak reed in Thy service; grant that inviolably attached to Thy commandments, I may be made worthy of Thy glory. Amen.

Meditation XCIII.

CONTINUATION OF THE DISCOURSE OF JESUS CHRIST, AFTER THE DEPARTURE OF THE MESSENGERS SENT BY S. JOHN BAPTIST.

Jesus discovers here divers movements of His divine Heart. 1. a movement of indignation against those cities which did not respond to His grace; 2. a movement of praise and love towards God His Father; 3. a movement of love towards all men. S. Matt. xi. 20—30.

FIRST POINT.

A movement of indignation against those cities, which did not respond to His grace.

1. Jesus manifests the greatness of that crime. *Then began He to upbraid the cities wherein most of His mighty works were done, because they repented not. Woe unto thee, Chorazin! woe unto thee, Bethsaida! for if the mighty works which were done in you had been done in Tyre and Sidon, they would have repented long ago in sackcloth and ashes.* Jesus continues to complain of the conduct of the Jews. Seized with a movement of indignation mingled with grief and compassion, and addressing Himself to the cities which had not profited by His discourses, nor by the miracles which He had wrought there, He reproaches them with their sin of unbelief; a sin so much the more enormous, in that He had bestowed upon them signal graces, chosen favours in abundance, and in preference to other cities. Woe be to you, He says, ungrateful cities! because if the wonders which had been done in the midst of you, and which you misuse, had been done at Tyre and Sidon, idolatrous and corrupt cities, they would long ago have embraced the repentance, which I have preached to you in vain. You would have seen their inhabitants, humbled and contrite, clothed with sackcloth, and lying in ashes. Guilty of the same crimes, do we not deserve the same reproaches and the same anathemas? Let us

count, if we can, all the graces which God has bestowed upon us, all the means of salvation which He has procured for us; what use have we made of them? what profit have we drawn from them? We reject them, those graces, and we count as nothing the contempt with which we treat them. Ah! they would have converted and sanctified a multitude of those to whom God has not granted them; and we, ungrateful that we are, we think ourselves perhaps even innocent, after having neglected them.

2. Jesus sets forth to us what will be the punishment of this crime. *But I say unto you, It shall be more tolerable for Tyre and Sidon at the day of judgment, than for you.* Yes, at the day of judgment, ungrateful and impenitent cities will be treated with more rigour, will be condemned to greater punishments than heathen cities, and the most wicked cities which shall not have received the same graces. Alas! this great day is always out of our thoughts, and yet we ought always to have it before our minds, since everything will there be known, everything will be judged. At that day, we shall have to answer not only for the sins which we shall have committed, but also for the graces by which we have not profited. We pity the misfortune of those who are born out of the fold of the Church, and out of the pale of true religion, and they are to be pitied indeed; their sins cannot but draw down a miserable fate upon them in the day of judgment: but a thousand times more terrible will be the lot of bad Christians, a lot more terrible in proportion as they shall have misused greater grace. Let us examine our hearts and let us fear; for what use do we make, for the most part, of the blessings, the graces, and the gifts which God showers down continually upon us? What will be then our fate at the great day of judgment? Let us labour to avoid it, whilst we can, by a sincere repentance.

3. Jesus sets forth to us the source of this crime. *And thou, Capernaum, which art exalted unto Heaven, shalt be brought down to hell; for if the mighty works*

which have been done in thee had been done in Sodom it would have remained until this day. *But I say unto you, That it shall be more tolerable for the land of Sodom in the day of judgment than for thee.* Capernaum was a rich and opulent city. It comes to pass but too often that the wealth and splendour of a city inspire its inhabitants with a secret pride, which makes them despise the duties of religion and neglect the care of their salvation. Alas; everything becomes a source of pride; science, merit, fortune, nobility, reputation, even the holiness of our calling, everything inspires that pride which hardens the heart, and which makes persons believe themselves to be innocent, even whilst they are neglecting the greatest graces; thence arises that fatal calm, in which the mind is steeped till it no longer feels the necessity of repentance. But in the day of judgment, all this glory which dazzles us will be swept away, the intoxication of this pride will be dispersed; Jesus Christ will ask of us a rigorous account of the graces which we have despised, and He will exercise upon them a vengeance perhaps more fearful even than upon the crimes, the enormity and infamy of which cause us the greatest horror now.

SECOND POINT.

Movement of love and praise in the Heart of Jesus Christ towards God His Father.

1. Jesus blesses His Father for the Infinite Wisdom with which He governs mankind. *At that time, Jesus said, I thank Thee, O Father, Lord of heaven and earth, because Thou hast hid these things from the wise and prudent, and hast revealed them unto babes. Even so, Father: for so it seemed good in Thy sight.* God shews forth His justice and His mercy equally towards mankind: His justice towards the proud, whom He gives up to the blindness of their false wisdom; His mercy towards the humble, to whom He discovers the precious truths of salvation. I adore Thy judgments, O my God!

and I acknowledge with my Saviour, their equity and wisdom. Thou willest to have it thus, I will say to Thee at all times; Thou hast ordered it thus, I yield to Thy holy will, which is none other than my salvation. Far be from me all other knowledge and all other wisdom, which would only serve to blind me and to make me proud. Let others pride themselves in their worldly studies, which they care for only in order to display their talents and their learning; let others glory in their talents for increasing their wealth and their credit, in satisfying their ambition, in carrying out their wishes, and in procuring for themselves every kind of pleasure; as for me, Lord, I will know Thee only, Thy Will alone, and that whereby I may work out my own salvation.

2. Jesus thanks His Father for the abundance of the gifts which He has bestowed upon Him. *All things are delivered unto Me of My Father: and no man knoweth the Son, but the Father: neither knoweth any man the Father, save the Son.* Jesus Christ, as the second Person of the Holy Trinity, is in all things equal to His Father: but besides that, Jesus Christ, as man, of a reasonable soul and human flesh subsisting, has received from God His Father, the fulness of all His gifts, as much in that which regards the gift of knowledge, as in that which regards His power. I rejoice, O my Saviour, that God Thy Father has placed no limits to the precious gifts which He has bestowed upon Thee. Thou knowest all things, and Thou canst do every thing; nothing is hidden from Thee, and nothing is impossible to Thee: Thou alone hast a perfect knowledge of the heavenly Father, of His will, His designs, and the knowledge of the highest seraphim is as nothing compared to Thine. Ah! who can know Thee, O Jesus, what Thou art in Thyself, and what is the sublimity of Thy divine greatness? The angels wonder at it, without being able to comprehend it. God alone, Thy Father, from whom Thou dost derive it, knows it perfectly. All that I can do then, O my Saviour, and my

God, is to prostrate myself before Thee, to acknowledge my own nothingness, and to worship Thee.

3. Jesus gives praise to His Father for the power which He has given Him to communicate His knowledge to mankind. *Neither knoweth any man the Father save the Son, and he to whomsoever the Son will reveal Him.* It is not for Thyself alone, blessed Jesus, that Thou hast received the knowledge of all the mysteries of Divinity: Thou dost glory in the power that Thou hast to reveal them to whomsoever Thou willest. And, in truth, Thou hast revealed them by faith to all Christians who make a profession of believing them: but Thou hast also another manner more secret and more intimate by which Thou dost reveal them, which Thou dost reserve for the chosen souls whom Thou dost favour. Oh! happy those on whom Thou dost bestow such favours. How pure and full of delight is the knowledge which Thou dost communicate to them! They know God, Thy Father, they are penetrated with His divine Presence, which makes a deeper impression on their hearts, than does the presence of objects of sense to their eyes: they know Thee Thyself, O divine Jesu! they see what they owe to Thee, and that they are in Thee, and by Thee; and with what love does not the revelation of these mysteries enkindle them! Ah how fully does it compensate to them for the loss of the vain pleasures of the world, and of its vain amusements? O Jesus! if Thou wouldest deign to shed upon my soul one single ray of this divine knowledge, I should love thee with more ardour, I should serve Thee with more fervour: but why should I not hope for this from Thy mercy? Thou hast declared to us that Thou hast the power of revealing Thy divine secrets to those whom Thou willest, only in order to excite our ardent longings, and to lead us to desire to be made partakers of them. I ask this therefore, of Thee, O divine Saviour: behold me at Thy feet: enlighten my soul, enkindle my heart, that I may long for and love none but Thee.

* THIRD POINT.

Movement of love in the Heart of Jesus Christ towards mankind.

By this movement of His infinite love, Jesus invites us all, 1. to come to Him; 2. to learn of Him; 3. to submit ourselves to Him.

1. Jesus invites us to come to Him. *Come unto Me, all ye that labour and are heavy laden, and I will give you rest.* How can we come to Jesus? We come to Him by prayer, and the oftener we draw near to Him, the more confidence shall we have in Him. When is it more especially that Jesus invites us to come to Him? It is when we are in sorrow and in affliction, weighed down with labour and anxieties, groaning under the burden of our bodily and spiritual miseries. Ah! such is not the condition in which the world invites us to come to it. Then, even our most faithful friends weary soon of the recital of our misfortunes: and those whom we thought to be beholden to us, disown and forsake us. A man who is in affliction bears his misfortune with him every where, and becomes irksome to every one. It is Thou alone, O Jesus, Who art the faithful Friend, Who art always ready to hear us and to receive us. By what hope does Jesus invite us to come to Him? By the promise which He makes to us that He will comfort us in all our sorrows, that He will wipe away our tears, and soothe all our sufferings. How, after so true a promise, can we still persist in seeking for our consolation from created beings? No, no, they are too feeble to deserve our confidence: they can indeed bring us some distraction from our troubles, but this distraction, though it may hide for a moment the wound of our hearts, does not heal it. Thou alone, O Jesus, canst penetrate to this heart, canst hear its voice, know its miseries, comfort, and heal it. I come then to Thee, O tender and faithful Friend, O charitable Physician, O Almighty Saviour! I come to Thee, wearied with the tumult of the world and of my passions, laden with

the weight of my iniquities; comfort me, deliver me, solace me.

2. Jesus invites us to learn of Him. *Take My yoke upon you, and learn of Me; for I am meek and lowly in heart, and ye shall find rest unto your souls.* How can we learn of Jesus? We learn of Him by conversing with Him, by studying Him so to say, by meditating on His words, and by considering His actions. What do we learn from Him? That He is full of sweetness and humility; that He is good and compassionate; that He is not a hard and unreasonable master, but One Who is filled with tenderness, and who only desires to load us with benefits. Let us then submit ourselves to His commands, follow His laws, embrace His doctrine, and imitate His example. Alas! how long have we not been in the school of Jesus Christ, without having yet learnt this lesson, so simple and so easy, of gentleness and humility! We have then learnt nothing yet; for this lesson is the foundation and the summing up of all religion. If we are still to be seen filled with pride and haughtiness, quick-tempered and impatient, prompt to take revenge and self-willed in our conduct, censorious in our words, and hasty in our actions, to what school do we then belong? Ah! it is not to that of Jesus Christ, but to that of the world; for this is not the teaching of Jesus Christ, but of the world. We are the disciples of the world, and not of Jesus Christ. What is the fruit of the lessons of this divine Saviour? Repose of soul, tranquillity of mind, peace of heart. In vain shall we seek for this repose elsewhere than in meekness and humility; we shall only find every where else trouble, disquiet, uncertainty, cares and distresses. Let us be meek and patient, humble and submissive; then, firm in our faith, peaceable in our conduct, in quiet trust in an overruling Providence, we shall enjoy a perfect calm which nothing can trouble.

3. Jesus invites us to submit ourselves to Him. *Take My yoke upon you; for My yoke is easy, and My burden is light.* What is the yoke and the burden of

Jesus? His yoke is His commandments; His burden is His cross. At these words nature shudders. But we will not let ourselves be deceived; the devils, evil passions, sin have their yoke and their burden. It is not a question of choosing between carrying the yoke or not carrying it, but of choosing between carrying the yoke of Jesus Christ, or of carrying the yoke and the burden of sin. Wherefore does our Lord say to us, *Take My yoke upon you?* It is in order to declare to us that He leaves us a free choice to take it up or not to take it up. His yoke is not a yoke of bondage, but a yoke of liberty and deliverance. We are born under the yoke of the devil, of sin, and of evil passions. It is only by taking up of our free will the yoke of Jesus Christ, that we can free ourselves from this hateful and cruel bondage. Our Lord says to us, *Take upon you,* bear My yoke, carry it, as if to make us understand that as we take it of our own free will, so we ought to carry it openly and cheerfully; that we ought to make a pleasure and an honour of it, and put our joy and our glory in it. What does our Lord promise to those who shall take His yoke and burden upon them? He promises them that they shall find the yoke full of sweetness, and the burden infinitely light. How can that be? It is, that under this yoke and this burden, we are in a state in which God wills us to be; it is, that our Blessed Saviour will help us to bear the yoke and the burden by His grace, and lastly, that in so doing we are supported by the hope of an immortality of happiness to come. On the contrary, under the yoke of sin, we are without hope, without comfort, and necessarily tormented by the fear of an avenging God. This promise of the Saviour is confirmed by experience; the more faithfully we keep His commandments, the more we mortify our evil passions, the more we do violence to ourselves, the more truly we repent, the more shall we experience the sweetness which belongs to His service.

Prayer. Oh blessed yoke of my Saviour, I have been happy when I have borne thee, and I have only ceased to be so, when, deceived by the enticements of a false happiness, I have submitted to the yoke of my passions. Yoke of iron, overpowering weight, how long shall I groan under so hard a bondage? Deliver me from it, O my Saviour! break my bonds, restore me to liberty, I only ask to consecrate myself to Thy service, and to devote myself entirely to the faithful observance of Thy holy commandments. Amen.

Meditation XCIV.
THE WOMAN THAT WAS A SINNER AT THE HOUSE OF SIMON THE PHARISEE.

The Gospel offers to us here a picture of penitent love: it proposes to us for our meditation; 1. its characteristics; 2. its justification; 3. its reward. S. Luke vii. 36—50.

FIRST POINT.

The characteristics of penitent love.

1. It is active to seek for an occasion of manifesting itself, and of obtaining forgiveness. *But one of the Pharisees desired Him that He would eat with him. And He went into the Pharisee's house, and sat down to meat. And behold, a woman in the city, which was a sinner, when she knew that Jesus sat at meat in the Pharisee's house, brought an alabaster-box of ointment.* One can believe that all which S. Luke relates here took place in the city of Nain, and was the fruit of the discourses which Jesus Christ had just uttered there. There was present at that pathetic and touching discourse, filled as it was with the tenderest invitations to sinners, and of threats against impenitent hearts, a woman, whose bad life was notorious, and was the scandal of the city. This woman was touched by His Words, she became aware of the danger of her condition, she was seized with horror at her sinful life, and resolved to quit it without delay. She did not doubt that He Who had

changed her heart, and of Whom she had heard so many wonders, was the true Messiah, and that He had the power to forgive her her sins. Animated by this faith, she sought for an opportunity to manifest her grief, and to ask for grace from Him; and in order not to lose so precious a moment, she carefully kept in sight Him, from Whom she hoped for so great a blessing. At this same discourse, a Pharisee, named Simon, had been present, who was more just in his judgement, and less prejudiced against Jesus Christ than the other Pharisees; he was edified by our Saviour's words, and whether out of regard towards the new prophet, or in order perhaps also to observe Him more closely, he invited Him to eat with him in company with several other Pharisees. Jesus, Who had designs of mercy both on the Pharisee and on the sinner, accepted the invitation, and the woman, who was attentive to observe all that took place, was aware of it. O my God! how great is Thy mercy, how worthy of admiration is Thy Providence, and how important it is to be attentive to its ways in order to respond to its designs!

2. Penitent love is prompt and ardent to seize the first occasion which presents itself. *And stood at His feet behind Him.* As soon as the woman knew that Jesus was to eat meat at the Pharisee's house, she did not lose a moment, she did not await a more favourable opportunity; she hastened to her home, and fetched thence a box of precious ointment, and betook herself to the Pharisee's house. The shame of appearing before an assembly to whom she was known as an open sinner did not intimidate her; the fear of what would be said with regard to her conduct, or the reproaches of her companions in guilt on her change of life, did not keep her back. Having no other shame save for her sins, no other love than that of her Saviour, she enters into the banqueting-hall, and places herself behind Him, from Whom she awaits her salvation. Jesus, according to the custom of the country, was lying on a sort of couch, with His face towards the table, and His feet turned to

the outside, uncovered and without wearing any sandals. It is at these adorable Feet that the penitent stands in the humblest and most reverential attitude: and there, without being seen of the Saviour, although she was in sight of all the other guests, she manifests her grief and love.

3. Penitent love is careful to make good use of the opportunities which it finds. *And began to wash His Feet with tears, and did wipe them with the hairs of her head, and kissed His Feet, and anointed Them with the ointment.* The penitent sinner, placed at the Feet of Jesus, penetrated with the most lively grief, and burning with the deepest love, found herself unable to utter a single word. In a moment, her eyes are bathed with tears; she delights to shed them on the Feet of Him from Whom she looks for grace. Her tears become so abundant that the Feet of Jesus are as if they were bathed with them; she dries them with her hairs, kisses them with reverence, and waters them with the precious ointment which she had brought with her. Oh true penitent, how eloquent is your love! What heart could not but be moved at your tears, and not weep with you? Alas! I have sinned more than you, for I have misused greater graces than you; ought I not then to shed a torrent of tears at the Feet of my Saviour, especially since those Sacred Feet have been pierced for love of me? O generous woman! your penitence is a true sacrifice, a perfect holocaust! What fitter way could there be of repairing the disorders of your past life, than by employing all that ministered to your sins as means to your reconcilation! You sacrifice to a grief that is but too just, all that has served to nourish your passion, or to enkindle it in the heart of others. You offer to God what you have employed hitherto in a criminal manner in order to lead others astray. Your eyes have been the organ of evil desires, and you disfigure them by the abundance of the tears you shed; you extinguish the impure and contagious fire of their glances in the waters of repentance; you fix upon the Feet of Jesus

their ill-regulated movements, which formerly were the instruments of sin, and they have now no motion save that of grief. Your mouth which has been defiled, is now purified by the kiss of reverence which it gives to the Feet of Jesus, the kiss which is the token of your reconcilation with God. That hair which you have adorned with so much care, and made use of to draw down admiration on yourself, now dishevelled and disordered only serves you to wipe the Feet of the Saviour which you have watered with your tears; those perfumes with which you have embalmed a sinful flesh of which you have made an idol, you pour them now on the lifegiving Flesh of Him, Who alone is worthy of all our homage; and thus you offer to the Lord as a holocaust all that has contributed to your sinful pleasures. How great is the peace of your soul amidst this complete sacrifice! Never have you found as great satisfaction in crime, as you now taste a sweetness in the exercise of penitence. Nevertheless your Saviour does not look at you, He does not speak to you; but you are content that He does not repulse you; you esteem yourself too happy in that by permitting you to testify your love to Him, He appears to accept it. And, in truth, without apparently responding to the generosity of your actions, your Incarnate God supports their fervour. Do not grow weary then; without uttering a word, cease not to solicit the grace you desire; continue to prepare your heart for it; soon Jesus will speak, His eyes will be turned towards you, and the words which He will address to you will set the seal to your happiness.

SECOND POINT.

Justification of penitent love.

Now when the Pharisee which had bidden Him saw it, he spake within himself, saying, This man, if He were a prophet, would have known who and what manner of woman this is that toucheth Him: for she is a sinner. The Pharisee, who was a spectator of that which was taking place, was inwardly offended, not at the woman herself, as that which she was doing was not entirely unwonted, but at Jesus, Who allowed Himself to be approached by a person, who was well known for the disorderly life she led; for it was amongst the Pharisees, a point of religion not to suffer the companionship of sinners. This man, he said to himself, not being an inhabitant of this city, may very likely be ignorant of the evil repute of this woman; but if he were a prophet, he would know through supernatural enlightenment, that this woman is a notorious sinner, and He would not permit her thus to approach Him. Alas! how little it needs to lower in our minds the good opinion we have of others, however well founded that may be. Jesus had compassion on the error of the Pharisee: He willed at the same time to enlighten him, to comfort the penitent woman, and to teach us.

1. The Pharisee is enlightened. *And Jesus answering said unto him, Simon, I have somewhat to say unto thee. And he saith, Master, say on.* After this interchange of civilities which was fitted to arouse the attention of the bystanders, Jesus explains Himself thus, *There was a certain creditor who had two debtors: the one owed five hundred pence, and the other fifty; and when they had nothing to pay, he freely forgave them both. Tell me therefore, which of them will love Him most? Simon answered and said, I suppose that to whom he forgave the most. And He said unto him, Thou hast rightly judged.* The design of the Saviour was to make it felt that God was in reality less loved by the proud Pharisee than by the humble sinner. With this view, he sets forth a parable, in which He represents Simon and the sinner, under the character of two debtors, both equally insolvent, and He represents Himself under the figure of the charitable creditor who remits to both the entire debt. He had brought the Pharisee to agree that the one who ought to love best the liberal creditor was the one to whom he had remitted most, and on this decision, this is the conclusion which He drew from it;

you judge that the love which gratitude inspires is proportioned to the greatness of the benefit which has been received, your conclusion is just: but if you judge that in the order of nature, after the remission of the debt and the gratuitous gift made of it by a creditor to two debtors, whose debts are unequal, the one whose debt is the most considerable must love the most; so also in the order of grace, you must remark the same in spiritual debtors, that is to say in penitent sinners, before their debts, that is, their sins are remitted to them. The most guilty are generally the most fervent: they have the deeper love, because they are laden with a heavier debt: and because they hope for or obtain a greater mercy. In order to convince you of it, I need only to compare you with this woman whom you despise. *And He turned to the penitent woman,* who had been waiting, longing, for one look of pity, *and said unto Simon, Seest thou this woman? I entered into thine house, but thou gavest Me no water for My Feet; but she hath washed My Feet with tears, and wiped them with the hairs of her head. Thou gavest Me no kiss; but this woman since the time I came in hath not ceased to kiss My Feet. My Head with oil thou didst not anoint, but this woman hath anointed My Feet with ointment. Wherefore I say unto thee, Her sins which are many are forgiven:* you must judge, according to your own decision, that so it must be, *for she loved much,* as she hath testified by her deeds of which you have just been the witness; *but to whom little is forgiven, the same loveth little.* The Pharisee answered nothing; but he must have clearly seen that Jesus not only knew the woman, but also that He had penetrated into the secret thoughts which he had had. He ought to have perceived that Jesus was He whom the Prophets had foretold, that is to say, the Messiah Whom God, His Father had entrusted with all supreme power, and the power of forgiving sins. Happy if this salutary instruction led him to love with more ardour, Him, Who had enlightened him with so much wisdom, power, and goodness! Happy shall we be, if we love perfectly a God, Who has made grace and happiness the price of an affection, the most natural to man, and that to which he is the most sensible and most keenly alive.

2. *The penitent is comforted.* What was the transport of joy of this weeping woman, when Jesus turned Himself round towards her, and that she heard Him, not only approve of that which she had done for Him, but also praise and extol it, and Himself relate what had taken place in all its details, and with all the circumstances connected with it! Ah! who would not hasten to serve so good a Master, Who sees all, and Who rewards us for all that we do in His service?

3. *We receive instruction ourselves.* Let us learn from the Pharisee not to despise any one, nor to compare ourselves with others save only in order to humble ourselves. Alas! in how many respects are we not inferior to those over whom we give ourselves the preference! Often even at the Table of the Lord, the righteous man is less fervent than the newly converted sinner. Let us learn from the penitent woman to mourn over our sins, with compunction at the feet of our Saviour, to employ in His service and in deeds of penitence those members of our body which we have hitherto employed in sin, and to make use of in relieving His suffering members, that wealth which has only ministered till now to our luxury and vanity. Let us learn from our Saviour, that He is that charitable and compassionate creditor, ready to forgive us all, if we will only entreat Him with importunity; that we are His debtors, that our debts are our sins, with which we are all laden, some more, some less. Let us learn from the Saviour that He is rich in mercy, but that He requires from us that we should love Him so much the more ardently, as we have offended Him so much the more grievously; and that on these conditions, not only will He not condemn us at the last day, but that He will plead our cause in the face of the assembled universe.

THIRD POINT.

Reward of penitent love.

1. The forgiveness of sins. *And He said unto her, Thy sins be forgiven.* The Saviour makes known to this woman, that God has mercy on her. He does not content Himself with having already declared her forgiveness to Simon. He desires to give to herself the full and complete joy of her forgiveness; He wills that she should taste the ineffable peace of a soul returned to grace, and that she should learn it from His own lips. *Thy sins are forgiven.* O powerful and consoling words! It is Jesus Christ, Who still pronounces them by the mouth of His ministers, and they have the same power on us if we receive them with truly penitent hearts. The Pharisees who were present murmured at them in secret. *And they that sat at meat with Him began to say within themselves, Who is this that forgiveth sins also?* This Pharasaical spirit still prevails amongst us: it prevails still in several who are not content to murmur in secret, but who complain loudly, and seek to trouble the peace of the Church. The ministers of Jesus Christ cannot exercise too great precautions in their dealings with sinners, avoiding, on the one hand, too easy an indulgence which should encourage a sinner to continue in sin, but at the same time, avoiding an excessive rigour with regard to a penitent whose heart has been touched by grace, and who has turned to the Father of mercies with a spirit of contrition and love, of trust and humility.

2. The reward of penitent love is salvation and the health of the soul. Our Lord did not will to reply to the inward murmurings of the Pharisees, nor to discover their thoughts. His charity made Him speak and be silent by turns. He passed over the want of good dispositions which He beheld in the Jews, and gave to the penitent woman the joy of a good conscience. *And He said to the woman, Thy faith hath saved thee.* There is in the soul, as in the body, a state of strength and health, which is more than mere exemption from sickness.

This spiritual health and strength, which is one of the results of true penitence, renders the soul fit for the exercise of virtue and constant in the practice of virtue. If pious souls, who often approach to the Blessed Sacrament, find themselves still in a state of langour and feebleness, it is owing to their want of faith. Let them examine themselves if no human considerations enter into the spirit of the *faith* in which they frequent this Sacrament; if custom, habit, vanity do not animate them; if they go there with firm *faith* in the presence of Jesus Christ to heal and to bless them? Ah! how many blessings are often lost, for want of this practical faith; how many sins, how many profanations do we not commit to which we wilfully blind ourselves! The penitent woman sees only in Jesus Christ the Messiah promised to Israel, her Saviour and her God, and it was this *faith* which saved her. She was, perhaps, the only one, at least she was the first, who sought Jesus Christ only for the forgiveness of her sins.

3. The reward of penitent love is peace of heart. The last words which the Saviour says to this happy penitent set the seal to her happiness and her perfect reconciliation. *Go in peace.* Oh sweet peace! Oh happy fruit of true repentance! The greatest sinners experience its happiness, when after having sounded the depth of their conscience, without any self deception, and penetrated with sorrow and love, at the feet of an offended God, after having overcome all false shame, they lay bare their sins without dissimulation. But how does it happen sometimes that pious souls, who fear sin more than death, are sometimes deprived of this sweet peace, and are on the contrary, filled with the most lively disquietude respecting their sins? Ah! it is an artifice of the enemy of peace, who troubles these souls with needless scruples, in order to deprive them of the fruits of their repentance, in order to hinder them from making advances, to give them a distaste of virtue, and, if he can, to make them turn back again. Disquieted souls, resist the enemy of your salvation by a perfect confidence in

your Saviour's mercy and goodness. You have done what you could, to regain the graces you have lost; you have sought, by repentance, to make amends for the past. Well then, why should you spend yourselves in anxious scruples, when you ought to spend yourselves in love? If you believe that your sins are forgiven, why do you not take pains to testify your gratitude? If your sins are forgiven, your disquietude only offends Him Who has forgiven them; if they are not, your disquietude will not obtain their pardon, but love alone can effect this miracle, and supply that which has been wanting in your repentance. Less disquietude as regards the past, and more fervour with regard to the present. Love much; love is the surest mark of the remission of sins. Love and enjoy the peace which penitent love procures.

Prayer. Let Thy love, O my God, be then the principle and soul of my repentance: let my grief be that I have offended a God so good, a Father so tender and so beneficent. Grant that I may love Thee much, because I have sinned much: grant that I may receive at Thy hands the forgiveness of my many sins, because I have loved Thee much. Kindle in my heart that fire of divine love, which made in one moment, of the vilest and most despicable of women, the object of Thy tenderness: which by purifying her, made her worthy of Thee, so that I may partake in the reward of her love both in time and in eternity. Amen.

Meditation XCV.

OF THE HOLY WOMEN WHO MINISTERED UNTO JESUS WHILST HE WAS ENGAGED ON HIS MISSIONS.

Consider, 1. the benefits they received from Christ; 2. the gratitude which they testified to Him during His life; 3. the attachment which they cherished for Him after His death. S. Luke viii. 1—3.

FIRST POINT.

Of the benefits which they received from Christ.

And it came to pass afterward, that He went throughout every city and village, preaching and shewing the glad tidings of the kingdom of God: and the twelve were with Him: and certain women who had been healed of evil spirits and infirmities, Mary called Magdalene, out of whom went seven devils.

1. The first benefit which these holy women received from Christ, was the healing of the body. They had been healed of their sicknesses, and some of them had been delivered from evil spirits. The healing of the body, is, of all the benefits of God, that of which we are the most sensible, and which most naturally excites us to gratitude. How often have we not received this benefit from God, and in what have we testified our gratitude to Him! How often have we promised to God, in the time of sickness, that if He would restore us to health, we would employ it wholly in His service! How have we acquitted ourselves of this promise? Let us acknowledge our ingratitude, let us bewail it, and make the best amends we can for it.

2. Second benefit, the remission of their sins. The healing of the body which Jesus worked, was the figure of the healing of the soul, which He bestowed at the same time, as He makes known to us Himself, by declaring distinctly to several of those whom He had healed that their sins were forgiven. As the healing of S.

Mary Magdalene was as singular as her condition was surprising, the Gospel makes a special mention of her. We must not be surprised that this woman should have been possessed of seven devils, since we have seen elsewhere a man who was possessed of a legion of devils. Is it not truly to be delivered from evil spirits, when we are delivered from sin? Now, how often have we not received this great benefit from God? Has only one evil spirit gone out of us? Have not seven gone forth from us? Let us recall to mind, if we can, the number, the greatness, the diversity of our sins; and penetrated with gratitude to our Divine Benefactor, let us consecrate ourselves entirely to His service.

3. Third benefit, the gift of faith. It was not possible to have been miraculously healed by the Saviour without believing in Him. He even required faith in Himself as a condition of healing; how much more lively must this faith have become through the cure itself? This precious gift of the faith of Christ, we have received in our baptism, and from our earliest youth we have been instructed in the divine mysteries which this adorable faith contains, and in the eternal benefits which it promises to us: lastly, we have come into the world when this faith spreads its brightest light on all sides, and shines forth throughout the world: how have we profited by so great and so special a benefit? Have we honoured and defended it? Have we never blushed to confess it? Have we not run a risk of losing it, by joining in conversations, or reading books which we knew were likely to unsettle our faith, and prove dangerous to us?

SECOND POINT.

Of the gratitude they testified to Jesus during His life.

And Joanna, the wife of Chuza, Herod's steward, and Susanna, and many others, which ministered unto Him of their substance.

1. These holy women consecrated their worldly possessions to Him. Jesus was poor; He went about

accompanied by His twelve apostles, who were as poor as Himself. He never worked any miracles to supply His own private needs, nor for His own subsistence or that of His disciples. In the cities, He found those who thought it an honour to receive Him at their table, and others who gave alms to His apostles: but in the country places, and in the villages whither His zeal led Him, far from finding help for His own necessities, He only found poor, to whom He caused to be distributed the greatest part of the alms which had been given Him for His own use. It was especially then, that these holy women ministered unto Him of their substance, and provided Him with things needful for His wants: thus they co-operated in the establishment of the kingdom of God, and had a share in the ministry and rewards of the Apostles. If Jesus gives here in His own person, an example of disinterestedness to the ministers of His gospel, He gives us also, in the person of the holy women who succoured Him, an example of the manner in which we may testify our gratitude to Him. It is then in the order of the divine appointment, established by the example of Jesus Christ Himself, that as Christian women cannot teach the truths of the Gospel, having received neither the grace of the apostolic mission, nor the power of preaching the divine word, yet they can have a share in the ministry of the Gospel, either by their alms, or by the assistance which they give in providing for the needs of Christ's ministers. But it is for their needs alone, not for their luxuries and in order that they may live at their ease, that Christ permits that they should receive assistance, that they may not be chargeable to any one. S. Paul has set forth the justice of this kind of succour, although in general he did not make use of it. If we have sown unto you spiritual things, is it a great thing if we shall reap your carnal things. For it is written in the law of Moses, Thou shalt not muzzle the mouth of the ox that treadeth out the corn. Doth God take care for oxen, or saith He it altogether for our sakes? For our sakes, no doubt, this is written, that he that ploweth should plow in hope: and he that thresheth in hope should be partaker of his hope. Nevertheless we have not used this power: but suffer all things, lest we should hinder the Gospel of Christ. (1 Cor. ix. 9—14.) This great apostle worked with his own hands, that he might not, as he said, hinder the progress of the Gospel; but he preached to the Gentiles and lived amongst them, and Jesus Christ and the apostles lived in Judea and amongst the Jews.

2. These holy women consecrated to Him their persons. They did not content themselves with furnishing pecuniary succours only to their Saviour, they followed Him themselves, they repaired to places where He was likely to pass or to sojourn, they ministered to Him, and His disciples, they were present at His discourses, and were witnesses of His miracles, and thus by testifying to Jesus their gratitude, they received from Him fresh favours: and it is thus that we shall experience His favour and grace in proportion as we devote ourselves to His service.

3. These holy women consecrated to Him the affections of their hearts. It is through our hearts only that we can be pleasing to our Saviour. The three holy women who are here named were free from all domestic ties. Joanna was a widow and without children. Magdalene and Susanna were unmarried, and being free to act as they willed, they followed Jesus, and attached themselves to His service. Happy lot! blessed choice! how worthy of imitation by those who are situated under similar circumstances! Amongst the other women who followed Jesus and who are not named here, there were others who were bound by the ties of marriage. No condition of life is excluded from the service of God, from the hope of pleasing Him, and obtaining from Him singular favours. These holy women knew how to find the secret of consecrating themselves to the service of Jesus, without neglecting the duties of their station. We sometimes plead the perplexities of our station, in order to excuse ourselves for our remissness in the

service of God; but if our hearts were truly God's, we should find out a way of reconciling our various duties.

THIRD POINT.

Of their devotion to Jesus after His death.

1. They prepared to embalm His body. Although we shall enter more into detail on this subject in its own place, in the order in which the Evangelists relate it, yet we may say a few words respecting this point here in connection with the subject in hand. Observe first, that amongst these holy women, Mary Magdalene holds the first rank, and was as remarkable for her courage, her zeal, her constancy and love, as by the strangeness of the possession from which she had been delivered. Amongst the holy women, she was the first who went to the sepulchre, the first to whom our Risen Lord appeared, and the first to announce His resurrection to the Apostles. Joanna is also mentioned amongst those who went to the sepulchre, and made known the resurrection of the Saviour. We do not find any further mention of the name of Susanna; doubtless she was with Mary Magdalene and Joanna, when they wished to go and embalm the body of their divine Master.

2. They saw Jesus ascend into heaven. Bound to the apostles by the same sacred bond which had bound them to Christ, after having made known to them His resurrection, they continued in the same fellowship with them, and followed their steps, and returned with them into Galilee, whence they followed them to Jerusalem, and there on the Mount of Olivet, they had the ineffable consolation of seeing their Divine Master leave the earth and ascend up to Heaven.

3. They were present when the Holy Ghost came down on the Apostles. After the Ascension they continued in prayer with the Apostles till the day of Pentecost; they were witnesses of the descent of the Holy Ghost on the Apostles. These all continued with one accord in prayer and supplication, with the women, and Mary, the mother of Jesus, and with His brethren.

Lastly they reign now in heaven together with Jesus Christ.

Prayer. Can one wonder, O Jesus, that these holy women should have been unwilling to leave Thee after Thou hadst delivered them from the bondage of the devil? How blessed is Thy service, O my Saviour! Who could leave Thee to seek for another Master? Give us likewise grace to follow their good example, and to love and serve Thee as they did. Amen.

Meditation XCVI.

A SICK MAN WHO HAD HAD AN INFIRMITY FOR THIRTY EIGHT YEARS CURED BY JESUS CHRIST, ON THE SABBATH DAY, BY THE POOL OF BETHESDA IN JERUSALEM.

Examine the circumstances which precede, which accompany, and which follow this healing. S. John v. 1—16.

FIRST POINT.

The circumstances which precede this healing.

1. The season. It was the season of one of the solemn feasts of the Jews. *After this there was a feast of the Jews, and Jesus went up to Jerusalem.* We have seen, in the preceding meditation, how Jesus, accompanied by His twelve apostles, went through the towns and villages. It was in continuing this exercise of His zeal, that He came with them to Jerusalem. He had only appeared once in that capital since the commencement of His public ministry. He came there on this second occasion in order to spend there the feast which was being celebrated, in order to instruct the Jews, and to give to them fresh proofs of His divinity. Great festivals are seasons of special grace, salvation and instruction. Do we render ourselves in a fit condition to avail ourselves of the special privileges which such holy seasons bring with them?

2. *The place.* *Now there is at Jerusalem by the sheep market, a pool, which is called in the Hebrew tongue Bethesda, having five porches.* In this place there was a pool, that is a bath built near one of the gates of the city, and surrounded by five porches or covered galleries. This pool had the same name as the gate close to which it was situated, and the gate was called in Latin *Probaticus*, in Greek, with a word signifying *sheep*, and in Hebrew, *Bethesda*, which signifies place of provisions, because it was by that gate, that a large number of sheep, lambs, and other animals necessary for the sacrifices of the temple came in from the country. This pool represents to us naturally the baptismal fonts which are placed at the entrance of our Churches, where the consecrated water is, as it were, a bath for the purification of the soul, which draws its virtue from the merits of the Lamb without spot, Who is daily offered up upon our altars.

3. *The assembly.* *In these lay a great multitude of impotent folk, of blind, halt, withered, waiting for the moving of the water.* The porticos of the pool were filled with a great number of sick people of every kind, who were awaiting the moment of their healing. There were also assembled there a number of people in health, some of whom were engaged in giving assistance to, or comforting the sick, and others who came there to be witnesses of the miracle which God was about to work. If we had but as much zeal for the health of our souls, as for that of our bodies! But alas! how many there are who think that they require no healing at all?

4. *The virtue of the pool.* *For an angel went down at a certain season into the pool, and troubled the water: whosoever then first after the troubling of the water stepped in, was made whole of whatsoever disease he had.* It is not said here whether the angel only came down once in a year, and on one of the feast days mentioned here, or whether he came down in the same manner at all the great feasts. Whatever it may be, this miracle, the only one of the kind on record, was

only granted to the city of Jerusalem. It foretold the coming of the Angel, He Whom God was about to send mankind, in order to prepare for them in His Blood, a spiritual bath, wherein they might cleanse their souls from all their infirmities. But this salutary bath, which is that of baptism and repentance, is not now the privilege of one single city, nor of any particular period, or day, but everywhere, at all times, and every day, we may descend into it, and be healed. Do not let us then defer the moment of repentance, especially at those moments of grace, when by some profitable remorse, or by the voice of some minister of God the depths of our conscience are stirred up, and troubled. Ah! let us profit without delay by this blessed agitation, do not let us seek for calm, save in being healed, and do not let us lose by our delays, a favour of which others may know how to profit.

5. The malady of him whom Jesus healed. *And a certain man was there which had an infirmity thirty and eight years.* It appears as though he were a paralytic. But this we know for certain, that for thirty-eight years, he had been afflicted with this infirmity; a sad picture of an habitual sinner, who has languished long in sin without repentance. His misfortune is, that the longer he has put off, the longer he will put off. Nothing is so dangerous as delay in these matters, for we never can know how long the opportunity of repentance will be granted to us.

SECOND POINT.

Circumstances which accompany the act of healing.

1. The look of Jesus on the sick man. *When Jesus saw him lie, and knew that he had been now a long time in that case.* Precious look, look of compassion and love! Alas! if God does not look upon us in pity, if He does not prevent us by His grace, we can do nothing, we cannot even know the infirmities of our soul, nor desire its healing.

2. The question Jesus puts to him. *He saith unto*

him, *Wilt thou be made whole.* The Saviour, Who was not ignorant either of the nature of his disease, or of the character of his affliction, knew also as well how desirous of healing he was; but it was more fitting that he should be led himself to acknowledge to the Saviour the greatness of his desire, and the insufficiency of his own efforts. How often does not God say to us, *Wilt thou be made whole?* We desire it, doubtless, and with too much anxiety; but this desire which we feel for the sicknesses of the body, is it not often wanting with regard to the sicknesses of the soul? Nevertheless, without this desire, on our part, this spiritual healing cannot be effected. Now this desire includes a sincere detestation of sin, a strict self-examination, and an honest confession of the faults of which we feel ourselves to be guilty, with a resolution which is not vague and feeble, but firm and stable, not to sin any more. If it is thus that we desire to be healed, we shall be healed. If till now, we have not been healed, it is because we have not desired to be so. Let us ask of God for this desire, let us ask Him to increase it unceasingly in us, to strengthen and support us. He knows our infirmity, our weakness, and all that is in us, better than we do ourselves.

3. Answer of the sick man to Jesus. This man did not know Him Who thus interrogated him, and much less what he might hope for from him. *The impotent man answered Him, Sir, I have no man when the water is troubled, to put me into the pool: but while I am coming, another steppeth down before me.* A very natural picture of the distribution of the good things of this world, after which so many persons hasten and sigh for, but which so few obtain. They are not given to those who are in need and indigence, who have good will and use their best endeavours, to those whose services and talents merit them: no, favour, or credit dispose of them, and dispense them with a caprice which deceives often the expectations of those whose hopes seem to be the best founded. It is not thus with

the gifts of grace: he who desires them, who asks for them, who strives to acquire them, is sure to obtain them. Can we say that we have no one to help us? Alas! enlightened ministers are not wanting to us; but it is we who are wanting to them.

4. The command of Jesus, and the obedience of the sick man. *Jesus saith unto him, Rise, take up thy bed and walk.* These words are full of greatness and majesty: Jesus Christ utters them, the malady ceases, and the sick man is healed. *And immediately the man was made whole, and took up his bed, and walked.* In order to draw down upon ourselves spiritual healing, let us see how we obey the commands of our Saviour: the commands to arise, to come forth from that evil company, to break off that engagement, that habit, to separate ourselves from all dangerous intercourse, to renounce that besetting sin: the command to crush that intimacy, to restore that ill-gotten possession, to burn those books, those pictures, which lead us into sin; the command to walk in the paths of repentance and piety, to pray, to watch, to lead a Christian life, to do good works. If we do nought of all this, or at least, if we do not make a single effort to overcome our faint-heartedness, alas! we are not healed.

5. The observance of the day on which this healing was effected. *And on the same day was the sabbath.* The great feasts of the Jews lasted eight days, of which only the first and last were celebrated by the cessation of labour. The Saturday which fell during the feast was the most solemn day, and it was that which Jesus chose in order to work this miracle, in order that the repose of the sabbath might give leisure to a greater number of persons to be the witnesses of the miracle, and that the inhabitants of Jerusalem might be more disposed in consequence to believe in Him. But the chiefs of the people were to be offended at Him, to take occasion of it to decry Him, to persecute Him, and to make Him die. The designs of God in all which He does, being specially directed towards the benefit of

mankind, the abuse which the wicked make of them is
no reason to Him to change the order of His decrees.
The Lord regulates His actions on the principles of
His wisdom, and not on the malice of men, and there
is nothing to be surprised at in His so doing; but that
which is worthy of admiration, is, that, by ways far above
all created intelligence, He causes the malice of the
wicked to serve to their own punishment, to the increase
of His glory, and the advantage of His gifts. It is thus
that the offence which the Jews take at this miracle
will draw forth the sublime instruction which we shall
trace out in the following meditation, and that their
hatred against Jesus, and the death which they caused
Him to suffer, will bring about the salvation of the universe; an essential principle, which answers so many
presumptuous and impious questions, and which teaches
us not to reason about the works of God, but to profit
by them.

THIRD POINT.

Circumstances which follow this act of healing.

1. Consider in the man who was healed, his answer
to the hypocritical scruples of the Jews. The people,
witnesses of so sudden and perfect a healing, were
doubtless filled with admiration; but the Jews, that is
to say, the Pharisees, the chiefs of the people and of the
synagogue, who had been for a long time embittered
against Jesus, and who could not doubt any longer
that it was He, who, on His return from Galilee, had
worked this miracle, only drew attention to that which
could furnish them with a pretext for censuring the
act, and decrying Him Who was the author of it. They
first of all addressed themselves to *him that was cured*,
and they seemed almost to make a crime of his cure.
It is the sabbath day; they said to him; *it is not lawful for thee to carry thy bed.* *He answered them, He
that made me whole, the same said unto me, Take up
thy bed, and walk:* as if he had said, I do only that
which has been commanded me: it is He Who has healed

me, who has told me to take up my bed; since He has healed me, He knows what is lawful for me to do, and I obey Him. He Who is powerful enough to work a miracle, is doubtless enlightened enough to be able to instruct me. Change of life in a converted soul, is never without those who censure it and murmur at it: a retired life, a modest exterior, abundant alms, assiduity in prayer, frequent communions, all this excites the criticism of the worldly; but be firm, let the world say what it will, imitate this sick man, shew that you are healed, and answer to your censurers that you only do that which He has commanded, Who has healed you, and that you will obey Him.

2. Observe the answer of the man who was healed, to the malicious curiosity of the Jews. *Then asked they him, What man is that which said unto thee, take up thy bed and walk?* He answered that he did not know who it was, that he did not know who had healed him. *And he that was healed wist not who it was; for Jesus had conveyed Himself away, a multitude being in that place.* The vain scruples of the Jews had been distinctly refuted: here their malicious curiosity remains ungratified. They often met with similiar mortifications on the part of those whom Jesus had healed, which their pride never forgave. Jesus had given them an example of humility in concealing Himself from the applause of the people: but the virtues of Jesus, like His miracles, only irritated them the more.

3. Meditate on the gratitude of the man who had been healed towards God. *Afterward Jesus findeth him in the temple, and saith unto him, Behold, thou art made whole; sin no more, lest a worse thing come unto thee.* The first use which the paralytic man made of his health, was to go to the temple to thank God for it, and it was there that he received fresh favours. Jesus found him there, made Himself known to him, and gave him the counsel not to sin any more, lest any thing more grievous yet should befall him. Christian soul, purified by the all powerful grace of repentance,

beware lest you fall back into sin, for fear that something yet more to be dreaded should happen to you, that is to say, lest you should die in your sins. Let gratitude for mercies received, let the fear of falling back into sin, lead you often to the foot of the altar; it is there, that, growing more and more in the knowledge of Jesus Christ your Saviour, and enlightened as to the perils which threaten you, you will learn to be on your guard, and to persevere.

4. Remark the zeal of this man for the glory of Jesus. *The man departed, and told the Jews that it was Jesus which had made him whole.* Let us spread abroad the greatness of Jesus, His power, and His mercy, let us seek to win over all hearts to Him: if we do not succeed, yet our zeal will not be without its reward.

5. Let us tremble at the sight of the hardness of heart of the Jews. *And therefore did the Jews persecute Jesus, and sought to slay Him, because He had done these things on the sabbath day.* Remark here the difference which there is between an upright heart, and a heart blinded by passion. The first goes naturally up to that which is true and essential: the second only raises difficulties, and avoids tracing things to their origin. The sick man here mentioned, in speaking of Jesus, always calls Him *He that made me whole:* the others, on the contrary, speak of Him as *he that said unto thee, Take up thy bed, and walk,* and there they stop. When any one has taken up a prejudice against another, they never refer save that to which has an appearance of evil in him, and never speak of the good he does, which might serve as his justification, or at least as an excuse. Such is still the method adopted by unbelievers; they only dwell upon that in religion at which they take offence, and at which their limited reasons revolts, and they always forget that He Who has given us that religion is He, Who with a word, drove out devils, healed the sick, raised the dead, and rose Himself from the grave: nevertheless, so long as the truth of those attested facts shall endure, and cannot

be destroyed, the reasonings of the unbeliever will only merit contempt, and hurt none but himself.

Prayer. This paralytic, who had had an infirmity for so many years, O my God, is the figure of my soul, which has languished for so long a time in sinful habits, which is covered with mortal wounds. Deign to cast upon it, O divine Saviour, one look of Thy love, deign to deliver it from the yoke which weighs it down, and dishonours it. I desire to be healed; yea, Lord, I do desire it, I ask it of Thee with all earnestness; I hate the disease from which I am suffering, and especially that palsy which hinders me from acting, speaking, walking, and running in the way of Thy commandments; I turn to Thee with the fullest trust. Bid me then, as Thou didst this paralytic man, to rise, to take up my bed, and walk in Thy commandments. Amen.

Meditation XCVII.

DISCOURSE OF JESUS CHRIST TO THE JEWS, AFTER THE HEALING OF THE MAN WHO HAD BEEN ILL FOR THIRTY EIGHT YEARS.

JESUS DECLARES HIS DIVINITY.

Jesus manifests, 1. His equality with God His Father; 2. the difference of Person in the unity of nature and operation; 3. the union of humanity and divinity in His own Person; 4. the authority He possesses over all mankind. S. John v. 17—26.

FIRST POINT.

His equality with God His Father.

The chiefs of the Jews, when they knew that it was Jesus, Who had commanded the sick man, who had laid at the pool of Bethesda, to take away his bed on the the sabbath day, took the opportunity of this act, to persecute the Saviour, and they reproached Him publicly with this pretended breach of the law. Instead of reasoning simply and naturally thus: this man has dispensed with the observance of the sabbath, but he, to whom He granted this dispensation, is a sick man whom He has cured before our eyes of an inveterate malady: He has then the right to do the former, since He has the power to perform the latter act, and He is, as His works prove, the Messiah Whom we look for; those prejudiced minds were delighted, on the contrary, to have a pretext to calumniate a man whom they would not acknowledge as the Messiah, because, although He was of the lineage of David, He was poor, without pretentions, and did not answer to the ideas of pomp, and to the preconceptions which they had formed of a king, a warrior, a conqueror, who should restore the temporal power of Judah, who should break the yoke of the Romans, and subject the nations to themselves: because, far from speaking of victory, and preparing for triumphs, He only preached renunciation, and practised self-denial: because lastly, far from making Himself agreeable to those whom He found installed as rulers and teachers of the people, He discovered their ignorance, unmasked and brought it into discredit. Those proud and ambitious men, faithless depositaries of the teachings of their sacred writings, and corruptors of the tradition of their fathers, flattered themselves that in bringing grave reproaches upon Jesus respecting the pretended transgression of the sabbath, He would not answer it in a manner which should be plausible enough to take from the accusation what it might have in it that was specious, and that by that means, they would prevent the people from deserting them, and following after Jesus. They said to Him then, or at least used equivalent terms: you lay claim to work miracles, and yet you transgress the ordinances of Moses! you heal a sick man who has kept his bed for thirty eight years, and without respect to the sanctity of the sabbath day, you make him violate the law by commanding this disciple of Moses to carry his bed on his shoulders, in the sight of an infinite number of spectators! What can we think of your miracles, which you only work whilst disobeying God! How can we reconcile a power which can only come from heaven, with such want of submission to divine commands? Your miracles are only illusions, and you are not sent by God. *But Jesus answered them, My Father worketh hitherto, and I work.* The Jews felt well the full force of this answer, and *therefore they sought the more to kill Him, because He had not only broken the sabbath, but said also that God was His Father, making Himself equal with God.* It was as though Jesus had said unto them, I know that God is My Father, and that He is eternally in repose and in action. If it is said that He rested on the seventh day, that rest has reference only to the first creation of all things; but it is not to be understood of the continual cares of His Providence: unceasingly, and without interruption, His Word upholds all things, His Spirit animates every thing, His Power preserves every thing; He does not cease to do good on the sabbath day as on other days: if He ceased on that day to do good under the pretext that it was the sabbath day, that day would be the most fatal of days to mankind, and the end of the world; and it is thus that I act myself, being His Son, and of power equal to His. Neither He nor I are subject to laws, to time, and to place. Equally and always Masters of nature, so that we make ourselves obeyed by it, we are so also of the law, so that we can dispense with its observance. What majesty in these words! what instruction in this discourse! An apology so sublime ought to have made a strong impression upon the minds of the Jews, and filled them with an astonishment still greater than the healing of the sick man. Jesus there announced very clearly that God was His Father, not by adoption and by grace, but by being begotten of Him, and that He was at the same time equal to His Father. If that which Jesus said was true, then He was the expected Messiah. The declaration which He made of His Divinity to the Jews ought at least to have seemed to them worthy of their most religious attention, and of the most serious examination: but this sublime answer, far from calming those enemies of Jesus, far from suspending their pursuit until they should have sufficiently examined into the matter, only served to embitter them and to make them more enraged. Prejudiced by their hatred and their jealousy, they beheld only in the miraculous cure, an unpardonable infringement of the law; they only looked upon the answer as a horrible blasphemy. Already homicides in will, they formed a conspiracy to become so in deed: they swore to compass the death of Jesus, because He called God His Father in the most literal sense, and because He attributed to Himself an equality of power with God; or rather out of hatred to Jesus, because He was not the Messiah they desired, they would not ask Him for an explanation of the parodox which He advanced, since they feared to allow themselves to be convinced: they arose against Him, instead of seeking to be taught by Him, and they resolved that He should die as a corruptor of public morals, as a blasphemer, and a false prophet. In vain did the holiness of His life, and the greatness of His works speak in His favour; self-interest, passion, and prejudice would not permit them to clear up a truth which was offensive to them, and such will always be the misfortune of prejudiced and jealous hearts. We do not listen to the explanations of a man whom we hate: we take it for granted without listening to his defence, that he cannot have any good reasons to advance. Notwithstanding the peril with which Jesus was threatened, this divine Saviour, Who did not fear to die for us, and Who willed to teach us not to fear to die for Him, continued the sublime discourse which He had begun; a divine discourse, which we ought to meditate upon with the deepest reverence, and the most lively gratitude. There was no one save the Son of God, Who could make use of such adorable language: it belonged to the beloved disciple to gather up the words He made use of, to the Holy Spirit to enlighten us as to their meaning, and to the Church, the Spouse of Jesus, to transmit to us these doctrines of faith, and to perpetuate them until the end of time, in instructing us what we must believe with regard to the mystery of the Holy Trinity, and of one God in Three Persons, and of the mystery of the Incarnation, or of the Word made man, Who is Jesus Christ Himself, in Whom we acknowledge two natures, the Divine and the human nature, subsisting in one Person, Who is the Person of the Word or the Son, the second Person of the All Holy Trinity : so that Jesus Christ our Saviour is true God and true man, a God-man, and man-God. With this faith, we shall understand the words of Jesus which follow, as much as is needful to penetrate us with the idea of His greatness and His power, that we may hold fast to Him as to our God and our Saviour, that we may place all our hope in Him, that we may serve Him with all our powers, and love Him with all our hearts.

SECOND POINT.

Difference of Person in the unity of nature and of operation.

Jesus, continuing to answer the Jews, or rather in answering to their fresh murmurings, explains still more at length that which He had only as yet proposed to them, and *said to them, Verily, verily, I say unto you, The Son can do nothing of Himself, but what He seeth the Father do ; for what things soever He doeth, these also doeth the Son likewise.* The formula with which Jesus begins His discourse, *Verily, verily, I say unto you*, and of which He often makes use hereafter, serves to warn us of the greatness of the mysteries which He is about to reveal to us, and of the attention accompanied with faith, which we must bring to the subject. The first defence against the Jews which Jesus sets forth, is the impossibility, that as Son of God, He should either do any thing or say any thing of Himself; an impossibility which has nothing disadvantageous in it, nor partakes in any way of the dependence in which created things stand with regard to the Creator; it simply establishes a union so close between the Father and the Son, that it constitutes unity: it establishes so essential and so perfect a relation, that the Son only wills and thinks, says and acts, according to that which the Father wills and thinks; a relation so intimate, an union so inseparable, which springs, as S. John tells us in the first chapter of his Gospel, from the Son having been from all eternity in the bosom of His Father, where He has seen, and been partaker of all the hidden mysteries of His Father; whence this oneness of power, knowledge and action; whence these operations in common, of the Father and the Son; whence the development of the following truths. In the adorable Trinity, the Father is the principle, Who proceedeth from no one, and from Whom the other two Persons proceed; the Son proceedeth from the Father by the way of understanding, knowledge and generation; the Holy Spirit proceeds from the Father and the Son by way of love and inspiration; but these three Persons, really distinct amongst themselves, are what they are eternally and of necessity, without inequality or dependence, having the same nature, the same power, the same operation, and being all Three but one only and the Same God subsisting in Three Persons. Let us adore this Being in Three Persons; a Supreme Being, eternal, and incomprehensible, the sight and the possession of Whom are promised to us, and will make the bliss of the blessed in Heaven.

THIRD POINT.

Union of humanity with Divinity in the Person of Jesus Christ.

Jesus adds; *For the Father loveth the Son, and sheweth Him all things that Himself doeth; and He will shew Him greater works than these, that ye may marvel.* Jesus continues to reveal His divine greatness; He discovers their source, or rather He goes back still to the same source. Another principle, He says, of the Divinity of the Son of man, is the love which His Father bears Him. He is His Son, He loves Him with a sovereign love; this infinite love produces an infinite communication of power, wisdom, knowledge, and of all ineffable, and incomprehensible perfections. *And sheweth Him all things that Himself doeth.* Jesus Christ manifests besides here the union of humanity with Divinity in His Person; a union which is substantial in Jesus Christ, and terminates in that Person of the Word in Whom humanity subsists. Thus in Jesus Christ, there are two natures and but one Person; Jesus Christ is God from all eternity, and man in time, and this Godman Who has appeared on earth, Who has saved us by the merits of His Death, Who is now addressing the Jews and is the Object of their hatred, it is He Who is the Object of the love and of the tender regards of God His Father. This God His Father conceals from Him nought of that which He does, He unveils to Him all the mysteries of Divinity; He makes known to Him all that, as man, He must do for the salvation of the universe, for the foundation and government of the Church, of Whom He has made Him the Head. When then Jesus healed the sick man at the pool, He did it only by virtue of the knowledge, through the operation, and conformably to the will of His Father. His Father will make known to Him yet greater wonders than these which He will work, such as the resurrection of the dead, that our admiration may be raised, and that by this means, we may gain a more perfect acquiescence in the truths of the faith which are revealed to us. Let us admire, praise, and offer thanks to God our Saviour, and let us strive to imitate Him, by looking to God our Father in all that we do, and resolving to act only according to His will, which is made known to us in His commandments, and by the inspirations of His Holy Spirit.

FOURTH POINT.

Of the rights which Jesus Christ has with regard to mankind.

1. The power to raise the dead, and to work every kind of miracle. *For as the Father raiseth up the dead, and quickeneth them; even so the Son quickeneth Whom He will.* The resurrection of the dead is the explanation of those greater works spoken of in the preceding verse, and the preceding verse explains the words of this one, that *the Son quickeneth Whom He will,* that is to say, always conformably to that which His Father shows Him, and wills, since the will of Jesus Christ, in that He is God, is the same as that of the Father, and that His will, in that He is man, is always subject to and directed by that of God His Father.

2. The power to judge. *For the Father judgeth no man, but hath committed all judgment unto the Son.* Jesus came into the world to save men and not to judge them: but in the next world, God His Father has committed to Him the power of judgment. God the Father will not judge mankind directly by Himself, and in a visible manner; He will judge by that God Whom He has appointed for that purpose, as He has appointed Him to be our Saviour, and this Man God is His well beloved Son.

3. The right to be adored. *That all men should honour the Son, even as they honour the Father. He that honoureth not the Son, honoureth not the Father which hath sent Him.* O my Saviour, O my Judge, O Son consubstantial with the Father, true God and true Man! I adore Thee, I render Thee my deepest homage as I render it to God Thy Father, acknowledging that Thou art but One God with Him, my Creator, and the Sovereign Master of all things. No, they who do not honour Thee do not honour God Thy Father. Mankind, who lost the tradition in early times of Thy future coming, lost at the same time the knowledge of the true worship of a God, and worshipped only idols. Those, who

since Thy coming, have refused to acknowledge Thee, or have remained on in their superstition, have only practised an external worship, unworthy of God, without inward holiness, without justice, without purity. And how can God accept the worship of such men, vain and proud, who refuse to render Him the homage He has prescribed to them, of these men conceived in sin, and defiled by their own iniquities, who refuse to purify themselves in the Blood of the Victim which has been prepared for them, and reject the Mediator which He has sent them?

4. The right to teach. *Verily, verily, I say unto you, He that heareth My word, and believeth on Him that sent Me, hath everlasting life, and shall not come into condemnation; but is passed from death unto life.* Although he does not yet possess that blessed life, he has a right to lay claim to it, for he has in his faith the pledge, the germ and the first fruits of it. Jesus is the Word of God, the consubstantial Word of the Father! With what reverence ought we not to listen to His words! with what fulness of faith ought we not to believe His mysteries! with what care ought we not to put His teaching into practice!

5. The power to give life. *Verily, verily, I say unto you, The hour is coming, and now is, when the dead shall hear the voice of the Son of God; and they that hear shall live. For as the Father hath life in Himself, so hath He given to the Son to have life in Himself.* Jesus has the power to give life. The natural life which He gives to those whom He raises from the grave, the life of grace which He gives to those whom He raises out of sin, the life of glory, eternal life which He gives to those who persevere unto the end, and whom He takes out of this world whilst in the life of grace: life which He gives, not by a ministry such as that of the prophets and apostles, but by an essential power which He has received from the Father, by which He is Himself the principle of life, as well as His Father. He then who hears the voice of Jesus Christ, who is obedient

to It, and becomes united to Him, comes forth from the death of sin, and has already passed from death unto life; he has in himself the life of grace, which brings him out of condemnation, and gives him a claim to the eternal life of grace, of which it is the germ and pledge.

Prayer. O precious life of grace! of what avail is the life of the body to me without thee? O Jesus! cause my dead or languishing soul to hear Thy voice, that, entering on a new life, an inward life, a spiritual life, a life of faith, I may renounce for ever the life of the flesh, of the senses, of my passions, and of the world: a miserable life which is only truly death, and which leads to eternal death. May all my joy, O my God, be to honour Thee in time and in eternity. Amen.

Meditation XCVIII.

FIRST CONTINUATION OF THE DISCOURSE OF JESUS CHRIST TO THE JEWS, AFTER THE HEALING OF THE MAN WHO HAD HAD AN INFIRMITY FOR THIRTY EIGHT YEARS.

OF THE LAST JUDGMENT OF JESUS CHRIST.

Our Saviour furnishes us here with matter for six reflections on the last judgment. S. John vi. 27—39.

1. Who is He that shall be the Judge?

It will be Jesus Christ Himself. The Father has given into His Hands the power to judge, and to pronounce the final sentence which shall decide for ever the lot of mankind. *And hath given Him authority to execute judgment also, because He is the Son of man;* because Jesus is that Son promised to the first man, Who should repair the fatal consequences of his sin, that Son, Who being equal to the Father, has taken upon Him our nature, and made Himself like unto us, and has redeemed us at the price of His Blood; this First Born, this Chief, this King of men, it is He Who will be their Judge. How terrible it would be to have as our Judge, a God, outraged in His Majesty, in His Benefits, in His Love!

2. When this judgment will take place.

The time is not far distant. It will come at length, and to each one of us the time is at hand. *Marvel not at this*, that the Father hath given to the Son authority to execute a sovereign judgment: for *the hour is coming*, when you yourselves will be witnesses of it. Yes, *the hour is coming*, and even if this last judgment were not to come till after millions of centuries, the hour is at hand to each one of us, because we have only our life-time in which to prepare for it, after which we can add nothing, nor take away any thing from that which will form the matter of that judgment. Let us hasten then, whilst we live, to put ourselves into the state in which we should wish to be then.

3. Who are those who shall be judged?

Every body, the living and the dead; we who live, and those who are dead, we who shall die, and those who will succeed us, *in the which all that are in the graves*, in whatever part of the world their bodies may be dispersed, *shall hear the voice of the Son of God*, which will call them together from the depths of the earth, and will reanimate in a moment their ashes throughout the whole extent of the earth. The archangel whom He will send forth will make known to them His will, His commands, and will summon them before Him. Then, in a moment, in the twinkling of an eye, all the dead will rise. *And shall come forth*. None will be able to resist that Almighty Voice, all will appear to receive the last sentence of their eternal doom. O ye, miserable men, who have placed all your confidence in death; ye who hope, that in consuming your bodies, it will annihilate your souls, that it will bury together with the spoils of your mortality your names and your ill-deeds, Ah! this death will betray you; it will restore you at that great day, laden with all your iniquities; it will obey Him Who has conquered it, and will render to Him the deposit which has been entrusted to it until the day of His vengeance.

4. What will be the matter of that judgment?

Our works. *They that have done good. They that have done evil.* It is by our works that Jesus Christ will judge us, and not by our reputation, by the esteem in which we stand amongst men, by the edifying appearances which we have taken care to keep up, not by the confused reports, by the praises of flattery, or the calumnies of injustice. By our works, that is to say, by our actions, our words, our thoughts, our intentions, our desires, the use we have made of our time and our means of grace, the way in which we have employed the good and the ills of life; works which will be manifest, which will no longer be hidden in the depths of our consciences, but unveiled and public; works which will appear what they are, without its being possible for us not only to hide them, but to disguise them, excuse them, or justify them.

5. What will be the decision of this judgment?

Heaven or hell. *They that have done good, unto the resurrection of life: and they that have done evil, unto the resurrection of damnation.* There will be no middle course between resurrection to eternal happiness, or to eternal misery, because there is none between being righteous or sinful. Upon those who shall have lived good lives, the Sovereign Judge will pronounce a sentence of eternal life; upon those who have led evil lives, He will pronounce a sentence of eternal condemnation. Ah! we must be more deaf than the very dead themselves, if we do not awaken at these appalling words, if fear and hope do not equally animate us to repent, to avoid every kind of evil, and to practise every kind of good.

6. What will be the nature of this judgment.

It will be just, and according to the will of God. *I can of Mine own self do nothing:* says Jesus Christ. *As I hear, I judge: and My judgment is just; because I seek not Mine own will, but the will of the Father which hath sent Me.* It is Jesus Christ, as Man, Who will pronounce the last sentence; but it is divine justice which will dictate that sentence. What Jesus Christ hears, is what He sees in the Light of His Father. His judgment will be just, because it will be conformable to the will of God. It will be just, that is to say, it will be without mercy, without diminution of the penalty, without any alleviation: there will be neither prayer nor intercession there. It will be just, that is to say, it will be without regard to rank, dignity, nobility, talents, or powers of mind: there will be no place for any of these distinctions there. It will be just, that is to say, it will be proportioned to the merits or demerits of each one; it will correspond exactly to the threats or the promises which have been foretold, and there will be room neither for complaints nor for murmurings. It will be according to the will of God; consequently, it will be different to ours, which are founded only on our own will, our inclinations, our tastes, our love or our hatred; our self-interest, our own advancement, our policy, or our ambition; on the esteem and opinion of men, or the customs and maxims of the world, and not on the law of God, the maxims of the Gospel, and the rules of conscience. It will be according to the will of God; consequently, it will be immutable, eternal, irrevocable, and without appeal; consequently, the execution will be inevitable, and will be carried out by that same will Which has created Heaven and earth, Which has caused us to be born, to die, and to rise again, and to which nothing can resist.

Prayer. Oh day of judgement, equally desired by the good, and dreaded by the wicked! remain ever in my thoughts, so that thou mayest be the rule of my thoughts, of my actions, and of all my conduct. O

Jesus! Who art the Author of the natural life, which is common to all mankind, and of the life of grace which distinguishes Thy followers and Thy friends, grant that I may only make use of the one, in order to gain the other, and that by a holy use of both, I may attain to the life of glory. Amen.

Meditation XCIX.

SECOND CONTINUATION OF THE DISCOURSE OF JESUS CHRIST TO THE JEWS, AFTER THE HEALING OF THE MAN WHO HAD HAD AN INFIRMITY THIRTY-EIGHT YEARS.

Jesus proves His mission, 1. by the testimony of S. John, His forerunner; 2. by that of God His Father. S. John v. 31-41.

FIRST POINT.
Testimony of S. John Baptist.

1. Avowed testimony to Jesus Christ. *If I bear witness of Myself, My witness is not true. There is another that beareth witness of Me; and I know that the witness which he witnesseth of Me is true.* The wisdom of Jesus Christ appears here in the order and the succession of His words. His enemies to whom He had just announced His Divinity in so striking a manner, might object to Him, that, speaking thus in His own favour, He merited neither credence nor attention; therefore He employs, in order to convince the unbelievers to whom He was speaking, an authority already recognised, and which being without suspicion and incontestable, rendered His own witness incontestable likewise. In truth, what more powerful means of conviction could there well be? Never have two men so famous by the holiness of their lives, equally disinterested, standing also in so slight a relationship the one to the other, rendered mutually to one another so uni-

form a testimony, while each takes up such a different position. The one speaks of Himself as the Son of God and the Messiah; the other, when asked if he were not himself the Messiah, answers in the negative, and says, that it is He Whom he has already announced, and Whose shoe's latchet he is not worthy to loose; and the former, whilst sustaining here His own dignity, confirms the testimony of the latter. These are not the proceedings of complicity and of knavery. We have seen false teachers extol one another in view of a common interest or of a common fame to be gained; and we have beheld yet more often the chiefs of a party who profess to be sent by God to reform the Church, contradict and refute one another, and end by attacking one another by reciprocal anathemas. How worthy of admiration are Thy works, Lord! how worthy of belief are the witnesses which Thou dost bring to bear to attest to the truth of Thy words!

2. A testimony accepted by the Jews. *Ye sent unto John, and he bare witness unto the truth.* In other words, ye know the austerity of his life, and the character of his person. Ye have sent unto him to enquire of him, and to learn from his own mouth who he was, resolved to believe him on his word, and to acknowledge him for the Messiah, if he declared that he was the Messiah. What then did that man whom you look upon as the man of God answer? *He bare witness unto the truth.* In order to have some idea of the great deference which the Jews had for S. John, it is sufficient to see that Jesus Christ Himself referred to it, and that long after, S. John the Evangelist lays stress upon that testimony, from the very beginning of his gospel.

3. A disinterested testimony. John rendered it, not in behalf of himself, but in behalf of one with Whom he had had no intercourse, nor connexion, Whom he had only seen once, at His Baptism, and from Whom he had neither honours nor dignities to expect in this world: it was then evident that it was truth alone which could lead him to render this testimony.

4. *A witness not necessary to Jesus Christ.* *But I receive not testimony from men; but these things I say, that ye might be saved.* What greatness and charity in these words! I do not seek the testimony of men to give authority to My teaching; if I appeal to S. John Baptist, it is in order to overcome your prejudices, it is in order that at least you may lend credence to the words of a witness whom you have chosen yourselves, and which nothing can render suspected by you; I only speak of him in order to rouse you out of the prejudices which you have adopted, and which you urge upon others; I do so only in the desire which I have of your salvation; thus does Jesus Christ employ, in order to save us, every kind of means, even those which appear to be in some sort beneath His greatness. Animated with the same spirit of charity, if we dispute with unbelievers, or with those who have separated from the Church, let us not do so in the idea that Jesus Christ and His Church have need of our voices, let it be still less in order to gain an idle triumph over men who only merit our compassion, but let it only be in order that they, with us, may be saved by coming forth out of the paths of unbelief in which they are walking.

5. *Authentic testimony, which cannot be rejected.* John *was a burning and a shining light; and ye were willing for a season to rejoice in his light.* Whilst John was at liberty to preach publicly and to exercise his functions as forerunner, he was a light which burned and gave light; he carried fire into men's hearts, and light into their minds. Judæa gloried in the lustre of his preaching, and in the odour of his virtues; it esteemed itself happy to have produced so great a prophet. But what fruit have you gained from the teachings of a master so renowned? How long has the joy which you felt in possessing him lasted? You ceased to listen to him, as soon as he spoke to you of Me, and declared Me to be the Son of God. Jesus gives the name of a light to S. John, a light which was kindled at the light of Him, Who was essentially *the* Light of the world.

This divine Saviour has left in His Church a light, which has been equally kindled at His Light, and which is always shining, to enlighten our steps. True believers walk continually and surely in that light, a light so brilliant and so universally acknowledged, that there is no one, who may not follow it, so as not to stray from the right path.

SECOND POINT.
Testimony of God the Father.

However signal may be the testimony of S. John, it is as nothing when compared to that of God, which cannot but be recognised, 1. in the miracles of Christ; 2. in the miraculous voice of God; 3. in the divine Word of the Holy Scriptures.

1. In the miracles of Christ. *But I have greater witness than that of John; for the works which the Father hath given Me to finish, the same works that I do, bear witness of Me, that the Father hath sent Me.* The divine works, the wonders, the miracles which I perform, such are the witnesses whom you may question. Consult them, and they will tell you that God My Father has sent Me; for what can you oppose to the evidence of their witness? And in truth, what miracles equalled those of Christ! True miracles in the manner in which they were wrought; they were made public, and wrought with a single word, and by a single act of will. True miracles in the matter on which they were wrought; Jesus worked them on earth, and on the sea, on the sick and on the dead, on men and on devils. True miracles in the end for which they were wrought; Jesus worked them as proofs of His mission, of His doctrine and of His divinity. True miracles in their effect; after having examined them, discussed them, fought against them, the world has changed its religion; hundreds of idolatrous nations, given up to different kinds of worship, opposed to one another, yet more by their habits than by their climates, have been all reunited in Christ, have acknowledged Him as their God and their

Saviour, have bewailed the inconceivable blindness of those who refuse to own Him, and have not been shaken in their faith by this hardness of heart and this sinful obstinacy. If we are not eye-witnesses of the miracles of Christ, at least we see the effect which they have produced in the conversion of the world. He who should invite men to follow him in a different career, and who should do so by alleging the proof of miracles which he had worked, but yet should never work any, would never find any followers; he would not only be a deceiver, but a fool who himself shewed forth his own deceptions.

2. Testimony of God in His miraculous Voice. *And the Father Himself Which hath sent Me, hath borne witness of me. Ye have neither heard His voice at any time nor seen His shape. And ye have not His Word abiding in you, for Whom He hath sent, Him, ye believe not.* As though He would say, that is not all, I have other witnesses whom ye must hear. My Father, Who sent Me, has willed to bear an unanswerable testimony to Me; if you say that it is not God's voice which you have heard, that it is not He Who has appeared to you, I will answer you that ye yourselves prayed Him not to let you hear His terrible voice, and that no one can see Him and hear Him. This privilege is reserved to Me, Who never cease to see Him and to listen to Him, and He has given Me to you as a Mediator, in order to declare to you His will, and to announce to you His designs; nevertheless you reject Me, and join sin to your weakness, a wilful unbelief to the impossibility that exists that you should know Him in Himself. You fill up the measure of your iniquities. We shall one day see Him face to face, this God Who is now hidden from our sight; but till then we must walk in the obscure pathways of faith.

3. Testimony of God in His Word of the Holy Scriptures. *Search the Scriptures; for in them ye think ye have eternal life; and they are they which testify of Me. And ye will not come to Me that ye might have life.* You read the Holy Scriptures, you take them

about with you, you weigh the meaning of the words, you seek carefully for the most hidden meanings, convinced that you will find there the necessary doctrines to lead you to eternal life. Now these Holy Scriptures bear witness of Me. How then, since they refer you unceasingly to Me as to the Christ, since they set forth to you that it is I, Whom you must acknowledge as sent by the Father, how then do you refuse to seek for instruction from Me, and reject all the lessons and graces I desired to bestow upon you? Ah! you keep to the letter of the Scriptures, but you have lost their meaning; for if you read them with the attention which faith alone gives and requires, the light it gives would shew you the truth of which your passions deprive you, and which cause you to take offence at My Words; you would speak of Me, as the Scriptures speak. Such has been the blindness of the Pharisees, and such is still the blindness of those who separate from the Church. The old Testament, the law, the psalms, and the prophets set forth Jesus Christ so plainly, that one would have been tempted to think that an infinity of passages must have been inserted after the events had taken place, if, by a singular Providence, the Jews, the declared enemies of Christianity had not preserved these Scriptures such as Christians possess them. Now the Jews still now-a-days study these Scriptures; they search into them, they seek out the most subtle and hidden senses; they seek *life* there, and they will not see in them Jesus Christ, Who alone can give them *life.* Heretics of past ages have read the Scriptures of the New Testament, have studied them and interpreted them, but they did not will to read them in the light of the Gospel revelation, which alone could have given to them their true meaning, and enabled them to find *life* in them. Learned men criticise the Scriptures, and we continually hear them preached and explained; but how few seek Jesus Christ in them in order that they may *come to Him,* and *have life?* Ah! what a difference to this holy, pure, innocent, and inward life, which leads to a blessed and eternal life.

Prayer. O divine Jesus! give me that spiritual life, that life of grace and union with Thee. Alas! where should I go elsewhere to seek for that life? I find only every where else doubts, uncertainties, perplexities, devouring remorse, a continual death which can only lead me to eternal death. I must be my own enemy that I thus flee from Thee with so much obstinacy, when Thou dost call me with so much tendernesss, and only that Thou mayest make me happy. It would seem as though Thy happiness and Thy glory depended upon my fidelity in following Thee, so much assiduity dost Thou manifest in drawing me to Thee. This assiduity is only the effort of Thy love. Thou art infinitely great and infinitely blessed. Whether men adore Thee or blaspheme Thee, their homage and their outrages will alike turn to Thy glory, and it is they alone who are interested in the choice which they make. My choice is made, O divine Saviour; I come, I hasten to Thee with confidence in order to receive from Thee the life of which Thou art the Source. I cast myself into Thy Bosom, draw me more and more, so that, closely united to Thee, nothing may ever separate me any more from Thee. Grant that I may be according to my station, like S. John, a burning and a shining light, that I may burn, like him, with the fire of Thy love, with zeal for Thy commandments, and that I may give light to my neighbour by my words and by my example. Amen.

Meditation C.

CONCLUSION OF THE DISCOURSE OF JESUS CHRIST TO THE JEWS, AFTER THE HEALING OF THE MAN, WHO HAD HAD AN INFIRMITY FOR THIRTY EIGHT YEARS.

Jesus Christ distinguishes here four sources of unbelief in the Jews; 1. a want of love to God. 2. a positive aversion to God. 3. an immoderate love of the esteem of men. 4. their former unbelief. S. John v. 42-47.

1. A want of love to God.

But I know you, our Lord continues, *that ye have not the love of God in you.* Ah! if men had but this holy love, if they had but a sincere desire to know God, to love and please Him, how soon would the Jew acknowledge the Messiah, and the deist the truth of Christianity. What animosities would not be extinguished! what dissensions stifled, and what disputes ended, if this sacred love reigned in our hearts. Each one nevertheless gives himself credit for possessing it. We speak much of the purity of the Word and the worship of God, of the severity of the Gospel, the zeal of the law, justice, purity of life, and even of pure love; but with these words, with these external appearances, we may indeed deceive men; but as for Me, says Jesus Christ, *I know you that ye have not the love of God in you.* Terrible words which each one ought to apply to himself, and meditate on well. Ah! if I had in me that love of God, would my passions be still so little mortified? Should I have so much distaste for my devotional exercises, so much negligence in the fulfilment of my duties? O divine Jesus! Thou dost know me a thousand times better than I know myself; Thou knowest the depths of my heart; dost Thou behold there the love of God? Give it to me, Lord, that holy love, increase it, perfect it in me, that it may become alone the principle and motive of all my actions.

2. A positive aversion to God.

I am come in My Father's Name, and ye receive Me not; if another shall come in his own name, him ye will receive. You have so little love for God, My Father, that you will not acknowledge Me, Who come to you in His Name, and with His authority. Let another come forward whose mission comes only from himself, let him know how to dazzle you or to flatter you, you will support him by your approbation. And such is still the fatal frame of mind in which we are for the most part towards God. We reject with obstinacy all that comes from Him, and calls us back to Him, and the most evident proofs make no impression on us, whilst on the contrary, we embrace with ardour all that draws us away from God, even though that which is alleged is devoid of all proof and of probability. Let an unbeliever bring forward a statement, that it is our body which thinks, that we shall perish utterly, that God does not concern Himself with anything that takes place in the world, and that after this life, there is no other life for us to fear or to hope for, he is listened to, he is believed in, and he is never questioned whence he knows what he advances, from whom he has derived so monstrous a doctrine, and what are his guarantees for its truth. We are too apt to revolt against that which bears the seal of God, and which requires of us to submit our own judgment to His, whilst we are led away and charmed by all that draws us away from Him and flatters our love of independence. How greatly is such blindness to be feared! Disperse it, O God! take it away from the minds of those who refuse to acknowledge Thee, and permit me not to fall into it.

3. The love of the esteem of men.

How can ye believe which receive honour one of another and seek not the honour which cometh from God only? Do not think that I will accuse you to the Father; there is one that accuseth you, even Moses, in whom ye trust. How would it be possible for you to believe Me and to declare yourself for Me? You are jealous of the approbation of men, and you do not seek God's glory alone; you have a regard for the inclinations of those whom you know to be the arbitrators of public opinions and the dispensers of earthly honour. Now, as you will gain only repulse from men, if you make profession of belief in Me, for this reason you are unwilling to acknowledge Me, in order that you may not run the risks of a like brand. And it is thus that still we daily renounce true glory, which consists in humbling ourselves before God by a humble faith, in order that we may obtain the applause of certain persons who flatter us. To believe what our fathers have believed, to hold the same principles, to follow the same maxims, this is to remain in the crowd, ignored and unknown, without any other honour than *which cometh from God only.* But when we adopt the part of thinking differently to others, of denying revealed truths, and resisting lawful authority, then we make ourselves remarked, we make ourselves talked of; the lips and pens of others praise our mind or our talents; we strive in our turn, to sustain or increase that reputation by new excesses, and how can we, with such fatal dispositions, submit ourselves to the humility of faith? Oh human glory, esteem of men, human respect, how many unbelievers you have made, how many conversions you have hindered! Alas! let us who strive to believe with faithfulness, let us take care that this love of human glory does not corrupt our faith, our zeal, and all our actions. The Jews prided themselves on having Moses as their lawgiver; they ought then to have acted according to the spirit of the law which he gave, and received the Messiah Whom it foretold; but, on the contrary, they only prided themselves in Moses whilst going contrary to the spirit of the law, and persecuting the Messiah. Thus it will be this same Moses, in whom they gloried, who would accuse them before God, and condemn them. How many saints in whom we glory may become our accusers before God, especially those holy men, apostles and bishops, who were the first to bring the knowledge of Christianity to our shores, and who will rise up against us, and reproach us with having forsaken the faith they preached, changed their precepts, and degenerated from their virtues.

4. Former unbelief.

For had ye believed Moses, ye would have believed Me, for he wrote of Me. But if ye believed not his writings, how shall ye believe My words? In refusing to believe in Me, ye refuse to believe in Moses; for it is of Me that that ancient lawgiver prophesied, when he foretold that another prophet would arise from the midst of your brethren, to Whose voice you must hearken, and Whose lessons you must follow. He has pointed out to you in his writings, how you might distinguish the true from the false prophet, the man of God from the deceiver. If you read with attention what he has written, you will be convinced Who I am, you will recognize Me without difficulty in these prophecies, and in the rules which he has left you. But if, notwithstanding the evidence of the letter, you persist in supposing that the writings of Moses do not contain any prophetic oracles which should announce a Messiah such as I am, it is in vain that I tell you that it is of Me that he spoke, you would still refuse to believe in Me. Jesus had not till then unfolded, at least publicly, in so distinct and accurate a manner, the character of His mission, the nature of His power, and the divinity of His Person. Why then had not the Jews, the possessors of the holy Scriptures, recognized Him as the Prophet of whom Moses had written? Because they only spoke of Moses and the prophets out of vain-glory; they did not believe in them. And for the same reason, so many unbelievers quote the writings of the New Testament, but acknowledge no divine authority in them, and only quote them to suit their own prejudices, because they do not believe in them.

Prayer. Lord, I believe in Thee; I believe in Thy

holy Gospel, and in Thy Church. Make this faith to grow in me more and more, grant that I may embrace all the truths which Thou hast revealed to me even those which are the most opposed to my prejudices and my passions. Be Thou my Master now, O Jesus, that one day Thou mayest be my Mediator and not my accuser. Let Thy love be the principle of my affections, Thy Gospel the rule of my life, and Thy Glory the end of all my actions. Amen.

Meditation CI.

THE EARS OF CORN PLUCKED ON THE SABBATH DAY.

OF THE UNJUST CENSURE OF THE ACTIONS OF OUR NEIGHBOUR.

The Gospel discovers to us here 1. the passions which are the source of this unjust censure; 2. the reasons which justify our neighbour under this unjust censure; 3. the faults which we ought to avoid when it is necessary to justify ourselves from unjust censure. S. Matt. xii. 1—8. S. Mark ii. 23—28. S. Luke vi. 1—5.

FIRST POINT.

Of the passions which are the source of this unjust censure.

1. We censure without authority, and this is pride and presumption. *And it came to pass on the second sabbath after the first* [1], *that He went through the corn*

---

[1] This expression of S. Luke the *second sabbath after the first*, has given rise to a variety of interpretations; but we will only refer to three here. 1. The sabbath which fell within the Octave of the Passover, was the most solemn, and might be called *the first*. After that, the sabbath which fell in the Octave of Pentecost, was the most solemn; and it is that which S. Luke calls the *second sabbath after the first*. 2. The first sabbath of the first month of the year was called *the first*: the first sabbath of the second month was called the *second sabbath after the first*, and so on. But these two systems and many other like theories are not supported by any authority. 3. A third explanation would appear perhaps to be more simple. S. Luke at the beginning of this chapter, relates two facts which took place

fields; and His disciples plucked the ears of corn, and did eat, rubbing them in their hands. Such was the object of the censure of the Pharisees who were there present. They began at once to exclaim against the violation of the Sabbath. But, according to them, who was it who was violating it? It was the disciples of Jesus. And by what right did they censure their conduct. Alas! are those whose conduct we censure dependent upon us? Have we any authority over them? Are we their judges? By what right do we place them before our tribunal, and condemn them there? Ah! if we knew how to confine ourselves to that which concerns us, how many words would be kept back, how many sins avoided, how many better employed hours should we spend!

2. We censure without reason, and that is blind malice. The law which commanded them to prepare on the eve what was to be eaten on the Sabbath day, and which forbade them to dress any thing on that day, was it then violated by the action of the disciples? What labour was there in a dish which was provided for them by the hands of nature itself? Did a preparation which consisted in rubbing some ears of corn in order to draw from them the grains, deserve that name? But the eyes of ill-will see objects quite different to what they really are; they are wilfully blinded both as to the justice of the case, and as to the facts; they neither know what

on the sabbath day. The second which begins at verse 6, is undoubtedly more striking than the first, both by circumstances which accompany it, and from the impression which it must have made on the public, and from the confusion with which the Pharisees were covered by it. S. Luke, having to relate this striking miracle, which took place on the sabbath, places before it a less important fact, and he relates that this event took place on the *second Sabbath after the first*, that is to say, on the Sabbath before the second Sabbath of which he is about to speak immediately afterwards in verse 6. In the arrangement of the facts which we follow, we suppose that the plucking of the ears of corn took place as Jesus and His disciples were leaving Jerusalem, immediately after the feast which has just been spoken of in the healing of the sick man, and thus, in order to explain these words, *the second sabbath after the first*, we will adopt the third explanation which we have just given.

the action is which they condemn, nor the law by which they condemn it, nevertheless they decide the matter, and say boldly, *It is not lawful.* Nothing is innocent in the conduct of those whom they attack, nothing is excusable; every thing is worthy of blame. How many similar judgements and censures does not our malice cause us to pronounce every day? Let us be more just, do not let us suffer ourselves to be prejudiced by passion, and many of those whom we thus unjustly condemn will then be acquitted.

3. We censure without moderation, and that is hatred towards others. *And certain of the Pharisees said unto them, Why do ye that which is not lawful on the sabbath day?* The Pharisees, without being really offended at it, yet made a pretence, according to their wont, of being much displeased at it. It was neither respect for the law, nor the fear of bad example which made them take offence at it, as if religion were utterly overthrown by this act: it was not even the apostles whom they were anxious to attack, but it was in order to have a pretext for slandering the master, that they bethought themselves to trouble the disciples. It was not the alleged fault which displeased them, but the person of Jesus, Who was not a Messiah after their own will, and Who reproved them for their vices. Determined to rid themselves of Him in whatever way they could, they spied out every opportunity to bring Him into discredit with the multitude, whose esteem and affection were the only obstacles which they feared to meet with in the execution of their designs. If it had been one of their own friends who had committed this act, they would not have found any cause of complaint in it: but how otherwise could they get rid of a virtuous enemy, if they must needs wait to find crimes whereof to accuse him?

4. We censure without recalling our words, and this is jealousy, and a spirit of intrigue. The infringement of the law of the sabbath was one of the accusations which was most frequently brought forward against

Jesus Christ; He answered this accusation over and over again, and again and again the Jews brought forward this same accusation anew as something fresh. Of what avail are the most reasonable apologies to persons determined to make their enemies out as guilty? They will diminish nothing of the accusations they have once brought against them; they will renew them continually, and by dint of repeating them, they will make them believed by some, and they will poison the minds of others against them; a diabolical scheme which has been employed at all times by the enemies of God and of His Church. Jesus suffered Himself under these false accusations, and willed that thus it should be, in order to encourage His disciples not to relax their efforts through fear of calumny, but, on the contrary, to rejoice, when after the example of their Master, they should one day fall victims to their zeal.

SECOND POINT.

Of the reasons which justify our neighbour under this unjust censure.

1. Necessity and need. *And Jesus, answering them said, Have ye not read so much as this, what David did, when himself was an hungered, and they which were with him; how he went into the house of God, and did take and eat the shewbread, and gave also to them that were with him; which it is not lawful to eat, but for the priests alone?* As though He would say, Yes, without doubt, I see what My disciples do: but I do not see anything that merits your censure. They have done nothing contrary to the law in what they have done; but that which has kindled your zeal so strongly, is that it has been done on a sabbath day. What would you then have said, if you had lived in the time of David? for you who know the Scriptures, you have read what took place when Abiathar was high priest, when Abimelech the priest gave hallowed bread to the fugitive David and to those who accompanied

him. These loaves of shewbread, which had been placed before the ark, were consecrated ; David and his followers were neither priests nor Levites, and you know that it was strictly forbidden that any but the priests should eat of that bread; but was David reproached with this action as if it were a crime? Was not the necessity in which he was, considered a legitimate dispensation? Wherefore then should not the law of the sabbath day yield to the necessity in which My disciples are? Thus it happens continually that those who are in abundance, who are in want of nothing, and who have nothing to suffer, can make no allowances for the needs of their poorer neighbours. There are others, who with a robust temperament, unvariable health, and a strong constitution are able to endure an amount of severity and austerity, which makes them believe others to be capable of the same labours, the same self-denials, as they can bear, and they look upon the least relaxation as an infringement of the law. Let us put far from us such censures, let us seek to justify our neighbour instead of criticising him; let us have compassion on his weakness, let us not close our eyes to his necessities, and lastly, let us believe that he may have needs which are none the less real, because we do not always know them.

2. The service of God or our neighbour. *Or have ye not read in the law, how that on the sabbath days the priests in the temple profane the sabbath, and are blameless? But I say unto you, That in this place is One greater than the temple, But if ye had known what this meaneth, I will have mercy, and not sacrifice, ye would not have condemned the guiltless.* The priests in the temple do not keep the rest of the Sabbath, and yet they are guiltless of sin in so doing. The reason which excuses this apparent breach of the law, is that though the ministry which they exercise there, such as slaying the victims, skinning them, offering them up in sacrifice, and distributing them out, are in themselves servile works, yet they are the functions of their ministry which are destined for the service of God,

and required by the service of the temple. Now, if the law has neither force nor authority with regard to the ministry of the priests in the temple, with far greater reason has this same law neither authority nor force with regard to the ministry of My disciples, to whom it is impossible to obey the law, and at the same time to obey My Will, and do that which is pleasing to Me, for I, I am greater than the temple, I am the living temple, the God of the temple, and I look upon conformity to My Will, as preferable to the external worship of religion. Moreover do you not know that as God declared to the prophet Hosea, when these two laws, the law which regards the worship of God and religion, and the other which has to do with the works of mercy, and the duties of charity, are brought together so as to clash with one another, you are bound to put the law of charity before that of external worship and sacrifices! God is more mindful of the needs of your neighbour, His child and your brother, than He is to the marks you shew Him of your piety, by offering up victims to Him in sacrifice. God is love itself; He wills that you should be filled with love; that is the spirit which animates Him, and is therefore the spirit that should animate you; it is that which fills His heart, it should therefore fill your's. Now since the works of spiritual mercy are above legal observances, and positive commands, My apostles, occupied as they are in the instruction of their neighbour, and employed in My service, so that they have not the time to provide things needful for their subsistence, and to give thought for the morrow, may well be dispensed from the observance of the Sabbath. If they have strayed from the letter of the law, it has only been in order to fulfil the spirit; they are then innocent, and you are blameable in condemning them. Thus we have no right to exact from those who are devoted to the service of their neighbour, or are occupied in ministerial labours, that they should practise as strictly the same devotional exercises as others who have only the requirements of their own private devotions to attend to. He who exempts himself from some regular observances only through zeal for God's glory and out of love to his neighbour, when both are regulated by wisdom, is free from all blame, and merits no censure; and this is a second way by which we may make excuses for our neighbour.

3. The spirit and the end of the law. *And He said vnto them, The sabbath was made for man, and not man for the sabbath: therefore the Son of man is Lord also of the Sabbath.* The Lord, in appointing the rest of the Sabbath, had two ends in view: the first, to hinder men from giving themselves up wholly to their own interests, so as to neglect to render to God the honour and the sacrifice of prayer which are due to Him; the second, to prevent the labourer from being unduly oppressed by work through the hardness of his master. Thus God has appointed the Sabbath for the advantage of mankind, but the Lord did not make man for the Sabbath. He has never commanded, that in order to maintain the rest of the Sabbath, man was to deprive himself of necessary food. It is the same with all positive commands; the end of these commands, the intention of the Giver of the law, is not that they should be observed at the peril of life, health or property. Our Lord, in replying to the Pharisees with regard to the non-observance of the Sabbath, failed not to make known to them that as He was the Lord and Master of the Sabbath, consequently, He could dispense them from the obligation of its observance. But that was the essential point which they obstinately refused to admit, although our Lord proved His power by the most evident miracles.

THIRD POINT.

Of the faults which we must avoid, when it is necessary to justify ourselves under unjust censure.

1. Vanity and self love. We ought not to seek to justify ourselves save when charity and the fear of being

the cause of scandal require us to do so. It was for this reason that our Lord answered the censure of the Pharisees. When it is simply a question of ourselves, we ought to be silent, to forget ourselves, to suffer in patience, and to place our cause in the hands of Him Who knows our innocence; but how many there are who, full of themselves and their own self love, resent the least word that is said against them, although it be often one that does them no harm, spend themselves in excuses, and weary everyone by the recital of their self-justification.

2. Hatred and resentment. We ought not to look upon those who have censured us in anything as our enemies; and even though they should be so, far from hating them, we are bound to love them. We should only seek, in justifying ourselves, to disabuse their minds, to enlighten them, to gain them over. See with what charity our Lord profits even by the censure of the Pharisees, to reveal to them His greatness, His sovereign power and His divinity; how He brings them back to the duties of mercy, in order to inspire them with it.

3. Anger and animosity. Let our justification of ourselves be well-considered and just, and at a fitting time; but let it be without any bitterness or hastiness. Let us banish every injurious word from it, or any expression which can convey either contempt or affront. See with what gentleness, what calmness, and what mildness our Lord here replies to the Pharisees.

4. Revenge and accusation of others. The faults of our neighbour do not justify our own; nevertheless it often happens that the first means we employ to justify ourselves, is to accuse others. What arises from this? That if we had confined ourselves to our own justification, we might have extinguished the spark which was just kindled, whereas by attacking others and accusing them in their turn, we fan the flame of discord, and stir up a fire which nothing perhaps will be able to quench. Let us examine ourselves then closely in so important

THE EARS OF CORN PLUCKED ON THE SABBATH DAY. 145

a matter. Let us understand that censuring others, we render ourselves guilty, because it is always some wrong passion which is the motive of our censure; let us acknowledge that those whom we censure may have reasons for their acts which may excuse them, and let us take it for granted that some such reason exists, and abstain from censure; lastly, let us acknowledge the faults we commit ourselves, in seeking to justify ourselves.

Prayer. Ah Lord! far be from me that Pharisaical spirit, which condemns our neighbour on suspicions, or even on grounds which are good or at least doubtful! If I be the object of calumny, let me suffer with patience the envy or malice of others; grant that I may not be eager to justify myself, so that Thou, Who art wisdom and power, mayest justify me Thyself, when Thou seest fitting. In vain will men condemn me, if Thou dost justify me; in vain will they justify me, if Thou dost condemn me. Grant then that I may give no cause of offence by my conduct; but if others take offence without cause, that I may not be disquieted by men's judgement, and seek only to please Thee, Thee Who art the sole witness and the true Judge of my actions. Amen.

Meditation CII.

HOW WE SHOULD ACT UNDER CONTROVERSIES WHICH TROUBLE THE PEACE OF THE CHURCH.

1. The Pharisees here offer to us a type of unbelievers; 2. Jesus Christ presents here a pattern for the ministers of the gospel, 3. the man who was healed furnishes an example to believers. S. Matt. xii. 9-14. S. Mark iii. 1-6. S. Luke vi. 6-11.

FIRST POINT.

The Pharisees, a type of unbelievers.

1. The character of unbelievers, like that of the Pharisees, is to be invidious in their conversation. *And*

it came to pass also on another sabbath, that He entered into the synagogue, and taught; and there was a man whose right hand was withered. And the scribes and Pharisees watched Him, whether He would heal on the sabbath day, that they might find an accusation against Him. And they asked Him, saying, Is it lawful to heal on the Sabbath days? that they might accuse Him. The Pharisees watched attentively to see whether Jesus would perform this act of healing on the Sabbath day, because they had resolved to make a crime of this act; but fearing, that if the miracle was once performed, their accusation might come too late, they began by prejudicing the minds of the people beforehand, so that a sort of sedition might arise, of which they hoped that Jesus would become the victim. With this view, as soon as our Lord's instruction was concluded, and before the man with the withered hand could present himself to Jesus, they put to Him this invidious question, and asked Him whether it was lawful to work cures on the Sabbath day. The artifice of this question which they put to our Lord consisted in the vague and general meaning which it presented; the people, in this kind of statements would only seize upon the first point that struck them, (for example in this case, the sanctity of the Sabbath,) and would not perceive the false deductions which could be drawn thence. Is it not thus that error is always expressed; and is it not in the same spirit that insidious questions are often put, which seem outwardly to bear only the impress of piety, but which, under hidden snares, conceal monstrous errors? Let us mistrust all teaching which is not that of the Church, or of her authorised ministers.

2. The character of unbelievers, like that of the Pharisees, is to be crafty in their silence. *But He knew their thoughts, and said to the man which had the withered hand, Rise up, and stand forth in the midst. And he arose, and stood forth. Then said Jesus unto them, I will ask you one thing; Is it lawful on the sabbath-days to do good, or to do evil? to save life, or*

to destroy it? But they held their peace. Jesus, having put the question so as to be within the reach of the people, and having, in His turn, interrogated the Pharisees, they looked at one another, but no one made an answer. What is this silence? Is it the silence of reverence, of conviction and approbation, or of pacification? No; it is a silence full of craftiness, obstinacy, and ill-will. They see two answers to the question, and they will not give either. The one which would have best suited their feelings, would have been distasteful to the people, because guided by a right reason, they would not have been able to hear without indignation, that works of charity were unlawful on the sabbath day, and that it was more righteous to look on coldly and let a man die, sooner than lend him a helping hand in his danger. The other answer which was affirmative, would have been according to good sense; but it would have ruined their plans, and done away with their authority. Thus does error spread itself in many forms which have no stability; and when you think you have seized them, they escape you like a phantom which vanishes away. They are without foundation, and when examined into, they contradict themselves.

3. The character of unbelievers, like that of the Pharisees, is to be cruel in their plots. *Then the Pharisees went out, and held a council against Him, how they might destroy Him. And straightway they took counsel with the Herodians against Him.* The fury of the Pharisees is changed into extravagance and folly; seeing themselves covered with confusion before a numerous assembly, they go out quickly, and are filled with but one idea, namely how they should destroy Him Whom they hated, and to Whom they could no longer resist. They assemble together, and with what feelings? They ought to have been filled with admiration for this divine Saviour, for His wisdom, His gentleness, His power. But the unbeliever sees only in those who combat his errors that which is hateful. However wise, moderate, or irreproachable they may be, let them even

work miracles, their merits serve only to exasperate him; he pushes his resentment to the extreme of folly, extravagance, and fury. With whom do the Pharisees assemble together? With the Herodians. What! these strict observers of the law of Moses, so jealous of the interests of the nation, ally themselves with the courtiers of Herod, the enemies of the nation and of the religion of the Jews! But to whom will not people have recourse, and what resources will they not make use of in order to oppress an enemy? All will join together for that purpose. The different sects who are the most opposed amongst themselves will conspire unanimously against true religion; they will forget their own dissensions in order to attack the Church of Jesus Christ. These who call themselves the friends of truth, the promoters of reform, and the zealous supporters of law, will not blush to find themselves allied with irreligious men, even those who are subjects of foreign powers, and enemies of their nation, their government, and their religion. One might give, as a proof of the truth of the Church of Jesus Christ, that it is against her that every kind of unbelief is joined together. Lastly, for what purpose do the Pharisees assemble together? For the purpose of ridding themselves of Jesus Christ, by decrying Him in the first place, in order then to be able to take His life. That is a point upon which they need no further deliberation, as they have already made up their minds about it; the only matter for deliberation is the means by which their end is to be accomplished. It would not appear easy to cry down in the minds of the people a Man so holy, so irreproachable in life, so mighty in deeds and words; nevertheless, by dint of calumnies, of suspicions skilfully disseminated, of reports indistinctly scattered abroad, they accomplished their purpose, at least, in the capital. They joined their authority and the power they held to lying and hypocrisy, and by a deep and adorable Providence of God, the Innocent was sacrificed to the hatred of the guilty. Alas! how many victims has not this same spirit of error made during the different ages of the Church!

SECOND POINT.

Jesus a Pattern to the ministers of the Gospel.

1. He opposes wisdom to craftiness. Our Lord begins by deciding the too widely general question proposed by the Pharisees. *Jesus knew their thoughts.* This reflection ought indeed to arrest, or at least to disquiet those who still oppose themselves to the Church of Christ. They may be able to conceal their secret intentions and to deceive men: but Jesus knows and will make known one day the evasions and artifices in which they pride themselves. Jesus commands the man whose hand was withered, to rise, to draw near to Him, and to stand forth in the midst of the assembly. This movement alone served to answer the question. The sight of this afflicted man, so worthy of compassion, sufficed to turn the thoughts of the people towards the true object of the question, and to prevent them from letting themselves be carried away by a false idea of the observance of the sabbath. Then our Lord interrogated in His turn the Pharisees, and said to them, *Is it lawful to do good on the sabbath day, or to do evil? to save life or to kill?* The answer did not appear difficult to the assembly, but it was so embarrassing to the Pharisees, that they adopted the expedient of remaining silent. If the people had been asked, they would have answered without difficulty that not to *do good* to another, when there was an opportunity of helping another in distress would be to *do evil;* and not to *save* the *life* of any one, when it lay in our power, would be to *kill*, and that such wicked cruelty could not be in any way intended by the obligation laid on us of sanctifying the Sabbath day. Lastly, our Lord makes the question still more obvious by a comparison. *And He said unto them, what man shall there be among you that shall have one sheep, and if it fall into a pit on the sabbath day, will he not lay hold on it, and lift it out? How much then is a man better than a sheep? Wherefore it is lawful to do well on the sabbath-days.*

2. Jesus opposes firmness to their malice. *And when He had looked round about on them with anger, being grieved for the hardness of their hearts, He saith unto the man, Stretch forth thine hand. And he stretched it out: and his hand was restored whole as the other.* Firmness of Jesus in His looks. The Pharisees persisting obstinately in their silence, Jesus looked round upon the whole assembly with that air of majesty and noble assurance, which formed the consolation and the joy of His true disciples; and then turning towards the Pharisees, He looked upon them with eyes filled with anger which overwhelmed and confounded them. Firmness in His feelings. He was grieved at the blindness of their hearts; but He was in no wise dismayed at anything that they were capable of undertaking and of carrying out against Himself. Firmness in action. The taciturn behaviour, the air of discontent of the Pharisees did not hinder in any way the actions of Jesus. He speaks as a master, He commands the sick man to stretch out his hand, who obeys with confidence, stretches forth his hand, and at the instant it recovers its natural form. This firmness, which is especially suitable to the ministers of Jesus Christ, who are responsible to Him for the trust He has committed to their keeping, applies likewise in proportion to all true believers when they find themselves placed under circumstances in which they are called upon to defend the cause of religion and of virtue.

3. Jesus opposes retreat to persecution. The Pharisees, coming out of the assembly, held a council against Jesus, as we have already mentioned. *But when Jesus knew it, He withdrew Himself from them with His disciples to the sea.* As Jesus did not fear the fury of His enemies, He might at will have put a stop to its effects; He did not fear the death which they were preparing for Him, and was well resolved to give Himself up one day to it, but at this moment He was forming His Church, and especially those who were to bear rule in it, by His words and actions; He was teaching them, by withdrawing to the shores of the sea of Galilee that

it is sometimes prudent to yield to the storm, that they might withdraw themselves for a time in order to render greater services hereafter, being always ready to give their lives for their flocks, when the moment appointed by God should come, if, by His mercy, He found them worthy of so great blessedness.

THIRD POINT.

The man who was healed, an example to believers.

1. As for us, who are faithful believers, let us learn to know what is amiss in ourselves and not to concern ourselves respecting controversies which may arise in the Church. This man had his right hand withered and crippled. If by the right hand we understand that which is required of us to do to secure our eternal salvation, it will be easy for us to see that the infirmity of this man is our own, that our left hand alone has the power to move, and that the right hand has none; because all that we do is for earth, and we do nought for Heaven. With what intention do we think that this man repaired to the assembly where Jesus was with the Pharisees? Was it to listen to the disputes of these latter, and to know what it was that they had to bring forward in opposition to the teaching of the Saviour? No. Entirely occupied with his own infirmity, he only thought of obtaining a cure. Ah! wherefore then, in a condition which is far sadder than his, are we filled with other cares than he? Why all this avidity to hear all that passes in the world, to occupy ourselves with politics, and to devour all the gossip of the day? Why do we pride ourselves upon understanding all controverted points in matters of religion, and on being able to reason upon them? Let us rather occupy ourselves with our own faults, and seek to remedy them, let us study our own duties, examine our own conduct, learn to know ourselves, and think only of our own cure and our own salvation.

2. Let us know how to obey God's commands with-

out taking offence at the disputes which arise in the Church. After the questions put by the Pharisees, *Jesus saith unto the man which had a withered hand, Rise up and stand forth in the midst.* With what joy did he hear these words which announced to him his salvation! and with what promptitude did he obey them without concerning himself with the question of the Pharisees. Such is the example which we ought to follow: let us arise, Jesus bids us do so; let us come forth out of our indolence and our idleness. Let us begin seriously to work out our salvation, and let us learn from the Gospel what we must do to be saved. But, do you say, amidst all these troubles, you do not know any longer whom to obey. What, you do not know any longer whom to obey! but in the midst of all these difficulties, has any one told you that you need no longer obey Jesus Christ, fulfil the commandments of God, and follow the Gospel? Obey then Jesus Christ, obey them who have the rule over you, whom He has put in His stead, and to whom He says, *He that heareth you, heareth Me, and he that despiseth you despiseth Me.* Have these disputes altered the institutions of Jesus Christ, and the appointment of His Church? Has she no longer any appointed ministers? Is Jesus Christ no longer her Head? But you will add, these disputes cause a great offence. Doubtless they do so; but do not let yourself take offence at them: are you to wait, in order to be converted, till there are no more causes of offence in the world? Are you to wait, to labour at your salvation, until these controversies are brought to an end, until there are no more unteachable spirits to trouble the peace of the Church? Vain hope, frivolous pretext, chimerical pretension, which will not be able to excuse you before God. There will always be offences and disputes so long as the world lasts; and it is in the midst of these storms that you are commanded to rise, to stand firm, and to obey the voice of Jesus Christ, Who has promised that He will at all times, and every where, be with His Church unto the end of the world.

3. Let us begin to work, and let us cease to discourse on the disputes which trouble the Church. Jesus, having confounded the Pharisees, said to the man, *Stretch forth thine hand. And he stretched it forth, and it became whole as the other.* Leave it to those whose duty it is to refute error, and keep silence amongst your brethren: but edify them by works which prove to them your healing and your sincere conversion. *Stretch forth your right hand* which has been so long idle, and without motion; stretch it out over all that might prove hurtful to your salvation to destroy them; over those books, those papers, those pictures, to burn them; over these ill-gotten goods, to restore them; over that luxury, those adornments, to retrench them; over the bonds of a friendship which is too tender, or of a society which is dangerous to you, in order to break through them; stretch it out to all that is necessary for your salvation that you should embrace, to the duties of your station which you should fulfil, to the acts of repentance and devotion which you ought to practise, to that enemy with whom you ought to be reconciled, to that needy person whom you ought to relieve; stretch it towards Heaven, to ask of God the peace of the Church, the peace of the state, the peace of families, the conversion of sinners, the perseverance of the good, and for all believers, those graces of which they have need.

Prayer. Preserve me, O Lord, from the spirit of opposition to Thy divine truth. Give me the most lively horror of all that might turn me away from it. Make me to cling closely to that Church which Thou hast purchased with Thy Blood, and founded upon the Chief corner-stone, even Thyself, so that at the day of judgement Thou mayest set me at Thy right hand, and admit me to a share in Thine eternal kingdom. Amen.

Meditation CIII.

JESUS WITHDRAWS TO THE SHORES OF THE SEA OF GALILEE.

The sacred text seems to apply itself to set forth before us here the features of the gentleness of Jesus, and to show it to us as practised during the life of this divine Saviour, announced before His birth, and victorious after His death. S. Matt. xii. 15—21. S. Mark iii. 7—12.

FIRST POINT.

Gentleness of Jesus, as practised during His life.

1. With regard to these who had need of Him. 1. An attractive gentleness. The Pharisees and Herodians having joined together in order to deliberate respecting the way in which they might compass His death, *and when Jesus knew it, He withdrew from thence with His disciples to the sea; and a great multitude from Galilee followed Him, and from Judea, and from Jerusalem, and from Idumœa, and from beyond Jordan; and they about Tyre and Sidon, a great multitude, when they heard what great things He did, came unto Him. And great multitudes followed Him, and He healed them all, and charged them that they should not make Him known.* The withdrawal of Jesus, whatever pains He took to effect it quietly and silently, had more the appearance of a truimph than of a flight; bardly had He reached the shore, than He saw Himself surrounded by an innumerable crowd of people, who came not only from the neighbourhood of Galilee where He was, but also from Judea and even from Jerusalem, from Idumæa and other countries on the other side of Jordan, and from regions situated on the Mediterranean, and places in the neighbourhood of Tyre and Sidon. The fame of Jesus, the report of the miracles which He worked, the gentleness with which He received everyone attracted all these people to Him. Do we possess this same attractive gentleness? Does it not often happen, on the

contrary, that we drive people away from us by our peevish temper, our haughty and proud character, our contemptuous manner, and our abrupt ways, and that those who have need of our ministry, or our help, dare not approach us, or do so only with fear?

2. A patient gentleness. *And He spake to His disciples, that a small ship should wait on Him, because of the multitude, lest they should throng Him: for He had healed many, insomuch that they pressed upon Him for to touch Him, as many as had plagues.* As Jesus had already healed a great number of sick persons, who had come to Him, and that they perceived that it was sufficient only to touch His garments in order to be assured of a prompt cure, one can well imagine what must have been the anxiety of this multitude who were congregated around Him; each one made an effort to approach Him, in order to touch Him, to see Him and to hear Him. This eagerness often made them wanting in the reverence due to His sacred Person: but His goodness made Him so feeling towards the evils which they brought before Him, that although the crowd overwhelmed Him, He made no complaint; He only commanded His disciples to keep a boat in readiness, so that, if He were too closely pressed upon by the multitude, He might withdraw to it. Alas! how much less provocation it often takes to exhaust our patience, and to arouse our complaints and our murmurs? 3. A beneficent gentleness. *He healed them all.* Jesus did not withdraw Himself till He had healed all the sick, and if He made use of the ship which His disciples had prepared for Him, it was only apparently in order to dismiss all this multitude, who would never have left Him so long as He remained on the shore. If we have it not in our power to relieve our neighbour, at least we can receive him, and speak to him with gentleness; but when we can be of use to him, we have not the gentleness of Jesus Christ, unless we show it in our manner, in our words, and in our deeds.

2. Gentleness of Jesus Christ with regard to His

enemies. 1. A gentleness full of humility. *He withdrew Himself.* As He was Almighty, it would have been easy for Him to overturn the designs of His persecutors, and to make their envy recoil on themselves; but He chose rather to withdraw Himself, that He might not embitter further their angry tempers. We, on the contrary, do we not make a boast of never yielding, of resisting with all our might, and even beyond our power? 2. A gentleness full of discretion. *But when Jesus knew it.* He knew all, He knew that His enemies were assembled and deliberating at that moment how they should find means to destroy Him. He might have laid open to the eyes of all this multitude the mystery of iniquity which was being laid against Him; nevertheless, He does not speak of it, not a word escapes Him with respect to it. We, on the contrary, not only publish only too readily any plans which we may know to have been formed against us by our enemies, but we imagine designs to have been meditated against us, we give them credit for all that is the blackest and most odious, and relate it as if we had certain proof of it. 3. Lastly, a gentleness full of thoughtfulness, and consideration. *And charged them that they should not make Him known, And unclean spirits, when they saw Him, fell down before Him, and cried, saying, Thou art the Son of God. And He straitly charged them that they should not make Him known.* The glory of Jesus Christ sufficed to confound His enemies. The possessed of evil spirits prostrated themselves before Him, and by their mouths, the devil published that He was the Son of God. All those whom He healed made it a duty to exalt Him, and to make known their gratitude, by their praises; but Jesus forbade them all to speak of Him, and to make Him known, in order not further to embitter the jealous enemies whom He desired to gain. But we, do we not rather if we have some advantage, or if some fortunate success befalls us, desire that our enemy should know it, and do we not take a malicious pleasure in the jealousy and the spite which we imagine him to feel at it?

SECOND POINT.

Gentleness of Jesus Christ announced before His birth.

1. Announced as the Object of the affection and love of God. *That it might be fulfilled which was spoken of by Esaias the prophet, saying, Behold My servant, Whom I have chosen; My beloved, in Whom My soul is well pleased; I will put My Spirit upon Him, and He shall shew judgement to the Gentiles.* Thus God speaking of Jesus Christ by the mouth of the prophet Isaiah, makes known to us His high dignity under three terms. 1. He speaks of Him as *My servant Whom I have chosen.* It appertained to the greatness of God that this God-man should be His servant, and there was none other, Who was worthy to serve God, Who could render Him an obedience, yield to Him a homage, and offer to Him a sacrifice worthy of His infinite greatness. This Jesus Christ has accomplished, in that being God, equal to His Father, He has taken upon Him the form of a servant, in becoming man like us, and that clothed with our humanity, this Man-God has humbled Himself before the infinite Majesty of God His Father. 2. He speaks of Him, as *My Beloved in Whom My soul is well pleased;* insomuch that neither our services nor our homage, in a word, nothing that we could do would be able to please God save through this well-beloved Son, Who is pre-eminently His Servant; whilst, on the other hand, by the union which we have with Him, and our participation in His Merits, all that we are and all that we do becomes well-pleasing to God through Him. 3. Lastly He says that it is *upon Him* He *will put* His *Spirit.* God has given His Spirit to the sacred humanity of our Lord, and it is of this fulness that we receive. It is only by Jesus Christ, and for the sake of His merits, that grace is bestowed upon us, and the gifts of the Holy Spirit communicated to us. Ah! what an exalted idea we ought to have of our Saviour, and of ourselves in Him and through Him! But after that God has thus

made known to us the greatness of His Son, what does He tell us of His virtues in the same prophet, and in the same place of the prophecy? He speaks to us of His gentleness, and gives it to us as the distinctive characteristic of the Messiah, in order to make us understand that it ought also to form the characteristic of the Christian; that it is by it that we must resemble to Jesus Christ; that without it, we cannot serve God, or please God, or have any share in the communications of the Spirit of God.

2. Gentleness of Jesus Christ announced as the source of blessing to mankind. *Behold My servant Whom I have chosen: He shall not strive, nor cry; neither shall any man hear His voice in the streets. A bruised reed shall He not break, and smoking flax shall He not quench, till He send forth judgement unto victory; and in His Name shall the Gentiles trust.* Thus, 1. Wherefore should the nations trust in Jesus Christ? Because it is with gentleness that He shall preach His Gospel. The prophet, after having told us that this well-beloved Son will shew judgement to the Gentiles, that is to say, truth, righteousness, the true worship of God, the Gospel, the kingdom of God, passes all at once to the praise of His gentleness, in order to make us understand that it is with this gentleness that He will preach His Gospel, and that His disciples will preach it after Him, and that it is in the same spirit of gentleness that the Gospel ought to be received and practised. 2. The nations will trust in Jesus Christ, because He will administer justice to them; but as the prophet continues, He will do so without disputes, without strife, clamours, complaints or murmurs. He will not break the bruised reed, nor quench the smoking flax; figurative expressions, which set forth perfectly His extreme and unchangeable gentleness. And, in truth, if He lifted up His voice, it was not on behalf of His own personal interests, but solely against vice and its allurements. Such is the example which He has given us, such is our Pattern. 3. Lastly, the nations will trust in Him, because it is in His gentle-

ness that He will establish the foundation of their hope. Christian gentleness is not merely the effect of a happy temperament, much less of insensibility and dulness of disposition; it is to be found in those who are by nature the most ardent and the most lively, as well as in those of calmer and more equable natures. It feels the injustice which oppresses it; but it sighs before God alone, and entreats for the conversion of its persecutors, and makes no complaints before men in order to procure satisfaction for injuries done to it. It is at the same time the effect and the firmest foundation of hope. It is hope which has supported the martyrs in their torments, and it is patience in their torments which has strengthened their hope. What must not he suffer who has no hope? What can he hope for who cannot suffer any thing with gentleness and without complaint?

THIRD POINT.

Victorious gentleness of Jesus Christ after His death.

He will exercise gentleness, the prophet says, *till He send forth judgement unto victory.*
1. The justice of His law, in establishing His Gospel on the earth, and in making it triumph through gentleness. In the first place, over the malice of evil spirits by the destruction of idolatry. If the world has been purged from the impious and sacrilegious worship which it offered to devils, if the universe acknowledges now and adores but the one true God, is this owing to the reasonings of philosophers and the eloquence of orators? Is it not the death of Jesus Christ, the humble preaching of His Apostles, the patience of martyrs, Christianity, in a word, which, by its gentleness, has brought about this wonder, and has overthrown for ever the reign of evil spirits? In the second place, over the fury of tyrants, by the conversion of the rulers of the world. All the powers of the earth were leagued together against the Gospel, and they have invented a thousand unheard-of

tortures in order to torment and destroy the Christians. If Christianity now occupies the first thrones in the world, has it gained them by force of arms and by intrigues? Is it not by its gentleness, by its patience, and by the virtue of the blood of Jesus Christ that it has gained this victory, and brought about this prodigious change? Lastly over the violence of men's passions through their sanctification. The war of human passions against Christianity has been most obstinate; it still continues, and will continue till the end of the world. But how many victories has not Christianity gained, and does it not gain every day over evil passions? How many have come forth victorious out of the struggle, with palms and laurels, which their gentleness, patience, self-mortification and their holy lives have gained for them.

2. Jesus Christ will exercise gentleness until He makes the justice of His cause to triumph, by rendering at the end of time, an eternal and victorious judgement, by which, in the first place, He will manifest the truth of the doctrines which He has taught, and the precepts which He has given; the truth of His wisdom, of His providence, and of the abundance of His redemption; the truth of men's actions, of their motives, and of all the circumstances attending them. In the second place, He will punish with eternal punishment the wicked and sinners, those who have refused to receive His law or to practise it. Lastly, He will reward with eternal happiness the righteous, who shall have persevered with gentleness and patience in the practice of His commandments. Oh day of glory and of triumph for Jesus Christ and for Christians, for humble virtue, which has been hidden and persecuted, why art thou not continually before our minds, to sustain our faith, and reanimate our hope! The time of gentleness and patience will then have its end, and in its turn will come the time of justice and of triumph. But our self-love finds this end very far distant, since it does not come till death; we should like it to come in this life; we would willingly suffer for a time, if we were certain of being soon glorified, and of

seeing our enemies humiliated. How weak our thoughts are, how short-sighted our views, how limited our projects! God has designs for our benefit, which are far nobler, more vast, and more worthy of Him! let us strive to enter into them, and let ourselves be led by them. To suffer all our life, and to triumph throughout eternity, the first is an obligation laid on us, and the second is our hope!

Prayer. O Jesus! grant me to imitate that gentleness which is the ground work of my trust. Alas! how far removed am I from this virtue, of which Thou hast given me so constant an example! What gentleness hast Thou not shewn towards me, whether it be in sparing me when I was Thine enemy, or in succouring me when I have implored Thine aid! Ah! can it be that I shew so little tenderness towards others? Should I not take Thee for my Pattern, and can I, without that, have Thee for my Saviour? O divine Jesus, I join myself to that multitude of infirm and sick in the Gospels: let me approach Thee, let me touch Thee, and vouchsafe to heal me of my anger, my impatience, my murmurings, my spirit of pride and revenge, and of all that is in me that is opposed to Thy divine gentleness. Amen.

Meditation CIV.

OF PRAYER.

Jesus sets before us here, 1. the necessity of prayer; 2. the object of prayer; 3. perseverance in prayer; 4. the fruits of prayer. S. Luke xi. 1—13.

FIRST POINT.

The necessity of prayer.

It came to pass, that as He was praying in a certain place. The example which Jesus here offers us, makes us see the necessity of prayer, and destroys all the pretexts we make in order to dispense ourselves from its observance.

1. Jesus was Holiness itself, and yet He prays. How is it, that we, who are weakness itself, filled with passions, evil inclinations, and bad habits, can hope to avoid sin, and to continue in the practice of virtue, if we do not draw down upon ourselves from heaven, by the fervour of our prayers, the graces and helps of which we stand in need?

2. Jesus was the Essence of light, the Light of the world, and yet He prayed. How shall we, who are but darkness, and surrounded by objects which are ever drawing us away, pursued by hidden and crafty enemies, ever escape all the snares which are laid for us, and all the precipices on the edges of which we are walking, if we do not draw deeply from the wells of prayer, the light which is needful for us?

3. Jesus enjoyed the beatific vision, and was without interruption constantly united with God, and yet He made use of an appointed time, which He employed in devotion. How shall we, who live in a continual distraction of mind and heart, ever hope to enjoy the fruition of God, and to be united to Him, to have any feelings of devotion, faith, hope and love, unless every day we take a time, when, closing the door of our senses and of our hearts to all worldly objects, we are able to gather ourselves up entirely into the presence of God, to speak to Him, to listen to His voice, and to shew forth our love to Him?

4. Jesus was constantly occupied in furthering the glory of God His Father, and the salvation of men, and yet He laid aside His occupations, and took from His necessary repose, a certain time to be dedicated to prayer. And how shall we not take this time from a needlessly prolonged sleep, from occupations which are purely temporal, and often useless, from vain or dangerous pleasures, from hours even of weariness, in which we are unoccupied, and which we know not how to employ? Ah! do not let us seek any other cause of our frequent

falls, of our imperfections, of our want of virtue, and devotion, but in this want of prayer. *And it came to pass, that as He was praying in a certain place, when He ceased, one of His disciples said to Him, Lord, teach us to pray, as John also taught his disciples.* I cannot pray, you say. What, a thing which is necessary to you, appears to you impossible. Ah, say rather that you do not know how to pray. But it is that very thing which condemns you: for if you do not know, it is because you have never willed to learn, nor even tried; or if you have sometimes begun this holy exercise, thrown back by the first difficulty you have experienced, you have soon given it up. Have you then acted in this way, as regards so many other useless and even more difficult things which you have learnt? But if you do not know how to pray, whose disciples are you then? you are not the followers of Jesus, or of His holy forerunner: their first care was to teach their disciples to pray, and the first eagerness of their disciples was to learn from them. Let us then join ourselves to that disciple of Jesus, let us ask with him of that divine Saviour that He will teach us to pray, let us beg of Him to direct our conscience, and let us spare neither pains nor care to instruct ourselves in a matter of such importance to our salvation.

SECOND POINT.

The object of prayer.

1. The glory of God and the establishment of His kingdom. *Jesus said unto them, When ye pray, say, Our Father, Which art in Heaven, Hallowed be Thy Name, Thy kingdom come.* Here is the object or the end which we ought first of all to set before ourselves in prayer, namely, the glory of God, and the establishment of the kingdom of Jesus Christ on earth and in every heart.

2. Our temporal and spiritual needs. *Give us this*

day our daily bread. That is to say that which is necessary for the nourishment and support both of body and soul, for the attainment of every virtue, victory over our passions, the increase of grace, and our advancement towards perfection and in charity.

3. The forgiveness of our past sins. *Forgive us our trespasses, as we forgive them that are indebted to us.* In asking for the remission of our past sins, we ought to mourn over them, detest them, and make amends for them without ceasing: but whilst we ask daily of God to purify us more and more, we must remember the condition which He has laid upon us that we should forgive those who have offended us.

4. The avoidance of all sin for the future. *And lead us not into temptation.* We ought to ask of God to keep us from temptation, because we are feeble; if temptation presents itself, then let us ask Him to support us, that we may not yield to it, but that we may turn away from it with all our strength as from a snare, or a dangerous precipice. We ought lastly to foresee the temptations which may come upon us, in order to avoid them, and not to throw ourselves into them. Is it thus that we pray?

THIRD POINT.

Perseverance in prayer.

Our Saviour explains this point to us by an instructive and touching parable, when we see,

1. The motive for perseverance in the exercise of prayer, namely, our own needs and those of our neighbour, the charity we owe to ourselves, and that which we owe to others. He continues by saying to them; *If any of you shall have a friend, and shall go to him at midnight, and say unto him, Friend, lend me three loaves, for a friend of mine in his journey is come to me, and I have nothing to set before him?* Such is our state. Let us not suppose that we are able to feed

ourselves or feed others, unless we have recourse to that rich and powerful Friend, and unless we are assiduous in asking Him every day for the bread we need, and which we do not possess. Ah! if we were zealous for our own salvation, and that of our neighbour, we should not give up the use of prayer.

2. The difficulty of perseverance. The difficulty attendant on prayer is the reason why we do not persevere. It is in the night, and at midnight, that this man is obliged to go out of his house, to fetch bread from his friend. The night, that time that others employ in sleep, is the fittest time for prayer, and for divine communications; but it is inconvenient to our natural inclinations. Ah! how many people in the world spend their nights in feasting, dancing and amusements! and we have not the courage to consecrate one hour, or one half hour of our night in prayer, to overcome our weariness, fatigue, and idleness, in order that we may persevere in the exercise of prayer!

3. Another obstacle to perseverance, is the apparent uselessness of prayer. *And he from within shall answer and say, Trouble me not; the door is now shut, and my children are with me in bed; I cannot rise and give thee.* Such is the answer which God seems sometimes to make us, that is to say, heaven seems to be closed to our prayers, and we seem as if we ought not to expect any answer thence. The devil and self-love unite to persuade us that the wise delays of God are absolute refusals. It is useless for me, we say to ourselves, to pray; I am none the holier, I do not live any the better; the time which I spend in prayer is only wasted time, in which I feel only weariness and langour, and which I should do better to employ in some other way. Ah! do not let yourself be drawn away thus. If God does not answer your prayers at first, if prayer has no attraction for you, do not weary of it, do not let yourself be discouraged, continue to pray instantly, without giving up; cry yet louder, knock still more importunately. Far from abandoning the exercise of prayer, set yourself still more fervently to it.

4. *The reward of perseverance.* *I say unto you, Though he will not rise and give him, because he is his friend, yet because of his importunity he will rise and give him as many as he needeth.* Behold the reward of our perseverance, an excellent and much to be desired reward, which includes every thing which is needful for our salvation and sanctification; a reward assured and unchangeable, for He to Whom we pray is not only our Friend, but our Father. His delays are an effect of His wisdom, of His tenderness for us, and not of any difficulty which He has in granting our prayers. Lastly, let us remember that it is Jesus Christ Himself, Who, under the similitude of this parable, promises to crown our perseverance, that it is He Who adds; *And I say unto you, Ask, and it shall be given you; seek, and ye shall find; knock, and it shall be opened unto you.* He repeats it to us again and makes of it a general maxim to us, that we may never forget it. *For every one that asketh, receiveth; and he that seeketh, findeth; and to him that knocketh, it shall be opened.* Let us learn, from these expressions how much God inclines to hear our prayers, and how important it is that we should pray and persevere in the exercise of prayer.

FOURTH POINT.

Fruits of prayer.

1. These fruits are virtues, which are real and not only apparent. In the same way that an earthly father acts towards his children in the order of natural and physical life, so does God act towards us in the moral and spiritual order of things; and in this same moral order the world deals in a contrary way, with regard to the children of its generation. *If a son shall ask bread of any of you that is a father, will he give him a stone?* No, but he will give him real bread, which will strengthen and nourish him. In the same way, God gives us in prayer, real virtues, humility, obedience, faith, devotion, and charity. In the world, on the contrary, virtue

is but hypocrisy and ceremony; humility is only a compliment, obedience is yielded through interested motives, religion is assumed from human respect, and charity through vanity. Such is the bread with which the world nourishes its children. But under the semblance of bread, there is nothing but hardness, self-esteem, and self-love; with this appearance of bread, the soul remains in weakness and langour, and often falls into the corruption of death.

2. The fruits of prayer are true delights, and not such as are only deception. *Or if he ask a fish, will he for a fish, give him a serpent?* Nay, but he will give him a real fish, which will not only procure him a solid but a delicious nourishment. God, in the same way, gives us in prayer such superabundant graces as render the practice of virtue, not only possible, easy, and sweet, but even delightful, so that we can find true happiness in humiliation and self-abnegation, in crosses and afflictions. The world, which has never experienced any such joys, treats these holy comforts as chimeras and illusions, and promises true pleasures to those whom it gains to itself by its attractions; but what is this pleasure which the world offers, but an insidious and seductive serpent?

3. The fruits of prayer are healthful maxims, and not such as are poisonous. *Or if he ask of him an egg, will he give him a scorpion?* No, but he will give him a real egg, such as will afford him a wholesome and nourishing food. God fills our mind in prayer with maxims of salvation, on the shortness of life, on the difference between time and eternity, on contempt for the false goods of this world, on the happiness of the righteous; salutary and divine maxims, which contain the precious germ of a holy and perfect life, and which lead the soul to a happy immortality. But what are the maxims which the world gives to its children as regards pleasures, riches, honours, the use they should make of life, especially of the earlier portion of it? Poisonous and diabolical maxims are they, which like so many venomous scorpions fix themselves on the heart, infest and corrupt

it, spread their venom over all the actions of a person's life, and precipitate the soul into an inevitable and eternal death.

4. The last fruit of prayer is the spirit of goodness, and not of malice. *If ye then being evil, know how to give good gifts unto your children, how much more shall your heavenly Father give the Holy Ghost to them that ask Him.* God gives us every thing in communicating to us in prayer the gift of the Holy Spirit; Spirit of goodness and love, Spirit of strength and virtue, Source eternal and inexhaustible of all good. Ah! if we did but know the value of such an excellent gift, with what ardour, with what constancy should we pray for It, with what care should we not prepare ourselves to receive It. God gives It to those who ask Him for it, and does not give It to those who neglect to pray for It. But if God does not give us *His* Spirit, we cannot escape being delivered up to the spirit of the world; spirit of malice and corruption, spirit of error and falsehood, spirit of confusion and of trouble, source impure and unquenchable of disorder and of every evil thing.

Prayer. O holy exercise of prayer, wherefore have I neglected you so long, or practised you with such coldness! Ah! I have too truly proved by my experience, that without you, there is neither virtue nor piety; that without you, the soul is in trouble and sin, in a state of infirmity and langour, and often even in a state of death which may become eternal. Holy Spirit, Who art both the Author and the Reward of prayer, teach me to pray: pray in me, and I shall with Thee have all; the more Thou dost communicate Thyself to me, the greater will be my delight in prayer; the more I pray, the more wilt Thou give Thyself to me. Amen.

Meditation CV.

JESUS HEALS A MAN WHO WAS POSSESSED WITH A DEVIL, AND WAS BLIND AND DUMB.

1. Consider the healing of this man who was possessed-with a devil; 2. see in this man the type of the sinner; 3. observe the discourses of the by-standers with regard to this act of healing. S. Matt. xii. 22-24. S. Luke xi. 14-16.

FIRST POINT.

Healing of the man who was possessed with a devil.

1. *A prompt healing.* *There was brought unto Him one possessed with a devil, blind and dumb; and He healed him, insomuch that the blind and dumb both spake and saw.* The Saviour, after His own prayer, and the instruction given to His disciples on prayer, proceeded to accede to the requests of the people who presented to Him a man possessed with a devil, and who was rendered deaf and blind by it, and *He healed him.* The Evangelist could not better express to us the promptitude of the cure, than by these words, *and He healed him:* that is to say, the moment when the man who was possessed was brought to our Saviour was the moment of his healing.

2. *Miraculous healing.* This man was afflicted with three maladies at a time; he was possessed with a devil, was blind and dumb. His condition was worthy of compassion, and nothing less than a miracle could avail to bring him out of it; thus it was a miracle which the people looked for from Jesus, when they brought this unfortunate man to Him.

3. *Public healing.* It is in the presence of the multitude that this cure took place: it is the people who themselves bring to Jesus the object whom He knows, and whose sad situation He pities. It is this same people who are the witnesses of his sudden and perfect cure, who behold him having now his body whole, his mind

set free, his tongue unloosed, his eyes opened, speaking and acting like a man who is entirely healed. Let our hearts be penetrated with the thought of our Saviour, of His greatness, His goodness, and His power; let us join our admiration to that of the people, and let us yield ourselves up to the most tender feelings of reverence, trust, and love.

SECOND POINT.

This possessed man is the type of the sinner.

The condition of this possessed man represents to us the condition of a sinner who is in a state of mortal sin.

1. He belongs to the devil; he is his slave, he is in his invisible possession, which though insensible, is true, is real, and so much the more fatal, that if the sinner were to die in that state, it would be eternal.

2. He is blind; blind to the fearful state of his conscience, and to the perils of his condition; blind to the enormity of the sins which he has committed, and to the excesses to which his passion carries him away, and to which he is about to yield himself up; blind even to the temporal hurt which his sins cause him, whether in his body, his property, or his reputation.

3. He is dumb; dumb to pray, dumb to confess his sins, dumb to ask for help. If he speaks, it is only to those confidants of his passion, who are likely to encourage him in it, or to furnish him with the means of gratifying it; but he will employ all the care he can to conceal it from the wise and virtuous, who might discover to him the snare which was being laid for him, and the abyss of perdition to which he was being led on.

THIRD POINT.

Discourses of the bystanders with regard to this act of healing.

1. The discourse of the multitude. *And all the people were amazed, and said, Is not this the Son of David?*

The multitude, who were not prejudiced by any foregone conclusion nor blinded by any self-interest, and who witnessed the unheard-of wonders which Jesus had wrought before their eyes, could not restrain themselves from acknowledging Him as the Messiah, and crying out *Is not this the Son of David*, the promised Saviour, and Him Whom we look for? The cry of the multitude has prevailed, it is still to be heard now-a-days, and the evidence of the truth is forced from the lips of all who know what Christianity really is, and who have no prejudices to hinder them from acknowledging the truth. The more we search out the depths of the Christian religion, the more we study history, the more we are forced to exclaim, This is not the work of man, of deceit, or of fraud; it is the work of God, it is truth.

2. Discourse of the Pharisees. *But when the Pharisees heard it, they said, This fellow doth not cast out devils, but by Beelzebub, the prince of devils.* The Pharisees saw the miracle which had been worked in favour of the blind and deaf man who was possessed with a devil, and they heard the judgment which the people passed upon it. What could they find to oppose to so palpable a fact? It was not possible to deny the truth of it. They said therefore that Jesus had made a compact with hell, and that it was in the name of Beelzebub the prince of the devils, and by his power, that He drove out the other devils; an absurd and ridiculous evasion, which no one in the present day would dare to make use of; but is that which the free thinkers of our generation employ, namely the denial of facts which have been attested in the earliest ages of Christianity, and handed down to us, less absurd and ridiculous?

3. Discourse of the unbelievers. *And others, tempting Him, sought of Him a sign from Heaven.* The wonders which Jesus worked were, according to these Jews, only works of this earth, however wonderful they might be. These enemies of the Saviour insinuated then to the people, that, in order to be fully convinced of the truth of His mission, it was necessary that there should

be some phenomenon in the air, some prodigy in the sky, *a sign from Heaven.* Was it in order that they might believe in Jesus Christ that they made this request? No, it was in order to tempt Him; it was in order to see if He would grant them this request, that they might see if He had the same power in Heaven as on earth; or, if Jesus did not listen to their demand, as they must have expected that He would not, it was that they might construe His refusal into a proof of His want of power, and draw the attention of the people to it as such. Restless and frivolous spirits, who would have preferred vain and useless prodigies to those miracles of healing and blessing which Jesus wrought, and which characterized so well the true Saviour of men! Such are the straits to which the philosophers of our days are reduced; they are not satisfied with the miracles which are offered to them, they ask for fresh ones of which they would be the witnesses; as if they could believe in good faith that this were wise conduct and worthy of God, to lavish miracles at the senseless desire of each unbeliever! How consoling it is for the Christian to see all the enemies of Christianity reduced, at all times, to prove only their own folly, their malice, and their blindness!

Prayer. O Jesus, if I am not yet so hardened as to contest Thy miracles as the Jews did, or to deny them as unbelievers do, am I not guilty in Thine eyes of those evil passions which lead to this denial of Thee? Alas! Lord, am I not perhaps in that sad state of possession, of blindness, and of silence, in which this man whom we read of in the Gospel was? Does not the devil exercise over me the most absolute rule? Am I not dumb through shame or through obstinacy, so that I do not confess my sins, or pray to Thee with fervour? O Son and Lord of David! drive from my heart the evil spirit which tyrannises over me; open my eyes, unloose my tongue, and make me cling to Thee irrevocably in time and in eternity. Amen.

Meditation CVI.

ANSWER OF JESUS TO THE BLASPHEMY OF THE PHARISEES.

1. Jesus refutes here the blasphemy of the Pharisees; 2. He points out to them Who alone is the Author of the miracle which they contest; 3. He reproaches them with the enormity of their blasphemy. S. Matt. xii. 25—27. S. Luke xi. 17—23.

FIRST POINT.

Refutation of the blasphemy of the Pharisees.

1. Our Lord points out that there is a contradiction on the part of the Pharisees in this accusation. *But He knowing their thoughts, said unto them, every kingdom divided against itself is brought to desolation; and a house divided against a house falleth. If Satan also be divided against himself, how shall his kingdom stand?* These Pharisees, so unblushing in their jealousy, did not shrink from attributing the miraculous works of Jesus Christ to a secret understanding with hell. These slanderers, scattered amongst the different groups of spectators, where the event which had just taken place was the topic of conversation, insinuated every where that Jesus cast out devils by the power of the devils themselves. As this accusation, absurd as it was, might make an impression on the minds of the multitude, our Lord thought it needful to point out the contradiction into which His enemies fell, through the conclusion they thus drew. If a kingdom, He says to them, if a city, if a family is divided, it destroys itself, and cannot exist any longer. It is the same with the kingdom of darkness; if a devil drive out another devil, the devils must then be divided amongst themselves: and then how shall the kingdom of Satan be maintained? His empire must be destroyed, and fall into ruin, for its end is at hand. The accusation of the Pharisees with the contradiction it contains, is not one of the attacks made by unbelievers

of the present day upon the teaching of our Lord and Saviour, but who can count the numberless contradictions into which the enemies of Jesus Christ and His Church fall? They accuse religion of having incomprehensible mysteries; as if mysteries were not the mark of God's works, as if nature itself were not full of mysteries, as if those who find fault with such assurance, and without being supported by any authority, were not in themselves paradoxes, which are still more incomprehensible; for example a world and reasonable beings, which are created for a moment, and without any further aim; a God infinitely perfect, and yet Who displays in His works neither wisdom, goodness, nor justice. And amongst unbelievers there are as many systems as there are men, and as many contradictions as there are systems. Why should man take such pains to avoid the truth, whilst it is offered to him by Jesus Christ in a manner so evident and so perceptible?

2. Our Lord points out that there is, on the part of the Pharisees, partiality in their judgements. *And if I by Beelzebub cast out devils, by whom do your sons cast them out? therefore shall they be your judges.* The Jews, being possessed of the true religion, had also amongst them exorcists approved of by the scribes and by the Pharisees, who in the name of the true God, conjured the evil spirits and drove them out. 'Now,' our Lord answers, 'I do what your disciples do; it is the same God Whom they invoke, and Whom I acknowledge; it is by Him and in His power that I drive them out. You sanction the acts of your children, wherefore then do you refuse to acknowledge what I do? *Therefore shall they be your judges.* The wonders which they work are so many precedents for My miracles; the ministry which you have entrusted to them will form at the same time My apology and your condemnation.' Such are generally our judgements; we have respect of persons, we justify and we condemn at the same moment, and for the same action, two different persons. In those whom we do not love, good is an evil, the least failing is a

crime, their name alone decides us; what we blame in the one, we praise in the other; but a judgement in which there is so much partiality and injustice forms an apology for these whom we condemn, and the condemnation of those whom we judge. Do we not fall ourselves into this unjust partiality, when we praise or excuse every thing in ourselves, and blame everything in those who do not please us?

3. Our Lord points out to us that there is, on the part of the Pharisees, inconsistency in their reasoning. These wicked and envious men had nothing that they could bring against the conduct of Jesus Christ, they could not blame the action of driving out evil spirits, and yet they said that he who drove them out was himself given up to the devil, and possessed by him, and that the miracles he worked were the works of hell. Be consistent in your judgements, our Lord said to them; *Either make the tree good, and his fruit good; or else make the tree corrupt, and his fruit corrupt; for the tree is known by his fruit.* You desire to judge of My conduct; in order to do so with justice, you must confine yourselves to deeds and works, as one must necessarily judge of the goodness of a tree by the goodness of its fruit; it is by that, you must regulate your actions, and not by suspicions or by prejudices, by the malice and the injustice of your own hearts. Wherefore then is there amongst us that animosity in running down persons, whose lives are irreproachable, their faith pure, and their conduct blameless? Why, since you find nothing praiseworthy in them, should you go out of your way gratuitously to assign to them criminal intentions, or motives? It is with difficulty that we restrain our indignation against such slanderers: our Lord gives vent to His indignation in the strongest terms, because He willed to put a stop to the insinuations whereby they sought to mislead the people. *O generation of vipers!* He adds, *How can ye being evil, speak good things? For out of the abundance of the heart the mouth speaketh. A good man out of the good treasure of the heart bringeth*

forth good things; and an evil man out of the evil treasure, bringeth forth evil things. Wicked men, generation of vipers, like unto those from whom you spring, ye take delight in spreading poison on all around which is opposed to you! Whilst you are thus disposed and suffer yourselves to be governed by your own cruel jealousy, how could you speak a good word? How can your lips utter ought but calumnies and blasphemies? It is out of the abundance of the heart that your mouth speaks; what else could be expected to come forth from envenomed, jealous, and cankered hearts, save words of death, calumnies and blasphemies? Cease to hate Me, change your heart with regard to Me, and you will speak another language. The fore-runner of Christ had spoken with the same force, and nearly in the same words, against the hypocrites who corrupted the people, and turned them away from the truth. After such examples, ought we to fear, when the occasion presents itself, to let our zeal burst forth in order to close the mouths of those who only attack God's ministers in order to put an end to their ministry, and believers in order to destroy the true faith? But are we in no way partakers of the crime of these wicked men, whose hearts are thus corrupted, if we suffer empoisoned words to come forth from our lips, against God, the Church, or our neighbour?

SECOND POINT.

Jesus Christ declares that He is the sole and real Author of the miracle which gave occasion to the blasphemy of the Pharisees.

1. As Son of God, acting only by the Spirit of God, and in that, He is the object of our faith. *But if I with the finger of God cast out devils, if I cast out devils by the Spirit of God, no doubt the kingdom of God is come upon you.* Jesus drove out the devil out of the bodies of those possessed by him only by the Spirit of God, and in order to establish amongst men the kingdom of heaven, by the faith which persons ought to have

in Him, as Son of God, and as the Messiah. It is also by the Spirit of God that He drove out the devil from the souls of sinners, by destroying sin in them, in order to establish in their hearts the reign of God, of His grace, and His love. He who only abstains from sin from human motives, who only renounces one passion in order to yield to another, who only breaks through one old habit in order to contract a fresh one, does nothing more than change the evil spirit who has taken possession of him. Am I not of that number? Does God reign in me? Does the devil no longer exercise any empire there? Have I that faith which is victorious over the devil and the world?

2. As Saviour of men, stronger than the devil, their enemy; and in that He is the object of our hope. *When a strong man armed keepeth his palace, his goods are in peace; but when a stronger than he shall come upon him and overcome him, he taketh from him all his armour wherein he trusted, and divideth his spoils. Or how can one enter into a strong man's house, and spoil his goods, except he first bind the strong man? and then he will spoil his house?* This devil, this well armed man, had subjugated the earth, and was in the peaceful enjoyment of his victory. He reigned in the hearts of men; he had temples and altars erected to him by their hands, adorned without and enriched with the most precious gifts of nature; he extended his dominion even over God's own chosen people. But a stronger than he was now come, Jesus, our divine Saviour, who conquered him, bound and chained him; Who drove him out of the souls and bodies of men, Who overthrew his temples and altars.

3. As sovereign Creator of all creatures, on Whose side every one ought publicly to declare themselves; and in that, He is the Object of our love. *He that is not with Me, is against Me; and he that gathereth not with Me, scattereth abroad.* He who is not for Christ is against Him; there is no middle course between Him and the world, between the happiness of being wholly

His as His disciple, and the misery of being against Him as His enemy. As soon as the Gospel is made known, there is no choice left to men to be indifferent to it; it must be embraced, we dare no longer remain neuter. As soon as the commandments of God are known we may not any longer hesitate, consult the inclinations of others, await their approbation: we must obey. He who does not declare himself on the side of Jesus Christ does not love Him; and he that does not love Him, let him be anathema maranatha. (1 Cor. xvi. 22.)

THIRD POINT.

Jesus Christ reproaches the Pharisees with the heinousness of their blasphemy.

1. Jesus manifests the infinite mercy of God towards the sins of which men repent. *Wherefore I say unto you, All manner of sin and blasphemy shall be forgiven unto men. And whosoever speaketh a word against the Son of Man, it shall be forgiven him.* O ye, who groan under the tyranny of your sins! listen to these words of our Saviour, and rejoice at the thought of His infinite mercies. All sins shall be forgiven to men, however great, however enormous they may be; blasphemy against God, blasphemy against Jesus Christ, abuse of His Sacraments, profanation of His Body and Blood by unworthy Communions; every thing in a word, will be forgiven, if, with a truly contrite, humble, and penitent heart, you have recourse to that same Saviour Whom you have offended, and to those same Sacraments which you have profaned.

2. Jesus sets forth the terrible justice of God against those sins in which men harden themselves. *But the blasphemy against the Holy Ghost shall not be forgiven unto men. But whosoever speaketh against the Holy Ghost, it shall not be forgiven him, neither in this world, neither in the world to come.* The blasphemy against the Holy Spirit is the only sin which is not forgiven, that is to say, that obstinacy with which

men withstand known truth, the evidence of miracles, and the proofs of Christianity; those efforts which men make after having defiled themselves with numberless crimes, in order to quiet their consciences in the midst of their sins, by denying, against their own consciences, the existence of a Providence, of holiness, and of religion; that perversity of heart with which men close their eyes, against their own conscience and its remorse, to the light which shines around them on all sides, and wilfully determine to remain in error themselves and to draw others into it; such is the sin which shall not be forgiven either in this world, or in that which is to come. It is rarely that such sinners are brought to repentance, to open their eyes, and be converted; and thus they come into eternal punishment. A terrible truth, and one which will not fail of its accomplishment? A great number amongst the Jews who demanded the the death of Jesus Christ, the executioners who crucified Him, the soldier who pierced His side, and the centurion who commanded the guard, were converted; but the Scribes and Pharisees who blasphemed against the Holy Ghost, during the life of Jesus Christ, continued on in their blasphemies after His death, and died at last in their wilful blindness, and hardness of heart. Ah! if the frailty of our nature had made us commit such sins, if even we had begun to blaspheme against the Holy Ghost, do not let us be mad enough to close all return against ourselves, and to take from ourselves all hope, by persisting willfully in our blasphemies against that Spirit of holiness, Which could yet restore us to life, by wilfully refusing to listen to His voice.

3. Extreme rigour of the judgment of God against unrepented sins. *But I say unto you That every idle word that men shall speak, they shall give account thereof in the day of Judgment: for by thy words thou shalt be justified, and by thy words thou shalt be condemned.* When we shall appear before God in order to be judged, we shall have to render an account even of useless words which we shall have spoken without ne-

cessity and which shall have been of no advantage either to ourselves or our neighbours. Who would have thought that God would have thus entered into these details, and with such minute exactness, if we had not been assured of it, by our Lord Himself? But in a Divine judgment, nothing can escape, nothing is of little account: it is then for us to watch carefully over our words, since they must of necessity, enter into the sentence of our condemnation or of our justification. Now, if words are to be thus examined into with this rigorous exactness, how will it be with our actions, with the thoughts, desires, and all the motives of our hearts?

Prayer. Have mercy on me, O Jesus! have mercy on me! Alas! what will become of me in the day of Thy justice, if Thou dost not come to my succour. Ah! deign to communicate Thy Holy Spirit to me, that He may reign in my soul, and that the evil one may be driven thence for ever. The glorious victory which Thou hast gained over this enemy of my salvation inspires me with confidence. With Thee, what can I fear against this strong man armed? Let this furious lion cause his ravings to be heard, he will not terrify me; armed with Thy grace, I shall triumph over his fury! O God! be my strength and my support! O King of glory! I am Thine now and for ever. Fear, human respect, nothing shall be able to hinder me from declaring myself for Thee in time, so that I may be united to Thee in eternity. Amen.

Meditation CVII.

THE DEVIL RETURNING TO HIS FORMER ABODE.

Jesus sets forth to us under this parable; 1. the relapse of a soul into sin; 2. the relapse of a people into infidelity. S. Matt. xii. 43-45. S. Luke xi. 24-26.

FIRST POINT.

Of the relapse of a soul into sin.

1. Of the causes of the relapse. These causes are to be found in the conduct which the devil pursues, and which we ourselves adopt, after he has been driven out of our hearts. 1. The devil is restless, and we, we are quiet. *When the unclean spirit is gone out of a man, he walketh through dry places, seeking rest, and findeth none.* Our Lord compares the devil to a man, who having been driven out of a house of which he had taken unjust possession, goes to hide his disgrace in desert places, and does not know whither he shall withdraw himself. The devil, confused at his defeat, cannot endure the affront that he has met with; he feels the loss he has sustained, and he is in distress and agitation. As for us, on the contrary, we are quiet and indifferent; after some moments given to devotion, we think no longer of the happiness which we enjoy, in order to thank God for it, nor of the furious enemy who does not lose us out of sight, in order that we may keep on our guard; we allow ourselves to fall asleep in a fatal security, instead of which we ought to give ourselves no repose, but fear, watch, and pray without ceasing. 2. The devil makes a firm resolution, and we, we only form but feeble ones. *Then he saith, I will return into mine house from whence I came out.* The devil always looks upon that house as his own, and he calls it so. Resolved to do every thing and to undertake every thing in order

to make himself master of it for the second time, he dares to assert that he will return there, and looks upon the matter as certain. Ah! how much is wanting to our resolutions of this determination and resolution! It is only in half heartedness that we promise not to fall back into sin, and often we feel that our hearts are giving the lie to our words. Very far from feeling assured that we shall not again relapse into our former sins, we look upon it as but too sure that we shall fall back into them; or, if we do form some resolution which appears to us firm, alas! it lasts but a short time, every day it grows weaker, it lessens. Ah! we ought to renew it each day, many times a day, and always with the same fervour; we must oppose the firmness of the devil with firmness, and his determination with determination, and say to him, ' No, thou shalt not return into my heart, it belongs to God, and never shall be thine again; thou hast been driven from it like a usurper, and with the grace which He gives me Who has conquered thee, thou shalt never have possession of it again.' Ought not the very determination with which the devil seeks to claim the empire of our hearts, suffice to inspire us with a firm and courageous determination to refuse that which he tries to gain from us by force? 3. The devil comes to see in what state our heart is, and we, we neglect to examine in what condition it is. *And when he is come, he findeth it empty, swept, and garnished.* If the devil discovers a weak place any where in our hearts, it is there that he attacks it; if he finds there confusion and dissension, some ill-curbed passion, some ill-restrained inclination, these are so many advantages of which he makes the most, and which he does not fail to turn to profit; if he finds there anything which sullies our hearts, such as self-love, dislike of our neighbour, avarice, anger, love of pleasure, he claims them as his own, and as giving him the right to recover their possession; if he finds this heart unadorned, that is without strength, defenceless, and destitute of virtue, he returns there, and makes himself the master of it without a struggle; but if he finds it well armed, adorned with Christian virtues, and at peace, then he withdraws, not to renounce his enterprise, but to take new measures. It is then for us to examine daily our conscience most carefully, to discover in what state it is, and promptly to remedy any thing which might favour the designs of the enemy. 4. The devil does not reckon upon his own strength alone, but he goes to seek for help, and we, we count too much on ourselves, and on our own strength. *Then goeth he, and taketh with himself seven other spirits more wicked than himself.* When the devil finds our heart in a state of defence, he goes to seek seven other evil spirits, that is to say a great number of evil spirits, in order to be able to carry the place by storm: and he chooses those that are more wicked, more crafty than himself, that together they may employ all their strength and attack us on all sides, by joy and sorrow, by pain and pleasure, by adversity and prosperity, by love and hatred, by friends and enemies, by the attractions of the world and by its persecutions. Nevertheless the assistance which the devil has procured for himself would not give him any advantage over us, if we, on our part, after having done all that depends on ourselves, knew how to mistrust our own strength, and in this mistrust to implore the help of God by fervent and constant prayer. 5. Lastly, the devil attacks us with force and obstinacy, and we, we offer him only a feeble resistance and of short duration. The first assault often makes us lose heart. A longer resistance appears to us impossible; a life passed in struggles appears to us too rigorous a martyrdom. The eternal crown which is promised to us does not touch us. We yield, at least, for that time, flattering ourselves that we shall rise up again some day, and that then our courage will be more established, the struggle less severe, and the victory easier. Ah! how we delight to flatter ourselves, to deceive ourselves, and too early to ruin ourselves!

2. The misery of a relapse. *And they enter in and dwell there; and the last state of that man is worse*

than the first. The condition of a soul that relapses into sin is worse than its first state of sin. 1. By the heinousness of the fresh sins it has committed, which ingratitude for blessings received, broken promises, and the contempt of grace given, render so much greater. 2. By the number of its sins. Instead of one evil spirit, it often becomes possessed by seven; instead of one vice or one passion, it abandons itself to all its inordinate inclinations; instead of some sins of the same nature into which it fell but rarely, and not without remorse, it multiplies the acts of sin, and no longer knows their number. 3. By the difficulty there is in rising again after a relapse. The devils establish in that soul their dwelling as firmly as possible. The habit of sin is formed, and its chains are multiplied; the soul becomes more feeble, the light of faith is obscured, remorse is felt less often and is less poignant, grace abounds less, and conversion appears so difficult, that the sinner puts it off continually, and often ends by giving it up altogether. 4. By the facility with which a person falls back into sin. After a first deliverance, the person has probably resisted for some time against the temptation, or has made some struggle before falling back into sin; but if he does not rise again after the first fall, a second fall will quickly follow; and the oftener he falls back into sin, the shorter interval will there be between the repentance, and the relapse which follows. 5. Lastly by the delusions into which it is but too common for a person to fall. It is but too easy to accustom one's self to an alternation of sins and confessions; by that means, one finds a way in which to satisfy one's passions, and quiet one's conscience. The sin is committed without difficulty, because the person counts upon confessing it; he confesses his sin without difficulty, because he feels sure that he shall fall back into it; he feels the shame of his chains, but he hugs them in secret: he flatters himself in his imagination that they are broken, but in his heart he rejoices that they are not. Fatal delusion which leads so many sinners to the tomb, and from the tomb into hell! Ter-

-rible consequence of relapses, and often of the first relapse!

SECOND POINT.

Of the relapse of a nation into infidelity.

1. *Of the causes of relapse.* What our Lord has just spoken is not less applicable to an entire nation than to a particular soul; He applies the words Himself to the Jewish nation. *Even so shall it be also unto this wicked generation.* The Jewish nation had often fallen into idolatry, and been raised out of it again. The last idolatry, and the longest of all had been expiated by the Babylonish captivity, which was also the longest of all. This chosen people had come forth from it full of zeal for their religion, and of fervour, and God had renewed the miracles of His Almighty power on behalf of its reestablishment. When Jesus Christ came into the world, the Jews had for a long time begun to decline from this fervour. The impiety of the Sadducees, who denied the resurrection and the immortality of the soul; the pride and hypocrisy of the Pharisees, who corrupted the law of God, and wrested the meaning of it to their own profit: the corruption of manners which had crept in amongst every rank of life; the false ideas which had spread respecting the reign of the Messiah which they looked for, all this rendered this generation the most sinful of all those which had preceded it, and prepared the nation for that act of Deicide of which they became guilty. After this crime had been committed, great numbers of private persons so abhorred it that they became Christians; but the main body of the nation have persisted in it, and still persist in it, without acknowledging the hand of God, which, for so many centuries has been heavy upon it. Thus has been fulfilled in that ungrateful nation that which our Lord here prophesies. The history of the Jews, in this point, is the history of all those nations, who, after having renounced idolatry in order to embrace Christianity, have afterwards fallen

into schism or unbelief. The same causes which we have shewn above have precipitated them into this misery, that is to say, the malice and activity of the devil, who, in order to return into his former abode, has brought every thing to bear, the luxury of riches, the splendour of arts, the pride of knowledge, love of novelty, and so on. And as each person may contribute to the decay of the faith in a nation, so also each separate individual, each family may labour to preserve it, and to cause it to flourish anew. But to this end, 1. we ought to set an infinite value upon this precious gift of faith, to rejoice that we are members of the Holy Catholic Church, and thank God that He has caused us to be born in her bosom, and pity those who have not the same advantages as ourselves! What does it matter that a state flourishes though commerce, sciences and arts, if those flowers do not produce the fruits of faith. Happy is the country whose citizens belong to the heavenly kingdom! Every thing else is as nought, and cannot follow us beyond the tomb. 2. We ought often to make acts of faith, and renew in the presence of Jesus Christ our feelings of inviolable attachment to His Church, which He has purchased with His Blood, and built upon a foundation which cannot be shaken, though the waters rage and swell, and though the mountains shake at the tempest of the same. Let us examine ourselves whether we in no way open the door to the enemy, by reading publications which are directed against religion or the faith of Christ's Church, or by listening with pleasure to discourses in which holy things are ridiculed. We ought to pray daily for the preservation of the true faith in the nation to which we belong. 3. We ought to resist with firmness to every attack which is made against the true faith, without letting ourselves be dazzled by the intellect, the knowledge, and talents of whoever it may be who holds a contrary language. Our faith rests upon the word of God, and not upon the dogmas of human science and learning.

2. Misery of a relapse into infidelity. The misery

of a nation, which falls back into unbelief after having held the faith is the same as that of the Jews. 1. It is given up to a wilful blindness which no light can disperse. The Jew prides himself, in that, exempt from idolatry, he worships God, and obeys His commandments, and he will not acknowledge that to reject Jesus Christ is to reject God and His commandments. 2. In the same way he is animated by the implacable hatred of truth, which no reasonings can overthrow. The Jew perpetuates the same hatred against Christianity from generation to generation. 3. He is abandoned to an inconceivable hardness of heart, which nothing can overcome. We see individuals amongst them abandon Judaism and embrace Christianity, but as a nation, it remains unconverted, and obstinately refuses to walk in the paths of truth. Such hardness of heart is a curse from God, and a visible punishment of their apostacy. The present state of this nation, as our Lord says, is worse than their first condition, because the evil is greater, and appears to be without remedy and hopeless. Let us thank God for the light He has bestowed upon us, whilst we pray, fear, and keep on our watch.

Prayer. Defend me by Thy grace, O Jesus! Save me, O my God! and suffer me not to be lost by falling back into sin, and to add to my other unfaithfulnesses the ingratitude of a wilful relapse. Preserve me from so great a misfortune, so fatal in its consequences. Grant that I may not exercise less vigilance in saving myself, than the devil shews in his furious endeavours to lose me; grant that I may live and die in Thy holy grace and in Thy holy love. Amen.

Meditation CVIII [a].

EXCLAMATION OF A WOMAN ON THE BLESSEDNESS OF THE MOTHER OF OUR LORD.

Consider; 1. Her confession of Jesus, as Very God and Very Man; 2. The Conception of Jesus in the body would not have profited Mary, without the conception in spirit. 3. The whole perfection of the spiritual life is in hearing the Word of God and doing it. S. Luke xi. 27, 28.

FIRST POINT.

When the Lord Jesus was saying these things in reply to the blasphemies of the Jews, *a certain woman*, not rich, not powerful, not noble, but poor, of the crowd and of the common people and populace, *lifting up*, i.e., bringing up out of her heart, and steadily and loudly putting forth a *voice*, in praise of Christ and reply to the blaspheming Jews (for the common people are usually more devout than those in higher place), burst forth in praise of Christ against the reviling of the Jews. She could no longer endure the blasphemies of the Jews against Christ, and, against the blasphemers, put forth her voice in praise of Christ and His mother, extolling the conception of her Son, and the Birth after the flesh, and saying, *Blessed is the womb which bare Thee* the Blessed One through Whom we all are blessed, and *blessed the paps which Thou didst suck.* She blesses and praises the mother from the Son, and not vice versa, because grace and glory proceed from Him as their Source. The great truthfulness and confidence and faith and devotion of that woman appear in two points. First that she spake not silently and in a whisper: she feared not to raise her voice on high, for she was enkindled by the sweetness of Christ's words. Secondly at the very time when the Scribes and Pharisees were tempting the Lord, while they were blaspheming,

[a] substituted from Ludolphus, Life of Christ, part 1, chap. 75.

she with great boldness confesses the Son of God, so as to confound both the accusation of the Jews at the time, and the unfaithfulness of heretics in after time. She confesses against the blasphemers that He is true Son of God, of One Substance with the Father, in that she calls the mother *blessed* from her Son as the Source of her blessedness by reason of His Godhead: and she witnesses that He is true, and no phantom, Son of man, of one substance with His mother, in that she declares that He is borne from her belly, suckled at her breasts.

Spiritually that woman means Holy Church, which amid crowds of Jews, Pagans, and heretics confesses with believing voice the Lord Jesus Christ; by whose voice in truth the *blessed womb* of the Virgin Mary is proclaimed, which was made meet to bear the Redeemer of the whole world, as she says of herself, *From henceforth all generations shall call me blessed.* Let us therefore lift up our voice with the Catholic Church, of which this woman was a type; let us lift up our mind too out of the midst of the crowd and say to our Saviour, *Blessed is the womb that bare Thee, and the paps which Thou hast sucked.*

SECOND POINT.

Jesus, confirming the woman's speech and endorsing her praise of His mother and the faith and constancy of this woman and of others like her, said, *Yea rather, blessed are they which hear the word of God and keep it.* Whereby He shewed that the blessed Virgin had conceived Him, spiritually through faith and devotion, with greater bliss than through the bodily Birth. It is as if He said, 'As thou sayest, specially blessed is she whose womb bare Me: yet not only is *she* blessed, rather all *are blessed*, now in hope, at length hereafter in reality, *who hear the Word of God*, believing it in their heart, *and keep it*, fulfilling it in their actions. Blessed indeed and happy is My mother, who bare Me and suckled Me: yet happier and more blessed, for that she heard *the Word of God,* and on hearing, believed it, believing, kept it. For except she had done this, My mother could have been neither happy nor blessed. Whence Elizabeth said to her, *Blessed is she that believed, for there shall be a performance of those things which were told her of the Lord.* More blessed therefore is she, because she conceived the Word spiritually in her mind, received it by the hearing of faith, and kept it diligently and in heart in her life: because spiritual conception, whereby Christ is conceived in her heart, is more blissful than the bodily conception. For to *faith working through love* is vouchsafed eternal bliss, not so to conception or bearing without faith; because *without faith it is impossible to please* God. Hence according to S. Augustine, "More blessed is Mary in receiving the faith of Christ than in conceiving the flesh of Christ[b]:" and more blessedly conceived she God in her mind through faith, than in her body through the assumption of flesh. For " her nearness as a mother would have been of no profit to Mary, had she not borne Him in her heart, after a more blessed manner than in her flesh[c]." Hence S. Chrysostom says, "Neither to conceive Christ nor to bring forth that wondrous offspring is of any use, where virtue is not: for the conception would not have been any good to her except she had done all that she ought, and her giving birth would not have profited her had she not been wholly good and faithful."

THIRD POINT.

The whole perfection of the heavenly life is comprised in these two, to *hear the Word of God and* to do it. Whosoever therefore has pleasure in the blessedness of Mary, let him aim gladly to *hear the Word of God and* to *keep it,* and he shall be *blessed.* For whoever gladly hears *the Word of God,* conceives Christ: but if

[b] de Virginitate c. 3: see in S. Augustine's Treatises p. 209 O.T.
[c] ib. p. 210.

he fulfil it in act, he bears Christ: Him Whom Mary bare bodily, *he* bears spiritually. Whence S. Augustine, " He who *with the heart believes unto righteousness*, conceives Christ; and he who, *with the mouth confesses to salvation*, bears Christ. Wherefore the Lord saith elsewhere, *If any one shall do the Will of My Father, the same is My brother and sister and mother.*

The Word of God ought to be heard reverently because of its pricelessness. If any one had a particle of the Lord's vesture, or a Tear from His Eyes, or a drop of Blood from His Body, very reverently would he take and keep it: far more *the Word of God*, which comes forth not out of His Mouth only, but from the depths of His Heart. Again it must be heard patiently, not with languor, murmur or detraction. Further it must be heard obediently, so that he who hears may fulfil it in action. The bad ought gladly to *hear the Word of God*, that they may be corrected; for *the Word of God* is the soul's medicine against sin's sickness. The good too, who are in threefold case, ought gladly to *hear the Word*. For to beginners this belongs, that they may be instructed, and to them *the Word of God* is milk. To the more advanced also it belongs to *hear the Word of God*, that they may be guided in the way of spiritual progress. To the perfect too it befits to *hear the Word of God*, that they may be the more perfected: to them *the Word of God* is solid food. For *the Word of God* is heavenly manna, and agreeth *to every taste.* (Wisdom xvi. 20). Whence Origen says, Now therefore let us haste to take the heavenly manna, for that manna tastes in the mouth of each according to his longing. Thou therefore if thou receive *the Word of God* which is preached in Church, with all faith and with all devotion, the Word itself will be to thee whatsoever thou longest for. For example, if thou art in trouble, it comforts thee, saying, *A broken and contrite heart, O God, Thou wilt not despise.* If in prosperity thou joyest, it addeth thereto the joys of the things to come, saying, *Rejoice in the Lord, ye righteous, and shout for joy.* If thou art angry, it calms thee, saying, *Leave off from wrath and let go displeasure.* If thou art in sorrow, it heals thee, saying, *The Lord healeth all thine infirmities.* If thou art wasting in poverty, it comforts thee, saying, *The Lord raiseth up the poor out of the dust, and lifteth the needy out of the dunghill.* Thus then will the Word of the Lord give you in your mouth that taste you would have.

Prayer. O Lord Jesus Christ, grant me to hear Thy word in faith by believing, and to keep it in act by fulfilling: grant me to bear spiritually by hearing, and through keeping to feed that word of God. Grant me, O Lord my God, ever to prefer and put first spiritual work before every bodily affection, the work of God before human business, and altogether, the more helpful before the less helpful, Thou being my ruler, Thou my Guide. Grant me in heart, mouth, and work, to do Thy Will in precepts, counsels, and example; that I Thy servant may be made worthy to be well-pleasing to Thee, and at length by Thy grace to be numbered among the sons and heirs of God. Amen.

Meditation CIX.

JONAS GIVEN AS A SIGN OF THE RESURRECTION OF JESUS CHRIST.

The miracle of the resurrection of Jesus is, 1. the most efficacious to prove our holy religion; 2. the most easy to be verified; 3. the fittest for our edification. S. Matt. xii. 28—42. S. Luke xii. 29—32.

FIRST POINT.

The most efficacious miracle to prove the truth of our holy religion.

1. From the nature of the miracle itself. *Then certain of the scribes and of the Pharisees answered, saying, Master, we would see a sign from Thee.* We do

not know what it was that inclined some of the scribes and Pharisees to ask for a sign from our Lord, some new phenomenon, to prove the divinity of His Mission. They were well assured that He would not grant it them; but they hoped to draw some profit from His refusal. It was perhaps this demand which re-awakened the curiosity of the people, drew together a new concourse, and caused them to press around to hear the reply. *And when the people were gathered thick together, He began to say, This is an evil generation: they seek a sign; and there shall no sign be given it, but the sign of Jonas the prophet. For as Jonas was a sign unto the Ninevites, so shall also the Son of man be to this generation. For as Jonas was three days and three nights in the whale's belly, so shall the Son of man be three days and three nights in the heart of the earth.* The miracle of a man, who after having been buried, comes forth from his sepulchre by his own power, and full of life and glory, is it not a prodigy much more striking and more efficacious as a proof of the truth of our holy religion, than any which the Pharisees demanded, or any other which could be imagined? If, instead of forging for ourselves new systems of religion, we would meditate carefully on that which God has given us, we should see without difficulty that it is so much the greater, so much the holier, as it is above our wisdom.

2. By the prediction of the miracle. Isaiah had extolled it, David had foretold it, Jonas had given utterance to it in his own person: but above all Jesus Christ had announced it on several occasions, and in several ways, so that His enemies, even after they had beheld Him expire in torments on the Cross, feared still the effects of this prediction. Now a man who says, ' I shall be put to death, I shall be laid in the tomb, you will behold me dead and buried; but three days from thence I shall rise again, and you will see me living and glorified;' if that man carries out his words, he has a right to require of me what he will; I am ready to do and to

believe all that he will tell me. Wherefore then, ye freethinkers, who pride yourselves on your logic and your powers of reasoning do ye repeat unceasingly your declamations against our august mysteries, the objects of our faith? Are you ignorant that we believe that He, Who has taught us these dogmas, such as they are, and not such as you misrepresent them, rose again on the third day after His death, as He said that He would? Begin then, if you reason justly, by destroying this miracle, which is the foundation of our faith, and all else will fall to the ground of itself. But so long as the faith of this miracle lasts and that you can bring forward no proofs which can destroy it, your reproaches are vain, your reasonings only excite derision, and your scoffings prove perhaps even less the malice of your hearts than the want of uprightness in your judgements.

3. By the strangeness of the miracle. That a man should raise himself; that, by his own power, he should come forth triumphant from the tomb, can only belong to an Incarnate God, to the Son of God, to Him Who is the absolute Master of life and death, Who after having been three days in the tomb, passes forty days more on the earth with His disciples; Who, on the fortieth day, ascends to heaven, before their eyes, in order to send down upon them the Holy Spirit: and before that time, had shewn Himself to an unbelieving apostle, to bring him back to his belief in Him, and after that time, to a persecutor, to make of him an apostle; is an unheard-of wonder, without example, and without imitation; mythology has never dared to make pretence of any thing similar. Let the unbelievers of our days search then with care all that the different superstitions of the universe have invented that is most fabulous, and most absurd, and let them venture to compare it with our mysteries, with our dogmas, with our Sacraments. I will always ask them, Has the author of these superstitions risen from the dead? Has he given his resurrection as a proof of that which he has taught? Oh perverse and unbelieving generation, you ask for another sign; you

are not yet, you say, convinced! Ah! If other miracles were granted to you, you would dispute them one after another, you would slander them all, and you would yield to none. He whom the resurrection of Jesus Christ has not convinced will never be convinced; there is nothing left for him but to become more and more hardened, to multiply his crimes; and to be judged. As for us, let us thank Jesus Christ, and let us pray that our faith may be increased daily more and more.

SECOND POINT.

The miracle the easiest to be verified.

1. By the witnesses of the miracle itself. Witnesses in whom there could be no delusion by reason of the leisure which they had during forty days to assure themselves of the truth of the fact: by reason of the different ways in which they beheld Jesus risen, sometimes together, sometimes alone, sometimes by day, sometimes by night, speaking, eating, walking, letting Himself be touched, instructing them, reproving them, renewing His promises to them, and ascending up to heaven; then, by reason of the change they experienced in themselves, when the Holy Spirit, Whom He had foretold, came down upon them under visible symbols, and enlightened, and quickened them, and communicated to them the gift of tongues and of miracles. Witnesses amongst whom there could be no collusion on account of their immense number: for besides the apostles, the disciples and the holy women who saw Jesus risen, we must add the five hundred brethren of whom S. Paul speaks in 1 Cor. xv. as having seen Him at once, and not only they, but we must number among the first witnesses of the resurrection those who witnessed the miracles of the apostles themselves, and their immediate successors; miracles which were only a continuation of that of the resurrection, and which were only worked in order to confirm it; miracles worked in public in different cities, and before persons of different nations. What interest

moreover would these witnesses not have had in renouncing a Master Who had deceived them, and from Whom they had nothing further to hope or to fear! What interest would they not have had in rejecting a religion which was founded only on fraud and falsehood, and which could only bring upon them persecutions, sufferings and death! Witnesses, lastly, who had all the qualities that could be desired; honesty, holiness of life, disinterestedness, unanimity, boldness, strength, constancy to die with joy, even in the midst of the most terrible sufferings. None but the Christian religion has had martyrs who have died as witnesses for the truth of miraculous facts, which they had seen with their eyes, handled so to say, with their own hands, or learnt by a living tradition from those who had witnessed them.

2. The miracle the easiest to be verified by those even who contradicted the miracle. Those who out of pride, hatred, or jealousy had put to death the Messiah, were authorised to contradict His resurrection, and that was the contradiction of the Jews; those to whom the doctrines of Jesus Christ were a stumbling-block, because they attacked their prejudices, abolished their false gods, and condemned their evil passions, were equally interested in denying it, and that was the contradiction of the Gentiles; but this double contradiction is a new proof of the truth of the resurrection, because those who opposed it, whether Jews or Gentiles, brought forward no solid reason, nor any proofs which should give the lie to the witnesses against which they contended; whether it were because they only opposed to them, threats, exile, the loss of property, sufferings, death, and especially slander and falsehood; or whether it were that the more obstinate and cruel the contradiction was, the deeper did the interest in them become, and the more carefully were they examined into. Now, if it were only a matter of public facts, the verification of which was easy, who would have believed them, at the peril of fortune, honour, repose, and even life, if they had been false, or even doubtful?

3. The miracle the easiest to be verified by the results of the miracle itself. The results of the resurrection of Jesus Christ have been the conversion of the world. One may say that the great controversy respecting the resurrection of Jesus Christ has been judged, after hearing both sides, by the whole universe, and by the unanimous suffrage of all the nations who have had any knowledge of it; a judgment which has been pronounced, after all the particulars have been carefully examined into; a judgment not of speculation and of thought, but of practise and action. Not only have the nations received the religion of Jesus Christ, but, in order to receive it, they have renounced that which they already held, and have cast down at their feet the gods whom they worshipped, in order to serve and worship Jesus Christ, God made man for us, crucified and risen again; a judgment which still endures, to which we adhere ourselves, which we confirm by our own professions, and for the truth of which we should be ready to give our life. Imagine now any thing that you please, enthusiasm in the apostles, fanaticism in the people, marvels in paganism; quote the deification of Romulus, the wonders of Apollonius, and of a hundred others like him; the world has seen them, and it has judged them; what has it thought of them, what does it think of them? The world has become Christian, and is Christian; it has believed the resurrection of Jesus Christ, and believes in it still. The blindness of the Jews has only served to confirm its faith and its judgment. This homeless people, wanderers on the earth, bear witness, in spite of themselves, both of the authenticity of the prophets, and of the truth of all that we believe concerning the death and resurrection of Jesus Christ. Dare to deny, if you will, the authority of the Gospel, the truth of the history of all nations, this desperate resource will not suffice you still, and unbelief will not be able to maintain itself behind that entrenchment. The whole of Europe, to speak only of that part of the world which we inhabit, has become Christian; it has not always been so, how has it become Christian?

If all the facts upon which Christianity is founded are false, how is it that amongst all the people of Europe a false account of that great revolution only has been preserved, and that not a vestige of the truth remains? To pretend that it is the Christians who have falsified the facts, and substituted false histories, for the true one; ah! without examining here whether such a falsification could be possible, may we not say that this is not reasoning, but only taking for granted that which is called in question? for why should nations have become Christian, in such numbers, only to fabricate these false histories, to make them believed by their contemporaries, and to abolish all true history? Iniquity is then forced to contradict itself and to prove its own falsehood, when it persists in denying a fact so evident and so easily proved as that of the Resurrection. Let us add that all that we have just spoken of, had been foretold just as it took place, foretold by the old prophets and by our Lord Himself, namely not only His resurrection, but the witness which His apostles should bear to Him, the miracles by which they confirmed it, the contradictions they experienced, the victories they gained, the conversion of the Gentiles, the ruin of the Jews, their hardness of heart, their dispersion, such as we behold it with our own eyes. Oh my God! how unsearchable are Thy ways, how faithful are Thy promises, how convincing the evidence of Thy Gospel, how do they merit our faith! not only do they call for our belief, but they force it from us, they enrapture us, and an upright heart cannot resist them.

THIRD POINT.

The miracle the fittest to serve to our edification.

Signs such as the Pharisees required, and such as even devils have sometimes worked, are only exhibitions of vain-glory, without any results, and without any designs of wisdom. It is not thus that the Almighty acts; it is not in order to satisfy the idle curiosity of men, or to gain from them some barren admiration, that He works

His miracles. The resurrection of our Lord is not only the most striking miracle, the most solid proof, and the most complete and the easiest to be understood that we could desire; but it has besides infinite relations, and bears the impress of that holiness, goodness, and deep wisdom which characterize all the works of God.

1. Character of holiness, because Jesus has risen from the dead as our Example, that is to say, as the example of the spiritual life which we ought to live in Him, after having risen with Him. Jesus, in dying, has made sin to die in us, He has destroyed the life of sin, and in rising again, has given us the life of justification, the life of grace, the new life in which we are to walk. Our resurrection to a new life ought then to be like His, a manifest resurrection, sensible, and visible, and not hidden, obscure, timid, and apparent to no one; an eternal resurrection to last for ever, and not only momentary and of short duration. Is it thus that we have risen with Jesus Christ, and that we are living in His new life?

2. Character of goodness, because Jesus has risen as our Head. His glorious resurrection is the reward of His merits, and the pledge of His promises. He has risen; He is the Object of our faith; we shall rise again as He has done, this is the object of our hope; He has taken His own Body again, but in a very different state to that in which it was; He has taken it back again, glorious, immortal, impassible, incorruptible, endowed with gifts of subtility and activity, and in one word spiritual. We shall take back our bodies with the same qualities, and become partakers in the same glory. Oh sweet hope, Oh consoling thought, Oh powerful motive! Oh my body, my flesh, my senses! do not think that the hatred that I bear you will last for ever. If I keep you in servitude aud in privation, if I keep you back from pleasure, if I rejoice in sufferings which befall you, if I even inflict some on you, and rejoice even that you should languish, fail, and die, it is only in the hope of saving you from eternal punishment, and to procure for you

glory, liberty, and the delights of immortal life. Courage, yet a little while, this life will soon end; soon you will rest in the bosom of hope, until at last the day appointed, the happy day of reward arrives.

3. The character of wisdom, because Jesus has risen as our Judge. It is not only to true Christians that the mystery of the Resurrection of Jesus Christ is of interest, but it is so also to wicked men and to bad Christians; for if they can refuse to follow Jesus as their Leader, they cannot escape having Him as their Judge. Ah! scorn and railing will have no place then. It is no longer our indignation which the blindness of sinners and unbelievers excites in us, it is our compassion, our sorrow, and our tears. *The queen of the south shall rise up in the judgement with the men of this generation, and condemn them: for she came from the utmost parts of the earth to hear the wisdom of Solomon: and behold a greater than Solomon is here. The men of Nineve shall rise up in the judgement with this generation, and shall condemn it: for they repented at the preaching of Jonas; and behold, a greater than Jonas is here.* The queen of the south has come from a far distant country to hear the wisdom of Solomon, and we shut our ears to the teachings of Jesus Christ. The Ninevites, at the preaching of Jonas, repented in order to avoid a temporal misfortune; and we refuse to do so, when Jesus Christ Himself invites us to repent, and when we are threatened, if we do not do so, with eternal misery. The queen of the south and the Ninevites will rise up against us in the day of judgement; in other words, those who have been less favoured by heaven than we, who with less light, less teaching, and less knowledge, have believed with simplicity, and have lived innocent lives; all those whose instructions, advice, and good examples we have despised; those barbarous and savage nations, who will have received the faith in a teachable spirit, and have faithfully conformed their lives to it: such are the accusers who will condemn us at the last judgement.

Prayer. How many voices, O my God, will there not be raised against me, if I do not by a prompt repentance, seek to make amends for the abuse which I have made of Thy grace! Ah Lord, I do not ask of Thee for new wonders, more abundant helps, and greater graces, or greater knowledge. Alas! it is not grace, but faithfulness in using that grace which has been wanting to me. Grace has only been so weak in me, because I have been too faint-hearted. Could I then complain of that, which arises only from the perversity of my own heart? No, my Divine Saviour, I desire only to profit by that which Thou hast done for me, instead of asking Thee for fresh miracles. No, *no sign, but the sign of the prophet Jonas.* Grant that I may draw a holy profit from it, by learning from Thy Death and Resurrection to die to sin in order that I may live unto righteousness by a new life. Amen.

Meditation CX.

OF THE MOTHER AND BRETHREN OF JESUS.

1. His mother and brethren desire to speak to Him; 2. Jesus does not acknowledge His mother and brethren according to the flesh; 3. Jesus forms the closest bond of union with His disciples. S. Matt. xii. 40-50. S. Mark iii. 31-35. S. Luke viii. 19-21.

FIRST POINT.

His mother and brethren desire to speak to Jesus.

1. Their arrival. *While He yet talked to the people, behold, His mother and His brethren stood without, desiring to speak with Him.* These brethren of Jesus are believed to be the nephews of S. Joseph, the children of his sisters, and the reputed cousins-german of Jesus, as Joseph passed for His father, and the Jews generally gave to their cousins-german the name of brethren. If these relations were the same who had suspected some de-

lusion in the conduct of Jesus, and had wished to hinder Him, it is evident that in taking His mother with them in the hopes of better succeeding in their plans, they had not communicated to her their suspicions, but only their alarms, that is, the fear they had that the hatred of the Pharisees might lead to some excesses against Him. If it was thus, as we can only conjecture what was the object of the journey, the conduct of His mother deserves our admiration. She knew that her Son must die for the salvation of man; but she did not know the precise time, nor under what circumstances that death should come about. If this thought filled with bitterness every moment of her life, she was none the less attentive to what God would require of her in that great mystery in which she too was to take her part. She comes then full of tenderness and love for her Divine Son, but at the same time with a perfect resignation to the will of God, whatever that might be, and with the peace of heart which is the fruit of submission to His Will; and in her conduct, she sets us an example to do all that depends upon ourselves, and then, avoiding all haste and anxiety, to be perfectly resigned to all that it may please God to require of us.

2. The obstacle they met with. *And could not come at Him for the press.* Jesus was still in the place where He had healed the man who was possessed with a devil. An innumerable multitude besieged the house where He was, in such a manner, that His mother and His brethren could not penetrate through it so as to reach Him. What a spectacle for the heart of that tender mother! With what joy did she behold the earnestness of the people to hear the heavenly doctrines which her Son was teaching them? What thanksgivings did she not inwardly render to God! Let us rejoice likewise at all that is good and edifying in the Church. Let us thank God that so many faithful souls follow Jesus with fervour, and let us join ourselves to that multitude.

3. The message which they send to Jesus. *And standing without, sent unto Him, calling Him. And the*

multitude sat about Him; and they said unto Him; Behold, Thy mother and Thy brethren without seek for Thee, desiring to see Thee. It was doubtless the fear of what might happen to Him that induced His relations to send this message to call Him from the midst of this assembly. The messenger who was sent with the message having penetrated the crowd, came to announce to Him the arrival of His mother and of His brethren. Without the respect which they bore to the Teacher, the people might perhaps have broken up the assembly in order to satisfy their pious curiosity, and to see His relations; but they were desirous to await the answer which Jesus gave, and that was very different to what they had expected.

SECOND POINT.

Jesus does not acknowledge His mother or brethren according to the flesh.

And He answered them, saying, Who is My mother, or My brethren? And He looked round about on them which sat about Him, and said, Behold My mother, and My brethren. An answer full of mystery and of instruction.

1. To the Jews. Jesus implied by this answer that they were not to look on Him only as the Son of Mary, and as Man only, but to raise their thoughts higher, that they might acknowledge in Him the true Son of God. He willed to teach them that the claims of blood and of nature have nothing in common in His Person with the claims of the grace and of the faith which He came to preach and to establish; that He is the Heir of the promise, and the Head of the people of God, not because He was descended from Abraham, but because He had the faith, the spirit, and the obedience of Abraham.

2. Answer full of instruction to the ministers of the Church. Jesus, by His example and His words, teaches them here that in the exercise of their ministry, they

must not regard merely the ties of relationship founded on nature, and which are liable to change, but that spiritual relationship, which is infinitely above all other, and which ought to absorb every other feeling, namely the guidance and charge of those souls committed to their care; He teaches them that they must not let themselves be drawn away from the duties of their calling, by the inclinations of a purely human affection; that all their cares and all their tenderness must be devoted to those, the care of whose salvation God has committed into their hands; that nobility of blood, birth, rank are no longer to be of any consideration to them; that the office they bear as ministers of Jesus Christ is to supersede all these, and ought to make them forget them, and finally, that if their devotion to their calling is reproached as indifference, hardness or ingratitude, they must boldly declare in pointing to their flock, *Behold My mother and My brethren*, my relations and friends.

3. Answer full of instruction for parents and people. Relations ought to avoid becoming a subject of temptation, and an occasion of falling to the ministers of the Gospel, by requiring of them attentions, services, or consideration which are incompatible with their duties. They ought not to take offence, when on similar occasions they meet with refusals and even rebuffs. The people, on their side, ought not to regard in the minister of Jesus Christ, any thing save that which appertains to his ministry. Whatever his birth or family may be, it ought not to be made any account of, but all classes ought to respect him, and have a true and sincere regard for himself and the office he holds.

THIRD POINT.

Of the disciples of Jesus, and of the bond of union which He forms with them.

For whosover shall do the will of My Father which is in heaven, the same is My brother, and sister, and mother. *My mother and My brethren are these which hear the word of God and do it.*

1. The character of this union; 1. It is a close union. The relationships of parents, brother and sister, husband and wife, only represent in a figure the close and intimate bond which exists between Jesus Christ and a soul that waits upon Him fervently, and expresses only feebly the sweetness, the tenderness, the ardour of the love which follows from this bond of union. 2. It is noble, because in uniting us with Jesus Christ, it unites us with God, with the angels, and with the saints. Who would not despise, in comparison with this, all earthly relationships and friendships? 3. It is eternal. Death will put an end to every other, but it will set the seal to this, and will assure its perpetuity.

2. The foundation of this union; it is the goodness of God our Creator; it is His love towards us, which led Him to give His Only-Begotten Son to be our Redeemer; it is the merits of Jesus Christ, His Passion and Death, which have gained for us this great privilege; it is the grace of this divine Saviour, which raises us, and gives the merit to all our actions. What ought to be our gratitude for so many blessings!

3. The condition on which this union is offered to us is that we hear the Word of God, diligently seeking to become acquainted with the truths and precepts which it contains; that we do not sink into a shameful ignorance or an indolent indifference with regard to it; that we close our ears to the words of those who seek to lead us astray, and obey that Divine Word, believing firmly the truths it teaches, practising faithfully the laws it lays upon us; lastly that we seek, and love in every thing only the accomplishment of the will of God, of that God Who is so loving, Who is our Father, that Almighty God, Who reigns in heaven.

Prayer. Ah! Lord, can there be any thing to make me afraid in conditions so sweet? And what eternal regret would there be for me, if I should fail to fulfil them, since there would be neither heaven, nor God, nor a Saviour, nor hope further for me! I will then seek to stir myself up to the fervent and faithful fulfilment of Thy will, O my God! I will seek to encourage others also in it, and the attachments I form with them shall have no other foundation, and no other aim. What more powerful motive to follow Thy commandments, than to see the close union which Thou dost form with those who do Thy Father's will! Let It then be henceforth the rule of all my affections, and actions here below, that it may be my crown and glory in Heaven. Amen.

Meditation CXI.

JESUS, DINING AT THE HOUSE OF A PHARISEE, REPROVES THE VICES OF THE PHARISEES AND THE SCRIBES.

1. The vices for which Jesus reproves the Pharisees; 2. the vices for which He reproves the scribes; 3. the reproofs which He administers to sinners. S. Luke xi. 37-54.

FIRST POINT.

Of the inward faults for which Jesus reproves the Pharisees.

Let us examine whether these faults are not to be found in us, and if we do not deserve the reproofs which our Saviour here administers to us. It appears that our Lord continued His instruction for some time longer, after He had been told of the arrival of His mother and His brethren. *And as He spake, a certain Pharisee besought Him to dine with him; and He went in, and sat down to meat.* How much was wanting to render this Pharisee as well disposed as was that Pharisee at Nain! The Saviour also does not spare him any more than the rest who were invited to this repast, whether they were Pharisees, or scribes. He begins with the Pharisees, and reproves them,

1. With their folly in cleansing only the exterior without cleansing the interior. *And when the Pharisee saw it, he marvelled that He had not first washed before dinner. And the Lord said unto him, Now do ye Pharisees make clean the outside of the cup and the platter; but your inward part is full of ravening and wickedness.* As though He had said, I am not ignorant what you think of Me; but this is what I think of you. With all your zeal, and your regularity, you impose on the people and lead them astray by your affectations and your maxims. All with you consists in ceremonies and external practices; you subject yourselves in the most scrupulous way to ablutions, you take great pains in cleansing the outside of your cups and platters; but, under this appearance which imposes upon them, your hearts and minds, far from being pure, are filled with iniquity and rapine. *Ye fools*, He added, *did not He which made that which is without make that which is within also?* The sovereign God Who has created that which forms the exterior of a man, his members and his body, has He not also made that which is far more essential to man, and more closely bound up with him, his soul with all its powers? Yes, doubtless, the same God Who has given me my body has given me my soul; it is in vain that I occupy myself with cleansing the exterior of this body, in washing it, adorning it, embellishing it, if I leave my soul, my conscience, my heart, full of defilements and iniquities. Ah! it is inward purity which God requires, and of which He will demand a rigorous account.

2. Jesus reproaches them with their injustice and thefts. *Your inward parts are full of ravening and wickedness.* These Pharisees committed injustice and robbery in the exercise of their offices, in the administration of justice, in the management of affairs. Of what avail was it to wash the outside of the cup and platter, when they lived on the substance and steeped their hands in the blood of the people? Of what avail to wash with water hands, which were filled with rapine?

To what avail are the ablutions of the body, when the heart is defiled by insatiable desires to enrich itself, let it cost what it may? *But rather give alms of such things as ye have : and behold, all things are clean unto you.* Make restoration of your ill-acquired goods, retrench your luxury in order to give alms to the poor, and then, independently of all your external ablutions, all will be pure in you, body and soul; you will be pleasing to God, and edifying to men. Alas, how many Christians have no firmer grounds for their judgments, or are more enlightened in their conduct, or less superstitious in their practices than these Pharisees!

3. Jesus reproaches them with their blindness in priding themselves on their observance of the minutest details of the law, and of neglecting the fundamental and essential parts. *But woe unto you, Pharisees! For ye tithe mint and rue and all manner of herbs, and pass over judgement and the love of God : these ought ye to have done, and not to leave the other undone.* That is to say, you are scrupulously exact in paying the tithe of the smallest herbs that grow in your gardens: but justice and equity, the love of God and your neighbour, the works of mercy which God recommends you in preference to legal observances, you dispense yourselves from; not that you are to exempt yourselves from the payment of tithe; that is a duty which you must doubtless perform, but you must not make it an excuse whereby you may omit all the rest. How many in our days still fall into a similar blindness! Are we not ourselves of that number? We acquit ourselves with care of the external duties of religion, we even make a point to ourselves not to omit certain established pious practices, or such as we have voluntarily prescribed to ourselves, whilst we forget what we owe to our children, or to the servants in our employ; whilst we continue in habits of sin which destroy the love of God in our hearts. Is it not nevertheless justice and charity which properly speaking makes a Christian? Ah! let us not cease to inculcate this maxim in our own minds, and in those of

others, especially of those who depend upon us for instruction.

4. Jesus reproaches them with their pride and vanity. *Woe unto you, Pharisees! for ye love the uppermost seats in the synagogues, and greetings in the markets.* To aspire to the first places and to seek after the respect and homage of the people, how despicable is this pride, and yet how common! Ah! how many dissensions and how much havoc has not the jealousy of rank and authority, so contrary to the Spirit of God, caused?

5. Jesus reproaches them with their hypocrisy, so fatal to themselves, and so dangerous to others. *Woe unto you, hypocrites; for ye are as graves which appear not, and the men that walk over them are not aware of them.* Like unto sepulchres hidden just below the ground, the Pharisees were filled with corruption, without being in any way suspected of it. Alas! how many such hypocrites are there not among ourselves, severe towards others, zealous in their remonstrances, composed in their conduct, edifying in their words, orderly in their outward conduct, disinterested in public, mortified in all their actions, and speaking only of charity, holiness of life, and conversion, but yet whose consciences are filled with headstrong passions, with ill-regulated desires which tear their souls more than worms gnaw the body! If these tombs, these sepulchres covered from without, were opened, what a tainted odour would exhale from them!

SECOND POINT.

Of the vices with which Jesus reproaches the lawyers.

Let us again examine here if we are not defiled with any of these vices, and if we do not merit the same reproaches. Jesus spoke with so much authority, strength, and power, that the Pharisees, astonished, confused, disconcerted, and as it were thunderstruck, dared not answer a word. Only one of the lawyers, or doctors of the law, thought himself able to hazard his remonstrances.

Then answered one of the lawyers, and said unto Him, Master, thus saying Thou reproachest us also. But Jesus, turning His discourse against them, and sparing them no more than He had done the Pharisees, He reproaches them,

1. With their pitiless severity towards others. *And He said, Woe unto you also, ye lawyers! for ye lade men with burdens grievous to be borne.* It is only too natural to men to be severe upon others, and to lay upon them heavy burdens. People will not content themselves with keeping within the bounds of God's commandments, but seek for that which is impossible, and exact of others an imaginary perfection, and go beyond the truth; and the evils which result from this conduct are not only harshness, pride, self-love, and hypocrisy on the part of those who make this profession, but the offence which they give to others, who are thereby discouraged and often give up every thing in despair, and abandon themselves without remorse to all their evil passions.

2. Jesus here reproaches them with their blind indulgence towards themselves. *Ye lade men with burdens grievous to be borne, and ye yourselves touch not the burdens with one of your fingers.* How many there are who take to themselves the credit of an austerity which they are far from making a trial of! They add to the commandments, the yoke of which they render intolerable, and these very commandments they do not keep. Under the cloke of an affectation of modesty, and of apparent holiness, they pass their lives in self-indulgence, idleness, and pleasure, in a continual dissipation, and an habitual vanity and love of riches. Ah! if we only took care to confront ourselves often with the precepts which we dictate to others, how much should we find whereof to feel ashamed, and how should we fear the anathema which our Saviour here pronounces!

3. Jesus reproaches them with their cruel hatred towards the messengers of God. *Woe unto you! for ye built the sepulchres of the prophets, and your fathers killed them.* The scribes and lawyers sought for a pre-

text and an opportunity to put the Saviour to death. Jesus knew the plots which they had formed against Him, and it was in order to let them see that He knew them, that He turned against themselves the care they had taken to build up the sepulchres of the prophets. 'This care, which, had it been actuated by other feelings, would have been a work of piety,' added our Saviour to them, (we shall treat of it hereafter with greater detail) 'is nothing else than the continuation of the persecution of your fathers. You are of one accord with them, they killed them, and you build their tombs. But soon you will imitate your fathers yet more closely, soon you will put to death yourselves the Prophet Whom the wisdom of God has determined to send to you. But your cruelties and your murders will not remain unpunished.' The hatred which men bear to those who preach religion, who defend and uphold it, is always bloody. We may seek to hide from ourselves the feelings of our hearts, we may pretend to speak of gentleness, peace, and love, and raise monuments to the prophets who are dead, when we are ready to steep our hands in the blood of those that are living, and if that is not in our power, when we strive at least to calumniate them, to decry them, and to persecute them.

4. Jesus reproaches them with their presumptuous ignorance with regard to the Scriptures. *Woe unto you lawyers! for ye have taken away the key of knowledge, ye enter not in yourselves.* The scribes had taken possession of the key of knowledge, and yet would not enter into it, that is to say, that they arrogated to themselves the right of teaching and explaining the Scriptures, and they themselves would not seek for or acknowledge the characteristics of the Messiah which they had beheld united in the person of Jesus Christ. They take away the key of knowledge, and usurp the exclusive right of teaching, who interpret Scripture in their own way, and refuse to see in these same Scriptures, the revelation of the mysteries of our holy religion, the faith once delivered to the saints. "False teachers,

who privily bring in damnable heresies, even denying the Lord Who bought them."

5. Jesus reproaches them with their culpable malice towards others. *And them that were entering in ye hindered.* The Jewish people were disposed to acknowledge Jesus as the Messiah, and entered without difficulty into the proofs which He gave of His Divine mission: if the doctors of the law and the Pharisees had aided these good dispositions, all the nation would doubtless have acknowledged their Deliverer; but they, on the contrary, took all the pains they could to turn away the people, to deceive and blind them: they succeeded, by their hypocritical zeal, by their seditious cries, by their intrigues, their calumnies, and the abuse of their authority, to draw away the people against their natural inclinations, and to induce them to reject the Messiah, and demand His death. Woe be unto you, ministers of error, who ever ye be, who seize the key of knowledge, and do not enter in yourselves, and hinder others from entering in, who close the door, and keep back those who would return into the path of truth! Woe to you, ye senseless people, who suffer yourselves to be thus led away!

THIRD POINT.

Of the inward reproaches which He makes to the consciences of sinners.

The reproaches which Jesus utters here to the Scribes and Pharisees, He still makes to impenitent sinners by the remorse which troubles their consciences.

1. Divine reproaches. These inward reproaches set forth a God, and a Master to Whom we are compelled to listen, Whose voice, louder than that of thunder makes itself heard, even in spite of ourselves, fills us with awe and fear, overwhelms us, makes us feel our own nothingness and our sinfulness.

2. Unavoidable reproaches, reproaches which nothing can still but sincere conversion of heart. In vain would we, so to say, compound and make an exchange, do

some good works, practise some moral virtues, utter some sighs, repeat some prayers, give even some alms; if all that is not done in the sincere desire to obtain our conversion, if with all that we will not renounce our passions and our sins, we shall not stay the threatening voice of Him to Whom we dare not offer a deception. In vain would we seek to stifle It by dissipation, in the midst of festivities and crowds as well as in solitude, in broad day-light as in the darkness of night, It cries, It pierces, It thunders!

3. *Reproaches full of love.* Wherefore does Jesus speak with so much power to His enemies, if not to subdue these intractable hearts? Ah! if at that very moment, they had fallen at His feet, repentant and converted, they would only have received consolations from Him. Wherefore does God pursue us with such keen and biting remorse, if not to make us commune with our own hearts, and to draw us away from sin, that we may escape from eternal misery?

4. *Reproaches, the abuse of which only makes us more sinful.* *And as He said these things unto them, the Scribes and Pharisees began to urge Him vehemently, and to provoke Him to speak of many things, laying wait for Him, and seeking to catch something out of His mouth that they might accuse Him.* The Scribes and Pharisees, more hardened and embittered by the reproaches which Jesus had just addressed to them, only sought from that time forward and on every occasion during the rest of His life, to lay snares for Him; they attacked Him everywhere with insidious questions; they sought unceasingly to embarrass Him by a multitude of questions which were more captious one than the other, and not being able to flatter themselves that they could excite a disturbance amongst the people against Him, they employed all their efforts to surprise Him in His words, and to draw from His lips an answer which was capable of bearing such a construction as they could lay hold of, in order to accuse Him to the priests and magistrates, who on their part, only waited for a specious

pretext to condemn Him. A true figure of wicked men, who, angry at the remorse by which they feel themselves stung, seek only to tear out of their hearts God and the religion which causes them to feel these pangs of remorse.

5. Reproaches, which, if we despise, will become eternal. Ah! if we cannot endure now the disquietude which this secret and inward voice causes us which speaks to us only in the depth of our consciences, which only reproaches us with our sins, and shews us at the same time the way in which we can make amends for them, how shall we endure it when it will burst forth, when it will accuse us before the assembled universe, when it will condemn us to eternal punishment, and follow us there, without any other hope being left to us?

Prayer. What would have become of me, O God full of goodness, if by an excess of Thine ineffable love Thou hadst not troubled me so as to render me intolerable to myself, if Thou hadst not filled me, in spite of myself, with the wholesome fear of Thy judgements and of the eternity to come? But, Lord, in vain is my soul enlightened by the light of faith, if I do not make use of it to regulate the motions of my heart and my actions. Grant, O my Saviour, that by stirring myself up to the practice of that humility, charity, devotion, and love of God which were wanting to the Pharisees and the scribes, I may avoid the reproaches which Thou didst address to them, and the blindness and condemnation which were the fatal consequences of their hardness of heart. Amen.

Meditation CXII.

PARABLE OF THE SEED.

Examine 1. the parable itself; 2. the reason why the parable was spoken; and 3. the explanation of the parable. S. Matt. xiii. 1—23. S. Mark iv. 1—25. S. Luke viii. 4—18.

FIRST POINT.

The parable of the seed.

1. To whom is this parable spoken? To an infinite multitude of people, and in their person, to the entire universe, and to me in particular. *The same day went Jesus out of the house, and sat by the sea side. And great multitudes were gathered together unto Him so that He went into a ship, and sat: and the whole multitude stood on the shore.* Jesus, having left the city, perhaps on quitting the house of the Pharisee, went to the sea shore in order to teach the people there. The crowd was so great, that He was obliged to go up into a ship with His disciples, and it was from thence that He spoke several parables to the multitudes who were standing on the shore. Let us join ourselves to this multitude, and let us listen with attention.

2. What is the subject of the parable? *And He taught them many things by parables, and said unto them in His doctrine, Hearken; Behold, there went out a sower to sow, and it came to pass, as he sowed, some fell by the wayside, and the fowls of the air came and devoured it up. And some fell on stony ground where it had not much earth; and immediately it sprang up, because it had no depth of earth; but when the sun was up, it was scorched: and because it had no root, it withered away. And some fell among thorns, and the thorns grew up, and choked it, and it yielded no fruit. And other fell on good ground, and did yield fruit that sprang up and increased; and brought forth, some thirty, and some sixty, and some an hundred.*

3. What is the importance of this parable? Our

Lord, in order to make known its importance, began by demanding attention: *Hearken;* and He ends it by *when He had said these things He cried, He that hath ears to hear, let him hear.* In truth we may say that our salvation depends upon understanding this parable. It is not difficult, doubtless, to understand its literal sense, and to have a speculative knowledge of it, but to hear it with the ears of our heart, and to have a practical knowledge of it, is equally important and difficult to us.

4. The means by which to hear this parable to our profit, is prayer. *And when He was alone, they that were about Him with the twelve asked of Him the parable. And the disciples came and said unto Him, Why speakest Thou unto them in parables?* Let us then leave earthly things and join ourselves to the disciples and apostles, and ask of Him, *What might this parable be?* Let us draw near to Jesus in the silence of prayer, and ask of Him, by humble and fervent prayer, wherefore He speaks to us in parables, and pray Him to make known to us the meaning of this parable.

SECOND POINT.

The reason why this parable was spoken.

Before explaining this parable to His disciples, Jesus answered their first question: *Why speakest Thou unto them in parables?*

1. By pointing out to them the evil dispositions of that people. *He answered and said unto them, Because it is given unto you to know the mysteries of the kingdom of Heaven, but to them it is not given. Therefore speak I to them in parables: because they seeing, see not, and hearing, they hear not, neither do they understand. And in them is fulfilled the prophecy of Esaias, which saith, By hearing ye shall hear, and shall not understand: and seeing, ye shall see, and shall not perceive; for this people's heart is waxed gross, and their ears are dull of hearing, and their eyes they have closed; lest at any time, they should see with their eyes,*

*and hear with their ears, and should understand with
their hearts, and should be converted, and I should heal
them.* 'As for you,' Jesus said to His disciples, 'you are
destined to enter into the secrets of the kingdom of God,
and there is nothing in your hearts which puts an obstacle
in the way of your understanding them: but it is not so
with this people; they have hardened their heart that
they may not understand, have stopped up their ears
that they may not hear, closed their eyes that they may
not see, lest they might be converted and be healed; and
I, on My part, I speak to them in parables as to strangers, in order that they may not see, that they may not
understand, that they may not be converted, and that their
sins may not be forgiven them.' Terrible, but just judgment of God, Who proportions the light we receive to
the dispositions of our hearts, discovers truth to us in
proportion as we love it, and hides it from us in measure
as we flee from it! If then I understand the things of
God so little, if His Divine Word appears to me like an
enigma, where for the most part I see nothing, I understand nothing, it is because, called upon to understand
the Divine mysteries, I have not chosen to search them
out, for fear that I should be obliged to renounce objects which my heart cherishes.

2. Jesus answers their question by making known to
them their own happiness. *But blessed are your eyes,
for they see, and your ears, for they hear. For verily
I say unto you, That many prophets and righteous men
have desired to see these things which ye see, and have
not seen them: and to hear these things which ye hear,
and have not heard them.* In truth, the apostles were
blessed in having been called to follow Christ, in having
been chosen to be the witnesses of His miracles, and the
confidants of His secrets. Many prophets and righteous
men would have desired to share in their blessings.
They were blessed in having obeyed their call, and
followed Jesus Christ, and in not having put any hin-
drance in the way of the designs of mercy which He had
in store for them. Ah! how blessed is a soul, when,

faithful to the light which God gives it, it hears the words of life which He has left to us, it tastes the mysteries of the religion of Jesus Christ, nourishes itself with its faith, enriches itself with its blessings, supports itself by its faith, and lives only through love of it. Why should I not aspire to this happiness, since it is offered to me, and that I am called by preference to so many who have never had the same opportunities to attain to it, nor the same external means of grace, nor the same inward graces as I?

3. Jesus answers to their question by instructing them as to their obligations. *And He said unto them, Is a candle brought to be put under a bushel, or under a bed? and not to be set on a candlestick. For there is nothing hid, which shall not be manifested: neither was anything kept secret but that it should come abroad.* If Jesus explains to His apostles the meaning of the parables, if He places in their hands the torch, it is not in order that they should hide it: if He admits them to the intimate knowledge of His mysteries, it is not that they should bury it in silence. He has sown the seed of the Divine Word the first: their duty is, after His example, to sow it without sparing any pains, without being discouraged by their want of success, without choosing out the fields for themselves, without neglecting any part of it, without fearing perils, without changing or mixing the grain which has been confided to them. After this instruction, Jesus Himself points out to them the importance of it, and it is for each one of us, each according to our station, to seek to understand it well.

4. Jesus answers to their question by encouraging them with the thought of the rewards or punishments which God awards even in this life. *And He said unto them, Take heed what ye hear: take heed therefore how ye hear: for with what measure ye mete, it shall be measured to you: and unto you that have, shall more be given. For he that hath, to him shall be given: and he that hath not, from him shall be taken even that which he hath.* Let us then take good care in what

manner we hear, read, or meditate on the word of God, and what use we make of it. Behold the reward; the more lavish we are towards God, the more lavish God will be towards us; the more attentive we are to hear and to meditate on His word, the more faithful in keeping it, and generous in sacrificing every thing for it, the more do we enjoy it, love it, understand it, the greater treasures do we discover in it, the more grace, enlightenment and strength do we gain from it : we have an abundance of supernatural treasure which we enjoy with delight, and which we see increase daily. Behold, on the contrary, the punishment; he who rejects the Word of God, who does not make it bear fruit in himself, who gives the lie to it by his conduct, and violates its precepts, little by little wearies of it, the light that is in him becomes darkness, and his fervour diminishes from day to day; he begins no longer to understand anything of the ways of God, and ends by total estrangement from them. He flatters himself that he still holds the faith, often when it has been taken from him, and sometimes he actually glories in possessing it no longer, and in persecuting those who keep it. A punishment much to be feared of which we see examples but too often. Alas! O my God! if by Thy mercy, I have not yet come to this excess of blindness, am I not in the way which leads thither? Dost Thou not deal with me already according to Thy justice; dost Thou not avenge the abuse which I have made of Thy divine Word? Ah! I have no longer the virtues, nor the fervour, nor the spiritual knowledge which I have formerly had ; all these blessings have been taken away from me, it is then time that I should seek to recover them. Thou dost give me still this hope, O my God! Thou dost encourage me to labour thereat and I ask of Thee the help of Thy grace that I may have good success!

THIRD POINT.

Explanation of the parable.

And He said unto them, Know ye not this parable ?

and how then will ye know all parables? Hear ye therefore the parable of the sower. Jesus condescends to explain to us Himself His own parable; without His help, how could we understand this and the other parables. He exhorts us to be attentive: let us then hearken to Him with reverence, and pray Him to give us a teachable heart that we may profit by His lessons. *Now the parable is this; The seed is the word of God.* The rest of the parable presents to us the character of four sorts of persons who hear this Divine Word.

1. The first are too dissipated, and this is what is meant by the road-side where the seed falls. *And these are they by the way-side, where the word is sown; but when they have heard, Satan cometh immediately, and taketh away the word out of their hearts, lest they should believe and be saved.* What is it to be dissipated? It is to hear, to read, to meditate with distraction, with negligence, without searching out what we have heard or read, and without making any application to ourselves of the Divine Word; it is, after having heard it, to neglect to put it in practice, to lose the remembrance of it, not to think any more of it, to open our hearts to all the objects which present themselves, to give access to a crowd of thoughts, desires, plans which succeed one another continually; it is to give oneself up to frivolous amusements, to useless novelties, to the enjoyments of the day, to the tumult of the world. What is the evil of this dissipation? It is that it comes from the evil one, that it is one of the most dangerous of his artifices: for while we are distracted, the devil, more prompt than the birds of the air, more watchful for our ruin than we are for our salvation, takes away out of our heart, without our perceiving it, the Divine seed, salutary thoughts, holy inspirations, good desires, and good resolutions. What is the consequence of this misfortune? It is that we soon lose our fervour, our earnestness, even our faith, and lastly our soul. This is whither our enemy seeks to lead us. Let us then open our eyes to his malice and artifices, while it is yet time, and let us understand of

what importance it is to us to watch over our hearts, and to be gn a serious, and recollected life.

2. The second are superficial, and this is what is signified by the stony ground where there is little earth. *He that received the seed into stony places, the same is he that heareth the word, and anon with joy receiveth it; yet hath he not root in himself, but dureth for a while; for when tribulation or persecution ariseth because of the word, by and by he is offended.* What are the indications of a superficial character? Excess of fervour at the beginning, especially when it is accompanied with a determination to be guided by a person's own judgment; excess of vanity, which makes him wish to appear to surpass others; of presumption, which makes him rest too much upon his own strength, and be too self-confident. What forms this superficial character? A fund of secret and hidden hardness, which a person has not taken pains to destroy, and which prevents the Divine Word from taking deep root enough, a sinful heart which is not overwhelmed with grief, softened by tears of penitence, touched by the flames of Divine love, and has not been exercised sufficiently by meditation nor penetrated deeply enough by the truths of salvation. What is the end to which this character leads? To inconsistency, to infidelity, to apostacy: the least object, the least temptation, the first occasion, the smallest petty interest, a word of raillery or criticism dries up in a moment all that appearance which had no roots. Fervour of a day, faith of the time and the moment; continual variations, perpetual inconsistency, is not that my character?

3. The third are too much occupied with the cares of this life, and this is what is signified by the thorns in the midst of which the seed falls. *And that which fell among thorns are they, which hear the word, and the cares and riches and pleasures of this life, and the lust of other things entering in, choke the word, and it becometh unfruitful.* What are these cares of this life? Its riches and pleasures, and honours: deceptive posses-

sions, seductive objects, which enkindle covetousness, and for which we form plans, abandon ourselves to enterprises, and are continually making exertions. Why are these cares compared to thorns? Because, like them, they prick the heart in a thousand ways, by fears, disquietudes, labours, sorrows; because if they are allowed to grow, they reproduce themselves and multiply without end: because they cross one another, are interwoven and gather strength, so that a person no longer finds the means to set himself free from them, and to recover his liberty? What is the effect of these cares of life? They stifle every good feeling, and the desire to labour at our salvation. We understand the importance of this matter; we feel the emptiness and falseness of all earthly possessions, we lament, we sigh, we desire, but we have not the time. Ah! unhappy that I am! it is not time that fails me: if I would tear out these thorns from my heart, confine myself to the duties of my station, renounce all that is only *the cares of this world*, I should have time left to pray, to meditate, and to seek to attain unto perfection.

4. The fourth are well disposed, and this is what the good ground into which the seed falls signifies. *And they which are sown on good ground, are they which in an honest and good heart, having heard the word, receive it, keep it, and bring forth fruit with patience, some thirty fold, some sixty, and some an hundred.* In what do these dispositions consist? They consist in a good, upright, sincere heart, a friend of all that is true: in a wise, attentive, recollected heart: in a pure and teachable heart, which is not defiled by crime, nor given up to the violence of its passions. What is the effect of these dispositions? With these dispositions we love the word of God, we comprehend it, we draw practical conclusions from it, we keep it in our minds, we never lose the remembrance of it. What does the word of God effect when it is received with these dispositions? It fructifies and does not remain idle: it bears the fruits of virtue, of zeal, and edification; it fructifies with patience, with-

out trouble, without haste, without ostentation. Its fruits, often concealed, only shew themselves on occasions when it is needful for the good of our neighbour that they should appear; it fructifies in diverse manners, according to the talents, the grace, and the faithfulness with which it is received, but always in abundance, bearing in some, a hundred for one, in others sixty, in others, thirty. Do we see ourselves amongst this number? After so many graces, so much teaching, so many Sacraments received, where are the fruits?

Prayer. O my God! in what confusion of face I am! have pity on me, Lord, change my heart, give me a new one in which Thy word may dwell, take root, spring into freedom, and bring forth the fruits of salvation which Thou dost look for. Amen.

Meditation CXIII.

PARABLE OF THE FIELD IN WHICH SEED HAS BEEN SOWN.

This field may be considered 1. as the natural field; 2. as the field of the Church; 3. as the field of our own hearts. S. Mark xv. 26-29.

FIRST POINT.

Of the natural field.

Jesus said again to His disciples, So is the kingdom of God, as if a man should cast seed into the ground, and should sleep, and rise night and day, and the seed should spring and grow up, he knoweth not how. For the earth bringeth forth fruit of herself; first, the blade, then, the ear; after that, the full corn in the ear. But when the fruit is brought forth, immediately he putteth in the sickle, because the harvest is come. It is an object well worthy of our admiration, if we will reflect upon all that takes place before our eyes in the productions of this earth. A man cultivates a field, and he has no need to look after it, except at two seasons of the year, in spring-time when the seed is sown, and at harvest time; all the rest of the time he is not occupied with it; he sleeps by night, and rises by day, and is engaged about other things. The earth works for him, firstly in its bosom, far from the ken of human sight; there, it warms the seed, softens it, develops it, moistens it, and receives its roots and nourishes them. Some time after, she works within sight, and rejoices the heart, and flatters the hope of the master. At first, it is only the blade which springs up, then the ear shews itself, lastly the grain forms in the ear, it fills out, it turns yellow, then the corn is come to maturity, it is the time of harvest. The master reappears, cuts down the corn, and fills his barns. O great God! who would not admire Thy works? What goodness, what wisdom, what power in that natural order of Thy providence, but at the same time what incomprehensibility! No! certainly, the labourer does not know how all that is brought about; and he needs not after all to know it. But the greatest geniuses, the most subtle philosophers do not know any more. They do not know the relationship of this seed with all nature, with the earth which receives it, with the clouds which water it, with the sun which warms and ripens it, with the body of man which is nourished by it, and which changes it into its own substance. They do not know the minute mechanism of so many different operators, and yet, in spite of all that, we desire to penetrate the dealings of God in the super-natural order of things, to comprehend the secrets of His reign, the mysteries of faith, and to sound even the abyss of His Being! Let us renounce such useless and dangerous researches; let us content ourselves, like the labourer, with sowing during this life the seed of good works, as God commands us, that we may reap the fruit which He promises us at the time of harvest.

SECOND POINT.

Of the field of the Church.

Let us apply this parable to the Church of Jesus Christ, which is the field of the Lord, and the kingdom of God upon earth; Jesus Christ will shew Himself visibly and publicly only twice on the earth; at the one time, to sow the seed of the Gospel there, and at the other to gather in the harvest. The first period has passed. Jesus has planted the seed, and with what care and labour, with what fulness and abundance! Now, seated at the right hand of His Father, He is in the fruition of His glory, and without appearing to take any heed of what is taking place on the earth. He awaits the fruit of His word, of His grace, of His Spirit, of His Sacraments, and of the merits of His Death, which He has bequeathed to His Church! This Church produces virtues, forms saints, and does her appointed work, but He does not appear. This Church is exposed to persecution, dishonoured by crime, torn in pieces by schisms, trampled under by heresies, blasphemed by unbelief, and yet Jesus does not appear. Arise, O Lord, why dost Thou appear to sleep? Art Thou ignorant of what is going on in the field of Thy Church, or art Thou insensible to it? Thine enemies are taking advantage of Thine absence, and are ravaging Thine inheritance. Shew Thyself and they will be confounded, and every thing will be restored to order. No, He will not appear, for thus it has been ordained and foretold. Let us then keep ourselves from murmuring or from taking offence at it. Notwithstanding this apparent absence, and in the midst of all these disorders, the field is bringing forth fruit, it is being covered with a rich harvest, which is ripening and coming on to perfection. When the time of the harvest shall have come, when the number of the elect shall be fulfilled, then the Master will reappear, and will gather in His Harvest, will accomplish His Words, and will reward those who have remained faithful to Him. Let us labour, and take heed that we belong to this number.

THIRD POINT.

Of the field of our heart.

Let us apply this parable to ourselves who are the kingdom of God. We have received the Divine seed into our hearts, we have been instructed in the commandments, the doctrine, and the mysteries of Jesus Christ, we have been prevented by His grace, the sources of which are always open to us in His Sacraments. Was there ever land better cultivated, and more richly sown? The time of harvest, for us in particular, will be that of our death. Then the Master will appear, and what will He find in us? Deceptive plants, desires and plans not carried out, sterile ears of corn, beginnings without perseverance, empty, light, spoilt, mixed, rotten grain, acts of virtue without perfection, without inward spirit, without any other motive than human respect, caprice, self-interest and vanity. Let us hasten then that the Divine seed should bring forth more fruit in us. The time of the harvest comes, it is at hand, and when it is come, we shall not be able to escape the sickle of the Reaper, nor change the nature of the harvest.

Prayer. Cause, O my God, that the good grain which Thou hast sown in me may shoot forth, grow, and ripen. May my heart, like a fertile soil, watered with the blessings of Thy right Hand, warmed by the fire of Thy Holy Spirit, stand firm against impetuous winds, the storms which the devil stirs up there, the violent passions which gain the mastery over it, that, sheltered by Thy grace, it may produce a full and abundant harvest. Amen.

Meditation CXIV.

OF THE PARABLE OF THE GRAIN OF MUSTARD SEED.

The grain of mustard seed is 1. the figure of Christ; 2. the figure of religion; 3. the figure of grace. S. Matt. xiii. 31, 32. S. Mark iv. 30-32.

FIRST POINT.

The grain of mustard seed, a figure of Christ.

Jesus put forth another parable unto them, (His disciples) *saying, Whereunto shall we liken the kingdom of God? or with what comparison shall we compare it? The kingdom of God is like the grain of mustard seed which a man took and sowed in his field, which, when it is sown in the earth, is less than all the seeds that be in the earth, but when it is sown, it groweth up, and becometh greater than all other herbs, and shooteth out great branches; so that the fowls of the air may lodge under the shadow of it.* If Jesus Christ asks to what He shall compare the kingdom of God, it is in order to awaken our attention, to testify to us the zeal which He has for our salvation, and the care which He takes to choose out images which are within our reach, and the most fitting for our instruction. *The kingdom of heaven is like a grain of mustard seed.* When it is sown, it is the smallest of all grains; but when it has developed to its full size and growth, then it becomes the largest of all plants, and puts forth branches so strong and tufted, that the birds of the air come and perch on its branches and rest in its shadow. Let us then apply the parable to Jesus Christ Himself. The obscurity of His birth, the labours of His life, the ignominy of His death made Him to be looked upon as a worm of the earth, the opprobrium of men; but from this field where the grain of mustard seed has been sown, from this garden, from this tomb where Jesus was buried, He has come forth triumphant and glorious, the Hope of all nations, the Bliss of saints, the glory of angels. Let us seek to make ourselves of little account on earth, and to be like unto Him, and in Heaven we shall be exalted with Him. He that humbleth himself shall be exalted, our Saviour says. Happy those pure and fervent souls, who, like the birds of the sky, rise above the earth, to rest themselves on the branches of this Divine tree, hide themselves in the wounds of Jesus and even in His sacred heart! There, inaccessible to the passions which agitate the earth, to the insatiable desires which burn and dry up the heart of mortals, they taste in the love of their Saviour, and in the shadow of His All-powerful Arm, an unchangeable rest, a delicious nourishment, and the assurance of eternal bliss.

SECOND POINT.

The grain of mustard seed, a figure of the Church.

Let us now apply the parable to the Church of Jesus Christ on earth. What could there have been weaker in its beginning, from the number and rank of the persons who composed it, by the humbleness of its faith, by the gentleness of its maxims, by the severity of its morals, by the contempt in which it was held by mankind, by the persecutions which tyrants have excited against it, and under which it has been so to say, so long buried? Nevertheless this grain of mustard seed has sprung up, has put forth blossoms, has grown from century to century, has become a majestic tree, which has extended its branches to the extremities of the earth, and has covered the entire world with its shadow. Under this shadow, the most powerful monarchs have laid down their sceptre and their crown, and have found in the humility of the Gospel, a glory far more solid than that which surrounds their throne; under this shadow the most sublime geniuses have humbled their intellects, and have found, in the submission of faith, truths more consoling than those which had formed the object of their vain researches; under this shadow, the most notorious sinners have immolated their hearts and their passions, and they have found in the restraints of penitence, delights far purer than those which they had sought for in the paths of iniquity. Let us then ourselves withdraw ourselves under the shade of this Divine Tree; let our glory then be in the practice of the Gospel, our knowledge in submission to God's will, our happiness in the mortifications of the Cross.

THIRD POINT.

The grain of mustard seed, a figure of grace.

We may besides apply the parable to the grace of Jesus Christ in our hearts. The first grace which begins our conversion and the work of our salvation is sometimes imperceptible. A good thought, a holy inspiration, a secret impulse, a work that has reference to God, either read or heard, an accident, a holy example, an act of resistance to temptation, or of avoiding an occasion of sin, a step in the right way, it often needs no more. What increase does not this first grace receive when we are faithful in corresponding to it! It grows, it is strengthened, it extends itself, and produces numberless virtues, sublime virtues, solid virtues, which adorn and edify the Church. How many souls come and rest themselves, and nourish themselves on the branches of this fertile tree. They find there consolation, counsel, vigour, strength and courage. Ah! if we did but know whither that good motive which urges us might lead us, or that call of God which presses us, if we did but know the designs that God has for us, all the good that He wills to do by us, and the height of holiness to which we might attain, if we would listen to His voice, we should take great care not to resist it. But alas! how often has He not offered us His grace, and we have rejected it? Ah! let us be wiser for the future. Let us take this precious grain which His mercy still offers us, let us sow it in the field of our hearts, let us cultivate it with care; however small it may appear to us, it is the germ of all that is the greatest.

Prayer. Thy ways, O Lord, and Thy designs are often hidden; grant then that I may not despise any longer the instructions which Thou dost give me how I may attain unto salvation, nor the means which Thou dost employ for my conversion. Yes, my God, I will reverence all that shall come to me from Thy Hand, and all who shall speak to me in Thy Name. I will be faithful in cherishing the first seed of Thy grace that Thou dost sow in my heart, so that it may bring forth fruit to Thy glory. Employ, O divine Jesus, in order to establish Thy kingdom firmly in my heart, the same power which Thou hast made use of to extend Thy Church throughout the earth. Grant that like this grain of mustard seed, that is to say, humble like Thy first disciples, little in my own eyes, and content to be so in the eyes of men, deeply humiliated, and crushed, and despising myself with my whole heart, I may become a tree rooted in charity and humility in the field of Thy Church, and worthy to be one day transplanted to Thy dwelling place in glory. Amen.

Meditation CXV.

PARABLE OF THE LEAVEN.

This parable is capable of two interpretations. Consider first, the first meaning which may be given it, then the second meaning that can be applied to it, and, lastly the prophecy which belongs to all these parables. S. Matt. xiii. 33—35. S. Mark iv. 33—35.

FIRST POINT.

Of the first meaning of this parable.

The kingdom of heaven is like unto leaven, which a woman took, and hid in three measures of meal, till the whole was leavened. This parable signifies the preaching of the gospel accompanied by the gifts of the Holy Spirit. The wisdom of God planted the gospel in Palestine, that land of promise and of blessing. It is there that this precious leaven began to ferment, it is from thence that the fermentation has spread into the three parts of the then known world, and which our Lord has willed perhaps to point out by the three measures of which He has specified the number. This world weighed down to the earth, knowing no other possessions than those of earth, and worshipping no other God than idols of metal or of stone, has been stirred up, moved, raised above itself; it has renounced its passions, it has destroyed its gods, it has adored its Creator, it has acknowledged its Saviour, it has turned its looks towards heaven, and it has laboured to render itself worthy of Him by its virtues. What a miracle, what a striking wonder of the Almighty power of God! The fermentation still continues, it has spread over the new world, and it will last until the entire universe shall have felt its salutary effects, and the number of the elect shall be accomplished. Advance this great work, Lord; support Thy Church, which has received from Thee this precious leaven, and which has the charge of spreading it everywhere. Give unto her faithful workmen, capable of carrying out her charitable labours, and to us teachable hearts to receive this leaven, with eagerness mingled with fear, lest it should be taken again from them, and which give it scope to work in all its force and efficacy.

SECOND POINT.

Of another meaning of this parable.

This parable may be applied to the Eucharistic bread which the Church gives us, and which she puts within us as a sacred leaven which should sanctify all the powers of our soul, all the senses of our body, all the actions of our life, which should penetrate us, change us, incorporate us into Itself, transform us, make us one flesh and one spirit with It, and render us mystic bread worthy of the table of God. Ah! how far am I from feeling in myself those Divine effects! I am always bowed down towards things of earth, always lukewarm and languishing about the things of God. Is there not some evil passion in me which I have not mortified, some bad habit which I have not broken through, some sin which I do not detest and hate? Take away from me, O my divine Saviour, all the evil leaven out of my heart, that it may yield itself up entirely to the Divine operation of Thy grace and of Thy sacraments.

THIRD POINT.

Of the prophecy which belongs to all these parables.

All these things spake Jesus unto the multitude in parables; and without a parable spake He not unto them; that it might be fulfilled which was spoken by the prophet, saying, I will open my mouth in parables; I will utter things which have been kept secret from the foundation of the world. And when they were alone He expounded all things to His disciples. The parables of Jesus Christ were prophecies; and by an admirable disposition of divine wisdom, they had themselves been prophesied beforehand, so that, by a marvellous agreement of the two Testaments, it might be seen that the Christian religion was the work of God, that it embraced all time, and extended from the beginning to the end of it. Jesus foretold incredible events, which appeared destitute of all likelihood, respecting the establishment of His Church, and the progress of His Gospel. He spoke to a people who were certainly not in a condition to understand His words, nor disposed to believe the events which they foretold; on the other hand, it was needful that these events should have been foretold, in order that they might not appear to be the effect of chance. The Saviour was then obliged in order not to expose these truths to the scorn and raillery of His hearers, to conceal them under figures and emblems which they could not fathom, and He reserved the explanation of their meaning to better disposed and more teachable disciples. What is most worthy of admiration is that this very disposition of the people, this conduct which our Saviour would adopt with regard to them, His goodness is instructing His apostles, and through them His Church to the end of time, should all have been foretold. For us, who are placed now-a-days under the most favourable circumstances, we see the accomplishment of the prophecies of Jesus Christ, their connection with ancient prophecies, the chain of events which have taken place on the earth, which have signalised there the power and wisdom of God, and discover to us the depth of His eternal counsels. Can there be a sight more divine and more full of delight? Ah! where are our faith, our gratitude and our love? Jesus spoke according to the capacities of the people, by which is not meant that He spoke to them according to the capacities of their minds, but according to the dispositions of their hearts. It is thus that He still speaks to us. If we do not understand anything of the mysteries of God, and of the truth of the Gospel, it is not our minds that are at fault, but our hearts. Let us seek to purify these hearts, and we shall then understand, and Jesus Christ Himself will explain to us what it is needful for us to comprehend.

Prayer. Far be it from me, O Lord, ever to mix strange leaven with the leaven of Thy Gospel. Preserve me from hypocrisy, from the love of the world, from its fatal maxims, from its corrupt inclinations, from its contagious examples, which are a leaven which corrupts the heart, and hinders the effect of the divine leaven. Do Thou stir Thyself, O my God, this precious leaven in the depths of my heart; that it may change me, that it may sanctify me. Let the holiness of the religion which I profess be every where visible in me, so that this grace of election which I have received from Thee may turn, not to my condemnation, but to Thy glory and my salvation. Amen.

Meditation CXVI.

PARABLE OF THE TARES.

Of the mixture of the wicked with the good. 1. Whence this mixture comes; 2. wherefore God permits this mixture; 3. how this mixture will end. S. Matt. xiii. 24—30. and 36—43.

FIRST POINT.

Whence this mixture comes.

1. It does not come from God. *Another parable put He forth unto them, saying, The kingdom of Heaven is likened unto a man which sowed good seed in his field. But while men slept, his enemy came and sowed tares among the wheat, and went his way. But when the blade was sprung up, and brought forth fruit, then appeared the tares also. Then the servants of the householder came and said unto him, Sir, didst not thou sow good seed in thy field? from whence then hath it tares? He said unto them, An enemy hath done this. Then Jesus sent the multitude away, and went into the house, and His disciples came unto Him, saying, Declare unto us the parable of the tares of the field. He answered and said unto them, He that soweth the good seed is the Son of man: the field is the world; the good seed are the children of the kingdom, but the tares are the children of the wicked one; the enemy that sowed them is the devil.* Let us join our prayers to those of the apostles, and let us pray our Lord to explain this parable to us, Who has Himself set before us these important truths. Let us consider, in the first place, what Jesus has done in order to form those who are righteous on the earth, and for us in particular, in order that we might be of that number. What Sacraments, what teachings, what grace has He not given us! Is it not to this divine Saviour, to this God of all mercy that we must betake ourselves, if there are amongst us

yet, any faint hearted souls, sinners, ungodly men! Let us consider, in the second place, what is a righteous man on the earth. He is a child of the kingdom, a child of God, a living member of Christ destined for heaven. Ah! blessed state! Such have we become by Baptism, we have been restored to this state by repentance, we have been strengthened in it by the Eucharist; let us now strive to remain in it until death. Let us consider, in the third place, what is a sinner on the earth. He is a child of the devil, shut out whilst he remains in that condition, from all claim to the kingdom of heaven; the slave, the instrument, the sport of the devil, the accomplice of his rebellion, and destined to the same punishment with him. Ah! let us come forth out of so deplorable a condition, and let us return to Jesus, Who still offers unto us assured means whereby we may be restored to our privileges as children of God.

2. This mixture comes from the devil, as an enemy who is a deceiver. This impostor leads us astray by flattering us; he entices us into sin by proposing to us pleasures, riches, honours, and perfect happiness; and we believe this deceiver, who only seeks to despoil us of a kingdom, to deprive us of our crown, in order that he may cast us down into hell.

3. This mixture comes from the devil, as a watchful enemy. Whilst men sleep, the evil one watches, he is on the watch for the right moment, and knows how to bide his time. Woe to the pastors who are asleep and to all to whom is entrusted the guidance of others, if they sleep instead of watching! and woe to ourselves, if we give an opportunity to the enemy by our negligence in prayer, in self-examination, and in avoiding occasions of sin!

4. This mixture comes from the devil as a hidden enemy. This enemy comes by night, and after having sown the tares, he withdraws, and does not appear any more. Who would not feel a horror of the devil, if he could see him? Who would not repulse him with indignation, if he did but remember that it is he who sug-

gests those thoughts of revenge, who presents to our minds those immodest thoughts, who holds forth to us those flattering discourses, who writes those poisonous books, who has drawn those lascivious pictures or composed those voluptuous songs? But he hides himself, and only lets his agents appear in his place, those whom he has seduced, and of whom he makes use in order to seduce others: let us mistrust then the artifices of this hidden enemy!

SECOND POINT.

Wherefore God permits this mixture.

1. For the perfection of the good. Let us take up the parable again. When the master of the field had heard from his servants that his enemy had sown the tares in his field, his *servants said unto him, Wilt thou then that we go and gather them up?* Such are men; such is their eager and indiscreet zeal, which is anxious to exterminate every thing, to pull up every thing; but God does not act thus. Their master answereth them: *Nay; lest while ye gather up the tares, ye root up also the wheat with them. Let both grow together until the harvest.* Let us observe here that the roots of the tares are so interlaced with those of the wheat, that the one cannot be pulled up without the other. In the same way, in the deep counsels of the wisdom of God, Who knows how to draw evil out of good, the malice of the wicked is bound up with the virtue of the good in such a manner, that were the former taken away, the latter would lose much of its lustre and its merit. In truth, 1. the corruption of the world gives to virtue a solidity and a lustre which it would not have had without that. The world is unfaithful to God: it only presents souls rebellious to their Creator, who have thrown off the yoke of His obedience and trodden under foot all His commandments; but what glory is there not in remaining faithful to Him in the midst of so general a defection, of daring to declare ourselves for Him, in making an open profession of obeying Him, and in walking with a firm and

equal step in the narrow way of His commandments! Such is the spectacle which religion offers to us: we see examples of solid piety in the midst of a corrupt world, and even amidst the general licence which prevails in it. 2. The offences which abound in the world do but give birth to sublime and unknown virtues, which would never have existed without them. The world is filled with objects of offence; it only offers seductive and contagious examples: every thing in it is a snare to innocence and virtue. But what have these offences produced? They have peopled deserts, they have caused places where virtue may take refuge to be built even in cities; they have raised up saints without number, who have enlightened, taught and governed the Church. Without these offences and dangers of the world, the Church would not have been adorned with so many different religious institutions which form its glory and its ornament, and which have not ceased continually to lead towards Heaven pure souls who have lived whilst on earth a heavenly life. 3. The hatred and persecution of the world have raised virtue to a pitch of holiness to which it would otherwise never have attained. This world is a tyrant which hates and persecutes virtue. Those who seek to lead a religious life in it, are sure to meet with scorn and contempt. What heroic patience do they not need in order to preserve charity and gentleness in the midst of so violent a persecution! Have not the holiest ages of the Church been those of persecution? Would heaven have had martyrs, if earth had not had tyrants? Let us adore this infinite wisdom of God, which has known how to bring such great good out of so great evil. Let us enter into the dealings of Providence, and profit each according to our own station, by the advantages with which this mingling of good and evil furnishes us. There are mixed states of life in which all these advantages seem united. We are sufficiently spread over the world, to have an opportunity of rendering to God a signal testimony, and of giving to that world proofs of incorruptible holiness of life;

we are perhaps sufficiently retired from the world to be able to practise sublime and hidden virtues, and lastly, we are perhaps sufficiently hated by the world to have some part in the crown of martyrs.

2. God suffers this mixture for the conversion of sinners. *But He said, Nay, lest while ye gather up the tares, ye root up also the wheat with them.* The tares sufficiently resemble the wheat, that till both are ripe, one may mistake the one for the other: but in the moral sense, it is still more easy to be mistaken in them, because tares cannot become wheat; but the sinner may be converted, become a saint, and one of God's elect. It is for that reason that God leaves him his free will on the earth: and that which ought to induce him to change, is, in the first place, the goodness of God which endureth yet daily. *Wilt Thou then that we go and gather them up? but He said, Nay:* Ah! words full of sweetness and tenderness! Where should I be, Lord, if these words of clemency had not come forth from Thy mouth to hinder all the creatures which had risen up against me? It is these words which have saved me from that danger in which I should have lost my life, which has healed me from that sickness which was about to become mortal, which has preserved me from a thousand accidents which I could not foresee, and has preserved me unto this moment. Thou dost give me time to return to Thee, and in order to give it me, Thou hast suffered in silence my faint-heartedness and my luke-warmness in serving Thee; Thou hast borne with my sins, my unfaithfulness, my relapses, my excesses of every kind. Ah! I have already offended Thee too much and abused Thy goodness; I come back to Thee, O my God, penetrated with the deepest sorrow, and resolved to employ the rest of my days in serving Thee faithfully, and in repairing the disorders of my past life. In the second place, the example of the good which urges him on. What is a sinner? He is the tares of the field of the Lord, the disgrace of religion, the opprobrium of nature, the child of the evil one, the enemy of God and of the Saviour, and an object

of horror to the angels. Ah! if God had not over and over again stayed the anger and indignation of those blessed spirits, they would long ago have rooted him out from the earth which he dishonours. The good on the contrary, are the precious wheat, the glory and delight of the master of the field; they are the children of God, destined to reign eternally with Him in Heaven. The world itself cannot refuse them its esteem and approbation, and prevent itself from envying their lot. And why envy it? We can be what they are; let us profit by their example, it is for that that God leaves us still on the earth. In the third place, the justice of God which threatens them. *Let both grow together until the harvest.* Cowardly and sinful soul, impenitent and obstinate sinner, do not deceive yourself, the patience of God has its limits; your pleasures, your acts of injustice, your blasphemies, your crimes will also have an end, beyond which you will not be allowed to continue on in your evil life! Multiply then your sins as much as you can, you will be permitted to go on, but only *till the harvest*, and no longer: till death, after which all will be over for you: then there will be no further repentance, conversion, grace, or mercy for you. Let us prevent that terrible moment, which will be followed by eternal despair!

THIRD POINT.

What will be the end of this mixture.

The punishment of the wicked, and the reward of the good. *In the time of harvest I will say to the reapers, gather ye together first the tares, and bind them in bundles to burn them; but gather the wheat into My barn.*

1. Of the punishment of the wicked. The terms of the parable will suffice to make us understand the rigour of this punishment, but let us see how our Lord explains it. *The harvest is the end of the world: and the reapers are the angels. As therefore the tares are gathered and burned in the fire; so shall it be in the end of*

the world. The Son of man shall send forth His angels, and they shall gather out of His kingdom all things that offend, and them which do iniquity: and shall cast them into a furnace of fire; there shall be wailing and gnashing of teeth. It is Jesus Christ Himself Who explains to us thus His parable: there can be in this explanation neither error, nor exaggeration: so let us examine into the punishment of the wicked. 1. The place of the punishment, a furnace. Is there any solitude, slavery, subjection which would appear hard to me, if it would save me from being eternally condemned to so fearful a prison, or to so terrible a dungeon as this furnace? 2. The instrument of the punishment, fire. Are there any pleasures or sensual indulgences, or delights, which I could not renounce, is there any kind of self-mortification, or crucifixion of my body, or act of penitence, which I would not willingly embrace, in order to avoid this devouring fire! 3. The effect of this punishment, rage and despair. Weeping and gnashing of teeth, despair, cursing God, cursing themselves the authors of their own misery, and giving themselves up to transports of eternal rage and fury, such will be the condition and the occupation of the damned! What a chaos, what horror, what an abode! Is there any thing I ought not to be willing to suffer here below in order to avoid it? Contradictions, unjust quarrels, the wearisome temper or proud harshness of others, ill-treatment, nothing of all that can appear insupportable to me in comparison with these gnashings of teeth, which are the portion of the damned? Now, who will be thus thrown into this burning furnace? All the wicked, without distinction of station or rank; kings, merchants, nobles, the great and powerful, the rich, the wise, they are no longer anything. Are you righteous, or are you sinners? That is a point which appeared to you light or of no consequence on earth; but here it is the only point, which decides every thing. If you are wicked, you are only the tares which are condemned to the fire. Priests, laymen, poor, feeble, afflicted, rich, healthy, great, are you righteous or sinners? It is a point to which you have not given on earth all the attention which you ought; but if you have not fulfilled the duties of your station, and profited by your sufferings, if in one word you are sinners, you are only the tares condemned to the fire.

2. Of the reward of the good. *Then shall the righteous shine forth as the sun in the kingdom of their Father.* Consider their reward, 1. in their persons. How different they will be from what they were on earth! There will not be the least imperfection either in soul or body; there will be nought in them but what is glorious and full of beauty. The brightness of the sun is only a feeble figure to express the splendour with which each of them will be surrounded. 2. In their abode; it will be the kingdom of God their Father, in Heaven. If the earth, although under a curse, yield still to the fortunate ones of this life, so many different charms, what will it be with the heaven, which the wisdom of God has formed to be the eternal dwelling place of His cherished children, where nothing is wanting, where every thing abounds? 3. In the object of their blessedness, which will be God Himself, the Infinite Being and source of all bliss. They will enjoy Him, they will see Him, they will love Him, and be partakers of His bliss in the ineffable delights of eternal love. But for whom will this lot so enviable be reserved? For the righteous, and by this title only can it be obtained. Of whatever rank, of whatever condition in life we may be, let us live in righteousness, let us fulfil the duties of our station, let us observe the commandments of God, let us practise Christian virtues, let us persevere in piety and devotion, let us die in the love of God, and Heaven is promised to us. And what other interest have I then in this world, and of what importance is all else to us, if only I live and die in the grace of my God? Here then is the solution of that strange scene which takes place on the earth, and of this mixture of the good and the wicked; a scene which has been such a stumbling block to free-thinkers, and which has sanctified all rational minds and teachable hearts. Such a solution

as is truly worthy of the majesty, greatness, wisdom, and magnificence of God.

Prayer. Thou dost add, Lord, in conclusion, *Who hath ears to hear, let him hear.* Ah! who would not rather be awakened out of his supineness by the interpretation which Thou dost give Thyself of the parable which Thou dost put forth to us? Let the ungodly man close his ears that he may not hear Thee, let the free-thinker divert himself so that he may not reflect upon it; as for me, O my God, I ask of Thee a teachable heart that I may profit by so important a lesson, by a truth at the same time so terrible and so consoling. Detach from my heart all that passes away with time, that I may understand and taste that which is eternal. Ah! Lord! may Thy justice appal me, may Thy commandments serve as my rule, so that, walking in light, I may attain to Thy glory. Amen.

Meditation CXVII.
PARABLE OF THE HIDDEN TREASURE, AND THE PRECIOUS PEARL.

After our Lord had explained to His Apostles the parable of the tares, He continued to instruct them by several other parables which will form the subject of this meditation and the following. Let us apply ourselves to develop in this one, 1. the parable of the hidden treasure; 2. the parable of the precious pearl. S. Matt. xiii. 44—46.

FIRST POINT.
Parable of the hidden treasure.

Jesus said to His Apostles; *Again, the kingdom of heaven is like unto treasure hid in a field; the which when a man hath found, he hideth it away, and for joy thereof goeth and selleth all that he hath and buyeth that field.* We may apply this parable to the treasure hidden in the Church of Christ. What did it not cost to the early believers to gain possession of this field, and to preserve it, to become members of this Church, and to persevere in its faith! They were obliged to renounce not only their worldly possessions, their rest, their good name, but often even their lives; and they did not fear to sacrifice all in order to continue in that faith, without which it was impossible to please God: in that Church, out of which they could not look for salvation. Those who are not within the fold of Christ's Church ought to imitate their generous self-sacrifice in order that they may enter into it; for us who have been born in her, how great is our ingratitude if we are not filled with thankfulness, and if we do not praise God for so great a blessing every day of our lives? But what is our folly, if we neglect this treasure which is in our possession, and which belongs to us: if we will not give ourselves the trouble to look for it, and to dig for it so as to discover it, and appropriate it to ourselves. What happens nevertheless? Like the first master of the field in the parable, and less excusable than him, we have not even a value for this treasure, we do not think of it, we are little attracted to the field where it is hidden, to the Church and the Christian faith, we are ready to abandon both one and the other, and the salvation which depends thereupon, as soon as pleasure, human respect, fortune or ambition require it. How often perhaps have not we even sold this treasure for so vile a price?

2. We may apply this parable to perfection hidden in the religious life, and in estrangement from the world. He whom God calls to perfection, whether by a special call, or by the life of the ministry, or by a religious life, or by a powerful attraction to an inward life, and to exercises of devotion and penitence, even in the midst of the world; he understands that it is a treasure he has found. Now, what is his joy at so happy a discovery! He takes care not to make it public, not to display it; he hides it in his bosom, he only communicates it to discreet and enlightened persons, who can aid him by their counsels, to gain possession of the field wherein his treasure is. What ardour, what eagerness, what holy and lively impatience to bring to a termination

all temporal business, to see the happy moment arrive in which he may give himself to God, and serve Him with entire freedom! Let us recall that happy time, if we have ever experienced its happiness. Did we find any difficulty then in separating ourselves from that which was dearest to us, and in making the sacrifices which our vocation required? No, doubtless; we would have sacrificed a thousand worlds in order to obtain the treasure so long desired. We were right, the treasure which we gained was of more value than a thousand worlds, more than all created things. But have we preserved these feelings, this esteem in which we held this treasure, this joy in having obtained it, this generosity in sacrificing everything in order to fulfil worthily its duties? The treasure has not changed, it is the same, and is always capable of enriching us, and satisfying all the desires of our heart. What misfortune for us if this treasure had still remained a hidden treasure to us! Ah! if that is so, let us commune with ourselves, let us not abandon the field which we possess; the treasure is there, we know it: let us seek, let us dig, let us pray, meditate, and work; we shall find it again, and a holy joy will take the place in our hearts of weariness and distaste.

3. We may apply this parable to ourselves, by considering, in this man spoken of in the gospel, 1. his happiness. He finds a treasure, and a treasure which he was not seeking for, of which he did not even think; and such is our happiness. Without having sought for it, without even having thought of it, we find ourselves members of the Christian Church, and we know all the blessings of which we have been made partakers. With how many graces does not God prevent us, with how many holy desires does He not inspire us! Let us learn to know our own happiness, and let us be filled with gratitude. 2. The prudence of this man. Having discovered this treasure in a field which did not belong to him, he puts it back in its place, hides it anew, and covers it with earth. This is what humility ought to do in us; it ought to hide the graces bestowed on it,

the gifts of God, and its good works. He exposes himself to have them stolen from him, who is imprudent enough not to hide his treasure. 3. His joy. Let us give ourselves up to the feelings of joy which the blessings merit of which faith makes us possessors, and which it gives us the right to hope for. 4. His courage. He sells all that he has, and buys that field. The knowledge of the treasure is not to be bought; faith, grace are given to us gratuitously; but the possession of the treasure, of the field where it is, of the kingdom of heaven, of eternal life, of the crown of righteousness, must be purchased. Do not let us deceive ourselves, it must cost us something. It would be to deceive ourselves grossly to persuade ourselves that heaven will be given to us gratuitously: it must be purchased at the price of our evil passions, of our vicious inclinations, of which we must rid ourselves; at the price of all the feelings of our heart, of all the actions of our life which we must consecrate to God and His Love; at this price, heaven is ours! Oh! blessed exchange, blessed acquisition!

SECOND POINT.

Parable of the pearl of great price.

Again, the kingdom of heaven is like unto a merchant man, seeking goodly pearls: who, when he had found one pearl of great price, went and sold all that he had, and bought it.

1. Apply this parable to the Church of Jesus Christ, to religion, to the Christian faith. Let us consider, in the first place, what should be the search after true religion. When a person is not born a Christian, however little he reflects upon a point which is of so great importance for eternity, he cannot but feel many disquieting thoughts. At the beginning of Christianity, many great philosophers and deep thinkers, having made trial of various sects, and finding none in them which could satisfy them, were won over by the Christian doctrine, embraced it, clung to it, and have become the glory and

ornament of the Church by their works. It would be the same with unbelievers, and philosophers of later days, if they would seek the truth with hearts as upright and intentions as pure as those earlier philosophers; but people do not seek the truth, because they hate it, and fear the just consequences of it, because they cherish error, and love delusions. Let us consider, in the second place, the truth of the Christian religion, and of the Catholic faith. As soon as we know the truths of Christianity, all doubts cease; the truth shews itself with a splendour which disperses all the darkness, and brings a perfect calm to heart and mind. All there is reasonable, all is proportioned on the one side to the needs and weaknesses of men, and on the other, to the nobility of his feelings and the extent of his desires. With regard to precious pearls, if one is not a good judge of them, one may be deceived by their respective beauties, whilst we only see in them common ones; but whilst among these there may be one of a perfect beauty, whoever will examine it attentively will distinguish it at once from all the rest. The misfortune of man is that he has no attention or activity but for the things of this life, that he only fears to be deceived in that which touches his temporal interests, and is lukewarm and indifferent to all that regards God and his own salvation; an indifference which goes as far as to make many unbelievers say, that all religions are good, and that we can be saved alike in all. Ah! he who speaks thus does not know himself; he who speaks thus knows not true religion. When he has it, he feels he has the truth, and the truth is one. *One Lord, one faith, one baptism.* For us who are born within the Church's pale, let us love it, let us study it, and cling to it more and more. Consider in the third place, what is the price of true religion and of true faith. If there are many who do not know the truth for want of research and attention, there are many others who do not embrace it for want of generosity and courage. The truth of religion and of faith is a truth of practice which requires the greatest sacrifices. We must submit the prejudices of our minds, the inclinations of our hearts, our pride, to the humble confession of our faults, repentance, fastings and abstinences. We must conquer the human respect which keeps us back, break the bonds which hold us, sometimes even give up fortune and our earthly possessions. Woe be to him who hesitates to gain even at this price, this pearl of great price which would enrich him for eternity! For us, let us love the faith into which we have been baptized, and let us pray to continue in it; but above all let us join to it the good works which it commands, without which it would only be a dead faith, a lost pearl to us, the loss of which would render us still more guilty.

2. Let us apply this parable to the true happiness of man, which consists in the love of God, and the state of grace. Consider, in the first place, what ought to be the search after true happiness. Every one desires to be happy; even the Gospel exhorts us to seek after happiness; but it warns us to seek for true happiness where only it is to be found. A man who seeks for pearls and traffics in them seeks only for good and fine pearls: why then should we seek for a happiness, which we have so often experienced to be false, defiled, impure, incapable of satisfying our hearts, and which can only cause us shame, trouble, and remorse? Let us reject, as men who know what they are about, and will not be deceived, those fictitious pearls, those false brilliants, which only merit contempt, and the acquisition of which, far from enriching us, can only bring ruin upon us. Consider, in the second place, where true happiness is to be met with. True happiness is only to be found in the love and grace of God. Ah! how happy is he who has made the discovery of this pearl of great price, and who knows its beauty and its value. Our hearts are made for God alone; it is in God, in His grace and love that they can alone find the rest they seek for in vain in the love of created things; it is to say too little, that they find there delights, sweetnesses, charms, in one word, bliss beyond all expression, with the sweet hope of which death cannot deprive them, but which it will on the contrary, consummate, and of which, it will render the duration eter-

nal. Consider, in the third place, the price of true happiness. The love of God, in which alone consists true happiness, is only acquired at the price of every other affection, at the price of all which we possess, or of which we hope for the possession, at the price of all the affections of our hearts. We seek in vain to retain ought, or to alter the conditions offered to us: the price is fixed. We shall never have this inestimable pearl until we have given up all for it. Whilst we are disputing and tormenting ourselves, we are losing precious moments, we are diminishing by so much the duration of our possession, and perhaps the time will come to a close, and shall we lose all the other possessions which we desire to obtain, without having gained the one which alone can remain to us and satisfy us? Ah! do not let us fear: when we are asked to give up all, it is not in order to impoverish us, it is in order to enrich us; it is not to deprive us of any happiness, it is to take away from us whatever hinders us from enjoying perfect, sovereign, and infinite happiness.

Prayer. Give me, O my God, that true wisdom, which can esteem and seek for things according to their true value; that true prudence, which prefers salvation before all else; that true generosity, which sacrifices every thing to Thy love. It is to faith and confidence, to prayer and faithfulness, that Thou dost grant both the precious pearl, and the hidden treasure, that is to say, Thy kingdom; grant that I may neglect none of these means in order to procure it. Amen.

Meditation CXVIII.
PARABLE OF THE NET.

This parable represents to us, 1. the state of the Church at the present time; 2. the state of the Church at the end of the world; 3. the state of the Church in the next world. S. Matt. xiii. 47—52.

FIRST POINT.

Of the state of the Church at the present time.

Again, the kingdom of Heaven is like unto a net, that was cast into the sea, and gathered of every kind, which, when it was full, they drew to shore, and sat down, and gathered the good into vessels, but cast the bad away. This vast net is the Church, which by the preaching of the Gospel gathers together men of all kinds, the good and the evil. Here below, all is mixed, all is hidden; the good cannot be distinguished with certainty, nor what is the degree of their goodness; nor who are the wicked, and what is the degree of their wickedness, and still less those who will persevere in their goodness or their wickedness. That which is said of the Church in general, is true of each profession in particular. Whence let us draw three conclusions.

1. A truth which we must know, namely that we are not out of the pale of the Church although we are sinners. The Church on earth is not composed only of the righteous, or of those only who are elect. Sinner though I may be, I am still in the Church, and I may yet be converted and saved; but I am not saved because I may have embraced a holy calling, although I am in the Church. A person may be lost in whatever position in life he is in.

2. A fault which we must avoid. The evil which appears in the Church ought neither to surprise me nor to cause me to take offence, since it is foretold. The Church of Christ is not the less holy in herself: the ministry is not the less in itself a holy calling because there are those in it who are unworthy or live evil lives. This evil is the sad apanage of humanity, it is an inevitable misfortune amongst mortals endowed with free-will. I must not take upon myself to judge any one, or make a separation which belongs only to God, and which has nothing to do with the present state of the Church, while it is still on the earth.

3. One important point to which we must attend. That which alone concerns me, is to see whether I am amongst the number of the good, and to use all diligence that I may be found amongst that number; to become

better and holier whilst there is yet time, for that which is now hidden and mingled will not be so always, and soon the net will be drawn up, that is to say, the separation of the righteous and the wicked will take place irrevocably.

SECOND POINT.

Of the state of the Church at the end of the world.

So shall it be at the end of the world; the angels shall come forth, and sever the wicked from among the just, and shall cast them into the furnace of fire; there shall be wailing and gnashing of teeth. When the net is full, it will be drawn up. When God shall have executed His designs upon the earth, in favour of His elect, the world will come to an end. Jesus Christ seated with His apostles, who have cast the net, around Him, will judge, pronounce the sentence, and a new order of things will begin.

1. That which was hidden will be manifested. Neither hypocrisy, nor even charity itself will be able to throw a veil over any thing, or to disguise it. The truth will appear in all its completeness; and with it, on the one side, what terrors, what abominations, what monsters, will then appear! and on the other hand, what beauty, what wonders, what enchanting objects! How shall I then appear? What I now am, and what I take so much care not to appear to be.

2. That which was mixed will be separated. The angels will come and separate the sinners from amongst the righteous: the sacrilegious priests, from amongst the saintly priests: the unjust magistrates from the midst of the upright magistrates: corrupt Christians from those that are fervent; the foolish virgins, from those that are wise; the unfaithful wives, from those that are faithful; worldly women, from amongst Christian women; in a word, the damned from amongst the elect. Ah! who would be able to endure the shame of such a separation? Let us separate ourselves now from sinners that we may not be separated then from the righteous.

3. That which was united in one common centre will be divided and placed at the two opposite extremities. The good and the wicked, the good things and the evils of this life were united on earth; then the division will take place, and every thing will be put in its place, in an infinite and eternal opposition; the sinners in the burning furnace in hell: the righteous in Heaven, in the delights of Paradise; on the one side, evil things will be gathered together as the portion of the wicked; and all good things as the portion of the righteous.

THIRD POINT.

Of the state of the Church in the world to come.

1. Consider what will be then the misery of the wicked. The wicked who shall have disowned or dishonoured their Baptismal privileges in her, will be excluded for ever from her, and given up for ever to torments, tears, regrets, rage, and despair; such will be their eternal occupation.

2. Examine what will be the happiness of the good. The good, who then alone will form the Church triumphant of Christ, will live in the delights of Divine love, and of a blessed and glorified life which will never have any end; such is their eternal lot.

3. Conclude from these two truths what is the true interest of those who are still living on the earth. Their true interest, is to take to heart these truths, that they may understand their full meaning. *Jesus saith unto them, Have ye understood all these things? They say unto Him, Yea, Lord.* Our Lord puts the same question to us still. Now have we sufficiently understood these truths, in order to see that the point in question here concerns us, what we are in this first condition of the Church, what we shall appear at the second, and where we shall be eternally in the third? Have we sufficiently understood them, that we may feel that we have only an uncertain time and the short space of our life in which to prepare ourselves for this terrible event? Have we understood them so as never to forget them, to draw

from them results in our practice, in order to make them the rule of all our thoughts and of all our actions; so as to be penetrated with them, so as to be able to instruct in them all those who are committed to our charge : so as to bring to bear to this end all our knowledge, all our zeal, all our care? *Then said He unto them, Therefore every scribe which is instructed unto the kingdom of Heaven, is like unto a man that is a householder, which bringeth forth out of his treasure things new and old.* That is to say, learn from My example who it is who is qualified to teach in the Church of Christ, and to become a useful guide to his brethren; he ought to resemble a householder, who draws out of his treasure things old and new. Entrusted with the charge of providing for his house, this man has always made provision beforehand for all needful purposes; there are some which he makes long before he has need of them, there are others about which he is occupied daily; such is the model of a skilful and zealous minister of the Church. He must never be taken by surprise. He must have treasure and a store whence he draws forth the truths necessary for the support of his people. He must possess ancient truths, and fill himself continually with new truths; sometimes making use of that which he has gathered in the Old Testament, sometimes of that which he meditates on and learns daily in the New Testament. This tender father, after having drawn from these divine sources, must offer to his children, with gentleness and without respect of persons, the milk and the wine of wisdom according as they are able to bear them, according to their needs, according to the different dispositions of their hearts. He must employ for their instruction all his powers of mind, all his studies, all that he has read in ancient and modern books, in sacred and profane authors, all his talents, and all his diligence; he must make use of all that is most forcible and most gentle, most sublime and most familiar, most terrible and most winning, in order to inculcate the important truths of salvation.

Prayer. O my God, why can I not answer Thee as the apostles did, *Yea, Lord,* I have understood them, these truths which Thou hast taught me for my salvation! But if I have understood them, why then have I not practised them? O my soul! thou art convinced of these great truths; and how couldest thou doubt them? It is Christ Himself Who explains them to thee in the clearest and the most precise manner; but if thou dost not doubt them, what then must thy insensibility be that thou dost not conform thy conduct to them? O Divine Jesus! enlighten my mind, or rather inflame my heart; engrave there deeply Thy divine words, vouchsafe to communicate to it such love for these holy truths, that I may call them to mind and practise them on all occasions, so that, living as a true Christian, I may not be rejected at the day of judgment. Amen.

Meditation CXIX.

JESUS MAKES A SECOND JOURNEY TO NAZARETH.

Consider here 1. the admiration of the Nazarenes; 2. the offence they took; 3. the gentleness of Jesus in the midst of the Nazarenes. S. Matt. xiii. 53—58. S. Mark vi. 1—6.

FIRST POINT.

Admiration of the Nazarenes.

1. A forced admiration which does not do away with hatred. *And it came to pass that when Jesus had finished these parables, He departed thence. And when He was come into His own country* (Nazareth, where He had been brought up) *His disciples followed Him and He taught in the synagogues, when the sabbath day was come, and many hearing Him were astonished at the gracious words which proceeded out of His mouth, and said, Whence hath this Man this wisdom, and these mighty works? From whence hath this Man*

these things? and what wisdom is this which is given unto Him, that even such mighty works are wrought by His Hands? Jesus, accompanied by His disciples, went from Capernaum to Nazareth, His own country, not in order to seek relaxation from His labours, but in order to continue them. On the days of assembly, He was to be found in the synagogue, and He taught the people with that wisdom, that authority, and that majesty so full of gentleness, which gained Him all hearts wherever He went. The Nazarenes knew the wonders which were published of Him, they had even seen Him work some miracles in their midst, and they could not refuse Him their admiration; but their hearts were alienated from Him, and they could not see without a secret jealousy one of their fellow citizens so distinguished and so raised above them. The ungodly man cannot help being struck with admiration at the doctrine and the precepts of Christ; but he hates them. The condition in which Christianity on the one hand, and Judaism, on the other, are to be found at the present time after the lapse of seventeen centuries, the victories which the Christian religion has gained over idolatry, so as to bring it to nought, are an object of admiration even to the unbeliever, and that in spite of himself; but he hates that very religion which he is forced to admire. As for us, let us admire and love the wisdom of God, and His works, His commandments and His religion, which are alone worthy of our admiration and our love, and out of which there is nothing but folly, weakness, and vanity.

2. A barren admiration which does not change the heart. The Nazarenes admired and were not converted; they admired, and were contented to descant on them. We imitate them but too much; every body delights to talk of a celebrated preacher, of his talents, his learning, his eloquence, but nobody thinks of profiting by the truths which he sets forth. We praise a well-written book, and admire its style and the thoughts it contains; but we do not change, we reform nothing in our conduct, we become no better. Vain admiration,

which only makes us more guilty and inexcusable. Is it with as barren an admiration that we listen to a man, or that we read an author, who would teach us the way to aggrandise or to enrich ourselves?

3. A malicious admiration which degenerates into contempt. These Nazarenes exclaimed with a kind of transport, Whence hath this man this deep knowledge, which accompanies His words, and regulates His actions? All is great in Him, His appearance, His discourses, His actions. Besides which, He has worked many miracles. *Whence hath this man,* from whom has He received this doctrine, this wisdom, this power of working at His will so many and such astonishing wonders? They knew doubtless what the scribes and Pharisees thought of it, they had often heard them say that all this came from the devil; and if they dared not express themselves as openly as they, perhaps they were not far from thinking as they did; at least this air of astonishment which they shewed, these exclamations which they repeated, only arose from a depth of malice, and jealousy, and had no other object but to draw down contempt upon Him, Whose miracles the entire people, and they themselves admired. Is it not by a similar artifice that unbelievers exalt sometimes the greatness or sublimity of our mysteries, only with the design of rendering them contemptible or incredible? Is it not by the same artifice that we sometimes praise in an exaggerated manner those whom we wish to lower in the esteem of others, that we praise with an air of surprise and astonishment, the force, the eloquence, which a minister of the Church shews either in his discourses, or his writings, only in order to take away the merit of them from him, in order to insinuate that the glory of them belongs to another? As for us, let us admire, let us adore the doctrine of Christ, and let us make it the rule of our faith and of our conduct.

SECOND POINT.

The offence of the Nazarenes.

1. The offence of pride. *Is not this*, they said, *the carpenter's son? Is not His mother called Mary? and His brethren James, and Joses, and Simon, and Judas? And His sisters, are they not all with us? Whence then hath this man all these things? And they were offended in Him.* And how could the pride of the world be able to esteem Him, Whose family was of so little distinction in the world? But, O eternal Wisdom! it was in order to confound that pride of the world, that Thou didst choose such a family, and that Thou didst not blush to appear there with Thy disciples. This pride still reigns in me, if I regulate my esteem upon the splendour of birth or the advantages of fortune; if I pride myself on an illustrious birth, or blush at an obscure one; if I ignore my relations, because they are poor, or feel impatient if reminded of them; if I like to recall the origin of others in order to equal them to myself, or to raise myself above them; if I seek to gain honour by the intercourse of the great, and if I fear to dishonour myself by that of those of lower position. Yes, Mary, thou art His mother, and thy humility has drawn down upon thee this honour! Oh happy Joseph, who in the midst of thy laborious and innocent occupations, hast merited, by thy virtues, to become the husband of Mary, and to pass for the father of Jesus! Oh happy Christian family, where work preserves innocency, and which, without distinction in the world, is distinguished before God by its faith and piety!

2. The offence of the Nazarenes, an offence of unteachableness. The doctrine of Jesus was sublime, His wisdom worthy of admiration, His mission authorised; but it needs but little to offend unteachable hearts; the most frivolous pretext suffices to shake off the yoke of obedience, and to resist the most lawful authority. If in that superior who has the rule over us, if in that

preacher who speaks to us, we would only regard the person of Christ, and the authority of God with which he is invested, how many questionings should we not spare ourselves, how many investigations, which are less the effect of a vain curiosity than of wilful unteachableness! Let us obey, let us be teachable, it is to God Himself that we obey.

3. The offence of the Nazarenes, an offence of unbelief. This offence is the more sinful, in that it is the more unreasonable. The Nazarenes admired the doctrines of Christ, they agreed to the greatness of His miracles, and they refused to believe in Him, because they knew His family, and knew His relations living amongst them in moderate circumstances. But was not that the very thing which evidently proved that His wisdom and the virtue of the miracles which they acknowledged in Him could only come to Him from God, and that they must therefore needs believe in Him? What is it which still offends unbelievers? The poverty of Jesus, the humility of His life, the shame of His death, the severity of His precepts, which appear to them impossible to practise; the sublimity of the mysteries which He taught, and which are incomprehensible; the greatness and the number of the miracles which He has wrought, and which appear to them incredible. But if all that has been believed by the whole world; if in spite of all that, the world acknowledges Jesus as its God; if with all that, His religion has triumphed over all the powers of earth, that which is made a subject of offence, is it not precisely that which has established the truth of the faith, and which makes its foundations such that they cannot be shaken? But the unbeliever does not reason, he seizes upon the object which offends him, fixes his attention upon it, he does not relinquish it, he returns unceasingly to it, without being willing to listen to any thing, to weigh any thing, or to confront any opposition; it is thus, O adorable Wisdom, that Thy wonders blind the proud, and fill the humble with light and consolation.

THIRD POINT.

Gentleness of Jesus in the midst of the Nazarenes.

1. In His words. *But Jesus said unto them, A prophet is not without honour, save in his own country, and in his own house.* Jesus made them no answer save by this proverb. The reproach was doubtless very gentle for so guilty an ingratitude, and such outrageous contempt; nevertheless does it not appear as if our Lord sought yet more to soften it, by making it general and avoiding any direct application of it? What an example to us of patience and gentleness! what an important lesson for the labourers of the gospel! If they only seek the glory of God and the salvation of souls, they must be content to go where Providence fixes their lot, and if they experience persecutions and injustice in the exercise of their ministry, they will find comfort in the thought of what the Son of God experienced from the hands of men.

2. In His actions. *And He did not many mighty works there, because of their unbelief. And He could there do no mighty work, save that He laid His hands upon a few sick folk, and healed them.* If the unbelief of the Nazarenes put a stop to the course of the power of Christ, constrained His mercy, tied, so to say, His Hands, and hindered Him from working amongst them many miracles and many acts of healing, it did not prevent Him from healing the small number of those who presented themselves to Him with faith, and in a teachable spirit. If, amongst Christians, there are so many sinners who wallow in their crimes, who live and die in them, without obtaining from the Saviour the healing of their souls, it is their want of faith alone, and their incredulity which hinder the course of His benefits and the operations of His all-powerful grace. But let not the great number of those who are wanting in faith, diminish our faith, but on the contrary let it increase it. Let us be of that small number who know how to profit by the goodness and power of the Saviour.

Let us pity the lot of those wilfully sick souls: and let us on our part address ourselves to the Heavenly Physician of our souls in order to obtain from Him their cure. How many wonders would He not work in our behalf, were it not for this depth of unbelief which we cherish in our heart, and which checks the outpouring of His Spirit, and the abundance of His grace.

3. In His feelings. *And He marvelled because of their unbelief. And He went round about the villages teaching.* What were the feelings of Jesus on quitting unbelieving Nazareth? Were they feelings of indignation, of contempt, of vengeance? No, but of surprise, of compassion and gentleness, to see Himself compelled to leave it in its unbelief, in order to carry the gospel elsewhere.

Prayer. Alas! Lord, am I not an object of astonishment to Thee? Ought I not to be one to myself? shall I not be one to the whole universe at the day of judgement? How, I, with so many helps, so much instruction, so many Sacraments, so many means of grace, should be still so weak, so imperfect, so far removed from holiness! Still so many failings in myself: still so few virtues in me! Ah! it is faith which is wanting to me; it is my want of faith which render all the means of salvation useless and inefficacious to me. Heal me then, O my God! enlighten me, break my bonds, fill me with that faith which obtains from Thee the most miraculous cures. Render me docile by rendering me humble; do not permit me to abuse any longer Thy gifts which would only serve to render me more guilty, but grant that only striving how to make of them a holy use, I may gather fruit from them, that is to say my salvation and Thy glory. Amen.

Meditation CXX.

BEHEADING OF S. JOHN BAPTIST,
ON IMPURITY.

Consider first, the first effects of impurity in Herod, then the last excesses to which this vice leads him, and lastly, the trouble and remorse which this evil passion stirs up in him. S. Matt. xiv. 1—11. S. Mark vi. 14—28. S. Luke ix. 7—9.

FIRST POINT.

The first effects of impurity in Herod.

1. An unbridled lust which nothing could check. *For Herod himself had sent forth, and laid hold upon John, and bound him in prison for Herodias' sake, his brother Philip's wife; for he had married her.* Herod, tetrarch of Galilee, loves the wife of his brother Philip, tetrarch of Iturea, and is loved by her. He gives himself up to this shameful affection, and soon he carries off his wife from his own brother, marries her publicly, and we see him at the same time a seducer, an adulterer, and incestuous, without decency, the voice of nature, or public opinion being unable to put a bridle on the passion of this monster of impurity whose very name is still held in horror amongst us. Ah! let us dread the first and faintest attacks of so dangerous a fire, whose violence surmounts every thing, and finds no obstacle capable of arresting its course!

2. An obstinate hardness of heart which nothing can overcome. *For John had said unto him, It is not lawful for thee to have thy brother's wife. And when he would have put him to death, he feared the multitude, because they counted him as a prophet.* A prophet, a man greater than the other prophets, the greatest and holiest of men. John the Baptist reproves Herod for his impurity; he makes him hear the truth in these distinct terms, 'Prince, it is not lawful for you to have your brother's wife.' The prophet's reproach does not touch him, and his boldness irritates him. Herod forms

the design of putting him to death in order to deliver himself from his importunity; but he feels that an attempt upon the life of this holy man is capable of exciting a popular sedition. There is no evil passion which is more ungovernable than that of impurity: it inveighs, it persecutes, it hates and pursues, even to the death, the charitable and zealous physician who desires to heal it. So it is still with sinners who have abandoned themselves to this passion, if they were not kept back by fear, they would steep their hands in the blood of those who oppose themselves to their crimes. But neither the hatred nor the threats of sinners ought to hinder those, who, by their office, are called upon to reprove them. Neither the rank, the position, nor the character of a person ought to dispense them from so doing; their silence would be an act of cowardice. Herod, in the paroxysm of his passion, would gladly have been freed from so zealous a censor; but when his fit of fury was spent, he could not withhold his esteem from S. John; he respected his holiness of life, he admired the intrepidity of his courage, he even listened gladly to him, and in many things he followed his advice; but when it touched on the essential point, he would hear nothing; passion destroyed his regard for him, or suspended its action, impurity stifled the voice of his conscience, and the tetrarch continued on in the sins in which he hoped to find his happiness. Such is the hardness of heart which this shameful vice produces, and which those experience but too vividly, who have the misfortune to abandon themselves to it.

3. A complete blindness which nothing can disperse. *Therefore Herodias had a quarrel against him, and would have killed him, but she could not; for Herod feared John, knowing that he was a just man and holy, and observed him; and when he heard him he did many things, and heard him gladly.* If the anger of Herod against S. John Baptist was short lived, that of Herodias was not so. The more natural gentleness is to a person of her sex who has preserved purity and in-

nocence, so much the more furious is the fury and the cruel revenge of one who has transgressed the bounds of modesty. The servants of God have not a more dangerous enemy, than a bad woman who is powerful and who has taken offence. Herodias, not having been able to obtain the king's consent to the death of John Baptist, this unprincipled woman resolved to execute, so to say by herself, independently of the royal authority and even against his will, the plan of revenge which she projected. She had a quarrel against him, of which Herod was not ignorant; and this timid although enterprising prince, who was at the same time vicious and yet equitable, instead of driving far from him this woman, who was the cause of such opprobrium to him, contented himself with frustrating her measures, arresting the effects of her violence, and watching over the safety of the prophet. But in what did these shameful compromises end? In adding lastly sacrilege to all his other crimes, in depriving the man of God of his liberty, in causing him to be arrested, laden with fetters, and shut up in a narrow prison; perhaps he flattered himself that he only acted thus in the prisoner's behalf, in order to save him from the fury of Herodias. It is thus that passion blinds a man, and that without perceiving it, he hastens by rapid steps towards the precipice from which he imagined that he was moving away. Preserve me, O Lord, from so deplorable a blindness, and from the infamous passion which gives rise to it.

SECOND POINT.

The last excesses of impurity in Herod.

The last excess to which Herod lends himself is the murder of S. John Baptist, accompanied by circumstances which we cannot recall even now without horror.

1. What was the occasion on which it took place? *And when a convenient day, for the design of Herodias, was come, that Herod on his birthday made a supper to his lords, high captains, and chief estates of Galilee,*

and when the daughter of the said Herodias came in and danced and pleased Herod and them that sat with him, the king said unto the damsel, Ask of me whatsoever thou wilt, and I will give it thee. And he sware unto her, Whatsoever thou shalt ask of me, I will give it thee, unto the half of my kingdom. Who would have thought that this feast day would have been *a convenient day* for fury and revenge, an opportunity which would lead Herod into the greatest of all crimes, would engage him to shed the innocent blood which he had respected till then? But who can answer for himself, and of what may he not become guilty, when to the abundance of good cheer, to the magnificence of the scene, are joined the snares of a shameless woman, who is without decency, and who knows how to enhance her attractions by attire which is as immodest as it is brilliant, and to make use also, in order to seduce, of all that music has that is most enchanting, and dancing that is most voluptuous. The daughter of Herodias entered into the banqueting hall, and danced there with so much grace, that she received the applause of all the guests, Herod especially was charmed with it; in his judgement, the merit of such a dance surpassed every thing else, and he could not recompense too highly her who had executed it. In the first burst of this mad delight, he leaves to her the choice of her reward, and promises her with an oath that she shall obtain all that she shall ask for, even if it were the half of his kingdom. Herod, where is your reason? Do you remember who is the person to whom you make this promise, and to what you are pledging yourself? But in the intoxication of pleasure and of passion, every thing is forgotten, and reason no longer makes itself heard. Christian mothers, take a lesson from this, and beware into what society you permit your children to enter.

2. What was the way in which it was carried out? Observe first how the demand was suggested by the mother and proposed by the girl. *And she went forth and said unto her mother, What shall I ask? And she said, The head of John the Baptist. And she came in*

straightway with haste unto the king, and asked, saying, I will that thou give me by and by in a charger the head of John the Baptist. The daughter of Herodias, assured by the oath of the king that she should obtain whatever she should ask, only takes a few moments to deliberate on the choice. From the banqueting hall, she goes into the apartment of her mother to consult her, and to know what she should ask; the latter answers in a few words, and without hesitation, *The head of John the Baptist.* Herodias, dost thou dare to make such a proposition to thy daughter? Will thy daughter have the hardihood to repeat it? Will Herod have the patience to listen to it, and can it be executed on a day set apart for public rejoicings? What! you prefer the death of a just and innocent man to the half of a kingdom. Is that the care you take of the interests of your daughter? What have you then to fear from that man? He is in chains. But the king respects him, and must you not fear to displease him? Whilst Herod is loading you with benefits, you are turning them against himself. Do you not fear that his love for you will be changed into hatred? And you, O daughter of the most cruel of women! do you not shudder at so bloody a request? will you dare to make such a fearful demand of the king? do you not fear to bring dishonour upon yourself in the eyes of so numerous a court? Will you let so favourable an opportunity pass by, of gaining some advantage to yourself? And what good will accrue to you from the unjust death of an oppressed and innocent man? Will you make no representation to your mother? No, the daughter, already too much resembling her mother, abandoned to the same excesses, and agitated by the same passions, returns suddenly into the assembly, presents herself there with effrontery, and says to the king with audacity, *I will that thou give me by and by in a charger the head of John the Baptist.* What expressions! what horror! what a family! what monsters! But let us follow this tissue of iniquities, and see how this proposal is received by Herod. *And the king was exceeding sorry; yet for his oath's sake, and for their sakes which sat with him, he would not reject her.* Herod ought to have been filled with anger and indignation; he was only sorry. Was this the feeling which a demand so unjust, so indecent, so barbarous, and so little suited to the circumstances of the day and the place ought to have excited in the heart of Herod? He may have indeed wished to save John Baptist from motives of policy, and a remains of equity: but his cowardice took from him the strength to refuse it, added to which the shame of recalling his words after a public oath, and the fear lest his refusal should be looked on as timidity, mingled with his affection for his brother's wife, and triumphed in his want of moral courage. What idea could he form then of religion, if he could believe that an oath could oblige him to a crime? What a scruple to fear to violate an unjust and indiscreet oath, and yet not to fear to cause to be put to death an innocent man, a holy man, and a prophet! He feared what those present might say. But would they not have been eager to praise his wisdom and his equity, if they had seen him firm in his refusal? Would they not have felt that an oath cannot oblige a person to do any thing which is in itself unjust, to that which reason, nature, and God's law forbid; that his promise was general, that his oath only extended to that which could be done in accordance with the laws of justice and conscience? But no, the real cause of this mad superstition of Herod, of his ridiculous fear, of so much weakness, and so much cowardice, is the impure love which reigns in his heart. Carried away by passion, he fears to offend her who is its object. Thus this shameful vice, which degrades every heart that abandons itself to it, renders this prince imprudent and blind, contemptible and cowardly, unjust and timid, inhuman and barbarous; thus did it lead him on to excesses of which he believed himself incapable, and which but a short time before would have been abhorrent to him.

3. How was it executed? *And immediately the king*

sent an executioner, and commanded his head to be brought; and he went and beheaded him in prison, and brought his head in a charger, and gave it to the damsel, and the damsel gave it to her mother. Here then is shamelessness triumphant in the person of Herodias, if one may call a triumph of shamelessness that which can only produce the greatest horror of it. All the wishes of this shameless woman are punctually executed. The bloody head of the prophet is placed on a charger, and given into the hand of her daughter, who carries this barbarous present to her mother, who feasts her eyes on it fearlessly and with content. What an object of pleasure to a woman! How many horrors in so few moments! Thus dies the forerunner of the Messiah, a victim of impurity; thus dies the man of God, the messenger of heaven sent to prepare the ways of the Lord, and to restore piety and religion in Israel. Oh depths! oh abyss! oh impenetrable dealings of Providence! let our mouth be silent, let our reason submit, let our heart adore! Every law is violated in this death. The preacher of repentance is sacrificed to impurity. A prince, intoxicated with pleasures, and given up to the most shameful passion, causes the declared enemy of pleasures and of vice to die in the most unworthy manner; he causes him to die in prison, which was contrary to the law of Moses, which prescribed that the guilty should be executed in the presence of the people: he causes him to be put to death, without having judged him, without having even brought any accusation against him, or let him undergo any trial. This command of the king is barbarous in all its details: every thing that passion leads a man to do is barbarous likewise. The very day on which Herod has received the gift of life, he takes it away from John the Baptist; he celebrates the anniversary of his birth by the death of the most innocent of men. O day for ever memorable! which the universe will celebrate until the end of time, but in execration of the cruel Herod and his accomplices, and in honour of the glorious and saintly forerunner.

THIRD POINT.

Trouble and remorse of impurity in Herod.

1. His fear that John had risen from the dead. *At that time, Herod, the tetrarch, heard of the fame of Jesus, and he said unto his servants, This is John the Baptist; he is risen from the dead, and therefore mighty works do shew forth themselves in him, others said, That it is Elias, And others said, That it is a prophet, or as one of the prophets.* But when Herod heard thereof, he said, It is John whom I beheaded: he is risen from the dead. Herod had desired to stifle a voice which reproached him with his incest, and now a thousand voices rise up in the depth of his heart, and reproach him with his murder. S. John is present day and night to his eyes, and he seems to see him every where. The rumour of the miracles which Jesus wrought having reached him, he cries out, seized with terror, 'It is John Baptist whom I have caused to be put to death: it is himself,' he says to his servants, 'who is risen from the dead, and this is why he works all these miracles. It is a second life which God has given him, with a power which he had not in the first.' Thus the saints, even after their death, make their persecutors to tremble. God avenges the innocence of His servants who are unjustly oppressed; He justifies them even by the lips of their persecutors. 'If God recompenses thus the virtue of John Baptist,' continues Herod within himself, 'what punishment does He not reserve to my crimes?' His servants sought to reassure him. Some said it was Elias, others that it is a prophet who was working these wonders, as some of the old prophets had done, and that there was nothing in this to be alarmed or surprised at, but nothing calms the fears of Herod. *But when Herod heard thereof, he said, It is John, whom I beheaded: he is risen from the dead.* A guilty heart cannot be quiet and free from remorse; it takes always the side of divine justice against itself. It may de-

ceive itself in the object of its fears; but it cannot reassure itself. In vain does the unbeliever arm himself with unbelief, in vain does the shameless woman arm herself with shamelessness, the miracles of Jesus will always create torments in their hearts. It is not only the reputation of Jesus, it is His religion, His worship, His Divinity which is acknowledged by the universe, the weight of which overwhelms him, and troubles the tranquillity which he affects. In the court of Herod, no one thinks of the Messiah: the idea of Him would have been yet more appalling than that of John risen from the dead. Ah! let us not imitate these men so wilfully hardened in their blindness; let us recognize our Saviour by the works of His power. If we are living in sin, let us yield to our remorse, let us have recourse to His mercy; if His grace has preserved us from it or delivered us, let us thank Him, and pray Him to continue to support us in the paths of innocence or repentance.

2. His perplexity to know, which was Jesus. S. Luke relates the preceding incident to us in a different manner. He tells us that it was only as doubting the fact, that Herod tells his servants that John the Baptist was risen from the dead; but this version of S. Luke is not the less instructive to us for that reason. *Now Herod the tetrarch heard of all that was done by him, and he was perplexed, because it was said of some that John was risen from the dead; and of some, that Elias had appeared; and of others that one of the old prophets was risen again. And Herod said, John have I beheaded; but who is this, of whom I hear such things?* Herod was by turns the sport of his own thoughts, and of the different opinions of his courtiers. Some thought as he did, that it was John Baptist who had risen from the dead; others said that Elias was expected, and that it was apparently he who was beginning to appear: others lastly thought generally that it might be one of the old prophets. Herod, surmounting sometimes the fear that he had of John Baptist, came back to the impious

system of the Sadducees, that the dead could not rise, that the soul is material, and that all dies with the body. 'I have caused John Baptist to be beheaded,' he said to himself, 'I have seen his head separated from his body, he is dead, it cannot then be he.' But after having thus assured himself that it could not be the resurrection of John, he was not any the more calm; the miracles took place, they existed, they were published abroad; 'Who then is he,' added this prince, 'of whom I hear such wonderful things?' This was what he desired to know, this was what caused his perplexity of mind; and that which will form the perplexity of all ungodly men unto the end of time, and will torment them unto death. Yes, ungodly men, deny what you will, stifle the inward motions of your conscience, and renounce the purest light of reason, the question will yet always remain, Who is He Who has founded the Christian religion, Who has banished idolatry from the earth, Who has brought to mankind so pure a morality, and Who has taught them truths so sublime? Ah! Lord, Who art Thou? Thou art my God and my Saviour, in Whom alone holiness and peace, truth and life are to be found; out of Thee there is nought but crime and corruption, trouble and despair.

3. His desire to see Jesus. *And he desired to see Him.* What was this desire in Herod? It was not the desire to know the truth, to learn his duties, to correct his faults; but to satisfy his curiosity, to quiet his troubled conscience, and to reassure himself in his crimes. The time is coming when he will see Jesus, not such as he desired, astonishing mankind by the prodigies of His power, but such as he deserved, blinding the proud Jews by the hidden mystery of His humiliations. He saw Him, and by a judgement deserved by him, and a punishment worthy of God, in the Incarnate Wisdom he perceived nought but folly. Alas! what is still this desire amongst ungodly men! They tell us, they would see Jesus and His miracles. Hypocritical desire and full of impiety! If they would, they might see Him with us in His Gospel, in His promises, in His threats, in

His holy religion, in His Church, in the Sacrament of His Body and Blood, in faith, in prayer, in meditation, in purity of heart. It is there that the believer, that the pure heart seeks to see Jesus and that it sees Him in truth; such as Jesus wills that we should see Him. There we see Him with a vision proportioned to our condition, but full of light, peace and consolation; we see Him in a manner which honours Him, draws down His graces upon us, and gains a reward from Him. A day will come when we shall see Him, no longer working miracles in order to confirm His Gospel, but exercising His justice in order to reward those who shall have been faithful to it, and to punish those who shall not have believed in it.

Prayer. Do not thus avenge Thyself, Lord, for my resistance to Thy grace, and my want of faith: rather triumph over them by Thy grace. Make me taste the truths which the carnal man cannot taste, that I may never be offended at the sufferings of Thy servants, nor intimidated if I am called upon to suffer for Thy Name. And grant that I may be on my guard against those passions which caused the death of Thy forerunner S. John Baptist, the greatest and holiest of men, the friend of the Bridegroom, the martyr of purity; grant that I may bear in mind in temptation those needful words which his lips uttered in vain to Herod; *It is not lawful for thee,* so that I may be enabled to triumph over the enemy of my salvation, and to have my portion in that glory in Heaven into which He has entered. Amen.

Meditation CXXI.

THE FIRST MULTIPLYING OF THE FIVE LOAVES.

This multiplying of the five loaves may be regarded as a figure of the Paschal Communion. We may consider in it, 1. the fervour with which we ought to prepare for it; 2. the faith with which we ought to receive the Communion; 3. the fruit we ought to draw from it. S. Matt. xiv. 12—21. S. Mark vi. 29—44. S. Luke ix. 10—17. S. John vi. 1—13.

FIRST POINT.

Of the fervour with which we ought to prepare ourselves for the Communion.

The disciples of S. John, having buried the dead body of their master, came to find Jesus at Capernaum, whither He had returned, and made known to Him that which He already knew by Himself. This divine Saviour listened with goodness and sorrow to the tragical circumstances of the death of His forerunner, and comforted the afflicted disciples. The apostles, on their part, came to render Him an account of their labours, and of the success of a mission which they had just concluded. He instructed and encouraged them. He willed to procure for them some moments of relaxation; but this short interval was for Him only a continuation of labours. Capernaum was not a place where repose could be found. The house in which Jesus dwelt was always so filled, that neither He nor His disciples had even time to take any food. *Come ye yourselves,* this divine Master said to them, *apart into a desert place, and rest awhile;* They took ship therefore, and the desert place which Jesus chose was that of Bethsaida, on the other side of the sea of Galilee, or of Tiberias, also called the lake of Gennesaret. Bethsaida was situated to the east of the lake, towards the north, and the desert was at some distance from the city. Jesus, in this journey, had another yet deeper design which He did not discover to His apostles. *And the passover, a feast of the Jews was nigh,* and we may believe that He willed, on this occasion, to give to them an image of the Christian Passover, in which the Lamb of God would be offered up under the forms of bread and wine. Let us profit by that which is about to take place here for our instruction, and let us observe first of all the fervour of the people.

1. This fervour consists in desiring and seeking Jesus. The people perceived that Jesus had embarked, and saw the direction He was taking; the rumour thereof spread throughout the neighbouring cities, and immediately an immense crowd of people, men, women, and children, all resolved to join Him by crossing the Jordan at the point of the lake. Some did so with such promptitude, that they reached the place before Him. Jesus saw with joy this multitude who had thus prevented Him; He came out of the ship, and whilst waiting till the rest of the people who were hastening up should be assembled, *Jesus went up into a mountain, and there He sat with His disciples,* and that was all the rest they took. Jesus had not long been there before He *went forth and saw a great multitude* waiting for Him with impatience. Have we the same fervour as this people in seeking Jesus, and in preparing ourselves to receive Him as our Food ? What negligence, what faint-heartedness! How many receive Him without any desire, without preparation, without any love ! How many dispense themselves from receiving Him on the least pretext ! Ah ! fervour surmounts all obstacles, it finds nothing wearisome, nothing impossible.

2. This fervour consists in having an entire confidence in Jesus. When all this multitude had arrived in the plain, there were assembled there about *five thousand men beside women and children.* It was the confidence which they had in the power and goodness of Jesus which attracted them, and the many miracles which they beheld Him work for the relief of the sick ! And in Whom could they better place their trust? Trust in

this divine Saviour is a sure means of obtaining graces from Him. *When Jesus then lifted up His eyes, and saw a great multitude, He was moved with compassion toward them, because they were as sheep not having a shepherd.* The idea that these people had formed of Jesus was very far removed from that which they ought to have had, and the motive which attracted them was far from being as perfect as it should have been: but how much does not Jesus graciously forgive to those who seek Him with care and confidence?

3. This fervour consists in listening to the instructions of Jesus. This tender Shepherd having come down to the people, *began to teach them many things;* He spoke successively to the different groups who assembled around Him; and He *spake unto them of* many things which concerned *the kingdom of God,* that is, of repentance, faith in the Messiah, and the establishment of His Church. With what attention, with what eagerness did they not listen to Christ: Alas! in the holy season of Lent which precedes the Christian passover, the Church multiplies its services and its instructions: how do we profit by them? We ought to devote as much time as possible to meditation, to reading the Bible, to prayer, and to give more care to our devotions during that holy season; and each time that we prepare to receive the Holy Eucharist, how do we acquit ourselves of this preparation?

4. This fervour consists in asking for our healing, and in receiving it from the hands of Jesus. To the instruction which He gave, followed according to His custom the healing of the sick, *and He healed them that had need of healing.* Such ought to be the fruit of religious teaching; each one ought, before eating the Heavenly bread, to prove himself, to examine the state of his soul, to present himself to Jesus, to lay before Him his infirmities so as to obtain from Him their cure.

SECOND POINT.

Of the faith with which we ought to receive the Communion.

1. In difficulties. If there is no mystery which demands more faith than that of the Divine Eucharist, never also did our Lord put the faith of His apostles more to the proof than when He was about to give them a sensible image of that adorable Sacrament. Jesus had been occupied from the morning when He had arrived in the desert, in instructing the people and healing the sick. These exercises of charity and zeal occupied Him until it was nearly night; the sun was already going down, before the Saviour spoke of sending away all the multitude, and before the people, transported with delight at hearing Him and seeing Him, appeared to bethink themselves of withdrawing thence. Not only were they fasting, but they were at too great a distance from any place to be able to get food. *When the day began to wear away, then came the twelve, and said unto Him, This is a desert place, and the time is now past; send the multitude away, that they may go into the villages, and buy themselves victuals.* The more reasonable the representations of the apostles appeared to them, the more must the answer of Jesus have surprised them. *But Jesus said unto them, They need not depart; give ye them to eat.* Never had the apostles heard anything from the lips of their Master, which was so directly opposed to the light of their own reason. *And they say unto Him, Shall we go and buy two hundred pennyworth of bread, and give them to eat?* Our Lord saw their perplexity, but He did not will yet to relieve them from it. It was, even in order to keep them still in this perplexity, that lifting up His eyes on this great multitude, *He saith unto Philip*, who was of Bethsaida, as also were Andrew and Peter, *Whence shall we buy bread, that these may eat? And this He said to prove him; for He himself knew what He would do. Philip answered Him, Two hundred pennyworth of bread is*

not sufficient for them, that every one of them may take a little. From this perplexity our Lord permitted them to fall into one still greater, but which brought them nearer to the end to which He desired to lead them. Apparently taking no notice of the project of buying food, which the apostles had proposed as the only means of providing for the sustenance of the multitude, *Jesus saith unto them, How many loaves have ye? go out and see.* These words must have appeared to them yet more incomprehensible than the former; they obeyed without making any reply, and if their search did not help them out of their difficulty, at least it served to warn the people of the design which Jesus had of feeding them, and to prepare them to acknowledge the greatness of the miracle which was soon about to be worked. The apostles returned to Jesus, and said to Him, *We have here but five loaves, and two fishes; and Andrew, Simon Peter's brother,* explains how they had been found, and saith, *There is a lad here, which hath five loaves, and two small fishes*; but he adds at once to Jesus, what use can you make of them? How can you distribute so small a quantity amongst so many people? *What are they among so many?* Thus, the more they reflected on it, the more impossible did the matter appear; in the same way, with regard to the great mystery of our altars, we ought not to reflect, but to believe in the power of Jesus, to Whom nothing is impossible.

2. The consolations of faith. Then Jesus said, *Bring them,* the five loaves and two fishes, *hither to Me. And He said to His disciples, Make them sit down by fifties in a company.* This order being executed, Jesus lifted up His eyes to Heaven, gave thanks to God His Father, for the power which He had granted Him, and blessed the loaves and fishes; then He broke the bread, and divided the fishes, and gave them to His disciples, so that they might distribute them to the multitude. It is thus that our Lord confirmed the faith of His disciples and His Church, that He gave them the knowledge of His Almighty power and prepared them for the great mystery

which He was about to institute to be the food of Christians. We who now behold the Church spread throughout the universe, with its appointed pastors and ministers from whom it receives the Heavenly Bread, can we not but see here with wonder and admiration the foreshadowing and prophecy of this great event, and not feel a sweet consolation thereby which makes us love and value our holy religion?

3. *The assurances of faith.* The apostles distributed the gifts of God, and in their hands, without their being aware how it was brought about, this miraculous food was multiplied by the blessing of the Lord, so that they were enabled to give five thousand men without including women and children, as much bread and fish as each desired, and at the end there was enough left to fill *twelve baskets full* of the fragments which were picked up. If this figure of the Eucharist was so striking a miracle, shall we persuade ourselves that the Eucharist itself contains none? And when our Lord tells us that it is His Body and His Blood that He gives us, shall we, for want of faith, or in order to satisfy our imagination at the expense of our faith, elude the meaning of these words, and believe that He gives us only the figure of His Body and His Blood. Nay, Lord, taught by Thee, by Thy apostles and Thy Church, my faith is stronger; it is beyond my senses, and my reason, and imposes silence on them. I believe things as Thou hast told them to me, as Thy Church teaches them, however incomprehensible they may appear to me, and I am ready to seal with my blood these precious truths.

THIRD POINT.

Of the spiritual food, and of the fruits which we ought to draw from the Communion.

1. *And they did all eat,* because they felt their needs, and knew the excellence of the bread which was offered to them. Placed in the desert of this life, what kinds of needs do we not experience? Estrangement from

God, dryness in devotion, inconsistency in the practice of good, frequent falls on the least occasions. The Bread which is offered to us is far above that which this people partook of. And of how many mysteries is It not the summing up? Of how many graces is It not the source? With what earnestness, with what ardour, and longing ought we not to desire It, to ask for It, to receive It? Shall we see others feed on It, and not desire ourselves to have some share in it?

2. *With what feelings they ate.* If ever a pure and modest joy prevailed in a repast, if ever guests were penetrated with gratitude and love towards a Host so liberal and beneficent, it was doubtless on this occasion that all these feelings burst forth; and how much more ought our's to break forth in the Eucharistic banquet! What a subject of wonder and joy, that on earth we posess our God, Who is in Heaven: that in the midst of the desert we receive our Saviour, Who is seated at the right Hand of God; that His Flesh and Blood become the Sanctuary of His Divinity! Ah! who am I, O my God! that Thou shouldest work so many miracles for me? Thou didst employ all Thy power, Thou didst heap miracle upon miracle, Thou didst overthrow all the laws of nature in order to overstep the space there is between Thyself and me, in order to come and give Thyself wholly to me. What gratitude can equal Thy benefits, and by what love can I respond to such love?

3. *And were filled.* All went away from that repast filled, contented, and strengthened. If such are the effects which this miraculous bread produced, how much more virtue has not the Eucharistic Bread! We are not *filled,* we are not nourished in eating the Divine Eucharist, when we eat It with distaste, with constraint, and in doing violence to ourselves, when we eat It without gaining strength to do right and avoid evil; when we remain always in the same state of spiritual weakness, in the same state of imperfections, in the same bad habits; when we eat It, and yet sigh after the poisoned food which the world, the flesh, the devil, and sin offer to us; when

we eat It without feeling an ardent desire to feed on It continually in order to renew our happiness, and to sustain our strength. In the life of the soul as in that of the body, there is no state so sad or so dangerous, as that of a person who does not eat, who only eats with distaste, to whom food is repugnant, to whom it does not profit.

Prayer. Alas! am I not, O my God, in that fatal condition, and what is yet more to be dreaded, am I not so without being aware of it, without feeling any anxiety about it? Lord, vouchsafe first to instruct and enlighten me, then to heal me, and lastly, to feed me and to satisfy me with Thyself, so that I may feel a distaste for all that is of this world. Amen.

Meditation CXXII.

JESUS AVOIDS BEING MADE KING.

Consider 1. the error of the people with regard to the kingship of Christ; 2. the danger which the apostles ran, and to which we are ourselves exposed, of falling into this error of the people; 3. the means of preserving ourselves from this danger. S. Matt. xiv. 22, 23. S. Mark vi. 45, 46. S. John xiv. 14, 15.

FIRST POINT.

Error of the people with regard to the kingship of Jesus Christ.

Then these men when they had seen the miracle that Jesus did, said, This is of a truth that prophet that should come into the world. When Jesus perceived therefore that they would come and take Him by force, to make Him a king, He departed again into a mountain Himself alone. These men, who were fed in the desert in so miraculous a manner, and beheld all the miracles which Jesus wrought, said among themselves, This is indeed the prophet who was to come, the Christ, the Messiah we looked for. So far their reasoning was just; but the Messiah was to be king of Israel, and it was on that point that they were mistaken. It was a temporal kingdom, an earthly kingdom, that they thought belonged to the Messiah. Full of this idea, they resolved to raise Jesus on the throne, to proclaim Him king, and they would have executed their plans without delay, if Jesus had not disconcerted their measures by withdrawing Himself from them. How weak and limited the ideas of men are! They are confined only to things of this earth. It is an earthly king that the blinded Jews promise themselves and that they expect. Every one would hasten to acknowledge and follow such a king. But Thy throne, O my God, is at the Right Hand of Thy Father. Thy Kingdom is in heaven, and Thy reign shall have no end. Such is the kingdom which I desire, and to which my heart aspires. None other can satisfy me. Thou wilt only wear on the earth, O divine Jesu, a crown of thorns, Thou wilt have no other sceptre than a reed, no other throne than the Cross; it is by this way of humiliations and sufferings that Thou wilt enter into Thy glory. I will follow Thee, O my glorious Redeemer! a thousand times too happy if I suffer some moments on earth that I may reign eternally with Thee in heaven.

SECOND POINT.

Danger to the apostles and ourselves of falling into the error of the people.

The apostles may indeed have heard the discussion of the people; but they did not know, as Jesus did, what was their intention. If they had known it, they were not sufficiently spiritual-minded to perceive the error, and had not a sufficient spirit of self-abnegation not to be tempted by the hope of present fortune and distinguished rank around the new king. They would have infallibly joined the people, and added to the tumult. It was in order to avoid this, that when they had gathered up the remains of the repast *Jesus constrained His dis-*

ciples to get into a ship, and to go before Him unto the other side, while He sent the people away. It was not without regret that the disciples obeyed; they were loth to separate from their Master, and it was already very late. Nevertheless the command was absolute, and they yielded to it without delay and without reply. Jesus commanded them to precede Him only to the other side of the district, which was at the foot of the lake, between the desert and Bethsaida, where He would join them. The danger which Jesus feared for His apostles is still to be feared for us. Although we are disciples of Jesus Christ, although we have been taught that we shall reign with Him in Heaven, we are always tempted to establish His kingdom on earth; we feel that we are made to be happy, and our heart which is eager for every kind of happiness, is only ambitious of riches, pleasures, repose, exaltation, preferment and the esteem of others. Faith tells us that we shall have perfect happiness in heaven, and all that heart can desire; but our impatience precipitates us, the good things of this world dazzle us, the example of worldly people leads us astray, and thus each one of us seeks in his own manner, to find his happiness, and so to say, his kingdom on earth, often at the risk of losing that of heaven. Have I not fallen myself into this error? Ah, Lord, deliver me from so fatal a delusion, tear me away from the seductive sweetness of earth, cast me into the midst of the waves, expose me on a sea of tribulation; let my life be agitated by violent storms and continual tempests which shall fill me with distaste of this world, and make me sigh after heaven, and put my whole happiness and all my hope in Thee!

THIRD POINT.

Means whereby to escape from this danger.

We find this means in the example of Jesus Christ. *And when He had sent the multitudes away, He went up into a mountain apart to pray; and when the evening was come, He was there alone.* When He had sent away His apostles, He gave command to the five thousand Galileans to withdraw, who having observed His proceedings, and having perceived that His apostles had gone away, withdrew, and put off the execution of their plan to the morrow. But Jesus left them, and went away into the mountain, where He passed the night in prayer. Let us admire this conduct of our Divine Master, and let us take Him for our model. Let us put away from us all that might flatter us, lead us astray, or engage our hearts; let us withdraw from the tumult of the world, and of our own evil passions; let us keep ourselves in retirement, where, alone with God, we may implore His succour, and meditate at our leisure on the vanity of the things of this world, may be penetrated with eternal truths, and turn all our thoughts and all our hopes towards that heavenly country.

Prayer. Inspire me, O Lord, Thyself, with this love of retirement and prayer. Detach me from the world, and from all that captivates my heart in it. Draw me, so that, despising all that is not of Thee, I may seek after and labour only to gain the abode of Thy glory and of eternal repose. Amen.

Meditation CXXIII.

JESUS WALKS ON THE WATER.

1. Jesus permits His disciples to be in trouble, and thereby He sets forth to us the contradictions which we must expect in His service; 2. Jesus walking on the water, comes to find His disciples, and thereby teaches us of the progress which we should make in His knowledge; 3. Jesus heals the sick in the land of Gennesaret, and thereby sets before us an example of the faith which we ought to have in Him. S. Matt. xiv. 24—36. S. Mark vi. 46—56. S. John vi. 16—21.

FIRST POINT.

Jesus permits His disciples to be in trouble, and thereby He sets forth to us the contradictions which we must expect in His service.

1. *The necessity of contradictions.* Who would ever have imagined, on seeing the disciples embark at the express command of Jesus, that they were about to meet with a stormy and angry sea, impetuous and contrary winds? But nevertheless this is what befell them. When Jesus had commanded them to go before Him unto the other side of the lake, as far as Bethsaida, they had uuderstood that after having sent away the multitude, He was about to take that short journey by land, and that they would take Him up on the coast of Bethsaida, and that then they should cross the lake with Him in order to go to Capernaum ; but it was not to be thus. The disciples, having embarked, wished to coast along the shore ; but the contrary wind prevented them, and threw them out into the open sea. To the absence of Jesus and the horror of the night was joined a violent tempest, the sea became furious. They might have found their safety in the port of Bethsaida ; but it was in vain they rowed and struggled against the waters, they could not gain the shore; and after an obstinate endeavour throughout the night to reach the land, they found themselves at break of day only a league from the place they 'had started from. Jesus saw their perplexity, and read their hearts ; He did not delay to come to them and deliver them from their trouble. Thus, Oh faithful but tempted souls, you think yourselves, in the moment of storms or of trials, either ready to perish or already lost ; but take courage, the calm will return ; Jesus is present, although hidden : He is about to reappear, and never will you have made a more rapid, surer, or more prosperous course.

2. *Designs of God in contradictions.* Who would have thought, in beholding the labours of the apostles during the whole night, their danger and the uselessness of their efforts, that that was the means which God had chosen for the execution of His will, to make His power and glory shine forth, to strengthen the faith of His disciples, to increase their zeal, and to load them with consolation ? Oh my God ! how great Thou art, how

blind we are, and how far above our thoughts are Thy thoughts! It is thus, that, on the stormy sea of the world, Thy Church is exposed to persecutions, that the righteous find themselves surrounded with perils, that the minister of Christ is a prey to contradictions. It is thus that our own heart, envelopped in darkness, agitated by external temptations, and by its own evil passions, sets itself unceasingly against the desires which we have to serve Thee, and to belong wholly to Thee; but Thou willest to have it thus, that Thy glory may be promoted, and Thy servants may reap the advantage from them: may Thy holy Name be blessed!

3. The duty of a person under contradictions. He must redouble his efforts, labour without relaxation, and without discouragement, however great, however long may be the trials to which he may be put. He ought to remember that Jesus sees his sorrows and difficulties and will put an end to them at the time and in the way that He sees fitting. He ought to perceive, that he is only fulfilling his duty by his labours, although he may not be able to procure the success which he desires. He ought to be assured that if he is faithful in that which God requires of him, Jesus will calm all his troubles, and crown his labours and his patience. Is it with such courage, O my soul, is it with these feelings that thou dost support thyself in the midst of the waves by which thou art agitated, that thou dost struggle against the winds which oppose thy course towards heaven, thy salvation, and thy sanctification?

SECOND POINT.

Jesus, walking on the water, comes to find His disciples, and thereby instructs us in the progress which we ought to make in His knowledge.

1. The first degree of the knowledge of Jesus, is that of conversion; a knowledge which is at first feeble, and often filled with fear. *And about the fourth watch of the night He cometh unto them,* as He had said unto

them, but not at the hour they had expected Him, and much less in the way in which they had expected Him. He came to them on the sea, as He would have come on dry land, *walking on the sea.* Master of the whole of nature, the liquid and agitated element became firm and motionless beneath His feet. The apostles, by the dim light of day which was just beginning to disperse the shades of night, perceived something which appeared on the water, walking. They all gathered together to see what it was; but they had no conception that it was their Master, Whom they had so long expected, and Whom they so ardently desired to possess. *They supposed that it had been a spirit,* a spectre, and *they were troubled.* It appears at first that the imaginary spirit made as though it *would have passed by them;* but when they saw Him walking on the sea, and drawing near to them, *they cried out for fear,* their fear was redoubled. But Jesus had pity on their weakness, and *spake unto them saying, Be of good cheer: it is I: be not afraid.* We may apply this to the fears which a soul experiences which seeks to be converted and to turn to God, and which begins to come forth from the darkness of unbelief, of sin, of worldliness, of a lukewarm and dissipated life. By the feeble light which dawns upon its eyes, it distinguishes objects but ill, it takes alarm at every thing, and imagines that all it sees are but spirits and delusions. Take courage, timid soul: it is Jesus Who is coming to you.

2. The second degree is that of beginners: this is the degree of fervour. S. Peter, always full of ardour, hearing the voice of His Master, makes proof of his tender love for Him. *Lord, if it be Thou, Peter answered Him and said, bid me come unto Thee on the water. Jesus saith unto him, Come.* Peter, then animated by a lively faith *came down out of the ship,* and *walked on the water to go to Jesus.* Blessed fervour, by which a soul offers itself generously and without reserve to do all that God wills for it, by which, from the moment that the Lord speaks, it no longer looks upon any thing as impossible,

and is ready to undertake every thing that comes before it. Peter advances towards Jesus; *but when he saw the wind boisterous, he was afraid: and beginning to sink, he cried, Lord, save me. And immediately Jesus stretched forth His Hand, and caught him, and said unto him, O thou of little faith, wherefore didst thou doubt?* It was neither the violence of the wind nor the nature of the water, which made S. Peter sink; the sea only began to give way under his feet when his trust became weakened, and that forgetting he was near Jesus, he was afraid. It is not long before our fervour is put to the trial: but if we let ourselves forget that all we have comes from God, if we cease to rest upon His all-powerful Arm which supports us, we shall be discouraged at the least temptation, we shall yield under the weight of our own corruption, and we shall perish infallibly, if by our cries we do not promptly draw down the help of Him Who alone can save us.

3. The third degree is that of perfection; it is the degree of enjoyment and rest; Jesus might have continued the journey with S. Peter, walking on the sea; but He returned with him to the ship, and entered it with him. *And when they were come into the ship*, as soon as this divine Master had joined His apostles, *the wind ceased*, the sea became perfectly calm, and this became a new subject of astonishment to His disciples; as if all these new miracles ought to have surprised them after that of the multiplying of the five loaves, of which they had just been the witnesses; but their minds were so narrow and their hearts so blinded, that they gained no enlightenment from any of the actions of our Saviour, and they continued to wonder at each fresh miracle. *They were sore amazed in themselves beyond measure, for they considered not the miracle of the loaves: for their heart was hardened.* This is the failing of those, who letting themselves be guided rather by sense and imagination, than by faith and reason, believe one mystery because it is revealed, and yet cannot bring themselves to believe another, although equally revealed. The

apostles, overpowered by so many wonders, *came* to throw themselves at the feet of Jesus, *and worshipped Him* with the deepest reverence, and the most lively gratitude, *saying, Of a truth Thou art the Son of God.* We cannot draw near to Jesus with faith and love without soon experiencing the effects of His goodness. By a new wonder, the ship, as it were, guided by Jesus Christ, and almost without effort, advanced with such promptitude, that *immediately the ship was at the land* (of Gennesaret) *whither they went.* We may see here the advantages which those enjoy who have supported with fidelity the trials through which God has made them pass; these advantages are the presence of Jesus Christ, calm and peace, the light of a pure and serene day, lively feelings of faith, and trust, and lastly an easy progress in holiness. We advance not only without effort, but with inexpressible consolations. Why then are there so few who attain to that happy condition? It is because there are so few who will to support its trials; we willingly undergo far greater difficulties in order to procure for ourselves the advantages of this world; but we are faint-hearted and indifferent with regard to the advantages which are to be found in holiness and perfection. One day, but too late, we shall see the difference of the prize to which we might have attained.

THIRD POINT.

Jesus cures the sick in the land of Gennesaret, and thereby sets before us an example of the faith which we ought to have in Him.

1. A prompt and entire faith. Jesus landed early in the morning, not at Capernaum, but farther on in the land of Gennesaret, whence He repaired the same day by land to Capernaum. *When they were come out of the ship,* the inhabitants of Gennesaret *knew Him* for one sent by God, for the prophet of Galilee, and they hastened to meet Him. Why do not our hearts thus fly towards Jesus, as soon as we enter His holy Habitation,

as soon as at the words of Consecration, He descends upon the Altar, and comes to fill our hearts with blessings, and to dwell with us, and make Himself one with us! Let us kindle our faith at these blessed moments, let us acknowledge, adore, and love so great a God, so powerful, so liberal and so beneficent a Saviour.

2. Active and charitable faith. *And when the men of that place had knowledge of Him, they sent out into all that country round about* to make known that He had come to Gennesaret, in order thence to pass to Capernaum. There was a general stir throughout the neighbourhood; *and they began to carry about in beds those that were sick, where they heard He was; and brought unto Him all that were diseased.* How praiseworthy was this charity for the sick, and how it must have touched the heart of Jesus! Ah! if we had the same zeal for the salvation of our brethren, if we did but profit by all occasions to bring them to commune with themselves, to make them know their sicknesses, and to engage them to have recourse to Him Who alone can heal them, how useful would our charity be to them, and how helpful to ourselves!

3. A faith which was reverent, and full of trust. *And whithersoever He entered into villages, or cities, or country, they laid the sick in the streets,* and implored His help. Seeing that He only passed through that country, *they besought Him that they might touch if it were but the border of His garment* as He passed by; Jesus permitted them to do so with ineffable goodness; He allowed them to approach Him, and almost to overpower Him, with such confidence did His gentleness inspire every one. The success of some encouraged others, and no one availed themselves of the condescension of Jesus without obtaining the accomplishment of his desires: *and as many as touched were made perfectly whole.* Such was the triumphant march of Jesus on His return to Capernaum, a triumph to which the triumphs of the most famous earthly emperors cannot be compared, a divine triumph over sea and land, by

which this divine Saviour confirmed the faith of His apostles, in order to enable them to hear, without fear, the sublime and unheard of mysteries which He was about to announce at Capernaum. For us, who believe in these mysteries, who have them so to say in our possession, who touch not only the hem of His garment, but His very Flesh and Blood, and who feed upon Him, how much greater is our happiness, how much more perfect ought our love to be!

Prayer. O my God! fill my heart with that divine love, that it may obtain from Thee the entire healing of my soul. *Thou art of a truth the Son of God.* Yea, Lord, Thou art; I confess it with Thine apostles, and I adore Thee with them. Have pity on me, hold out to me a helping hand as Thou didst to S. Peter; *Lord save me,* I will say to Thee unceasingly as he did. Make me to hear in the depths of my soul those consoling words which Thou didst address to him, *It is I, be not afraid;* vouchsafe to make me hear those words in all the trials to which Thou dost put me, in all the opportunities with which Thou dost furnish me of advancing in holiness, in prayer, in Communion, and above all, in the hour of death. Amen.

Meditation CXXIV.

DISCOURSE OF JESUS IN THE SYNAGOGUE AT CAPERNAUM.

Consider, 1. the promise which Jesus makes here of a Heavenly bread which gives eternal life; 2. the faith required in order to to receive this Heavenly bread; 3. the manna of the Hebrews, a figure of this Heavenly bread. S. John vi. 22—34.

FIRST POINT.

The promise of Heavenly bread.

1. The place in which this promise was given. It

was in the synagogue at Capernaum, in the assembly which was held on the eve of the Sabbath, that is to say on Friday evening. Jesus had multiplied the five loaves on Thursday evening, on Friday morning He healed the sick in the land of Gennesaret, and betook Himself on the same day to Capernaum, before the Sabbath began. As soon as He had arrived, He went to the assembly in order to teach there. Thus, Jesus in employing every moment of His life for the relief of those in distress, or in need, or in the instruction of the people, gives a lesson to the labourers of the Gospel that there should be no moment left unoccupied in their lives.

2. *Of those before whom Jesus made this promise.* It was in great measure before those in whose behalf He had multiplied the five loaves; perhaps even He worked that miracle in their presence only in order to prepare their minds for the instruction which He was about to impart to them. He had left them the previous evening, on the other side of the lake, when they were desirous to proclaim Him king; and in truth, as soon as it was day, they assembled in order to carry out their intentions. *When the people which stood on the other side of the sea saw that there was none other boat there, save that whereinto His disciples were entered, and that Jesus went not with His disciples into the boat, but that His disciples were gone away alone,* they concluded that Jesus must be on that side of the lake. Nevertheless, as in spite of all their researches, they could not find Him, they determined to return. *Howbeit there came other boats from Tiberias,* that very morning, of which several made use in order to return across the lake, others took their journey by land in order to regain their homes, and besides those who belonged to Capernaum, there were others who came to *Capernaum seeking for Jesus.* Jesus was in the synagogue at the moment of their arrival; and what was their surprise in seeing Him! If Jesus had spoken to this people only of self-abnegation, of bearing their

Cross, who amongst them would have taken the trouble to seek Him and to follow Him?

3. *Whence Jesus took the opportunity to make this promise.* It was on account of the zeal which the people of Capernaum made use of to find Him. *And when they had found Him on the other side of the sea, they said unto Him, Rabbi, when camest Thou hither?* Jesus, without satisfying their curiosity, and confining Himself to the dispositions of their heart; *answered them and said; Verily, verily, I say unto you, ye seek Me not because ye saw the miracles, but because ye did eat of the loaves, and were filled.* That is to say, instead of looking upon My miracles as the works of a God, and as the proof that I am the Messiah, you only regard the earthly profit which may accrue to you thence; you only follow Me out of carnal and interested motives. And in truth, such was the disposition of mind too purely human with which part of the Galileans to whom Jesus had so long preached the Gospel, and on whom He had lavished His miracles, still regarded Him. These carnal men did not refer these miracles to their real aim, which was to make them believe in Him, Who wrought them as in the Son of God, so that they should receive from Him on His word, the precepts of faith and doctrines which He gave them; they only regarded, on the contrary, their temporal utility. In witnessing them, they promised themselves in Christ Who wrought them, a powerful king who should render them happy on earth, and should raise again the glory of their nation above that of all the nations of the earth. It was in order to wean them from so dangerous an error, that Jesus reproached them in so severe a manner for the low and interested motives which made them act thus. Let us beware what are the motives which lead us to follow Christ, or which lead us to embrace a religious life, or to practise works of piety, and see whether we too are not influenced by human motives?

4. *In what terms Jesus makes this promise to them.* He adds, *Labour not for the meat which perisheth, but*

for that meat which endureth unto everlasting life, which the Son of man shall give unto you: for Him hath God the Father sealed, that is to say, ye carnal and worldly men, who are so little awake to the necessities of your souls, you are only touched by the needs of your bodies, the fruitfulness of your flocks, and the glory of your nation! But this is not the fruit which I await from My labours. If you desire to please Me, raise your minds to higher thoughts, labour to procure for yourselves not that material nourishment which perishes, but that spiritual food, whose fruits will last to eternity. It is I, the Son of Man, Who will give to you this food, I, Who am marked with the seal of God the Father. This seal of God, is the Holy Spirit, the voice of the Father Who has declared that Jesus is His Well Beloved-Son, to whom men owe a complete obedience! the prophecies which characterise the Messiah; lastly the miraculous works which the Father has given to His Son the power of working; a truly divine seal, which cannot be mistaken and with regard to which there can be no deceit. The food which leads us to eternal life, and which Jesus assures us here that He will give, is the Divine Eucharist, for which the divine Saviour prepares men's minds little by little, of which He develops insensibly the nature and the effects, and which He declares, at the end of this discourse, to be His Flesh and His Blood. Let us labour then to procure this celestial Food which gives eternal life. Alas! we often take so much pains to procure for ourselves perishable goods, and we will do nothing to gain those which are eternal. What is this fortune, this happiness, this glory, in which we delight ourselves, and which we seek with so much exertion? And when we should prepare ourselves to receive the divine Eucharist, the source of all blessings, then we say we have neither the time nor the will! What folly! what blindness!

SECOND POINT.

The faith needful in order to receive the heavenly Bread.

1. *The necessity of this faith.* The Capernaites did not see yet in what this food was to consist which Jesus promised to them! but that which He had said to them about it sufficed to make them desire it; it was only needful now to know what they must do in order to obtain it. *They said then unto Him, What shall we do that we might work the works of God?* that is to say, works agreeable to God, by which we might make ourselves worthy of this food? *Jesus answered and said unto them, This is the work of God that ye believe on Him, Whom He hath sent.* In truth there is no mystery which requires so much faith as that of the Eucharist. The other mysteries offer perhaps less difficulties, because they have spiritual things as their object, because they are, so to say, farther removed from us and out of our reach; but this is within our hands and under our eyes; it relates to a Divine Presence hidden under the outward forms of bread and wine. Not only must we submit our reason, silence our imagination, but we must contradict even the testimony of our senses. Nevertheless if faith in Christ is necessary in order to believe this mystery, we must acknowledge also that it suffices. From the moment that I believe that Jesus is the Son of God, the Incarnate Word, God Himself, He has the right to tell me all that He wills; I shall believe Him without any difficulty and without any doubt. My senses, my imagination, my reason are nothing in comparison of His word and of the teaching of His Church. Let us then strengthen ourselves in our faith, and let us be unshaken in that faith; without it, we have nothing; and with it, when it is a living faith, we have all.

2. *Motives of this faith.* To believe in some one, to believe in something without sufficient ground, is the distinguishing mark of superstition, of false religion, of heresy, even of unbelief; but the Christian faith has

victorious motives to which a reasonable man cannot refuse his assent. Amongst the inhabitants of Capernaum, there were many unbelieving persons, who sought besides to justify their unbelief. Their prejudices even led them to ask of Jesus what miracles He would do that they might believe on Him. *They said therefore unto Him, What sign shewest Thou then, that we may see, and believe Thee ? what dost Thou work ?* But as the miracle of the multiplying of the five loaves was too recent for them to deny it, they thought they should elude the proof it gave of our Lord's divine ministry, by opposing to it the miracle of the manna, under Moses. *Our fathers did eat manna in the desert,* say they; *as it is written, He gave them bread from Heaven to eat.* The comparison of these two miracles was, according to them, decisive in favour of Moses ; Jesus had only fed five thousand men, and Moses more than sixty thousand ; Jesus only fed them one day, and Moses during forty years ; Jesus only gave them an earthly and human bread, barley bread, and Moses, bread from Heaven, bread of angels. These unbelievers like those of our days reason ill, and impose on mankind in two ways. 1. If it were a question of the comparison of bread, it would have been necessary to compare the bread of Moses, not with that Jesus had multiplied, but with that He had promised to give, which they could not do, because they did not know what it was yet, and this is what our Lord is about to do Himself in His answer, as we shall see. If it regarded, as indeed the matter in question was, the miracles which Jesus wrought in order to merit the faith which He required men to have in Him, it was useless to compare the miracles of Moses with those of Jesus ; both were attested and established ; they had equally the seal of God set upon them, they were an incontestable proof of the truth. Their difference consisted, 1. In the end for which they were wrought. Those of Jesus were worked as a proof of His divinity, in order that men might believe that He was the promised Messiah, the Saviour of men, the Son of God : those of Moses, in order that the Egyptians and the Israelites might know that it was the Lord who had brought His people out of Egypt, and Who was leading them. 2. In the authority with which they were wrought. What title did Moses take in the midst of the wonders which he worked? *And what are we*, he and Aaron said to the Israelites, *that ye murmur against us? Your murmurings are not against us: but against the Lord.* But Jesus takes upon Him every where the title of Son of God, of Judge of the quick and dead, the Chief of all men, the title of Son of man, the Repairer of all the evils which the sin of the first man has caused. 3. In the manner in which these miracles were wrought. Moses sighed before the Lord, and the Lord made known to him the wonders which He was about to work through His ministry. Moses executed the commands of the Lord, and the Lord worked the wonders which He had promised: but Jesus received from His Father all power to work the works which He performed; thus He makes use of this power with an entire freedom, on all sorts of occasions, and over every kind of material thing; one word, one look sufficed to Him: the sick are healed, the devils flee, the winds are calmed, the water is changed into wine, the loaves of bread are multiplied, the sea becomes calm, and firm: and when He raises the dead, He says to them, Arise, it is I Who command you. Not only does Jesus make use of this power Himself, but He communicates it to whom it pleases Him; and when His disciples work the same wonders as He did, they declare that it is in His name and His power that they work them. What a comparison of Moses with Jesus, of the servant with the only Son; of a man with the Man God, of the creature with the Creator. I adore Thee, O Jesus! O Son of God! O my Saviour! I adore Thee, and I acknowledge Thy sovereign power! What! at Capernaum even do they still dare to ask, what miracles Thou doest? Let us rather say, Alas! that even amongst Christians, though Thou art risen from the dead, and Thy Church is founded on the ruins of idolatry and Judaism, and that it has continued for nearly eighteen centuries, there are still those amongst us who ask for miracles, or who dare to compare those which Thou hast wrought with those of paganism, which offer only fabulous miracles. Ah! if Thou didst will to be king on the earth, to dispense riches and pleasures amongst Thy subjects, Thy miracles would not be disputed; but Thou art the God of holiness, the King of the life to come; Thou dost require that we should yield our submission to a doctrine which humiliates our minds, or lays a restraint upon us, and this is the cause of our unbelief.

THIRD POINT.

Manna of the Hebrews, a figure of heavenly bread.

Then Jesus said unto them, Verily, verily, I say unto you, Moses gave you not that bread from Heaven; but My Father giveth you the true bread from Heaven. For the bread of God is He which cometh down from Heaven, and giveth life unto the world. The figure ought to bear some relation to the reality; but the reality ought to be above the figure.

1. The manna came down from Heaven, from the lower and aerial Heaven, from the Heaven of the clouds, like the rain, but not from the highest Heaven where God dwells and communicates His glory to the blessed. Now it is from that true Heaven, from the Bosom of God Himself that the Eucharistic Bread comes down to us, which God gives us, and which Jesus here promises, when He says that He is *the true Bread from Heaven*.

2. The manna is called the Bread of angels, because it was not made by the hand of man. The Eucharistic Bread is the Bread of God, which came forth from God, formed by the Word of the Incarnate Word, and by the operation of the Holy Spirit, containing God Himself, the humanity of Jesus with His Divinity. It is the Bread of angels, because, like the Blessed, they feed on It in Heaven by intuitive vision and beatific love, whilst

we feed upon It on earth by faith, in receiving it under the outward forms of the Sacrament.

3. The manna fell from Heaven by its own weight, like an inanimate body, as the rain falls, and it only fell in the morning at the same time as the dew: but the heavenly Bread is a living bread which came down from Heaven of its own free will, and by its own motion into the womb of a virgin, and which descends daily upon our altars.

4. The manna supported life but did not give it. It had a delicious taste, and in it were to be found every taste that could be desired: but all that had regard only to the life of the body, and the taste of the senses, and consequently was perishable. But the Bread of heaven gives to the soul a celestial and Divine life, and fills it with holy delights, which are the foretaste of a blessed eternity.

5. The manna was only for one nation and for one period; the heavenly Bread is for the whole world, and will be to the end of the world. This adorable Bread has been distributed to all the faithful who are spread over the world, during seventeen centuries, and it will be thus distributed until the end of the world. Although the Capernaites formed as yet but a carnal idea of this Divine Food, they did not fail to pray, *Lord, give us evermore this Bread.* Let us utter the same prayer as they, but with more faith and ardour. Woe be to us, if we ever come to experience a distaste for this heavenly bread, and eat it only with weariness, or deprive ourselves of it in order to feed upon objects of sense or of our own evil passions. The Hebrews grew weary of this manna, and desired other meat, and their desires were granted; but a prompt and cruel death was at the same time the punishment of their wrongful distaste, and of their depraved desires.

Prayer. O Jesus! I pray Thee, but in a different way to what the Jews did, *give* me *this Bread* so excellent and so needful to my soul, this Bread which is nought else than Thyself, give It me always, and grant that I may never set any obstacle in the way of Thy liberality. Grant me, in order to render myself worthy of it, a lively and active faith, firm and enlightened, humble and reverent, animated with confidence and love, submissive to Thy will, and zealous for Thy glory, grateful for Thy benefits, and persevering in the fulfilment of Thy commandments. Amen.

Meditation CXXV.

FIRST CONTINUATION OF THE DISCOURSE OF CHRIST ON THE EUCHARIST.

Jesus declares that He is Himself the Food which He has promised, and the Bread of Life which came down from Heaven. Consider 1. the unbelief of the Jews; 2. the conduct of Christ in order to overcome their unbelief; 3. the murmurs that they utter against the Saviour; 4. the answer of this Divine Saviour to their murmurs. S. John vi. 35—47.

FIRST POINT.

Unbelief of the Jews.

1. Jesus reproaches them with it. After the Jews had asked to have ever more this Heavenly Bread, Which giveth life, *Jesus said unto them, I am the Bread of life: He that cometh to Me shall never hunger, and he that believeth on Me shall never thirst.* At this declaration of the Saviour, the Jews, evilly-disposed as they were, must have been surprised, and thus they gave no credence to it; perhaps even, they showed in their expression of countenance, outward marks of their incredulity. However that may have been, Jesus, Who saw their hearts, added, *I said unto you, That ye also have seen Me, and believe not.* What blindness could be more deplorable! What incredulity could be more criminal then to have had thus Jesus Christ within their sight for so long a time, to have been witnesses of so many

miraculous works and yet not to have believed in Him? As for me, O my Saviour, I have never seen Thee, and I believe in Thee with all my heart; I have only seen Thee under the forms of bread and wine, where Thou hast hidden Thyself, in order to bestow Thyself upon me; it is enough for this mortal life, enough for my salvation, enough for my consolation, enough to exercise my faith, to nourish my hope, and to enkindle me with Thy love.

2. Jesus discovers to the Jews the source of their unbelief. That which kept them back from believing in Jesus Christ, was the base and interested motives for which they followed Him, and which they would not renounce. They only sought in Him a temporal king, Who should render them happy on earth, and it was in this hope that they referred to the miracles which they saw Him work. They ought when they saw His miracles, to have followed in a teachable spirit, the outward voice of His Person, and the inward voice of grace: but self-interest, avarice, ambition stifled in them all teachableness; and these same Capernaites, who, when convinced by the miraculous multiplication of the loaves with which they had been filled, sought for Jesus Christ on the very morning of that same day, in order to place the crown on His Head, showed themselves in the evening invincible to persuasion, because it was no longer a question of giving themselves a liberal and magnificent king, but of believing the word of a man, who without being willing to be made king, laid claim to be regarded as the Messiah, and the Son of God. It is only those nevertheless who seek Jesus with an entire faith and perfect docility, whom this God-Saviour calls as given by His Father, led and brought by Him to His Father, and they alone find in Him what they seek for in Him. They believe with an unshaken faith all that He says to them; they are not discouraged either by the purity of His doctrine, or by the incomprehensibility of His mysteries; it suffices to them that He has spoken, for them to yield Him belief, and they find rest, consolation, and

life in their faith. *All that the Father giveth Me*, adds Jesus, *shall come to Me ; and him that cometh to Me I will in no wise cast out.* Let us often examine what it is that leads us to Jesus; whether it be the Father Who leads us thither, whether the motives which lead us to profess Christianity, to receive the Sacraments, to practise acts of devotion, to listen, read, and meditate on the Holy Scriptures, come from God, and whether it is not merely custom, habit, human respect, the spirit of criticism, or regard for our own interests and reputation which lead us to do so.

3. Jesus puts forth to the Jews the remedy for their unbelief. This remedy was to change their ideas, and to pray the Father of lights to illuminate them. Faith is a gift which God only grants to humble and teachable spirits, a gift which we must ask of Him with trust and humility. Miracles and the most undeniable proofs of religion make no impression on a proud heart, which clings to earth, and closes itself obstinately against the inward graces which prevent it and plead with it.

SECOND POINT.

Jesus encourages the Jews to come forth from their unbelief.

1. Jesus encourages them to believe in Him, in assuring them of His goodness. *He that cometh to Me, I will in no wise cast out.* Nay, Lord, Thou dost not reject, or drive away any who come to Thee, whom Thy Father presents to Thee, who are led to Thee by pure motives, and with the intention of receiving Thy instructions and profiting by them; Thou dost receive them, on the contrary, with love and good-will; Thou dost admit them into the secrets of Thy mysteries; Thou dost make them taste of truths which overwhelm them with delights, and Thou dost give them hopes which transport them out of themselves. Ah! wherefore do I not go to Thee with confidence and teachableness! why am I not earnest in following after Thee? Why do so

many other objects and the distractions of my own heart draw me away so often from Thee!

2. Jesus encourages the Jews to believe in Him, in manifesting to them the will of God His Father. *For I came down from Heaven, not to do My own will, but the will of Him that sent Me.* It is the duty of a messenger to conform himself in every thing to the will and intentions of him who sends him. The human will of Jesus could not withdraw itself from this obligation, because in Him the Divine will and the human will belonged to the same Person. *And this is the Father's will Which hath sent Me, that of all which He hath given Me, I should lose nothing, but should raise it up again at the last day.* The will of God towards mankind is that all should acknowledge Him Whom He hath sent to them, that they should address themselves to Him, and hearken to Him as His well-beloved Son and their only Mediator. It is for this reason that He has authorised His mission in so striking and indubitable a manner. The will of God towards His Son, Whom He has sent to us, of which our Lord here speaks to us, is that all those who, convinced by the testimony of the Father, and obedient to the outward and inward voice of the Father, shall come from Him and be thus presented to the Son by the Father, the Son will receive them, will instruct them, form them, feed them, preserve them, neglect none of them, let none of them perish, and raise them up at the last day, in order to give them back into the hands of the Father; such is the economy of our salvation. Thus, the will of God the Father and the human will of God our Saviour are united on this point, and will that all men should be saved and come to the knowledge of the truth, that none should perish, but that all should be converted and repent. If we perish, it is then through our own fault, and our loss comes only from ourselves: to impute it to God, to insinuate that even Christians, if they are finally lost, have not received from God the necessary means of salvation, is blasphemy. If this error is put before us as a mystery, it is a mystery of

iniquity which the Church rejects, and which ought to be abhorrent to us. The true and great mystery which is worthy of our adoration, is the goodness of our God, and of our Saviour, Jesus Christ, His Son, Who entreats us to save ourselves, and gives us the most abundant means of procuring our salvation.

3. Jesus encourages the Jews to believe in Him, in putting before them the rewards of faith. Jesus repeats to them, *and this is the will of Him that sent Me, that everyone which seeth the Son and believeth on Him, may have everlasting life; and I will raise Him up at the last day.* Have I rightly understood these august words? Is it to me they are addressed? An eternal life, a glorious resurrection for whoever believes in Christ! Rejoice, O my soul! my body, thrill with joy, thy happiness is assured: O sweet hope! thou shalt be my strength and my consolation in all the temptations of life, and thou wilt not abandon me even when I shall be in the arms of death. At this last moment, I hope to receive Thee once more, O celestial Bread, as the last pledge of the accomplishment of Thy promises; after which, reposing myself on Thee, my soul, separated from my body, will be united in Thee until Thou shalt join them together again, and that both having served Thee on earth, shall reign eternally with Thee in Heaven.

THIRD POINT.

Murmurings of the Jews: the character of unbelief.

1. Unbelief is audacious in its discourses. *The Jews then murmured at Him.* Unbelief and unteachableness raise their voices, while obedient children keep silence. Murmurings, complaints, cries are the first weapons which error makes use of against the authority which condemns it. It would willingly make believe, by the haughty tone it assumes, and the noise it excites, that right and the majority are on its side; but the voice of lawful authority, more simple and majestic, is easily

distinguished from all these senseless clamours, and claims the respect due to it.

2. Unbelief is malignant in its observations. In that wonderful discourse of our Lord, the Jews only found one sentence, which appeared to them capable of criticism; They *murmured at Him, because He said, I am the Bread which came down from Heaven.* They paid attention neither to His preceding miracles which He recalled to them, nor to the reproach of unbelief which He made them, nor to the will of God which He explained to them, nor to the great rewards which He promised them; one single word arrests them; *He said, I came down from Heaven.* This offends them; they imagine to find absurdity in these words; here is sufficient to excite their murmurings and to make them forget all the rest. Ah! let us not imitate them. Let us cling closely to the Holy Scriptures, to our holy religion, to all that edifies us, and let us profit by them; if we meet with anything which we do not comprehend, either let us pass it by with humility, or let us seek for instruction in a teachable spirit.

3. Unbelief is false in its reasonings. *They said, Is not this Jesus, the Son of Joseph, whose father and mother we know? how is it then that He saith, I came down from Heaven?* Such is that which appeared to the Jews an invincible demonstration: and unbelievers, ungodly men, and heretics have never brought forward anything more plausible against our sacred mysteries. Thus, a supposed false statement, one single point on which a person is ignorant, is to overthrow the whole. Ah! of how much are we not ignorant! Why should we always employ ourselves in reasoning on matters which are far above us, whilst incontestable facts which are within our reach prove evidently the truth which is announced to us, and the infallibility of the authority which instructs us.

FIRST POINT.

Answer of Jesus to the murmurs of the Jews.

Jesus therefore answered and said unto them, Murmur not among yourselves. Jesus did not refute the false reasonings of the Jews: it would have been needful, for that purpose, to reveal to them another mystery which they were still less capable of understanding, and less disposed to believe; He contented Himself with putting a stop to their murmurs, and continued His discourse.

1. On the necessity of grace in order to attain to faith. *No man can come to Me, except the Father which hath sent Me draw him; and I will raise him up at the last day.* We cannot come to Jesus and believe in Him, unless God His Father draw us. God draws us to Jesus by the outward voice of prophecy, and miracles, and by the inward voice of His grace. Let us acknowledge that we owe our faith to God, let us meditate more and more on the Holy Scriptures, let us ask of Him fresh helps, and fresh grace, so that we may believe in our holy faith, and become daily more and more strengthened in it.

2. On the necessity of our correspondence to grace in order to attain to faith. *It is written in the prophets, And they shall be all taught of God. Every man therefore that hath heard, and hath learned of the Father, cometh unto Me. Not that any man hath seen the Father, save He which is of God, He hath seen the Father.* The law of Jesus Christ, the law of the Gospel is not like the law of Moses, intended for one single nation, for one single province of the earth. The voice of God is addressed to all mankind, and instructs them all; the prophets have announced it in more than one place, and in more than one manner; but all do not yield to this voice; some will not hear it, others will not listen to it, or understand it, keep it in their minds, and follow what it bids them; but those who hear it and follow it must come to Jesus, to Whom it leads them. God does not

need to shew Himself to mankind in order to make them hear His voice; he who has an upright heart, hears it; if we listen to it in a teachable spirit, it will guide us to Him Who Alone has seen the Father, Who knows all His secrets, and can instruct us in them. In vain does the deist glory in knowing God, and in following the religion of nature; if He listened to God with a sincere heart, he would soon believe in Jesus Christ.

3. On the reward of faith. *Verily, verily, I say unto you, He that believeth on Me hath everlasting life; and I will raise him up at the last day.* The reward of faith is then a glorious resurrection at the last day, and a life of eternal happiness in Heaven. Our Lord does not cease to repeat it to us; can we weary of hearing it, of thinking of it, of meditating on it, and of labouring so as to make ourselves worthy of it? Ye, who lay claim to be the partisans of reason and of nature, who dare to treat the Christian religion as superstition, what recompence do you promise to your followers? Total annihilation at death; and moreover this fearful promise is founded on no other proof, save on the desire you have that thus it should be. But is this desire then more conformable to nature than the desire of a life of eternal happiness? Ah! this desire of annihilation cannot be the desire of any but an enemy of God, who hates God, and fears His vengeance; but it is a desire as inefficacious as his hatred against God is powerless. Commune with yourselves, return to God; the way of eternal life is still open to you; if you refuse to enter into it, you must expect to be the victims of eternal punishment and of eternal despair.

Prayer. O my Saviour! I believe that Thou art this Bread which came down from Heaven: this living Bread which is at the same time Food and Drink and which alone can always satisfy the hunger and quench the thirst of those who receive It worthily. What happiness for my soul to be able to feed on this Divine nourishment! Make me to taste of its fruits, O my God; come into my heart in order to establish Thyself there, to regulate its motions, and to draw me more and more to follow Thee, to draw me after Thy Cross, and hereafter to bring me into Thy kingdom. Amen.

Meditation CXXVI.
SECOND CONTINUATION OF THE DISCOURSE OF JESUS ON THE EUCHARIST.

Jesus sets forth the manner in which this food which He has promised is to be partaken of, namely, by eating His Flesh, and drinking His Blood, and He instructs us successively in the reality, the necessity, and the efficacy of the Communion. S. John vi. 48—59.

FIRST POINT.
Of the reality of the Communion.

1. A reality clearly set forth. After Jesus had explained what was the faith which He required from the Jews, in order to receive the Bread which He had promised them, and which was to give life unto the world, He repeats that which He had added, that He was Himself that living Bread which came down from Heaven; *I am that Bread of life*, and in order to convince them that it was a question here of a real eating, He recalls to them what they themselves had said, that their fathers had eaten manna in the desert. *Your fathers*, added Jesus, *did eat manna in the wilderness, and are dead. This is the Bread which cometh down from Heaven, that a man may eat thereof, and not die. I am the living Bread which came down from Heaven; if any man eat of this Bread, he shall live for ever.* The difference which He sets down here is not that the manna was eaten, and that the Bread which He promises is to be taken only in spirit and in faith; on the contrary in speaking of the second Bread, He employs always the same expression of eating, and repeats it twice; all the difference then that He places between the two kinds of bread, is that those who have eaten the first are dead,

and that he that shall eat the second shall not die at all, but shall live eternally. After this preliminary, if we may so venture to speak, our Lord concludes the revelation of the nature of the Bread which He is about to give us to eat and which will give life to the world, by adding, *and the Bread Which I will give is My Flesh, Which I will give for the life of the world.* This adorable Flesh is doubtless to be sacrificed on the Cross for the salvation of the world, and the Divine Eucharist is essentially bound up with this sacrifice; but the death of the Son of God is another mystery of which our Lord is not speaking here. It is not now a question save of the Bread which He is about to give us to eat in the place of the manna which the Hebrews had eaten in the desert, and He assures us that this living Bread is His own Flesh. Yes, O my God, Thou hast said it, Thy Church teaches it me, and I believe it with a firm faith, which nothing shall ever be capable of shaking.

2. A reality which is disputed with boldness. *The Jews therefore strove among themselves, saying, How can this Man give us His Flesh to eat?* How can He? A bold question to put when it is God Who speaks, and His Son Who instructs us. But alas! what are the effects of this hardihood. The first is error. He, who, instead of believing, seeks out in his own mind how the mystery set before the eyes of faith can be accomplished, will meet only with error and absurdity. What! how can the human mind penetrate the ways of God? The Capernaites could not imagine any other way of eating the flesh of Christ, than that in which one eats the flesh of animals, and such an idea revolted them. If we see how, under the forms of bread and wine, Jesus gives us His Flesh to eat, we feel sometimes, and in spite of ourselves, doubts as to this great mystery, these arise only because we seek to imagine to ourselves how this great mystery is brought about. Let us drive away from ourselves such thoughts, let us believe all and imagine nothing. The second effect of this temerity, is the discord which arose in their feelings towards one another. *The*

Jews strove among themselves. Some said one thing, some another. We have seen this dissension exist amongst the two principal chiefs of the so-called Reformation. After fifteen centuries of an unanimity of faith amongst Christians with regard to this august mystery, Luther and Calvin arose as reformers; both of them looked upon themselves as sent by God, with a special mission, and both contradicted one another directly on this point. Luther, contrary to the faith of the Church, maintains that the bread remains unchanged, and in contradiction to Calvin, that the Body of Christ, is really present. Calvin in opposition to the Church and to Luther, maintains that the bread is only a figure and representation of the Body of Christ, Who is absent from it, and as far removed as the Heaven is from earth. It is thus that Calvin, with a word, imagines to destroy the mystery which he has desired to understand, but has failed to do so. How is it that the anathemas which these two reformers have mutually hurled at each other, the invectives and the abuse which they have poured on one another, have not opened the eyes of their followers? How could these two parties join, unless they changed their opinions? How, in becoming united in this manner, could they have flattered themselves that they held the faith of Christ, which is one, and indivisible? O incomprehensible blindness! Incredulity far more absurd and sinful than that of the Capernaites! The third effect of this temerity, is apostacy. The disputes of the Jews ended by separating them all alike from Christ, Whom they had hitherto followed with so much ardour; they were united on this point. And it is thus that heretics and unbelievers, unite in separating from their mother, the Church, in hating her and fighting against her with all their strength; but their efforts are powerless, and they only serve to strengthen the claims of this Spouse of Christ, the only depositary of the truths and the mysteries of her divine Spouse.

3. *A reality authentically confirmed.* If the dispute of the Capernaites had arisen only out of some error,

for example, as Calvin maintains, because of their misconception of the teaching of the Saviour, because they thought that He would really give them His Flesh to eat, instead of speaking of a metaphorical eating which took place by faith, our Lord, in His reply, would have needed to set them free from their mistake, and draw them from an error to which the expressions He had made use of had given rise, and His charity was so great, that we cannot doubt He would have done so. But if the question which they put came from their unbelief, and because they would not believe in a real eating, because they could not understand it, there remained nothing for our Lord to do but to confirm what He had already said, and to exact a faith which submitted itself to His Word; and this is what He did throughout the remainder of His discourse, with a force which heresy could not elude. He employs an asseveration to strengthen what He has said: He makes use of threats and promises, in order to make Himself believed. To His Flesh which must be eaten, He adds His Blood which must be drunk, and He declares that His Flesh is truly a food which is eaten, and His Blood truly a drink which is to be drunk. To eat His Flesh, to drink His Blood, are expressions which He employs henceforth on every occasion, and which He repeats five times, recalling once more the eating of the Manna as the figure of the eating of which He speaks. *Then Jesus said unto them, Verily, verily, I say unto you, Except ye eat the Flesh of the Son of man, and drink His Blood, ye have no life in you. Whoso eateth My Flesh, and drinketh My Blood, hath eternal life; and I will raise him up at the last day. For My Flesh is Meat indeed, and My Blood is Drink indeed. He that eateth My Flesh, and drinketh My Blood, dwelleth in Me, and I in him. As the living Father hath sent me, and I live by the Father; so he that eateth Me, even he shall live by Me. This is that Bread which came down from Heaven; not as your fathers did eat manna, and are dead; he that eateth of this Bread shall live for ever.* Who can help seeing in these words the real doctrine of the Presence of Christ invincibly proved by expressions so forcible, and repeated so often? Who could persuade himself that these expressions are only made use of in order to express the faith which we should have in the mystery of the Incarnation, or in that of the death of Jesus Christ? What relation is there between expressions which relate to eating the Flesh of Jesus Christ, and believing in His Incarnation, between eating the manna, and believing in His death? Ah! it is only through a deficiency in our faith, it is only because we will not humble our minds before an incomprehensible mystery, that we prefer so forced an explanation to expressions so clear and so natural. I believe, O my God; I believe in Thy Word, I believe with all Thy Church, and I detest those misinterpretations of this holy mystery, which the mind of man has only invented in order to conceal its own weakness, its pride, and its unteachable spirit.

SECOND POINT.

Of the necessity of the Communion.

Verily, verily, I say unto you, Except ye eat the Flesh of the Son of man, and drink His Blood, ye have no life in you. With regard to these words of our Lord, we may put three questions;

1. Upon whom this threatening of our Lord falls? It falls directly on those, who not believing in this mystery, refuse to participate in it through the Communion, and such was the disposition of mind in which the people of Capernaum then were; or on those, who, not believing in it, receive a barren empty Communion, which does not convey to them the Presence of Jesus Christ in His Body and Blood, and such is the communion of the Calvinists. It falls also on those who neglect to seek instruction, and defer too long their first Communion; but it does not fall on those, who through accident, have been hindered from so doing; their will has sufficed in this

case as in that of Baptism; it does not fall either on those, who having received Baptism, have not attained to a sufficient age to become communicants. This threat does fall on those who do not approach to the Communion, through their own fault, at all appointed seasons, and as often as their soul's health requires it. On this point, there should be neither idleness nor precipitation; but in all things we should seek to conform ourselves to the rules and the practice of the Church. Ah! if we loved Christ as we should, or in proportion as we love our life, we should not need to be solicited to draw near often to it.

2. Wherefore does our Lord distinguish here His Body and His Blood? It is because the food which He promises us is a complete and entire nourishment, containing food and drink, and because at the same time this nourishment ought to be a participation in the sacrifice which He is about to make of His Life on the Cross, by a violent death and the shedding of His Blood. The consecration of the Eucharist is a true sacrifice, which renews in a mystical and unbloody manner that of the Cross, by the separation of the symbols, the one which under the form of Bread, conveys to us, by virtue of the words of consecration, the Body of Christ, and the other, under the form of wine, His Blood. This consecration can only be legitimately effected through the action of the sacrifice itself, and the Communion is a participation in the sacrifice offered up on the Cross, which is none other than Jesus Christ Himself, and it is especially by this participation in the Communion that we have a share in the sacrifice. What could not have been done with regard to the sacrifice of the Cross, was done at the Last Supper, and is done in the Holy Communion. It is not necessary, though much to be desired, that all the faithful should communicate daily; they may content themselves with communicating spiritually by the affections of their hearts: but every time they do communicate, whether by joining in deed, or in spirit, in the act of the sacrifice, it is always with refer-

ence to the sacrifice; it is a participation in the sacrifice offered on the Cross. Oh! how great is our Christian religion! What sacrifice like that of a God to a God, and what happiness for a Christian to feed upon this Divine Victim, to eat His Flesh, and drink His Blood, under these simple symbols of bread and wine, which nevertheless are filled with grace and truth. These two kinds of bread and wine have been established for a more perfect representation, both of the sacrifice on the Cross, and of the spiritual refreshment and support of the soul; the Victim of this sacrifice, and the Source of our spiritual food in this Sacrament being Jesus Christ Himself; and he who partakes of it in faith satisfies therefore his spiritual hunger and thirst.

THIRD POINT.

Of the efficacy of the Communion.

1. The Communion confers on us immortality. Not a natural immortality, for it does not prevent our bodies from dying, and our souls cannot die in the natural order which God has established, but a supernatural immortality, by which our souls will live in blessedness, and be united to our bodies in order to enjoy an eternal felicity. The manna, which was only a bodily nourishment, did not bestow a natural immortality, much less could it bestow a supernatural immortality, which is of an order far superior to the manna. Every one will rise again, in truth, by an act of the Almighty power of God; the wicked in order to receive condemnation, and the righteous an eternal reward; but those who shall have worthily received the Communion, and who have not lost, through their sins, the fruits of their Communion, will have a special title to the resurrection by virtue of their Communion. It will be the Flesh of Jesus united to their flesh, it will be Jesus Himself, on Whom they will have fed, Who will raise them up again at the last day and will quicken them. From this present time, they receive this life through the Communion:

they have in themselves the seed, the germ of it, which death, and the corruption of the tomb cannot destroy, and which will develop itself at the last day through a glorious resurrection, and a life of eternal happiness.

2. The Communion gives us food. The effects of food are to appease the desires and the torment which hunger and thirst cause us, to heal our present languor and weakness; to strengthen us for the future against languor and weakness, to put us in a state of health, vigour, activity and joyousness; lastly to make us firm and to add to our life, so to say, until we shall have attained to a perfect age. Such are the effects of the Divine food of the Eucharist with regard to the supernatural life of the soul, provided always that we make a right use of it, and partake of it at fitting times. Let us seek then to render ourselves worthy to partake of it as often as we can, and do not let us wait until we have attained to perfection in order to draw near to it. This would be to confound the means with the end, and to reverse the order which Jesus Christ has established.

3. The Communion unites us to Christ. A real and positive union. It is not only by a moral union, by charity, etc. but by a real and positive union, by food. An ineffable union, the effect of the greatest love and the greatest charity; a union of which no natural union can give us any idea. The union of created beings, the union of hearts, the union of minds, the union of wills, do not approach to that union which is effected by the Communion. Jesus, after having loved us so as to suffer death for us, finds yet another way by which to testify His love to us, by uniting Himself intimately to us, and He gives us the means whereby we may shew our love to Him and become intimately united to Him, by incorporating Himself in us and incorporating us into Himself. A continual union, which is not for some moments only and at the moment of Communion alone, but which is permanent and always abiding. As the food which we convert into our own substance remains in us, exists in us, and becomes ourselves; in the same way,

but in an infinitely higher way, this Divine food, which changes us into Itself, causes us to be united to Him, so that He dwells in us, and we in Him, so as to make us but one with Him. If this union is the effect of love, how much ought it to increase love! O chaste Spouse of our souls! what delights dost Thou not make those feel who, faithful to this holy union, avoid not only that which might break it, but that which might impair it ever so little and displease Thee. Lastly, eternal union. Every other union will be dissolved, at least at death; but this union, victorious over death, will continue to shine forth in the glory of eternity.

4. The Communion communicates to us the life of God Himself. From all eternity, the Word was in God, and it was God; life was in Him; a life which was common to the three adorable Persons of the All-holy Trinity; the life of God, a life Divine, essential, uncreated, eternal. The Word was made Flesh, was made man, and has communicated to the flesh and the sacred humanity with which it has clothed itself, the Divine life which was in Him. As then God the Father has life in Himself, in the same way He has given to the Son to have life in Himself. And with regard to ourselves, God has also given to us eternal life, that life which is in His Son; we have this eternal life, because we have the Son, because we believe in the name of the Son, and that, following the commands which the Son has given to us, we eat His Flesh, and drink His Blood, and by partaking of them by faith, we are in the Son of God, Who is the true God and eternal life. It is thus that God communicates to us His Life by His Son. If this communication which God gives us of Divine life is above our senses and our understanding, it is none the less real, it is none the less worthy of admiration, it is only the more desirable and the more to be esteemed. O ye lovers of life, who desire to live eternally, here is the true and only means. No, there is no manna on the earth which can give you eternal life; if your name were to live on the earth to the end of the world, it would not be you

who would live, and this imaginary life would end with the world; it is only the *Bread Which came down from Heaven* Which could give you a life which would continue after your decease, and which after the end of the world, would still last on during all eternity.

Prayer. O incomprehensible mystery! O prodigy of love which love alone could understand! O heavenly Bread, Source of peace and life, assured Pledge of salvation and of immortality! O Divine Communion, how precious are Thy advantages, and how full art Thou of blessings and favours! What glory, O Jesu, to the faithful soul which is united to Thee! By Thine adorable Flesh, we are united to Thee, and to the Father Which hath sent Thee. Divinity hath given new life to Thy sacred Flesh, and we, through partaking of It, have become " partakers of the Divine nature." With what ardour shall I not then approach to Thee, O Lord! Thou shalt be the Bread of my soul, Thou shalt be the life of my members. Ah! the graces and the infinite Blessings which Thou dost communicate shall be to me powerful motives to draw near more often to Thee, and always in a worthy manner. O Jesus! do not suffer that by a prodigy of insensibility, I should remain cold and languishing when I receive the Sacrament of Thy love. Amen.

Meditation CXXVII.

OF THE RESULTS WHICH THE DISCOURSE OF OUR LORD ON THE EUCHARIST HAD.

1. The disciples murmured, and Jesus replied to their murmurs; 2. Jesus added reproaches to His answer, and His disciples forsook Him; 3. the Apostles remained faithful to Him, and Jesus foretold to them the treachery of Judas. S. John vi. 59—71.

FIRST POINT.

Murmurings of the disciples and the answer of Jesus.

Murmurs of the disciples. *These things said He in*

the synagogue, as He taught in Capernaum. Many therefore of His disciples, when they had heard this, said, This is a hard saying, who can hear it? If our lips have not uttered this blasphemy against the Divine Eucharist, how many times has not our heart rendered itself guilty of the same murmurings, sometimes against one point of the law, sometimes against a commandment of our Saviour, when it has been a matter of doing violence to ourselves, of fighting against some evil passion, of suffering some injury?

Answer of Jesus. *When Jesus knew in Himself that His disciples murmured at it, He said unto them, Doth this offend you? What and if ye shall see the Son of man ascend up where He was before? It is the spirit that quickeneth: the flesh profiteth nothing: the words that I speak unto you, they are spirit and they are life.* This answer of Christ's has two parts; the first proposes a fresh mystery, which contains a proof, a difficulty, and an explanation of that which He had said, that He was the living Bread Which came down from Heaven, and that this Bread was His Flesh which they must eat. *Doth this offend you?* He asks. *What and if ye shall see the Son of man ascend up where He was before?* Our Lord does not explain this further to His disciples, except by these words, 1. He offered to them a proof of His Divinity. In truth, the Ascension of Jesus Christ into Heaven, which took place in the presence of His apostles and of His disciples, was a very solid and consoling proof to them and the whole Church that He had descended from Heaven, that He was the Son of God, and that all that He had revealed and taught was of an incontestable truth. Let us often have recourse to this proof in order to find support in temptations, which come to us against the faith. 2. Jesus announced to them a fresh difficulty. It was in truth, as if He had said to them; Now that you see Me present, you cannot believe that I can give you my Flesh to eat, how will you then believe it when I shall have ascended up to Heaven, and have left My sojourn on earth? To those who will to believe, the Ascension of Jesus Christ is a proof of all the mysteries of religion, and consequently, of that of the Eucharist; but to those who only choose to reason, it is a fresh difficulty, which overwhelms their feeble reason. It is thus that with one and the same word, the wisdom of God consoles the humble believer, and blinds the proud enquirer into His mysteries. Calvin found himself reduced to this difficulty, which led him to put forth this blasphemy, that Christ is as far removed from the Eucharist, as the Heaven is from the earth. His followers do not cease to bring forth the same difficulty, without considering that having been foretold by our Lord, it is turned into a proof against themselves, and that they are thereby convinced of being amongst the number of His unbelieving and murmuring disciples. 3. Jesus gave them an explanation of it. His disciples as well as the Capernaites, could not conceive a real eating, such as Jesus taught, without imagining at the same time, a bloody and carnal eating of flesh divided and cut into pieces; and this is that which offended them. Our Lord, by the mystery of His Ascension, turns away their thoughts, from so gross a conception of it, and the sense of His Words is, Believe without hesitation what I have just said to you; if the proofs which you have in My miracles do not yet suffice to you, you will have a more complete proof one day in My Ascension. Believe without reasoning; otherwise that which appears difficult to you to believe now will become far more so after My Ascension; believe without imagining any thing; a time will come, namely, after My Ascension, when these carnal imaginings of your's can no longer find place. Let us believe ourselves in this manner, and let us enjoy the happiness which our faith procures to us.

The second part of the answer of our Lord shews us how that which He has spoken of, the necessity of eating His Flesh, must be explained; *it is the spirit that quickeneth; the flesh profiteth nothing.* We may attach two meanings to these words, which, although different, lead us to the same end. 1. By these words *the flesh profiteth nothing*, we may understand that mere carnal understanding, the light of our senses, and the natural manner of conceiving things, is of no avail; that, in the mysteries of God, flesh and blood, human reason and natural enlightenment see nothing; that *it is the spirit* of God *that quickeneth*, that gives power to believe His mysteries, that gives power to understand them, and to taste of them. Let us ask of God this quickening spirit, this spirit of purity and faith, and let us be guided only by its Light. 2. By this word *the flesh*, we may understand a real flesh, a real body. Our Lord had told the Jews that His Flesh gave life, that he who ate of It should have eternal life, and they understood these words of a dead flesh, such as we ordinarily partake of. He warns them here that that neither must nor could be understood in that manner. A dead body has no life in it, how then could it give life; the man who enjoys the possession of life, does not draw that life from the body, but from the spirit which quickens the body. The flesh does not contribute any thing to the life; the spirit has it independently of the body. If then we receive life by eating the Flesh of Jesus Christ, it is because in eating It, we partake of the Life with which It is animated, and that It receives, not from Itself, but through Its union with the soul of Jesus Christ, and with the Person of the Word. Who is Life uncreated, and eternal. Now what happiness for us and what glory! our Lord adds in the same meaning; *The words that I speak unto you, they are spirit, and they are life;* that is to say, they ought to be understood according to the spirit of God, and of faith and not according to flesh and blood, and according to the limited understanding of human reason; then you will find there the life which they promise. My discourses have all reference to life; and My words promise you eternal life; they promise you then all the spirit, which is the principle of life; you must not then understand them as you would as if they were spoken of a dead body, or of a body separated from the spirit.

The answer of our Lord cannot be understood of the figure of His Body, in the sense in which the Calvinists employ it. 1. Because in this case, the answer of Jesus Christ would not any longer be an explanation, but a formal retractation of that which He had said, which it would be impiety to believe. 2. If, in that which had preceded, Jesus had only intended to speak of the figure of His Body, He would have said so clearly here, because, in that case, the error of His disciples being innocent, it would have gained, from the goodness of the Saviour, a precise explanation which would have hindered them from leaving Him. How full of wisdom and truth are Thy words, O Jesus! What greatness and strength, glory and happiness, sweetness and consolation do not true believers receive from them!

SECOND POINT.

Reproaches of Jesus and the desertion of the disciples.

The words which Jesus was about to add, and the conduct of the disciples prove to us clearly that faith is rare, that it is a gift of God, and that it is indivisible.

1. Faith is rare. *But there are some of you that believe not*, our Saviour continues. *For Jesus knew from the beginning who they were that believed not, and who should betray Him.* What a subject of fear and self-examination offers itself to our consideration here! We all make a profession of being Christians, of being disciples of Christ; but how many among us are there not who have no faith, who have not a firm and unshaken faith, a lively faith which regulates their minds, their heart, and their actions; a faith which they dare to defend and maintain when occasion offers, and for which they are ready to suffer or to die? Am I of the number of those who believe in Thee? am I not of the number of those who do not believe? Thou dost know, O my God! Thou dost know every thing, the present, the past, and the future, Thou dost know who they are who will persevere unto the end, and those who

will not persevere. Thou dost know who will remain faithful unto Thee, and who will betray Thee, who will return unto Thee after their estrangement, and who will be overtaken in their sins, and die in them; but Thy Divine knowledge does not in any way hinder the free will of man; it does not prevent Thee from furnishing him with every means whereby he may believe and be saved, as also it does not prevent him from making use of these means. It is not then what Thou dost know which should alarm me, but what I am and what I do. I ought to know that Thou knowest every thing, that with Thy grace I can do all, that Thou dost pour out Thy grace in abundance, and dost never refuse it to him that asks it of Thee. Yes, Lord, it is not Thy grace which is wanting to us, it is we who are wanting to Thy grace; it is on Thy grace alone that our hope is founded; it is our sinfulness alone which we need to fear. Let us triumph over both our sin and our fear; give us faith, perseverance in the observance of Thy commandments, and the practice of Thy holy love.

2. Faith is a gift of God. Our Lord had already said so, and He repeats it here. *And He said, Therefore said I unto you, that no man can come unto Me, except it were given unto him of My Father. From that time many of His disciples went back and walked no more with Him.* Precious gift of faith, gift which is offered to all, and received by a small number. Many follow Jesus as His faithless disciples did, through the hope of the temporal advantages which might be found in His service, but not in the spirit of the true faith which makes us look upon Jesus as the Son of God, sent to deliver us from our sins, in order to reveal to us the conduct and designs of God, in order to teach us what we ought to do and to avoid, to love and to hate, to hope and to fear. O Heavenly Father! give me this inestimable gift of faith which leads me to Thy well-beloved Son, which brings my spirit and heart into subjection to Him, and which binds me to Him, so that I may never again be separated from Him.

THIRD POINT.

The faithfulness of the apostles, and the prophecy of the treachery of Judas.

That which follows will instruct us in the motives which ought to hinder us from forsaking Jesus Christ.

I. The great number of those who do forsake Him. *Then said Jesus unto the twelve, Will ye also go away?* Jesus addresses to us also the same words. Let us think with grief how many there are every day who forsake Him, without speaking of the multitude of those who have never willed either to follow Him or to know Him, how many Christians have separated from Him through schism or heresy, or through sin and evil lives; how many in all ranks of life, amidst the people, and amidst His disciples; how many, after having followed Him with fervour, basely forsake His service! But Jesus had need of no one. Were the number of deserters still greater, He will change nothing in His doctrine, in His morals, in His mysteries, because all this building is founded on the immutable truth, on the incorruptible holiness, on the essential wisdom of God Himself. But this great number of deserters ought to make us more fervent, and to make us cling still more closely to our Divine Master. Their desertion ought to render our fidelity more glorious and more meritorious. Would we confound ourselves with this multitude of base souls, of corrupt men, plunged in crime, the shameful slaves of their own evil passions, without faith, without law, without life? No, Lord; the greater the number of those who forsake Thee is, the more sure is their ruin, and the greater horror do I feel of them! Far from following them, why cannot I, by my faithfulness and fervour, repair the outrages which they offer Thee? Why cannot I bring them back to Thee, or at least hinder others from following their example, and forsaking Thee?

2. Second motive; the comparison of the masters whom we can follow. Simon Peter answers in the name of the others: *Lord to Whom shall we go? Thou hast the words of eternal life.* In worldly affairs, we do not determine on any course without previous reflection; we compare the profits, we make calculations, we compute, and then we choose what appears to be the most advantageous. Is it only in matters of salvation that we blindly take the most important steps, without regard as to the consequences they may have? But who are these masters then whom we may follow? The devil, the world, the flesh, self-interest, ambition, our evil passions, sin, this profligate man, that atheist. Now, what do they promise us, and what promise are they in a position to keep? If we have not ourselves made trial of them, let us ask those who follow them. But Jesus promises us eternal life; He alone has been able to make so glorious a promise, and He alone can perform it. Let us then say with S. Peter, " *Lord, to Whom shall we go? Thou hast the words of eternal life. And we believe and are sure that Thou art that Christ, the Son of the Living God.*" Yes, we have been born in this faith of the Holy, Catholic and Apostolic Church: we have been brought up and taught in it; all that we have read, seen and heard, has strengthened our faith in it, and we await the accomplishment of the promises which are given to this faith, after we have been faithful in the practice of the holy commandments which it lays upon us.

3. Third motive, the special graces which we have received from God. *Jesus answered them, Have not I chosen you twelve?* This choice of a free preference merited well that the apostles should remain faithfully attached to Him. But is this mark of acknowledgement wanting in ourselves? Ah! let us think of all the special graces which God has poured down upon us from our very birth. How often, after those first blessings of our birth in a Christian country, and our admission by Baptism into the Christian covenant, has He not

chosen us out specially from amongst others, to lavish favours on us which He has not granted to them? He has chosen us to live, whilst many others have been taken out of this world; He has ordered that we should receive a more Christian education and more careful teaching, whilst others have been left exposed to ignorance, and to the errors of the world; and if we are priests, He has chosen us to serve Him in a more perfect and intimate manner, whereby we are more closely united to Him. Ah! what gratitude should not such singular graces awaken in us, and how should they kindle our fervour! But let us beware lest we turn them into an excuse for relaxation or self-glorification! Whatever grace of election we may have received, we can abuse it, and be unfaithful to it; and if we do, our crime will be so much the greater, and our damnation so much the more terrible. And in truth, let us listen to what Jesus adds; *Have not I chosen you twelve, and one of you is a devil?* Who would not tremble at such words? *He spake of Judas Iscariot, the son of Simon; for he it was that should betray Him, being one of the twelve.* Judas, do you recognize yourself under this character? you, an apostle, you, one of the twelve whom Jesus chose, you will betray Him, you will be the shame and disgrace of the band of apostles to whom you belong, the object of horror to all Christians, and a victim of hell! you imagine yourself very far removed from such guilt; but already your faith is beginning to waver, your fervour to diminish, and your eyes are cast with longing towards the acquirement of earthly wealth. Ah! the year will not have come round again before your crime will be consummated. The day on which Jesus promises the gift of that Bread from Heaven, He foretells your treachery, and the day on which He shall fulfil His promise, will be that on which you will accomplish His prediction.

Prayer. Alas! O my God! dost Thou not behold in me dispositions of mind as fatal as those of Judas? Thou hast chosen me, and called me, and I draw near to Thy table, and partake of the Bread of Heaven, with other holy souls; but am I not *a devil*, although I am in their midst? Turn away from me, O my God, such misery, and grant that I may die soon than ever be faithless to Thee. Amen.

Meditation CXXVIII.

PHARASAICAL SUPERSTITION.

The Gospel offers us here for our consideration, 1. the malice of the Pharisees; 2. the reply which Jesus makes to them; 2. the warning which He gives to the people; 4. lastly, His instruction to His disciples. S. Matt. xv. 1-20. S. Mark vii. 1-23.

FIRST POINT.

Malice of the Pharisee.

1. They seek to criticise. *Then came to Jesus scribes and Pharisees, which were of Jerusalem.* Jesus had not been up to Jerusalem this year to the feast of the Passover, but His fame having been heightened there by the report which the Galileans who went up there gave of His wonderful works, some of the scribes and Pharisees who belonged to Jerusalem, deputed perhaps by the rest, betook themselves to Galilee in order to examine more closely into His conduct, and to seek at least to lower the esteem in which He was held amongst the people. Are we not of the number of the Pharisees? Does not the good which is spoken of another become to us a motive for examining into their conduct with a spiteful and jealous eye?

2. They make a trifle into a great crime. *And when they saw some of His disciples eat bread with defiled, that is to say, with unclean, hands, they found fault. For the Pharisees, and all the Jews, except they wash their hands oft, eat not, holding the tradition of the elders. And when they come from the market, except*

they wash, they eat not. And many other things there be, which they have received to hold, as the washing of cups, and pots, brasen vessels, and of tables. Such then is all that the Pharisees and scribes of Jerusalem after having well examined into their conduct, could find to bring against the disciples of Jesus: it was enough to let them loose against them, against their Master, and to cause to fall upon the Saviour a grave accusation. What a specious colouring did they not give to such an innocent omission! To whom did they not speak of it, as of an overthrow of ancient discipline, and ancient tradition! Is it not thus that we exaggerate the faults of others, real or imaginary, especially when those are concerned who make a particular profession of following Christ?

3. They utter their reproaches and their accusations in public. *Then the Pharisees and scribes asked Him, Why do Thy disciples transgress the tradition of the elders, but eat bread with unwashen hands?* The scribes and Pharisees, not content with having blamed in their private conversations the conduct of the disciples, and having sought to bring discredit on the Master, wished to render their accusations public, to throw Jesus into perplexity, and to cover Him with confusion in the presence of the whole assembly. They took therefore the opportunity of an occasion on which He was publicly instructing the people, and they drew near to Him, and put this question to Him with an air and a tone of usurped authority which they thought justified by the reputation in which they stood, and which they exercised over all the disciples of Moses. If questions are put only for the sake of receiving instruction, nothing can be more desirable; but most often these questionings are only made use of as a means of giving offence, or of bringing another into discredit.

SECOND POINT.

Answer of Jesus Christ to the Pharisees.

1. Jesus reproaches them with the transgression and

setting aside of the law of God. *But He answered and said unto them, Why do ye also transgress the commandment of God by your tradition? For God commanded, saying, Honour thy father and mother; and He that curseth father or mother, let him die the death. But ye say, Whosoever shall say to his father or his mother, It is a gift, by whatsoever thou mightest be profited by me; and honour not his father or his mother, he shall be free:* and will satisfy the requirements of the commandment. *And ye suffer him no more to do ought for his father and mother; making the word of God of none effect through your tradition, which ye have delivered; and many such like things do ye.* One of the commandments which God had delivered by the mouth of Moses, a commandment which was written in the heart by the finger of nature, enjoined upon children to honour their father and mother, to respect them, to obey them, to provide for them, if it were necessary, and to assist them in their needs. The law even added that he who should curse his father or mother, or should speak abusive words to them, who should make use of any marks of contempt towards them, or forsake them in their necessities, should be put to death. But these false teachers, on the contrary, taught that those who made gifts to the temple, fulfilled the law, and that they were free from all obligations to them, if they only expressed the wish that this gift might be profitable to them, and that it might render the Lord propitious and favourable to them. Thus, these doctors of the law, instead of encouraging the people in the observance of the law, turned them away from it by the interpretation which they made of it. This was only one example which our Lord quoted of their false teachings; for He adds, *and many such like things do ye.* How many, amongst Christians, fall into this fault of the Pharisees? how many are so much occupied with certain practices of devotion, that they neglect the law of God in the essential points which regulate their duties and their obligations? A person may be retiring in his outward appearance, whilst he is full of pride within;

he may impose hardships on his body, whilst he gives way to his temper; he may have appointed hours for prayer, but may be quite without gentleness, charity, or humility; he may subject himself to some external practices of devotion, and yet violate in their observance, the very law of which he wishes to pass as the strict observer. False and Pharasaical piety!

2. Jesus reproaches them with their hypocrisy. *Ye hypocrites, well did Esaias prophesy of you, saying, This people draweth nigh unto Me with their mouth, and honoureth Me with their lips; but their heart is far from Me.* When I consider myself, can I not in truth say that it is of myself that the prophet has spoken? What fair words! what a specious appearance! what external professions! But my heart, Ah! how far is it from God! If I were to ask my heart a hundred times a day, Where is it? a hundred times I should find it far from God. If I were to ask myself in my devotions, in all that I do, where my heart was, I should always find that it was far from God. Ah! how many of my actions are devoid of the spirit of recollectedness and devotion which ought to animate them! Hypocrite that I am, shall I never remember that God sees my heart, and that, without the homage of the heart, nothing can ever be pleasing to Him.

3. Jesus reproaches them with superstition. *Howbeit in vain do they worship Me, teaching for doctrines the commandments of men. For laying aside the commandment of God, ye hold the tradition of men, as the washing of pots and cups; and many other such like things ye do. And He said unto them, Full well ye reject the commandment of God, that ye may keep your own tradition.* The religious worship of the Pharisees was reduced to frequent ablutions of their cups and their pots, and of other similar practices; they preferred these works of supererogation to the precepts of God, or rather, in enhancing the value of the one, they lessened and did away with the other. The Gospel has set us free from Judaic superstitions, as from heathen superstitions. The

Church offers to God a pure worship, without permitting any modification either in faith or morals. But in the midst of so pure a worship, let us examine whether we have not our own private superstitions, somewhat similar to those of the Pharisees, if we do not cherish some particular scruples, and if we do not violate without remorse the precepts of the law, the duties of Christianity, the obligations which our station in life imposes on us, the precepts of subordination, charity, and humanity. Let us take care nevertheless, our private devotions may be our own, but faith is from God.

THIRD POINT.

Warning of Jesus Christ to the people.

And when He had called all the people unto Him, He said unto them, Hearken unto Me every one of you, and understand; there is nothing from without a man, that entering into him can defile him; but the things which come out of him, those are they that defile the man. If any man have ears to hear, let him hear. When Jesus had humbled the pride of the Pharisees and scribes of Jerusalem, and had reduced them to silence, He recalled the people to Him, and said unto them, in the presence of their teachers; Nothing which is outside of a man, and enters into him by his lips, can defile his conscience; that which defiles it is that which is in him, that which having been conceived in his corrupt heart, is expressed without. After this short warning, Jesus sent away His auditors, leaving those to meditate on the meaning of His words, who, as He often said, had ears to hear. It is not difficult for us to understand that the things we eat could not of themselves defile us; but as the Saviour adds, that that which defiles a man is that which comes forth from his heart, such as evil desires, and all manner of excesses, of which intemperance is one of those most to be condemned, it follows that the things we eat may defile us, 1. if we take them without gratitude to Him Who gives them us, without love to Him, and without regard to His presence; 2. if we take them, not in order to relieve our wants and to repair our strength, but in order to satisfy our sensuality, especially if this sensuality leads us into expenses and scandalous profusion, and beyond our power; if, when this sensuality is not satisfied, it causes us moments of impatience and anger, makes us burst forth into complaints and murmurs; if this sensuality renders us hard towards the poor, so that we refuse even to relieve them with the remains of those earthly possessions with which God has filled us; 3. if we take them with excess, against the commands of God; 4. if we take them without necessity, on days which the Church sets apart as days of fasting or abstinence.

FOURTH POINT.

Instruction of Jesus Christ to His disciples.

1. On the offence which the Pharisees took. 1. A hypocritical and unjust offence, to which no regard ought to be paid. *And when He was entered into the house from the people, then came His disciples, and said unto Him, Knowest Thou that the Pharisees were offended, after they heard that saying?* No one more easily takes offence, or gives way to more bitter complaints, than those who are reproved for errors which they spread abroad. To unmask their hypocrisy, is according to them, to violate the law of charity; to attack their doctrines, is to contradict Scripture, and to destroy tradition, Vain clamours! Pharasaical offence, which ought not to slacken the zeal of those whose duty it is to guide others, and to guard the faith committed to their charge. 2. Vain offence, which ought not to be feared. *But He answered and said, Every plant, which My Heavenly Father hath not planted, shall be rooted up.* However enraged the enemies of the faith may be, and to whatever excess of vengeance they may be capable of going, we must not fear them. They may calumniate us, persecute us, tear us in pieces, or even take

away our lives. They have put to death the Son of God, His apostles, and their successors; but the Church of the Son of God, established by His apostles, continued on by their successors, is this plant which our Heavenly Father had planted Himself, and which will last as long as the world shall continue. As for those plants which God has not planted, they will be rooted up, and will disappear from the earth, or will grow only outside the field of the Lord. Where are now the scribes and Pharisees with all their traditions? where are now so many heretical sects which have prevailed formerly, and have troubled the Church? They exist no longer, and those who trouble it now, or who will perhaps trouble one day this holy Church, will share the same fate. 3. A blind offence, which we must abandon to its own sinful blindness. *Let them alone: they be blind leaders of the blind. And if the blind lead the blind, both shall fall into the ditch.* There are those who wilfully blind themselves to the truth, and who are followed by others who wilfully shut their eyes to the character of those they follow. What is then to be done in such a case? After having patiently reasoned with them, answered their objections, spoken, exhorted, and used all the means in our power, there remains nothing more to be done than to submit to the dealings of God's Providence, who permits the offence, and to leave these blind leaders with their followers to perish, if they will.

2. Instruction of Jesus Christ as to the meaning of these parables. His disciples asked Him the meaning of this parable. *Then answered Peter and said unto Him, Declare unto us this parable. And Jesus said, Are ye also yet without understanding?* Alas! does not this reproach apply to ourselves also? Since we have been in the school of Christ, have we not continued in ignorance and without understanding? We have a speculative understanding of the signification of the words; but we have not a practical knowledge of the sense which they contain. What we know of them is superficial, does not penetrate to our heart, nor banish from our mind the

false maxims of the world, and the delusions of self love. Let us ackowledge at least our ignorance, and ask with Saint Peter for the enlightenment which we need.

3. Instruction of Christ respecting that which defiles a man. *Do ye not perceive, that whatsoever thing from without entereth into the man, it cannot defile him; because it entereth not into his heart, but into his belly, and goeth out into the draught, purging all meats? And He said, That which cometh out of the man, that defileth the man. For from within, out of the heart of man, proceed evil thoughts, adulteries, fornications, murders, thefts, covetousness, wickedness, deceit, lasciviousness, an evil eye, blasphemy, pride, foolishness, all these evil things come from within, and defile the man; but to eat with unwashen hands defileth not a man.* We can easily understand that the food which a man takes does not defile him, and does not enter into the substance of his soul; but it is of extreme importance for us to consider the details into which our Lord enters respecting all which defiles a man, and renders him impure in the eyes of God. *Evil thoughts:* they defile a man, if they are not disowned as soon as they are conceived, rejected with horror and driven away by prayer and contrary thoughts. *Evil eye,* the evil looks of anger and indignation, of envy and jealousy, of disdain and contempt, of curiosity and dissipation, of sensuality and impurity. *Blasphemy,* words which are offensive to God, and hurtful to our neighbour. *Pride* and its consequences, presumption, vanity, disobedience, and independence. *Foolishness,* that is to say, impiety, idolatry, incredulity, heresy and all the other disorders of the human mind. Such are some examples of that which cometh forth from the heart of man, and of that which defiles it.

Prayer. O my God! What is the heart of man, and what is mine in particular? By how many acts of impurity is it not defiled in Thine eyes! Who could wash it from so many sins, but Thine adorable Blood Which was shed for me? Who could purify it, but the fire of Thy Holy Spirit, and of Thy Divine love? O Heart of

Jesus! purify my heart. O Heavenly Father! turn away Thine eyes from my heart, that Thou mayest see in me only the Heart of Jesus, Thy well-beloved Son, to Whom I unite myself, and to Whom I cling that I may never be separated from Him any more. Amen.

Meditation CXXIX.

OF THE FAITH OF THE WOMAN OF CANAAN.

Admire, 1. her fervour; 2. her constancy; 3. her reward. S. Matt. xv. 21—28. S. Mark. vii. 24—30.

FIRST POINT.

The fervour of her faith.

1. A generous faith which adores the true God in the midst of a Gentile people. *And from thence Jesus arose and went into the borders of Tyre and Sidon, and entered into an house, and would have no man know it: but He could not be hid. For a certain woman of Canaan, whose young daughter had an unclean spirit, heard of Him, and came and fell at His feet: and she besought Him that He would cast forth the devil out of her daughter. The woman was a Greek and Syrophenician by nation.* Jesus had only a year more to remain on the earth. He willed, before going up to consummate His sacrifice at Jerusalem, to go through several parts where he had not yet shewn Himself. We suppose that it was from Nain that Jesus set out, and that, going northwards, He came into the tribes of Asshur, as far as to the confines of Phenicia. Tyre and Sidon were the two principal cities of that province, and their inhabitants who were Gentiles and idolaters, were called sometimes Canaanites, because they were descended from the Canaanitish nations, and sometimes Phenicians and Syrophenicians, because Phenicia which they inhabited,

was a province of the ancient kingdom of Syria. The woman in question here was of that country, and consequently a Canaanite, originally from Phenicia, or Syra Phenicia, and descended from heathen and idolatrous parents. It is to be presumed that this woman worshipped the true God, that she had renounced the worship of idols, and that she was awaiting the Saviour promised to Israel. How estimable is such a faith in the midst of Gentile belief, and of idolatry! How heroic it is! how precious in the eyes of the Lord. It is thus O my God, that Thou dost know how to preserve to Thyself everywhere faithful souls. In the midst of the greatest corruption of the world, in the midst of the licence of the army, Thou hast upright and sincere hearts, whom the contagion of bad example has not infected, and who serve Thee with fervour. What glory and what happiness for them! But what disgrace to me, if in the midst of Christianity, of holiness, and of fervour, I live as a heathen, or serve Thee with cowardliness.

2. A solid faith which bears up under afflictions. This woman had a daughter, the object of her tenderness, who was possessed by a devil. What an ever renewed sorrow, and as terrible as it was sad, must it have been to this tender mother to witness thus her daughter cruelly tormented by this impure spirit? Alas! this afflicted mother knew that the Son of David was in Galilee, that He was healing the sick there and driving out devils; she would have desired to have been able to convey her daughter thither, or to go there herself in order to solicit her cure; but the distance did not allow of her bringing her sick daughter there, and the disease was too severe for her to be able to leave her for so great a length of time. To what a dreadful extremity was she not then reduced! But how deep are Thy ways; and how worthy of adoration, O my God! Who would ever have thought that an affliction so cruel and so humiliating, that a condition so distressing and one apparently so hopeless should become the source of happiness to her, that it should render her one of the most celebrated women in

the world, whose happiness the Church would not cease to celebrate until the end of time?

3. An attentive faith which recognizes Jesus Christ even when He wills to be hidden. The Saviour did not wish that His arrival should be made known abroad, nor that any one should know that He was in this place inhabited by Gentiles, because He did not yet manifest Himself to them, nor communicate to strangers the cures which His mercy had poured out as yet only on the children of Israel. But if the commands which He had received of His Father did not allow of His going forth to seek the Gentiles, His mercy did not suffer Him either to reject them. Hastening as He did after those who fled from Him, how should He flee from those who came to Him? O Jesus! it was not Thy will that every one should be in ignorance of Thine advent; Thou didst know that there was one faithful soul there, who had need of Thy succour, who would discover Thee. Perhaps, alas! Thou didst come there only for her sake, and did order Thy steps only in her behalf. Thus dost Thou often hide Thyself from lukewarm, cowardly and indifferent souls; but dost prevent attentive and fervent souls, in order that their faith may discover Thee, and lead them to Thee. O Jesus! Thou art still a hidden God in the Sacrament of Thy Body and Blood; but the faith which discovers Thee there acknowledges Thee there, and falling low at Thy Feet, embraces them, and obtains from Thee its desires.

4. An active faith which finds Jesus even when He does but pass by. With what eagerness did not this woman hasten to find Jesus, as soon as she heard of His arrival! Alas! how different is our faith! How languishing it is! We grudge the trouble it takes us to leave our houses, and to betake ourselves to the House of God, and often we will not give ourselves that trouble. The opportunities of salvation offer themselves to us, we feel the need we have of them, and we let them escape: we wait for more favourable circumstances, and whilst we delay, the moments of grace vanish, the times

when our Saviour visits us pass by, our plans of conversion come to nought, our healing is not effected, and we remain to the day of our death, the slaves of the evil one, to be hereafter eternally his victims in hell.

SECOND POINT.

The constancy of her faith.

Never did any one find in their dealings with Jesus so much severity, nor so many obstacles to be surmounted as this Canaanitish woman.

1. First obstacle, the difficulty of approaching Jesus; she overcame that difficulty by her cries. *And cried unto Him, saying, Have mercy on me, O Lord, Thou Son of David; my daughter is grievously vexed with a devil.* A most touching prayer, which we ought ourselves often to repeat, Have mercy on me, O Lord, Thou Son of David; my soul is grievously vexed.

2. Second obstacle, the severity of the silence of Jesus; she overcame that by her perseverance. *But He answered her not a word. And His disciples came and besought Him, saying, Send her away: for she crieth after us.* Jesus appears insensible to so touching a prayer, He does not turn even His eyes towards her who thus invokes Him with her cries, He opposes to her fervour an apparent indifference, more discouraging even than a positive refusal. Nevertheless this afflicted mother does not let herself be discouraged, she continues to cry out, and to repeat without ceasing, *O Lord, Thou Son of David, have mercy on* my daughter and on *me.* The apostles, wearied out at this woman's cries, or touched by her constancy or her misfortunes, take her part, and approaching to Jesus, pray Him to yield to her importunity, to grant her petitions, or to listen at least to her request, for she ceaseth not, they say, to cry after us. In truth, these cries, on the one hand, betokened the greatness of her suffering, the liveliness of her faith, and signalised her constancy, and on the other hand, they might perhaps discover the arrival of the

Saviour in that spot where He wished to pass through unknown; it was therefore needful to put a stop to the cries of this woman, which could only be done by granting her petition.

3. Third obstacle taken from the mission of Jesus; she overcomes it by fresh entreaties. *But He answered and said, I am not sent but unto the lost sheep of the house of Israel.* When the Canaanitish woman saw that the apostles took up her cause, what hopes must not have filled her breast! With what attention did she not await the reply of the Saviour! But what must have been her surprise and her grief, when she heard Him utter these crushing words, *I am not sent but unto the lost sheep of the house of Israel.* Unfortunate mother, have you rightly heard the words of Jesus Christ? It is no longer by His silence that He expresses Himself; His Words are clear and precise; what hope can remain to you? Withdraw, go and weep over your lot and that of your daughter, there remains to you no other comfort than your tears and your despair. Ah! we should not have required as much to induce us to adopt such a fatal course! but the Canaanitish woman does not act thus. The earnestness of her desires and of her faith is only enkindled by obstacles, she sets aside all that hinders her from penetrating to Jesus, she throws herself at His Feet, and she will not leave Them till she has obtained the fruits of her petition. She renews her prayer with greater earnestness than before, and says to Him; Lord, Thou knowest my sorrow, Thou seest my trust; *Lord, help me.* Ah! if we did but know how to pray after this manner, with a like faith, a like fervour, a like trust, and a like perseverance, should we not obtain all that we desire?

4. Fourth obstacle, the harsh and discouraging words which Jesus spoke to her. She overcomes them by her humility. *Jesus said unto her, Let the children first be filled; for it is not meet to take the children's bread, and to cast it unto the dogs.* What an answer from the lips of the best of Masters, of the tenderest of Fa-

thers? Nevertheless our Lord, in uttering it, suffered her to remain at His Feet; this was an inestimable favour, which she regarded as the assured pledge of the miracle which she solicited. The expressions which Jesus Christ made use of, did not offend her; true humility takes offence at nothing; she did not find them too severe, she acknowledges that they are befitting to her, and she finds in them a ground for the granting of her request. In the ways of God, there is nothing so blind as pride; nothing so clear-sighted as humility. Perhaps even she understood from that moment that our Lord was expressly providing her with an opening, by these very expressions so hard in appearance, and was Himself suggesting to her a sure means whereby to disarm Him. And in truth, the grace of this Saviour God, by pouring unction into the heart which He seemed to will to wound, was furnishing her with a favourable opportunity. *She answered and said unto Him, Yea, Lord;* it is not meet to take the children's bread, and to cast it unto the dogs; *Yet the dogs eat of the crumbs which fall from their masters' table;* no one grudges them *the children's crumbs.* Now such is my condition, such is my position, such is the entire object of my request, pour down with abundance Thy fulness on the descendants of Abraham, as for me, I do not aspire save to the least of the blessings which Thou dost lavish on them. How pleasing was such an answer to the Heart of Jesus! Ah! if we did but know this divine Heart well, how we should love It, what trust should we not have in It? It belongs to humility to make it known to us. I will prostrate myself at the Feet of my Saviour in His holy House, and there I will ask Him for the salvation of my soul. If He does not hearken to me, I will raise my voice yet louder; if He rejects me I will persevere; if He reproaches me with my sins and my acts of perfidy, I will acknowledge them; if He says that Paradise is not for a sinner like me, I will answer, It is just, O Lord; but Thou didst come to call sinners, Thou didst come to heal the sick, to deliver those who were possessed of devils, to sanctify and save those who believe in Thee, who acknowledge the need which they have of Thee, who put their trust in Thee, who implore Thy succour and hope for it. Such is my condition, such is my position, and the sole object of my desires. Lavish Thy favours on those faithful souls who merit them; I do not lay claim to such benefits, but when Thou hast filled the children of the House, will there not remain some crumbs which Thou wilt deign to bestow upon me?

THIRD POINT.

The reward of her faith.

1. Jesus praises it. *Then Jesus answered and said unto her, O woman, great is thy faith:* Oh divine Saviour! how great must the satisfaction have been to Thy divine Heart to be able to praise the faith of this woman, which Thou hadst put Thyself to such severe trials! Oh woman! how great is Thy happiness, to hear Thy faith praised by Him Who had thus put it to the proof, and Who knows the depths of all hearts! Thou hadst rightly judged Him, when thou didst not suffer thyself to be discouraged by any thing, and when thou didst not fear to be either importunate or indiscreet. Alas! it is not thus with me: I am discouraged by every thing, I yield to the least importunity, I shrink back at the least dryness which I experience; thus, instead of the praise which thou didst draw down on thyself, I deserve only reproaches for my want of faith. Alas! how timid, feeble, and languishing my faith is!

2. Jesus bestows on her the favour she demands. *Be it unto thee even as thou wilt. And her daughter was made whole from that very hour.* She desired the deliverance of her daughter, and, at that very moment, her daughter was delivered from the evil one by whom she was tormented. Our desires are generally the measure of the graces which the Lord bestows on us for the salvation of our souls; we ask for victory over our passions, and the acquirement of graces, but we desire neither the

one nor the other, and it is done unto us even as we will. The first condition of a holy prayer, and that which most often is wanting to it, is that we should desire to obtain that which we pray for.

3. Jesus assures her of the deliverance of her daughter. *For this saying go thy way;* because you have prayed with humility, and persevered with constancy, your prayers are heard, *the devil is gone out of your daughter.* Could the devil, that spirit of pride, hold out against so humble an answer? It is humility which begins, which sustains, and which crowns prayer; without it, we begin ill, we do not persevere, and we obtain nothing.

4. Jesus dismisses her, and she returns home, where she finds her daughter delivered from the evil spirit. *Go thy way: and when she was come to her house, she found the devil gone out, and her daughter laid upon the bed.* Impatience or weariness often cause us to leave off our prayers abruptly, without our being, so to say, dismissed from them, by the call of duty, or of charity towards our neighbour: and we find no benefit from our prayers, we find no change, no healing effected in ourselves, and the evil spirit reigns there still. The woman of Canaan, on returning to her house, finds her daughter quietly laid on her bed, and enjoying the greatest calm. Such is the happy condition of a soul delivered from the evil spirit by a sincere conversion and confession. What was the joy of the mother and of the daughter! With what feelings of gratitude did the mother relate, and the daughter hearken to all that had taken place in her behalf! What thanksgivings! what renewed fervour! what transports of joy! Would they ever forget so signal a favour? And we, ungrateful that we are, so often delivered from sin and Satan, nothing moves us, nothing excites our gratitude and our fervour, nothing can rouse us out of our forgetfulness of God, and of the languor with which we serve Him.

Prayer. O Jesus! grant that my gratitude may be greater, my faith more lively, my desires more holy, more ardent, more constant, so that I may receive from Thee the precious benefits of Thy mercy in time and in eternity. Amen.

Meditation CXXX.

JESUS HEALS A DEAF AND DUMB MAN, AND SEVERAL OTHER SICK AND INFIRM PERSONS.

Consider, 1. the healing of the deaf and dumb man; 2. the healing of several other sick and infirm persons; 3. the applause given to Jesus. S. Matt. xv. 29—31. S. Mark vii. 31—37.

FIRST POINT.

The healing of a deaf and dumb man.

1. What was the infirmity of this man? *And again, departing from the coasts of Tyre and Sidon, Jesus came unto the sea of Galilee, through the midst of the coasts of Decapolis. And they bring unto Him one that was deaf, and had an impediment in his speech.* Consider in this man three infirmities, and in his infirmities, let us consider our own. 1. He was deaf. And we, are we not also deaf to all that regards our salvation, deaf to the law of God, and to the precepts of the Gospel, deaf to the voice of conscience, and to Divine inspirations, deaf to warnings and remonstrances, to the reproaches of men, and the threatenings of God? Alas! have we not often our ears open to vice and to error? do we not listen with pleasure to that which offends against modesty, sins against the law of charity, attacks religion, or flatters our self-love and our vanity? 2. He was dumb. And we, what use do we make of our words? Are we not dumb when it is a question of disclosing our faults, and confessing them; dumb, when we should sing praises to God, speak of Him, pray to Him, bless Him, offer Him thanks; dumb in supporting the interests of virtue, piety, faith, charity, religion, when they are attacked in our presence: in one word, are we not dumb

whenever we ought to speak, and do we not abound in words on all occasions on which we should be dumb? 3. And we may well suppose, that this man felt most keenly the weariness which his condition caused him, and that his family experienced likewise a bitter sorrow at it. As for us, we cannot deny the weariness which the state of lukewarmness in which we live causes to ourselves; but if we did but know the harm which we do to others, whom we might serve and edify, if we did but know the grief which we cause to all those who take an interest in our welfare, we should throw ourselves at the feet of Jesus, and pray Him to have compassion on us.

2. What did Jesus do in order to heal this man? *And they beseech Him to put His Hand upon him.* This laying on of hands would doubtless have sufficed for the healing of this afflicted man, but not for the instruction which our Saviour wished to take this opportunity of giving. *And He took Him aside from the multitude, and put His fingers into his ears, and He spit, and touched his tongue; and looking up to Heaven, He sighed and saith unto him, Ephphatha, that is, Be opened.* Nothing that our Lord did was without reason; and He probably acted thus; 1. for the instruction of the spectators. The Jews had perhaps become too familiar with the miracles which they saw Him do; they only beheld in Him His Humanity, and they did not raise their thoughts to His Divinity. Jesus was willing perhaps to temper the splendour of His Power, and to make the by-standers understand that He derived it from God His Father, and that it cost Him groans and sighs, without any thought of that which it was soon about to cost Him. Do we not let ourselves treat the Holy Sacrament of the Altar, and the holy mysteries of our religion with too much familiarity? Do we not too easily forget what they have cost Jesus Christ, and that they are the price of all His Blood? 2. For the instruction of His Church. Jesus willed to teach her that all that came from Him was of a virtue effica-

cious for the salvation of our souls; He willed that one day she should imitate Him, and that, in the administration of holy things, she should make use of ceremonies fitting to instruct her people, to signify the effects of the grace conveyed, and that, in these august ceremonies, the acts of her ministers should be regarded as their own. What respect do we pay to the ceremonies of our Church, and in what spirit do we join in them?

3. For our own instruction, and in order to make us understand that he who is deaf and dumb to the things of salvation, is more difficult to heal than we should imagine, that it is needful that he should go away from the multitude, and that he should seek for retirement, and should commune deeply with himself; that he must close his ears to the suggestions of the flesh, the world, and the devil, in order to fill them with Jesus Christ, His doctrines, His precepts, and the truths of salvation; that he must change his tastes, that he must no longer seek after the things of this world, but only after those of God: that he must raise his eyes towards Heaven, whence he must look for help, that he must weep, sigh, and groan with Christ, if he desire to have his prayers granted; and lastly, that Jesus Christ must speak, command, and apply to him the virtue of His merits.

3. What were the proofs of the healing of this man? *And straightway his ears were opened, and the string of his tongue was loosed, and he spake plain.* We see this man come back; he hears, he answers, and speaks with perfect facility; he was perfectly healed. People see us returning from the House of God, from the Altar, from Confession, or from a retreat, or a mission: but what change has taken place in us? Are we healed, or are we not the same? It is only by our words, by our discourses, that others can judge of us. If our conversation is not better than before, then we hear no better: if we still speak only the language of frivolity and trifling, of criticism and slander, of ill-temper and anger, of the world and our own evil passions, and never speak that of piety, of virtue, and of edification, we are not healed,

we are dumb and deaf, as infirm as we were before, and the want of effect of the remedy which we have taken gives room to fear that our malady is incurable, and that we shall never be healed of it.

SECOND POINT.

The healing of several other sick and infirm persons.

Jesus, after the healing of the deaf and dumb man, rejoins the people. *And He went up into a mountain, and sat down there; and great multitudes came unto Him, having with them those that were lame, blind, dumb, maimed, and many others, and cast them down at Jesus' feet: and He healed them.* Three objects call forth our admiration here.

1. Jesus seated on the the ground on this mountain, as it were, on the throne of His mercy, full of gentleness and sweetness, full of power and goodness. There, He invites all men to come to Him; He permits them to draw near to Him, He offers them a remedy for all their ills. Such He is still in our midst on His Altar: let us profit by His Presence there, and let us hasten to Him with fervour and with confidence. A day will come when He will show Himself on the throne of His justice, seated on the clouds of Heaven, full of Majesty and Glory, and then He will punish the wicked who have refused to acknowledge Him or abused His favours: let us prepare ourselves for that great Day, by making a holy use of those which yet remain to us to spend on earth.

2. Let us admire this multitude of sick and infirm persons who surround Him. Oh such attendants are worthy of the Saviour of men! The kings of the earth could not countenance such a retinue; they would feel themselves dishonoured by it, because they would shew forth their weakness and powerlessness to help: there is none but Jesus alone, Who could be honoured by it, because there is none but He, Whose glory it would cause to shine forth. Let these sick and infirm Whom this Blessed Saviour healed in such multitudes increase our

confidence, and urge us to have recourse to Him, in order that He may work upon us the miracles which He has wrought on so many sinners.

3. Let us admire this same multitude of sick and infirm perfectly healed. *Insomuch that the multitude wondered, when they saw the dumb to speak, the maimed to be whole, the lame to walk, and the blind to see.* What a spectacle it was in truth! Never has earth beheld one so magnificent. All these blind see, these lame walk, these dumb speak, these sick persons are in full health, and experience no weakness, nor any languour. O King of glory! O Saviour of men! who would not admire the greatness of Thy charity and of Thy power? Shew forth to Thy Church the like cures, or rather those that are yet more touching, by the healing of souls, and the conversion of sinners. Grant me grace myself to set forth Thy goodness by my conversion, and may it edify others as much, as my sins have been to them a cause of offence.

THIRD POINT.

Applause given to Jesus.

1. Applause which was refused. *And He charged them that they should tell no man: but the more He charged them, so much the more a great deal they published it.* Jesus refuses the applause which is offered to Him, and we seek for it. The refusal which Jesus makes, only increases this applause, and becomes a new subject for admiration and praise; the desire for praise which we shew diminishes that which we receive, is often the reason why it is denied to us, turns to our own confusion, discovers our vanity, and suffices even in the eyes of men, to efface the merit of our best actions. The refusal of Jesus was sincere, and our refusals are often only artifice and hypocrisy.

2. Applause which was deserved. *And the more He charged them,* so much the greater did their admiration

become. *And were beyond measure astonished, saying, He hath done all things well; He maketh both the deaf to hear, and the dumb to speak.* It is only in doing good that we can justly merit applause and praise. God will only reward good works at the last day. We do not merit them then by beauty, nobility of birth, and wealth, we do not merit them by knowledge, intellect, or talents. We merit them still less by doing evil, by slandering our neighbours, by mortifying them, by decrying them by some wittiness, or some well-written work, by answering with scorn, or shewing ourselves hardier than others in committing sin, or transgressing God's commands. What untruth, what treachery, and flattery, what injustice and folly are there in the applause which we give to one another, and in that which we receive!

3. Applause glorious to God. The people, in admiring and publishing abroad the wonders which Jesus wrought, *glorified the God of Israel.* The praise which is bestowed upon good actions is an act agreeable to God, when he that bestows it and he that receives it, refer it entirely to His glory. But alas! too often the fault of him that praises, is, that he stops short at the creature without raising his thoughts to the Creator, admiring the gifts of God without thinking of Him Who is their Author; and the fault of him who is praised, is, that he finds satisfaction in himself, as if that which was praised belonged to him, by which he usurps the glory of God, or at least appropriates a part of it, instead of referring the whole to the Lord. Ah! let us only have God in view, let us praise Him in everything, let us glorify Him in everything, let us thank Him in everything, and acknowledge that to Him alone belong all honour and glory,

Prayer. Grant, O Lord, that I may not be dumb when I ought to pray to Thee, to thank Thee, to praise Thee, to confess in Thy Presence my miseries and my sins, to edify my brethren, to reprove them with gentleness, and to console them with kindness. O Jesus!

say with power to all the powers of my soul, *Be opened;* so that being opened only to Thee, they may be filled by Thee, and remain for ever closed to all that is earthly. Amen.

Meditation CXXXI.

SECOND MULTIPLYING OF THE LOAVES OF BREAD.

OF TRUST IN GOD.

The knowledge, the goodness, and the power of God; these are the foundations of our trust in Him. S. Matt. xv. 32—39. S. Mark viii. 1—9.

FIRST POINT.

Of the knowledge of God, the first foundation of our trust in Him.

In those days the multitude being very great, and having nothing to eat, Jesus called his disciples unto Him, and saith unto them, I have compassion on the multitude, because they have now been with Me three days, and have nothing to eat: and I will not send them away fasting . . . . . And if I send them away fasting to their own houses, they will faint by the way; for divers of them came from far. During the three days since our Lord had returned from the borders of Tyre and Sidon, and whilst He had remained in the neighbourhood of the lake of Gennesaret, the multitude who had gone thither to seek for Him, had never left Him. It was doubtless towards the end of the third day that Jesus gathered around Him His disciples, and set before them the condition in which this multitude were, a condition which He knew perfectly. The past, the present, and the future, nothing could escape His Divine knowledge.

1. The past. Jesus recalls to His disciples that it is

already *three days* that this multitude have been following Him; He knows how long it is that we have served Him, and even the moments are counted. This Divine Saviour added: and *divers of them came from far.* Not only does He count the time, but He knows besides the value of our services; He knows all that it has cost us to come to Him, the temptations which we have withstood, the obstacles we have surmounted, the sacrifices we have made for Him. Not a single step has been taken by us for His sake, that He has not witnessed, and which He does not keep in remembrance. Ah! how sweet it is to serve such a Master, and what a very different master the world is! Nevertheless we put our trust in the world, and we place only a timid confidence in the Lord our God.

2. The present. Jesus tells His disciples that this multitude are in extreme need, and that there is nothing for them to eat. In whatever situation we may find ourselves, God sees us and knows our sorrows; He knows our misery and our indigence, our losses and our misfortunes; our afflictions and our sufferings, our sicknesses and our grief, our temptations and our weakness, our temporal and spiritual wants. Men do not know them, they cannot see all their extent, and often even they do not choose to believe them. Why then should we always place our trust in men, and not in God Alone, since He Alone knows all the bitterness of our condition; why should we not seek for consolation from Him? why not seek our consolation even in our trust, and in the thought that God knows all and sees all?

3. The future. Jesus points out to His Apostles the danger that there would be in sending away this multitude without having given them something to eat. It is usually the future which causes us the greatest disquietude, it is the future that the devil makes use of the oftenest in order to trouble us and discourage us; but why do we disquiet ourselves about a future respecting which we are ignorant? God Alone knows it, let us

SECOND MULTIPLYING OF THE LOAVES OF BREAD. 347

leave to Him the care of it. Not only does He behold the future, but He beholds it as regards ourselves: He sees that which may happen to us either of joy or sorrow: and He knows how to keep far from us that which might be hurtful to us, and to procure for us that which may be advantageous to us. Let us then place all our trust in Him: by so doing, we shall honour Him, and find peace of mind in ourselves. Trust in God is the most glorious worship that we could render to Him, and that of which He is the most jealous, and it is the source of the truest and most solid happiness to ourselves, by the peace which it procures for us, and the blessing it draws down upon us.

SECOND POINT.

Of the goodness of God; second foundation of our trust in Him.

1. A compassionate goodness, which is touched by our needs. Men often see our wants, and are insensible to them: it is not thus with the Heart of God. Jesus, having called His disciples around Him, said unto them, *I have compassion on this multitude.* Their condition touches Me with compassion. Oh loving Saviour, Whose heart is sensible to all the miseries of mankind! Wilt Thou see mine without being touched by them?

2. A judicious goodness, which discerns our needs. What is it that touches the heart of Jesus, and draws down His compassion? It is the necessities of mankind, and not their cupidity, avarice, or ambition. In vain do we implore His help in order to satisfy our love of luxury, our sensuality, our projects of fortune and elevation: such a disposition of heart would serve rather to kindle His Anger towards us, than to excite His Compassion. But when we are really, according to our station in life, in need and in distress, do not let us doubt that He is aware of it. What is it that touches the heart of Jesus? Need suffered for love of Him, because we have willed to remain with Him, and to be faithful in

keeping His holy laws; for if, in order to avoid falling into want, we break His laws, if we are so eager in the pursuit of self-interests, that we employ on them the time that should be spent in prayer, in good works, or in the worship of God: if we permit ourselves sordid and unlawful gains, and if we make use of theft, fraud, and similar artifices: if we will not yield to the guidance of God, preferring our own will to that of those whom He has placed over us, from that time we are no longer with Him; and, if we suffer, we do not suffer any longer for Him. If the distress in which we find ourselves proceeds from our own negligence and idleness, from waste or extravagance, from self-indulgence in habits of luxury, then we have only ourselves to blame for it, and we cannot hope to draw down upon us the compassion of our God, save by returning to Him by a sincere penitence. Lastly, what is it that touches the heart of Jesus? Want borne with constancy and perseverance; for if we disquiet ourselves on account of difficulties which have not yet come to us, if we murmur from the first moment that troubles befall us, we are not worthy of the mercy of our God. It is an enduring constancy and perseverance which touch His Heart, and draw down the tenderness of His commiseration upon us.

3. An efficacious goodness, which wills to succour us in our needs. Jesus, having represented to His Apostles that the multitude who followed Him had nothing to eat, after having said to them that He was touched by it, added *I will not send them away fasting, lest they faint in the way.* Hearken to this word, all ye who follow Jesus, and who are faithfully attached to Him. Yea, in His service you will have to suffer; He will try your fervour and your constancy up to a certain point; but He knows how far your strength will hold out, and He will not suffer that you should be tempted above your powers of endurance. Every thing seems to fail you, your condition appears desperate to you: friends, relations, all seem to have forsaken you; your God will never forsake you, and He wills that you should find

succour. But whence will this succour come? Such is the reply which the apostles made to Jesus. In the desert in which we are, whence shall we find bread to feed so great a multitude? Whence the succour will come to you, you do not know, you cannot foresee; but does it not suffice to you that you know that God wills that it should come to you, that God does not will that you should be abandoned in your distress? Rest then quietly in the Bosom of His infinite Goodness, persevere in the feelings of an entire trust in Him, and you will not be deceived.

THIRD POINT.

Of the power of God. Third foundation of our trust in Him.

And His disciples answered Him, From whence can a man satisfy these men with bread here in the wilderness? And He asked them, How many loaves have ye? And they said, Seven. And He commanded the people to sit down on the ground: and He took the seven loaves, and gave thanks, and brake, and gave to His disciples to set before them; and they did set them before the people. And they had a few small fishes; and He blessed and commanded to set them also before them. So they did eat, and were filled; and they took up of the broken meat that was left seven baskets. And they that did eat were four thousand men, besides women and children: and He sent them away. What a miracle! what liberality! what abundance! But this prodigy of power, God renews it still daily in three manners.

1. In the general order of nature. Every year, the earth is covered with new productions in order to furnish all our needs: the plants are renewed, the animals are multiplied, the fields bear increase. A prodigy so much the more worthy of admiration as it is the more constant; a prodigy which ought to penetrate us with the highest idea of the Power of God, and fill us with the tenderest

gratitude. But ungrateful and unthankful as we are, we only regard in this prodigy our own interest, and laden with the blessings of the Lord, we forget the powerful Hand which lavishes them upon us. While we are awaiting this yearly renewed blessing, we are disquieted, mistrustful, and murmuring: when we are in the enjoyment of it, we are ungrateful towards God, hard towards the poor, unjust towards those who have a claim on any portion of the blessing which we gather up. Do we think then by this means to draw down the blessings of God on our labours and our harvests? Have we not, on the contrary, reason to fear lest our cupidity and our ingratitude draw down upon us His curse?

2. The prodigy of power is renewed daily in the particular order of Providence. God hath secret resources on behalf of those who trust in Him; He does not always employ miracles in order to succour us, or rather the miracles which He employs are not always such as dazzle our eyes by their splendour; they are the miracles of a watchful Providence, and so much the more worthy of admiration as they are the more concealed. We find still upright and charitable persons, who give to the poor, comfort the unhappy, lend a helping hand to all good works, and yet who nevertheless do not come into need themselves. The more they give, the more they have, without knowing how, or whence it comes: every thing prospers, and their worldly possessions seem to multiply under their hands. What they give is like a seed which produces hundredfold: it is the effect of the trust which they have in Him Who is all Powerful, and Whose Providence governs all things, provides for all.

3. This prodigy of power is renewed daily in the order of grace. The miracle of the multiplication of the loaves was the figure of the Bread of the Eucharist. With what profusion has not the Lord provided for the nourishment of our souls? Not only does He give us His grace, but He gives us Himself, the Author of all grace. If we are weak and languishing, it is our own fault. Is the Heavenly Bread wanting to us, and is this Bread

Which giveth strength, wanting in strength? It is we who are wanting to Him, who are wanting to ourselves, whom we suffer to die of hunger in the midst of abundance, either because we refuse to eat this Bread which is offered to us, or because we do not eat It with the needful dispositions of mind.

Prayer. O my God, Thou seest all my temporal and spiritual needs, Thy goodness is touched by them, and wills to relieve them: Thy power is infinite, and nothing can resist Thee. In whom shall I hope then, if not in Thee? Ah! Lord, the more pressing my necessities are, the more languishing my soul is, the more will I place my trust in Thee. Amen.

Meditation CXXXII.

THE PHARISEES ASK FOR A SIGN.

Jesus, having *sent away the multitude, entered into a ship with His disciples, and came* towards the north of the lake, *into the coasts of Magdala and Dalmanutha,* two neighbouring cities, situated on the same lake. Hardly had He arrived on the shore, than the Pharisees come to seek for Him. Consider, 1. the conduct of these Pharisees with regard to Jesus; 2. that of Jesus with regard to them. S. Matt. xvi. 1—4. S. Mark viii. 10—13.

FIRST POINT.

Conduct of the Pharisees with regard to Jesus.

1. Their determination in pursuing Him. As soon as Jesus had arrived in the country of Magdala, *the Pharisees came forth, and began to question with Him.* Wherefore this eagerness of the Pharisees in betaking themselves whithersoever Jesus goes, if it be not for the purpose of contradicting Him, and seeking to take Him in His Words? They did not fear for that purpose to associate themselves with *the Sadducees,* they agree on this point with those who hold opinions the most opposed

to theirs, and whom they detest the most heartily. In this union of the hypocrite with the impious man in order to fight against Jesus Christ, is it not easy to recognise the conduct of the libertines and unbelievers of all ages, how they make common cause, and cabal together to fight with relentless pursuit against the Church of Jesus Christ and her teaching, against humility, virtue and piety. Thus does it often happen that a common passion will join together, against a good man, wicked persons, however divided they may be amongst themselves, and that, in order to ruin a rival, a person will beg for the assistance of a wicked person whom he detests in his heart.

2. The folly of their demand. And *tempting, desired Him that He would shew them a sign from Heaven.* To what end do they desire a sign from Heaven? What use, what wisdom, what virtue would there be in this sign? Ah! how far above man's wisdom is the wisdom of God! how far above the means which our presumption dares to suggest to Him, or to demand of Him, are the means which He employs? *A wicked and adulterous generation,* says Jesus Christ, *seeketh after a sign; and there shall no sign be given unto it, but the sign of the prophet Jonas.* The sign placed in the person of Jonas, Jesus dead and risen again, such is the sign given by the wisdom of God, which merits all our faith, which ravishes all our love, which is the remedy for all our evils and supplies all our needs. I accept, O my Saviour, this sacred sign, this adorable sign of Thy Cross, this sign of Thy ignominy and of Thy glory, of my redemption, and of my salvation. Let this sign be imprinted on my forehead, and engraven in my heart, let it be the beginning and end of all my actions, let it be the source of all my undertakings.

3. The malignity of their intention. Wherefore do they address themselves to Jesus, dispute with Him, demand of Him a sign? *Tempting Him.* In order to oppose this sign, if He grants it: in order to decry Himself, if He refuses it. And in truth, would they not have

said, in seeing this prodigy, what they said of the other miracles of Jesus Christ, that He only wrought them in the name of the prince of the devils? This was the second time that they demanded a sign from Heaven. They knew well that it would be refused, and they had not forgotten the reply which Jesus had already made to a similar demand; but the enemies of Jesus and of His Church are never weary of repeating the same objections, the same calumnies, the same blasphemies. Woe to those who only read, who only study religion, and only speak of it, in order to take offence at it and to blind themselves! As for us, let us seek only to strengthen ourselves in the Christian faith, and we shall find wherewithal to render ourselves proof against doubt.

4. Their wilful ignorance. *He answered and said unto them, When it is evening, ye say, It will be fair weather: for the sky is red. And in the morning, It will be foul weather to-day: for the sky is red and lowering; ye can discern the face of the sky, but can ye not discern the sign of the times.* That is to say, it is very surprising that you should know how to judge of the weather which is coming by certain signs which you see in the sky, and that you should not be able to know that the time has arrived for the Messiah to make His appearance, by the certain signs which you have of it in the preaching of John Baptist, by the miracles of which I have made you the witnesses, by the details of the prophecies which are accomplished in Me, and are pointed out by the exact calculations of the times marked by the prophet Daniel. This is what the Jews and unbelievers cannot even yet perceive. Every branch of science is known, except the knowledge of Jesus Christ and His Church, the knowledge of salvation and of eternal happiness. Oh accursed and adulterous generation! have I no share in these reproaches! how many useless things do I not glory in knowing! how many needful things do I not refuse to learn!

SECOND POINT.

Conduct of Jesus with regard to the Pharisees.

1. He mourns over their condition. *And He sighed deeply in His spirit, saying, Why doth this generation seek after a sign?* The demand of the Pharisees is full of injustice and malignity. Jesus, in rejecting it, cannot restrain Himself from pitying them, and mourning over them. Such is, Oh my Saviour, the Goodness of Thy Heart ; Thou art grieved to find even in Thine enemies, obstacles to Thy benefits. How often, O Jesus! have I not given Thee reason to sigh! let me at least mourn with Thee, over myself, and over those who sin against Thee!

2. Jesus refuses them the sign which they demand. *Verily I say unto you, There shall no sign be given unto this generation.* They ask a sign from heaven; they wish to choose one at their will, and to subject Me to their caprices; but they may ask for it, and make complaints, *no sign shall be given* to them. What a difference between a nation who seek Jesus out of love and attachment, and the Pharisees who seek Him in order to tempt Him and confound Him ; thus does He grant to the needs of this nation a miracle which they do not ask for, and He refuses to the unbelief of the Pharisees the sign which they ask of Him. The unbeliever desires new proofs in order to believe ; it is a new heart which he should ask for, and his prayers would be heard. God does not change the order of His decrees according to the desires of the wicked, and according to the caprice of men: it is for us to conform ourselves to His will, and to enter into His designs, Who, if we will, will turn every thing to our gain; but do not let us expect that He should bend them at the will of our pride and of our evil passions.

3. Jesus utters severe reproaches against them. *A wicked and adulterous generation!* Happy still in his misery is he who listens to the reproaches which his conscience makes to him, and who does not seek to stifle

them. Remorse is the last resource of the sinner, and the last act of God's mercy towards him.

4. *Jesus leaves them and withdraws Himself.* *And He left them, and departed; and entering into the ship again departed to the other side.* This Divine Saviour, having done amongst these Pharisees that which His divine ministry required of Him, left them in haste. Fatal lot of a blind and hardened sinner, who, by his contempt and resistance to grace, forces Jesus Christ to abandon him.

Prayer. Where should I be, O my God, if Thou hadst abandoned me so soon as I had merited it? Ah! my Divine Redeemer, do not punish me in so terrible a manner. Remain with me, or command me to go to Thee; but do not suffer that I should ever have the misery to lose Thee. Grant that I may mourn with Thee over the hardness of my heart, that I may profit by the signs, the wonders, the glorious miracles of Thy Divinity, and that I may accomplish with fidelity all that Thou dost require of me. Amen.

Meditation CXXXIII.

JESUS PASSES FROM THE COASTS OF MAGDALA OVER TO BETHSAIDA.

Consider here, 1. the oversight of the Apostles; 2. the reproaches which Jesus makes to them; 3. the warning which He gives them. S. Matt. xvi. 5—12. S. Mark viii. 14—21.

FIRST POINT.

Oversight of the apostles.

1. *This oversight makes them afraid.* *And when His disciples were come to the other side, they had forgotten to take bread, neither had they in the ship with them more than one loaf. Then Jesus said unto them, Take heed and beware of the leaven of the Pharisees and of*

the Sadducees. And they reasoned among themselves, saying, It is because we have taken no bread. At this word of leaven, the apostles were thrown into consternation, they remembered that they had forgotten to take bread ; and without paying any attention to the instruction which Jesus was giving them, they took notice only of the reproaches which they imagined that their Divine Master implied by His Words. Do we not fall ourselves into the same fault, when instead of preparing ourselves for the Communion by fervent acts, or of enjoying the delights of the Presence of Christ after the Communion, we are only occupied with looking into ourselves, with recalling the sins which we fear to have forgotten ? We imagine that our Lord reproaches us for them ; we become troubled, and we lose by that means a part of the benefits which we might have gained.

2. This oversight throws them into perplexity. Thinking only of the word of leaven in its natural sense, they fancied that Jesus forbade them to buy bread from any one who was of the sect of the Pharisees, of the Sadducees, or Herodians, and they did not know how they would be able to make this distinction. Such are often the scruples of certain souls, who, not disclosing their sorrows, or not acquiescing in a teachable spirit to the judgment of those set over them, imagine commands to exist where none are given, and things to be sinful which are not so.

3. This oversight throws them into distrust. They feared, that restrained by the prohibition which they believed themselves to have received, they would not be able to find bread to eat, and that they would be in want. Such is the ordinary source of distractions, the necessities of this life, the cares of our business, the fear of failure. Ah ! how carnal minded we still are ! how far from being spiritually minded ! our mistrust and our fear do not procure for us the success of our worldly affairs, and they take from us the spirit of devotion with which all the rest would prosper.

SECOND POINT.

The reproach which Jesus makes to the apostles.

1. He reproaches them with their want of penetration and understanding. *Which when Jesus perceived, He saith unto them, O ye of little faith, why reason ye among yourselves, because ye have brought no bread? Perceive ye not yet, neither understand? have ye your hearts yet hardened? Having eyes, see ye not? and having ears, hear ye not?* Objects present themselves to you, and you behold them without reflecting on them. My words strike your ears, and you take them always in a carnal and material sense. You never raise your thoughts to the spiritual meaning which they contain. We understand, it is true, the metaphorical sense of the expressions of which our Lord makes use; but do we penetrate well into the meaning of this sense which we understand: do we apply it to ourselves, reflect upon it, relish it? Does not our heart remain always in the same state of blindness, although our hearts may be enlightened? Have we not eyes without being able to see and ears, without hearing?

2. Jesus reproaches them with their want of faith and trust. *O ye of little faith.* It is easy to see that all the reproaches which our Lord here makes to His Apostles fall principally on their want of faith and confidence. That is also almost always our principal fault. We constantly lose sight of the goodness and power of our Saviour and we abandon ourselves to a state of weariness, of distaste and discouragement. How displeasing to Him are such feelings, and how they wound His Love.

3. Jesus reproaches them with their want of memory, and their prompt forgetfulness of the past. *Do ye not yet understand, nor remember when I brake the five loaves among five thousand, how many baskets full of fragments took ye up? They say unto Him, Twelve. And when the seven among four thousand, how many baskets full of fragments took ye up? And they said,*

Seven. And He said unto them, How is it that ye do not understand that I spake it not to you concerning bread, that ye should beware of the leaven of the Pharisees and of the Sadducees. The remembrance of the past, if we did not lose it, or if we took care to recall it often would be to us a source of enlightenment, and a pressing motive for avoiding evil, and for practising good. If we did but bear in mind the number and grievousness of our sins, we should not find it difficult to bear anything in a spirit of penitence. If we did but remember the sorrow and remorse which sin has caused us, and all that it had cost us to get free from it, we should not be likely to fall again so easily into it. If we remembered the dangers we have run, the accidents which have befallen us, or which have frightened or startled us when they have happened to others: if we bore in mind the truths with which we have been penetrated, the peace and sweetness which we have tasted in the service of God, all the blessings which He has so liberally bestowed upon us, surely nothing would be capable again of diminishing our fervour, and the remembrance of them would suffice alone to rekindle it. The reproaches of Jesus were efficacious, because, although animated by zeal, they were just, full of charity, and instruction. If the reproaches we make to others have not the same success, it is because they are not administered in the same spirit, and do not possess the same qualities.

THIRD POINT.

Warning which Jesus gives to His Apostles.

Then understood they how He bade them not beware of the leaven of bread, but of the doctrine of the Pharisees and of the Sadducees. Let us profit also by this instruction which is intended for every one, and for all generations. Let us be attentive, let us arm ourselves, and be on our guard;

1. Against the doctrine of the Pharisees, that is to say of those hypocrites, who, in order to set themselves

off, exaggerate the teaching of the Gospel, who make an outward profession of severity, whilst they dare openly to oppose its ministers, and to decry its supporters; of those men whose piety is false, superstitious, and devoid of that spirit of charity which is the foundation of all true religion.

2. Against the doctrine of the Sadducees, that is of those impious men, who go to an excess opposed to that of the Pharisees, who do not distinguish virtue from vice, acknowledging no other substance than the body, no other life than this present life, no other happiness than sensual enjoyments, no other end than themselves.

3. Against the doctrine of the Herodians, who, differing little from the Sadducees, acknowledge no other god than fortune, no other Messiah than the sovereign, no other law than human respect, no other maxims than those of the world, no other merit than that of favour. The names of those men whom the Saviour points out here are changed, but their modes of life and thought are not. These actors have passed away: but the personages remain, and their passions, under different names, continue to play the same parts. The world is filled with persons resembling those of whom our Saviour warns us to beware. What will become of us, if we live carelessly and thoughtlessly, if we read, if we listen to every thing, and exercise no discernment, and feel no mistrust? Each of these three sects is dangerous: but all three are always ready to join together against Christ and His Church, against religion and good men.

Prayer. Inspire me, Lord, with that true and solid piety which can only come from Thee, and lead to Thee. Preserve me from the leaven of the Pharisees, the Sadducees and Herodians, by putting Thy truth into my mind, and Thy divine charity into my heart. Let Thy doctrines be in me like a sacred leaven which changes me entirely, and, raising my mind and heart above the things of earth, may render them worthy of Thy grace in time, and of Thy glory in eternity. Amen.

Meditation CXXXIV.

HEALING OF A BLIND MAN AT BETHSAIDA.

OF THE SPIRITUAL LIFE.

The healing of this blind man, and the circumstances which accompany it, furnish us with the features, characters, and conditions which 1. the purgative life, 2. the illuminative life, and 3. the unitive life, ought to have. S. Mark viii. 22—26.

FIRST POINT.

Of the purgative life.

Three things are necessary in the purgative life. 1. Prayer is necessary in order to enter upon it. *And He cometh to Bethsaida: and they bring a blind man unto Him, and besought Him to touch him.* A person is blind when he is living in sin, when he is in a state of lukewarmness or indifference, when he is leading a dissipated or worldly life: in either of these states, he does not know as he should, either God, or Christ, or the end for which he is created, or the Christian duties which he ought to perform. Jesus Christ alone can cure this blindness: but how shall the blind person go to Him? He must be led to Him, Jesus must be prayed to for him. Pray then, fathers and mothers, for your children: pray, fervent and zealous souls: speak, exhort, lead to Jesus these blind souls, and implore them to pray for themselves. Ah! how many sinners have been converted, and have become saints through the prayers of righteous souls! Others have prayed for us, let us pray for others.

2. There must be separation from the world in order to persevere in it. *And He took the blind man by the hand, and led him out of the town.* Whoever is truly touched with the desire to return to God, to purify himself from his sins, to be enlightened, and to become holy, ought to begin by going *out of the town,* that is to say,

he ought to separate himself from the world, and renounce its pleasures, its amusements, its tumult. We are out of the town and separated from the world, when, retired in our homes, occupied with the duties of our station, we only mingle in the world when charity or necessity calls us thither, remaining always with our hearts separated from it, separated from its pleasures, its pomps, its maxims, and its vices. We are out of the town and separated from the world, when, retired within our own hearts, far from the noise of worldly affairs and of our evil passions, we mourn over our past disorders, entreat God for the forgiveness of them, and prepare ourselves for the account which we must render to Him of all the actions of our life.

3. We need the Hand of the Saviour in order to advance in it. *And He took the blind man by the hand.* If Jesus Himself does not take us by the hand, and lead us, whither shall we go, and what progress can we make in holiness of life? How shall we attain to the conquest over our own unwillingness, and surmount the obstacles which the world and the devil unceasingly oppose to our welfare? What powerful graces, what singular events, what tokens of a loving Providence combine to detach a soul from the world, and to attach it only to Christ! Let us recall with gratitude and compassion all that God has done for us in this way. Happy they who let themselves thus be led! What delights do they not taste, what virtues do they not acquire, what progress do they not make in the life of the Spirit! Ah! when shall I enjoy so sweet a repose in silence and retirement from the world?

SECOND POINT.

Of the Illuminative life.

Three virtues are especially recommended in the Illuminative life. 1. The exact observance of the practices of religion. Jesus, having come forth from the town, and finding Himself alone in the country with His disciples, and the blind man whom He was leading by the hand, *spit on his eyes, and put His hands upon him.* Jesus applies His virtue to the signs which He thinks fit to establish : it is for us to reverence them, to admire His power, and to thank Him for His goodness. There are pious practises established and made use of amongst religious persons, whereby to advance in holiness, which may appear small and contemptible in the eyes of men, but let us beware of judging them according to worldly ideas; they may be more efficacious than we think for, to bring the flesh under subjection, to put a bridle on the senses, and to humble the mind. If this blind man had refused to allow our Saviour to spit on his eyes, or to lay His Hands on them, what should we think of him, save that he would have been destitute of sense, and that he would have remained for ever blind ? There are too many such senseless persons who despising the experiences of the saints, and neglecting to put their recommendations into practice, remain in blindness as a punishment of their pride.

2. Candour in rendering acconnt of one's conscience. *Jesus, having taken His hands off the blind man's eyes asked him if he saw ought ; and* the blind man *looked up, and said I see men as trees walking.* Jesus did not will to heal this blind man all at once, as He had healed so many others, in order to teach us that He is the Master of His own gifts and graces, and that He communicates them in proportion as He pleases. Perhaps also in that He conformed Himself to the weakness of the faith of the sick man, who had not himself asked to be healed ; and as we have often said, faith is the measure of the gifts of God. However that may be, our Lord willed that he should declare himself to what point he could see, in order that he might understand, on the one hand, how much he had already received, and on the other, what was still wanting to him ; in order that gratitude, animating his faith, and especially his desire, he might become capable of an entire cure. Such is the fruit we draw from the caudour with which we open our hearts

to God, and lay bare the depths of our inward soul to Him. We begin to learn truths before unknown, which we then first begin to taste. We are humbled to find that at first we see these truths only in a confused manner, in the shade, in the distance, and mingled with chimeras which our mind produces, and which our ignorance cannot disperse. Then we learn to pray to know them better, and as we follow on to know the Lord, we desire, we hope, our false ideas are enlightened, and the phantoms which have wearied our imaginations vanish.

3. Perseverance in religious exercises. After the answer of the blind man, our Lord *put His Hand again upon his eyes, and made him look up; and he was restored, and saw every man clearly.* There is this difference between the eyes of the body, and those of the soul, that the first have a sphere of natural and limited activity, beyond which they cannot act or acquire any degree of perfection, but the eyes of the soul can attain perfection to an infinite degree, and daily acquire new degrees of perfection and light. The same truths of salvation and faith are seen by a person of interior life, or by a saint, in a far more elevated and more perfect manner than they are by the ordinary class of believers. The way in which to acquire this increase of enlightenment, is to profit well by the light that a person has, to acknowledge that Christ alone is the Source, both of that which we possess, and of that which we hope for; it is to believe that what we possess is but little in comparison with that which is wanting to us, with that which we should have, if we were but more faithful in responding to the grace already given, in comparison with that which is enjoyed by an infinity with others, less favoured than ourselves, but who are yet more faithful. Lastly, the means of acquiring this increase of enlightenment, is to persevere with fervour in the exercises of devotion, to continue to apply to ourselves the merits of Christ, through the Sacraments of His Church, in the sole desire to please Him, and to attain before our death, to the degree of perfection which He destines for us.

THIRD POINT.

Of the unitive life.

Three points are to be observed in the unitive life. 1. The love of retirement. After that Jesus had healed the blind man, *He sent him away to his house, saying, Neither go into the town, nor tell it to any in the town.* He who desires to be united to God, and to remain united to Him, ought to withdraw into his house, into his oratory, into his heart; there he ought to occupy himself with the Presence of God, with prayer, meditation, reading, and all the duties of his station. Ah! how often should we require to have the words, Go to thine house, repeated to us. Perhaps we weary of our homes, and do not know how to occupy ourselves in them: or perhaps we are only in our homes, in order to stir up disagreement, and discomfort there, to disturb their peace and bring discord into them. Alas! if we loved our souls, if we sought to please God, our homes would be our delight, and we should make the delights of our homes.

2. Rare intercourse with the world. *Neither go into the town.* Our Lord does not by this, forbid us all intercourse with the world. However retired we may be, necessity, charity, or the duties of our station must lead us into occasional intercourse with it; but when not called into it by either of these motives, let us keep at home, occupied with God, and the duties of our calling. He who loves to frequent the world in order to see it, and to be seen by it, in order to participate in its pleasures and its distractions, cannot remain united to God, nor can he avoid a great number of faults; he runs even an evident danger of soon learning to think like the world, of adopting the vices of the world, and of being lost with the world.

3. Discretion in words in frequenting the world. *Neither tell it to any in the town.* Our Lord commands

the blind man whom He had healed, to say nothing of that which had taken place. But, Lord, without his uttering a word, is it not sufficient that he should enter into the town, for it to be seen that he is no longer blind, and that Thou hast healed him? Doubtless; but Thou willest not that he should publish abroad the news by which his healing has been effected. And it is in that he ought to be our example. Let us shew forth in our works the change which grace has wrought in us; but there would generally be pride in publishing it by our words. If we are obliged to return into the world, let our whole conduct shew to it that we are cured of ambition, of vain-glory, of self-love, and of love of pleasures; that we see the dangers with which they are filled, and that we seek to avoid them; let it understand that it is not fear or hypocrisy, affectation or ill-humour, but the grace of God which has changed and healed us. As regards the manner in which we have been healed, we ought not to speak of it to others who are only too much inclined to ridicule that which is not conformable to their ideas. We must seek only to edify them, and to lead them towards virtue, by holy conversation, and still more by good examples. But what a scandal would it not be, if we show ourselves as blind as they, and subject to the same foibles. However blind people may be with regard to themselves, they are very quick-sighted with regard to those from whom they have a right to look for edification.

Prayer. Make me docile to these holy truths, O my God. Disperse all my darkness by the operation of Thy grace, that I may walk with joy in the way of the precepts which Thou dost here give me. Take me thyself by the hand, O Jesus! and lead me out of the town. Alas! miserable that I am, how often hast Thou not willed to lead me thither, and I have not been willing to follow Thee! How often hast Thou not willed to take me by the hand, and I have drawn it back in order to hide myself from Thy tender pursuit, O my Saviour, and have stretched it out towards a vain and deceptive world! To-day, I hold it out towards Thee, O charitable and powerful Physician! Lead me, enlighten me, that I may see Thee, that I may know Thee, and that I may love none but Thee. Amen.

Meditation CXXXV.

CONFESSION OF S. PETER.

Examine, 1. how it was made; 2. what was its reward; 3. why Jesus forbid that it would be made public. S. Matt. xvi. 13—20. S. Mark viii. 27—30. S. Luke ix. 18—21.

FIRST POINT.

How the confession of S. Peter was made.

1. *That which precedes it, is prayer. And Jesus went out from Bethsaida, and His disciples, into the towns of Caesarea Philippi: And it came to pass as He was alone praying, His disciples were with Him: and He asked them.* After Jesus had sent away the blind man healed, He continued on His way with His apostles, going over the villages and towns till He came to the neighbourhood of Caesarea Philippi, a town situated in the north of Palestine, near the source of the Jordan, and a different place to the Caesarea of Palestine, which is situated on the Mediterranean Sea. When He drew near this place, He retired into an out of the way place, where He took with Him only His Apostles; the people, who had joined Him on the way, waited for Him in the open country, and the disciples, who were closer to Him, observed Him in silence whilst He prayed. When Jesus was about to choose His apostles, He began by prayer. It is by prayer that Jesus formed the plan of His Church, and of the hierarchical order, which He has established in her; it was of her that He was conversing with His Father; it was for that Church that He was praying, and about her that His thoughts were occupied,

till He had gained her for Himself by the shedding of His Blood; it is thus by prayer that this holy Spouse became united to her celestial Spouse: it is by prayer that she becomes fruitful, that she gives us life and nourishment, and that she enriches us with all her treasures. Children of prayer, what ardour have we in prayer?

2. That which gives occasion to it, is a particular conference. His prayer finished, Jesus comes to find His disciples, and as He was walking with them, the people only following at a little distance, He began to converse with them, and to ask them questions, *saying, Whom say the people that I am? Whom do men say that I, the Son of man, am?* How useful and touching our conversations would be, if we were engaged only in speaking of Jesus Christ, of His mysteries, of His doctrine, and of the interests of His glory! *They answering said, John the Baptist; but some say, Elias; and others say, that one of the old prophets is risen again.* Alas! how inclined the spirit of man is to error and how naturally opposed to the truths of salvation! How can it be, that, amidst this people so assiduous to hear Jesus Christ, and spectator of His miracles, the opinion the most commonly held should not be that He is the Christ Who is expected? Some few have recognized Him; but the greater number prefer to launch out into all sorts of chimeras and extravagant theories, sooner than acknowledge a Messiah, Who is not such as they desire. The humility and holiness of Jesus Christ, such is that which still now-a-days prevents the world from acknowledging Him: but let us be content to leave the world to wander amidst its systems, and chimeras: let us seek for truth in the teaching of the Church, and never separate ourselves from the faith of her first pastors; for it alone can disperse our errors and calm our disquietudes.

3. That which accompanies it, is a lively and well considered faith. Jesus *saith unto them, But whom say ye that I am? And Peter answereth and saith unto Him, Thou art the Christ, the Son of the living*

God, that is to say, the Messiah. This confession of
S. Peter was remarkable for the faith which accompanied
it, and which merited to be praised and rewarded by the
Saviour. It was not the first time that Jesus had been
called Son of God. Not only did the devils generally
call Him thus, but Nathanael had given Him this Name
in a first movement of admiration. The apostles had
also given it Him, with one accord, when hardly recovered from their terror on the lake of Tiberias. The
day after the first miracle of the multiplication of the
loaves, after the wonders of the Sea of Tiberias and of
the country of Gennesaret, S. Peter, still penetrated
by the events which had just preceded, made the same
confession in the name of the other Apostles which he
here makes. But perhaps the feelings of surprise, joy,
admiration, and fear, which had, as it were, forced this
confession from them, on several occasions, had also
diminished its value. Here there was nothing of that
kind, their minds were calm, and it was faith alone
which prompted this confession. I join myself to Thy
blessed Apostle, O Jesus, and prostrate at Thy Feet, I
acknowledge Thee to be the Messiah, the Christ, the
Anointed One of God; for the Son of God, not by adoption, but by nature. I acknowledge in Thee the Incarnate Word, the Divine and human nature subsisting
in one Person, the second Person of the Ever Holy
Trinity. I acknowledge, that according to Thy human
nature, Thou art truly man like unto myself, and according to Thy Divine nature, truly God equal to the Father,
and one God with the Father and the Holy Spirit. I
acknowledge Thee for my King, for my Saviour, for my
Meditator, and for my God, in Whom I place all my
hope, and to Whom I consecrate all the affections of my
heart.

SECOND POINT.

What is its reward.

The reward of the confession of S. Peter is the praise

bestowed on him by Jesus, and the revelation which He makes to him respecting the future of His Church.

1. Jesus makes known to him what is the source of the faith and doctrine of His Church. *And Jesus answered and said unto him, Blessed art thou, Simon Barjona: for flesh and blood hath not revealed it unto thee, but My Father Which is in Heaven.* The Christian faith has its source in Divinity: what it teaches us has been taught by Christ Himself. The Son of God, sent by the Father, has announced to us the truths of revelation; the Holy Spirit, sent by the Father and the Son, has developed those truths and has confirmed them to us, and preserves in His Church this precious deposit. The dogmas of faith owe nothing to human industry: they are not the systems of philosophers, or the informal and timid productions of the meditations of learned men; it is a body of essential truths which make known to us Jesus Christ, and through Him God His Father, which set before us our duties, and the happiness of our eternal destiny with the means whereby to attain it. Oh divine knowledge, in comparison with which all other knowledge is but as darkness; O blessed Apostle, to whom the Heavenly Father has made a revelation so important, and who wert the first to confess the Son of God in a manner to deserve His praises! O how blessed were the other Apostles to have been united with S. Peter in this confession of faith! and how blessed are we ourselves, who hold still even now the same doctrine, the same faith, the same language as they!

2. Jesus makes known to S. Peter and the other Apostles what would be the stability of His Church. From the first time that Jesus had seen Simon, He had changed His name to that of Peter, and from that time, he had been called generally Simon Peter: our Saviour here alludes to this change of name; Thou shalt be called Cephas, which is by interpretation, a stone. No one, had known the signification of this change of name, but our Lord here gives the explanation of it Himself. *And I say also unto thee, That thou art Peter; and upon*

this rock I will build my Church, and the gates of hell shall not prevail against it. The name of rock, or corner-stone is a metaphorical expression which has diverse significations, according to the persons to whom it is applied. Jesus Christ is the corner-stone and the foundation of the Church; the apostles and prophets, are the foundation of the Church. The Church, that company of faithful believers, represented here under the figure of a building which belongs to Christ, and of which He is the architect, was not properly speaking to be formed until after the descent of the Holy Spirit when Jesus should be no longer on the earth. The Church built on this stone, has lasted for eighteen centuries; against this stone all the efforts of hell have raged in vain. This stone has resisted everything and has crushed everything that opposed itself to it; it has crumbled to powder the false gods of idolatry, and overthrown the tyrants who protected it; it has dispersed and driven away heresy. This Church forms one Body, of which Christ is the Head; it is spread over the whole world, and its members are united together in one common bond of union under their one Head. What a misfortune it is for those who do not belong to this Church: let us thank God that we are members of her: let us cling more and more to this unshaken stone: let us never go astray from the faith she teaches, and let us live in a manner worthy of our faith.

3. Jesus declares to them what shall be the power of His Church. Jesus had always called His Church the kingdom of Heaven, and it is thus that He calls her also here. It is a kingdom that God His Father has given to Him, and which He has gained at the price of His Blood; He alone is the King, the absolute Monarch. It is the kingdom of Heaven, essentially allied to this eternal kingdom, prepared for the righteous in Heaven, and entirely separated and independent of the kingdoms of this world, the administration of which God has given to the kings of the earth. This kingdom of Heaven only has to do with man, as a being destined to serve God,

to become sanctified, and worthy to enjoy the fruition of God throughout eternity: but this kingdom of Heaven, how shall it be governed on earth, when its King has ascended to Heaven: who shall govern it in His place while this world lasts, and with what power shall it be governed? Our Saviour reveals this to us here under two metaphors. Continuing to speak to S. Peter, He said to him, *I will give unto thee the keys of the kingdom of Heaven.* It is then to S. Peter and the other Apostles that our Lord, on leaving His sojourning place on the earth in order to return to the bosom of His Father, will give the keys of His Church; it is they and their successors who will hold the place of Jesus Christ, and to whom will belong the universal care of the whole Church. But what is the power which Jesus Christ confers on His Church? *Whatsoever thou shalt bind on earth, shall be bound in Heaven, and whatsoever thou shall loose on earth shall be loosed in Heaven.* This power of loosing and binding is sometimes called the power of the keys: and this power was granted to all the apostles, and through them to their successors to all ages. It is impiety and hardness of heart alone that can despise these spiritual bonds, granted to His Church by Jesus Christ with so much goodness and mercy and which are none the less formidable, because they are invisible. Be for ever blessed, O my Saviour! that Thou hast given to the pastors of Thy Church so merciful and so gracious a power. Full of confidence in Thy promises, I will submit myself to Thy ministers; knowing that when I seek for absolution from my sins at their hands, with sincerity and true contrition of heart, Thou dost ratify and confirm their deed. What a consolation! what inward joy! what happiness for a miserable sinner like myself.

THIRD POINT.

Wherefore Jesus forbids His disciples to publish abroad this confession of S. Peter.

Then charged He His disciples that they should tell

no man that He was Jesus the Christ. It is not that He wished men to be ignorant of it: S. John Baptist had announced it and shewn Him forth as such: He Himself had proved by His words that He was such, and He declared it openly, more or less plainly, according to the disposition of His auditors, and according to the laws of His divine Wisdom. The people, ill-disposed and little attentive, did not understand that which He had announced to them regarding His Divinity; His enemies understood it, and reproached Him with it as a crime. Since His miracles had become known abroad, and had drawn down upon Him the jealousy and hatred of the chief priests, it was not possible any longer for them to publish clearly that He was the Son of God, without exposing themselves to certain death. It was therefore under these circumstances that our Lord willed that His apostles should content themselves with setting forth as they had done the near approach of the kingdom of God, the necessity of preparing for it by repentance, and that He forbade them to tell any one that He was the Christ. For this we may consider three reasons.

1. First reason, taken from the dignity of this mystery. The great mystery of the Incarnation, the master-piece of the wisdom and power of God, the foundation of the redemption of mankind: this mystery, after having been announced in part by the forerunner, was in its nature too Divine and too sublime to be worthily published by any other than by the Incarnate Word. According to the decrees of eternal Wisdom, the public confession of the Divinity of Christ was to be sealed by the blood of Him Who should make it, and it could not be more worthily sealed than by the Blood of the God-man Himself. No creature would have been worthy to shed his blood for this sublime truth, before Christ had gained for him that grace, and given him the example by shedding His own.

2. Second reason, taken from the course of events. If, before the death of Jesus Christ, the faith of people had been turned towards the great mystery of His Divinity,

I cannot avoid accepting one or the other; I must either be saved or damned, there is no middle course in this matter; before long I shall be either the one or the other, and at my death my lot will be as irrevocably fixed as is that of all who are already dead. In any other matter I may refuse to take a part, and remain either neuter or indifferent; but here the alternative is fixed by that sovereign Power to Whom nothing can resist. Oh men! of what then are you thinking? Of what have I myself thought till now?

3. The necessity of the destination of all creatures. God has made them all in order to help us to attain to our end; if some of them seem to turn us away from it, it is only in order to try our virtue, and to give us an opportunity of testifying our faithfulness. If we abuse them, they will one day rise up in arms against us, and contribute to our punishment; but if we make use of them according to the appointment of the Creator, bearing patiently with some, employing others with moderation, and courageously abstaining from those of which we are forbidden to make use, they will all one day bear witness in our favour, and contribute to our eternal happiness.

4. The necessity of the means which lead us to our destination. He Who has established the term of our destination, has regulated the way which leads us thither with an independence which is an essential attribute of His, and without consulting us. Whoever desires *to save his life* in this world, that is to say to preserve his life, and the advantages of that life, at the expense of his faith, who seeks to satisfy his soul, that is, his own inclinations, tastes, and likings; who desires to enjoy the pleasures and comforts of this life at the expense of the commandments of God; whoever sets his happiness in the enjoyments of this life, living only for its pleasures, with no hopes, thoughts, or fears for any other, will find that he has lost his soul for eternity. But, on the contrary, he who is willing *to lose his life* for Jesus Christ and His Gospel, who would rather die than give up his

faith, who would renounce everything, deprive himself of every thing sooner than violate one single precept of the Gospel; he shall *find his life,* that is to say, he will save it, and will enjoy for ever in Heaven a life of bliss. Such is the immutable order according to which we must regulate our actions, but which we cannot change. We cannot look for happiness both in this life and in the next: we must choose between them, and God will keep His Word. All the pretexts which the world brings forward in contradiction of truth are frivolous; they may blind men, but they cannot change the decrees of eternal Wisdom.

THIRD POINT.

Importance of salvation.

For what is a man advantaged, if he gain the whole world, and lose himself, or be cast away?

1. The matter of salvation is the only important one, because it is the only one in which man himself is concerned, his soul, his being. If he loses this, it is not his property which is lost, his employment, his occupation, credit, glory, reputation, health, life; it is not all that, it is himself who is lost. The affairs of this life do not regard the personality of man, his life, his soul; at most they regard some possession which belongs to him, which surrounds him, and which may perhaps be of some transitory use to him; but with regard to that which is really the man himself, all this counts for nothing, and all these matters concern him not. Nevertheless these are what we look upon as the great business of life, and with which we occupy ourselves entirely. So long as we succeed in these matters, we are contented, we do not trouble ourselves whether we lose ourselves; what folly!

2. The matter of salvation is the only important one, because it is the only one of which the loss or gain depends upon each one of us in particular. There are

business matters, in which it is necessary, in order to succeed, to have the concurrence of several persons; but here I only need myself. In other matters, others can act for me, supply that which is lacking in me of strength, knowledge and talents: they can spare me all the trouble, and I may succeed in a matter without mixing myself up in it. But in the matter of salvation, as it is myself alone who am concerned, so it is I myself alone who must act; I must then instruct myself in the knowledge of salvation, the means to be employed, the dangers to be avoided, and the obstacles to be surmounted in order to succeed in them. I must then act myself. It is I who must repent, practise holiness of life, exercise good works, avoid all occasions of evil, and conquer temptations. Another may indeed pray for me, exhort, direct and help me: but he cannot supply my place: it is I who must be penitent, humble, gentle, chaste, just, holy, pure and innocent. If we fail in other matters of business, it is often not our fault, because we have met with unsurmountable obstacles; but here, we have no such excuse; in worldly matters, it may be others who are alone to blame; but in this matter, there can be no one to blame but ourselves. Others may indeed have solicited or incited us to evil, and urged us on in sin, that is their sin, and not ours; but if we have followed their examples, listened to their solicitations, yielded to their promises, or to their threatenings, that is a matter which regards our salvation, not theirs.

3. The matter of our salvation is the only important one, because it is the only one the gain or loss of which cancels the gain or loss of all besides. If I am saved, all is saved, all is gained for me. What matters it to me then if I have been poor, miserable, ruined, despised, slandered, infirm, ill-treated or persecuted? all that is nothing, I am saved. If all that has contributed to my salvation, it has been a true happiness for me. Salvation gained makes up for all other losses, it repays us for every thing, repairs all other sorrows and misfortunes, and contains within itself every blessing we could

desire. If I am lost, all is lost for me. Alas! of what avail is it to the damned, who burn in the flames of hell-fire, that they have possessed great wealth, have swum in a flood of delight, have satisfied all their evil passions, have been praised, applauded, admired, esteemed, sought after, raised to high dignities? Could they have possessed the entire world, what would that have availed them? Salvation lost brings with it the loss of every thing, and annuls all else. What folly then to run such a risk! What folly then to lose every thing, not for *the whole world* even, but for just some petty self-interest, just the pleasure of a moment, and not only that, but often in squandering in its pursuit, health, property, and good name! Ah! fools that we are, shall we never raise our thoughts above this miserable and short life?

4. The matter of salvation is the only important one, because it is the only one the loss of which can neither be repaired, nor the success of which can be destroyed. Salvation lost, all is lost, and for ever. Salvation gained, all is gained, and for ever. In the affairs of this life, we may repair our losses, we may also gain on the one hand what we have lost on the other, as we often lose on one occasion what we had gained on another. It is not the same in the matter of salvation: once decided, it is decided for ever, without any resource or any indemnification for him who has lost it, as also without any fear or danger for him who has gained it. *What shall a man give in exchange for his soul?* When any thing has been lost, it may be recovered, or redeemed, or something else may be given in exchange for it; but when the soul is lost, what can be given in order to recover it? What equivalent can be given for it? What is there in the world of which the price can be compared with the price of the soul? And what can be given when nothing yet remains, and what is there remaining to him who has lost his soul? Has he not lost all in losing himself? And to whom is it to be given? He who has possession of the soul in hell requires nothing, and has need of nothing. The loss of the human race, through

the sin of Adam, has not been irreparable. If man, lost through sin, had nothing whereby to redeem himself, God gave him a Redeemer, through Whose Infinite Merits the loss might be repaired, the price of Redemption paid. The exchange has been made. Blessed exchange! God hath laid the sins of guilty man upon His Innocent Son. The temporal death of this Well-Beloved Son has delivered sinful man from eternal death; a merciful agreement, which is an invention of Divine Wisdom, in which the Justice of God has won the victory and His Mercy has triumphed; in which the Re-redeemer has gained an eternal glory, the favour of God His Father, the love of angels and men, and the adoration of all His creatures; in which men have found their salvation, the price and ransom of their souls, and the remedy for all their ills. Sinner though I be, whatever crimes I have committed, I will not then despair; I have wherewith to repair my losses; I have in the Blood of my Saviour, the price of my offences, the satisfaction for my sins, the ransom of my soul. It is on the earth that this Blood has flowed, and it is on the earth that this exchange was made, this Redemption effected: and it is on the earth, that whilst I live, I ought to profit by It, and apply the merits of It to myself; for if I die without having profited by It, I am lost; since in hell there is no Redeemer more, no Saviour more, no further exchange, no further ransom. Oh infinite loss! Oh infinite misery! Have I ever seriously thought what it is! On the other hand, if I profit by the blessings of Redemption, if I die in the favour and love of my God, I am saved, and in Heaven, no more sins, no more danger, no more fear, no more precautions to be taken, no more temptations to be overcome.

Prayer. Oh infinite happiness, oh eternal happiness, oh unchangeable and never ending happiness! thou shalt be from henceforth and alone the object of my desires, and the mainspring of my actions. Amen.

Meditation CXXXVIII.

CONTINUATION OF THE INSTRUCTION GIVEN BY OUR LORD TO THE PEOPLE.

OF THE SOLEMN DECISION OF THE MATTER OF SALVATION, OR OF THE DAY OF THE LAST JUDGMENT.

The day of judgment will be a day of glory, a day of confusion, a day of justice, a day of indubitable certainty. S. Matt. xvi. 27, 28. S. Mark viii. 38, 39. S. Luke ix. 26, 27.

FIRST POINT.

Day of glory.

The Son of Man shall come in His own glory, and in His Father's, and of the holy Angels. Jesus Christ never spoke of the ignominious judgment which He must undergo on earth, and which was to cost Him His Life, without speaking of the glorious day, when He shall come Himself to judge all men, at the end of the world, in order that the thought of that great Day might lead us to adore His Cross, and help us to bear our own. Jesus calls the glory and majesty in which He will appear at the last day *His own glory*, the *glory of His Father*, the *glory of the holy Angels*. Ah! if we could form to ourselves some idea of this glory, how vile and contemptible would all the glory of men appear to us, and what ardour should we not feel in the service of so great a King!

1. Jesus will come *in His own glory*, that is to say, in the glory which beseems Him as Son of Man, First-born of the children of men, and of all creatures, as Son of God made Man, as God-Incarnate, the King of men and angels, the King of Heaven and earth, the immortal and eternal King. Now what is all the splendour and all the majesty which surround the greatest Kings, in comparison with that of the King of kings,

and of this sovereign Judge of all the kings of the earth? Nevertheless the majesty which accompanies them dazzles us, inspires us with respect and fear, renders us submissive to their will, and desirous to please them. And Thou, O King of kings! Thou art offended, outraged, despised, blasphemed, insulted even in Thine own Temple, in Thy very Presence, and on Thine Altars! Ah! if Thou didst but suffer one single ray of Thy glory to shine upon these rash profaners. Thou wouldest see them trembling, dismayed, prostrate at Thy feet and ready to execute Thy commands; but Thy own servants would be terrified at the manifestation of Thy glory. How would they dare to draw near to Thee, and speak to Thee of their love? Moreover, even the homage which these impious men would render to Thee would not be worthy of Thee: it would be the result of their terror, and Thou willest that it should spring from our faith alone! I believe then, O my Saviour, in that awful Majesty and Glory which is befitting to Thee, and which, out of condescension for me, Thou dost hide from my eyes. I believe, and in this faith, I submit myself to Thee, I declare myself for Thee, I desire to love Thee and to obey Thee, as if I saw Thee in all the splendour of Thy glory.

2. Jesus will come *in the glory of His Father*, that is to say, in the glory with which God has clothed Him as His Word, as His Well-Beloved Son; Heavens, fold yourselves up; stars, disappear; what is the splendour with which the power of God has adorned you in comparison with that which He has given to His Son, Whom He hath appointed Heir of all things, by Whom also He made the worlds, Who is the Brightness of His glory, and the express Image of His Person? God His Father has crowned Him with glory and honour: He has put Him above all which He has created; He has put all things under His feet, and has made nothing that is not put in subjection under Him. The angels themselves have received the command to adore Him, to acknowledge Him as their Creator, as the Creator of

the Universe; such will Jesus appear in the Glory and Majesty of His Father. Happy then in that day they who shall have served, adored and loved Him.

3. Jesus will come in the glory *of His holy Angels*. A numerous and brilliant court sets forth the glory of kings, it makes known their greatness, and manifests their power. But what a difference between the court of the kings of earth, and that of the King of Heaven! The former, feeble and mortal men, have only men like themselves, weak and mortal like themselves, to form their court; but the Son of man, Jesus, God made Man, has as His courtiers and ministers the immortal angels, of whom one alone has more knowledge, strength, and power than all mankind put together. The kings of the earth, sinners and subject to sin, have as their courtiers only men, sinners like themselves and subject to sin; but Jesus has in His court holy angels, all whose thoughts, affections, and actions are holy. The kings of the earth have at their court their own subjects, to whom they have given favours, employments, and graces: but they have given them neither being, nor the qualities of mind which recommend them; the court of Jesus is composed of His angels and they are pre-eminently His Angels, because it is He Who has created them, Who has given them that sublime intelligence, and that vast power which raise them so far above men. They acknowledge that they only exist by Him, that they are nothing without Him, that they have received everything from Him, that He is their God, their Creator, their Master, and that they are bound to employ all they are and all they have to the promotion of His glory and the honour of His service. But what is the number of these blessed spirits, attentive and ready to execute the supreme orders of their Sovereign? Their number is innumerable, and S. John, in the Revelation, speaks of them as "the number of them being ten thousand times ten thousand, and thousands of thousands," who surround His Throne. O King of Glory, how great Thou art, and how great Thou wilt appear at the last day!

Who would not then fear Thee, who would not serve Thee, who would not dread to displease Thee, who would not despise all that is on the earth, in order to devote himself only to Thee and Thy service?

SECOND POINT.

Day of confusion.

Whosoever therefore shall be ashamed of Me and of My words in this adulterous and sinful generation, of him also shall the Son of Man be ashamed when He cometh in His Glory. Jesus will cover with confusion at that great day, and will be ashamed to acknowledge those who shall have been ashamed to declare themselves on His side, that is to say, to fulfil His Commandments, and to submit themselves to His Law. Now, of these we may distinguish two sorts.

1. The first reject Christ in His Gospel through love of this world, its possessions, pleasures, and greatnesses. They prefer the present gratification of their passions to the hope of good things to come, the passing splendour of this corrupt world to all the glory of the future life. Neither the promises nor the threats of Christ touch them: they will not venture to trust in Him, and renounce, at His Word, the false happiness of this perishable world in order to gain the true happiness of eternal life. But what will be their confusion, when they shall see Christ in His Glory, and shall understand the consequences of the senseless choice they have made; when they shall compare this world which they have loved, with the new world which will open to their eyes!

2. The second are those who are ashamed of Jesus Christ before men, and are afraid to practise the precepts of His Gospel through human respect; sometimes it is the Faith, and sometimes it is virtue which they betray. They fear for their fortune, their repose, their reputation. They wish to be as others, they do not like to be singular; they omit to do what is right from fear,

and they do evil out of a yielding spirit. It is necessary to speak and act as others do, in order to avoid malicious remarks, and the censures of others. Conscience murmurs at such conduct, but men applaud; what men, and what applause! But then Jesus, in His glory, surrounded by His holy angels, will condemn and will reject with opprobrium, both those perverse men who have made themselves feared and those cowardly deserters who have feared them rather than God.

THIRD POINT.

Day of justice.

And then He shall reward every man according to his words. Let us weigh these four words.

1. *Then.* Do not let us be surprised at the injustice which we see prevail on the earth. The reign of justice has not yet come; we may form some idea of it, but the knowledge, power, and in most cases the will to execute it is wanting to us. Glory and rewards are often given to those who merit them the least, whilst those who deserve them the most are put on one side, and often find themselves oppressed and despised. Do not let us complain uselessly of this want of order, but let us seek only not to fall into it ourselves; let us bear it patiently. God bears with it Himself. His day is coming, and *then* He will repair the injustice, and will re-establish order. Let us not seek our reward in this world, we shall seek it in vain, and what we do for a temporal reward may make us lose our eternal reward. Let us await with patience God's own good time, let us refer our cause to Him, and *then* our patient waiting will not be in vain.

2. *He shall reward.* Who? Jesus Christ Himself, Who here assures us that He will do so, our God and our Saviour. *He will reward* as God, as Saviour, the good who have served and loved Him, with a happiness pure in its enjoyment, immense in its greatness, eternal in its duration; and the wicked, who have despised and

outraged Him, with a punishment, which is incomprehensible in its nature, infinite in its extent, and eternal in its effects.

3. *Every man.* To the great and small, the rich and the poor, the learned and the ignorant, the sovereign and the lowest of his subjects, to *every man* in particular, separately, and not confusedly, to a nation, a generation, a class, a society, a congregation, but to *every man* of each nation, of every class, of every society, out of the whole congregation, to myself in particular, and considered alone without any other relationship. No more countenance, or help, or support from others; *every man* for himself, and nothing besides.

4. *According to his works,* Not according to the position he holds, or to his intellect, his talents, birth or reputation, but *according to his works,* such as they are in themselves, not such as they have been thought of by men, praised or blamed, extolled or denied; *according to his works,* his private works as well as his public ones, his most secret works as well as those best known; *according to his works,* that is to say, his thoughts and words, his actions, and desires; *according to his works,* with all their circumstances, those which in some degree extenuate their guilt, or increase their virtue, the intention with which they have been accompanied, and all the consequences which they may have had. O my God, where shall I hide myself in that great day, and where wilt Thou find in me ought, save works of iniquity, works of abomination and iniquity? Unhappy that I am! I have not even made a beginning of the practice of good works. Let us begin from this day forth, O my soul, let us labour for the last day, and let us never lose it out of sight.

FOURTH POINT.

Day of indubitable certainty.

Without bringing forward here the proofs which we might draw from the depths of our own hearts, from the disorder which prevails here below, from the necessity of a judgment, from the very nature of God, let us confine ourselves to the words of our Lord. *Verily, I say unto you, There be some standing here, which shall not taste of death, till they see the Son of man coming in His Kingdom.* Jesus, in order to confirm what He had just spoken of the glory of His last Advent at the end of the world, foretells to His audience, events which would take place at a nearer date, and He concludes this discourse by assuring them that some amongst them would not die without having seen them. This prophecy was fulfilled by three marked events.

1. The Transfiguration, at which three of the apostles were present, and which took place six days after this discourse.

2. The public preaching of the Gospel by the power and virtue of the Holy Spirit, Whose descent on the apostles took place within the year.

3. The triumph of the Gospel over the unbelief of the Jewish people, the establishment of the Christian religion on the ruins of Jerusalem, of its temple and its religious ceremonies, by the power of Jesus Christ, and the wonders which caused the enterprise of the Romans against that unbelieving and deicidal nation to prosper. This event took place about 40 years after this discourse, in the year 70. A.D. S. John the apostle lived more than thirty years afterwards, and consequently, others amongst those who here heard the prophecy may have also been witnesses of it, as well as S. John, and may have been able to recall to mind, in seeing the events, the words of Jesus Christ Who had foretold them. As for us, who acknowledge Jesus Christ, behold and adore Him reigning in His Church, who see His reign established by innumerable prodigies of His Almighty Power, and His Church subsisting for so many centuries; who behold the Jewish nation dispersed over the world, bearing every where the opprobium of their crime and being able to go nowhere where they do not behold Him, Whom they rejected as their king, reigning: as for us who are witnesses of so many wonders, can we but believe, and

this faith yet tender would have suffered too great a shock, at the time of His passion, and of His death, with the risk of never being re-established. Were not even the apostles themselves offended, was not their faith shaken, and they themselves discouraged, when Jesus revealed this mystery to them?

3. Third reason, taken from the witness of the apostles. The testimony of the apostles would not have had that force of proof which it had after His Death, His Resurrection, His Ascension, and the Descent of the Holy Spirit. There was nothing super-human, and such as had not been seen on more than one occasion that disciples, whether deceivers or deceived, should publish the works of their master, whilst they were living with him, in order to draw down upon him and upon themselves credit and consideration; but that disciples should publish the Divinity of their Master, and should not publish it until after His death, expecting only death themselves as the reward of their zeal, is Divine, and such as had never yet been seen; and in consequence of such a witness the world has been converted, Christians have freely offered and shed their blood, for the confession of the name of Jesus Christ.

Prayer. Ah! wherefore can I not shed mine in so sacred a cause! Why can I not join mine to that of so many martyrs, to Thine own, O Jesus! At least, I will make it an honour to myself to set forth on every occasion Thy holy religion, to defend it according to my power, and to justify it by the holiness of my life, that I may obtain the reward which Thou hast promised to those who shall believe in Thee. Amen.

Meditation CXXXVI.

JESUS FORETELLS HIS PASSION TO HIS APOSTLES.

Consider 1. the circumstances of this prediction; 2. the terms in which it is expressed; 3. the opposition which S. Peter makes to its accomplishment. S. Matt. xvi. 21—23. S. Mark viii. 31—33. S. Luke ix. 22.

FIRST POINT.

The circumstances of this prediction.

1. At what time does Jesus utter it? *From that time forth began Jesus to shew unto His disciples,* the mystery of His passion, *how that the Son of man must suffer many things.* It is after having confirmed His Apostles in the faith of His Divinity, and at the very time that they made a profession of their belief in Him. If He had made this declaration sooner, it might have discouraged them, and perhaps, separated them from Him: do not let us then separate these two mysteries, the one of glory, and the other of humiliation. A God made man, an Incarnate God, what a mystery! But this God-man suffering and dying, what a still greater mystery! In these two great mysteries joined together, what wisdom, what greatness, what love! My Saviour is God, and my God dies for me! What a ground of hope! At this thought, with what feelings ought not my heart to be penetrated!

2. To what end does Jesus make this prediction? It is in order that the mystery of the Cross, which His disciples were soon to have under their eyes, might not destroy in their minds the mystery of His Divinity which they could not see, but on the contrary, might confirm it. If the Jew, the philosopher, the unbeliever bring forward the ignominious death of Jesus Christ as an objection against Christianity, I will answer them always, ' But long before it took place, Jesus foretold the time,

the place, the manner. The prediction of this death takes away from it all difficulties; and far from troubling my faith, it confirms it, especially being joined to the prediction of a resurrection soon to follow, which has not been proved true any less than the prediction of His death.'

3. To whom does Jesus make this prophecy? To His Apostles, to those who follow Him, and who are the most closely attached to Him. O blessed those with whom Jesus converses of His Passion and His Death! Happy those who taste Its mysteries, who meditate on them, and fill their minds, and nourish their hearts with them! What sweetness do they not find in them! what strength, grace, and comfort do they not draw forth from them!

4. In what place does Jesus make this prediction? It is in solitude, when withdrawn from the multitude. And what hinders us from withdrawing ourselves thus and retiring with Jesus, and separating ourselves for a few moments from the crowd, in order to meditate at our leisure on that which His love has made Him suffer for us.

5. In what manner does Jesus make this prediction? *And He spake that saying openly.* In clear and precise terms. The forerunner had announced that death under the figures of a lamb and a victim: our Lord had announced it Himself several times to all the people, and in the presence of His enemies, but under the figure of Jonas, under that of the temple, and of the brazen serpent raised by Moses; here He speaks to His friends, and He speaks to them without a parable, and without figures, because the time is drawing near, and that it was needful that they should be instructed. In all this conduct, Jesus causes His Divine Wisdom to shine forth, and strengthens our faith more and more by strengthening that of His Apostles.

SECOND POINT.

The terms of this prediction.

From that time forth began Jesus to shew unto His disciples, how that He must go unto Jerusalem, and that the Son of man must suffer many things, and be rejected of the elders and of the chief priests, and scribes, and be slain, and be raised again the third day. Let us take each of these words.

1. *He must.* God the Father had thus appointed it. A supreme command and one which was very severe, but still a command of sovereign Wisdom, which united the claims of the severest justice with the favours of the tenderest mercy. God is so compassionate towards mankind, that He willed to give them His Son as their Redeemer: but He is so jealous of the claims of His justice, that in reparation for sin, He requires the death of this well-beloved Son. Ah! do not let us form our ideas of the goodness of God according to our own corrupt inclinations. The goodness of God is not such that we may despise and outrage it with impunity. A God Who dies, such is the Victim Whom His justice requires; A God, Who has died for sinners, and through Whom He accepts the repentance, the sufferings, and death of sinners: such is the excess of His mercies. But for sinners who should refuse to profit by the merits of Jesus Christ, and who should pretend to take advantage of them in order to sin with greater security, alas! there is for them only a hell without mercy, and an eternity without end.

2. *He must go.* Yes, in order to obey the commands of God His Father, Jesus will go of His own free will; He will repair punctually and without resistance to the place which is appointed for Him, although He knows that He is to die there. What pretext shall we find after such a signal act of obedience on the part of God, wherewith to cover our disobediences?

3. *He must go to Jerusalem.* Jesus was born in a stable in the small town of Bethlehem. He had passed

all that part of His Life that was not public in a still more obscure town. He had worked the greater part of His miracles in the depths of Galilee: but the capital is to be the theatre of His Death, in order that, on the one side, nothing might be wanting to the glory of His triumph, and that on the other, the certainty of the facts, namely, of His Death and Resurrection, should be so strongly attested, that the most distant posterity might never be able on any grounds to contest its truth.

4. *He, the Son of Man, must.* It is as *Son of man* that Jesus suffers and as Son of God that He saves us by His sufferings. He suffers in His Humanity and His sufferings are raised to an infinite price by His Divinity. It is by the union of these two natures in one single Divine Person, that Jesus is our Second Adam, the Repairer of the disobedience of the first Adam, that He is the Head and First Born of men, and that He forms a new generation of men redeemed and regenerated by the virtue of His Blood. Let us then lay aside the old man, let us renounce the inclinations of the first Adam, formed of the earth, in order to clothe ourselves with the new man, and to attach ourselves to the second Adam, Who came down from Heaven.

5. *He must suffer many things.* O Jesus, how much dost Thou include in these few words! Thou *must suffer many things!* Thou dost spare Thy apostles here the detail of them: could they hear them without horror, and can I think of them without shuddering at them? Alas! Lord, would it not suffice that Thou shouldest suffer a little? would not this little have been superabundant, and of an infinite price? But love cannot content itself with a little. Thou didst will, by Thy sufferings, to bear witness to Thy love, both to God the Father to Whose glory Thou didst make amends, and to sinners, whose loss Thou didst repair, and therefore nothing appeared too much to Thy love, nothing ever has been able to suffice in order to satisfy it. Ah! if after so many sufferings on the part of our Saviour, we do not enter into the grievousness of sin, the rigour of

divine justice, the necessity of suffering and of repentance; if we are not comforted in our afflictions, reassured in our fears, detached from all sensual indulgences, enemies of our flesh, unshaken in temptation, moved, touched, penetrated with the most ardent love, we have never meditated as we ought on all that Jesus has suffered for love of us. To *suffer many things*, such is the joy of a Christian: if we complain of them, let us compare these *many things* with those of our Master, and that which we call many things will appear to us to be very few.

6. *He must be rejected*, declared not to be the Christ, and condemned because He said He was. Ah! after such an Example, let the world reject, say of me what it will, treat me as it pleases, if only I belong to Jesus Christ.

7. *He must be rejected by the elders*, who were the senators or members of the great council or Sanhedrim in which all matters of religion were decided upon, and the greater number of whom were of the sect of the Pharisees: *and chief priests*, who were also members of the great council; *and by the scribes* who were the doctors and interpreters of the law, in order that all that there was that was greatest, most elevated in rank, or by their dignities, and held in the highest esteem by their teaching, might concur in this solemn and decisive judgment. Now, how is it after that, that Jesus has been acknowledged to be the Christ, not only by several Jews, but by the entire world?

8. *He must be put to death.* Death is the last effort of human power in him who causes to be put to death and the end of all subjection to human power in him who is put to death. Shall the enemies of Jesus Christ then triumph, and shall He have no more power when He shall have been put to death? Doubtless, if His Power is only human; but if He is God, He and His servants will triumph after death, and those who shall have brought about their death shall be confounded.

9. *And be raised again the third day.* Here is a

prediction which man has never made, nor dared to make; it belonged to a God Alone to announce a like event. The term was not long, and if there were a mistake, the error at least could not last long. This it is which abundantly repairs or rather efficaciously anticipates the offence of the Cross. Jesus suffers and dies: I am no longer dismayed by it, He will rise again: His disciples suffer and die for Him with joy; I have no difficulty in believing it, they will rise again with Him. Oh world! thy power only extends thus far, it is enclosed within the narrow limits of this short life. Death is its term, beyond which thou dost acknowledge that thou canst do nought: but the power of my divine Saviour extends beyond death. I will live then for Him, I will suffer for Him, I will die like Him, that I may rise again and reign eternally with Him. Such are the three great mysteries of Jesus Christ, His Divinity, His Death, His Resurrection; such are at the same time, by participation, the three great mysteries of the Christian; his Baptism, which makes him a child of God: his death to the world, which makes him an object of contempt: his resurrection, which makes his hope, and which will make his eternal happiness.

THIRD POINT.

Opposition of S. Peter to this prophecy.

S. Peter, full of love for Jesus Christ, but little instructed in His ways, struck by the first words of His Master, and but little attentive to His latter words, could not restrain his zeal. Not only was he taken by surprise, but he was moved and distressed, and rebelled against them; and taking Jesus aside *he began* in this first moment of his grief *to rebuke Him, Be it far from Thee, Lord: this shall not be unto Thee. But when He had turned about and looked on His disciples,* who were doubtless of the same mind as S. Peter, *He rebuked Peter, saying, Get thee behind Me, Satan, thou art an offence unto Me: for thou savourest not the things that be of God, but the things that be of men.* Let us examine here three things.

1. Whether we do not imitate S. Peter, and if we do not deserve the rebuke which Jesus administered to him. And in truth, 1. What savour have we for *the things that be of God*, mortification, repentance, humiliation, prayer, Communion, in a word, all the exercises of religion? What savour, on the contrary, have we not for *the things that be of men*, that men seek after, honours, pleasures, wealth, distinctions, amusements, dissipations? 2. Are we not a cause of offence to some of our brethren? Do we not turn them away by a false love, or by earthly inclinations, from *the things that be of God*, that is to say, do we not keep them back from exercising works of piety, or from leading holy and regular lives? do we not carry on in the world the office of Satan? do we not turn others away from the practice of good, by our raillery, our sarcasms, our contempt, or by the abusive things we say? do we not lead them to do evil by our flatteries, our solicitations, our promises, our example?

2. Do we imitate our Lord? Do we make use of His answer, *Get thee behind Me Satan; thou art an offence unto Me*, 1. with regard to those who, out of a false tenderness, seek to oppose themselves to our true happiness, by keeping us back from the service of God, in whatever way He calls us; 2. with regard to those, who because they savour not the things of God, seek to turn us away from the practices of penitence and devotion: 3. with regard to those who seek to lead us astray, and place us in danger of falling into the snares of Satan. To all such persons, let us answer with our Lord, let us *rebuke them, saying, Get thee behind me;* you force me to treat you as enemies. I belong no longer to you, as soon as you seek to hinder me from belonging to God.

Prayer. Yea, Lord, such shall be the firmness with which I will seek to overcome all the obstacles which the esteem and the false friendship of men can offer me in the fulfilment of my duties, in the sacrifices which Thy commandments require. I will hearken no longer to vain pretexts, to frivolous interpretations, to fatal counsels in order to dispense myself from their observance. I will break off, if it must needs be, from those who are the dearest to me, and this sacrifice, oh my God ? do I not owe it to that which Thou art about to make of Thy life, the obstacles to which Thou dost here set aside, so as to treat with severity even a cherished apostle who seeks to turn Thee away from it ? O Jesus ! raise me, as Thou didst S. Peter, above flesh and blood, that I may have no relish but for the things of God, and no contempt but for the things of earth. Amen.

Meditation CXXXVII.

INSTRUCTION GIVEN BY JESUS CHRIST TO THE PEOPLE.

ON SALVATION.

Jesus sets forth here, 1. the difficulty, 2. the necessity, 3. the importance of salvation. S. Matt. xvi. 24—26. S. Mark viii. 34—37. S. Luke ix. 23—25.

FIRST POINT.

Of the difficulty of salvation.

And when He had called the people unto Him with His disciples also, He said unto them, Whosoever will come after Me, let him deny himself, and take up his cross daily, and follow Me. Here then are four things which Jesus Christ requires of us for the work of our salvation.

1. Will. A free will which men can neither give nor force. Grace even, which alone can give the will to work out our salvation, does not compel man, but always leaves him his liberty, which, unhappily for him, he but too often abuses. To wait for a grace which

should work every thing in us, without ourselves, is to confound redemption with creation, eternal life with natural life. Without then waiting any longer, let us make up our minds to-day, and let us say with all sincerity, I will seek to work out my salvation. A fervent will; let us see what men do when they desire a thing, the merchant who desires to become rich, the warrior who desires to acquire glory, the courtier who desires to rise to a higher position, every one who has an aim to which he desires to attain. The will which animates them makes them undertake every thing that leads to their end, and avoid all which turns them away from it; they find nothing impossible, nothing desperate, nothing difficult in order to arrive at their aim. A constant will; it never leaves them, it is with them every where, it directs them in everything. Whatever other occupation they may be engaged in, they never lose out of sight the object they have in hand; all their efforts tend thereto, and they draw nearer unceasingly to it. Such ought to be in us the will to work out our salvation.

2. Self-denial. The unchastened love of ourselves, which hinders the love which we owe to God, is the source of all sin; and the abnegation of self, in order to seek ourselves only in God and for God, is the remedy for it. This abnegation of self has different degrees; the first excludes all mortal sin, and puts us in a state of mind in which we would rather die than disobey God, or lose His grace: the second excludes all venial, known, and deliberate sin; the third has to do with the imperfections and the artifices of self love which creep in every where, even into the practice of virtue itself. The further we advance in this last degree, the greater are the peace we enjoy, and the inward freedom, and the consolations of the Holy Spirit. If then we are still subject to any sin, to any evil passion; if any thing hinders us from advancing in the paths of virtues and of the spiritual life, it is because we have not yet understood and practised these words of our Lord: *let him deny himself.*

3. *To take up his cross.* There are crosses of various kinds. Some are extraordinary, and only exist in times of persecution, and consist in tortures and death; such was the Cross our Lord bore, and such are those which the holy martyrs bore after Him. We ought like them, to be ready to die for the faith, and to strengthen ourselves so much the more in this holy disposition, as we might be called on to do so at a time we least expected it. Some crosses are ordinary, and to be met with at all times; and amongst these, there are some which are necessary and involuntary; such are, on the part of nature, the discomforts of life, bodily infirmities, the weaknesses of old age, the rigour of the seasons: on the part of fortune, losses, disgraces, need, indigence, the disarrangement of our affairs, and other such like mischances: on the part of men, their hatred, contempt, persecutions, failings, characters; on our own parts, our tempers, our evil passions, our faults, and our relapses. When they present themselves to us on all sides, and are such as we cannot avoid, and which we are constrained to bear, Ah! what an advantage to ourselves if we accept them in a right spirit, and as Christians! And what does it avail to us if we bear them as heathen, murmuring at them, and rebelling against them. They only become so much the heavier, because thus borne they are without unction in God's sight, and on our part, without any motive or hope of reward. Lastly there are voluntary crosses imposed upon ourselves of our own choice: such are the mortifications and self-denials which each one lays upon himself; a rule of life to which we subject ourselves: such is sometimes the weariness or distaste which we experience in a course of a practices or occupations which we have voluntarily adopted; and which we ought to bear with the more joy, because they are our own choice, and we have embraced them of our own accord. Do not let us repent of them, but let us persevere courageously in them, and we shall die in them with happiness.

4. *To follow Christ.* To deny oneself, to do violence

to oneself, to suffer, to bear our Cross, is not enough, if it is not done for Christ, walking in His steps, and uniting ourselves to Him. But also, in suffering for this Divine Saviour, let us remember that He is at our head, that He has suffered more for us than we could ever suffer for Him; let us remember that if we follow Him in His Life and in His Death, we shall follow Him also in His Resurrection, His Ascension, His Kingdom. Let us choose now, and see what it is that we desire. *If any man will*, the road is traced out, the way is open, and the goal known. *Whosoever will save his life shall lose it; but whosoever shall lose his life for My sake and the Gospel's, the same shall save it.* There are in the economy of our salvation four things which are absolutely necessary, and independent of ourselves.

SECOND POINT.

The necessity of salvation.

1. The necessity of our being. We did not give ourselves life; it is God Who gave being and life to all men, and to me in particular; it is He Who has regulated the time, the place, the duration of it, and all the circumstances attending it. It did not depend upon myself to remain in a state of nothingness, or to come out of it, and it does not depend upon myself whether I remain among other living beings, or return to dust. He willed that I should be an immortal soul: it is so, and it will be so. If I wished that it should be otherwise, if I complained that it was thus, wishes and complaints would alike be useless, and would only serve to render me sinful, and would add impiety to ingratitude.

2. The necessity of our destination. God, Who did not consult me in order to create me, has not consulted me either, in order to give me an end; this end is, an eternity of bliss, if I obey His commandments in this life, or if I disobey them, an eternity of misery in hell. Heaven or hell, happiness or misery, such is my destination; I may choose between these two alternatives, but

await with an entire certainty the last coming of Him, Who in foretelling it, has foretold all that we see with our eyes? and if we believe it, can we do ought but prepare ourselves for it with all the care that depends upon ourselves?

Prayer. O Jesus! what could be more capable of animating me to embrace Thy cross, to be and to appear to be Thy disciple, to practise Thy commandments, and to lead a truly Christian life, than this certainty of Thy second coming, than the just belief that I have that Thou wilt one day come to pronounce *according to* our *works,* the judgment of eternal life, or eternal death? What consolation then for me, if I have the happiness to find in my Judge, Him to Whom I have sought to conform myself during my life! Grant me this grace, O my Saviour, that I may have a share in that glorious testimony which Thou wilt one day bear to Thine elect before the entire universe. Amen.

Meditation CXXXIX,

OF THE TRANSFIGURATION OF OUR LORD.

Consider, here, 1. our Lord; 2. Moses and Elias; 3. the apostles; 4. the words which the Voice of God caused to be heard. S. Matt. xvii. 1—8. S. Mark ix. 1—7. S. Luke ix. 28—36.

FIRST POINT.

Of our Lord.

1. How He prepared for His transfiguration. *And after six days Jesus taketh Peter, James, and John his brother apart, and went up into an high mountain to pray.* 1. Jesus chose only three of His apostles to be the witnesses of His transfiguration. Visions and revelations are not granted to everyone, but only to some privileged saints, according to the choice and good plea-

sure of the Saviour. Let us extol these holy Apostles for the choice which the Lord made of them in order to manifest His glory to them: but let us beware of desiring similar favours for ourselves, but rather on the contrary, let us judge ourselves as utterly unworthy of them. Let us only beseech Him for the grace to profit by the wonders revealed to them, and pray that we may be penetrated, like them, with the greatness and splendour of His glory. 2. Jesus led them up on a high mountain which tradition has always regarded as Mount Tabor. If, as some have asserted, there was no mountain of that name in the neighbourhood of Cesarea, towards the source of the Jordan, where Jesus had delivered the preceding discourse, we may presume that the six or about eight days which had elapsed since then, had given more than sufficient time for this Divine Saviour to repair to Tabor, situated on the confines of Galilee and Samaria. However that may be, it was on a mountain that Jesus worked the greater part of His great mysteries, in order to shew us what should be the elevation of our heart above earthly things, an elevation without which we can neither meditate with profit on these mysteries, nor relish them aright. 3. Jesus goes up on a mountain *to pray*, and it was during His prayer that God His Father conferred on Him honour and glory, and bore witness to His supreme authority. It is only in silence and in prayer that Jesus manifests Himself to us. If we were faithful to these holy practices, what enlightenment should we not receive as to the greatness of Jesus, and the necessity of obeying Him!

2. In what manner was Jesus transfigured? *And as He prayed, He was transfigured before them, the fashion of His countenance was altered, and His face did shine as the sun, and His raiment was white as the light, white as snow, so as no fuller on earth can white them.*

1. In the splendour of His face. His face appeared quite transformed, and appeared to have nothing earthly

in it. It became quite radiant with glory, and shining like the sun. The Divine light which issued from It spread forth brilliant rays to a distance, the splendour of which, equally bright and full of sweetness, charmed the eyes without dazzling them. Oh! the glorious sight! Blessed are the eyes which beheld Thee, Lord, in Thy glory! Disappear from sight, terrestrial beauties! What are ye with all your allurements and your artifices? What are ye? Dust and ashes, in comparison with Jesus, my Saviour. O my heart, if splendour and beauty have charms for you, attach thyself to Jesus, love Jesus only, Who is the Brightness of the glory of God, and the Express Image of His Person.

2. In the splendour of His raiment: His garment appeared resplendent, and of a whiteness equal to snow. This mingling of light and whiteness formed the most ravishing colours, so as to delight all eyes. No, there is no kind on earth which could equal its sweetness, its magnificence and its beauty. In vain does luxury exhaust its resources in the endeavour to dazzle our eyes, and surprise our hearts. Let it join together all that art and nature can furnish it with: let it join to the most brilliant colours the richness of gold and the brilliancy of jewels; what is all that, save a mass of corruptible matter, a frivolous and childish adornment which can only corrupt the heart that takes pleasure in it, and which admires it!

3. In the glory of His soul. All that outward and ravishing splendour with which Jesus was surrounded was only but a slight emanation of the Heavenly glory which His blessed Soul enjoyed, admitted as it was to the intuitive vision of God from the first moment of Its creation, and of Its substantial union with the Word. It is not thus with the splendour which men procure for themselves. What shame and disgrace does it not sometimes conceal! How often is not the soul which exists in a body, endowed with all external qualities, and adorned in magnificent garments, only an object of horror? How senseless then is he who fixes his atten-

tion on this vain splendour, and lets his heart grow attached to it? But happy he who clings to Thee, O Jesus! Thy glory is not a borrowed one; it belongs to Thee of right; Thou didst conceal it during Thy sojourn on earth, in order to teach us, and to die for us; Thou didst manifest once in order to sustain our courage, and animate our hope; Thou dost hide Thyself in the Sacrament of Thy Body and Blood, that Thou mayest become our Food; Thou dost manifest Thyself in Thy Kingdom in all Thy fulness to be our Blessedness for evermore. Oh! what motives are not these to make us love Thee! O my soul, detach thyself then for ever from earth, in order to love Jesus only, in order to hope only in Him, and to long only for Him.

SECOND POINT.

Of Moses and Elias.

1. *Of their appearance. And behold, there talked with Him two men, which were Moses and Elias.* Moses, the lawgiver of the Jews, and Elias, the father of the prophets, come to render homage, and at the same time, to bear witness to Him Who is the Fulfilment of the law and of the prophets, to Him Who made truth to take the place of the shadows and figures of the law, and events, to succeed to the promises and prophecies of the prophets. Let all adore Thee, O Jesus! let every thing render homage to Thee. Thou art the End of all things; and every thing has reference to Thee. Promised from the beginning of the world, announced until the time of Thy Coming, preached every where after Thy return to Heaven, Thou art the Author and the Accomplisher of the faith of all time.

2. *Of their glory. Who appeared in glory,* that is to say, they were invested with the splendour of Christ, radiant with the glory which was reflected in them from Him Whom they foretold. The nearer we draw near to Jesus, by meditating on His glory, and imitating His virtues, the more shall we partake in His glory.

3. Their discourse. *And spake of His decease which He should accomplish in Jerusalem.* They talked with Jesus; and of what did they speak whilst in that glorious state? of the death which He was about to undergo at Jerusalem, by which He should accomplish the will of His Father, the salvation of mankind, the types and figures of the laws, and the prophecies spoken by the prophets of old, of which no circumstance, no single detail of ignominy and cruelty was to be spared Him. O Jesus! is this then a subject which can be pleasing to Thee, and respecting which Thou shouldest take pleasure in conversing with Thy friends, even in the midst of Thy glory? Ah! I understand, O my Saviour! it is that in speaking to Thee of Thy death, they speak to Thee of Thy love! and wherefore then, ungrateful as I am, do I not speak to Thee unceasingly of it, I, who have been the object of this great love, and who reap all the fruits which it has brought forth? Wherefore when I join in commemorating Thy Blessed Sacrifice and Death on the Cross, and kneel before Thy Holy Altar, am I not wholly penetrated by the remembrance of it, inflamed, taken out of myself? O Death, O Sufferings, O excess of Love, shall I never repay Thee but by an excess of ingratitude?

THIRD POINT.

Of the Apostles.

1. Of their sleep. *But Peter and they that were with him were heavy with sleep.* When Jesus, having reached the mountain, began to pray, his three chosen companions began also to pray with Him; but soon, overcome with fatigue, they allowed sleep to gain the upper hand over them, which thus hindered them from witnessing the first beginnings of the Transfiguration, and caused them to lose a portion of this magnificent sight. Jsus dealt tenderly with their weakness, and did not permit them to be entirely deprived of it. Alas! how

often does not sleep make us lose the graces and favours, which others more fervent than ourselves have the happiness to enjoy! If it is a sleep of weariness and weakness, Jesus is merciful enough to pardon it; but if it is a sleep of idleness, of cowardliness, of distaste for holy things, of forgetfulness of God, or of weariness in His service, we must not be surprised, if we have no insight into the truths of salvation, and into the mysteries of Christ, or if we have no love and no relish for them. Let us then arouse ourselves out of so fatal a sleep; let us resume our practices of meditation and prayer, and we shall be enlightened.

2. Of their awakening. *And when they were awake, they saw His glory, and the two men that were with Him.* What was their surprise! with what feelings of fear, of joy, and admiration were they not agitated, when they saw the glory and the majesty of the Saviour in the midst of these two venerable persons who were with Him! What will be the surprise and the despair of a sinner, when he shall feel the weight of that Majesty which he has outraged, and of that Power which he has despised! What will be the joy and the admiration of the righteous man, when he shall behold the glory of His Saviour Whom He has adored, loved, and served! What will be the astonishment of all created beings, in the day of the Universal Resurrection, when they shall see Jesus, in the glory of His Saints, come with the majesty of a sovereign Judge, in order to decide upon their eternal fate! O Jesus! before that terrible day, awaken my soul from its state of slumber, that it may know Thee, serve Thee, and love Thee.

3. Of the words of S. Peter. *And Peter answered and said to Jesus, Master, it is good for us to be here: and let us make three tabernacles; one for Thee, and one for Moses, and one for Elias. For he wist not what to say; for they were sore afraid.* After that the Apostles had contemplated the glory and the majesty of their divine Master, and had heard His conversation with Moses and Elias, they understood that these latter

were about to separate from Jesus. Then Peter, always impetuous whenever the glory of his Master was concerned, cried out, Lord, how blessed we should be, if Thou wouldest permit us to remain here with Thee! Consent that we should set up in this place three tabernacles; the one shall be for Thee, the second for Moses, and the third for Elias. But Peter, as well as his companions, agitated by conflicting movements of surprise, fear, admiration and joy, at the same time frightened, dazzled and enchanted with the greatness and the novelty of the scene, was beside himself, and did not know what he was saying. This earth is not the place of happiness; if God sometimes causes us to feel the sweetness of His Presence here below it is a passing favour which is only bestowed upon us in order to encourage us to work and to suffer for Him.

FOURTH POINT.

Of the voice of God.

While he yet spake, behold a bright cloud overshadowed them; and, behold, a Voice out of the cloud, Which said, This is My Beloved Son, in Whom I am well pleased; hear ye Him. And when the disciples heard it, they fell on their face, and were sore afraid.

1. Of the fear which this Voice caused to the Apostles. Peter had hardly uttered his request, than a new spectacle offered itself to their eyes. A brilliant cloud appeared suspended over their heads, and attracted their admiration and attention. This bright cloud lowered itself slowly towards the ground, and enveloping Jesus and themselves as it were under a shining pavilion, they were completely surrounded by it. At this sight, the fear of the Apostles increased still more, and it was brought to a height by a Heavenly and Majestic Voice, which, coming forth from the cloud, made Itself distinctly heard in their ears. It was then, that, yielding to their fear, they fell down with their faces to the

ground, not knowing what was about to become of them. Ah! Lord, if Thy Voice is so terrible to Thy friends whom It is about to instruct, what will it be to thine enemies, when It shall come forth in order to condemn them?

2. *Of the words which the Voice uttered.* These are the words of God Himself, proceeding forth from the Dwelling place of His Glory, and addressed to all mankind, when giving to them Jesus Christ as their Master; *This is My Well-Beloved Son in Whom I have much pleasure:* on Whom all my affection rests, and in Whom I delight; *hear Him,* with the submission and in the teachable spirit which the Master Whom I give to the universe, has a right to expect from you. In these words, we find an instruction and a command; an instruction which teaches us that in God's sight, there is nothing great, good, estimable, worthy of His approbation, or His love save Jesus Christ, and he who is united to Jesus Christ, and that which is done for Jesus, by His Spirit and by His Grace: an instruction which teaches us that all that is not of Jesus Christ, all that calls itself worldly glory and greatness, whatever it may be, is as nothing in God's sight, that no mention will be made of it throughout eternity, and that it is often only sin and abomination in His Eyes. Do we regulate the esteem in which we hold persons and things by this rule? In these words, we have also a command by which we are bidden to hear Jesus, to believe in His doctrine, to practise His commands, to imitate His Example, to follow His precepts, and live according to His Spirit. Now, is it Jesus to Whom we hearken? or is it not rather the devil, the world, ourselves, our evil passions and temper? Do we hearken to Jesus, when He tells us to renounce that sin, to break through that evil habit, to resist that passion, to stifle those motions of our heart, to repress our senses, to restrain our looks, to control our tongue; when He tells us to avoid distractions, to keep ourselves collected, to give ourselves up to prayer, to meditation, and other devotional exercises? Do we not

stifle His voice within us, do we not close our eyes that we may not hear Him, and do we not openly resist It when we do hear It? If it is thus, how shall we present ourselves then before this God Whom we have thus outraged, and how shall we be received by Him?

3. Of the end of this vision. *And Jesus came and touched them, and said, Arise, and be not afraid. And suddenly, when they had looked round about, they saw no man any more, save Jesus only with themselves,* the voice having ceased to make Itself heard, the cloud was dispersed, the vision came to an end, Moses and Elias disappeared, and Jesus resumed His ordinary Form. Nevertheless the Apostles remained still prostrate on the ground, and did not venture to lift their eyes; but this Divine Master drew near to them, and *touched them and said, Arise, and be not afraid.* Reassured by the words of the Saviour, they arose, and having looked round about them, they saw no one with them save Jesus only, and He restored to His wonted condition. Blessed they to whom Jesus says, *Arise, and be not afraid.* Blessed he who is with Jesus, who in every thing and every where, sees Jesus only, and acts only for Him!

Prayer. O Jesus, Thou art my only Master, and what blessedness is it not for me to be Thy disciple! Grant that I may hearken to Thee in a teachable spirit; grant that I may never hearken to any voice which is opposed to the truth, that I may believe with a firm faith all that Thou hast taught me, that I may practise all that Thou dost command me; make me to live in continual expectation of that day when Thou wilt change my body, vile and abject as it is, in order to make it like to Thy glorious Body, that I may have a share in the happiness and glory of which Thou dost give us a foretaste in Thy glorious transfiguration. Amen.

Meditation CXL.

CONVERSATION OF JESUS WITH THE THREE APOSTLES, AS THEY CAME DOWN FROM MOUNT TABOR.

Observe 1. the command which Jesus lays on His apostles; 2. the question which the apostles put to Jesus; 3. the answer which this divine Saviour makes to them. S. Matt. xvii. 9-13. S. Mark ix. 8-12. S. Luke ix. 36.

FIRST POINT.

Of the command which Jesus lays upon His Apostles.

And as they came down from the mountain Jesus charged them, saying, Tell the vision to no man, until the Son of man be risen again from the dead.

1. The reason of this command. It is probable that Jesus gave this command in order not to expose the truth of so great an event to unbelief, doubts, criticism, especially on occasions where the malignity of the Jews turned everything into poison, and where the Apostles themselves, still carnal minded and imperfect, did not relish the things of God; but after that this divine Messiah had been received up into the abode of His Glory, and had sent down His Holy Spirit on His disciples, and that He had shed out upon them the fulness of His gifts, then their witness would no longer suffer any difficulty, and it would be convincing.

2. The obedience of the Apostles to this command. *And they kept it close, and told no man in those days any of those things which they had seen.* The Apostles kept silence we are told, respecting that which they had seen during the time in which it had been forbidden them to speak of it. Doubtless the extraordinary events which succeeded one another so rapidly, the difficulties, the questionings and even the trouble which the greater number of our Lord's discourses caused amongst them occupied their minds to such a degree, as to render their

obedience comparatively easy to them, and they even appear to have forgotten for a time the grand spectacle which they were forbidden to publish abroad; but after His Resurrection the remembrance of it returned to the Apostles' minds, and with what rapture did they not speak of it? *We beheld His Glory*, says S. John at the beginning of his Gospel, *the Glory as of the only-Begotten of the Father full of grace and truth.* And S. Peter, in his second Epistle exclaims, We do not set before you unknown gods, as do the Gentiles, *we have not followed cunningly devised fables*, of gods whom none has ever seen, gods of whom long genealogies are related, and learned fables are told, which never had any one as eye-witnesses. As for us, we speak to you of the presence, and of the life of Jesus Christ, *when we made known unto you the power and coming of our Lord Jesus Christ, but were eye-witnesses of His Majesty. For He received from God the Father honour and glory, when there came such a voice to Him from the excellent glory, This is My beloved Son in Whom I am well pleased. And this voice Which came from Heaven we heard when we were with Him on the Holy Mount*, and it is after having been spectators of His greatness, after having seen with our eyes the splendour of His glory, and having heard with our ears the Voice of the Father on the holy mountain. O my soul! such is then the God Whom thou servest, in Whom thou believest, in Whom thou hopest; what ought to be thy joy, thy fervour, thy love, in the service of so great and so tender a Master.

3. The perplexity of the Apostles respecting this command. *And they kept that saying within themselves, questioning one with another what the rising from the dead should mean.* It was not the command which Jesus laid on them not to publish abroad that which they had seen, which perplexed them, it was rather the permission that He gave them to publish it after He had risen from the dead. They understood nothing of these last words. They believed indeed that

Jesus would restore the kingdom of Israel, that He was its King, and would cause Himself to be acknowledged as such; but they did not imagine that that could be after His death, and never man, in truth, has ever formed a like project of royalty. They knew well that all men should rise at the end of the world; but Jesus spoke to them of His Resurrection as of an event that was near at hand, and which He would survive, and this was a new source of perplexity and of questionings amongst themselves, the answer to which they could not solve. Ah! how blind we are with regard to God's works, if faith does not enlighten us! How far above our feeble understanding are the ways of God! No, no, the Christian religion is not a human invention, it is not a tissue of learned fables, composed and arranged by the mind of man; the Majesty of a supreme Being makes Itself felt everywhere, and the Wisdom and Power of Him Who has created the world, ordered the duration of time, and disposed of all events, as of all parts of the universe.

SECOND POINT.

Of the question which the Apostles made to Jesus Christ.

And they asked Him, saying, Why say the scribes that Elias must first come?

1. Of the object of their question. It was the doctrine which the Pharisees and scribes taught with respect to Elias. These false doctors, the enemies of Jesus Christ and His kingdom, made an erroneous application of the prophecy of Malachi, *Behold, I will send you Elijah the prophet before the coming of the great and dreadful day of the Lord.* According to these words, they said, he has not come, he has not appeared, God has not sent him; consequently this Jesus to Whom you hearken, and Whom you follow, is not the Messiah under Whom this great and terrible day of the Lord of which the prophet speaks shall appear. There will always be those who will interpret the Scriptures according to

their own fancy, conformably to their own pre-conceptions, their prejudices, their evil passions. Such questionings are but too often the effect of pride, presumption, and sometimes even of unbelief. It is for us to receive the truths of religion in a believing and not in a doubting or questioning spirit, for he that believeth, he shall know of the doctrine, whether it be of God or no.

2. Of the occasion on which the question was asked. The Apostles proposed their question in these terms, *Why then say the scribes that Elias must first come?* This question might be taken in connection with the appearance of Elias which had just taken place, and in this sense the Apostles would have enquired if this apparition was then the fulfilment of that which the scribes were in the habit of saying, and of that which the prophet had foretold? It might also have reference to the command which had been given them not to speak to any one of the vision which they had had, as though they had said, If we might be allowed to speak, we might reply to the Pharisees that Elias was indeed come, and that we have seen him. Must we then leave them to say that Elias has not come, and answer them nothing? Finally, it might be connected with the withdrawal of Elias, as if they had said; Elias only appeared for a moment and then he has disappeared. What must we then think of what the Scribes and Pharisees say? Are they mistaken, or will Elias indeed return before Thou dost re-establish the kingdom of Israel? The greater the knowledge which God bestows upon us, the more difficulties do we perceive which we are incapable of solving. We are not forbidden to seek for a solution of our difficulties, but we must do so with reverence and humility, and not in a spirit of contradiction or disputing, or of self-sufficiency.

THIRD POINT.

Of the answer of Jesus Christ to the Apostles.

1. Of the future coming of Elias. *And He answered*

and told them, Elias verily cometh first, and restoreth all things: and how it is written of the Son of man, that He must suffer many things, and be set at nought. That is to say, it is true that Elias must first come: that is foretold of him, that from his coming, he will seek to renew in mankind their first innocency, to recall to the children the piety of their ancestors, and to restore the practices of repentance, faith, and all virtues in their pristine vigour: but do not imagine that he will do so without being despised of men, without having to endure many insults, and without exposing himself to much bad treatment. Destined to prepare the ways of Jesus Christ, he will have a fate similar to His. But this Elias who is to come before Me, and prepare the hearts of the children of Israel for the establishment of My reign, this Elias has come in the person of S. John Baptist. Thus the error that the scribes committed was that they adhered too much to the literal wording of this prophecy, and understood of the person of Elijah himself, that which was only to be understood of the spirit and virtue of Elijah. There is generally more curiosity than usefulness in these researches after that which will take place at the end of the world: thus our Lord always recalls His Apostles' minds to present events, to His Death and Passion. That which ought then to interest us most deeply, is that our Lord has suffered for us, and that those who have announced it, whether before, or after His Coming, have all suffered persecution: and that if we desire to live as true Christians, we must expect persecution.

2. That the coming of Elijah was already past. *But I say unto you, That Elias is come already, and they knew him not, but have done unto him whatsoever they listed, as it is written of him. Likewise shall also the Son of man suffer of them.* The first crime of the Scribes and Pharisees was that they had not recognized the coming of Elias in the person of S. John. Their pride, jealousy, and hatred towards Jesus had blinded them. It is true that S. John, when question-

ed respecting this matter answered them that he was not Elias; but in telling them that he was the voice foretold by Isaiah, he gave them a sufficient clue to direct them, and if they had had upright hearts, they would have gone to Him to Whom S. John Baptist referred them, and they would have learnt from Him what He thought of S. John. Their second crime was that of persecuting S. John, ill-treating him, banishing him, and perhaps even taking part in the circumstances which led to his death. Their third crime, which was soon about to fill up the measure of their crimes, was the death of the Messiah; it was to this that our Lord here leads the minds of His disciples. Do we not recognise in all this the sin of the world, in which we perhaps are partakers? Much talking about religion, but at the same time, we refuse to acknowledge the teachers whom God sends to us to make known this very religion to us, and to teach us how to practise it. We do not seek to distinguish between false and true teachers; we hate, persecute or decry those, who, in the spirit of S. John, or of Elias, preach boldly against abuses or against sin; and we exalt those who preach peace when there is no peace, and leave us quietly in our sins and errors: conduct which ends in making us lose all faith and religion, and leads us to consider every form of religion alike good, and to practise none.

3. Of the understanding of the disciples. *Then the disciples understood that he spake unto them of John the Baptist.* We ought also to understand it ourselves, for it is the third time that we see this prophecy of Malachi quoted, and each time applied to S. John Baptist; the first time by the archangel Gabriel when speaking to Zacharias; *he shall go before Him in the spirit and power of Elias, to turn the hearts of the fathers to the children, and the disobedient to the wisdom of the just: to make ready a people prepared for the Lord;* the second time by Jesus Christ, in speaking to the people; *But what went ye out for to see? a prophet? yea, I say unto you, and more than a prophet. For*

this is he of whom it is written, Behold, I send My messenger before Thy Face, which shall prepare Thy way before Thee; and the third time again at the time when He here gives a more particular instruction to His three most chosen disciples. The Wisdom of God has given sufficient light to enlighten upright hearts, and obscurity sufficient to blind presumptuous spirits. Do not let us occupy ourselves with that which will take place at the end of the world, and at the last coming of the prophet Elias, so that we forget to fix our thoughts on the last day of our life, which may not be far distant, and on the care we should take to profit by the instructions which God gives us through the teachers of His Word whom He sends to prepare us for that last day. Our Elias, our S. John Baptist, is that zealous preacher, that watchful pastor, that instructive book, those good thoughts: how do we profit by them?

Prayer. Grant, Lord, that I may profit by all the graces which Thy Love lavishes on me; grant that all may be renewed, if not throughout the world, yet at least in my heart, that Thou mayest reign there in time and in eternity. Amen.

Meditation CXLI.

DELIVERANCE OF A YOUNG MAN POSSESSED FROM HIS INFANCY BY A DEAF AND DUMB SPIRIT.

The sacred text furnishes us here with some most solid subjects for reflections, 1. on faith; 2. on the ruling passion; 3. on prayer; S. Matt. xvii. 14—20. S. Mark. ix. 13—28. S. Luke ix. 37—44.

FIRST POINT.

Of faith.

1. Of faith becoming weakened. 1. Of the causes which lead to it. The first is, holding intercourse with

those who are unbelievers. *And it came to pass, that, on the next day, when they were come down from the hill, much people met him. And when He came to His disciples, He saw a great multitude about them, and the scribes questioning with them.* The nine apostles whom Jesus had left at the foot of the mountain were still filled with that faith, by the power of which they had, in the name of their Master, driven out evil spirits, and worked so many miracles during the course of their mission; but unhappily for them, during the absence of Christ, and as soon as the morning had come, before He had descended from the mountain, the scribes, His enemies, had come in search of them, and entered into dispute with them. Our faith must be well assured, before we venture to expose ourselves to the arguments of irreligious or free-thinking persons. However much we may uphold the Faith and the cause of religion against its adversaries, it happens but too often that we come forth from these disputes, or from the reading of books which advocate these opinions, with our own faith weakened and almost tottering. Our safest way is to impose silence on these enemies of religion and of morals, to avoid any encounter with them, and to put aside all dangerous books, lest we be tempted by them, unless the duties of our station compel us to do so, and then, in that case, we must fear, pray, and watch. The second cause of our faith becoming weakened, is the greatness of the obstacles we meet with. *And when they were come to the multitude, there came to Him a certain man, kneeling down to Him, and saying, Lord, have mercy on my son; for he is a lunatic, and sore vexed, for oft times he falleth into the fire, and oft into the water. And I brought him to Thy disciples, and they could not cure him.* The apostles had undertaken this cure, but with a feeble, languishing faith. Surrounded by a crowd of people, observed and perhaps defied by the scribes with whom they had just been disputing, when they saw this young man who was possessed, and had learnt the length and duration of his possession, they may have begun to mistrust as it were, their own powers, in the face of the scribes, and in such a frame of mind were they likely to be able to work miracles? Alas! does not our faith often become weakened in like manner? Do we not mistrust the promises which Christ has made to His Church, when we see the ravages which the devil effects? Do we not often allow ourselves to think that all is lost, and that there is no remedy for the evils we see around us, and does not this mistrust give rise in us to many doubts as to religion itself? Are we not tempted to believe that truth is no longer to be discerned, that every thing is a matter of indifference, and that all religions are alike? 2. Of the offence which is caused by the weakening of our faith. Faith does not grow weak without causing an offence which communicates itself insensibly to others, if we do not promptly bring some remedy to bear. We see here the contagion which spread through the weakening of the Apostles' faith, and the fatal impression which it made first of all on the Apostles themselves. Notwithstanding their secret mistrust which they did not suffer to manifest itself in their actions, they come forward, and command the devil, in the name of their Master, to come forth from the possessed; but this command, given with a faltering faith, had no effect. The apostles were astonished thereat, and doubtless their faith received a new shock. The contagion of this weakened faith spread itself next to the father of the child. He had come there in the hope of finding a certain remedy for his misfortune; but when he saw the devil resist even to the command of the apostles, he knew no longer what to hope or to fear, nor whether the Master would have more power than His disciples; and this contagion spread further over the people. Accustomed, as he was, to see all nature obey the Name of Jesus, it must have been a great cause of astonishment and offence, when he saw that Name invoked in vain, and his faith could not fail to be shaken at it. Lastly, it was a subject for scandal to the scribes themselves, who drew from it a motive for triumph, and for hardening themselves yet more in unbelief. Each one ought to examine themselves here, and see whether he, in his station of life, does not contribute to the weakening of faith in others; if he speaks and acts always as if he were really persuaded and penetrated with the truths of the faith. How much would the faith of each one be strengthened, if believers would encourage one another by good examples! But how easily does faith become extinguished, when we, far from helping one another on, are really only a stumbling block in each other's paths. 3. Of the effect which most commonly ensues on faith growing weak, namely, consummated unbelief. Jesus, having heard from the lips of the father of the one who was possessed, that His disciples had been unable to cure him, and knowing the dispositions of heart of the by-standers, cried out, *Oh faithless and perverse generation! how long shall I be with you? how long shall I suffer you?* We see, in these words, how much want of faith offends and outrages the Majesty of God. How terrible is the threat which He utters, of abandoning those who allow their faith to grow cold! A threat which did not fail to be executed on the Jewish nation: a threat which has since been executed on several Christian nations; a threat, lastly, which is executed daily on a number of individuals. Let us fear for ourselves, and let us strive to re-kindle faith in our own hearts, and in that of others.

2. Of faith becoming weakened. The most effectual means whereby to re-kindle our faith, are 1. The presence of Christ. *And straightway all the people, when they beheld Him, were greatly amazed, and running to Him saluted Him.* Wherefore are this people seized with astonishment? Doubtless, because they did not look for Jesus at that particular moment, nor so early in the morning: perhaps also the scribes may have taken advantage of His absence to calumniate Him, and to assure the people that they would see Him no more. Wherefore are this people seized with fear? Doubtless the enemies of Jesus feared lest their calumny should recoil on

themselves, and lest they should be covered with confusion by the display of a new miracle; perhaps the friends of Jesus Christ feared lest they should have deserved His reproaches by their mistrust; perhaps even some yet weaker in their faith, feared lest His Power should fail as well as that of His disciples, in overcoming a malady so violent and so inveterate. However that may have been, all hastened to meet Him, and to salute Him. *And He asked the scribes, What question ye with them?* To this question, no one ventured to reply. Apostles, scribes, people, all keep a gloomy silence, which is only broken by the prayer of the afflicted father. The silence which His enemies maintained proved their weakness. 2. The actions of Jesus Christ. After the afflicted father had set before Jesus the sufferings of his son, and the powerlessness of His disciples to cure him, after Jesus had expressed His sorrow and His displeasure at the want of faith which He met with, He said, *Bring him hither unto Me,* and in speaking to the father, *Bring thy son hither.* In vain does the devil use his last efforts and tear the child in the most terrible manner. Jesus speaks, threatens, commands, and He is obeyed; the unclean spirit is compelled to come out of the child, and Jesus gives him back to his father perfectly healed. Everyone was amazed, and everyone praised the greatness of God, and wondered at the miracles which Jesus wrought. Ah! how firm and unshaken would not our faith be, if, instead of listening to and reading so many vain and frivolous discourses, so many systems of religion which rest on nothing, we would give ourselves up to meditate on the actions of Jesus Christ, if we would love them, reverence them, and seek to be penetrated by them! Our faith, thus nourished, would gain new strength each day, instead of becoming daily weaker. 3. The words of Jesus Christ to the father of the child, which precede the miracle. This father, having shewn his want of faith by saying to Jesus, *if Thou canst do anything, have compassion on us, and help us;* Jesus said unto him, *If thou canst believe, all things are pos-*

sible to him that believeth. How comforting are these words! Let us ask with faith, and we shall obtain our petitions. Afterwards, Jesus having told His disciples that they had not been able to work this miracle on account of their want of faith, adds, *Verily I say unto you, If ye have faith as a grain of mustard seed, ye shall say unto this mountain, Remove hence to yonder place : and it shall remove ; and nothing shall be impossible unto you.* Powerful words made use of by our Lord in order to express the almighty powers of faith, and to shew us plainly how little we possess. What miracles has not this faith accomplished, whether in the physical or in the moral order of things! Without speaking here of the former, how many sinners have we not seen, who, by the power of faith, have been won over from pride to humility, from self-indulgence to self-mortification, and from anger to meekness. Let us then pray both for ourselves and others with that faith to which all things are possible.

SECOND POINT.

Of the ruling passion.

The possession of this child may be regarded as the figure of a heart which is taken possession of by one ruling passion. Let us consider here all its characteristics.

1. The author of this possession. This child might appear at first sight only to have a natural disease, namely, epilepsy: but if we observe more attentively, we shall perceive that he was really possessed by the Evil spirit. It is the devil, our declared enemy, who enkindles in us every evil passion, it is he who tempts us, who urges us on to sin, who puts bad desires into our hearts ; and if we once give him an entrance into our hearts, he seeks to establish himself there, to strengthen himself, and to take possession of all our senses and all our thoughts. He takes advantage of our natural dispositions, of our tempers, and our various characters ;

he conceals himself there in such a manner, that we mistake his operations for our own acts and deeds, and in obeying his suggestions, we fancy we are only following our own natural inclinations. We lay the blame on our natures, and on the Author of our Being, we plead them as an excuse for our faults, as a motive for continuing in evil, and a reason for persuading ourselves that it is vain to attempt to correct our faults; but the evil lies in our own wills, which we allow to be carried away by the artifices of the devil.

2. The torments of this possession. The state of this child excited at the same time horror and compassion. When the evil spirit seized it, he *teareth him and he foameth again, and gnasheth with his teeth, and bruising him, hardly departeth from him;* it threw him on the ground, and shook him with violent convulsions so that it seemed as if he would tear him to pieces, *ofttimes he falleth into the fire, and oft into the water*, where without prompt succour, he could not but perish. In the midst of these torments, this child uttered terrible cries; and *wallowed, foaming on the ground*. Who cannot but see in this sad picture the fearful torments which an ungoverned passion produces in him who gives himself up to it? Ah! what struggles take place in him who is the unhappy victim of such passions! Fury, hatred, fear, anger, repentance, despair agitate him by turns, and cause him to endure numberless tortures; and the struggle which reigns within is plainly depicted in his outward appearance.

3. Intervals of this possession. The devil gave this child some intervals which caused it another kind of torment through the knowledge which came to it of its disease, and through the fear of its return. Evil passions have also their intervals; to make a merit of it would be pride; to congratulate ourselves upon it as if it were a cure, would be deceiving ourselves: we ought to profit by them, in order to consider the greatness of the evil, to humble ourselves, to pray and prepare ourselves by every means to withstand the return of temptation.

4. *The danger of this possession.* The design of the devil in this possession was to destroy the child. It is only in order to cause us to perish eternally that the devil enkindles and foments these evil passions within us. It is not in order to render us happy that he incites us to sensuality, or in order to enrich us that he persuades us to commit acts of injustice, or to gratify our tempers, that he inspires us with feelings of revenge; all that he seeks is to bring about our eternal destruction, that is his only object, and the rest is of very little interest to him. But since we know his designs, do not let us be senseless enough, and so much our own enemies, that we suffer ourselves to be deceived by him.

5. *The character of this possession.* Jesus asked this father how long his son has been subject to this malady. *How long is it ago since this came upon him?* and his father answered, *of a child.* Let us examine what is the ruling passion which prevails now with us, and let us ask ourselves how long we have been subject to it, and perhaps we shall find that it is also from our childhood. Woe be to those, to whose charge the education of children is entrusted, if they do not employ all their care in seeking to repress in them their evil passions, in guarding them as far as they can from all occasions of yielding to them, and instructing them in the necessity of overcoming evil inclinations, and resisting temptation. Woe be to the child, who having contracted any evil habit, does not strive to get rid of it, as soon as he is of an age to know what is right. If he delays to correct himself of it, he will never correct himself; from childhood people put off till youth, from youth to a more advanced age, and from riper years to old age; and then they despair of being able to correct themselves, and finally die in them. We have then nothing left to us, but to begin at once and strive with all our might to root out the evil passion which we know to be in us, and which rules in our hearts.

6. *The effects of this possession.* The father knew that there were two results of his son's possession: the

first was the instability, the changeableness, the variableness of his possession, which made him say that he was *lunatick;* the second, his powerlessness to speak, which made him say that his son *had a dumb spirit.* We can easily perceive these two results in a person who is a slave to any evil passion; on the one hand, he is inconstant and passes rapidly into the most opposite extremes, and so to say, *falls oftimes into the fire, and oft into the water,* sometimes indulging in excessive merriment and dissipation, and sometimes being of a moody and sombre melancholy which makes a person insupportable to themselves; on the other hand, he is dumb as to the cause of his trouble, dumb to discover his malady and to ask for deliverance from it, dumb in prayer, dumb in confession of his sin, dumb in all that might procure his healing. Our Lord sees in this child a third result of the possession which the father had perhaps not perceived, namely, deafness. *Thou deaf and dumb spirit, I charge thee, come out of him, and enter no more into him.* This is the most terrible and most pernicious effect of yielding to evil passions. One may speak to that sinner whom one sees walking in the paths of iniquity, or of lukewarmness, or indifference; one may exhort him, or entreat him, but he is deaf, and does not hear; nothing profits him. The names of God, Saviour, virtue, duty, salvation, judgment, Heaven, and Hell, sound in vain in his ears; they cannot penetrate into them, they present no idea to his mind, and make no impression on his heart. A terrible state, which we cannot even conceive to ourselves! But Thou Who dost behold it, oh Divine Jesus, Thou alone canst deliver from it. Command then *this deaf and dumb spirit to come out* of my soul, and then it will hear Thy Word, it will speak, it will bless Thy holy Name, and will praise for evermore Thy exceeding mercy.

7. The difficulty of the cure. The father had in vain presented his son to the Apostles, they could not heal him. When Jesus *was come into the house, his disciples asked him privately, Why could not we cast him*

out? *And Jesus said unto them, Because of your unbelief;* and, *This kind can come forth by nothing, but by prayer and fasting.* First difficulty, want of faith. Faith is equally opposed to despair and presumption. Jesus Christ is all-powerful: He can do all things, therefore let us never despair; we can do nought, let us then not rest either on our good resolutions or on ourselves; but let us do all that depends on ourselves, and let us await the success of our undertakings only from God. Second difficulty, the want of prayer and repentance. In order to effect a complete cure, we must employ prayer and meditation, and join to it fasting, repentance, and mortification.

8. The healing of this possession. It was effected in spite of the resistance of the devil by the Almighty power of Jesus Christ, and the cure was a permament one. When this child was to be presented to Jesus, the devil tormented it in a more fearful manner than he had yet done. Do not let us be surprised at any artifices which the devil employs, in order to keep us back from a sincere confession of our sins. These are the last efforts which he can make: do not let us yield to him, cost it what it may. Jesus spake the word, and the devil was forced to come forth. How this mircle should animate our confidence! What have we to fear, when we have so merciful and powerful a Saviour! The devil made a new effort, he uttered a terrible cry, and rent the child with so much violence, that he fell to the ground as if dead, *insomuch that many said, he is dead.* Such is often the opinion of worldly men, when any one seeks truly to turn to God. *But Jesus took him by the hand, and lifted him up; and he arose, and He delivered him again to his father.* This child, whom the world looked upon as dead, and whom the father wept over as dead, became the consolation of his parents, their joy and glory. Lastly, the child was for ever delivered from this evil spirit, for our Blessed Saviour's command to the evil spirit was, *I charge thee, come out of him, and enter no more into him.* Speak thus, O my God, to the

evil spirit that has possession of me, and grant me grace that I may never recall him, and never open to him again the door of my heart.

THIRD POINT.

Of Prayer.

We find here an example in prayer which we ought to follow. Let us particularly observe in this afflicted and suppliant father,

1. His ardour and his humility. He comes forth from the multitude, he draws near to Jesus, he prostrates himself at his feet, he raises his voice, he cries; *Lord, have mercy on my son; Master, I beseech Thee, look upon my son; have compassion on us, and help us.* Is it thus that we pray, either for others, or for the salvation of our own souls?

2. The motives with which he supports his petition. On the one hand, the greatness of the malady, a terrible, inveterate malady, a malady incurable by any but Jesus; on the other hand, it concerned an *only son.* Have we not the same reasons for our petitions? Our soul, our salvation, our eternity, the *only* important matter is at stake; now how is it with our soul, and the matter of our salvation, or of our eternity? Alas! is not every thing in disorder, at the will or discretion of the enemy?

3. His faith. It was feeble, and yet Jesus did not reject it: on the contrary He encouraged it, and this became a new subject of prayer to the father, a subject equally of prayer to us. Let us acknowledge, with this afflicted father how little faith we have. Touched by the words which Jesus had spoken, he *cried out, and said with tears, Lord, I believe; help Thou mine unbelief.* Like him, let us cry, let us sigh, let us weep over our unbelief, and let us pray Jesus Christ to assist our weakness, and to increase our faith.

Prayer. Ah! Lord, *I believe* then Thou canst heal me; but *help Thou mine unbelief.* Make me believe and pray in a more fervent and more lively manner.

Raise me up out of the despondency into which the evil spirit casts me down; drive him out of my heart. Have pity on me, succour me, open my ears, loosen my tongue, take me by the hand, grant that I may remain for ever firm in following Thy commands; from this moment, I commend to Thee my spirit, I place it in Thy Hand; heal it, purify it, sanctify it, so that I may serve Thee faithfully in time, and bless Thee in eternity. Amen.

Meditation CXLII.

JESUS FORETELLS FOR THE SECOND TIME HIS PASSION TO HIS APOSTLES.

Consider here, 1. the circumstances; 2. the terms of this prophecy; 3. the impression which it made on the apostles. S. Matt. xvii. 22, 23. S. Mark ix. 30—32. S. Luke ix. 43—45.

FIRST POINT.

Of the circumstances of this prediction.

And they departed thence, and passed through Galilee; and He would not that any should know it. But while they wondered every one at all things which Jesus did, He said unto His disciples, Let these sayings sink down into your ears; for the Son of man shall be delivered into the hands of men; and they shall kill Him, and the third day He shall be raised again.

1. The humility of Jesus Christ. Whilst all men were in admiration, and praising God for the great wonders which they had seen Him work, this Divine Saviour turns away the mind of His disciples from this applause in order to occupy them with the thought of His humiliations. In truth, how vain is the applause of men in itself; how hurtful to those who dwell upon it! how fickle it is! Those who praise us to-day, are ready and prepared to condemn us to-morrow.

2. Instruction given by Jesus Christ. This Saviour

God sets off then from the place where He had been transfigured, and where He had delivered the possessed of the devil. He crosses a part of Galilee in order to repair to Capernaum, but without remaining in any place, not wishing His journey to be made known. Nevertheless His zeal did not remain unemployed; if He did not exercise it in behalf of the people, He exercised it in favour of His disciples. He instructed them as to the great mystery which He had come to accomplish on the earth. Alas! they were not yet in a condition either to understand it or to profit by it, but they would be one day. Thus we ought to cast our bread on the waters, knowing that we shall find it after many days; we should instruct, each according to our several capacities, those whom we have any opportunity of benefitting; however hopeless the task may appear at the time, believing truly that what we say to them at one time will bear fruit at another. Jesus instructed His Apostles with regard to the mystery of His Death, and that of His Resurrection, two very different events, but essentially bound together. Such is the plan of the Christian religion. It presents at one and the same time truths which are the most repelling to human nature, and those which are the most attractive; it warns us that we must suffer, die to the world, die to ourselves, die, if it be needful, amidst opprobrium and sufferings, but in order to rise again, to live and reign eternally.

3. Recommendation given by Jesus Christ. The Saviour was not content only with instructing His disciples, He recommended them, before giving them this instruction, to mark it well, and to engrave it deeply in their hearts. It was in truth for them, and is also for us, a very remarkable fact, that our Lord should have foretold here His Death and Resurrection in so express and precise a manner. He does so when nothing special seems to call it forth, He does so in the midst of the miracles which He wrought, and of the praises which were given to Him. How then could this death be anything but a cause of offence? Could it be the effect of

weakness in Him to Whom all nature and even the evil spirits obeyed, in Him Who foretold and announced it, in Him Who, in announcing it, has at the same time, foretold His Resurrection, and given but three days as the term of its fulfilment, that is to say sufficient time in order to verify His death? O holy religion! O Saviour, Who art always adorable even in the midst of opprobrium and torments! Thy death can only be the work of Thy Divine power, and the masterpiece of Thy wisdom.

SECOND POINT.

Of the terms of this prediction.

Jesus foretells three things;

1. He foretells that *He shall be delivered into the hands of men;* Ah! who will deliver Thee, O Jesus? Alas! it is an apostle, one of those who hear this discourse, and who have just been witnesses of the extent of Thy power. Who will deliver Thee up? Thyself, Thine obedience to the commands of Thy Father, and Thy love for us. Who will deliver Thee up? My sins, myself, and the love which Thou hast for me. The Son of man, the Master and chief of men, the Son of God *into the hands of men*, given up to their mercy, their hatred, their fury! What depths of wisdom and love!

2. Jesus foretells that He shall be put to death. Such is then the use which men will make of the power which will be given them over Thee, O my Saviour. They will have Thee in their hands, not in order that they may acknowledge Thee, offer Thee their vows, and render Thee their homage, but in order to outrage and torment Thee; their fury will only be assuaged by Thy death, the justice of Thy Father will only be satisfied by Thy death, our salvation will only be consummated by Thy death, Thy glory will only be made perfect and Thy love satisfied by Thy death. Let me die then with Thee in order to satisfy the justice of Thy Father which I have offended, in order to testify my love to Thee. O death of my Saviour! Thou art my life, my strength, my consola-

tion, the foundation of my hope, and Thou shalt be the pattern of that spiritual death to which I dedicate myself at this moment, and for the rest of my life.

3. *Jesus foretells that He will rise again the third day.* If the death of Jesus appears to dim His glory, to render His doctrine doubtful, His promises uncertain, the miracle of His Resurrection re-establishes all. O mystery full of love and hope, of sweetness and delight! Courage, O my soul! let us suffer, let us die with our Saviour; in three days we shall rise with Him. Rejoice, O world, triumph, satisfy thy passions and thine appetites, abuse thy power, and the benefits which God lavishes on thee, but in three days, thou wilt no longer exist, thou wilt pass from a temporal death to an eternal one, where one of thy greatest torments will be to know that this Jesus Whom thou didst not will to know or follow, that those faithful disciples of Jesus whom thou hast despised or persecuted, will now enjoy a glorious resurrection, and a life which shall never end.

THIRD POINT.

Of the impression which this prediction made upon the minds of the Apostles.

1. *They understood nothing of it. But they understood not this saying, and it was hid from them, that they perceived it not.* Their ignorance was excusable, and our Lord did not reproach them with it; it will last yet longer, until the entire fulfilment of the prediction, till the fire of the Holy Spirit shall have consumed the veil which was on their hearts. They acknowledged Jesus as the Son of God, as their King, as He Who should restore the kingdom of Israel; but they were ignorant of the nature of that kingdom, and of the manner in which it should be established. They were far from thinking that it was by His death that the King of Israel should conquer His kingdom, and enter into His glory, deliver His people, sanctify them, and render them partakers of His Heavenly inheritance. But have not we,

who are instructed in these truths, also a veil over our hearts which hides them from us, which hinders us from thinking of them, from penetrating into them, and drawing from them treasures of grace, enlightenment, consolation, strength and love?

2. They were very much grieved at it. *And they were exceeding sorry.* Although they did not understand what our Lord said to them, yet they knew for certain that it was of death, outrages, and sufferings that He spake to them; and they perceived well that He spake to them of it as of an event near at hand, and this thought filled them with grief, a grief which was caused by their love; besides, what our Lord added concerning His Resurrection did not enlighten them, and consoled them but little. Can any one love our Saviour and not feel sorrow at the remembrance of all that He has suffered for their salvation? Should not love make this remembrance always present to our minds? Blessed sadness, the bitterness of which purifies the heart, and inflames it with a holy love! Could I give myself up to dissipation and pleasure, to vanity and sensuality, to anger and impatience, when I consider my Saviour in opprobrium, in torments, and expiring on the Cross?

3. They dared not ask Him. *And they feared to ask Him of that saying.* They were desirous to know whether these words were to be taken literally, and whether it was a real and true death which they were to expect; they were also desirous to know how the promises concerning the re-establishment of the kingdom of Israel were to be accomplished; but they did not venture to put these questions to Him, whether out of the fear of finding themselves deficient in understanding or faith, or from fear lest truths yet more sorrowful than these which they thus dimly perceived should yet be set before them. Do not the same reasons sometimes hinder us in our enquiries after truth? Do they not often keep us back from consulting our own consciences? We often dare not contemplate Jesus Christ crucified, lest the remembrance of His sufferings should condemn our luxury,

our worldliness, our sensuality, our self-indulgence. But this God, crucified for us, if we fear to question Him now, He will question us one day, and after having marked out for us by His example the path of salvation, He will ask us how we have followed it. Let us ask Him now, this Saviour and God, and if He teaches us truths hard to nature, do not let us grieve; let us think of the glory of the resurrection, of the happiness of life eternal, which will be the reward of our fidelity in following Him, and of the conformity which we have borne to Him.

Prayer. Oh Jesus, Who didst die and rise again for me! O Lord of the living and the dead, cause me to feel how much I owe to Thee, that Thou didst effect my salvation by Thy death, how deeply I ought to cherish Thy sufferings, since it is through them that I hope to be made a partaker in Thy glorious life, and lastly how much I am bound to follow Thee by an exact, continual, and persevering practice of Christian mortification. Amen.

Meditation CXLIII.

TRIBUTE IS DEMANDED OF JESUS.

1. Jesus was exempt from paying the tribute; 2. Jesus pays the tribute for Himself and S. Peter. S. Matt. xvii. 24—27.

FIRST POINT.

Jesus exempt from paying tribute.

1. An exemption which was real and well founded. In order to understand all that is about to follow, we must suppose here, that Jesus, after having foretold His death to His Apostles, these latter, seeing Him absorbed in a profound meditation on the designs of God His

Father, followed Him at a little distance, and continued to muse together over that which He had just spoken to them: that this Divine Saviour reached the house of S. Peter, where He was wont to lodge, before them, and it was doubtless at that moment that *when they were come to Capernaum, they that received tribute money came to Peter, and said, Doth not your Master pay tribute? He saith, yes. And when he was come into the house, Jesus prevented him, saying, What thinkest thou, Simon? of whom do the kings of the earth take custom or tribute? of their own children, or of strangers? Peter saith unto Him, of strangers; Jesus saith unto him, Then are the children free.* This tribute was imposed on every family, and it appeared to those who collected it, that Jesus, being at the head of His twelve Apostles, who thus represented a family, was under the obligation to pay it. They did not venture nevertheless to demand it of Jesus Himself; but addressed themselves to S. Peter. Jesus was without any doubt, exempt from it; if this tribute was raised in the name of Herod or of the Romans, Jesus was of the royal line of David; if it was raised, as has been thought was more probable, in the name of God, and for the requirements of the temple, Jesus was the Son of God, the Lord of the temple, and the true Temple Itself. He was then exempt from paying tribute, and His exemption was real and well founded. As for us, by what title do we exempt ourselves from the duties of our Christian religion, from the observance of the obligations it lays upon us? Do we excuse ourselves an account of our age, our occupations, our position, our deserts? What is there in all this too often, but self-deception, pride, self-love, and imaginary hindrances?

2. An exemption which was kept secret. Jesus makes it known only to S. Peter for his instruction and for our's. We, on the contrary, like to make a display of any fancied advantages we may possess; we speak of them to every one in a self-gratified tone and are indignant if any one refuses to acknowledge our claims; we bring

them forward on every occasion, and weary every one with our pretensions.

3. *An exemption of which Jesus does not avail Himself.* Although He had shewn that He was exempt from paying the tribute, He did not dispense with the payment of it, but commanded, as we shall see, S. Peter to satisfy their demands. How His example confounds our pride! yea, Lord, Thou art exempt from all, above all, independent of all; but in order to set me an example, and to overcome my disinclination, Thou dost submit to every thing, and dost refuse no mark of submission or dependence. How then shall I dare again to reply that I am under no obligation, when some good work lies within my power, or some work of charity or devotion is required from me. Is this the example which my Saviour has given me? Is this the language of a disciple of Jesus Christ?

SECOND POINT.

Jesus pays the tribute.

Notwithstanding, continues Jesus, *lest we should offend them, go thou to the sea, and cast a hook, and take up the fish that first cometh up: and when thou hast opened his mouth thou shalt find a piece of money: that take and give unto them for Me and thee.*

1. *Jesus pays in order not to give offence.* The claims of Jesus had not yet been published, and made known to all the world, and therefore in order to avoid giving offence, He wills that the tribute should be paid. It is an offence not to be willing to submit to lawful authority; we are in duty bound to honour and obey all those in authority over us, and to submit ourselves to all those who have the rule over us.

2. *Jesus pays as God,* if we may so speak, that is to say, by means of a miracle. Wherefore was a mira-

cle employed? Because neither Jesus nor S. Peter had wherewithal to pay. What an instance we have here of the poverty in which our Blessed Saviour was pleased to live! And wherefore this particular miracle? In order to make us understand the greatness of the power of Jesus, which extends not only over all the earth, but even to the depths of the sea, Who knows how to make Himself obeyed, not only by devils, but by the most senseless of animals. What must have been the astonishment of those who had demanded the tribute, when they saw whence the payment was drawn! Let us admire and praise the infinite Power to Whom every thing is subject. Jesus pays the tribute in order to give us the example of submission and dependence, but He pays it as God in order to shew us His Independence, and to give still more weight to His example.

3. Jesus pays the double of that which is demanded of Him. The stater was a piece of silver which was worth four drachms, and only two of them were demanded of Him; He confirms by His example that which He had taught, If any one will take away thy coat, let him have thy cloke also. S. Peter obeys without reply, without any delay, and without any doubt. Let us imitate his obedience.

Prayer. [a] O Almighty God, Who by Thy Son Jesus Christ didst give to Thy Apostle, S. Peter, many excellent gifts, and commandedst him earnestly to feed Thy flock; Make, we beseech Thee, all Bishops and Pastors diligently to preach Thy Holy Word, and the people obediently to follow the same, that they may receive the crown of everlasting glory, through Jesus Christ our Lord. Amen.

[a] Collect for S. Peter's Day substituted for original.

Meditation CXLIV.

QUESTIONS OF THE APOSTLES ON THE SUBJECT OF PRE-EMINENCE.

1. Jesus teaches us how to avoid even thoughts of ambition; 2. He teaches us what is the value of humility. S. Matt. xviii. 1– 5. S. Mark ix. 33—36. S. Luke ix. 46–48.

FIRST POINT.

Of ambitious thoughts.

1. Thoughts opposed to the spirit of Christ. *Then there arose a reasoning among them, which of them should be greatest.* Ambitious thoughts stifle every feeling of piety and humanity, and are often a great stumbling-block. Jesus had just foretold to the Apostles His coming death, and they had been distressed at it; but ambition soon turned their thoughts away from these sad thoughts in order to fill them with hopes which were more flattering. They had not well understood all that Jesus had spoken to them concerning His death and resurrection, and they did not venture to ask Him the explanation of it; but what they were anxious to ascertain, and what appeared to them of far greater moment, was, to discover who amongst them would succeed to the highest place, when Jesus should have taken possession of His Kingdom. Alas! what piety can there be towards God, and what humanity towards mankind, when a person is governed by ambition? Shall Apostles, who have forsaken all, to follow a Master Who had given them so many lessons and shown them so many examples of humility and self-renunciation, cherish such thoughts? O pride! how art thou rooted in the heart of man! thou art to be found in the lowliest conditions of life, as also in the holiest! Ambition is not the virtue of heroes, it is the vice of all mankind. Every one, in his station and in his sphere, seeks to raise himself up above the rest. The Apostles, occupied by these thoughts, suffered Jesus

to advance in front of them, and they followed at some distance, discussing this question, and making valid their pretensions. Their dispute was keen, lasted some time, and was brought to no conclusion. How many wars, how many quarrels, how many disputes among mankind have had no other source than the desire to know *which of them should be greatest.* Take away the desire of domination, of making a name in the world, of rendering oneself worthy of praise or applause, or of humiliating one's rivals, or surpassing one's equals, and you will cause all disputes to cease, and all the causes of offence to disappear which are their unfortunate consequences. Ah! let us detest the odious vice of ambition, and let us watch that it does not enter into our hearts.

2. Thoughts known by Jesus. *But He, knowing their thoughts.* It would seem that the Apostles withdrew to a distance in order to give free vent to their disputes respecting their respective claims. Jesus *read the thoughts of their hearts.* In vain do we turn away from the thought of God in order to dwell on our own greatness; in vain do we hide from men the pride and vanity which are the motive-springs of our actions; in vain do we dissimulate to ourselves the spirit of ambition, and the desire of predominance which prompt our actions; in vain do we adorn ourselves with the glorious titles of justice, zeal, truth and religion, God sees the depths of our heart, its secret thoughts, its most hidden motives, and He sees there nought but pride, vanity, and ambition. Let us examine ourselves, let us purify our hearts in the presence of Jesus Christ, in the eyes of Him, from Whom nothing is hidden, nothing is obscure.

3. Thoughts brought before the tribunal of Jesus Christ. *And He came to Capernaum; and being in the house, He asked them, What was it that ye disputed among yourselves by the way? But they held their peace; for by the way they had disputed among themselves who should be the greatest.* The Apostles then arrived at Capernaum, and entered into the house where Jesus Christ was. Then this Divine Saviour asked them

of what they had spoken on the way, since He had left
them alone, after having announced to them what He
had yet to suffer for the glory of His Father, and the
salvation of the world; they looked at one another, and
as criminals when brought before their judge feel at the
first question put to them that their crimes are discovered,
so did this first question of our Lord's fill the Apostles
with confusion, and they remained there utterly disconcerted and unable to utter a single word. What answer
had they to give, they, His Apostles, formed in His
school, which was that of humility, save to acknowledge
the disputes into which their vanity had led them, their
ambitious thoughts, to lay bare the unworthiness and
baseness of their feelings. And what shall I answer to
Jesus, when, brought before Him, He will ask me what
has been the subject of my conversations, with what I
have occupied myself on the fleeting journey of this life,
I, a Christian, I, His disciple, baptized with His Baptism,
instructed in His mysteries and His doctrine? What
shall I answer with regard to so many thoughts, so many
actions, so many desires, not only vain, base, despicable,
and unworthy of a Christian, but vile, abominable and
unworthy of a human being? Ah! Lord, I am quite
covered with confusion at the remembrance of them;
pardon Thou me, O Jesus, at the tribunal of Thy mercy,
before I am cited to appear at the tribunal of Thy
justice.

4. Thoughts which we take great care to conceal
from the knowledge of men. If there is no thought
which is more familiar to us than to wish to rise above
others, there is none which we more carefully conceal
from others, since it would not fail to draw down upon
us their contempt and hatred. The apostles, questioned
by Jesus, are at length compelled to break their silence. But let us see, how ambition, which can support
its pretensions with so much tenacity, can also disguise
itself most skilfully. In order to reply to their Master's
questions, the apostles themselves put one to Him. *At
the same time came the disciples unto Jesus, saying,*

Who is the greatest in the kingdom of Heaven? It would appear from these words as if they would imply that this had been the subject of their disputes by the way; but what a difference there really was! Here, it is only a question generally put, there each set forth his personal claims; here, it is a question of pure speculation, there it was a matter which touched each of them closely; here it is an edifying question, there it was a lively and scandalous dispute, in which there was no mention of the kingdom of Heaven, but which only concerned the point as to who amongst them should be the greatest. How hidden and full of artifice is vanity? We put sometimes similar questions which appear to have no reference to ourselves. We ask what is the most perfect way of life, what is the most praiseworthy conduct, and what are the most meritorious acts, but we do not ask these questions for any other purpose than to raise ourselves up above others, and nourish the vanity and ambition which reign in our hearts.

SECOND POINT.

Of the value of humility.

1. Humility is the measure of greatness in the kingdom of heaven. *And Jesus sat down, and called the twelve.* Let us also listen with the attention and respect which the Divine Master Who is about to speak deserves, and let us bear in mind the divine truth He is about to utter. *And saith unto them, If any man desire to be first, the same shall be last of all, and servant of all.* Noble and holy ambition, to desire to be great in the kingdom of Heaven. This is the way whereby to attain to it, a sure means, for it is Jesus Christ Himself, the King of Heaven, Who gives it us; a means which is in our power, and which no one can take from us. This means does not consist, in words of mere ceremony, and sometimes of vanity, but in putting ourselves in the last place, in being contented to be placed there, in desiring to be there and to

remain there. It consists, further, in yielding to others in everything, in looking upon ourselves as the last of all; it consists, in ministering to others in every way we can, and looking upon ourselves as the servants of others. We must be little in the eyes of the world, and in our own eyes; but the more we humble ourselves, the more we shall be exalted, and the greater shall we be hereafter. Do we believe this truth?

2. Without humility, we cannot enter into the kingdom of Heaven. *And Jesus called a little child unto Him, and set him in the midst of them, and when He had taken him in His arms, He said unto them, Verily, I say unto you, Except ye be converted, and become as little children, ye shall not enter into the kingdom of Heaven. Whosoever therefore shall humble himself as this little child, the same is greatest in the kingdom of Heaven.* It is to us all that these words are addressed, whatever rank we may occupy, however great, however learned we may be, were we chosen apostles of Jesus Christ. If we are not converted, if we do not renounce these projects of fortune and greatness, these desires of esteem and pre-eminence, these ideas of comparing ourselves with others, these murmurings, these complaints of the want of regard shown towards ourselves, these flattering thoughts of our own knowledge and merits, we shall not enter into the kingdom of Heaven. Look at this child, see its innocence, its candour, gentleness, docility, simplicity and obedience. No disquietude for the future, no projects of ambition and fortune. He believes what he is told, he says what he thinks, he goes where he is led, he does as he is told. How different to ourselves! Nevertheless, if we do not become like him, we shall not enter into the kingdom of heaven; but on the other hand, the more we strive to resemble him, the greater we shall be in the heavenly kingdom.

3. Humility is a virtue which delights our Saviour's heart. *And when Jesus had taken him in His arms.* Who would not envy the blessedness of that child? Jesus did not grant the favour of this embrace merely

on account of the tender age or disposition of this child, but for the sake of the virtues of which it was the image and type. He who strives to acquire these virtues, he who has made himself a child, by acquiring the virtues of a child, has the same claim to the favours which Jesus bestowed on this little child; he enjoys His embraces, and receives from Him the most signal favours. Let the world then forget or despise me, the love of Jesus Christ will be an abundant consolation. Let the world grant me its esteem and its favours, the love of Jesus Christ will enable me to detach myself from them. In the Arms of Jesus, I shall be alike insensible to the praise or contempt of men! oh blessed childhood! form it within my heart, O Jesus, the humblest and sweetest of the children of men!

4. Humility raises us up to Jesus Christ, up to God, His Father. *Whosoever shall receive one of such children in My Name, receiveth Me, and whosoever shall receive Me, receiveth not Me, but Him that sent Me, for he that is least among you all, the same shall be great.* It follows thence that all the good we do to a humble person, who has become a child for Jesus Christ's sake, and all the help that we bestow on him, is accepted by Jesus Christ, as done unto Himself, and not only as done to Himself, but even as done to God Himself, His Father, Who sent Him on the earth to save us.

Prayer. What motives are there not, O my God, to make me love Thee, to practise humility, and to make me love, and esteem it in others? Grant, Lord, that I may be gentle and humble of heart after Thy example: that I may be so, not out of necessity and in a murmuring spirit, but out of a feeling of true humility; that I may love to be dependent, to obey, to be counted as nothing, and to remain in this state of lowliness, until it please Thee to raise me to heaven, and to make me partaker there of true greatness. Amen.

Meditation CXLV.

OF ONE WHO DROVE OUT DEVILS IN THE NAME OF JESUS.

ON ZEAL.

This circumstance sets before us the characters, 1. of imperfect zeal; 2. of indiscreet zeal; 3. of enlightened zeal. S. Mark ix. 38—41. S. Luke ix. 49, 50.

FIRST POINT.

Of imperfect zeal.

And John answered and said, Master, we saw one casting out devils in Thy Name; and we forbad him, because he followeth not with us.

1. There was good in this zeal. A man who did not follow Jesus Christ, who was neither of the number of His Apostles, nor of His disciples, nevertheless cast out the spirit of darkness, in the name of Jesus. Perhaps he had beheld the empire which the Apostles exercised by virtue of this Sacred Name, and without knowing or seeking to know anything further in the matter, he invoked with faith the same Name, and worked the same miracles. How powerful is this Name! how holy It is! how terrible It is, and how feared in hell! Let us adore It with reverence, and put our trust in It. If a stranger employs it with so much success, shall we fear to employ it in vain, we who belong to Jesus, we who are His disciples and members?

2. There is something incomprehensible in this zeal. How could it be that a man who worked miracles in the Name of Jesus should not desire to see and hear Him? how was it that he did not desire to follow Jesus, and be numbered among His disciples? The heart of man is indeed incomprehensible. We often meet still with those who are zealous for the salvation of others, but have no thought for their own; who know how to

lead others into the way of perfection, and yet neglect to enter it themselves: who teach others the practice of prayer and mortification, and yet practise neither the one nor the other. Am I not of this number? Is my zeal perfect? Is it well ordered, and do I begin with myself?

3. We must not seek to check this zeal, but to perfect it. We are not to put a stop to this zeal either in ourselves or in others; but we must labour to make it perfect, not contenting ourselves with calling on the name of the Saviour, but by applying ourselves to practise His commandments, to follow His maxims, and to imitate His example.

SECOND POINT.

Of indiscreet zeal.

1. This zeal is rapid in its decisions. Indiscretion in zeal is generally the fault of beginners. Those who have least experience are the least embarrassed in passing judgment, and the promptest in their decisions. The apostles had only entered on their first mission when they met this man who cast out devils in the Name of Jesus: they came to a conclusion at once; they judged that it was their duty to oppose him, and they forbad him to undertake any thing similar for the future; but they were wrong in so doing. What harm did this man do, and what good could arise from this prohibition? If we could only give ourselves time to reflect, and to examine these two points, before we pass judgment on any one, our decision would be less prompt, but it would be safer and better considered. If the apostles, who were men sent by Jesus Christ, nevertheless judged amiss in the case of this man, should we not fear greatly lest we also err!

2. Indiscreet zeal is often ill founded. The only reason which determined the apostles on forbidding this man to continue to cast out devils, was because the man did not follow Jesus along with them. *He followeth not with us.* And such is often the only reason which

leads us to blame, or to hinder the good that others do or might do. We do not see him with us, we say; he does not belong to us, he does not follow us. But far from that being a just reason, it is only a pretext wherewith to cloak our ambition, pride, jealousy, and the desire we feel of making our authority and our own deserts felt. How many evils may not this party-spirit cause in the Church; one body assumes to itself an exclusive privilege of doing good, and seeks to exclude others from contributing to the common welfare, by putting a wrong construction on their efforts, or seeking to diminish the esteem in which they are held.

3. Indiscreet zeal seldom takes counsel from others. Whether all the apostles met this man, or only some few, it is certain that those who met him were of the same mind, and had no doubt as to the step they took; that it never occurred to them to consult their Master, either before they issued their prohibition to him, or even when they returned to Jesus. It was only after the lessons of humility and charity which Jesus had just given them that S. John began to fear that he had done wrong, and related the matter to our Lord, as it had taken place; and he then saw by our Lord's reply, that they had acted too hastily, and that they ought to have asked for counsel before taking upon themselves to rebuke the man. Presumption, confidence in one's own powers are very dangerous in the exercise of zeal. He who does know how to doubt, and suspend his decision, who has not sufficient charity to fear lest he may injure his neighbour by deciding too precipitately, cannot fail to commit great faults, to hinder much good, and to cause real evils.

THIRD POINT.

Of enlightened zeal.

1. Enlightened zeal refers all to the glory of Jesus Christ. *Jesus said, Forbid him not; for there is no man which shall do a miracle in My Name, that can*

lightly speak evil of Me. The time was not distant, when nearly the whole world would be let loose against Jesus. Now, it was not morally possible, that this man, who cast out devils, in the Name of Jesus, would change so suddenly, would declare himself against Jesus, and join himself to his enemies. Let us then have the glory of Jesus Christ always in view, let us seek it alone, and we shall learn to rejoice with S. Paul in all that promotes it, in whatever manner it may come to pass, and from whatever source it may come. Would to God, said Moses, that all the Lord's people were prophets, and that the Lord would put His Spirit upon them.

2. Enlightened zeal refers everything to the spread of Christ's Church. *He that is not against us is on our part.* Our Lord had said on another occasion, *He that is not with Me is against Me.* These different ways of speaking are verified in a contrary sense, according to the different occasions to which they are applied. We may say that on that occasion our Lord was speaking of a person's inward dispositions, but here He speaks of external works. The time was soon about to come in which the Apostles and the Church would have to endure a general persecution from the Jews. Under these circumstances, all were to be looked upon as friends who did not declare themselves avowedly as enemies; and far from reproaching them even with their indifference, they ought rather to bear them good will for it; with much greater reason ought they then not to oppose the zeal of this man, which might turn to good. We are no longer placed in the same circumstances, but we should learn from these words of our Lord that all which can serve to the spread of the Faith, and the edification of our neighbour merits our esteem, support and favour.

3. Enlightened zeal refers everything to oneness with our neighbour. *Whosoever shall give you a cup of water to drink in My Name, because ye belong to Christ, Verily I say unto you, he shall not lose his reward.* The third motive which ought to engage us to desire that everyone should labour to contribute to the glory

of God, of His Christ and of His Church, is the advantage which each one draws, who co-operates in this good work. If it be but a glass of water which is given to one of the members of Jesus Christ, because he belongs to Jesus Christ, out of affection for the doctrine of Jesus Christ, for the sake of His Church, He assures us Himself that he will not lose his reward; with far greater reason therefore should he not lose it, who glorified the Name of Jesus, by invoking it against the evil spirits. What great virtues have not been gained, what great merits have not sprung from beginnings of but small value, which have drawn down graces, whose progress has become immense. Let us then encourage ourselves and others in the practice of every kind of good works, since we serve so merciful a God, Who recompenses so abundantly whatever is done for Him, however small.

Prayer. Ah! Lord, grant that I may neglect no good work which lies within my power. If I cannot perform those which are the greatest in Thy sight, yet grant that I may practise with fidelity those which belong to my station and my calling, that I may sanctify by the purity of my intention, my commonest actions. Far be from me that ambition which refers everything to self, that jealousy, which, under the appearance of zeal, prefers to see that left undone which it cannot do itself, rather than to leave others free to accomplish it. O my God! grant that I may have Thy glory only in view and that I may look upon all those who are joined together in this one aim, as being united to myself in one common bond of love and charity. Amen.

Meditation CXLVI.

OF OFFENCES.

Consider 1. the misery of him who causes the offence; 2. the care we ought to take to guard against offences; 3. the crime of him who causes the offence. S. Matt. xviii. 6—14. S. Mark ix. 42—47.

FIRST POINT.

Of the misery of him who causes the offence.

To the zeal which each one ought to have to extend the kingdom of God, and which God will not leave without reward, Jesus opposes the offence which destroys the kingdom of God, and which God will not leave without punishment. *But whoso shall offend one of these little ones which believe in Me, it were better for him that a millstone were hanged about his neck, and that he were drowned in the depth of the sea. Woe unto the world because of offences! for it must needs be that offences come; but woe to that man by whom the offence cometh!*

1. Of the necessity of offences. This necessity comes from the malice of men, and from the plan of wisdom according to which God governs the world. Men, being what they are, naturally prone to evil through original sin, free nevertheless, and with a freedom strengthened by the grace of the Saviour, on the one hand, God, according to His plan of wisdom, leaving men to act according to their own free wills during the short space of their lives, without hindering or interrupting the exercise of their liberty, it is not possible but that several amongst them should abuse this very liberty in order to give themselves up to evil; that in time, they should form the greater number, and that they should strive to render others imitators of their crimes. We must not be surprised that there should be offences, we must not be offended at them, or murmur against the wisdom of God, and distress ourselves, and imagine that all is

lost, that God does not behold what takes place on the earth, or that all is indifferent to Him. Offences follow in the order of the Providence of God respecting mankind. God has willed to crown in Heaven those noble souls who, by His grace, become conquerors, who have generously declared themselves on His side, and who have really striven for Him. Offences contribute to manifest the constancy, the virtue, the zeal of faithful souls. Offences then enter into the scheme of this Infinite Providence, Which includes equally the freedom of action and its necessary effects, and makes every thing subservient to His glory and to the happiness of the righteous.

2. Of the place where offences prevail. They prevail in the world, it is there that they have erected a throne, and that they exercise their empire. Every thing in the world tends to lay a snare in our path, to form an occasion of falling, and offers a constant and entire opposition to the precepts of the Gospel. We find everywhere causes of offence, temptations to evil in all we see and hear. Do not let us be surprised then that our Saviour uttered these warning words against it. *Woe unto the world because of offences!* If the duties of our station require us to mix in the world, let us be on our guard that we are not carried away by its precepts and maxims, and draw down upon us this curse.

3. Of the punishment of offences. If offences are necessary, if the wisdom of God permits them and is glorified by them, wherefore does God punish them? It is that the wisdom of God, which permits them and is glorified through them does not destroy on that account the wickedness of him who deserves punishment, any more than it destroys the virtue of him who keeps clear of these causes of offence and merits a reward. The good which God draws out of evil justifies the wisdom of His ways, and not the wickedness of him who commits the evil. Therefore woe be to him who offends against the least of His children, the lowest of those who believe in Him. It were better for him that he had been thrown into the depths of the sea with a millstone

about his neck, than that he should be cast into hell fire, where the fire is not quenched. *Woe then to that man by whom the offence cometh!* Woe be *to that man* who corrupts the young, and teaches them the evil they do not know! *Woe to that man* who leads astray innocence by entreaties, threats, promises or by bribes. *Woe* to him who turns others away from the paths of virtue and piety, by satires and railleries! *Woe* to him who writes books against religion or morals, or who disseminates them! *Woe* be to him who leads others astray by means of unseemly pictures, or of impious or impure songs! Lastly, *woe* be to him, who causes offences, of whatever nature they be, or who, having it in his power to hinder that evil, does not do so effectually, or use his utmost efforts to do so! Let us examine whether we have not ourselves been a cause of offence to others! Let us weep bitterly over our faults, let us repent of them, and try in every way we can, to repair the evil we have done.

SECOND POINT.

Of the care we should take to guard against offences.

This care consists in avoiding, fleeing, and cutting off all occasions of falling which our Lord sums up under three heads, under the figures of the hand, the foot, and the eye.

1. Of the hand. *If thy hand offend thee, cut it off; and cast it from thee,* if you desire to enter into heaven, and not to fall into hell-fire. By these words, Jesus condemns the immodest hand, whose actions will be punished by hell-fire; the covetous hand, always closed to the necessities of a neighbour, but always opened to theft, rapine, injustice, usury, fraud; the angry hand, always ready to strike, to injure, to do hurt, and to revenge: the idle hand, which does no useful thing, and practises no good work, has no motion but for pleasure, and frivolous amusements.

2. *Of the foot.* *If thy foot offend thee, cut it off, and cast it from thee,* if you desire to enter into heaven, and not to fall into hell-fire. This foot signifies the places to which we go, of unlawful pleasures, and dissipation; this foot signifies the persons we frequent, persons who are likely to lead us astray; persons, whose morals are corrupt, and who may infect us with the same contagion; persons, whose conversation is repugnant to modesty, piety, or charity; this foot signifies the persons, in whose wrong doings we connive, if for worldly reasons, or motives of policy we find it convenient to cultivate their acquaintance. Let us cut off, let us cast away this foot which offends, rather than to *be cast into everlasting fire.*

3. Of the eye. *If thine eye offend thee, pluck it out, and cast it from thee,* if you desire to enter into heaven, and not to fall into hell-fire. This eye, which you must pluck out, are looks of distraction on all that presents itself, which extinguish fervour, devotion, the love of God, and the spirit of recollection and prayer; immodest looks, which may kindle a flame that may not be quenched again; unguarded looks, either on persons, pictures, or engravings, the sight of which may make dangerous impressions on the senses and on the heart: looks of passion on lascivious books and objects, such as would excite impurity, and nourish adulterous, criminal, or sacrilegious fires; looks of envy on the property of another, or his advantages, or successes, in order to undervalue them, or deprive him of them; looks of curiosity or ill-will upon the actions of others, in order to blame them, to criticise them, or decry them.

What our Lord says here of the hand, the foot, and the eye, is not less to be understood of all the other senses, hearing, smell, taste, the tongue, the heart, the imagination, memory, thought, mind and will. From whatever side the offence comes, all that is an occasion of falling to us must be cut off without any reserve, under pain of our being for ever shut out of heaven, and cast down to hell. A vast subject for self-examination, and an important matter for reflection! If we would but take care to cut thus at the root of the evil, salvation would be neither as difficult, nor as uncertain, nor as hazardous as it is.

THIRD POINT.

Of the crime of him who causes the offence.

1. The man who causes the offence offends the heavenly Angels. *Take heed that ye despise not one of these little ones; for I say unto you, That in heaven their angels do always behold the face of My Father which is in heaven.* This child whom you despise, this servant, that young person, whom you think that you can sin against with impunity, and make the accomplices of your crimes, do you know well who they are, Whose they are, to Whom they belong, and who they are who protect them? They are the children of God, and the angels of heaven are commissioned to defend and protect them: each of them has a guardian angel, who watches over them without losing sight of God. These angels see you; and what must be their grief, when they see you endeavouring to ruin that which they take so much care to preserve? Will they not entreat the God, in Whose Presence they dwell continually, to take vengeance on you? Ah! imitate rather these blessed angels, and seek to join them in their work, seek to protect the innocent, and to remove all stumbling blocks and causes of offence out of their way. Thank God that He sends His angels to minister unto us; and reverence these holy, powerful, and blessed spirits.

2. The man by whom the offence cometh makes the redemption of the Saviour of no avail with regard to him against whom he sins. *For the Son of Man is come to save that which was lost.* Jesus came down from Heaven in order to save mankind; He came down from the bosom of His Father. He has, so to say, left the Heavenly court and the company of holy Angels to seek after this sheep that has gone astray; and when

He has found it, and rejoices over it, you, by your offence, you lay waste a harvest on which He had placed His most tender hopes. It was of these little ones, of these simple and innocent souls, that He hoped to form to Himself a new and faithful people; already He had purchased them at the price of His Blood, already He had consecrated and incorporated them by Baptism; He would have made Saints and elect of them, and you overthrow all His hopes, you destroy the fruit of His labours and of redemption. Do you now conceive what a crime this offence is? In a short time, the face of Christianity would be renewed, if it were not for the offence which is given to youth, and often to childhood even before the age of reason! Woe be to them who render themselves guilty of so great a crime!

3. The man by whom the offence cometh sets himself in opposition to the will of God, Who desires the salva- of mankind. *It is not the will of your Father Which is in Heaven, that one of these little ones should perish.* All that Jesus has done for the salvation of mankind, He has done in conformity with the will of God His Father, Whose only Son He is. This God, the Creator and Father of all men, Who has more specially become our Father through our adoption in Jesus Christ, wills not that any should perish. He wills that after having lived on the earth as worthy children, we should be partakers in Heaven, of His eternal inheritance, with His Blessed Son, and that united to Him and to our Saviour, we should enjoy an eternity of happiness in Heaven. Ah! what murder does not he commit, who opposing himself to this will of God, and uniting himself to the malice and jealousy of the Evil one, deprives a soul of so great blessedness, in order to precipitate it into the torments of hell fire. But does the man who thus causes the offence imagine that he will always be able to oppose the will of God? If this will of God for our salvation is conditional in this world, and demands a faithful co-operation on our part, that will of God which He has to recompense virtue and to punish

vice in the next world is absolute, and nothing can either oppose or resist it. If in the next world, he who has allowed himself to be led astray by the offences of others is punished in so terrible a manner, what will become of him who by his offences, has lost himself, and caused the loss of others?

Prayer. Ah Lord, grant that I may be the victim, not of Thine anger, but of charity, in burning with the fire of Thy love. Grant that, far from corrupting others, and becoming a cause of offence to them, I may seek, on the contrary, to preserve them from the corruption and offences of the world. Amen.

Meditation CXLVII.

OF HELL.

If the laws which our Lord has just given us respecting offences, appear to us severe and difficult to practise, the motives which He sets before us are powerful enough to cause every difficulty to vanish, since it is a matter, on the one hand, of gaining heaven, and on the other, of avoiding hell. Let us pause at this last motive; *Be cast into everlasting fire. Into the fire that never shall be quenched, where the worm dieth not. Into hell fire.* Such are the words of Jesus Christ, words which prove to us undeniably, that in the torments of hell there are three things, the fire, the worm, eternity; we will add to them the justice of this punishment. S. Matt. xviii. 8, 9. S. Mark ix. 43—48.

FIRST POINT.

Of hell fire, or of external sufferings.

1. Fire surpasses all other bodily sufferings. We are right in saying that there are torments in hell, since there is fire there. Think over all the diseases, all the sufferings which we can possibly endure in our bodies, they are nothing in comparison with the suffering which is caused by fire. Have we never experienced the sharpness of the pain in ourselves, or witnessed on others the terrible effects it produces? Any burning

thing taken up accidentally, a drop of boiling water, a spark which has fallen by chance on the hand draws forth cries and causes the severest sufferings.

2. Fire is the most fearful torture that human justice can employ. It is so terrible, that, if it is employed in its full strength, it cannot last long, and when people desire to prolong the suffering, it can only be used little by little. A man burned at a slow fire; this thought makes one shudder, and yet he only suffers in some part of his body. A man burned alive at a quick fire is a horrible spectacle, the sight of which is too terrible to witness; nevertheless he suffers only a few moments, and death soon delivers him from his tortures. But to be thrown into the fire, to be enveloped in it, to be penetrated by it, to be burnt in all the parts of one's body, without the body being consumed, or the suffering becoming deadened, without the possibility of death or an end to these terrible torments, what a condition, what a punishment! Ah, my God, who could live before Thee, who would not dread so powerful and terrible a justice?

3. Fire is the most terrible of all sights. A house has caught fire; it seizes all the parts of it, it gains all the stories; the flame, mingled with a black smoke, rises in eddies above the roof, and makes known afar the horror and the ravage which it is causing. Some unhappy people who are surprised by the fire, and are enclosed in the burning mass and surrounded by flames seek in vain for the means of escape; bewildered and knowing not in what direction their steps are turning, they run into the very death which they desire to avoid, they cross the flames only to fall into burning gulfs which open on each side, and where they perish miserably. Meanwhile the whole city is alarmed, and in motion; every one hastens thither, at the peril even of their lives, to bring them succour, to extinguish the fire, and to preserve the neighbouring houses. A feeble image, which but little resembles hell-fire. Unhappy victims of the justice of a Lord Whom you have despised, there remains no way for you to escape from the burning

flames, to get out of your fiery dungeons, nor even for you to die in them. You have neither help nor mitigation of your sufferings, nor even compassion to expect. The fire which devours you is of such a nature that it cannot be extinguished in you; you are yourselves the immortal aliment on which it feeds and the breath of the anger of your God Who has kindled it will be eternal as Himself.

4. Fire is the element against which we take most precautions. See with what care we guard against it, with what quickness we extinguish a spark that falls, or pick up ashes that spring out from burning wood; how watchfully we examine that all risk of fire is avoided, before we take our sleep. Ah, we say, no one can take too many precautions against fire. Senseless that we are! We take no precaution, we have no fear, no disquietude with regard to hell fire! With doubts upon religion, with known and grave sins on our conscience, we remain perfectly tranquil, and give ourselves up to sleep as if there were nothing to fear. We are on the brink of this fearful gulf, and yet we laugh and amuse ourselves, and take delight in throwing ourselves into it, and dragging others with us. What folly, what madness! Does our Lord say too much when He says; *If thy hand or thy foot offend thee, cut them off, and if thine eye offend thee, pluck it out.*

SECOND POINT.

Of the gnawing worm—or inward suffering.

The torment of fire, in this life, absorbs all the faculties of the soul, and takes away from it all power of occupying itself with any other object; it is not thus in hell. As the fire fills all the faculty which the soul has of feeling, its two other faculties feeling and will, preserve all their powers in order to cause it a new kind of torment, which is this gnawing worm with which it is devoured, and of which the suffering is beyond all that we could conceive or express. *Their worm dieth not.* Three kinds of reflections overwhelm the damned soul.

1. Reflections as to the present. The damned soul turns its thoughts to the present, to all that surrounds it, and it beholds only torments, and the utter impossibility of avoiding them or of alleviating their severity. Sometimes it regards them as cruel, unjust, and curses its Creator, and its Saviour; sometimes it acknowledges their justice and equity; it conceives all the horror of the crimes with which it is defiled, and turns its fury against itself; at other times it compares its own state with that of the blessed; it knows that this same God Whom it has rejected, communicates Himself to others in all the splendour of His glory; that, whilst it feels the weight of His avenging Hand, that same Hand is putting forth all Its Power to make others blessed, and that while it is plunged in an abyss of fire and torments, they swim in an ocean of delights of which the ineffable sweetness can never be changed. And amongst those blessed citizens of Heaven, it counts up some which it has known, with whom it has lived, whom it has perhaps mocked at, despised and insulted; it recognizes there relations, friends, who have had its salvation at heart, and have done their best to draw it thitherwards with themselves. With what longing does it desire to partake of this blessedness. Ah! interest yourselves then on my behalf, it cries, and draw me out of this fearful gulf. Vain desires, useless cries which do not reach to them, to the glorious abode of the blessed. There, absorbed in God, calm in their happiness, they think no more of that soul; they have no further remembrance of it. Transported there with hatred and fury, it would annihilate every thing if it could, the Creator and all created beings, Heaven, hell and itself with all the universe; but it feels its powerlessness, it gnaws itself, it tears itself, it spends itself, and bemoans to itself its most cruel torment.

2. Reflections as to the future. It casts its thoughts on to the future, and sees there only a boundless abyss,

an endless continuation of the same tortures, without any hope that they will either come to an end or change, or be lessened. No more help, no further remedy for them, no further consolation, or compassion; there is no power capable of succouring or delivering them; there is no strength in nature save to torment it, and to perpetuate its torments; and who can express the rage and despair which such an assurance causes?

3. As to the past. It reads in the past that it is through its own fault that it has fallen into this abyss of torments; it recalls to mind the means of grace it has had whereby to escape from it, the religious instructions, the corrections, the good examples with which God provided it: it acknowledges that it has neither been taken by surprise, nor deceived, that it knew all what it now suffers, that it thought of it, meditated on it, that there was a time when it walked in the right way, when it depended on itself to persevere in it, that, having sinned, it might have returned to God by repentance, and have regained the grace it had lost. Ah! blessed time thou art no longer, thou wilt never come back. 1 am plunged in sovereign misery, and I was made in order to enjoy sovereign happiness; I might have been in Paradise, and I am in hell; all is lost for me, and 1 am without any hope. It meditates on the vanity of the objects which it preferred to God, and which have been the cause which brought it into all this misery. World, pleasures, riches, sensual enjoyments, transitory life, where are ye? Is it then possible that ye have seduced me, that it is for you that I exposed myself to these torments, and finally have fallen into them? O regrets, O grief, O tears of blood! But vain regrets, fruitless tears, gnawing worm which will never die! I am damned, I am lost, and my loss is irreparable.

THIRD POINT.

Of the eternity of hell.

I. With relation to the damned. 1. It fills up the

measure of their misery, because it renders their sufferings infinite. The least and the slightest pain, even an uncomfortable position, were it even without inconvenience, if it was to last for ever, would be an infinite evil. What is then this *fire that is not quenched*, and this *worm that dieth not?* An eternity! who can hear that word without shuddering? The thought of it is so terrible, that it is sometimes dangerous for the mind to seek to search too deeply into it. 2. The eternity of hell fills up the measure of the misery of the damned, because it is known by them. In sharp pain the first anxiety we feel is to know when the pain will cease. If it last ever so short a time, we desire death, and are irritated by its continuance. But the first thing of which a damned soul becomes aware in entering hell, is that it will never come out again. 3. The eternity of hell fills up the measure of the damned, because it is always present to their minds. A damned person cannot any longer deceive himself as to the duration of his sufferings: he cannot suffer without at the same time knowing that he will suffer eternally. Thus we may say that at each moment, he suffers an eternity of torment. O God! what vengeance! how terrible are Thy judgments!

2. Of the eternity of hell with regard to ourselves. 1. It is an object of faith. Jesus Christ has clearly revealed it in His Gospel. To deny this eternity, is not to destroy it, it is only to draw it down on ourselves, to make sure of it; for we must at the same time deny Jesus Christ, and His Gospel. This eternity is incomprehensible; but such are all objects of faith, because they turn upon the nature, the designs, and works of an Infinite and Incomprehensible Being. All the works of this Infinite Being participate in His Infinity, and are according to their nature, works of an Infinite Love, Mercy, Liberality, Justice, and Severity. Let us adore, fear, and love this Infinite Being, let us profit by His love and His mercy, so that we may escape the punishments of His Infinite Justice. 2. The eternity of hell is a subject of fear to us. To fear hell, to fear

eternal damnation, to fear sin which alone leads to hell, to fear God, Who punishes sin with such severity, and Who alone can cast us down into hell: these are the things we have to fear. And who would not fear Thee, O terrible God! and how can it be that men fear so many things on earth, and yet do not fear hell. How is it that men fear other men so much, and yet do not fear God? Blindly senseless in this have I been myself! am not I so still? Why are there so many damned in hell? because they have not feared. Let us fear Him with an efficacious fear, which shall be the basis of all our actions, of all our deliberations, of all our undertakings, of all the movements of our hearts. The fear of the Lord is the beginning of wisdom.

3. The eternity of hell is a motive of fervour and love. I have merited hell, and God has preserved me from it! If I had died at such a time, under such circumstances, my soul would have been lost, I should be now in hell, and there would be no more hope for me. There are now in hell those who have died at a younger age than I, and to whom there remains no hope of escape. Why then am I not there? by what excess of goodness, by what special favour, O my God! hast Thou preserved me from so great misery? Thou dost reject these souls, whilst Thou dost invite me to come to Thee; Thou dost make known to them that there is no further redemption for them, whilst Thou dost offer me the Blood of Thy dear Son. They are plunged in the fires of Thy wrath, and I am surrounded by the fires of Thy love. An eternity of misery is their irrevocable portion, and an eternity of blessedness is offered to me. Thou dost invite me to partake in it. Hell has closed upon them, and Heaven has opened for me. Alas! they complain of it; Thy goodness to me excites their murmurs, their blasphemies, and yet it does not excite my love! Ah! I love Thee, O God, my Deliverer, O God, my Protector! I love Thee, I bless Thee, I admire Thee, and I am ready to do all that lies in my power to prove my love to Thee. Thou hast delivered me from hell,

and how can I find anything difficult in thy service? If one of these unhappy victims of hell could come back on the earth, would he find anything hard in the exercise of virtue, and in the constant practice of all his duties?

FOURTH POINT.

Of the equity of the punishment of hell.

1. Examine to what this punishment is proportioned.
1. It is proportioned to the grievousness of the sin. We are not to judge of sin according to our own prejudices, passions, senses, nor according to the judgment of the world, but according to the light of faith. Sin offends God, it is a disobedience to His known and declared will, a transgression of His sovereign and absolute commands; a transgression, a disobedience committed in His presence and in His sight, notwithstanding His threats and His promises, and in order to commit which we have been obliged to make use of His own blessings, of our being, our body, our soul, and of the other creatures which He had given us in order to serve Him, and which we hold only from His liberality. Thus the most odious titles belong to sin, such as those of ingratitude, hatred, contempt, insult. Now the heinousness of an offence increases in proportion to the difference which exists between the position of him who offends, and the one who is offended. God, being Infinitely above man, the offence which man commits towards God is of a heinousness in some sort infinite; thus the interminable duration of the punishments of hell gives them a sort of infinity which corresponds to the heinousness of the sin.
2. The punishment of hell is proportioned to the needs of our condition on earth. Filled by passions within us, surrounded by objects which cause offence without us, we have need of a bridle which should be powerful enough to restrain us. If, notwithstanding the belief in hell which exists, the world is so corrupt, what would it be without that? We see plainly that the unbeliever,

who seeks to weaken or to destroy this belief, speaks only on behalf of vice. It belonged therefore to the wisdom of God, as well as to His justice, that there should be a hell: it belonged likewise to His Mercy, for if there was only a Paradise, and no hell, how few would make use of the self-restraint needful in order to gain Heaven! How many saints have owed their conversion, their final perseverance, and all the perfection of their love to the thought of hell! How many martyrs have there not been who have been supported in the midst of the greatest torments by the remembrance of the torments of hell! Let us profit also by the remembrance of it, let us thank God that He has given us so powerful a spur, so efficacious a means whereby to serve Him, and to gain eternal happiness.

2. Consider to what the punishment of hell-torments is not proportioned. In the first place, it is not proportioned to the pleasure which is to be found in sin. The philosophy of unbelievers is also here at fault. It is not the pleasure, which God punishes in hell, it is the sin. Virtue has its pleasures, which are a thousand fold sweeter than those of sin. Diminish then, as much as you please, the pleasure which the most voluptuous heart can enjoy, you are right: say that it does not appertain to the goodness of God to punish by fearful and eternal torments, a pleasure which is but of such short duration and so slight, in one sense you are still right; but, the more vain and momentary this pleasure is, the more sinful is it in you to have preferred it to the obedience you owe to the commands of your Creator: commands which are absolute, and accompanied by such heavy threatenings, and rewards so magnificent, and it is this malignity of sin which God punishes. The more vain, and transitory this pleasure is, the more it is mingled with troubles and pains, the more senseless you are to have preferred it to the will of God, to the joy of Heaven, and to have exposed yourself, for so slight a gratification, to eternal suffering in hell; and that is the conclusion that you should draw. Oh pleasures of sin! ye

cannot seduce a heart which is filled with the thought of hell, ye cannot tempt him who is penetrated with the fear of God, and with the severity of His punishments! Can the pleasure of a moment, followed by an eternity of torments have any attraction for me any longer! could I ever again consent to it, and yield myself up to it?

3. The punishment of hell is not proportioned to the sufferings of virtue. That which the Gospel enjoins us which is the hardest to endure, the most rigorous act of repentance, duties which are the most repugnant to us, or the severest persecutions, all that is nothing in comparison to the tortures of hell. You find the practice of virtue difficult; you cannot inconvenience your mind in order to meditate and pray, restrain your senses so as to preserve a spirit of recollection, mortify your carnal affections in order to keep your body in temperance, soberness, and chastity, and how then will you be able to support the severity of hell-fire? You grow weary, you turn back, you have no power to persevere in that which is good, and how then will you endure the weight of the eternity of hell? If a soul could be drawn out of hell, think you it would find the sufferings brought on it by a holy life unendurable? Keep in mind then these words of our Saviour, where continuing to employ the same figures, He says, *It is better for thee to enter into life halt or maimed, rather than having two hands or two feet, to be cast into everlasting fire.* Yes, doubtless, it is better to be in Paradise without having tasted the sinful pleasures of the world, than to be in hell after having been satiated with them. It is to us all that Jesus Christ addresses these words, let us not forget them, let us repeat them to our soul, when the opportunity offers itself to make some sacrifice: *It is better* for thee, O my soul, to deprive thyself of that gratification, and to save thyself, than to enjoy it and be lost eternally.

Prayer. Ah, my God, strike here below, burn, cut away, if only Thou wilt pardon me in eternity. Nothing is difficult, when it is a question of escaping hell fire. Grant, oh God, that that sin, which eternal flames cannot expiate in me after my death, may be effaced in this life by tears of repentance. Amen.

Meditation CXLVIII.

PARABLE OF THE SALT.
RECAPITULATION OF THE PRECEDING DISCOURSE.

Jesus Christ makes use often of the comparison of salt, and applies it to different subjects. He seems to distinguish here four different kinds: 1. a salt of punishment and torment; 2. a salt of mortification and repentance; 3. a salt of wisdom and discernment; 4. a salt of concord and union. S. Mark ix. 48, 49.

FIRST POINT.

A salt of punishment and torment.

One of the properties of salt is that it preserves. When our Lord tells us that *every one* (i. e. all who are damned) *shall be salted with fire,* He sets before us the universality, immensity and eternity of the torments of hell.

1. The universality. Let us not disdain to meditate on a metaphor which our Lord has deigned Himself to set before us, in order to bring the subject more forcibly before our minds, and to lead us to do all that lies in our power to escape this fearful punishment. Let us see how meat which any one desires to preserve is prepared with salt. A person takes care to fill up every part with it, and to see that the salt penetrates every where into the meat, both without and within, and he covers it all over with the salt, and lastly plunges it into the salt. Such is the picture which we can set before ourselves of the sufferings of the damned. No single sense, no single part of his body, no faculty of his soul will be exempt from torment.

2. *The immensity.* But what a fearful and infinite torment! It will not only be a biting and pungent salt, but a burning, seething and devouring fire, which will cause the keenest suffering to the damned in all his members. This fire will be applied to him, he will be covered by it, he will be plunged into it.

3. *The eternity.* Lastly this fire will be like the salt which preserves intead of destroying; it will burn, and will not consume. The damned, imperishable, always existing, will be the eternal aliment of this fire: he will be the immortal victim of the justice of a God Whom he has despised, Whom he has offended, Whom he has willed neither to fear nor to love.

SECOND POINT.

A salt of mortification and repentance.

Every sacrifice shall be salted with salt. Another property of salt, is to consume what is corrupt, in order to preserve the rest in its integrity. The law commanded that salt should be added to all that was offered to God in sacrifice, and God calls it the salt of the covenant. In the new Covenant we ourselves are the victims which God requires. This covenant which was completed on the Cross, warns us that the salt of the new covenant, which must be applied to every sacrifice, is crosses, sufferings, tribulation, self-denial, and acts of penitence: a salutary salt, the poignant operation of which consumes only that which is corrupt in us, and which might be the cause of our ruin. But what is the passing pain which the mortification of some evil passion, and the cutting off of all which is a cause of offence to us, in comparison with the eternal fire which threatens us? For we cannot escape from undergoing either the one or the other, though we have it in our power to choose which it shall be. We must be either the victims of the merciful justice of Almighty God through repentance here on earth, or the victims of His rigorous justice in hell. Here it is only a temporal and purifying salt: yonder, it an eternal, burning and preserving fire. Towards which are we inclining? Oh, Lord, apply to me this salutary salt; whatever it may cost me, humble my pride, repress my avarice, crucify my sensuality, consume my self-love, so that my soul, thus purified, may be pleasing in Thine eyes like a holy victim, without blemish, and be, in the abode of Thy glory, entirely absorbed and consumed in the fire of Thy love.

THIRD POINT.

A salt of wisdom and instruction.

Salt is good: but if the salt have lost its saltness wherewith will ye season it? A third property of salt is to season food, to give it flavour and relish.

1. The excellence of instruction and of zeal. There is nothing so valuable in the Church as zeal for instruction, whether by word of mouth or through written books. It is that which makes us take delight in works of piety, in the performance of our duties, and in the exercise of self-denial. We ought earnestly to seek for this sacred salt, and those whose office it is to distribute it and who are qualified to do so, must not refuse to make others partakers in it.

2. The dangers of instruction. This precious salt may lose its strength, or even become a poison, as much to those who distribute it as to those who receive it, either through the dogmas of false doctrine, or through public scandals which bring discredit on the ministry, or through secret motives which corrupt the intention of the minister, and hinder the fruit of his labours.

3. The evil of instruction, if it be once corrupted. Salt gives to food its relish: but if the salt have lost its own flavour, how shall it impart that relish to it? If the teacher be in error, what teacher shall instruct him? If the preacher, the minister yield to his passions, to human interests, to vanity, ambition and to vice, who shall preach to them, who correct them? Ah! whoever has the office of teaching others should do so with zeal as

regards others, but with fear, circumspection and wisdom as regards himself.

FOURTH POINT.

A salt of concord and union.

Have salt in yourselves, and have peace one with another. A last property of salt, is to coagulate, to unite, to draw together, to condense. Peace and union is the essential character of the Church, and each one should seek to contribute to it; a union of the ministers of the Church in the doctrine they preach, and in their manner of preaching it: a union of the people to whom they preach in the submission and teachableness due to lawful authority: a union of all hearts in charity, disinterestedness, humility, and gentleness. Thoughts of ambition had lately troubled the union of the apostles; Jesus recalls them to sentiments of peace, and what He says to them, let us apply to ourselves, *Have peace amongst yourselves.*

Prayer. Ah! Lord grant it to us, this peace so much to be desired, grant it to the Christian people, grant it to Thy Church; open the eyes of those that trouble her, make them to see how grievous a thing divisions are, so that united all together in one common faith, under our one Lord and Master, we may serve Thee with joy and faithfulness. Amen.

Meditation CXLIX.

OF OFFENCES RECEIVED.

Consider, 1. what ought to be our conduct with regard to offences which we have received; 2. what power the ministers of God have to repress these offences; and 3. what indulgence we ought to show with regard to the offences we receive. S. Matt. xviii. 15—22.

FIRST POINT.

Of the conduct we ought to adopt with regard to offences which we have received.

1. First step; we must reprove in private him who has sinned against us, and who has offended us. *If thy brother shall trespass against thee, go and tell him his fault between thee and him alone: if he shall hear thee, thou hast gained thy brother.* Whether his fault consist in some omission with regard to yourself, in some injury or personal offence; or whether it consist in something reprehensible that you have remarked in his conduct, in his morals or his faith, and which might become a scandal; whether, on the one hand, you are his equal, or on the other hand, you are his superior or his pastor, you have two shoals to steer clear of; the first, to leave your neighbour to continue in this condition through indifference, or lack of zeal for his salvation; the second, to follow your own tempers or passion, instead of charity in the means you employ in order to correct him, to bring about a reconciliation with yourself, and to recall him to his duty. That which charity, or a prudent zeal requires of you, is that, without waiting that he shall acknowledge his fault or make advances to you, you should go and seek him out yourself; that, face to face, you should reprove him with gentleness, should represent to him his fault, and bring him to look into his own heart. If he listens to you, it is a brother that you gain, that you have saved from the paths of perdition, that you have won over to yourself, to whom you have restored peace of mind, and whom you have

brought back into the way of salvation. Can there be a more powerful motive to engage you to take this step? What hatred, what enmities, how many law-suits, how many causes of offence would not be stifled at their birth, if men would but follow this first rule of brotherly correction; but revenge, pride, self-love delight in noise and display, whilst people flatter themselves that they are acting thus only out of zeal and love of justice.

2. Second step: to reprove the guilty person in the presence of witnesses. *But if he will not hear thee, then take with thee one or two more, that in the mouth of two or three witnesses every word may be established.* We must omit nothing on the one hand, in order to gain a brother; and on the other, in order to avoid publicity; if the first step has proved insufficient, take another, go and find him in company with one or two others, who are capable either of making an impression on him, or of bearing testimony against him. Perhaps this form of justice, which spares his reputation and his weakness, will arouse in him a salutary fear, and that, being no longer able to deny either his fault, or his resistance to the voice of correction, he will finally resolve to repair the first, and thus avoid the consequences which the latter may bring with it.

3. Third step; to denounce him to the Church. *And if he shall neglect to hear them, tell it unto the Church; but if he neglect to hear the Church, let him be unto thee as an heathen man and a publican.* If the guilty man will hearken neither to your counsel, nor to the remonstrances of these whom you have brought with you; if he persists in his hatred, in his evil courses, or in his errors, do not then fear to denounce him publicly. Zeal for the particular welfare of the guilty man, and love for the public welfare of the Church oblige you to do so. Lastly, if he will not listen to the Church, look upon him as a heathen man and a publican; hold no intercourse with him, keep yourselves apart from him, abandon him to his own intractable spirit, keep up no fellowship with him.

SECOND POINT.

Of the power given to the ministers of Jesus Christ to repress offences.

1. *Of the power granted to the Church of Christ.* Jesus, then addressing Himself to all His apostles, said to them, *verily, I say unto you, Whatsoever ye shall bind on earth, shall be bound in Heaven: and whatsoever ye shall loose on earth, shall be loosed in Heaven.* Let us thank our Lord that He has granted to His Apostles, and in their persons, to their successors, a power so sublime, so needful for the preservation of good order, and for the maintenance of the Faith. Our Lord continues to explain further this power which He has bestowed upon His ministers. *I say unto you that if two of you shall agree on earth as touching anything that they shall ask, it shall be done for them of My Father Which is in Heaven.* The promise which our Lord makes, that His Father will hear their prayers, and will confirm their judgments, when called upon to decide in any difficult cases is in this as well as in several other cases, conditional, and presupposes that on their part, there is nothing which puts an obstacle in the way of its performance: it assures them of the gracious designs of God, of the efficacy of the merits of His Son, and points out to them the nature and the source of their power and authority, which demands on our part reverence and submission: but it does not guarantee them absolutely and without condition freedom from all error or mistake.

2. *Of the power given to faithful members of the Church of Jesus Christ.* *For where two or three are gathered together in My Name, there am I in the midst of them.* By these words, Jesus confirms the promise made to His Apostles, as though He would say to them, How shall not your prayers be heard, since wherever there are even two or three gathered in My Name, there am I present in their midst? By these

words, we are also encouraged to join in the assembling of ourselves together for prayer, for worship, to betake ourselves to the House of Prayer; to join in prayer with others in order to ask of God some special petition for ourselves or others; lastly, to meet together in our own families for prayer, in a spirit of union, peace and concord. Jesus assures us that He will be in the midst of those who are thus joined together in His Name. What joy for us to know Thee thus present with us, O my Saviour! to be able to render Thee there our homage and to offer to Thee our prayers. What condescension dost Thou not manifest in that Thou art willing thus to be present amidst Thy servants, to comfort, strengthen, hear their prayers, and grant them their petitions! But how shameful in me, if, whilst Thou art thus in our midst, I am only present in body, whilst my thoughts wander, my mind is distracted, if I am every where else save where Thou art! Where can I find greater happiness than with Thee? Moreover, have I nothing to ask of Thee? have I no needs? have I nothing to attach me to Thee? have I nothing to hope or to fear from Thee? Ah! fatal absence! Whilst my soul is wandering far from Thee, others are with Thee and in the enjoyment of Thy Blessed Presence; Thou dost reward their fervour and their faithfulness, Thou dost communicate Thyself to them, and Thou dost grant them the desires of their hearts. Prayer is to them a time of delight, they come forth from it with unwillingness, and return to it with eagerness; as for me, on the contrary, prayer is a time of weariness, of which I look forward with anxiety to the end; I come forth from it in a state of distraction, I feel nothing but distaste for it; a just punishment of my faint-heartedness.

THIRD POINT.

Of the indulgence we ought to shew towards offences which we receive.

1. Question put by S. Peter to our Lord. *Then*

came Peter to Him, and said, Lord, how oft shall my brother sin against me, and I forgive him? Whether the offence given by our neighbour have been against God, or against ourselves, whether it is a matter of granting him pardon on his repentance, on our own part as private persons, or on the part of God, as His ministers or His judges, let us not follow our own ideas, our own passions, or the motions of our indiscreet zeal; let us put far from us all severity, rigour, bitter reproaches, or accusations: let us consult our Lord, and ask Him, with S. Peter, how many times we ought to forgive, and how often we should bear with acts of unfaithfulness, and relapses into sin.

2. Suggestion made by S. Peter. He suggests himself the answer to his demand, and adds, *till seven times?* Sometimes we refer a matter which concerns us to God, and without awaiting His answer, we make an answer to ourselves, we follow our own judgment, whilst we flatter ourselves that we are only acting according to the will of God. We often consult wise and pious men, more from the desire to bring them over to our own opinions than from a wish to follow theirs. S. Peter thought that he was allowing a great deal, and seems to have doubted whether the forgiveness of offences should be extended as far as seven times. Alas, how weak are our ideas, and how limited are our conceptions of holy things! Let us hearken what our Heavenly Master will say; let us behold the vast extent of His divine charity.

3. Reply of Jesus. *Jesus saith unto him, I say not unto thee, Until seven times; but, Until seventy times seven.* That is to say, your forgiveness must be boundless and without measure, as often as your brother shall sin and shall repent. S. Peter gave very narrow limits to Christian charity, whilst imagining that he had extended it within a very large margin; but the charity of God towards us is infinite, and it must serve as a rule for that which we must manifest towards one another.

Prayer. Oh infinite charity! oh inexhaustible patience of my God! Ah! where should I be, Lord, without that divine Word of forgiveness which has come forth from Thy lips, and has been treasured up by Thy Church? Where should I be after so many relapses, if Thy mercy were not infinite, if Thou hadst not revealed to Thine apostles all the wondrous immensity of Thy forgiving love? With what long-suffering, with what gentleness should I not then extend to others that forgiveness which I have received so abundantly from Thee? With what generosity and patience should not I endure, and be willing to forgive, the offences committed against myself? Enlarge my heart, O Jesus! fill it with that charity, which knowing neither bounds nor measure, wearies not, and is never exhausted. O my Saviour! how gentle, patient, and merciful Thou art! Grant that I may follow Thy gentle will and put its commands into practice. Amen.

Meditation CL.

PARABLE OF THE CREDITOR AND DEBTOR.

OF THE PARDON OF INJURIES.

This parable contains, 1. the goodness of the master towards the servant who owed him a debt which he could not pay; 2. the cruelty of the servant towards a fellow servant who likewise owed him a debt which he could not pay; 3. the justice of the master towards the unmerciful servant. S. Matt. xviii. 23—35.

FIRST POINT.

The goodness of the master towards his servant.

1. *The debt of the servant.* *Therefore is the kingdom of Heaven likened unto a certain king, which would take account of his servants; and when he had begun to reckon, one was brought unto him, which owed him ten thousand talents.* It is to-day, in this retreat, at this holy season, in this prayer, that God

wills to *take account of* us; do not let us refuse to meet Him, the opportunity is a favourable one; a day will come when we shall be forced to render up an account, whether we will or not, when we shall not find the same resources and the same advantages which we now have; therefore let us render Him our accounts in all good faith now. What have we done with the goods which the King our Master has put into our hands? To what purposes have we employed this body, this soul, this mind, this heart, this wealth, these talents, these graces, these instructions we have received, these Sacraments of which we have been partakers? Let us acknowledge with confusion that we have abused all these goods, that we have appropriated them to our own use, that we have only made use of them for our own advantage, that we have wasted them, and that we owe to our King an immense sum which far exceeds our powers to repay.

2. The sentence of the master. *But forasmuch as he had not to pay, his lord commanded him to be sold, and his wife, and children, and all that he had, and payment to be made.* This was the lawful claim of the master, and this command was just. If God were to exercise His rightful claims upon us, we should not only be sold, but, after having been stripped of all the goods which we have abused, we should be abandoned for ever to those to whom we have sold ourselves, to the devil, and to hell, in order that we may there pay our debts by an eternal punishment. Terrible sentence! Woe be to him, who receives such a sentence at the day of judgement, because then it will be irrevocable! Happy he who meditates upon it now, because our Lord only speaks to us of it, in order to furnish us with the means whereby to escape the execution of the sentence.

3. Prayer of the servant. *The servant therefore fell down, and worshipped him, saying, Lord, have patience with me, and I will pay thee all.* The servant, having heard this overwhelming sentence, does not lose courage, and yield to a fruitless despair. He throws him-

self at his master's feet, he entreats him, he conjures him; Master, he says, do not treat me with rigour: have patience, grant me a little time, and I will pay thee, I will satisfy all thy just claims. Oh how foolhardy is he who waits to make this prayer till he is on his death-bed, when there is no more time. Ah! it is now, it is to-day, while the day of salvation lasteth, that we must make this prayer, if we desire to be heard. To-day then, however great our debt may be, however grievous, however numerous our sins, let us humble ourselves before God, let us prostrate ourselves at His Feet, and there, let us weep, sigh, acknowledge our faults, entreat for time to repair them, and promise with sincerity to employ the rest of our life in the earnest endeavour to defray the debt we owe.

4. The clemency of the master. *Then the lord of that servant was moved with compassion, and loosed him, and forgave him the debt.* The master, seeing at his feet this servant, was touched with compassion and granted him more than he asked; he revoked the sentence which he had pronounced upon him, and which condemned him to perpetual slavery, he sent him away free, and remitted him all his debt. Is it not our Master, our King, our Judge Who has Himself set forth this parable to us? It contains then nothing that is exaggerated, nothing that is magnified. Yes, the greatest sinner, the most infamous and scandalous sinner, who has offended and outraged God in a thousand ways, and as far as he could, from the moment that he humbles himself in all sincerity, Jesus has compassion on Him; as soon as he entreats for grace and pardon, Jesus sets him free; as soon as he promises to make what amends he can for the transgressions of his past life, Jesus forgives him the debt. Oh infinite goodness, clemency, and love of our God! how can we not love Thee? How after a pardon so generously granted can we still offend Thee? Ah! it will be indeed our fault, if at the Judgment day, we are still laden with debts.

SECOND POINT.

Cruelty of the servant towards another servant.

1. His meeting with another servant. *But the same servant went out, and found one of his fellow-servants, which owed him an hundred pence.* The opportunity was favourable to this man to shew himself worthy of the acquittal of his debt which he had received, by forgiving in his turn the debt which was owed to himself. And what was this debt in comparison to that from which he had been discharged? Alas! it is sometimes when we leave the Church, when we come from the holy Table, on the very day when we have ourselves received special graces, that an opportunity presents itself to us to testify to God our gratitude and faithfulness, to practise some act of holiness, love, patience, or gentleness: to resist some violent temptation; but if, instead of availing ourselves of this opportunity, we shew ourselves ungrateful and perfidious, what judgment can be formed of our conversion?

2. The inhumanity with which he exacts the payment. *He laid hands on him, and took him by the throat, saying, Pay me that thou owest.* This recital inspires us with horror, but is it not thus that the wealthy often treat their poorer neighbours? Is it not thus that haughty, proud, vindictive persons require satisfaction or reparation for supposed injuries? Have we nought wherewith to reproach ourselves on this head?

3. The contempt with which he treats his request: *and his fellow-servant fell down at his feet, and besought him, saying, Have patience with me, and I will pay thee all. And he would not: but went and cast him into prison, till he should pay the debt.* The debtor no sooner got free from the hands of his creditor than he threw himself at his feet, and prayed him to grant him a little delay, promising him to repay him shortly. It was the very same request which this creditor himself had made to his master, and which had been received so favourably; but this hard-hearted and

cruel man remained always pitiless, and unmoved; he does not relinquish his claims, and giving his debtor over to the hands of justice, and putting the last stroke to his ingratitude and cruelty, he caused him to be cast into prison, where he commanded him to be kept until he should have paid his entire debt; a very inhuman proceeding, at which one cannot restrain a feeling of indignation. But we who pray to God every day, and who have unceasingly need of His help, of His mercy and forgiveness, if we examine in what manner we receive the prayers and the excuses of others, we shall find perhaps that we have more share than we think for, in the indignation which this unmerciful creditor deserves.

4. The report which is made to the master of it. *So when his fellow-servants saw what was done, they were very sorry, and came and told unto their Lord all that was done.* God does not need to be told of that which takes place; He sees every thing, He is attentive to the tears which the poor and oppressed shed; but the indignation of the saints, and of the angels in Heaven, the sighs and groans of the righteous on earth, who are witnesses of acts of cruelty and inhumanity, do not cease to appeal to His vengeance. Let the hard and unmerciful man learn that Divine justice cannot fail, sooner or later, to burst upon him, and in a manner so much the more terrible as it shall have been longer suspended.

THIRD POINT.

Justice of the master with regard to the unmerciful servant.

1. The citation of the servant. *Then his lord, after that He had called him.* Terrible summons, supreme command which no one can resist! Rich, great, powerful, kings, emperors, potentates, masters of the world, your Master calls you, not with that Voice of grace and mercy with which He has so often called you to His love, to the observance of His commands, and which you have always despised, but with that Voice of power

and absolute sovereignty, by which He drew you out of nothing, and gave you the life and all the blessings which you have abused. He calls you; appear before Him, and render Him an account of your conduct. Shall we always behave ourselves as though we had no Master above us? Shall we live always as though we were never to die? I return to Thee, Lord, by my repentance, and by my tears; forgive me as I forgive others, grant me mercy before that terrible day when Thou wilt call me, and when I shall find at Thy hands only severe and inexorable justice.

2. Reproaches made to the servant. *Then his Lord said unto him, O thou wicked servant, I forgave thee all that debt, because thou desiredst me; shouldest not thou also have had compassion on thy fellow-servant, even as I had pity on thee?* What answer have I to give to so just a reproach, and so overwhelming a parallel drawn between the conduct of my Heavenly Master towards me, and mine towards my fellow creatures. I, your Master and your God, I have remitted to you, my creature and my slave, numberless and heinous offences; and you have not been willing to remit to your brother a light offence, which however grave you may suppose it to be, is as nothing on his part in comparison with those which you have committed against Me! I, your Master and your God, have hearkened to your requests, and have dealt bountifully with you, I have restored you to My love and favour; and you have rejected with harshness the advances which your brother has made towards a reconciliation, you have nourished a mortal hatred against him, and preserved an implacable enmity! I, your Master your God, have had compassion upon you; I have pardoned your inconstancy, your inattention, your frivolity, and your weakness; and you have not been willing to make excuses in one of your fellow-creatures for the least error; you have cherished in your heart secret aversions, and antipathies towards others which have often found a vent in your actions and in your words!

3. *Punishment of the servant. And his lord was wroth, and delivered him to the tormentors, till he should pay all that was due unto him.* Let us bring before our minds that this anger is that of a God, that these ministers who execute His justice are the devils, that these torments are hell fire, and that the term of payment is an eternity which has no end?

4. *Application of the parable. So likewise shall My Heavenly Father do also unto you, if ye from your hearts forgive not every one his brother their trespasses.* It is thus, concludes our Blessed Saviour, that My Heavenly Father will deal with you, if ye, to whom He has pardoned and to whom He pardons every day so many sins whereby ye offend against Him, do not willingly forgive your brethren the debts which they have contracted towards yourselves. See here, what a source of consolation is opened for mankind, and what depths of mercy for even the greatest sinners, did they but know how to avail themselves of them! But, in spite of the promises and of the threatenings of Jesus Christ, what do we behold around us in the midst of Christianity? Righteous men owing little and forgiving every thing, whilst the unrighteous who owe to Almighty God a heavy debt which one shudders to think of, and who have within their reach wherewith they might win for themselves the pardon of their offences, cannot make up their minds to pardon others ought whereby they have offended against them. Be it far from us to fall into such a deplorable mistake! Let us be ready and willing to forgive; but in forgiving, let us do so heartily and freely; let us beware that whilst appearing to become reconciled to our brethren, there does not remain in us a germ of coldness, alas! not far removed from hatred. Let us under these circumstances question our heart, and search well into all the feelings which it conceives, all the thoughts and words which come forth from it, and not judge ourselves only by those words or actions of mere ceremony in which often the heart has no share.

Prayer. O Lord, could I then treat my brethren with hardness, after having received at Thy Hands the most exceeding long-suffering? Thou dost pardon, O my God, the greatest faults, Thou dost pardon me them entirely, and should I be inexorable towards the slightest faults, which are committed against myself? Should I exact the minutest satisfaction for them, and even when I make a semblance of forgiving them, should I still maintain feelings of indifference or coldness towards those who have offended me? Should I pretend to dispense myself in any thing from the duties of charity which Thou dost lay upon me towards my brethren, after Thou hast Thyself set no bounds to Thy charity towards myself? Be it far from me such injustice! Nay, Lord, Thou dost give us Thy precious Blood, that we may by applying the Merits of It to our sinful souls, gain the remission of all our sins; I will avail myself of this powerful and effectual means of salvation; I will banish henceforth from my heart every feeling of resentment towards my neighbour, that so I may find at my death, mercy and pardon at Thy Hands, and that Thou mayest deal out to me the same tenderness and goodness of this master, this king in Thy Holy Gospel under the figure of whom Thou Thyself art set forth. Amen.

Meditation CLI.

A CITY OF SAMARIA REFUSES ADMITTANCE TO JESUS.

Let us examine that which precedes, that which accompanies, and that which follows this refusal. S. Luke ix. 51—56.

FIRST POINT.

That which precedes this refusal.

When the time was come that He, [Jesus,] *should be*

received up, He stedfastly set His Face to go to Jerusalem. The days of the Passion and Death of Jesus were not far distant, and there were not more than about six months to the time when He must needs accomplish His Sacrifice. Although this journey was not the last that He would have to make to Jerusalem, He regarded that city only as the scene of His Sufferings and His Death. The courage and firmness of His Soul did not permit nevertheless that He should shrink from this place where His Sacrifice was to be completed. He set out then from Capernaum in order to repair to the capital with a calm and stedfast countenance, which showed plainly how far raised above the events which there awaited Him He was. This courage, this assurance of Jesus ought to give us courage and strength amidst injuries, sufferings and death. Let us go whither God's commands call us; whatever struggles we may have to undergo, whatever opprobrium or sufferings may be in store for us, let us strengthen our hearts with the thoughts of His passion, and march forward with courage. When the time of our departure from this world shall approach, let us fortify ourselves with the strength of our Divine Master, against the pains of death and the terrors of judgment. To allow ourselves to be cast down by fear at such a moment, would be to be wanting in trust in our Redeemer. Let us throw ourselves into His Hands while there is yet time, and rest assured that He is able to sustain us, to make us triumph over all our enemies, and to lead us by a holy death to the abode of glory, whither He has entered Himself only in order to call us to follow Him.

SECOND POINT.

Of that which accompanies this refusal.

1. An unjust refusal. *And sent messengers before His face, and they went and entered into a village of the Samaritans, to make ready for Him; and they did not receive Him, because His face was as though He*

would go to Jerusalem. The Samaritans could not endure, that the Jews should, in contempt of the new Temple that had been built in Samaria, hold exclusively to that which Solomon had built at Jerusalem by God's command, and which Ezra had rebuilt by the same command. It is thus that the world despises, rejects and persecutes those whom it beholds constant in the duties of religion, and following out faithfully the ancient customs of the Church, and of the faith. The true believer should neither be surprised, nor offended at this contempt, nor should his faith be shaken by it.

2. A refusal which was an insult to Jesus, because He only demanded a lodging, which had been never refused to Him in any other city; because this refusal was made apparently in the name of the whole city, its inhabitants, and its magistrates; because it was made to Jesus, accompanied as He was, by His disciples, and in the presence of many witnesses; lastly, because it did not take place until after Jesus had sent messengers to announce His coming; so that they could not excuse themselves on the ground of ignorance or of misconception; and consequently the affront was offered to Him in His own Person, knowing Who He was. The claims of the Samaritans were unjust in themselves, as far as the Jews were concerned, but they were far more so with regard to Jesus, Whose doctrines and miracles proclaimed Him as the Messiah, alike expected by Jews and Samaritans. O Jesus! to what insults dost Thou not expose Thyself for our instruction, and in order to serve us as an Example? But have not I also committed this outrage against thee? Alas! how often have I not closed the door of my heart against Thee, in order that sin, my evil passions, and all the false maxims of the world might reign there! I was not ignorant Who Thou wert? a Christian education had taught it me only too well, a thousand warnings received from Thee had announced Thy coming to me, but I feared because Thou didst will to save me, and I willed to lose myself. Pardon my blindness of heart; come to me, O divine Jesus; come

and dwell in my heart, establish there Thy dwelling place, and leave me no more.

3. *A refusal infinitely prejudicial to this city.* Although Jesus had left Capernaum in order to go to Jerusalem, His intention was not to repair thither at once, nor to be present at all the approaching festivals. Perhaps if the Samaritans had received Him, He might have tarried for a while in their city, and made it the centre of the mission which He was about to carry on: but if He had only passed through their city, what blessings would not His Presence have procured for them! Of what blessings does not he deprive himself, who refuses the entrance of his heart to Jesus, or drives Him thence by sin, after having received Him there by grace!

THIRD POINT.

Of the consequence of this refusal.

1. *The indignation of the two apostles. And when His disciples James and John saw this, they said, Lord, wilt Thou not that we command fire to come down from Heaven and consume them?* Jesus had already given to these two Apostles, the name of Boanerges, or sons of thunder; they manifest here all the signification of that name. They knew that the power of their Master was far superior to that of Elias, who had caused fire to come down from Heaven on those who had insulted him; but they did not know the spirit of Jesus, which, in this point, was entirely opposed to that of Elijah. Are there not still sons of thunder, who seeing the outrages committed daily against Jesus Christ, His Church, and His Sacraments, desire miracles of power in order to avenge the cause of God, whilst it is miracles of humility, of patience, and of gentleness which Jesus requires of His servants, in order to give them the victory? Where should I be, Lord, if Thou didst arm thyself with the thunderbolts of Thine anger whenever I deserved that they should fall on me? Thy patience has overcome my obstinate resistance to Thy grace, Thy gentleness

has triumphed over my ill will; be Thou for ever blessed; this triumph is the only one worthy of Thee. Reign then, O gracious King! reign over a heart which having deserved only Thy wrath, has been subdued only through Thy benefits.

2. *Answer of Jesus to the two apostles.* *But He turned and rebuked them, saying, Ye know not what manner of spirit ye are of.* The spirit of the new law, to which S. James and S. John belonged, far from permitting us to do evil to those who refuse to do us good, commands us to do good to those who do us evil: that is what neither an apostle nor a true Christian can be ignorant of. Our Lord adds, *For the Son of man came not to destroy men's lives, but to save them.* Oh words full of gentleness and love! How gracious is He Who *is come* only *to save* us! Ungrateful hearts! how can we not love Him! Madman that I am! why should I refuse to follow Him Who only desires to save me, whilst I yield myself up to him who seeks only to lose me eternally, and to bring me into damnation.

3. *Jesus withdraws to another place.* *And they went to another village.* Jesus leaves Samaria, and retires to another village of Galilee. Oh fortunate place, which profited by the infidelity of a proud city, and which had the happiness to possess Jesus!

Prayer. Alas! of what avail to a city, to a kingdom, to a state, are their glory, their riches, and their splendour, if Thou art not known there, O Jesus, if Thy holy religion is banished from it? Let me rather dwell, O my Saviour, in the poorest dwelling, where Thou art known, loved and served. What shall it profit a man to be great, learned, rich, powerful, if he have not faith, if he have not, Lord, Thy grace and Thy love? Let me be the least amongst men, and the most despised, if only I possess Thee within my heart. O divine Jesus! do not forsake me in anger and remove Thyself from me; but if Thou art outraged by others, come to me, redouble Thy graces in my heart, that I may redouble my fervour and my love towards Thee. Amen.

Meditation CLII.

OF THE APOSTOLIC CALLING, AND OF THE PRIESTLY VOCATION.

1. The difficulties of the undertaking, and the means whereby to surmount them; 2. the dangers of failing in carrying out the designs of God, and the means whereby to avoid them; 3. the perseverance which a person ought to have in his vocation, and the means whereby to persevere in it. S. Luke ix. 57—62.

FIRST POINT.

Of the difficulties of the undertaking and of the means whereby to surmount them.

And it came to pass, that as they went in the way, a certain man said unto Him, Lord, I will follow Thee whithersoever Thou goest. And Jesus said unto him, Foxes have holes, and birds of the air have nests; but the Son of man hath not where to lay His Head. If there should be any one who feels himself drawn towards the calling of the ministry, or if he feels himself led to embrace a religious life, let him ponder well the following truths.

1. He should consider well beforehand what are the privations of the profession he is about to embrace. Bodily privations. There will be many things, which although innocent in themselves, you will be called upon to give up. You will find many bodily fatigues in the exercise of your ministry, many acts of self-denial, labours, watchings, and fastings. You will find also mental privations. Earnest study, continual application, cares, anxieties, weariness, distaste, humiliations, contradictions. Such is what you must expect. If you enter the ministry from ambitious motives, in order to gain a life of ease and comfort, to spend your time in repose and tranquillity, you expose yourself indeed to live a most miserable life, to profane the holiness of your calling, and to lose your own soul. If you do not feel that

you have sufficient courage to endure these privations, do not enter on the life of the ministry, but content yourself with living a Christian life in the world; if this condition of life is not so high a condition, yet it will be more safe for you.

2. After you have once entered on this ministerial life, you must bear with courage the privations of the calling which you have embraced. These privations are not beyond your strength, you ought to have counted the cost, you knew what they would be: of what then have you to complain? These privations are even less than those which you might have expected. What is it that excites your discontent and your murmurs? A trifle, a mere nothing in comparison to that which you might have expected to suffer. These privations are not too great for you to bear: you found them endurable when you pictured them to yourself before you undertook them: you endured them joyfully at the commencement of your ministry; have you then less courage now, than at first? Recall your first fervour, and your courage will surmount your present privations.

3. Before and after you enter upon the work of the ministry, you must bear in mind and never forget that in all the privations that we may be called upon to endure, Jesus is our Example, our Support, our exceeding great Reward. He is our Example; we suffer nothing that the Son of man has not suffered for us, and far more besides. He is always at our head; should not His example raise us above ourselves and above all our difficulties? He is our Support; the world sees the crosses those have to bear who follow the Saviour, but it does not see the unction of grace which supports their courage, and makes them find ineffable delights even in their very trials. He is our great Reward; the sufferings are but of short duration, death will put an end to them. This death, so terrible to worldly minded men, will be to him who shall have given himself up to the service of Christ, full of comfort and followed by eternal happiness. O hope, what power dost thou not pos-

ness! With what strength, with what generous purposes hast thou not inspired millions of souls who have suffered and given up all for Jesus Christ! The world, on the contrary, has its crosses which are often far heavier than those which Christianity lays upon us; but in overwhelming us with troubles, it does not teach us the manner in which we may support them patiently, and with profit to ourselves. That which we suffer for the world, we suffer without any motive, without comfort, without hope.

SECOND POINT.

Of the dangers of failing in carrying out the designs of God, and the means whereby to escape them.

And He said to another, Follow Me: but he answered, Lord, suffer me first to go and bury my father. And Jesus said unto him, Let the dead bury their dead, but go thou, and preach the kingdom of God.

1. The danger there is before entering on the life of the ministry. A first danger comes from distraction of mind, which hinders a person from hearing the voice of God. He to whom Jesus said, *Follow Me*, was with Him, he was amongst the number of His disciples, he followed Him, and made a profession of being attached to Him. How can we know what God wills us to do, if we never seek His Presence, if we never listen to Him, if we remain always at a distance from Him, in a continual state of distraction, without communing with ourselves, without prayer, self-examination, or Communion? A second danger comes from our making a pretext of our worldly occupations in order to delay obeying God's voice; a fatal delay, when it comes, as it generally does, from a wavering will. He whom Jesus called only asked for time to bury his father: whether his father was only aged, ill, and that he wished to delay until his death: or whether he was already dead, and that he asked for the time needful to attend his funeral, Jesus did not grant him this delay. Happy if he was

teachable and obedient, if he obeyed without delay. A third danger comes from the love of this world, which causes us to stifle God's voice within us. How many have heard this Voice of Jesus, *Follow Me*, that is to say, follow Me into retirement, follow Me in the way of repentance, follow Me in the labours of the ministry! But the world has raised a contrary and more flattering voice, Follow me into repose, to pleasures, to honours. The first Voice has been stifled in order to listen only to the second; this latter has been followed, it has deceived us; how shall we correct the error into which we have fallen, and repair our fault?

2. After having entered on it, we still run a risk of being wanting in the spirit and duties of our vocation. The first danger comes from faint-heartedness, from idleness which prevents us from studying what our duties are, and fitting themselves to carry them out, or makes us disinclined to fulfil them, lest the exertion and the labours, for which they call, trouble the shameful repose to which we yield ourselves. A second danger comes from the distractions of needless occupations, or those which do not appertain to our calling, which we take up in order to gratify our own inclinations, and which even if innocent in themselves, are carried on by us at the expense of occupations which are far more serious, useful and suitable, if not even essential to our calling. *Let the dead bury their dead:* leave to the world the business, the occupations, the amusements of the world, and think only of the weighty and serious matters which you have taken upon yourself; namely to follow Jesus Christ, and to gain the kingdom of Heaven. A third danger comes from timidity and mistrust of self. What do you fear? Do you think, if you seek God only, that He will not give you strength to bear the burden He lays upon you. It is He Who says to you, *Go;* wherefore do you stay? It is He Who says to you, *Preach the kingdom of God*, wherefore then are you silent? Announce it by preaching, by exhortation, let your whole life announce it, let all your actions and

your words, let your behaviour and manner persuade, edify and touch men's hearts; your calling requires it, and even the world expects it of you. Leave the dead to bury the dead; forsake these frivolous conversations, these worldly discourses which lend only to distraction; leave them to the world and its followers: as for you, occupy yourselves only with things pertaining to the kingdom of God, with endeavours to bring men into it, and to make them love it. Alas! how many shortcomings on this head, do we not need to bewail and amend!

3. Whether before or after entering on this course of life, the means whereby to avoid all these dangers is to meditate on, and never to forget the benefits, the glory, and the blessedness of one's vocation. 1. Consider unceasingly the singular benefit, whereby God has testified towards you, without any merit on your part, a special predilection, by choosing you from amongst so many others, who would have been more faithful than you; He has passed them by, and it is to you that He has spoken, by saying to you, *Follow Me.* What gratitude does not such a benefit require of you! If you refuse to respond to such love, you have reason to fear that God may leave you, and on your refusal, may call in your stead others who are more faithful than you. 2. Meditate on the glory of your vocation. What is there more glorious than to be specially dedicated to the service of Jesus Christ, united to Him, set apart only to serve Him, associated in His ministry and His labours? And what a disgrace would it not be to refuse so glorious a destiny, only in order to occupy yourself with temporal and trifling matters, which in the sight of God are of no price! 3. Recall to yourself continually the blessedness of your vocation. Mark what a difference there is between two persons who have embraced the same mode of life, of whom one has been exact, and the other negligent in the fulfilment of his duties. But let not him who has refused to obey the call of God which is clearly set before him, expect to find happiness elsewhere. His want of faith-

fulness in corresponding to God's call will be a constant source of torment to him; it will mingle with his pleasures and his sorrows, in his successes and his falls; it will trouble him and overwhelm him at the last moment of life, unless by God's mercy, he have wept over his shortcomings in this life, and bewailed them here, so that they may not rise up against him in judgment hereafter!

THIRD POINT.

Of the perseverance a person ought to have in his vocation, and of the means whereby to persevere in it.

And another also said, Lord, I will follow Thee; but let me first go bid them farewell which are at home at my house. And Jesus said unto him, No man, having put his hand to the plough, and looking back, is fit for the kingdom of God.

1. Before entering on the ministry, you must renounce all that is contrary to the spirit of the ministry. You must not seek for riches, honours, pleasures, and the things which the world offers you. You must be ready, in conformity to the spirit and end of your calling, to forsake all at the voice of God, to go whither He calls you. It must also be a prompt renunciation. It must also be a courageous renunciation. He that loveth father or mother more than Me, is not worthy of Me. You must be prepared to give up every thing, at His call, and to make of yourself a generous sacrifice, to follow Him, to live only for Him, and to cling to Him with all your heart and soul.

2. After you have entered on the ministry, you are no longer permitted to look behind you, in order to consider those objects which you have renounced. One single look might shake your constancy, might take from you the crown of perseverance, and deprive you of the fruit of that which you have already gained. It may be *looking back* in action, whereby you look back upon former pleasures, and return again to the world and its

claims, and feel a distaste for the duties of your calling. Or it may be *looking back* in thought, by which you recall too often those things which you have left behind, whether in order to exalt yourself above others, or to indulge in thoughts of vanity or self-love, or to persuade yourself that you have already done much, and that there remains nothing more to be done. Or it may be a *looking back* of the affections, whereby you sigh after those things which you have left, and think others happy who still enjoy the honours and pleasures of this world, and regret that you have entered on a stricter mode of life; by which the heart retracts the sacrifice it has made, and falls into a species of apostacy.

3. Whether before or after entering on the duties of the ministry, if you desire to persevere, you must look before you. When the labourer has put his hand to the plough, he thinks only of directing and advancing his work. After his example, look before you, and think of the work you have undertaken, your own sanctification, and that of others, evil passions to be mortified, vices to be rooted out, virtues to be practised, perfection and union with God to be attained. What a noble, what a holy occupation! Look before you, and behold Him Whom you follow, Whom you have taken as your Guide and your Example, He will never lead you astray, He will never forsake you. Look before you and see the end of the work which is at hand, death which will soon destroy every thing, the judgment which will decide every thing, eternity which will punish or reward every thing. With this fixed and continued look, you will never go astray, you will never relax in your efforts, you will never grow faint-hearted.

Prayer. What blessedness, if I can attain to this point, before life comes to an end! Happy, a thousand times happy, if when I reach that end, my life has been spent in the service of my Lord! Grant me this grace, O divine Jesus. Amen.

Meditation CLIII.

THE CHOICE AND SENDING FORTH OF THE SEVENTY DISCIPLES.

Let us learn here 1, what is the preaching of the Gospel; 2. what is the misery of those who reject it, 3. what is their crime. S. Luke x. 1—16.

FIRST POINT

Of the preaching of the Gospel.

1. What are the means which the disciples of Jesus Christ have employed in order to convert the world to Christianity? *After these things the Lord appointed other seventy also, and sent them two and two before His Face into every city and place, whither He Himself would come. Therefore said He unto them, The harvest truly is great, but the labourers are few: pray ye therefore the Lord of the harvest, that He would send forth labourers into His harvest. Go your ways: behold, I send you forth as lambs among wolves. Carry neither purse, nor scrip, nor shoes; and salute no man by the way. And into whatsoever house ye enter, first say, Peace be to this house. And if the son of peace be there, your peace shall rest upon it; if not, it shall turn to you again. And in the same house remain, eating and drinking such things as they give; for the labourer is worthy of his hire. Go not from house to house. And into whatsoever city ye enter, and they receive you, eat such things as are set before you; and heal the sick that are therein, and say unto them, The kingdom of God is come nigh unto you. But into whatsoever city ye enter, and they receive you not, go your ways out into the streets of the same, and and say, Even the very dust of your city, which cleaveth on us, we do wipe off against you; notwithstanding, be ye sure of this, that the kingdom of God is come*

nigh unto you. The mission with which Jesus here entrusts His disciples, as also that one with which He, on another occasion, entrusted His apostles, was only a slight sketch of that which both were to carry on after His Resurrection, throughout the world. Consider, 1. their number. They were only a small number, and yet they were to disperse, and go forth only by twos. This was probably in order to give no offence, to cause no fears. 2. Their strength. It is that of sheep in the midst of wolves, that is to say a patience, a gentleness which exposes itself to every thing, which resists nothing, which suffers not only without defending itself, but even without complaining. 3. Their wealth. It is the most entire abnegation of all things, having neither even scrip nor purse, and being simply clothed. 4. Their credit. They have neither friends nor protectors, and must not even think of seeking to gain them for themselves. 5. Their entrance into a city and into a house. It is entirely pacific, they come to preach peace, and they bring it to those who love it. 6. Their manner of life. It is as simple as their clothing, without any affectation of austerity, or desire for good living. 7. Their talents. No other knowledge than the knowledge of Jesus Christ, no other eloquence than that of preaching that the kingdom of God is at hand, that the Messiah is come, that men must repent and embrace the Gospel. 8. Lastly, their works. Ah! they are supernatural, and can only come from a Divine power; to heal the sick and infirm, with whatever disease, infirmity or possession they may be afflicted, to heal them in a moment, without any remedy, with a single word and in the Name alone of Jesus.

2. What effect have these means produced? By these means the only true God has been known upon earth: His Son has been adored as making but One with the Father and the Holy Ghost; all the mysteries of His Humanity have been believed, all the dogmas which He has taught have been received, all the tenets of His moral law have been embraced, and Christianity has

been established in the universe, and has reigned there for several centuries in the order in which we behold it to-day. What has become of that multitude of false gods which were worshipped in every nation? What has become of their temples, their priests and their altars? What has become of their defenders and protectors, the philosophers and tyrants of past ages? All have vanished, and it is through the instrumentality of the disciples of Jesus Christ that these changes have been effected, through the means alone that Jesus Christ here puts into their hands. The fact speaks for itself, exists, and cannot be denied. If miracles have been employed to bring it about, the work is divine; if the miracles are denied, how then can the fact be explained? It would be itself more marvellous than the greatest miracles. What blessedness to belong to so holy a religion, to know its divinity, to practise its duties, and to await its rewards!

3. With what feelings should not the condition in which the Church is at this present time inspire us, compared to the condition in which she took her beginning? When we reflect upon the prodigious change that has taken place, when we see the Church of Christ spreading and making her voice heard throughout the world, we may indeed exclaim, The finger of God is here. When we think upon the sufferings, privations and martyrdoms of the early Christians, and compare the present state of peace and prosperity of the Christian Church, we cannot but feel ourselves penetrated with transports of joy, and gratitude. We do not fear to apply to this event, the words of the Blessed Virgin Mary in her hymn of praise, "He hath put down the mighty from their seat and hath exalted the humble and meek."

SECOND POINT.

Of the misery of those who have rejected the preaching of the Gospel.

In the abuse which is made, or in the little profit

which is drawn from the gifts and graces of God, three degrees of sinfulness may be distinguished to which correspond three degrees of punishment.

1. The first degree of sinfulness is represented by a city which would not receive the disciples of Jesus Christ. *But into whatsoever city ye enter, and they receive you not, go your ways out into the streets of the same, and say, Even the very dust of your city which cleaveth on us, we do wipe off against you; notwithstanding, be ye sure of this, that the kingdom of God is come nigh unto you. But I say unto you, that it shall be more tolerable in that day for Sodom, than for that city.* This first degree of punishment is reserved for those who do not will to be instructed in the faith and in their duties, who do not attend the services of the Church, and who neither use private prayers, meditation, nor spiritual reading, and who stifle in their hearts even all the right impulses which are stirred up within them by God's grace. Their punishment is, that the light they despise is withdrawn from them, that they remain in their ignorance, their wilful blindness, their prejudices, their forgetfulness of God; but at the great day of judgment, Sodom will be treated with less rigour, and the most enormous crimes will be punished less severely than this refusal to open their eyes to the Light, than this contempt of the grace offered to them, than this sin of voluntary blindness.

2. The second degree of sinfulness is represented by the cities of Chorazin and Bethsaida, in which Jesus had worked so many miracles. *Woe unto thee, Chorazin! woe unto thee, Bethsaida! for if the mighty works had been done in Tyre and Sidon, which have been done in you, they had a great while ago repented, sitting in sackcloth and ashes. But it shall be more tolerable for Tyre and Sidon at the judgment than for you.* This second degree of punishment is reserved for those who having been instructed, so to say, in spite of themselves, who, placed in the midst of the light, are neither ignorant of the Gospel nor of the obligations which

it lays upon them, and yet nevertheless live as if they did not know how they ought to live, who abandon themselves to their evil passions and to the inordinate desires of their heart, who have at the least only a dead faith without works, who only maintain some deceptive appearances of devotion and piety, some outward observances of religion. They practise neither self-denial nor repentance; they shudder at the very idea of either of these virtues, and imagine to themselves that they need them not, but at the great Day of judgment, Tyre and Sidon, heathen and idolaters, will reproach them with their ingratitude and folly; their punishment will be infinitely more severe than that of those heathen cities.

3. The third degree of sinfulness is represented by the city of Capernaum, where Jesus made His usual abode when engaged in preaching. *And thou, Capernaum, which art exalted to Heaven, shalt be thrust down to hell.* This third degree of punishment belongs to those who, favoured by more singular graces, called to a higher state of perfection, forget the holiness to which they are specially pledged, and lead a profane life. Raised up to Heaven by the sublimity of their calling, they creep upon the earth by a manner of life which is of this earth, earthy, and differs in nothing from the followers of the world. The nearer they have been brought to God, the greater will be their fall. They will be cast down to the lowest depths, below the greatest sinners. Proud of the height to which they have been raised, they feed their own vanity thereby, instead of employing all their energies to respond to their vocation, and to fulfil its duties faithfully. They do not perceive the abyss which they are digging for themselves, and which will be so much the deeper, the more exalted they have been. Ah! woe be to me, who have refused so many graces, and have abused so many others! Ungrateful cities, hardened and impenitent, ye are more guilty than heathen cities, and I am more guilty than you. Repentance, then, O my soul; repentance in dust and ashes; external repentance, inward repentance, this is the only way which

remains open to thee, whereby to appease the anger of thy God, justly incensed against thee.

THIRD POINT.

Of the crime of those who have rejected the preaching of the Gospel.

He that heareth you, heareth Me; and he that despiseth you, despiseth Me; and he that despiseth Me despiseth Him that sent Me. This judgment of Jesus Christ extends to all time; it regards the successors of this mission of the disciples, as well as the disciples themselves, and is equally true, whether applied to those who minister to us now on God's behalf, or to those to whom Jesus Himself applied it, whom He then sent forth to teach and to preach. Such then is the crime of him who despises the voice of those whom God has appointed to instruct and guide him.

1. It is the crime of the unbeliever and of the deist. He follows only what he terms natural religion; he goes direct to God the Father, he worships Him, and despises all the rest as superstition. But is it for him to regulate the worship which is due to God? If God the Father wills to be honoured in His Son, is not despising the Son despising the Father also? Thus the unbeliever who despises the Son is despised of the Father. He remains plunged in a profound ignorance; he knows not what he should do or avoid in this world, nor what he should fear or hope for in the next; he is unceasingly the puppet of his own thoughts, which change at every moment, and will never cease to torment him, until he fall into the avenging hands of the God Whom he has despised.

2. It is the crime of the Jew, who, closing his eyes to the wonders displayed in the Coming of Christ, and the establishment of His Church, makes a profession of believing only in the promises of God, and refuses to believe in their accomplishment, which he beholds with his own eyes. He looks for the Messiah Whom God has

promised, and rejects Him Whom God hath given him. Is it not to despise thereby the very God Whom he boasts that he adores?

Prayer. O my God! give me that simplicity and faith, that teachableness of spirit so needful in order that I may profit by the truths which Thou hast taught me, or in which Thy ministers instruct me on Thy behalf. Amen.

Meditation CLIV.

RETURN OF THE SEVENTY DISCIPLES.

The Gospel teaches us here, 1. what was the joy of the disciples; 2. what was the joy of Jesus Christ; 3. what ought to be the joy of Christians. S. Luke x. 17—24.

FIRST POINT.

Of the joy of the disciples.

1. *A joy which was well grounded.* *And the seventy returned again with joy, saying, Lord, even the devils are subject unto us through Thy Name.* Was it not indeed a matter worthy of joyful wonderment that men, such as the disciples, should have authority to command the evil spirits, and that these proud beings should be constrained, by the Name alone of Jesus, to obey them? Those who labour for the salvation of souls with zeal, fervour, and in the Name of Jesus, experience often this holy joy which compensates them well for their fatigues. They behold with joy and humility the most obstinate demons yield to the name of Jesus, the most hardened hearts become converted, seek reconciliation with their foes, make restitution of the goods of others, and renounce the sensual enjoyments of the flesh in order to embrace the hardships of a life of repentance.

2. *A joy increased by the revelation which Jesus makes to them.* *And He said unto them, I beheld*

Satan as lightning fall from Heaven. Under this figure, Jesus makes known to His disciples that the power of the devil is destroyed, that his kingdom is at an end, and that the kingdom of God is about to take its place. He announces to them by this figure, although they did not then comprehend it fully, that the worship of the evil one was about to be annihilated, and idolatry banished from the earth; that the worship of the True God would be spread over the world and received every where, and the Name of Jesus would be known, adored, and invoked by all nations. What joy for us to behold the accomplishment of this prophecy? What confidence ought we not to place in the Holy Name of Jesus as a sure defence against the power of evil spirits! But what would be our misery, if the devil, driven out from Heaven and earth, should find a refuge in our heart; if, his temples and altars being destroyed, he should find them anew within us; if he were worshipped in the secret depths of our souls; if, whilst professing to abhor him with our lips, we should yet serve him by our works, our thoughts, and our desires!

3. A joy confirmed with regard to the future. *Behold, I give unto you power to tread on serpents and scorpions, and over all the power of the enemy; and nothing shall by any means hurt you.* Several holy men, such as S. Paul, made use of this power literally. But this power is the type of a yet more sublime power which protects the Church of Christ from all the assaults of the Evil one, so that neither persecution, nor the attacks of wicked men, nor schism, nor heresy, can shake the foundations upon which she is built. All her children participate also in this power, so that neither the temptations of the flesh, nor the snares of the devil, nor the attacks of man, can hurt those who invoke the Name of Jesus, and who put their whole trust in Him.

4. A joy directed towards another object. *Notwithstanding, in this rejoice not, that the spirits are subject unto you; but rather rejoice, because your names are written in Heaven.* The joy which is caused by the

success of any thing which we undertake for God is lawful; but it may become dangerous, if we allow ourselves to rest too much upon it. We ought to dwell more on that which God has done for us, and for our salvation, than on that which He has done through us for the salvation of others. We should, by far greater reason, banish from our hearts all frivolous or criminal joy, which is caused only by human success, temporal advantages, or successful crime. Ah! do not rejoice that your names are written among the great, the learned, the rich of this world; that they are written among the lists of the honours, the dignities, and the favour of the princes of the earth; that which should fill you with ineffable joy, and with which your thoughts should be unceasingly occupied, is that your names are written in Heaven, that you are numbered amongst Christians, children of God, members of Christ, inheritors of the kingdom of Heaven, friends of God. What infinite blessedness, if, faithful to your vocation, you continue therein, and your names being written in the Book of Life, you do nought which may draw down upon you the misery and the shame of having your names wiped out of it.

SECOND POINT.

Of the joy of Christ.

1. His joy is in God His Father, Whose judgments He adores and praises. *In that hour Jesus rejoiced in Spirit, and said, I thank Thee, O Father, Lord of Heaven and earth, that Thou hast hid these things from the wise and prudent, and hast revealed them unto babes; even so, Father, for so it seemed good in Thy sight.* Jesus was always animated by the Holy Spirit, of Whom, in that He was Man, He had received the Fulness, and of Whom, in that He was God, He was the Essence conjointly with God His Father. He willed, at this time, to manifest to His Apostles and to His disciples, and by them to ourselves, in the most intimate

manner, the motions of His Heart. He therefore yielded Himself to a holy transport of the Spirit Which animated Him, and giving utterance to His feelings of joy, He exclaimed as He had done on a somewhat similar occasion, O absolute Master of Heaven and earth! I perceive that Thou hadst concealed Thy holy truth from the wise and learned of this world, in order to reveal them to humble and innocent souls, who are little in their own sight. Yea, my Father, I adore Thy judgments, I acknowledge their equity and wisdom. Thou hast willed it to be thus, Thou hast thus ordained it, and thus it will be; I acquiesce in it, I assent to it, Blessed be Thou for ever. Let us strive to enter into the feelings of the Heart of Jesus, because it is for this purpose that He reveals them to us; let us praise God, let us bless God for the justice which He exercises towards the proud, and for the goodness which He manifests towards the humble. Let us become humble ourselves, and let us be, by the innocency of our lives, and the simplicity of our faith, of the number of those babes to whom God wills indeed to communicate Himself.

2. The joy of Christ is in His Sacred Humanity, of Which He acknowledges that all the gifts come from God His Father. *All things are delivered to me of of My Father; and no man knoweth Who the Son is, but the Father; and Who the Father is, but the Son, and He to whom the Son will reveal Him.* The gifts which Jesus Christ has received from God His Father are, 1. a boundless power over all creatures, 2. a dignity which makes Him God, subsisting in the Person of the Word, true Son of God, having only God for His Father both in time and in eternity; a dignity so sublime, that no one but God Alone can perfectly comprehend this mystery, and all the greatness of Jesus Christ, His Son; 3. a knowledge proportioned to His dignity and His Power, by which He has received from God His Father, the knowledge of His secrets and His designs, which None other but Himself could have; thus the knowledge of the prophets, the power of Moses, the dignity of

Aaron, of the kings and patriarchs of the Old Testament, all this was as nothing in comparison with the dignity, power and knowledge of Jesus Christ. They were His servants, and He is the Son of God. As for the Angels of Heaven, God said to them, Behold My Son; Let all the Angels of God worship Him. (Heb. i. 6.) Ah! what should be our joy to have such a Head, such a Master, such a Saviour!

3. The joy of Christ is in His Church, to whom He communicates all these gifts. *And he to whom the Son will reveal Him.* Jesus Christ communicates to His Church all the gifts which He has received from God His Father, as though He had only received them for our sakes. He communicates to her His Power by granting her the gifts of miracles, and the power to remit or to retain the sins of her members; His knowledge, by giving her the gift of faith; His greatness, by humbling Himself and offering Himself up for us, by uniting Himself to us that we may become the children of His Father by adoption, and by being not ashamed to call us brethren, so that He becomes one with us and we with Him, which He operates in us specially in the Sacraments of Baptism and the Holy Eucharist. Jesus takes delight in His power to communicate to us all His powers; it is this which makes Him rejoice in Spirit. How great and how good Jesus is! What thanks should we not render to God that He has thus given us His Son, and in giving Him to us, has freely given us all things! What thanks should we not render to this Son, so worthy of our love, that He has thus given Himself to us!

4. The joy of Christ is in each faithful soul, which prepares itself to receive these divine communications. *And he to whom the Son will reveal Him.* Jesus is the absolute Master of His own gifts: He communicates them to whom He wills, at the times and in the manner which pleases Him; but it comes to pass only too often that we deprive ourselves of these intimate communications through our own fault, our distractions, and our

frivolity. Let us acknowledge and weep over the blessings we have lost; let us return to our Saviour, and pray to Him, and become to Him a cause of rejoicing and not of sorrow.

THIRD POINT.

Of the joy of Christians.

And He turned Him unto His disciples, and said privately, Blessed are the eyes which see the things that ye see; for I tell you, that many prophets and kings have desired to see those things which ye see, and have not seen them; and to hear those things that ye hear, and have not heard them. Our joy ought to be in the special privileges of our Christian covenant. In order to understand aright what they are, and to learn their true value, we need not fear to compare ourselves with so many others who have been less favoured by God, since this comparison ought only to increase our gratitude, to excite our watchfulness, and to humble us, instead of making us proud.

1. Let us compare ourselves, with regard to our birth, with those who were born and who lived before the coming of Jesus Christ. The earth, then covered with darkness, stained with crimes and idolatry, presented only a fearful sight. The knowledge of the true God was, as it were, confined to a corner of the world, to the nation of the Jews alone. The righteous men, the patriarchs, the prophets, the holy kings of this chosen people sighed for the coming of Him by Whom the whole world was to be redeemed, instructed, and sanctified. Now we see with our eyes what these holy men could not see, namely the worship of God and His Christ established amongst all nations, Christianity spread over all the earth, making every day fresh progress, and announced to the most barbarous and most distant nations. The Jew beholds it himself, but with eyes which nothing can open; he beholds it, but as he beheld the Messiah Whom he crucified; he beholds it, but not in order to

yield to the truths displayed before him, but to be himself an evident proof of it, and to be a confirmation of it at the very time that he is fighting against it.

2. Let us compare ourselves with regard to the place of our birth, with those who have been born in the countries of unbelievers or of the heathen. There are many nations still plunged in the most deplorable blindness, of whom some, such as Mohammedans, will not hear of Christianity, although living in the midst of it; and others who sometimes allow it, and sometimes persecute it, and others again who are still ignorant of it, and to whom it has not yet been preached, such as are some savage nations who as yet are hardly known. What is then our happiness that we are born in a Christian land, where the true light shineth, in a country where it reigns, and where so to say, we have sucked in its Christian doctrines with our mother's milk? Instead of making so great a blessing the subject of gratitude, the impious man makes it, alas! sometimes a ground of offence, and a reason for his unbelief; instead of profiting by it, of thanking God for it, he makes a pretext of it to accuse his Creator, and to reject the gift which He offers him. Fools that ye are! is it for you to penetrate the secrets of divine Providence, and do ye not fear that the Lord will justify the equity of His judgments? Is it thus that ye act in the abundance of earthly possessions? Do ye deprive yourselves of them, because others have them not? Will ye always abuse your reason, and be guided only by the instinct which ye have in common with brute beasts? As for us, let us shew forth more faith, let us thank God with a holy joy, and the deepest gratitude.

3. Let us compare ourselves with regard to the family in which we are born, with those who are not members of the Church. Many families, many sects, who retain the name of Christians, have broken off from the Church, and do not hold her faith or her teaching. What a blessing for us that we are born within her bosom? We see this Church, founded by Jesus Christ and His Apostles, continue on for nearly two thousand years, often

attacked, but always victorious. We see her members
baptized into the same Holy Faith, the Cross of Christ
openly preached, the Sacrifice of His death perpetually
pleaded, the Sacrament of His Body and Blood administered.
We behold Him, hidden under the forms of
bread and wine, present to our faith, offered to our longing
hearts, and communicating Himself to our souls. O
blessed are the eyes, which, enlightened by the light of
faith, can behold and enjoy this most touching, enrapturing
sight.

4. Let us compare ourselves, with regard to our particular
vocation, with those to whom God has not vouchsafed
a like vocation. If God has graciously called us
into the ministry, or led us to embrace a religious life,
or if in the world, He has inspired us with the desire to
lead a retired and regular life, apart from the world and
its corruptions, what ought to be our joy, and how happy
we ought to esteem ourselves! What privileges and
what blessings we have that others have not? What
truths do we not feed upon, and what mysteries do we
not enjoy, of which the world seems to be ignorant?
What goodness does not God shew forth towards us?
Let us rejoice in so many blessings, and let us thank
Him Who is the Author of them, but let us not forget
also that He will one day require us to render Him an
account of the use we have made of them.

Prayer. Yea, Lord, I will render Thee a continual
homage of love and gratitude, for all the benefits which
Thou dost so bounteously bestow upon me, and especially
that Thou hast made known to me the hidden things of
Thy Kingdom. How great is this grace, how perfect!
O Jesus! Thou hast asked for me that I should become
a partaker in this grace, Thou hast procured it for me,
Thou hast thanked Thy Father that He has prepared it
for me and given it unto me. I will join unceasingly
my thanksgivings to Thine, I will return thanks through
Thee to God the Father, for all that He has bestowed
upon me in Thee. Grant me so to relish the Holy
Mysteries which Thou hast revealed to me, that I may

never seek for any other joys save those with which they inspire me. Amen.

Meditation CLV.

JESUS QUESTIONED BY A DOCTOR OF THE LAW.

OF THE LAW OF GOD.

We see here in what consist the study, the summary, the practice, and the difficulties of the law of God. S. Luke x. 25—29.

FIRST POINT.

Of the study of the law of God.

And behold, a certain lawyer stood up, and tempted him, saying, Master, what shall I do to inherit eternal life? This lawyer, seeing the high reputation which Jesus had acquired throughout Palestine, wished to put it to the proof, to fathom His powers, and to try either to embarrass Him or to lead Him to advance something which might be turned against Him. It was doubtless on a Sabbath day, when Jesus was teaching the people in the synagogue, that this lawyer got up in the midst of the assembly, and proposed a vague and general question to which it was not easy to give a complete and precise answer. But Jesus, in order not to commit Himself, and to leave His adversary to make the first advances himself, *said unto him, What is written in the law? how readest thou?* How many persons still put the same question as this lawyer! We hear them say sometimes, I desire to know what I must do in order to be saved? what must I do to be saved? Vain and useless questions! As if we did not know, as if God had left us in ignorance, as if we had not His commandments. But with regard to this holy law, here is our crime.

1. We do not read it. We will not even listen to those who are appointed to explain it to us, and to in-

struct us in it. If we were to ask many persons, What must you do to be saved? *what is written in the law* on this subject? What does the Gospel say on this important question? what are the rules given in it for your condition in life? Alas! they know nothing which it behoves them to know concerning their salvation, they never read the Word of God, and yet it concerns their eternal life or eternal death, and they are utterly indifferent! They will read books which treat of their bodily health, the means whereby to acquire wealth, or books of amusement, these they will read; but those books which speak of salvation, and teach the way whereby to gain eternal happiness, these are neglected. O fatal mistake! O deplorable blindness! Let us then not pass a day without spiritual reading, let us meditate on God's Holy Word, and study diligently those things which concern our salvation.

2. We read the law of God amiss. *How readest thou?* It is a question which may be put to you in another sense than that in which Jesus put it to the lawyer. If the word of God is read, it is often read only out of habit, negligently, hurriedly, with disinclination, and only in order to be able to bear witness to oneself that it has been read, and that one has thereby fulfilled that obligation. Some pages of it are rapidly glanced over, without reflection on what is read, without giving oneself time to consider the occasions and the way in which one may put it into practice. Or it is read merely in an intellectual manner, in order to become acquainted with the facts it contains, or the knowledge it imparts, not in order to learn from it one's duties or the will of God. It is sometimes read in a spirit of criticism and censure, which leads a person to deny the facts, or to seek for difficulties or contradictions, in order to reassure himself in his irreligion, or to confirm himself in his prejudices, or to find whereon to support his doubts; he interprets every thing according to his own fancy, and turns every thing to favour the errors he has already adopted. Such readings are barren, profane and impious:

3. We read all that is contrary to the law of God. *What is written in the law? How readest thou?* If it be a question of the law of God, we are entirely ignorant; but if it be a matter of that which is contrary to the law of God, we read every thing, we know every thing; romances, plays, satires, pamphlets against religion, and morality, against the Church, infidel books, these we read. We have time to read them, we can buy them, we know where to find them; but we have neither time nor inclination to read religious books. Is it for this that God placed us on the earth? Is this the use we make of the life which He has given us? But, when summoned before His tribunal, He will put to us this question, *How readest thou? What is written in the law?* what will be our surprise, our despair, and our shame!

SECOND POINT.

Summary of the law of God.

And he answering, said, Thou shalt love the Lord with all thy heart, and with all thy soul, and with all thy strength, and with all thy mind; and thy neighbour as thyself. Such was the answer which the lawyer made to Jesus, and which Jesus approved; such is the abridgment of the law of God, and in which all is contained.

1. He loves God *with all his heart*, who loves nothing above God, nothing as much as God, nothing but in God and for God; nothing which he is not ready to lose, to quit, to sacrifice in order to please God, or rather than offend God; who has no love, nor hatred, nor desire nor fear, no inclination nor dislike, but in reference to God and according to God's will.

2. He loves God *with all his soul*, who is ready to yield up his life for God, to suffer all kinds of torments, to deprive himself of every kind of pleasure rather than lose the grace of God; who, in order to please God, banishes from his soul every thing that might displease God, and who regulates all the impulses of his soul according to the will and good pleasure of God.

3. He loves God *with all his strength*, who for the glory of God, spares himself neither labour nor trouble; who sacrifices time, health, and rest, and employs all his talents, powers, influence, in His service.

4. He loves God *with all his mind*, who applies himself to know God and His will, who receives with reverence and submission the truths which God has revealed to mankind, who studies the Word of God, meditates on its mysteries, commands and rewards; who makes a study of other sciences and knowledge only so far as they are in accordance with God's Holy Word, and makes use of them only for God, who forms no projects or designs but in reference to God, and the interests of His glory, who banishes from his mind, from his imagination, and from his memory, every needless and dangerous thought, every idea that is capable of sullying it, or of turning it away from God, and uses all his powers of mind for God's glory, who sees only God, and loves to think only of God. Alas! how far am I from this perfection of divine love. Every thing in me is soiled and corrupted by self-love, and the love of the creature. When shall I love only Thee, O my God! when will my heart, my soul, my body, and my mind be perfectly subject to Thee, and be able to answer Thee that I love Thee?

5. He *loves his neigbour as himself*, who manifests towards his neighbour the same esteem, affection, good-will, respect, attention, and regard that he wishes him to shew towards himself; who speaks to him or speaks of him as he would desire that he should be spoken to himself, or be spoken of by others; who bears with his faults, who conceals or makes excuse for his failings, who praises what is praiseworthy, who takes his part, and supports his interests, as he would desire that others should do on his behalf; lastly who renders him all the services which he would desire that others should render him. A vast matter for self-examination and reform, a large subject for grief and confusion.

THIRD POINT.

Of the practice of the law of God.

1. *How necessary it is.* And He said unto him, thou hast answered right; this do, and thou shalt live. It is not then enough to answer well, to know much, to teach well, to speak well, to write well, we must *do* well. Ah! how many deceive themselves on this point? Am I not of those to whom S. Paul speaks, Thou therefore which teachest another, teachest thou not thyself; you do what you say you are forbidden to do, and you do not do that which you say you are commanded to do.

2. *In what it consists.* In the exercises of devotion which form the spiritual life. All that the masters of the spiritual life teach us in accordance with the Gospels all the practices which they recommend, all the virtues which they exhort us to acquire, tend to make us practise the great precept of the love of God and our neighbour. Prayer, meditation, spiritual reading, frequent communions, victory over our passions, mortification of our senses, humility, obedience, keeping under our bodies, detachment, gentleness, resignation, patience, all is directed towards this end, to form in us the love of God, to increase it, to perfect it unceasingly, and to make the love of our neighbour, as it were, familiar to us; it is the end which we ought to set before us, to which we should aspire, and to which all our efforts should be directed. How do we apply ourselves to these holy exercises? If we neglect them, do not let us be surprised that this love of God and our neighbour is not in us, or that it is feeble, languid, and always ready to become extinguished. Let us put our hand to the work; let us *do*, let us act.

3. *What is the reward?* This do, and thou shalt live. You will live in this world with a spiritual life, an inward life, a life of love, a life of delights, which will compensate to you abundantly for all your self-denials; a life which the world does not know, and which is sometimes unknown even to those who have left the

world, because after having left it, they have not left themselves in order to love God alone. You will live in death itself; and when your last hour shall have arrived, you will live by an increase of joy and of consolation, and by the sweet transports of a hope full of immortality. Lastly, you will live in a blessed eternity, in the delights of a divine, perfect and consummated love. Can our heart be cold and indifferent when a reward so noble, so desirable, and so full of delights is offered to us?

FOURTH POINT.

Of the difficulties of the law of God.

The lawyer, seeing that Jesus had made him answer himself to the question which he had proposed to Him, was embarrassed; but, in order not to appear so, and in order to shew that he was right in putting this question, *willing to justify himself*, he particularised one point, and proposing a new difficulty, as if it were something which was very embarrassing in the law of God, he asked; *But who is my neighbour?* It is easy here to trace the spirit of pride and unteachableness, antipathy and jealousy, of subtilty and disputation which prompted this question. Alas! how many disputes have not arisen amongst ourselves respecting this precept of the love of God! disputes which have enlightened the mind less than they have offended against the love of God itself, and the love of our neighbour. Might one not say to these reasoners, Leave there your subtleties, and apply yourselves to love God with all your heart; exhort, lead, persuade others to do so as much as you can. But no; they persist in disputing, and in setting forth their arguments in order to perplex you. They demand that you should distinguish in this law, what is only a precept and a counsel, and what is an absolute necessity, and if you undertake to answer their arguments, what vain and insidious questions will they not add? If you answer that you abide on these points by the decisions of the Church, that you hold what she holds and condemn what she condemns, they will not yet hold their peace; they will ask you what this Church is, where she is, in whom she dwells, in what she consists. The answer is easy to be found by those who do not wilfully close their eyes; but these questioners *will to justify* themselves, instead of submitting themselves to lawful authority. Let us avoid those kind of men who only love to make disturbance and disputes; let us go to God with simplicity, and serve Him with joy; let us ask of Him His holy love, and labour to make each day fresh progress in it.

Prayer. Spread abroad in my heart, O my God, this spirit of love, without which I cannot be either truly holy or eternally happy; without which I cannot please Thee in this world, nor possess Thee in the next. Grant that all my thoughts and all my actions may be sanctified by Thy divine love. Amen.

Meditation CLVI.

PARABLE OF THE SAMARITAN.

OF THE LOVE OF OUR NEIGHBOUR.

Consider here, 1, the want of charity, and what is the source of it; 2. the charity of the Samaritan, and what was the character of it; 3. the charity of Jesus towards us, and what has been the abundance of that charity. S. Luke x. 30—37.

FIRST POINT.

Of the want of charity, and what is the source of it?

The lawyer, having asked Jesus who was his neighbour, and whom he ought to comprehend under that title, Jesus answered him in this instance, by a parable, which, in instructing the lawyer in several truths, forced him, for the second time, to answer himself his own question. *And Jesus, answering, said, A certain man went down from Jerusalem to Jericho, and fell among thieves, which stripped him of his raiment, and wounded him, and departed, leaving him half dead. And by chance there came down a certain priest that way: and when he saw him, he passed by on the other side. And likewise a Levite when he was at the place, came and looked on him, and passed by on the other side.* A natural picture of the want of charity which prevailed then, even amongst the priests and Levites of the Jewish people. But in this picture do we not recognize ourselves? The cause of this inhumanity which is in us, and of our want of charity, does it not arise from the same principles, or rather from the same vices, which are;

1. Pride. This man who was covered with wounds, and lying by the roadside stripped and naked, was of the same city as themselves; he was their fellow-citizen. How many claims were not added to those of nature, to arouse their pity, and to induce them to assist him? But he was only a man, unknown, without title, rank, or position, and they were priests, Levites of a tribe honoured and distinguished above the rest, consequently they contented themselves with giving a glance at him, and passing on. It would be beneath their dignity to stay any longer, and so they continued on their way. And is it not with the same look of pride that we witness the misery, the nakedness, the wounds, in a word, the wants of the poor? We do not deign even to listen to their sorrows, to comfort them at least, in words. If it was a great, a distinguished man, who claimed our assistance, we should hasten to his help, we should consider it an honour to shew our generosity: but for this man of the scum of the people, what glory would redound to us to have succoured him in his needs? Alas! how often has not pride hindered us from comforting an afflicted spirit, a wounded heart, and from healing the sores which perhaps we have caused ourselves!

2. Self-interest. This man had been robbed, despoiled, and he had nothing left. He could only be helped at

the expense of the person who gave him that help, and there was no return to be looked for. At that price, no service. When it concerns a person from whom one has anything to hope for, one is liberal, generous, even affectionate, and anxious to help; but do we hope for no return, then there is no help offered, we find we have not even the time or the leisure to stay to do a kindness. How many works of charity do we not say we cannot perform, which we would willingly do, if they concerned a person on whom depended our future? An affable air, engaging manners, gentle words, obliging services, all these would cost us no trouble, if our self-interest were at stake; but let it be charity which asks them of us, and at once they become an impossibility.

3. Hardness of heart. This man was in a state to excite compassion. Was it possible to see him without being touched by him? But, not only do pride and self-interest render men hard and insensible to the misfortunes of others, there are some hearts which do not allow themselves to be touched by anything. We have not yet arrived at that point doubtless, and we should have been touched with compassion on the present occasion; but on how many other occasions do we not shew this insensibility, this hardness of heart! We see our neighbour in trouble, in distress, and we make a mock of him; in infirmity, in sickness, and we laugh at him; in depression and grief, and we insult him; our witticisms, our sarcasms offend him, wound him, distress him, and yet we continue to annoy him; far from healing his wounds, as might perhaps have been easy to us, we add wound to wound, and we are not touched at his misery but rather glory in so doing. Let us fear lest this insensibility, this hardness which we shew towards our neighbour should recoil upon us, lest they should shut up the bowels of God's mercy towards ourselves, since He has said that He would treat us, as we treat others.

4. Self-love. Not only was this man in a condition to excite compassion, but his condition was one also to

call forth horror, half dead as he was, lying, covered with blood and wounds. What a sight for men filled with self-love and of refined natures! All that either of them could do, was to endure for a moment the sight, and then to pass on. Those who have need of our help revolt our nature, inspire us with disgust; they have bodily and spiritual infirmities; they have their tempers, they have their failings, they have manners which shock us and revolt us. But these are failings which we must endure, our repugnance must be overcome, in order to be truly charitable. If we shew zeal and care only towards those who please us, and with whom our natures harmonize, it is no longer charity, it is self-love.

SECOND POINT.

Of the charity of the Samaritan, and what were its characteristics.

But a certain Samaritan, as he journeyed, came where he was; and when he saw him, he had compassion on him, and went to him, and bound up his wounds, pouring in oil and wine, and set him on his own beast, and brought him to an inn, and took care of him. And on the morrow when he departed, he took out two pence, and gave them to the host, and said unto him, Take care of him; and whatsoever thou spendest more, when I come again, I will repay thee. Charity worthy of admiration! let us gather up all the features of it, which our Lord has singled out with so much care, and if we may venture to say so, with so much condescension, in order to put them before us in this short parable.

1. An universal charity. He does not consider that this unfortunate man is a Jew, he does not give heed to the antipathy which the diversity of nation, of country, of religion, caused, and often causes; it was a fellow-creature, that was sufficient for him.

2. A compassionate charity. He could not endure the sight of this Jew, thus wounded and forsaken, without being touched with compassion.

3. An active charity. He does not content himself with a barren expression of compassion, with useless speeches, or with wishing him or asking for him God's help; however hurried he may have been, he gets down from his horse; whatever repugnance he may have felt, he approaches the unhappy man, he washes his wounds, he bathes them, he assuages the pain, and stops them from bleeding.

4. A generous charity. This Samaritan had provided himself with wine and oil, doubtless for his own use; but his charity made him forget his own requirements, and he rejoices to have in his abundance the means, whereby to minister to the needs of some one in misfortune.

5. A painstaking charity. Not only does he sacrifice what he has for his own use, but he puts himself to inconvenience, and fatigues himself in behalf of the afflicted man. He puts the sick man on his own beast, he follows him on foot, and himself accompanies him until he has found an inn to which to take him.

6. A persevering charity. When there, he does not forsake him. Whether his own affairs suffer in consequence or not, the care of this unfortunate man has become his only occupation. He causes everthing to be given to him that he needs, and he stays with him for the remainder of that day, and all the following night.

7. A charity which anticipates future needs. Who would not have thought that this charitable Samaritan would have exhausted all his charity, and fulfilled all the duties which it could possibly prescribe to him? No; he does not rest there, he bethinks him of the future. On the morrow, being obliged to set out on his journey, he leaves money with the master of the inn, in order that he may provide what was needful for the wounded man. He begs him to spare nothing, and if the sum he leaves with him, should not prove sufficient, he promises on his return, to repay him all that he shall have spent in addition. After this touching picture of charity, at which the lawyer must have been moved himself, Jesus asked him, *Which man of these three, thinkest thou, was neigh-*

bour unto him that fell among the thieves? There could be no possible doubt, and the lawyer was compelled to reply, *He that shewed mercy on him.* Go, then answers the Saviour, *and do thou likewise.* It is to ourselves that Jesus addresses these words: let us go and do as this pious Samaritan; let us be charitable and beneficent towards every one, without distinction of country or religion, because in his need, every one is our neighbour and has a claim on our assistance.

THIRD POINT.

Of the charity of Jesus towards us, and with what lavishness He has bestowed it on us.

We cannot read the parable of the good Samaritan without perceiving that Jesus has therein represented Himself under the most loveable lineaments.

1. How did Jesus Christ come to us? It was not chance which led Him thither, but love. If He has been a traveller on this earth, it is for our sakes that He undertook that journey. He knew where we were, and from the Highest Heavens He came down to us. He knew in what condition we were, how cruelly we had been treated by the Evil one, with how many wounds we were covered, and that without Him we must perish eternally. He knew who we were, how sinful we were, that we had fallen into so wretched a condition only through our own fault, and in sinning against Him; that we were slaves who had revolted, and had actually taken up arms against Him, and persisted in continuing in our rebellion. It is then that He came down to us, not in order to punish us, but in order to save us. Not only did He come down from Heaven to earth in making Himself Man, but this God-made-Man has submitted His Humanity to all our weaknesses, to all our miseries, in order to apply to us a more efficacious and prompt remedy. It is by taking our wounds upon Himself that He has healed them, by taking upon Himself our debts that He has paid them, by taking upon Himself our

sins that He has expiated them. O Heavenly Love!, who can comprehend Thee!

2. How has Jesus Christ dealt with us whilst He has been with us? It is not one day only, but all His life that He has laboured for us. He has spared neither care, nor fatigues, nor benefits; He has sacrificed His repose, His reputation for us; He has even given His Blood for us, and lastly, He has succumbed under the weight of His charity, and given Himself up to die in order to deliver us from death. Can we think of it without dying of love for Him? At least, let us live for Him, and let our life be employed only in serving and loving Him.

3. Where has Jesus Christ placed us before leaving us? In His Church, which He has founded and purchased with His Blood for the salvation of all mankind; and in this Church, what abundance of blessings has He not gathered up as in a store house? His grace and His merits, the price of His Death and of His Blood are there communicated to us by the Sacraments. What remedies against all our evils! what preservatives against all dangers! what a pure Table full of delights hast Thou not prepared for us! what Bread and what Wine for our Food! what abundance of knowledge for our instruction! and to all these blessings, He adds the Spirit of truth, which assures to us the real possession of all these blessings till the end of the world. Ah! it is then through our own fault, and not through any fault on His part, if we are not healed, if we do not live.

4. What has Jesus Christ promised to do on His return? Not only will He demand an account of that which has been done for us; but moreover, He commends us to the cares of the ministers of His Church in such a manner, that in enjoining them to let us want for nothing, and to provide us abundantly with all we need, He declares to them that He will regard as done to Himself all that they will have done or left undone on our behalf; that their negligence on a point which

touches Him so closely will be punished with an everlasting punishment, and that their cares and their labours will have an everlasting reward. That which He says to His Ministers, He says also to each one of us, who ought to have the same care one for another, to be a mutual help and comfort one to the other, so that unity, peace and concord should reign in His Church, and that each one, finding in it the helps he needs should have also opportunities whereby he may gain that which He has promised on His return. Oh return which is too easily forgotten! O divine Charity! descend into our hearts, and from the Heart of Jesus, spread thyself in our hearts, that we may all love one another as Thou hast loved us.

5. What ought to be our gratitude? The parable says nothing of the gratitude of the unfortunate Jew who was so generously assisted; this was not the occasion on which to speak of it, and Jesus willed only to speak to us of the love which He bore towards us; but in carrying on the parable, let us employ ourselves in thinking of the love which we owe to Him. What must have been the feelings of this unhappy man, when he saw the kind and generous care taken of him by a man to whom he was not only a stranger, but more than that, a Jew, an object of aversion and hatred, and one from whom no return could be looked for? Would it have been too much for him to do, to give himself up to his service, to dedicate to him a life which he owed only to him? Can one believe that he would ever forget this benefit which he had received from him, but that rather he would publish it abroad, and seek for every possible occasion wherein to testify to him his lively thankfulness?

Prayer. Ah! Lord, such are the feelings which my heart would have dictated to me, and with which, on a similar occasion, I should, methinks, have been penetrated. Oh! how much more ought I not to be filled with the like feelings towards Thee, my Saviour, Who hast set before me this parable, and Whose love has been so far more generous, and Thy benefits so far more signal than those which Thou dost here set forth! But if, in loving Thee as I ought, there is nought that I can do for Thee, shall I refuse to render services to my brethren whom Thou willest to put in Thy stead; and can I not but esteem myself happy, in serving and in sparing myself nothing for them, in order to testify to Thee some small portion of my gratitude? Ah! communicate it then to me Thyself, O Jesus! this love which never neglects the needs of others, sets aside no duty, despises no one. Amen.

Meditation CLVII.

JESUS AT THE HOUSE OF MARTHA AND MARY.

Observe 1. the happiness of Martha and Mary her sister; 2. the complaints of Martha against her sister Mary; 3. the decision of Jesus between Martha and her sister Mary. S. Luke x. 38—43.

FIRST POINT.

The happiness of Martha and her sister Mary.

Now it came to pass, as they went, that He entered into a certain village, and a certain woman, named Martha, received Him into her house. And she had a sister called Mary, which also sat at Jesus' feet and heard His Word. But Martha was cumbered about much serving.

1. What was the happiness of these two sisters? This happiness consisted in their union. A union founded on the proximity of blood; they were sisters, and lived as friends. How sweet a similar union is! but is it not sad that friendship has become so rare between brothers and sisters, when they have attained a certain age. A union strengthened by piety. They

were both fervent Israelites; they were looking for the Messiah, they were attentive to all that had been told them of Jesus, and were moved by it. Without true piety there is no solid union. A constant union notwithstanding the diversity of their characters. The two sisters, although united, had not the same disposition. Martha, on whom the care and management of the house devolved, liked an active life, and was never idle; Mary, loved contemplation, meditation, prayer, and religious exercises. Each followed their own likings and vocation; and this diversity, far from disturbing their union, preserved its harmony, and brought about mutual edification, and reciprocal esteem. Happy the family, the community in which such union reigns.

2. What was the special happiness of Martha? It was to receive Jesus into her house, and to employ all her activity in ministering to Him. She has consequently become an example for those who are engaged in domestic cares, who are occupied in ministering to, in waiting upon, or providing for the members of Christ, and in working for Him by working for them. These persons ought to imitate the fervour in work and the purity of intention of Martha.

3. What was the special happiness of Mary? It was to keep near to Jesus, and to listen to Him. If Martha received Him into her house, and worked for Him, Mary not only took part in this good work, but she sought besides to profit by the Presence of such a Guest, by listening to the Words which fell from His lips. In order not to lose any of them, she remained seated at His Feet, in the most humble posture, and in the deepest contemplation. In this she followed the steps of the Blessed Virgin Mary, who kept with so much care all His sayings in her heart. What hinders us from partaking in the happiness of Martha and Mary? We can by a fervent Communion, like the former, receive Jesus into our house; we can, like Mary, whether in the Communion, or at other times, sit at His Feet, listen to Him, and feed upon His Heavenly doctrine. If

we were faithful, how many happy moments should we not spend, what delights should we not enjoy!

SECOND POINT.

Complaints of Martha against her sister Mary.

1. *Complaints which are borne only to Jesus.* But *Martha was cumbered about much serving, and came to Him and said, Lord, dost Thou not care that my sister hath left me to serve alone? bid her therefore that she help me.* Far from this complaint which was addressed to Jesus being either sharp or bitter, we see in it, on the contrary, the expression of her love to the Lord, and of her friendship to her sister. If all our complaints were such as this was, if we only addressed them to Jesus Himself, if we only looked for the remedy from Him and by His command, they would be much more rare, and would never disturb either the peace or charity of others.

2. Complaints which do not hinder Martha in her work. Mary is seated at the Feet of Jesus, but as for Martha, she comes before Him standing, she comes direct from her work, she is about to return to it; her only object in coming to our Lord, is to induce others to work, and as it would appear, to animate herself and incite herself to greater diligence. Our complaints are far different, they discourage us, they make us faint-hearted, they reduce us to despair, and often make us give up our work altogether. Ah! if we did but think that it is for Jesus that we are working; that our work is our calling, our duty, our gain, we should not complain that all the work was left to us, or if we did complain, we should do so, like Martha, in a spirit of love, without ceasing to work, and with the intention of continuing our work with renewed fervour.

3. Complaints which did not offend Mary. Mary knew her sister, and saw well the motives which animated her; she does not place a false interpretation on her words; she sees in them neither want of reverence

for Christ, nor unkindness towards herself; she only sees in them the amiable character of her sister, always quick, active and zealous in serving others. Mary keeps silence, not a silence of ill-temper and displeasure, nor a silence such as persons keep who shew that they are exercising self-control in order not to give vent to their feelings, and in order to bear in patience, a silence which is often more offensive than an answer, but a silence full of gentleness, kindness and respect. She waits till He Who permits her to sit at His Feet, and to Whom this complaint of hers was addressed, should condescend to answer for her. If we only uttered complaints of others in the same manner as Martha, we should give offence to none, and if we received the complaints which are uttered against us as Mary did, we should preserve our peace of mind, and Jesus would take our defence upon Himself.

THIRD POINT.

Decision of Jesus between Martha and her sister Mary.

And Jesus answered, and said unto her, Martha, Martha, thou art careful and troubled about many things, but one thing is needful, and Mary has chosen that good part, which shall not be taken away from her. Let us remark with what gentleness, with what seriousness, and with what skill our Lord turns the complaint of Martha into an important instruction.

1. Observe the trouble of Martha. *Martha, Martha, thou art careful and troubled about many things.* This reproach applies to ourselves yet more forcibly than to Martha. We *are troubled*, because we occupy our minds with an infinity of things which do not concern us, which do not regard our station in life, or our occupation. We *are troubled* in our employments, and in our needful duties, either from a natural activity, which makes us act with too much impetuosity, or because we undertake more than we are able to carry out, and wish to do things otherwise than we can; or out of a spirit of va-

nity which makes us fear blame or disgrace if we do not succeed in them, which makes us seek for esteem, praise and approbation; or from self-love, by which we desire to be contented with ourselves, and that others should be so also. We *are troubled* in our devotions by chimerical fears and vain scruples which only serve to draw us away from God. If we would renounce all these useless cares, if we would seek God Alone, His glory and our salvation, our work would be quieter and more useful; it would not harden our heart, it would not harden our minds, and it would leave us all the time which was needful for us to devote to prayer and other spiritual exercises.

2. Meditate what is this one only necessary thing, of which Jesus speaks. *But one thing is needful.* A maxim, a sentence which is all important, a divine word, a two-edged sword, which cuts off on the one hand, all the superfluous cares of the present life, and on the other hand, sets before us the only real and lasting possessions of the future life. *But one thing is needful.* If we contented ourselves in the world with what was absolutely necessary for our support, our food and clothing, how many cares would not be spared, how many murmurs stifled, and how little would suffice to our needs; but we desire abundance, luxuries; and avarice never says, It is enough. *But one thing is needful*, and that is salvation; *needful*, because without it we must be sovereignly and eternally miserable; *but one thing is needful*, because every thing else can contribute in nothing to our happiness, and that it alone can render us sovereignly and eternally happy; it is also the only thing that every one can gain, and perhaps, alas! the only thing which men do not seek to gain, and for which they do not labour. O folly of mankind! Am I not myself of that number? Have I laboured in the matter of my salvation more than in any other? Is it to that, that I make all else subservient?

3. Consider what is *that good part* of which Mary made choice. *Mary has chosen that good part.* That

good part, is the care of one's salvation, seeking after the one thing needful, diligence in prayer, in contemplation, meditation, and self-renunciation of earthly things. He has chosen tha *good part,* that young man who gives up the world, who enters upon the ministry, in order to serve God alone, and to think only of his salvation. She has chosen that *good part,* that young person, who renouncing the vanities of the world, the hopes and longings of this life, gives herself up entirely to a life spent in the service of God, and in works of piety and devotion. Wise and happy he who has made so good a choice. *Mary has chosen that good part which shall not be taken away from her.* O fleeting possessions of this world; whatever love, or attachment we may have for you, you will be taken away from us, you will be torn out of our hands, we shall be separated from you for ever. Riches, pleasures, glory, honours, arts, sciences, sceptres, crowns, all will be taken away from us, and nought will abide with us.

Prayer. O Mary, the *good part* which *thou hast chosen* will *never be taken away* from thee. Thou wilt enjoy it with Him, Who Himself pronounced these blessed Words, the King of angels and men, and with all those holy souls, who like thee have had the courage to choose *that good part.* Alas! wherefore am I not of that number? Give me, Lord, a spirit of recollection, which shall precede, accompany, and follow all my actions; grant me a lively and active charity, which shall produce in my heart all the blessed fruits of action and of contemplation. Amen.

Meditation CLVIII.

DISCOURSE OF JESUS TO THE PEOPLE, IN WHICH HE AGAIN ENJOINS THAT WHICH HE HAD TAUGHT ELSEWHERE.

ON DIVERS POINTS OF THE MORAL LAW.

Jesus explains here, 1. what hypocrisy is; 2. what a Christian's fear should be; 3. in what his obligation to confess Christ consists. S. Luke xii. 1—12.

FIRST POINT.

Of hypocrisy.

Jesus, when He left Bethany, returned to Galilee. *In the meantime, when there were gathered together an innumerable multitude of people, insomuch that they trode one upon another, He began to say unto His disciples first of all, Beware ye of the leaven of the Pharisees, which is hypocrisy. For there is nothing covered that shall not be revealed; neither hid, that shall not be made known.*

1. Consider hypocrisy in the evil deeds which we take care to conceal. Vain precautions; often in this life the most shameful mysteries are discovered, and then, what trouble and bitterness does not this fear mingle with our pleasures. A pure and innocent life enjoys, on the contrary, an unchangeable peace. But even if we succeed in concealing them during this life, the great Day of judgment will come, when the secrets of all hearts will be laid bare; what will then be our shame, our confusion! If we take so much care to keep our evil actions hidden in this life, let us take still more care that they may remain concealed in the next life, by confessing them and repenting of them now.

2. Consider hypocrisy in works which are externally good, but corrupted by secret faults. Protestations of friendship, offers of services without sincerity, good

offices, warm professions, without affection, frequenting Church services and Communions without devotion, external marks of devotion, forms of prayer recited without inward prayer; what shall be said of so many ill-regulated motives and perverse intentions which form the spring of so many of our actions? Vanity, self-interest; how difficult it is to preserve ourselves from this Pharasaical leaven, which corrupts our holiest actions, and turns them into so many acts of hypocrisy! Now, all these faults, all these motives, these intentions, these most secret and most hidden thoughts of our heart, which we conceal so skilfully, which we veil under so fair an exterior, and which sometimes we conceal even from ourselves, will be discovered and made manifest, and what will then be our surprise and our confusion!

3. Consider hypocrisy in the doctrine which we retail in secret. *Therefore,* continues Jesus, *Whatsoever ye have spoken in darkness shall be heard in the light, and that which ye have spoken in the ear in closets shall be proclaimed upon the house tops.* Unbelievers, heretics, ungodly men, after the example of the Pharisees, disseminate in darkness, in private, in the circles of persons who are easily to be led astray, and already half corrupted, abominable maxims, principles which tend to extinguish every feeling of remorse or of modesty. They take good care not to give utterance to them in public, or if they do so, they retail them anonymously, and veiled under equivocal expressions which can be made to bear an apparently justifiable construction. It is not thus with the doctrines of the Church of Christ. Such as they are spoken in private, such they are preached on the roofs, in acknowledged writings, in the pulpits, and even on the scaffolds. He who is not ready to acknowledge his assent to them, and to maintain them before the whole world, and before each one in particular, is not worthy of them, and is disavowed by them. This is the example which the apostles and martyrs have left us, and which will find imitators to the end of the world, notwithstanding the opposition of many.

SECOND POINT.

Of a Christian's fear.

1. He does not fear the persecution of men. *And I say unto you My friends, Be not afraid of them that kill the body, and after that have no more that they can do.* The Christian does not fear the persecution of men, because that which he possesses, and that which he hopes for are beyond their power, and they can only have power over those possessions which he despises. They may deprive him of his offices and his employments, seize upon his property, carry him away from his native country, take away his liberty from him, torment him, and cause his death; after which, their power over him expires, and his happiness begins, never to end. Ah! how far are we from this Christian intrepidity, we, whom a word, whom a look causes to tremble, and who, out of human respect, fail in our most sacred duties, trangress God's commandment, and basely abandon the cause of Jesus Christ and the side of virtue!

2. He fears God. *But*, adds Jesus Christ, *I will forewarn you Whom ye shall fear: Fear Him, Which after He hath killed, hath power to cast into hell, yea, I say unto you, Fear Him.* Fear this God Whose power is eternal, and Who, after having sometimes punished in this world by a premature death, can also precipitate the sinner into hell for all eternity. Ah! this is indeed what we should fear. The fear of God is the beginning of wisdom and of holiness. Beware lest you shake this foundation by the maxims of a false doctrine, which the Gospel does not teach. The greatest saints have strengthened themselves in the midst of temptations, and even martyrs, at the sight of the tortures prepared for them, by the thought of hell. Love God, keep His commandments, serve Him with love; Who is more worthy of our love than He? But if some temptation presents itself to you which is capable of turning you away from that love, remember that this God is not less terrible than He is long-suffering, and

that one single mortal sin suffices to draw down upon you all the rigour of His justice. If we were truly penetrated with this fear, temptations would have no attraction, the world would possess no charms, the devil would be powerless, our evil passions would have no strength, repentance would have no hardships, and piety would be without any obstacles. When the unbeliever seeks to stifle the fear of God in men's hearts, is it in behalf of virtue that he speaks? No, he is in that, the abettor of all vices and of all crimes. He who makes a boast that he does not fear God, declares himself prepared, when the occasion presents itself, for the greatest crimes.

3. The Christian does not fear the most grievous events of life. *Are not five sparrows*, continues Jesus, *sold for two farthings, and not one of them is forgotten before God? But even the very hairs of your head are all numbered. Fear not therefore; ye are of more value than many sparrows.* The Christian, calm in the bosom of Providence, knows that God governs every thing, and that He takes care of all His creatures. If a sparrow is not excepted from His care, how then should He forget man, formed in His image, and for whose sake every thing else has been created? Not only each human being in particular, but all that belongs to them is present to His knowledge. Your health, your body, your soul, your worldly possessions, every thing is under His protection. Even the very hairs of your head are counted. Nothing can happen to us but by His permission, and nothing can happen to us, if we only will take it aright, but for our greater good. What shall we fear under so great and powerful a God, our Creator and our Father? Let us banish then these fears, this mistrust, which are an outrage to His greatness and His goodness; let us accept from His Hand with gratitude the evils as well as the good things of this present life; let us submit ourselves with reverence to His holy will, and let us be sure that the abundance of His help will always answer to the greatness of our trust.

THIRD POINT.

Of the necessity which is laid upon us of confessing Jesus Christ.

1. The reward or the punishment of those who shall have fulfilled or violated this obligation. *Also I say unto you, Whosoever shall confess Me before men, him shall the Son of man also confess before the angels of God, but he that denieth Me before men shall be denied before the angels of God.* To confess Jesus Christ is to declare oneself a Christian, to shew oneself as a Christian in the face of those who attack Christianity. The times of persecution of the Church have passed away; but in their stead more insidious and subtle attacks have arisen. The martyrs were called upon to confess Christ, to declare that they worshipped Him, followed His commandments, and renounced idol worship. Such is still our duty. It is not necessary for us to enter into disputations with those who blaspheme Jesus Christ, and outrage His Church, but the most unlearned woman, the simplest child can avow boldly their belief in the truths of Christianity, and it would be to betray our duty, if we should keep silence when we hear them attacked, although we may not be able to combat their sophisms. The day will come when Jesus, accompanied by His Holy Angels, will come to judge the living and the dead. What glory then, what happiness for us, if we have declared ourselves on His side! What shame and misery if we have shrunk back from so doing!

2. Punishment of those who have violated this obligation. *And whosoever shall speak a word against the Son of man it shall be forgiven him; but unto him that blasphemeth against the Holy Ghost, it shall not be forgiven.* There are some whose crime, however enormous it may be, is not without hope of pardon; such are they who speak or act against Jesus Christ without having a sufficient knowledge of Him, and without having had an opportunity of knowing Him; such

were several of the Jews, such were the Gentiles who knew Him only as man, and spoke disparagingly of Him on sundry occasions: such were even the executioners who crucified Him. We may add to this number those who now-a-days, without ceasing to acknowledge Jesus Christ, yet sin against Him through the frailty of their nature, carried away by their evil passions, led astray by evil example, or temptations. This is what our Lord calls *speaking a word against the Son of Man*. Such may and often do acknowledge their faults, return back from the path in which they have strayed, weep over their sins, gain the victory over them, and obtain their pardon. But to deny the mystery of the Incarnation, that fundamental operation of the Holy Spirit; to withstand the Christian religion, and to persist in so doing, notwithstanding the most evident proofs of its authenticity; to harden one's heart against the voice of conscience and of remorse, the inward voice of the Holy Spirit; to deny the work of the Holy Spirit in the Church of Christ, His strengthening, guiding, confirming Influences; this is what our Lord calls blaspheming against the Holy Ghost, and this is a crime from which one never beholds a sincere repentance. There were a great number of those who actually took part in the death of Jesus Christ, who were converted, there were some even among His executioners; but we do not know of one amongst those, who having wilfully blinded themselves, have counted the Blood of the covenant, wherewith they were sanctified, an unholy thing, and have done despite unto the Spirit of grace. O you! who enter into the world after having been carefully and Christianly brought up, persevere in innocence and in the practice of God's commandments, and sin not against the Lord; but if, unhappily, you sin against Him, do not close the doors against your return to Him, do not cast yourself into the abyss which you can yet avoid, do not join yourselves to the blasphemers and unbelievers, and seek for peace in the most terrible and senseless despair; acknowledge that you are a sinner, and avail yourself of the remedy that still remains to you in faith and repentance.

3. The help which the Holy Spirit gives in order to fulfil this obligation. *And when they bring you into the synagogues, and unto magistrates, and powers, take ye no thought how or what thing ye shall answer, or what ye shall say; for the Holy Ghost shall teach you in the same hour what ye ought to say.* Do not be discouraged at the thought of your want of ability, knowledge, or talents; remain only firmly attached to Jesus Christ, and His Church, and when the need comes, words will not fail you; the Holy Spirit will suggest to you at the time what you must say. Did this help fail the martyrs? Summoned before the assembly of an infuriated people, before magistrates clothed with power and authority, before governors surrounded by their satellites, even before emperors themselves, seated on their throne with all the paraphernalia of majesty, it was under these circumstances, that unlearned and ignorant men, that feeble women, that timid maidens have spoken, have confounded their oppressors, have disconcerted all their wisdom and set at nought their power. And if they could withstand such overwhelming adversaries, what are the enemies that you are called upon to oppose when compared to them? The most unlearned woman, if she is only a fervent Christian, need not be perplexed how to give an answer of the faith that is in her.

Prayer. Grant me grace, O God, to confess Thee in spite of all opposition, without seeking the glory that cometh of men, without fearing their power, without opposing to their artifices, artifices which are purely human, without seeking for any other wisdom than that which comes from Thee, and leads to Thee. Amen.

Meditation CLIX.

FIRST CONTINUATION OF THE DISCOURSE OF JESUS TO THE PEOPLE.

RESPECTING RICHES.

1. The desire of riches persuades a person of their necessity: 2. the possession of riches makes a person feel the vanity of them; 3. death amidst riches makes a person know their folly. S. Luke xii. 13—21.

FIRST POINT.

The desire of riches persuades a person of their necessity.

1. The effects of this persuasion. *And one of the company said unto Him, Master, speak to my brother, that he divide the inheritance with me.* This brother wished doubtless to take possession for himself of the entire heritage of his family, and to yield no portion of it to his brother. When a man allows himself to be possessed with the desire of riches, he comes to look upon them as the one thing necessary to which every thing else must be sacrificed. The first effect of this persuasion is injustice. He who desires to enrich himself does not fear to be unjust, when it lies in his power, and he finds an opportunity to be so; he is never an equitable judge between himself and his neighbour. He is never wanting in a pretext whereby to appropriate to himself and to retain the goods of others, when it lies in his power: and if a pretext fails him, he does not blush to employ force, violence, or an unjust detention. Such was this brother who kept back for himself an inheritance which he ought to have shared with his brother. The second effect of this persuasion, is the division that arises amongst families, the reproaches, bickerings, disputes, complaints, lawsuits, the hatred, and

even animosities between brothers and sisters, between those whom nature has united in the closest and most sacred bonds, and whose happiness and glory ought to be in their union. The third effect of this persuasion is, forgetfulness of God, and of their salvation. In this crowd of people who listen to Jesus with so much earnestness, do not seek the covetous brother; do not seek in our Churches, at the hours of public worship or of communion, those men greedy of wealth; other cares occupy them, and they would look upon the time employed in the worship of God, or in thoughts of Him, as wasted. The fourth effect of this persuasion is preoccupation of spirit. The brother wronged by his brother was amongst the number of the auditors of Jesus; but in hearkening to Him, with what objects were his thoughts occupied? He speaks to Jesus, but respecting what does he converse with Him? He asks a favour of Him; but what does this favour regard? O love of riches! thou pursuest those of whom thou hast taken possession, to the very foot of the altar, to the Feet of Jesus. He who is possessed by it, speaks, thinks, converses even with God, only of this one all engrossing object of his desires.

2. Example opposed to this persuasion. *And He said unto him, Man, who made me a judge or a divider over you?* It is the duty of the ministers of Christ to exhort us to disinterestedness, to peace, to concord, to the ways of gentleness and reconciliation; but it is not for them to mix themselves up personally in the petty details of our affairs, our claims, our interests. Not only would such a discussion be a needless waste of time, but there would be a risk of their losing thereby the trust, if they did not even incur the hatred, of one of the parties. There are judges to whom we can have recourse, there are arbitrators to whom we can refer our disputes.

3. Refutation of this persuasion. Jesus, then addressing Himself to all His audience, *said unto them, Take heed and beware of covetousness; for a man's*

life consisteth not in the abundance of the things which he possesseth. Abundance or superfluity does not serve to the support of life, because a person cannot make use of it all, and must needs leave some of it after he has supplied all his wants. This superfluity does not add either to health or to the amenities of life; it would tend rather to destroy health, by arousing within us imaginary needs, or making us commit excesses beyond our real requirements. This superfluity does not avail to prolong life; when the hour of death has come, this superfluity will not deliver us from it. How happy is he, who in his station of life, knows how to content himself with that which is necessary for himself, his family, and for the education of his children! How many crimes would be avoided, how many good works would be practised, how many anxieties would be spared! What peace of mind, what real happiness of soul would that not be! Let us then hearken to the lesson our Divine Master here gives us! Let us bring to bear all our care in order to preserve ourselves from this spirit of avarice, that is to say, from the love of riches, and that eager desire to increase our possessions, to raise ourselves above our station, to rise in the social scale, to equal those above us, and even to surpass them, when we think we have raised ourselves to an equality with them. It is not without reason that our Lord bids us *beware*, because this desire is natural to us, and creeps imperceptibly into our hearts. All the conversation we hear around us, all the maxims of the world and the examples it sets us, tend to excite in us this fatal desire from which very few know how to preserve themselves.

SECOND POINT.

The possession of riches makes us feel their vanity.

1. By the anxieties which it causes. Our Lord, continuing to address His audience, *spake a parable unto them, saying, The ground of a certain rich man brought forth plentifully.* What advantage did he gain from

this abundance? None, save an increase of anxieties. *And he thought within himself, What shall I do, because I have no room where to bestow my fruits?* See him then disquieted in mind by the thoughts with which he is agitated. *He thought within himself.* If he had been a good man, and one that feared God, at the sight of this heaven-sent blessing, he would have rejoiced in the Lord, and praised and blessed God, and have received this increase of his possessions as a gift sent by His Divine goodness; but instead of so doing, this rich man becomes pensive, anxious, on account of this unusually plentiful harvest; he concentrates his thoughts upon himself, and gives himself up entirely to his perplexities as to how to dispose of this increase. Do we always behold, a real and genuine joy on the face of a rich man, even when his fortune is prospering and increasing? The rich man in the Gospel, embarrassed and undecided, said, *What shall I do?* When a person has only a moderate fortune, he cannot understand this embarrassment of riches: there would appear to be nothing less embarrassing than riches, every one imagines that he would know how to make use of them, but experience teaches us that there is nothing which brings more solicitude with them. He only finds no perplexity, who neither loves them, nor esteems them, who neither seeks them nor desires them, and only accepts them, when God sends them to him, in order to employ them in accordance with His holy will. But this is not the position of the avaricious man; he is disquieted and knows not what to do with his wealth; and who would believe it, his very abundance is the cause of his disquietude. Of what then does he think *within himself?* On what does he deliberate so seriously? What is it then that disquiets him so cruelly? It is one thing which is wanting to him. *He thought within himself, What shall I do, because I have no*—What! is there any thing you have not? Have you not more than you hoped for, more than you can consume? And yet you are perplexed, you say, because you have no—Yes, it is this very abundance which disturbs me, which perplexes me, which straightens me, because I have not where to put my harvest, my granaries are too small. O unhappy man, who only thinkest of thyself, thou hast not where to put thine abundance; but are there no poor to support, no one in misfortune whom you can succour, no indigent families to relieve, no prisoners for debt whom you can release? Do the Churches, the Altars, the worship of God require nothing from thy gratitude? Be then, insatiable man, abandoned to thine anxiety, which is the just punishment of thy avarice, or if thou overcomest that, it will only be in order to fall into a still greater punishment.

2. The possession of riches makes a person feel the vanity of them by the occupations which it gives. The rich man comes to an end of his perplexity, and decides upon his course of action. *And he said, This will I do; I will pull down my barns and build greater; and there will I bestow all my fruits and my goods.* Is not that the first occupation of those who set their heart on riches? 1. It is an occupation of pride and display. The home of their fathers, where they have been born themselves, and where they have been brought up, does not suffice them; it humiliates them, it dishonours them. The father was content with a modest house, the son requires a superb palace. He imagines by this means to make the mediocrity of his birth forgotten, and to conceal the obscurity of his former station; he imagines to add lustre to his name in proportion as he extends his buildings, but he only excites against himself contempt and hatred; each one delights in recalling the remembrance of his first condition, and takes care to hand it down to posterity. 2. A ruinous and contradictory occupation. This man loves his riches, and in order to preserve them he spends them; he causes that which has been built to be demolished, and larger buildings to be erected. Thus, this which constituted the ground of the fears of this rich miser, that is to say the loss of his superfluity, is nevertheless that upon which he determines. How many persons has one not seen who having caused

vast granaries to be constructed, have not had anything to put into them! How many, who after spending their money in erecting and furnishing magnificent apartments, have not been able to enjoy them, but have had to give them up to their creditors! 3. An occupation full of distraction and irreligion. Whilst this rich man is occupied with his buildings, it would be useless to speak to him of prayer, of meditation, of Communions; he has no time for them. It would be useless to speak to him of good works, almsgiving, charity, he has not the means for them. Who would venture to answer for him even that he would commit no injustice, that he would pay those in his employ with exactness, that he would be just in his dealings with his workmen? Oh vain and deceptive riches! how fatal ye are to those who are engrossed by your possession! must we always be dazzled by your false splendour!

3. The possession of riches makes a person feel the vanity of them, by the projects which it causes him to form; chimerical projects, on which he feeds all his life, and of which he never sees the execution. When I shall have finished my buildings, this rich man said to himself, and when I shall have gathered in all my harvest and all my possessions, then *I will say to my soul, Soul, thou hast much goods laid up for many years; take thine ease, eat, drink, and be merry.* Such are the projects of the man who is greedy of riches, by which he promises himself, first of all, an abundance of possessions which fills his mind with anxiety. You see him to-day greedy of gain, eager in accumulating wealth, on the watch to take advantage of every means whereby he may enrich himself, occupied with trifles, alive to everything, making money out of everything, disquieted about all passing events, inconsolable if he lets the least opportunity escape him; but all this only lasts a certain time, and that until he has amassed a certain amount, after which he will say to himself, Now I have enough, I have sufficient for the rest of my life, I fear nothing more, I trouble myself about nothing

further. But alas! where are those who, contented with their future and satisfied with what they have acquired, have placed bounds to their cupidity? They promise themselves a perfect repose and exemption from all solicitude. To-day you behold them in perpetual motion, coming, going, working unceasingly, spending whole nights, and even anticipating the day, giving themselves neither rest nor relaxation; but all this is only in order to procure for themselves a perfect repose hereafter, in which they will be freed from further exertions, and be able to enjoy at their ease the fruit of their past labours. But alas! have we seen many who have attained to this condition of rest and tranquillity? Finally they promise themselves a life of good cheer and enjoyment. To-day you behold them depriving themselves even of the necessaries of life, and regretting the little that they are compelled to spend on themselves, they are sordid and sparing; but when they shall have amassed sufficiently, they will indemnify themselves for their privations, they will abandon themselves to luxury and the pleasures of the table, and they will spare nothing in order to provide enjoyments for themselves. Behold then the last term to which the hopes of the rich tend, and the most noble object of his desires, *to eat and drink.* O vanity of riches! does it require so much pains to attain to such an aim! The poor, in his mediocrity has long enjoyed this advantage, and he enjoys it with so much the more delight that he is far from placing his sovereign happiness in it.

THIRD POINT.

Death in the midst of riches makes a person know the folly of them.

But God said unto him, Thou fool! this night thy soul shall be required of thee; then whose shall those things be, which thou hast provided? So is he that layeth up treasure for himself and is not rich towards God. The rich man was feeding himself on his flattering hopes, when God, Whom he had entirely forgotten, and the thought of Whom never entered into his vast projects, overturned all his plans. Thus consider,

1. The folly of the rich man in amassing riches which he must leave behind him. Sure as we are that we must die, that we have only a short time to remain in this world, and that we shall pass from hence into another, there to dwell eternally, that, in this other world, we shall only carry with us thither our soul, with its crimes or its virtues; that the hour of our departure is uncertain and that it may take place at any moment, and that when that hour has come, and that God speaks the word, we must obey without delay, and appear before Him; certain as we are of all that, is it not a folly to occupy ourselves so seriously with the things of this life, to be so eager, to give ourselves so much trouble in order to procure wealth which we must leave behind, which we cannot carry with us, and which moreover would be of no use to us?

2. The folly of the rich, in that leaving his possessions behind him, he does not even know to whom he leaves them. How often does it not happen that a rich man has only amassed his wealth for strangers whom he did not know, for ungrateful heirs who insult his memory, for children who consume it in lawsuits, or for sons who waste their inheritance, spend their money lavishly, and alienate their houses or lands, or for those who are profligate and evil livers, and damn themselves in the abundance of the wealth which an avaricious father has left them, and who might have been saved had a virtuous father transmitted them his own good example, and the moderate inheritance of their forefathers! What folly then to have bestowed so much pains to accumulate possessions which prove so fatal!

3. The folly of the rich, in that the treasures which he leaves behind have prevented him from laying up other treasures which he might have carried with him. Such is then the lot of whoever layeth up treasures only for himself, without bestowing on the poor or employing

in good works, some portion of the wealth which God gives him, he dies rich in the eyes of men, and poor in the eyes of God, rich in the possessions he is obliged to leave behind him, and poor in those which he might have taken with him. O folly, which we cannot too much deplore!

Prayer. Ah! if this night Thou didst recall my soul. O my God, should I find myself *rich towards* Thee, rich in good works, rich in grace? Of what then have I been thinking till now? Alas! if the desire to amass earthly wealth, or any other care equally frivolous has hindered me from enriching myself with heavenly treasures, is not my folly equal to that of this rich man in the parable? Ah! Lord, it shall be so no longer, henceforth I will take warning by this rich man in the Gospel of whom Thou dost here speak, and I will strive to shew the same eagerness in gaining Heavenly riches, as he did in gaining earthly riches. Support this resolution by Thy grace, O my God! Grant that I may labour, that I may hope for, that I may lay up Heavenly treasures, so that I be content to die, and through Thy mercy find myself in the fulness of blessedness and delights in Thy Heavenly Kingdom. Amen.

Meditation CLX.

SECOND CONTINUATION OF THE DISCOURSE OF JESUS CHRIST BEFORE THE PEOPLE.

OF TRUST IN GOD WITH REGARD TO ALL THINGS NEEDFUL FOR THIS LIFE.

This trust ought to be founded, 1. on the wisdom; 2. on the power, 3. on the infinite goodness of God. S. Luke xii. 22—30.

FIRST POINT.

Of the infinite wisdom of God.

It adjusts every thing, and we owe it our admiration.

And He said unto His disciples, Therefore I say unto you, Take no thought for your life, what ye shall eat; neither for the body, what ye shall put on. Although this part of the discourse of our Lord was addressed more especially to the apostles and to the disciples, who were to carry out its precepts in the letter, it could not but be useful to the people who heard Him, and we ought to seek to profit by His words ourselves, by applying them to ourselves, in proportion to, and according to our different stations. Although our Lord only speaks here of trust in God with regard to food and clothing, we should understand it also as applied to the other necessities and requirements of life. But in order to strengthen ourselves in this trust in God, let us consider with what infinite wisdom God governs the world, preserves all the different creatures He has made, and adjusts every part of it. In this point of view,

1. Let us consider ourselves. *The life is more than meat and the body is more than raiment.* God has given us body and soul, our life and our being. That which is lacking to us, that which we need in addition, that which forms the subject of our fear and of our anxiety, is it something more considerable or more precious in itself than that which we have already received? Is it not an appointment of Providence itself, one of the demands which our nature brings with it? How then shall we fear that that Infinite Wisdom will refuse it us?

2. Consider the animals. *Consider the ravens, for they neither sow nor reap; which neither have store house nor barn, and God feedeth them. How much more are ye better than the fowls?* From the consideration of ourselves, let us pass to that of the animals which God has created; whether those which fly in the air, or creep on the earth, or swim in the waters. However prodigious may be the difference which exists between them, between their species, or their various requirements, between the food they live on, or the dwellings or the elements which are suited to them, do they

not find all that is necessary for their support? Has not the infinite Wisdom of God prepared for them all that they need? And, although they possess neither sciences nor arts, although they are all without reason, judgment, or foresight, does not this very Wisdom find the means whereby each should be able to provide for all their wants? Now, is there any comparison between us and animals? How then should this infinite Wisdom, which provides for all their needs, fail in providing for ours?

3. Consider the flowers. *Consider the lilies, how they grow; they toil not, they spin not; and yet I say unto you, that Solomon in all his glory was not arrayed like one of these. If God then so clothe the grass, which is to-day in the field, and to-morrow is cast into the oven, how much more will he clothe you, O ye of little faith?* From the animals let us come down to the plants and flowers which the earth produces. What a ravishing spectacle is that of a beautiful landscape, where trees and bushes, meadows and fields spread out before our view all that nature possesses that is the most transplendent. What exquisite perfumes, what splendour! And if we consider the objects more in detail, what delicacy of tints and outlines, what a variety of objects, what enchantment and what delight to the eyes! No, the wisest of men, the richest and most magnificent of kings, adorned in the most precious stuffs, dyed by art, embroidered with gold and enriched with jewels, has not found any clothing which can be compared in beauty to that of a flower. It is not you, brilliant flowers, who have bestowed on yourselves this radiant beauty, it is not your industry which has obtained it for yourselves, but this infinite Wisdom, which, lavishing its magnificence even on the most feeble beings, claims from us the tribute of our admiration and of our confidence. And what would it be, if we penetrated below the surface which adorns you and which dazzles us, and beheld the Divine skill which has given you birth, multiplies you, developes you, and causes you to wither? Oh God, so

many preparations, so much care bestowed upon grass which flourishes to-day, and to-morrow is cut down? O men of little faith! how could ye fear that the wisdom of God should forsake you, you for whom He has created the world, and to whom He destines Heaven.

SECOND POINT.

Of the infinite power of God.

It creates everything, and we owe it the acknowledgment of our own weakness. In order to convince us of the uselessness of our anxious thoughts, and our doubts,

1. Let us make trial of our own powers upon ourselves. *And which of you with taking thought can add to his stature one cubit?* Let us see, whether by dint of thought, of calculation, or by some invention, or any industry on our part, we could not, for example, increase our height by some inches. We are not even tempted to make a trial, and we should tax any one with folly who should seriously think of so doing. Let us then convince ourselves once for all of our weakness and powerlessness.

2. Let us carry on this reasoning a little further. *If ye then be not able to do that thing which is least, why take ye thought for the rest.* If we cannot effect anything on our bodies, which are a part of ourselves, by means of our thoughts, if we are forced to acknowledge that it would be folly to occupy ourselves seriously with such thoughts, what wisdom, what use, what efficacy can there be then in thoughts which are directed towards objects out of ourselves, which are above us, and unknown to us; as to these necessities of life which cause us such useless and uncalled for uneasiness, which require, in order to be satisfied, the concurrence of numberless different causes which we do not even know, and over which we are far from having any power? Nevertheless the world is full of persons, who, thinking themselves to be wise, busy themselves unceasingly, and converse seriously with others, respecting the seasons, winds,

rains, storms, the courses of nature, as if these thoughts were not as vain, as foolish, and as impotent as those which they might indulge in respecting the height of their stature.

3, Let us conclude from all this, and make a resolution never to distress ourselves again with regard to the needs of this life. *Seek not ye,* concludes our Saviour, *what ye shall eat, or what ye shall drink, neither be ye of doubtful mind.* Do not let us seek to search into a future which is not in our power, and let us not imagine that we can order the course of events which depend only on the Almighty power of God. Let us confine ourselves, according to our station of life, within the circle of daily occupations which God's good Providence has appointed for us, and without seeking to take a higher flight, let us leave the rest to that Infinite Power Which moves heaven and earth, and governs everything with a sovereign rule. It is in this perfect submission, in this acknowledgment of our own weakness, that we shall find our rest and happiness.

THIRD POINT.

Of the infinite goodness of God.

This goodness embraces all, and we owe it all our trust. *For after all these things do the nations of the world seek; and your Father knoweth that ye have need of these things.*

1. From the idea which we ought to form of God. We ought to look upon God as our Father, but also as a tender Father, Who loves us and desires our good; as an attentive Father, Whom nothing escapes, Who knows all our needs, and knows all that is useful to us; as an Almighty Father, Who makes both the actions of inanimate beings, and the will of free-agents to serve His purposes. Why should we disquiet ourselves under the Providence of such a Father? Has He not a claim upon our trust? And would it not be to outrage Him, to refuse to render Him that trust?

2. *From the example of the world which we are commanded to avoid.* *For after all these things do the Gentiles seek.* The notions which the Gentiles formed respecting Providence, are to be met with amongst Christians, or rather there are but too many Christians who only think of God in the same manner as the heathen do, who acknowledge no Providence, who regard only this visible world, and recognize in it only a blind nature, from which they have to look for no protecting care, no thought, no benefits, and from which, they have nothing to hope for, but, on the contrary, every thing to fear. Let us blush to think like the world, when we see that it adopts the reasonings of heathen.

3. *Of the object to which we ought to give our first cares.* *But seek ye first the kingdom of God,* concludes our Lord, *and His Righteousness; and all these things shall be added unto you.* What we ought to seek before every thing else, is the kingdom of God and His righteousness, the glory of God and our own salvation. Let us study the commandments of God, let us apply ourselves to observe them; let us practise works of charity, let us give up ourselves to prayer, let us be frequent in our Communions, let us set ourselves in earnest to acquire fresh virtues, and to gain the victory over our evil passions, and then let us not fear that the rest will be wanting to us. It is our God Himself, it is our Father, Who gives us His Promise. Let us trust then in His Word, let us rest upon His Infinite goodness, in all that concerns us, both in life and death.

Prayer. O my soul! be ashamed of thy vain and mistrustful disquietude under the government of a Wisdom which is Infinite both in its designs and in its purposes, in its measures and in the means which it adopts, and in the just proportion with which it carries out all its dealings. Rest thyself upon the Infinite Power of Thy God, without ceasing to labour thyself, under Its guiding hand, in a spirit of submission and of peaceful trust. Consider always, amidst the natural means whereby life and clothing are procured, Its beneficent liberality. And Thou, O my God, do Thou direct my thoughts and intentions towards the only really solid and eternal Good; grant that I may seek, before all things, Thy Kingdom and Thy righteousness, grant that I may love Thee alone here below, and may possess Thee for ever hereafter. Amen.

Meditation CLXI.

THIRD CONTINUATION OF THE DISCOURSE OF OUR LORD BEFORE THE PEOPLE.

JESUS STRENGTHENS HIS APOSTLES.

1. Jesus presents to them a solid consolation; 2. He gives them an essential counsel; 3. He sets before them an important maxim. S. Luke xii. 32—34.

FIRST POINT.

Jesus presents to His Apostles a solid consolation.

1. By the confidence with which He animates them. *Fear not;* that is to say fear not lest you should want for things necessary to support life; fear neither the power of men, nor the fury of evil spirits; fear not your own weakness, when you do not expose yourselves rashly, and without necessity, and when you place your whole trust in God: such ought to be the assurance of a truly Christian soul. But alas! if we examine ourselves seriously, we shall see that we are very far removed from this spirit of trust. How many puerile objects of fear present themselves unceasingly to our soul, trouble, and disquiet it!

2. Jesus presents to His apostles a solid consolation, by the name which He gives to them. *Fear not, little flock.* This name marked out the actual number of those who composed His Church, which was very small; but this little number was one day to become a great

multitude, and to embrace all the nations of the world. Nevertheless however widely extended this holy Church may be, how small the number of fervent Christians is in comparison with lukewarm and sinful Christians! Let us join ourselves to this small number if we wish to have any share in the favours which are promised to it. This name represented besides the principal virtues of the true children of the Church, which are humility, patience, and gentleness. It is by these that this little flock has triumphed over the whole world: have we these virtues? Lastly this name expressed the tenderness of Christ for His Church, He is her Shepherd, and she is His cherished flock; He knows how to distinguish the souls in it who serve Him with a generous fervour, and in all the purity of their hearts. Ah! how great is the affection, the tenderness which He has for this flock! Let us strive earnestly to be of that number, and let us neglect no means whereby we may attain thereto.

3. Jesus sets forth to His apostles a solid consolation by the reward which He promises them. *Fear not, little flock, for it is your Father's good pleasure to give you the kingdom.* Let us weigh all these words, *it is* the *good pleasure*. It is by an entirely gratuitous favour, it is in consequence of His love and condescension that He will put you in possession of it. *It is your Father's good pleasure*, and Who is this Father? God Himself, this Sovereign, Absolute and All-powerful Master, to Whom nothing can resist, Whom nothing can hinder from executing His will and from fulfilling His Promises, unless you render yourself unworthy of them. *It is your Father's good pleasure to give you*, not what you deserve; even your very merits are the gifts of His grace, and in crowning your merits, He crowns His own gifts. What misery for you, if you lose the gift of glory because you have rejected the gifts of grace! *It is your Father's good pleasure to give you the kingdom:* and what a kingdom? Ah! if it were a kingdom on earth, you would sacrifice every

thing in order to obtain it, and in order not to lose it; you would think of it day and night, it would be the sole object of your desires; you would sigh unceasingly for the happy moment which should put you in possession of it: every thing else would appear to you vile and despicable in comparison with it: you would form no projects in your mind but such as were worthy of the throne, and you would only nourish in your heart affections which were suitable to your high destiny. But you are destined to a heavenly kingdom, to an eternal kingdom. Do not grovel then on the earth, do not render yourself vile, do not degrade yourself. Let your thoughts be such as are worthy of *your Father*, worthy of the *kingdom* He has prepared for you.

SECOND POINT.

Jesus gives His Apostles an essential counsel.

1. To renounce the treasures of earth. *Sell all that ye have, and give alms.* The first disciples of Jesus Christ followed this counsel literally. But whether we are called or not to this degree of perfection, we have even in this counsel an essential precept, which is to detach our heart from all that we possess, and not to set our affections upon any earthly treasures. That which our Lord says of the treasure of wealth, ought to be understood also of every other treasure to which our hearts become attached. Beside the treasure of wealth, there are others of various kinds, and each one makes his own. There are treasures of science and learning, treasures of esteem and reputation, treasures of friendship and gratitude, treasures of favour and protection, treasures of ease and comfort, of pleasure and of sensuality. Let us follow the advice of our Saviour; let us renounce them all or let us retain only that which charity and the necessary duties of our station require of us. The more we shall practise this detachment of heart and this renunciation of things of this earth, the more we shall

enjoy inward peace, and the liberty of the children of God: an advantageous exchange, in which we give despicable things for treasures of an infinite price. Ah! it is only with God that we can make so priceless an exchange! Madman that he is who does not accept it!

2. Jesus gives His Apostles the essential counsel to lay up for themselves treasures in Heaven. *Provide yourselves bags which wax not old, a treasure in the heavens that faileth not, where no thief approacheth, neither moth corrupteth.* Riches distributed to the poor are a treasure in heaven. The knowledge of salvation and the knowledge of Jesus Christ, of His mysteries, of His commandments, are treasure in Heaven. Good works and virtues practised as in the presence of God and in order to please Him are treasure in Heaven. The time we take from our enjoyments in order to devote to prayer, to practise fasting and mortification, all these holy works are treasure in Heaven; such are the treasures which we should seek to amass, accumulate and increase daily.

3. What is the reason wherefore our Lord gives this counsel? Alas! do we not know it? must it be repeated to us unceasingly, and notwithstanding all that is told us about it, shall we be always so thoughtless, so foolish as to forget it again? It is that the treasures of earth have nothing that is noble or worthy of us, they are base, vile, and mean; far from filling or satisfying us, they impoverish us, they afflict and torment us. It is that the treasures of the earth have nothing sure or solid in them; manifold enemies seek to deprive us of them and succeed in so doing; our regrets, our despair, the misery we experience, are the just punishment of our imprudence. It is, lastly, that they have nothing durable or permanent; death takes them all away from us, or rather takes us away from them all, and there remains nothing to us. It is not thus with the treasures which we lay up in Heaven. They are noble, satisfying, elevating, they aggrandise, they fill our hearts; they are sure, no enemy can deprive us of them, and nothing can

corrupt them; they are durable and eternal, even death itself will put us in possession of them, and that for ever.

THIRD POINT.

Jesus sets before His Apostles an important maxim.

For where your treasure is, there will your heart be also.

1. Let us learn from this maxim to know ourselves. Do we wish to know where our heart is? Let us see where our treasure is, where we amass it, where we accumulate it, whether on the earth, or in Heaven. Do we desire to know where our treasure is? Let us see where our heart is, where our affections, desires, thoughts are; in what direction our heart perpetually turns, and so to say almost instinctively, if it is towards the earth or towards heaven; for these two things are mutually connected; and it is in vain that we would seek to deceive ourselves; where our heart is, there also is our treasure; and where our treasure is, there infallibly also will be our heart.

2. Let us learn from this maxim how to direct our conduct. Let us learn how important it is for us not to make a mistake in this matter, which is how to place our treasure and our heart aright. Since these two things are so closely allied, the mistake which we should commit in the one case would apply equally to the other case. If we make our treasure to consist in earthly and perishable things, our heart will be in them also, whence it will happen that our treasure will perish and our heart will be eternally rent from it; if, on the contrary, our treasure is heavenly and eternal, our heart will eternally enjoy it with security and felicity. Let us take good heed to it, and we shall not be mistaken.

3. Let us learn from this maxim to change ourselves. Do not let us pretend to change our heart without changing our treasure, nor to change our treasure without changing our heart; these two things are inseparable. Let us labour to change both at the same time.

In order to turn our hearts towards Heaven, let us lay up our treasure in Heaven, let us send thither our alms, works of charity, acts of humility, patience and mortification. In order to place our treasure in Heaven, let us turn towards Heaven the thoughts of our hearts, its desires and affections. Let us think often of that blessed dwelling place, of that immortal glory, of that eternal blessedness.

Prayer. Alas! how necessary this change in myself is; for my treasure and my heart are entirely on this earth! Assist me, Lord: for without Thee I cannot change myself. O God! if Thou wert my Treasure, how blest I should be! I should never feel distraction in prayer, I should have no difficulty in keeping myself recollected, and prayer would cause me no weariness. O Jesus! if Thou wert my Treasure, with what assiduity, with what reverence should I not come before Thee? My communions would be far more frequent and more fervent; I should no longer experience in them this coldness, this languor, this distraction which so grieves me. O my Saviour! O divine Jesus! be Thou my only Treasure, and let my heart be wholly Thine. Amen.

Meditation CLXII.

FOURTH CONTINUATION OF THE DISCOURSE OF OUR LORD BEFORE THE PEOPLE.

PARABLES UPON DEATH.

Under cover of these parables, Jesus teaches us here, 1, in what preparation for death consists; 2. what is the blessedness of the death for which one has prepared one'sself; 3. how great is the necessity to be always ready to die. S. Luke xii. 35—41.

FIRST POINT.

In what preparation for death consists.

1. In detachment from the things of this world. *Let*

your loins be girded about. The Jews wore a long robe, and in order not to be impeded by it, they gathered it up with a belt, when they had either a journey to make, or any labour to undertake. The first preparation for death, is to put ourselves in that condition in which nothing keeps us back, nothing impedes us. The garments which impede us, are worldly possessions, our evil passions, our unregulated affections, the love of ease and of objects of sense; now all these must be restrained, repressed, and so to speak, confined with the girdle of mortification and of detachment. Let us gird then this girdle upon our loins, let us detach ourselves from all the things of earth, and let us hold ourselves in readiness to quit it. Are we in this state of preparation and in this state of detachment?

2. The preparation for death consists in the practice of virtue. *And your lights burning.* This world is covered with thick darkness, and death is like a journey which is taken in a dark night. The lamp which should give us light, is faith and religion. He who has neither faith nor religion, has not the lamp in his hand, he knows not whither he goes, and cannot fail to fall into the precipice. He whose faith and religion is not the true one, established by Jesus Christ, follows a false gleam of light, and falls equally with the former into the precipice. He who has a dead, languishing faith, and is but little instructed therein, carries an unlighted lamp, and is hastening towards the precipice. Let us keep then our lamps lighted by assiduous study, and deep meditation of the mysteries and truths which the Gospel teaches us. The lighted lamp, which ought to be burning, is the love of God and of our neighbour in our hearts. Let us take care that this fire is not extinguished, and does not grow less, but rather let us strive each day to make it brighter and more burning. The oil which should keep our lamp always burning, is good works, and frequent acts of the virtues which befit our station, so that in sanctifying ourselves, they may lighten and edify others. Have we this lamp in our hand?

3. The preparation for death consists in a continual waiting for the day of the Lord. *And ye yourselves like unto servants that wait for their Lord when he will return from the wedding, that when he cometh and knocketh, they may open unto him immediately.* Our Lord is in Heaven, at the eternal Banquet of the Church triumphant; but without leaving it, He will come to us; we must always be in a state of expectation for His coming, and be ready to open the door of our hearts to Him. He knocks at our doors by sickness, and we open to Him, if we are in readiness, by a prompt resignation, and by the joy of being united to Him. Alas! men live on earth in continual expectation; but it is not the expectation of the Lord. Men expect age, health, strength; they expect places of trust, high positions; they expect the death of others, to occupy their vacant places, to succeed to the property of other men; what do they not not expect? Men expect especially a long life, some years more of life, and always an indefinite prolongation of life. But, in the midst of these frivolous expectations, the Lord Whom we do not expect comes; He knocks, and far from opening to Him quickly, we strive to close to Him the entrance, and to drive Him away; but He enters in spite of us, and He finds nothing in readiness, but every thing in confusion. What misery! O vain hopes, vain expectations, how many hearts have you not misled! Alas! have I not suffered myself to be led astray by them! Suffer it not, Lord! I am fully resolved, Thou Alone shalt henceforth be the sole object of my expectations. Yea, O my God, I look for Thee, I look only for Thee, I look for nought beside Thee. All that I do, all that I plan for the future, all with which I occupy myself, is only whilst awaiting Thy coming. I will sit loose to every thing; from the moment that Thou shalt knock, I will leave all, I will hasten to Thee, O my Saviour! I will open to Thee in the joy of my heart, and in the ardent desire to be united to Thee for ever.

MEDITATION CLXII.

SECOND POINT.

Of the blessedness of the death for which one has prepared one'sself.

Blessed are those servants whom the Lord, when He cometh, shall find watching! Verily I say unto you that He shall gird Himself, and make them to sit down to meat, and will come forth and serve them. And if He shall come in the second watch, or come in the third watch, and find them so, blessed are those servants.

1. Blessedness before the moment of death. With what consolation does not a fervent soul find itself filled on its death bed! Soon its sufferings will be passed, its struggles will be over; it beholds itself on the eve of eternal rest and happiness. Ah! how comforting it is for it to have learnt to despise all earthly possessions before they are taken away from it by death, and to have sought only to please that God Who is coming to it. With what joy does not that righteous soul behold its Redeemer come once more, in the Sacrament of His Body and Blood, to visit it, and to give it the assured pledge of a happy immortality. It is for the last time that it will behold Him under the mysterious veil which hides Him from human sight, soon it will behold Him unveiled in the splendour of His glory. Oh! how it will rejoice that it has given itself to Him! It is not thus with a worldly, sinful, lukewarm soul, whose heart has never been given wholly to God; on the contrary, how many regrets, what remorse, what fears will it not feel at that moment!

2. Blessedness at the moment of death. The blessedness of a good man in his death will be reflected on the bystanders. It is a true happiness to be a witness of the death of a fervent Christian. Whether death cuts him down in the flower of his age, and when the world offers him the most flattering hopes: or whether it carries him off at a more advanced age, when the heart has generally become more wedded to life, the joy which shines on his face, the ardour with which he longs for

his last Communion, the fervour with which he receives it, the words of comfort he utters to those who mourn to part with him, all these are an edifying and comforting sight. The air of content with which he yields up his soul into the Hands of his Maker bears witness to the feelings of faith, hope and love with which his heart is kindled. An odour of sanctity seems to be spread around him. The sacred fire which consumes him warms the coldest hearts, and makes them long to die so holy and so happy a death. The death of ungodly men is far different. Old and young have been known to utter terrible cries at the first announcement of approaching death, and it is with difficulty that they make up their minds to permit the ministrations of a priest; some even refuse obstinately to receive one, repulse those who speak to them of God, and either die in a state of hardness of heart, of insensibility, and of cynical indifference, and throw the bystanders into consternation, or they die with words of blasphemy on their lips, with transports of fury and despair, which fill the hearts of the spectators with fear, and cause them to flee in horror.

3. Happiness after death. The ghost is given up: the last sigh is breathed; that righteous and faithful soul no longer belongs to earth, there remains only on the earth the body it has indwelt, and which it will take again at the last day. What does it find at the moment when it is set free from the bonds of this body? It finds in God, the Master Whom it has served, Whom it has loved, Whom it has desired: but a Master full of goodness and of tenderness, a Master Who exacts no further service from it, but Who, on the contrary, wills to serve it Himself, and to introduce it to the Celestial Banquet in the abode of Glory, and Who employs His Almighty Power in order to render it happy, and to crown all its desires. Ah! the good, the tender Master Whom we serve, and Who here pourtrays Himself under such lovable characteristics! Happy, yea, once more happy indeed, are those servants Whom He finds, at

His Coming, faithful and watchful. Is life too long in order to serve such a Master? Are crosses, trials, self-denials, sufferings too severe when compared with the blessedness which they gain for us? O faithful souls who have given yourselves up to the service of Jesus Christ! do not let yourselves be cast down by the fear of death, as others who live for this world only. Await the day of your Master's coming with a holy impatience: think of it with joy, with transport; let neither the sins of your past life, which you have washed in His Blood, nor the lesser faults which through the frailty of your nature you commit, and for which you ask daily for His forgiveness, intimidate your heart, and go so far as to make you lose so sweet a hope. A firm confidence in the mercy of the Lord, and an ardent desire to be with Him, are more fitted to encourage you in His service, and are more pleasing to Him, than the servile fear to which you abandon yourself, which offends His goodness, which only serves to drive you away from Him, and to cast you down at the risk even of discouraging you. Say then often to yourself, *Blessed are those servants whom the Lord when He cometh shall find watching.* I trust, by the grace of my God, I trust to be of that number; what blessedness will that be for me!

THIRD POINT.

Of the necessity there is to be always in readiness for death.

1. Let us learn this necessity from a familiar illustration. *And this know, that if the goodman of the house had known what hour the thief would come, he would have watched, and not have suffered his house to be broken through.* If he knew the time, he would watch at that time; but not knowing it, what does he do? He takes care that his house is always in a good state of defence; and with this precaution, he rests tranquilly. If we knew the time when we shall die, we could put off our preparation to that time; but not knowing it,

let us imitate this householder, let us keep our conscience always in a good state, never allowing the devil, our enemy, and sin to enter into it, far less to dwell there; let us never be in a state in which we would not wish to die. When our conscience is thus set in order, and has nothing to reproach us with, then we may sleep quietly; then sudden death may come upon us, but we shall not die unprepared. Alas! when the preservation of earthly possessions is concerned, nothing is trusted to chance, our cares are unceasing, no precaution is considered too great; but when our soul and our eternal salvation are at stake, we take no thought, we are content to risk it; we are daily on the eve of eternal condemnation and yet we live in tranquillity.

2. Let us learn the necessity of being always ready to die, from our daily experience. *Be ye therefore ready also; for the Son of man cometh at an hour when ye think not.* Death surprises us by a thousand unforeseen accidents. One perishes in the waters, another in the flames; one falls and is killed, another is crushed under the ruins of a falling building or under a heavy weight which throws him down; such an one is killed by an enemy, or by an accident, or another dies of a fit, or through some sudden illness. The same day sees them full of life and health, and deprived of both; and these accidents surprise some on a journey, and others in their houses; some by day, and others by night. How many of our acquaintance have not died in this way? Were they prepared to die? Were they in a state of grace? Oh great God, how terrible is such a death for those who are only occupied with the things of this life, and who give no thoughts to their eternal salvation! Death surprises us by sickness. We do not know the time. We were occupied with our business, our projects, and our speculations; we were living in pleasure, perhaps in the indulgence of sinful habits, and when we were thinking of nothing less, we are struck down by illness; and what a time is that to prepare ourselves for death. We do not know the nature of our illness. We flatter

ourselves that it will pass away, that we have rallied from far more serious illnesses, that others have recovered from the same malady, and in this hope, we take no steps, we defer in sickness as we have done in health, and death comes. We are ignorant of the progress of our disease. After having experienced some fear of death, and made some preparations for it, we begin to feel better; the hope of life arises anew, and with it often, alas! all our evil passions; and when the sick man thought himself out of danger, a relapse comes suddenly, and he dies. Let us *be ready*, let us *be ready.* Shall we never understand the importance of this advice? Will our own daily experience never suffice to disabuse us? At such an hour as we think not, we die. Will this warning repeated so often, and confirmed by so many examples, never make any impression on us? If we are surprised without being ready, it will be doubtless through our own fault, but, alas! a fault which we can then no longer repair.

3. Let us learn the necessity of being always ready to die, by the application which we ought to make to ourselves of this truth. *Then Peter said unto Him, Lord, speakest Thou this parable unto us, or even to all?* It is a matter worthy of compassion, to see the use which is made of a truth so impressive as the uncertainty of death, and to see the way in which people apply this parable to themselves. In the first place they apply it without delay to their temporal affairs. They do nothing of any importance without taking their precautions against being overtaken by death, they take care to do everything, to sign everything, to make their will, because, as they say, no one knows what may happen, death may come at any hour; but is there no fear of being taken by surprise in our spiritual affairs, or are they not of sufficient consequence? Persons also apply this parable very willingly to others: they preach it, they inculcate it upon others, but they do not take it to themselves. They make the infirm health, or the weak constitution of this young person,

a matter of conversation: they notice the advanced and failing age of another, and say, They ought soon to think earnestly about death, and we, are we never to begin thinking of it? We only apply this parable to ourselves in a vague, undefined, and inefficacious manner. We sometimes make this reflection, that no one ever knows when they may die; after which we calm ourselves, as if at least one knew when one would not die, and it often happens that after so many warnings, after so many reflections, we still die without being ready.

Prayer. This instruction is specially addressed to myself. Without delaying any longer, I will then begin to put myself in the state in which I would wish to die, in the practise of the virtues, of the self-mortifications, and of the acts of devotion in which I would desire to die, in a word, to do that which I would wish to have done at my death. It is to delay too long, it is to risk too much to wait any longer. Amen.

Meditation CLXIII.

CONTINUATION OF THE DISCOURSE OF OUR LORD BEFORE THE PEOPLE.

PARABLE OF THE STEWARD.

Consider. 1. the faithful steward; 2. the unfaithful steward; 3. the difference which there is between unfaithful stewards. S. Luke xii. 43—48.

FIRST POINT.

Of the faithful steward.

1. His duties. *And the Lord said, Who then is that faithful and wise steward, whom his lord shall make ruler over his household, to give them their portion of meat in due season?* Anyone who has any power or rule over others is here represented under the

parable of this steward. Such are fathers of families, masters, magistrates, princes and especially the pastors of Christ's Church. The first duty of the steward, is fidelity, which consists in appropriating to himself nothing of the property which his master has confided to his trust, in not looking upon himself as having it in any way at his own disposal, in not seeking his own glory, or pleasure, or his private profit, but the glory, the good pleasure, and the interest of the master. The second, is prudence or the knowledge which is suitable for his condition. He ought to know all that is necessary in order to turn to the best account his master's property, he ought to know what works should be undertaken, and how to allot them to those over whom he has the command, and to give to each, work proportioned to his capabilities and his strength. The third, is exactness in providing for the needs of those whom he employs, in furnishing all the means, and conveniences, and in a word, providing for them every thing that could induce them, or encourage them to acquit themselves well of their tasks; he ought to furnish this assistance to them, not at the time that is most convenient to himself and that suits him best, but at the time agreed upon, and when they have need of it. How do we each one of us, in our station, fulfil these duties with regard to those whom God has committed to our charge? Alas! where is this faithful, prudent and attentive steward to be found? How small is the number in comparison with those who are unfaithful, and negligent! Am I not of the number of the latter?

2. The happiness of the faithful steward. *Blessed is that servant whom his lord, when he cometh, shall find so doing.* That is to say if he finds him in the actual performance of all his duties; but for that end, he must fulfil them, 1. with constancy and without interruption. He must not let himself be overcome by difficulties, cast down by weariness, conquered by idleness, or distracted by cares which are alien to his calling. 2. With application and without negligence. He must continue with

the same zeal, with the same ardour, with the same care with which he began, so that the master, when he arrives, may not find him either doing nothing, or not performing all his duties, or doing badly what he does. 3. With perseverance and without giving up any thing that he has undertaken. He must continue to labour with care to his last sigh, without ever leaving the post where God has placed him, either from fickleness, or weariness, or love of ease; or if he is no longer able to keep it, and infirmities or old age render him incapable of fulfilling its functions, he must recognize in that and follow out the will of the Master, who without doubt would be equally displeased to find him in a post where he could no longer be useful to Him, and in which he had only remained in order to enjoy the advantages attached to it, without being able to fulfil its duties.

3. The reward of the faithful steward. *Of a truth I say unto you, that He will make him ruler over all that He hath.* The master, who at his coming, shall find the steward of his house acquitting faithfully his duties, will testify to him his satisfaction thereat; and as a recompense of his fidelity and his prudence, will raise him to a higher place of trust, and will give into his hands the administration of all his property. Such is the reward which earthly masters can give, and those to whom they have entrusted a portion of their possessions may hope for; but the Master of Heaven, what will He do? What does he promise us Himself? The possession of *all that He hath*, the possession of His Kingdom, the possession of Himself. O reward well worthy of our desires, well worthy of our labours, and of our perseverance!

SECOND POINT.

Of the unfaithful steward.

1. His crime. *But and if that servant say in his heart, My lord delayeth his coming; and shall begin to beat the menservants and maidens, and to eat and drink, and be drunken.* The crime of this unfaithful

servant, with regard to his master, was to forget that he had one; it was to forget that this master was to return, or to persuade himself that he would not return so soon. Negligence in spiritual exercises, omission of prayer, of meditation, of spiritual reading, forgetfulness of God, forgetfulness of death, of its surprises and its consequences, are the first faults we commit, and the source of all other faults. We live as if we should never die, or we live as if death were always as far off from us. The crime of this unfaithful steward with relation to the other servants, was that he ill-treated them. He who forgets God, and the account which he will have to render to Him, follows in his conduct towards his neighbour no other rule than that of his own passions. The use he makes of his power, of his authority, becomes then a continual injustice. We are only too apt to favour, or support those who flatter us; whilst we do not fear to humiliate, vex, and annoy in manifold ways those who displease us. But the master beholds the injury which is done to them, He hears their groanings, and He will avenge the insults, the contempt, and wrong treatment which they have received from the unjust steward. Lastly, the crime of this wicked man with relation to himself, is that he yields himself up to luxury and idleness, to good living, gluttony and drunkenness, and employs the goods which his master had entrusted to him, and which were intended for far different uses, in order to satisfy the cravings of his own evil passions.

2. The misery of the unfaithful steward. *The lord of that servant will come in a day when he looketh not for him, and at an hour when he is not aware.* This Master will come; His return is inevitable, and how terrible will it be for him who will then have to give an account of so many malversations. This Master will come in a day when He is not expected, at an age when men thought there was nothing yet to be feared, at a time when they were still forming vast projects of fortune, pleasures, or elevation. This Master will come in an hour which men know not of, perhaps, alas! at the

very moment, when they have abandoned themselves with the greatest security to that which will draw down upon them the heaviest punishments. Here then is the answer to the question of S. Peter. All must watch, and be continually on their guard. This truth is addressed to every one, but more particularly to the ministers of Christ's Church. How sad it would be for him who should be the one to encourage others in being always ready, not to have been ready himself, and to have allowed himself to be taken by surprise!

3. *The punishment of this unfaithful steward.* *And will cast him asunder, and will appoint him his portion with the unbelievers.* His punishment will be in the first place to be separated for ever from the company of the blessed, where he would have taken his place amongst so many earnest ministers of Christ's Church, who have had a share in the labours, and now have a share in the glory of the first apostles. It will be to be banished from Christ's presence together with unfaithful stewards, with Jews, idolaters, unbelievers, evil spirits. What companionship for a minister of Jesus Christ, a successor of the apostles! Finally it will be to have his portion with them in their torments, and to suffer even yet greater in the same fires and in the same eternity.

THIRD POINT.

Difference between unfaithful servants.

1. *Of the servant who was most guilty.* *And that servant, who knew his Lord's will, and prepared not himself, neither did according to his will, shall be beaten with many stripes.* He, doubtless, is the most guilty, who, having been admitted to His Master's confidence, having been instructed in His designs, having known His intentions and learnt His will, has not had any regard for them, has done nothing of that which had been prescribed to him, and has equally despised His authority, His rewards, and His threats; thus he will be punished with more rigour and severity. Such were

the Jews, at the time of our Lord, in comparison with the Gentiles. They were instructed in the law of God and in the promise which He had made to send a Saviour into the world and instead of preparing to receive Him, they have crucified Him. Such are Christians, in comparison with infidels; such are, amongst Christians, the clergy, and those who have been educated with more care and better instructed, in comparison with uneducated persons, who have not been within the reach of Gospel teaching. If then we neglect to fulfil the will of our Master, which is so well known to us, let us acknowledge that we are guilty, and that we have deserved the most rigorous punishments.

2. Of the servant who was less guilty. *But he that knew not, and did commit things worthy of stripes, shall be beaten with few stripes.* He, doubtless, is less guilty, who not having been admitted to the secrets of his master, and not knowing in detail his intentions and his will, yet does things which deserve punishment, he shall be punished, but less rigorously than the first. Such were at the time of our Lord, the Gentiles in comparison with the Jews; such are unbelievers in our days when compared with Christians. If Jesus Christ has not been preached to them, they will not be punished for not having known and worshipped Him; but they will be punished on account of that which they have done against the natural light of their reason and their conscience. They are to be pitied in their ignorance, and we have here a mystery of the depths of knowledge and wisdom of God; but they are guilty in their crimes. As for ourselves, more favoured than they by a grace which we have neither been able to merit, and which we cannot esteem sufficiently, if we do not profit by it, we are infinitely more guilty, and our punishment will be in proportion more rigorous than theirs. Ah! what misery for me, if, after having been enlightened by the knowledge of the faith, I should be damned with the heathen, and tormented with far greater torments than they.

3. *A general rule of God's judgment. For to whomsoever much is given, of him shall be much required; and to whom men have committed much, of him they will ask the more.* Whether much or little has been given to us, an account will be required of us for all; we shall be asked what use, employment, profit we have made of all the gifts, natural or supernatural, which have been bestowed upon us, and of the time that we have enjoyed them. The account which we shall have to render will be so much the more rigorous in proportion to the amount that has been given us. Such is the entire answer which our Lord gave to S. Peter's question; an answer which deserves our deepest reflection in whatever station of life we may be; an answer which has made the greatest saints tremble, which has made them shrink back from high dignities, and has led them only to accept them out of obedience to God's will, though not without trembling and misgivings. He who accepts them in any other spirit, does not know the rigorous account which he will have to render of them.

Prayer. Oh my God! what account wilt Thou not require of me when I shall appear before Thee? Have mercy on me, O my Saviour! have mercy on me; I will strive to prepare yet more earnestly for Thy coming, so that it may not take me by surprise. I will take heed to my ways, weigh all my actions and count all my words, so that I may make a holy and faithful use of the means of grace which Thou dost bestow on me, and of the talents, the authority, and all the blessings and privileges which I have received from Thee. Amen.

Meditation CLXIV.

SIXTH CONTINUATION OF THE DISCOURSE OF OUR LORD BEFORE THE PEOPLE.

OF THE COMING OF CHRIST.

The Divine Saviour instructs us here respecting 1. the effects; 2. the knowledge of His Coming; 3. the particular judgment which He will exercise. S. Luke xii. 49—59.

FIRST POINT.

Of the effects of the coming of Christ.

1. Of the fire which Jesus Christ has brought upon the earth. *I am come to send fire on the earth, and what will I, if it be already kindled?* What fire has our Lord brought on the earth? The *fire* of divine love, in order to inflame men's hearts; the *fire* of the zeal of the glory of God, for the conversion of sinners and the sanctification of souls; the *fire* of persecution, in order to purify and perfect men in holiness of life. 1. The fire of divine love. Oh Jesus! Thou hast brought this sacred fire on the earth, Thou dost will that it should burn there, and inflame all hearts; why then is my heart so cold, so languishing? Wherefore does not this fire penetrate it, why does it not consume it? Thou willest that it should be kindled there; it is I then who do not will it. Miserable man that I am; I love better to yield my heart to numberless terrestrial objects which degrade it, debase it, and consume it; to earthly affections which corrupt it, rend it, and torment it, rather than suffer it to be inflamed with the love of God, which would be its glory, its joy, and its happiness. I acknowledge my crime and my folly. Suffer me, O my Saviour! to offer Thee this day my heart, corrupt and sinful as it is; purify it from all that can displease Thee, and kindle there the Heavenly fire which Thou didst come to bring upon the earth. Thou willest it, I will it also;

sustain the desire to be wholly Thine with which Thou dost inspire me, and in which I hope to die, and strengthen the resolution I have made to root out of my heart all that might be contrary to the growth of Thy love. 2. The fire of zeal. He who has not this zeal for the salvation of his neighbour, has not the love of God. Now, how are we each one of us exercising this zeal according to our station? Zeal is a devouring fire, which burns on all sides, which surmounts every obstacle, which never diminishes and is not extinguished, which increases and grows stronger unceasingly. 3. The fire of persecution. If the piety of which we make profession, if the zeal which we exercise draw down upon us unjust persecutions, let us rejoice at them; this fire is needful for us, and it is the will of the Lord, that it should be kindled, and should purify us; let us beware of seeking to extinguish it, by relaxing in our duties.

2. Of the baptism with which Jesus was baptised. *I have a baptism to be baptised with, and how am I straitened until it be accomplished.* 1. What was this baptism? That of His Blood wherewith He has been overwhelmed, a deluge of sorrows of all kinds in which He has been buried. O Jesus, can we think of it without being moved, and without loving Thee. 2. Wherefore has He received this baptism? In order that He may be the First to be consumed by the fire which He came to bring upon the earth, and in order to shew us how we ourselves should be consumed by it. He has been in His passion and in His death, the Victim of the love which He had for God His Father, Whose offended Majesty He desired to appease; the Victim of His zeal for us, whom He desired to deliver from hell; the Victim of the hatred of His enemies, which He wished to teach us to endure as He did. 3. Whence came this constraint which Jesus suffered until this baptism had been accomplished? It came from His love, and from the ardent desire which He had to accomplish His Sacrifice for our redemption. The short time He had yet to wait appeared too long for the ardour of His charity,

and this delay was a continual anguish to Him. What love, what zeal! How worthy of love is Jesus! How is it that we do not burn with love for Him, and with zeal for His glory!

3. Of the division which Jesus Christ has brought upon the earth. *Suppose ye that I am come to give peace on earth? I tell you nay, but rather division; for from henceforth, there shall be five in one house divided, three against two, and two against three. The father shall be divided against the son, and the son against the father; the mother against the daughter, and the daughter against her mother; the mother-in-law against her daughter-in-law; and the daughter-in-law against her mother-in-law.* The apostles and the Christians in the earliest times were the victims of this division. Following the example of Jesus Christ, inflamed with the love of God, and zeal for men's souls, they fell, as He did, under the sword of persecution. In the same family, composed of five persons, three were to be seen taking part against two, and two against three; and all that our Lord here speaks was the prophecy of the events which we find in history. The times of those bloody persecutions have come to an end. The world, by an unheard of miracle, by dint of slaying the Christians has become Christian itself, and the blood of the martyrs has cemented the foundations of the religion for which they died. To-day in the universe, Christianity is professed, there is no longer any division on this point. But he who loves God, and manifests zeal for his neighbour's salvation, would he not deceive himself, if he expected to enjoy a perfect peace. Alas! there must needs still be division, and separation. The good must declare themselves on the side of God. The wicked will never fail, on their side, to persecute the good, and to separate from them. Terrible separation, which is the image and the commencement of that which will be consummated at the last day, and which will be eternal. Let us not then fear this separation, let us not fear that sinners should separate themselves from us;

and if that is needful to our salvation, let us separate ourselves from them.

SECOND POINT.

Of the knowledge of the coming of Christ.

1. Of the attention which men pay to the transitory things of this world. *And He said also to the people, When ye see a cloud rise out of the west, straightway ye say, There cometh a shower; and so it is. And when ye see the south wind blow, ye say, There will be heat, and it cometh to pass. Ye hypocrites, ye can discern the face of the sky and of the earth, but how is it that ye do not discern this time?* People are prudent in temporal matters, they are skilful in human sciences; they know the heaven and the earth so far as the interests or amusements of this present time are concerned, they examine the course of the stars, they foretell their conjunctions, prognosticate seasons, announce events, reason upon every thing, and pride themselves upon their knowledge, and their enlightenment. What needless knowledge; what superfluous cares! O vain and superficial men, will you always occupy yourselves with chimeras, and neglect essential truth?

2. Of the want of attention which men pay to the things of God. *How is it that ye do not discern this time?* This time for the Jews, was that of the coming of the Messiah. The miracles which Jesus wrought, the oracles of the prophets which were accomplished in Him, the date of the events carefully marked out in the sacred Writings, the state of expectation in which they themselves were of the approaching coming of their Deliverer, every thing warned them to reflect on what was taking place, to examine what was written, and to acknowledge that they had reached the happy term of their deliverance, and that Jesus was their Saviour. But this was by no means their intention; they disowned the Messiah Whom they professed to await; they persecuted Him, they crucified Him. *This time*, which our

Lord warns us to discern, and which He exhorts us to reflect upon, is still for us the time of His First coming, the time of His grace and of His mercy, the time when He presses us to return to Him, when He offers us His merits, and the price of our redemption. *This time* is that of our present life. But this precious life, which is given us in order to know God and serve Him, in order to lay up treasures of virtues and good works, *this time* so short, on the right use of which depends eternity, in what do we employ it?

3. Of the way in which to repair our negligence. *Yea, and why,* continues our Lord, *even of yourselves judge ye not what is right?* Instead of occupying ourselves with objects which do not concern us, let us turn our thoughts towards ourselves. Let us begin by examining ourselves, then let us judge ourselves with justice, and lastly let us execute upon ourselves the sad judgment which we shall have pronounced. Alas! do we know Jesus Christ, do we believe in Him? Are we in His Church, that Church which acknowledges Him as her Head? Is our life comfortable to our faith? Are we just towards God? Let us judge by ourselves; should we like to be served as we serve Him? Are we just towards our neighbour? Let us judge by ourselves; should we like to be treated by others as we treat him? Are we just towards ourselves? Let us judge by ourselves, by our conscience and by our remorse. Alas! I am unjust, Lord; I am a sinner, a sinner more than others, and my repentance ought to correspond to the number and enormity of my sins. Such is the just judgment which we ought to pronounce against ourselves and which we ought to carry out. In vain do we hide our crimes from men, in vain do we stray from the paths of justice, if we refuse to enter them of our own will, the just Judge will drive us into them in spite of ourselves. He will unmask our hypocrisy, He will make known our crimes, He will judge them in His justice, and will punish them with the just punishment of which He will judge them worthy, which will be the eternal fire of

hell. Ah! let us anticipate this terrible judgment, whilst we have time; let us betake ourselves to His mercy and to repentance, and place ourselves at the tribunal of His justice.

THIRD POINT.

Of the particular judgment which Jesus Christ will execute.

Our Lord announces it to us here under a parable of which we might not understand the full meaning, if we did not know whom all the persons mentioned in it represent. *When thou goest with thine adversary to the magistrate, as thou art in the way, give diligence that thou mayest be delivered from him, lest he hail thee to the judge, and the judge deliver thee to the officer, and the officer cast thee into prison. I tell thee thou shalt not depart thence till thou hast paid the very last mite.*

1. Of the magistrate, and those who appear before Him. This Magistrate is our King, God Himself, Who summons us to His tribunal, and it is we all, who are going to appear before Him. Every day, every moment, that we live, is a step that we are in the way, that we take in order to repair thither, and we do not know if we are still far off, or if we are near. But what we have most to consider, is, that we are going there with our adversary, who will plead against us.

2. Of the judge and the officer. The Judge is the Son of God; and the officer or minister of justice is the evil one. It is then Christ Himself, Who, at the moment of our death, will judge of our eternal lot. He is an omniscient Judge, Whom nothing will escape, a severe Judge, Whom nothing will move, a powerful Judge, Whom nothing will resist, a just Judge, Who will decree to the righteous the rewards He has promised, and to the wicked the punishments which He has threatened them. Alas! the moment is drawing nigh which will bring me into the Presence of my Judge. What will be-

come of me, sinner that I am, insolvent debtor, covered with numberless crimes?

3. *Of the adversary.* Our adversary is conscience, our neighbour, the Judge Himself Whom we have offended. In this judgment, Jesus will be at once the Judge, the Witness, the Accuser, and the offended party. How terrible this judgment must be for sinners! But, O infinite goodness of God! Jesus teaches us Himself, the means whereby to avoid the rigour of it; and it is while we are *in the way*, while we are still in the enjoyment of this life, that we must *agree with* Him. *Agree with thine adversary quickly, whiles thou art in the way.* It is He Who invites us, yea presses us to do so; and yea, more than that, Who offers us Himself the means whereby we may gain a full acquittal of our debt, His Blood, His Death, His Merits, His Graces, His Sacraments, His Mercy. Oh senseless men! What can possess you that ye do not profit by an offer so generous, so advantageous, so full of tenderness and love, which would open to you the gates of Heaven, so that after you have departed this life, you might enter there without obstacle, and receive from the Hands of your Judge a favourable judgment?

Prayer. Grant, Lord, that before I appear in Thy Presence, I may repent truly of my past sins, and be washed and purified from them in Thy Precious Blood: that I may restore to my neighbour whatever I have taken wrongfully from him, may be reconciled with whomsoever I have offended, or who has offended me, that I may lead henceforth a pure, humble, repentant, and holy life; that I may rule my conduct according to the commandments of Thy Holy law, so that I may enter Thy Presence with Thee, not as my Adversary, but with Thee, as with my Master, Whom I love with tenderness, and Whom I will serve henceforth fervently, that I may find only in Thee, my God and my Judge, at that Day, a Mediator and a Saviour. Amen.

Meditation CLXV.

CONCLUSION OF THE DISCOURSE OF OUR LORD BEFORE THE PEOPLE.

OF THE PARABLE OF THE FIG-TREE.

The justice of God urges us to repent: 1. it urges us by the sensible effects which God points out to us; 2. it urges us by secret dealings which Jesus reveals to us. S. Luke xiii. 1—9.

FIRST POINT.

The justice of God urges us to repent by the sensible effects which God points out to us.

1. Let us examine how frequent these effects are. *There were present at that season some that told Him of the Galilæans, whose blood Pilate had mingled with their sacrifices. And Jesus answering said unto them, Suppose ye that these Galilæans were sinners above all the Galilæans, because they suffered such things? I tell you Nay: but except ye repent ye shall all likewise perish. Or those eighteen upon whom the tower in Siloam fell, and slew them, think ye that they were sinners above all men in Jerusalem? I tell you Nay: but except ye repent, ye shall all likewise perish.* At the time that Jesus was speaking to the people, it was announced to Him that Pilate had just caused a certain number of Galilæans who had come to offer their sacrifices in the Temple at Jerusalem, to be murdered there. To the recital of this tragical event, Jesus joined another, and recalled to their minds that which had taken place in the same city, when a tower of the fountain of Siloam had fallen, and crushed in its fall eighteen persons. How many similar accidents have we not known of, which have happened either to separate individuals, or to many hundreds of persons at once! Let us call them to mind, and say to ourselves; On what then is the security founded in which I live? May not that which has happened

to so many others happen to me at any moment? They did not anticipate them, any more than I do: they lived securely as I do; and yet they have been surprised, and have died without having a single moment in which they could know what had befallen them. And how, in the midst of so many perils which surround me on all sides, can I resolve to go on sinning? How can I live in sin, and continue in it a single moment? But, you will say, every body does not die through an accident. No, but I may die from one, and what matters it to me that others die otherwise, if I die in that manner?

2. Let us observe how terrible these effects are. When we hear of such events, each one reasons after his own fashion. Some speak of them as though they were heathen; they see only in them a concourse of natural causes and an effect of chance, without considering that all things are subject to God's overruling Providence, and that there is no chance in any thing; that in all things it is the will of the Lord which is being accomplished, and that all His judgments are full of equity. Others consider them from an entirely human point of view: they pity those who have perished so unfortunately; they think of the bereavement of a man's family, and the worldly loss they suffer, without thinking of his soul, and of the eternity which must follow. Alas! in what state was this soul? Was it in a state of grace, or of mortal sin? See in one moment his eternal lot decided; is not this enough to make one tremble? How often have I not been in such a state, that if the same accident had happened to me, I should have been lost for ever, I should have been damned! But God, in His mercy, did not suffer that it should be thus, and what is my gratitude? I am still uncertain as to what will happen to me, and what is my fear, what are my precautions? Am I going to run such a risk again? If I am taken by surprise, who shall I have to blame but myself? and what can remain to me save eternal despair? Others again reason respecting it in a superstitious manner, and this was the fault which the Jews

committed. They imagined that those who perished in this way were always the greatest sinners of a city, or a nation: but our Lord points out to them their error. Let us not judge any one, and let us tremble for ourselves. God, by the same accident, punishes the wicked and rewards the just man; all depends upon the state in which each one was when it befell them, and it is for each one of us to keep his conscience always in the state in which he would wish to die.

3. How instructive these effects are. Do not let us reflect upon what happens to others, except to draw from it instructions for ourselves. It is thus that our Lord, after having removed the erroneous idea which the Jews had formed with regard to these kinds of accidents, adds, *Except ye repent, ye shall all likewise perish.* You will all suffer a similar fate. These words were a prophecy to the Jews, which through their impenitence, was soon followed by its fulfilment, when almost all this perfidious nation perished by the sword of the Romans, or were buried beneath the ruins of the city and of the temple of Jerusalem. How many public and private misfortunes might not repentance turn aside? Let us take warning by others; we are perhaps more guilty than they, and our lot may be such as theirs. We may at least take warning by ourselves; and if we already begin to experience the effects of the wrath of God, let us hasten to appease it by repentance, and to divert from over our heads the last misfortunes which may perhaps be ready to burst upon them. If men are deaf to this voice, and multiply their evil deeds, let us be none the less earnest in our prayers both for ourselves and them. God wills sometimes to pardon the guilty for the sake of the righteous: but if His justice bursts upon them, we shall not lose the reward of our intercessions. Should we be involved in the same misfortunes, they will only serve to purify our virtues; should we be buried under the same ruins, our eternal salvation will thereby be assured.

SECOND POINT.

The justice of God urges us to repentance by the secret dealings which Jesus here reveals to us.

The threatenings which our Lord had just uttered in few words, He here enlarges upon at greater length in a parable, in which He discovers to us some important secrets of the Divine economy. *He spake also this parable; A certain man had a fig-tree planted in his vineyard; and he came and sought fruit thereon, and found none. Then said he unto the dresser of his vineyard, Behold, these three years, I come seeking fruit on this fig-tree, and find none; cut it down; why cumbereth it the ground? And he, answering, said unto him, Lord, let it alone this year also, till I shall dig about it, and dung it: and if it bear fruit, well: and if not, then after that, thou shalt cut it down.* Our Lord concludes His discourse by this parable, of which He leaves the interpretation to the investigation of His audience. We ought to apply it to ourselves, and we shall find in it six motives for repentance.

1. The benefits with which God has prevented us. *A certain man had a fig-tree planted in his vineyard.* This fig-tree represented the Jewish people on the earth and in the midst of other nations; it was Jerusalem in the midst of the chosen people, of whom it was the capital. This fig-tree is ourselves, made members of Christ in our Baptism, planted in His Church by faith, and perhaps associated in His ministry by the priesthood. Now, in whatever state of life we may be, we have been carefully trained there, watered by the graces of Heaven, and forearmed against the corruptions of the world. We pride ourselves on the enjoyment of all these advantages; but do we ever bethink ourselves of thanking Him from Whom we hold them? let us seek to profit by them by bringing forth fruits such as He has a right to expect from us? do we persuade ourselves that so many benefits impose no obligation upon us? do we think that after the goodness of God has been so lavishly bestowed

upon us, that His justice has nothing to demand of us in return?

2. *Our gratitude towards God.* *And he came and sought fruit thereon, and found none.* Such was the state of the Jewish nation, such was that of ungrateful Jerusalem at the time of the Messiah; is it not our state also? Is not this barren fig tree the figure of our ingratitude and our barrenness? Where are the fruits which we have borne? where are the good works which we have done? What virtue can the Lord find in us to-day? Alas! instead of the fruits of holiness, have we not perhaps brought forth the fruits of sin?

3. *The patience of the Lord towards us.* *Then said He unto the dresser of His vineyard, Behold these three years have I come seeking fruit on this fig-tree and find none.* It was the third year since our Lord had begun publicly to preach repentance, and yet neither the Jewish nation nor the capital had given heed to His Words. We do not count them; but God counts these years which we spend in idleness, in dissipation, in the forgetfulness of our duties, of our salvation, and in a complete barrenness. We forget what we owe to God; but He does not forget; we live as though we owed Him nought; but He comes to seek what we have owed Him for so long a period. He has been waiting patiently that we might bring forth fruits worthy of all the care He has bestowed upon us, and we have long deceived His expectations. Where should we be if He had punished us as soon as we had ceased to be faithful to Him. What patience to have borne so long with us! not only three years, but twenty years, thirty years, or perhaps longer. Hell has murmured at it, the devils have complained of it; the damned, many of whom are less guilty than we, and of whom some have been our accomplices, have blasphemed at God's long-suffering with us, and yet we are not touched by it, we are not penetrated with gratitude at it!

4. *The justice of God.* *Cut it down; why cumbereth it the ground?* Where should we be, what should

we do, if God had pronounced this sentence against us? With what terror should we have been seized, if we had heard these dreadful words! Unhappy that I am! it is perhaps to-day that God is about to pronounce them, and that His justice, wearied of my transgressions, my negligences, my uselessness, is about to give the absolute command that I should be pulled up from the place which another would occupy more profitably than I; that it is about to command that I should be cut off from a body which I dishonour, that I should be taken away from an office which I defile, a faith which I profane, a life which I abuse. Oh Lord; it shall be so no more, I will make a fresh beginning, I will search out the depths of my heart, and will humble myself with shame and confusion of face before Thee; give me Thy grace, O my Saviour.

5. *The mercy of God.* *And he answering, said unto Him, Lord, let it alone this year also, till I shall dig about it, and dung it; and if it bear fruit, well.* Who has then taken my cause in hand, who has pleaded for me thus, when I thought only how to lose myself! O Saviour of my soul; it is Thou Who hast satisfied by the merits of Thy death, the just anger of Thy Father. O mercy of Jesus! it is Thou Who hast come between my poor soul and the justice of God the Father, Who hast averted the thunderbolt ready to fall on my head, and Who, in the place of the punishment which I deserved, dost prepare for me new favours, dost bestow renewed blessings on me, and dost procure for me new means of salvation. Shall I still abuse all that? Do not suffer it, O my God; support me in the firm resolution I have made to profit by Thy mercy, and to be more faithful to Thee.

6. *The last limit of God's patience.* *If not, then after that, thou shalt cut it down.* Unhappy Jews, you would not understand the meaning of this parable, nor profit by this last year which was still granted to you, and you were cut off from the number of the nations. Wanderers upon the face of the earth, without

temples, without worship, without altars, you only exist in order to verify the prophecy which announced the punishment prepared for your impenitence. Alas! how many others likewise have not understood the meaning of this parable, have abandoned their faith, and been cut off from the number of true believers!

Prayer. O my God! do I then understand it myself aright? Where is this, the last limit of Thy patience on my behalf placed, after which there will be no further help for me? Perhaps I am approaching this limit, and that only this present moment remains to me. I will hasten to profit by it, I will return to Thee with all sincerity of heart, I will begin to serve Thee with fervour, and to bring forth the fruits which Thou dost look for in me. Thou dost suffer me still to hope in Thy goodness, I will delay no longer, I will not make the sad trial of the truth of Thy threats; I will love and serve Thee only in time and eternity. Amen.

Meditation CLXVI.

OF THE WOMAN WHO WAS HEALED ON THE SABBATH DAY.

Consider, 1. the infirmities of this woman; 2. her cure; 3. the question which the ruler of the synagogue put to Jesus respecting her. S. Luke xiii. 10—17.

FIRST POINT.

Of the infirmities of this woman.

And Jesus *was teaching in one of the synagogues on the Sabbath. And behold, there was a woman which had a spirit of infirmity eighteen years, and was bowed together, and could in no wise lift up herself.* The state of this woman was worthy of compassion; but alas, her infirmity was only a feeble image of that which is caused by sin.

1. What was the source of this infirmity? This infirmity came from the devil, *whom Satan hath bound;* and is it not also from him that all the evils of our soul come? is it not the suggestions of that enemy of our salvation that we follow, when we forsake God, and give ourselves up to sin? Ought not this thought alone to inspire us with horror and keep us back from sin? When God permits it, the evil one may have power over our bodies, without our being guilty; but it is only through our own fault and by our consent that he makes himself master of our souls.

2. What was the nature of this infirmity? This poor woman was bent down to the ground, a position equally painful and humiliating, the pain of which she could not bear, nor could she conceal her shame of it. Such is the sad condition of a soul which is steeped in sin; it sees only the earth and the mire, it is only occupied with shameful pleasures; it feels all the indignity of its criminal indulgences, and cannot prevent others from perceiving its grovelling propensities. Oh deplorable state! How can any one take pleasure in it? how can a person not fear to fall into it, or if unhappily, they have done so, how can they not seek to raise themselves out of it?

3. What was the character of this infirmity? *Eighteen years.* And how long is it since we have yielded ourselves up to sin? When a person commits the first sin, when he takes the first step in the paths of iniquity, he flatters himself that he shall not continue in it, that he shall soon give it up. Gross delusion! deceptive hope! Twenty, thirty, forty years pass insensibly in crime, and often a whole life.

4. What was the effect of this infirmity? This woman was so bent *that she could in no wise lift up herself*. Tell that sinner to raise his eyes to heaven, and to behold there a great and liberal God, Who employs His Almighty Power in filling with delights those souls which have been faithful to Him, and in compensating to them throughout eternity, for the vain pleasures and false en

joyments of which they have deprived themselves for a short space out of love for Him; tell him at least to consider there a just God, the Avenger of sins, who will condemn to eternal fires the guilty souls who have violated the holiness of His laws. He cannot raise his looks so high, he sees no other delights than those of earth, he knows no other pleasures than those of the flesh, he knows no other suffering than that of being deprived of them; the unhappy fruit of long continued perseverance in sin. Tell that soul, entirely occupied with herself, her vanity, her frivolous, sinful amusements, tell her to pray, to meditate, to think of God, and to place herself in His Presence; she does not know what you say to her, she understands nothing; she only sees the earth, she cannot raise herself higher; she makes some feeble efforts in vain; the habit is contracted, the habit holds her back, and she remains bowed down under the yoke, under the empire of the evil one.

SECOND POINT.

Healing of this woman.

1. Jesus sees her. *And when Jesus saw her.* This woman, in spite of her infirmity, had repaired to the synagogue in order to profit by the public instruction. Alas! we need no reason as strong as her's to keep us back from God's House. The least pretext suffices us, indeed we often absent ourselves without any pretext, out of pure idleness, from distaste for God's Word; and when we do go thither, in what frame of mind do we come there, in what state does Jesus see us? He saw this woman, and He saw her afflicted, humiliated, groaning under the weight of her infirmity, and desiring nothing so much as to be delivered from it. But how does he see us? He sees us in all the adornments of pride and worldliness, scandalising others by our irreverent and immodest behaviour; He sees us bowed down under the weight of our sins and of our evil habits, and cherishing them, and fearing nothing so much as to be

delivered from them. Ah! if we wish to be healed, let us come before Christ in a different manner, let us humble ourselves at the sight of our infirmities, and let us desire to be healed of them.

2. Jesus called her to Him. *He called her to Him.* What was the joy of this afflicted woman, when she heard herself called by that Voice so full of Power and sweetness! With what hope was not her heart filled! With what promptitude did she not obey so sweet a command! She does not fear to appear in the sad state in which she was in the midst of this numerous assembly, and to draw down upon her the looks of every one present. Love animates her and hope supports her. The same sweet and powerful Voice has been calling us for a long time. Why do we defer to obey it? What do we fear?

3. Jesus speaks to her and touches her. *And said unto her, Woman, thou art loosed from thine infirmity. And He laid His Hands upon her.* Jesus speaks to us by the lips of His ministers; He lays His Hands upon us; it is His merits which are applied to us; it is His Almighty Power which absolves us, and delivers us from the tyrannical weight of sin, under which we groan. Let us approach Him then with a sincere and contrite heart, and we shall find healing to our souls.

4. The woman is healed. *And immediately she was made straight, and glorified God.* A prompt, perfect, public, and lasting cure. At the moment that Jesus pronounced these words, and laid His Hands upon her, the woman felt herself healed; she arose without effort, she beheld her Deliverer, she thanked God for her miraculous cure: every one saw her in her altered condition, and glorified the Lord with her. When will others perceive in us so blessed a change? In vain do we flatter ourselves to have an inward healing, if our exterior is not changed, if our actions are the same, if our looks are always turned towards pleasures, towards the world and its vanities; if neither greater modesty, nor greater recollectedness, nor more devotion and love for prayer are

to be seen in us. The first effect of the inward healing of the soul, is change of life; and the first duty of a soul that has been healed, is gratitude towards God. If then we are healed and changed, if we feel our hearts loosened from earth and raised towards heaven, let us refer all the praise to Him, but let us remember also that it is not with the infirmities of the soul as with those of the body. This woman who was healed by the word of Christ had no reason to fear that the devil would have power to bind her anew, and bow her again to the ground. It is not thus with our soul; let her be healed again and again, she is always subject to debase herself, to stoop down, if we do not unceasingly implore the help of the All-powerful Hand Which has raised us up, if we do not unceasingly watch, and use every effort, by God's grace to remain in the blessed state into which He has brought us. Alas! O my God, how wretched I am! Whatever resolution I form, whatever effort I make, I find myself for ever grovelling on the earth; numberless earthly affections creep into my heart, and take entire possession of it, almost without my being aware of it. What can I do in my misery, but cry unceasingly to Thee, Help me, Lord; raise me up, O Lord, have mercy upon me.

THIRD POINT.

Of the indignation of the ruler of the synagogue.

1. He clokes his indignation under a false garb. This ruler of the synagogue was one of those proud and jealous Pharisees, to whom the growing reputation of Jesus gave offence, and whom His continual miracles angered beyond measure. But following the example of his colleagues, he concealed his indignation under the pretext of zeal against a pretended transgression of the law of God, because this healing had taken place on the Sabbath day. He did not dare directly to attack the author of this miracle, but addressing himself to the people with an imperious air; *There are six days*, he said to them, *in which men ought to work; in them*

therefore come and be healed, and not on the sabbath day. Let us learn from his conduct to mistrust the zeal which leads us so often to condemn the good works which others do. Let us search well into our hearts, and see whether our condemnation does not arise from a hidden spring of jealousy, and is not instigated by their superior success.

2. This candemnation is rebuked with severity. *But the Lord answered him, and said, Thou hypocrite, doth not each one of you on the Sabbath loose his ass or his ox from the stall, and lead him away to watering? And ought not this woman, being a daughter of Abraham, whom Satan hath bound, lo, these eighteen years, be loosed from this bond on the Sabbath day?* A comparison which would be easy of comprehension to the people, but very humiliating to the proud Pharisees. The characteristic the most marked of false zeal and Pharasaical piety is that which inspires us with harsh judgments of our brethren, when it renders us less compassionate towards the souls whom Christ has redeemed with His Blood, and who have long groaned under the slavery of the devil, than we should be towards the animals we employ for our own uses.

3. His indignation turns to his own confusion. *And when He had said these things, all His adversaries were ashamed.* And this is often the result, when the hypocrisy of those who make a profession of zeal for God's cause, which is only the mask for their own unworthy motives, is discovered. Such are the ordinary effects of envy; it rends us within, and fills us with confusion without.

4. This indignation serves only to increase the joy of the people, and their attachment to Jesus. *And all the people rejoiced for all the glorious things that were done by Him.* God permits often that calumny should serve to increase the glory of him that is calumniated. If it is praiseworthy to do good, it is far more so to do it amidst the opposition and contradiction of others; opposition does but recoil on the heads of its authors.

The happy simplicity of the people and of truly pious souls makes them take up the side of truth, and leads them to follow Jesus Christ, whilst the proud doctor is brought to shame and confusion.

Prayer. Look upon me, Lord, with the eyes of mercy. I am in a far more deplorable condition than that of this woman in the Gospel; I can in no way look on high: I follow blindly the bent of my own base and carnal desires; my soul is only occupied with things of this earth, and I remain always bowed down to earth. O Jesus! call me to Thee, or rather grant that I may be obedient to Thy voice which calls me. Touch my soul by Thy divine grace, touch my heart, and raise it towards the things of eternity, so that I may look only towards Heaven, whence cometh my help, and where I hope to reign with Thee. Amen.

Meditation CLXVII.
PARABLES OF THE GRAIN OF MUSTARD SEED AND OF THE LEAVEN.

The ungrateful city to which Jesus was slowly leading His disciples through all the villages and cities which lay on His way, was soon to make them witnesses of the bloody Death of their Master, and it was doubtless in order to prepare them for this spectacle of the Cross and the sight of His death, upon which the accomplishment of His promises depended, that He here offers them these parables, in which He sets before them anew the progress of the preaching of His Gospel, and gives them for their consolation, these two parables; 1. the parable of the grain of mustard seed; 2. the parable of the leaven. S. Luke xiii. 18—21.

FIRST POINT.

Of the parable of the grain of mustard seed.

1. Of the attention which this parable requires. *Then said He, Unto what is the kingdom of God like, and whereunto shall I resemble it?* Our Lord knew well under what figures He was about to convey the truths

which He would set forth; He had no need to enquire, or to consult any one on this matter. He speaks thus therefore only in order to draw forth the attention of those who were listening to Him, and of those who should meditate on His words. Let us ask of Him that respectful attention which shall impress these great truths on our minds, and penetrate our whole soul and heart with them.

2. Of the kingdom of God, expressed by this parable. *It is like a grain of mustard seed, which a man took and cast into his garden, and it grew and waxed a great tree, and the fowls of the air lodged in the branches of it.* This *garden* is that wherein the tomb of Jesus Christ lay, whence He came forth glorious and triumphant in order to be our Life, our Righteousness, our Hope. Are we of the number of those birds of the air, of those pure and holy souls who take their rest in Him, who seek in Him their refuge, who find in Him their strength, and put all their delight in Him? This *garden* is the world where Jesus Christ has placed His Church, so small and weak in its beginnings, and afterwards so triumphant and so widely spread. Do we love her, do we serve her, are we amongst the number of her members who edify others by our lives? This *garden* is our heart in which grace has been sown. What growth has it made in it? Has God's grace become there a fertile and spreading tree, in which we find our rest, our consolation, and where others may find help and encouragement? Or have we not rather stifled this precious seed? have we not hindered its progress by our multiplied infidelities?

3. Of the kingdom of the devil, expressed by this parable in a contrary sense. The devil, vanquished and banished from the earth by Christ, driven out of His Church, driven out of our hearts, returns thither in order to establish his kingdom which is opposed to the kingdom of God. Heresy in the Church, evil passions in a heart, both these have but feeble beginnings. It is only a very small and almost imperceptible grain; it

is only a seed which hides itself out of sight; but if we do not crush it at once, if we let it grow, it soon becomes a tree which stretches its branches wide, and to which not the birds of the air, but the reptiles of the earth, and the serpents of hell, that is to say, sins, impurity, blasphemies come, and where they come, not in order to take there their rest, but in order to bring confusion with them, and to trouble every thing, and to exercise there their excesses of fury and cruelty. Such is the difference between the kingdom of God, and that of the evil one; under which of these two kingdoms do we live ?

SECOND POINT.

Of the parable of the leaven.

1. Of the attention which this second parable requires. *And again He said, Whereunto shall I liken the kingdom of God?* Our Lord again arouses the attention of His auditors; let us also awaken ours anew in order to meditate upon this second parable, let us ask for the light we need to understand it aright, and for grace to profit by it.

2. Of the kingdom of God, as explained by this parable. *It is like leaven, which a woman took and hid in three measures of meal, till the whole was leavened.* These three measures of meal are the three parts of the then known world, Asia, Europe, and Africa. The Gospel has been made known in them, the Word of God has been preached, the Sacraments have been administered, and the fermentation of that leaven has produced an innumerable number of saints. Another and new world has been discovered, and there the Gospel has been preached, and this precious leaven has fermented there also, and has brought forth in this fourth part of the world the same virtues as in the old world. These three measures of meal, are also the three powers of our soul, where the grace of God, the Word of God, and the Sacraments have wrought a salutary fermentation, which elevates our senses, our spirits,

and our hearts, which unites us to God, transforms us into Him, and makes of us living bread meet to be offered to Him upon His sublime and eternal Altar. Let us receive this divine leaven with thanksgiving, let us give it free course in our souls, let us not hinder it, let us not disturb its action.

3. *Of the kingdom of the devil, expressed by this parable in a contrary sense.* If the preaching of the Gospel has been like a precious leaven, which has sanctified and still sanctifies the four portions of the world, there remains also always in the world an evil leaven of pride and concupiscence, which upholds the kingdom of the devil, and upholds in it all manner of impiety, unbelief, sin, schism, and heresy. Let us thank God that He has caused us to be born in a Christian country, where the leaven of God's Word still takes effect. Let us pray for those lands which have not yet received this precious leaven, for those which have rejected it, for those who have corrupted it, and let us tremble for ourselves. This evil leaven which introduces into men's hearts the kingdom of the Evil one is born within us. To this dangerous leaven is joined that of rising passions, evil examples, bad books, bad companions, evil conversation; let us be attentive and watchful over ourselves.

Prayer. Yea, Lord, I will apply myself earnestly to put far from me all that might weaken my faith, corrupt my heart, defile my senses, and bring me back under the empire of the devil, from which Thou hast delivered me by Thy grace. O my God, it needs, I know, but a little leaven to leaven the whole lump: but I will be instant in my watchfulness: sustain it, O Jesus! by the price and the merits of Thine Adorable Blood. Amen.

Meditation CLXVIII.

OF THE SMALL NUMBER OF THOSE WHO WILL BE SAVED.

Examine, 1. what we must do in order to be of that number; 2. the reasons which would exclude us from that number; 3. the despair of those who shall be excluded from that number. S. Luke xiii. 22—39.

FIRST POINT.

What we must do in order to be of that number.

And Jesus went through the cities and villages, teaching, and journeying towards Jerusalem. Then said one unto him, Lord, are there few that be saved. This Divine Saviour, without answering directly the question as to the great or small number of those who shall be saved, contented Himself with saying what was needed in order to be of that number; and that is in reality what is needful for us to know on that point. *He said*, unto those who were listening to Him, *Strive to enter in at the strait gate; for many, I say unto you, will seek to enter in, and shall not be able.*

1. Consider what is this *strait gate* by which we must enter Heaven. It is the Gospel, it is faith and the commandments of the Gospel. A very strait gate, for in order to pass through it, we must humble our minds, debase our pride, restrain our passions, our inclinations, our desires, our thoughts, our affections; we must despoil ourselves of all attachment to earthly things, to self, and self-love, in order to love God only, and to keep His commandments. Is this the gate through which we strive to pass, by which we hope to enter into Heaven?

2. See what are the efforts we must make in order to enter by this gate. They must be generous, constant, persevering efforts; efforts against the devil who drives us away from that gate as much as he can, some-

times by inspiring doubts into our mind, sometimes by exciting our evil passions, sometimes by attracting us to himself by flattering promises of wealth, pleasures, honours, which are not his to give; sometimes, by turning us away from the precepts of the Gospel, by filling us with unfounded fears, by exaggerating the difficulties to us, and by the impossibility which he assures us we shall find in carrying them out. Efforts against the world, which, in order to keep us away from that gate, retails out to us an easy-going and corrupt code of morals, quotes its own example, and then asks us, Shall we then all be damned? Efforts against ourselves; nature will complain, the flesh will rebel, our courage will fail us, every thing will suggest to us to take our ease, that a restraint so austere cannot last, and that it is not necessary. Do not let us suffer ourselves to be led astray, let us make an effort, let us break through every obstacle, and in spite of everything, let us pass through that narrow gate by which we enter into Heaven. If the passage is narrow, the end is eternal freedom; how ever narrow may be that passage, love can enlarge it, and grace will make it easy to us.

3. Observe who those are who seek to enter in and are not able. Those cannot enter that narrow gate, who do not seek it as they ought, and who do not use the necessary efforts in order to enter it. The Jews cannot enter it, who, obstinately attached to the law of Moses, refuse to know Him to Whom Moses directs them, Him Who is the End and Accomplishment of the law and the prophets. Unbelievers who know not the law of God cannot enter there. Christians who live evil lives cannot enter the strait gate, who, in order to gratify their passions, seek to join together the world and the Gospel, to belong sometimes to God and sometimes to the world, and to make of their whole lives a monstrous tissue of repentance and relapses, of devotion and of sin; or who delay to put themselves to any inconvenience for God, till they have no time left which they can abuse. Gross deceptions; how is it that there are so many who

yield themselves up to them? Let us reflect seriously upon the matter, let us never hope to enter Heaven by any other way than by the strait gate; do not let us think to be able to enter by that strait gate without great efforts, without doing great violence to ourselves, without gaining great victories over ourselves.

SECOND POINT.

Reasons which will exclude persons from that number.

Jesus, continuing the parable or allegory of the strait gate, represents God His Father, or Himself as reigning in Heaven, with the saints, under the figure of a master of a house at home with his children and friends, and refusing to open the door to strangers, who demand an entrance. This parable is well fitted to dispel our illusions and our pretexts, if we will be attentive to it; and although it was spoken specially to the Jews, it is easy to extend it to all sinners.

1. First answer given to sinners. *When once the Master of the house is risen up, and hath shut to the door, and ye begin to stand without, and to knock at the door, saying Lord, Lord, open unto us; and he shall answer and say unto you, I know you not whence ye are.* What surprise for men who had flattered themselves that they were in the right path, and truly religious. They will not be able to believe that they are to be treated thus, and they will persist in their intreaties.

2. Allegations of sinners. *Then shall ye begin to say, We have eaten and drunk in Thy presence, and Thou hast taught in our streets.* This would apply in the first place to the Jews, who might speak thus to Christ, with Whom they had lived, and Whom they had heard preach and teach in their synagogues, and streets. Christians will also say to Him, We have eaten and drunk at thy Table, we have received Thy Gospel, and it has been taught and preached amongst us. What then! will they exclaim, Thou dost not know us, we are un-

known to Thee? How dost Thou say that Thou dost not know whence we come. False pretexts, vain allegations, useless clamours! Alas! shall we wait until the last Day to undeceive ourselves? Must we blind ourselves until death and until the sovereign Judge has pronounced the irrevocable sentence of our damnation, which He seeks to warn us against by so many salutary warnings, and parables.

3. Last answer given to sinners. *But He shall say, I know you not whence ye are; depart from Me, all ye workers of iniquity.* This answer has two parts. 1. *I know you not.* You call yourselves disciples of Moses, but you have renounced the Messiah Whom Moses announced to you, and to whom His law pointed you. You call yourselves Christians, but you have followed the tenets of the world and the law of your own evil passions, in contempt of that of My Gospel, which has been unceasingly preached to you. *I know you not, I know you not whence ye are.* 2. *Depart from Me, all ye workers of iniquity.* The national iniquity of the Jews, was the deicide they committed in the person of Christ, in which all those of this nation participate, who still persevere in the same blasphemies. But how many alas! there are besides who give the bridle to their evil passions without remorse! How sad it will be for Christians, who have a clearer knowledge of the truth, and have been better instructed in God's commands, to find themselves in this respect as sinful, if not more so, than the Jews, and to hear the words, *Depart from Me, all ye workers of iniquity!* spoken to them. O terrible words, which I have only too well deserved to hear from the lips of my Judge!

THIRD POINT.

Despair of those who shall be excluded from that number.

There will be two causes or two sources of this despair of sinners.

1. The first cause of this despair will be the sight of

those who have lived before them. *There shall be weeping and gnashing of teeth, when ye shall see Abraham, and Isaac, and Jacob, and all the prophets, in the kingdom of God, and you yourselves thrust out.* The Jews will see Abraham, Isaac, and Jacob admitted into the kingdom of Heaven, together with all the prophets of the ancient dispensation, and they will find themselves excluded, because they have not believed in the Son of Abraham, promised to the patriarchs, and announced by the prophets as Son of God, God with us, the Messiah and Saviour of men. Christians who lead evil lives will see the Apostles, and saints whom they have revered on earth, together with all the martyrs who have sealed their adherence to the faith with their blood, and all the holy men of old, admitted into Heaven, and themselves excluded because they have failed to imitate their examples. Then there will be nought but tears, regrets, and gnashing of teeth; but it will be too late. Then there will be nought but rage, fury, and despair; but it will all be in vain.

2. The second source of this despair will be the sight of those who have lived with them, or after them. *And they shall come from the east, and from the west, and from the north, and from the south, and shall sit down in the kingdom of God.* The Jews will see the Gentiles, who knew neither Moses nor the prophets, and yet have acknowledged the Messiah, Jesus, Son of God; they will see them come in numbers from the four parts of the world, and sit down at the eternal banquet, in the kingdom of God, from which they themselves will be excluded. Those who have been made Christians in their infancy, will see there those who have been converted from heathenism and idolatry; priests will see laymen there, the rich will see the poor there, kings, their subjects, and masters, their servants seated at the heavenly banquet, and themselves shut out from it. Ah! who can picture to themselves what bitter regrets, what utter despair such a sight will cause to the heart of the damned?

3. *Conclusion. And, behold, there are last which shall be first, and there are first which shall be last.* Oh terrible change! Who would not fear, who would not tremble? Let us then not trust to our position, nor to our knowledge, nor to the graces we have received, nor to the advantages of our station. If we do not serve God with fervour, if we do not make an effort in order to enter by the strait gate, perhaps we shall see that sinner whom we have known, one day converted; that person whom we have looked down upon, but who was more fervent than we, admitted into Heaven, and placed among the ranks of the Blessed, and we ourselves cast into the lowest place into hell, a prey to eternal despair.

Prayer. Be it far from me, O Lord, that I should fall into such misery! I know Thy mercy, O God; Thou dost warn me here of the rigour of Thy judgments in order to lead me to avoid them. O Jesus! I detest mine iniquity. and I will, with the help of Thy grace which I entreat of Thee with all earnestness, strive to keep Thy holy commandments with so much faithfulness, that Thou wilt not disown me when death shall summon me to appear before Thee. Amen.

Meditation CLXIX.

ANSWER OF JESUS TO THE PHARISEES WHO TRIED TO FRIGHTEN HIM IN ORDER TO CAUSE HIM TO DEPART FROM GALILEE.

Consider, 1. the steadfastness of Jesus; 2. His compassion towards Jerusalem; 3. His threats and prophecies against that ungrateful city. S. Luke xiii. 31—35.

FIRST POINT.

The steadfastness of Jesus.

The same day there came certain of the Pharisees,

saying unto Him, Get thee out, and depart hence ; for Herod will kill thee. Aud he said unto them, Go ye, and tell that fox, Behold, I cast out devils, and I do cures to-day and to-morrow, and the third day I shall be perfected. Nevertheless I must walk to-day, and to-morrow, and the day following ; for it cannot be that a prophet perish out of Jerusalem.

1. The steadfastness of Jesus appears in the character which he depicts of Herod. Sometimes Herod desired to see Jesus in order to satisfy his curiosity, at other times he desired that He should be put to death, in order to obliterate entirely the memory of S. John the Baptist; but he feared to irritate the people by this fresh crime. Policy enthralled all the feelings of his heart, and dictated all his actions. But this policy, which was so much admired in this prince, by which he succeeded so skilfully in captivating the Jewish people, in procuring for himself the favour of the Romans, in order to profit by every thing, and make every thing subservient to his own ends and his own interests, this policy was, in the judgment of the Son of God, only narrowness of mind, meanness of purpose, which degraded him from the nobility of man, and lowered him to the condition of an animal whom instinct leads to employ cunning stratagems. And it is thus that the Sovereign Judge of men regards the potentates of earth who govern the world, and who conduct with the greatest skill the most important affairs of state, if they do not make religion, truth, and righteousness the basis of their policy and of their wisdom. In all conditions of life, men often pride themselves on this mean craftiness, which has only in view its own self-interest, and they believe themselves to be wise, when they know how to attain their ends, by whatever means they employ. Let us hold such a character in detestation; let us always act with sincerity and candour, and let us examine what character our wisdom bears in the eyes of this sovereign Judge.

2. The steadfastness of Jesus in the resolution which

He declares to change in no point the plan of His operations. Whatever might be the terror with which the Pharisees essayed to inspire him with regard to the violences of Herod, our Blessed Lord will continue to go and come whither it seemeth Him good, to instruct and comfort the people, and He will not depart from Galilee till the time that He Himself had fixed, namely in three days' time. It is probable that in the expression *on the third day I shall be perfected*, He referred to the end of His Life, which was not far distant. In this sense, this expression must not be applied to the death of Jesus, but to His Resurrection. It was the third day that He rose; and it is by His Resurrection that Jesus Christ was *perfected*, that the work of our Redemption has been *perfected*, and that He has become the Perfecter of our faith. By this steadfastness of soul of which the divine Saviour here gives the example to His ministers, He disconcerted all the craftiness of the Pharisees; for the reproach of cunningness which He had applied to Herod did not any the less fall upon them, although indirectly. The Pharisees of Jerusalem had formed a conspiracy, as we shall soon see, to cause Jesus to be seized on the first day of the Feast of the Tabernacles, a period which was close at hand. We may easily suppose that the Pharisees of Galilee, where Jesus then was, were aware of the plot which was being hatched at Jerusalem, and not being able any longer to endure the sight of His Presence which dazzled them, nor His Holiness which condemned their sinful lives, observed the actions of this God-Man in order to see whether He intended to betake Himself to Jerusalem for the feast. The time was drawing near, and He did not appear to be making any preparations for His journey, and this it probably was, that led them to give Him this information in order to hasten His departure. What disquieted them in His answer was that as He did not intend to set out till the expiration of three days, it would be difficult for Him to arrive at Jerusalem in time to be there on the first day of the Feast, and that, if He were not there on that day, the conspiracy might fall to the ground, as it did in fact, according to the designs of this Divine Saviour, Who had appointed that His Death should take place at the Feast of the Passover, and not at that of the Tabernacles, which was a far less solemn feast. O Eternal Wisdom! what can the malice and the cunning of Thine enemies bring about against Thee? Thou dost mock at their senseless projects, and Thou dost carry out, as it pleaseth Thee, the designs of Thine infinite mercy, on behalf of those who obey Thee? What have I to fear, and wherefore should I disquiet or frighten myself with regard to the dangers which threaten me? I am sheltered beneath the wings of Thy Providence, and nothing can happen to me save for my good, and by the appointment of Thine Infinite Providence, to which, in life and death, I will be perfectly submissive.

3. The steadfastness of Jesus in the knowledge which He shews of the evil designs of the Pharisees. *For it cannot be that a prophet perish out of Jerusalem.* It is as if He had said; In three days, after I shall have accomplished My ministry, not only shall I depart from Galilee, as you counsel Me, but more than that, I shall go to Jerusalem, as you desire Me; for unfaithful Jerusalem has for a long time reserved to itself the right of slaying the prophets, and it is in the same place, where it has always prepared for them a tomb, that I must die like them in the defence of truth and justice. By these words, Jesus shewed to the Pharisees that He read the depth of their hearts, that He knew what was being plotted against Him at Jerusalem, and that He saw the part they were taking in the matter. But He shewed them at the same time, that as the fear of Herod did not make Him hasten His departure, neither did the fear of the senate at Jerusalem hinder Him from repairing to that city, and that the warning they had just given Him could not impose upon Him. O Jesus! how great Thou art, how wise Thou art, how good, how generous! The death with which Thou art threatened

on all sides does not terrify Thee. In the midst of so many perils, Thou art steadfast and intrepid, not because Thou hast it in Thy power to escape death, but because Thou willest to suffer it for love of us. What can He fear Who desires only to die for us?

SECOND POINT.

Compassion of Jesus towards Jerusalem.

Jesus could not think of the death which He must suffer, nor of Jerusalem where He must suffer it, without being moved with compassion at the fate of that ungrateful city.

1. Compassion of Jesus over Jerusalem at the thought of its crimes. *O Jerusalem, Jerusalem, which killest the prophets, and stonest them that are sent unto thee!* Jerusalem had already shed the blood of several prophets; it was about to shed that of the Messiah; and afterwards that of His apostles and of His disciples. What misery for a city in which such hatred prevails, and with how many crimes is it not defiled! Let us deplore here the sins with which we ourselves are defiled! How many warnings, how many inspirations, what remorse do we not stifle in order to gratify our evil passions!

2. Compassion of Jesus over Jerusalem at the thought of the graces which it abuses. *How often would I have gathered thy children together, as a hen doth gather her brood under her wings, and ye would not!* How often has not God called us to Himself, how often has not Jesus desired to gather us under His wings, and we *would not!* How little have we known our real interests! How happy should we have been under the wings of Jesus, in prayer, in meditation on His commandments, and in the faithful practise of His holy will! There, we should have enjoyed a perfect peace and an entire security; and instead of that we have been agitated by remorse, fears, disquietude and anxieties. Under the wings of Jesus, we should have lived sheltered

from all dangers, out of the reach of the darts of the evil one, and inaccessible to the contagion of the world; and instead of that, we have fallen into many a pit-fall, we have been the prey of our enemies, and bad example has drawn us away. Under the wings of Jesus, we should have seen death approach with calmness, if not with joy, we should have been sheltered from the wrath of God and His vengeance; and instead of this, we face death only with fear, and perhaps see it approach only with feelings of despair.

3. Compassion of Jesus over Jerusalem at the thought of its reprobation. The sentence in which this reprobation is conveyed, contains God's justification, and the sinner's condemation, and these two things are comprised in these few words, *I would, and ye would not!* *I would*, and how often, and during how long a time, and by how many means! *And ye would not!* Here is God's justification, and here is the sinner's condemnation. God willed to preserve me from hell, God willed to give me His Paradise, God willed that I should live so as to be worthy of it; what has He not done for me that I might attain to it? And I, I *would not—I would not.* O prey, O despair, O thought more cruel than even the fires of hell. It is for us to see now if we will, or if we will not, yea or nay; but let us not deceive ourselves as to the way in which we will it.

THIRD POINT.

Threats and predictions of Jesus against Jerusalem.

1. For this life. *Behold your house is left unto you desolate.* This temple will be destroyed, God will forsake it, and He will take away from you His covenant. Your houses shall be overthrown, and you will be buried under their ruins, and your city shall become a waste and solitary place. Such is the vengeance which God poured down and still pours down upon unfaithful Jerusalem, because it shed the Blood of the Messiah, and would not profit by It. It is thus that God still pu-

nishes the unbelief, whether of an entire nation, by taking from it the gift of faith, or of a soul, by depriving it of the special graces which it has abused, and leaving it like a desert land, and a house which is falling into ruins.

2. *For the next life.* When Jesus was addressing His enemies, He was wont often to join the threatenings of the last judgment with the thought of His death, which has made us follow here the plan of those who apply to that last day the last words of this chapter, *Verily, I say unto you, Ye shall not see Me until the time come when ye shall say. Blessed is He that cometh in the Name of the Lord.* It is as though He would have said to them, You may try in vain to disown Me and blaspheme against Me, to cause Me to be put to death, and to remove from your sight My Presence which is hateful to you; but the day will come when every knee will bend before Me, when you will see Me in the glory of My Father, when you will be forced to acknowledge Me, and to cry out, Behold Him, the Blessed of God, He Who came in the Name of the Lord in order to save us, and Who comes to-day in the Name of His Father, and in His Own Name, in order to judge us and condemn us. Yea, that Great Day will come, when the Jew, the ungodly man and the sinner will be forced to render homage to Him Whom they have outraged.

3. *Remarks on these last words. Blessed is He that cometh in the Name of the Lord.* They are taken from the Psalm, in which, in a spirit of prophecy, David spoke of the Messiah, and gave thanks for the time of His coming. They were repeated by the acclamations which the people uttered at the triumphant entry of Christ into the city of Jerusalem, and our Lord does not quote them here without making allusion not only to the Psalm whence they are taken, but also to the people who would soon make them re-echo in the ears of the Pharisees of Galilee before His triumphant entry into Jerusalem, such as He repeated them, after the day of His triumph, to

the Pharisees at Jerusalem, with the same allusions, under the same circumstances, and with the same intention to make them fear the Majesty of His last coming. Let us repeat them with all the devotion of which we are capable, with the sentiments of humility aud gratitude which so great a blessing demands of us.

Prayer. Blessed be He that cometh in the Name of the Lord. Glory in the Highest! Be Thou for ever blessed, Lord, that Thou didst come upon the earth in order to save us, and dost descend upon Thine Altars to be our Food and Sustenance. May I bless Thee unceasingly here below, and praise Thee for ever in Heaven after that terrible day when Thou wilt come to judge us. Amen.

Meditation CLXX.

ANSWER OF JESUS TO HIS RELATIONS WHO PRESSED HIM TO GO TO JERUSALEM.

Examine, 1. the proposition which the relations of Jesus made to Him; 2. the answer which Jesus makes to them; 3. the effects which the absence of Jesus at Jerusalem on the day of the feast produced. S. John vii. 1—18.

FIRST POINT.

Of the proposition which the relations of Jesus make to Him.

I. In what place do they make it? In Galilee. *After these things, Jesus walked in Galilee: for He could not walk in Jewry, because the Jews sought to kill Him.* Jesus had been for some time going through Galilee, where Herod was reigning, and where the Jews who ruled at Jerusalem had no authority. He did not enter into Judæa, where they might have caused Him to be seized, because He knew that they wished to put Him to death. It was not fear of death which detained Jesus in Galilee, because He desired to die for us; but the day of His Sacrifice was appointed by the will of His Father, aud He would not anticipate the moment. He might have appeared in Judæa, and have delivered Himself from the hands of His enemies by miracles; but He willed only to make use of this Divine power, for the relief of the needy, and He preferred to give us an example of humility, patience, prudence, and submission to the will of God, rather than to lavish miracles which were not needful. Jesus was neither concealed nor idle in Galilee. He went over all the cities and the country, preaching and healing every where, and giving us in every place proofs and examples of His charity and zeal. Galilee was then a place both of refuge and of labour for Jesus: but at the same time it was a place of persecution. His relations probably spoke to Him on the same day, and in the same place as the Pharisees, who, in order to induce Him to depart from Galilee, had just told Him that Herod desired His life. O Jesus! what a cruel and unjust persecution arises on all sides against Thee! Thou dost edify, Thou dost teach every where with indefatigable care and zeal, Thou dost lade every place whither Thou goest with benefits; and nevertheless, in whatsoever country Thou dost direct Thy steps, men speak only of putting Thee to death. Ministers and disciples of Jesus Christ, can you, after this example, complain of the persecutions which you meet with so frequently in the exercise of your ministry, in the fulfilment of your duties?

2. On what occasion did the relations of Jesus make this proposition to Him? *Now the Jews' feast of tabernacles was at hand.* This feast, that of the Passover, and that of the Pentecost were the three great solemnities of the Jews: they were celebrated during eight days. The first day took the name of the Feast, and was called, for example, in this feast, the Feast of Tabernacles; it fell on the 15th day of the 7th month of the Jewish year, which would fall according to our reckoning, about the beginning of October. This solemnity was established in memory of the tabernacles

or tents under which the Jews had dwelt for forty years in the desert, and in order to thank God that He had brought them into the Promised Land. We are only in this world as in a desert, where we dwell in tents which have neither stability nor duration. Let us aspire unceasingly to the Promised Land of Heaven, to the Holy City, to the Heavenly Jerusalem, where our dwelling places will be fixed and eternal.

3. What were the motives which led the relations of Jesus to make this proposition to Him? *His brethren therefore said to Him. Depart thence, and go into Judæa that Thy disciples also may see the works that Thou doest. For there is no man that doeth anything in secret, and he himself seeketh to be known openly. If Thou do these things, shew Thyself to the world. For neither did His brethren believe in Him.* The first motive which made the relations of Jesus act thus was unbelief. They did not believe in Him, they did not look upon Him as the Son of God, and the promised Messiah. The second motive was ambition. Although they did not believe in Jesus, they could not hide from themselves the marvellous works which He did, and they wished to gain some advantage from them for themselves. They wished that He should go with them, so that the glory of His works might reflect upon them. Those who have least faith are often not the least disposed to profit, according to the views of their condition and self-interest, by the gifts of God, although they do not believe in them; it is not even because they have no faith, that they have ideas so contrary to the spirit of religion. The third motive was, as will appear by our Saviour's reply more clearly, that they had been tampered with by the Pharisees. The proposition which the relations of Jesus make to Him to depart from Galilee, and to go into Judæa is so similar to that which the Pharisees had made to Him, although it was grounded upon different pretexts, that it is hardly possible to doubt that these latter had inspired His relations with the idea. Those who have no faith pervert one an-

other more and more, and the simpler are often the dupe of the most wicked. Let us ponder within ourselves, O Jesus! do I indeed believe in Thee? Have I faith? If I had, should I act as I do? should I speak the words that I do speak? should I give the advice I give? should I pray as I do?

SECOND POINT.

Of the answer which Jesus makes to His relations.

It contains the reasons which He has for not going with them, and it shews plainly to His enemies that He is distinctly aware of all their designs. These reasons are;

1. The will of God His Father, which keeps Him where He is. *Then Jesus said unto them, My time is not yet come; but your time is alway ready.* It is the same answer that Jesus had given to the Pharisees, in telling them that the duties of His ministry would compel Him to remain three days in Galilee. Thus, this God-Man has no other rule for His conduct than the will of His Father. Those who follow only their own will are always ready to join in anything which might do them honour, or by which they might gain any pleasure; but it is not thus with him whose thoughts are of God and his duties; he never gives up his obligations, either out of an easy compliance with the wishes of others, or in order to please himself; his first care is to carry out the work which has been entrusted to him, and then to learn God's will with regard to that which remains for him to do. Happy dependence, which assures to the soul its true liberty, which makes life holy, and fills it with good works, and virtues.

2. The hatred of the world. His relations had said to Him, *Shew thyself to the world*, by which they meant to the multitude, who were gathered together in the capital, at Jerusalem, and Jesus answers them, *The world cannot hate you; but Me it hateth, because I testify of it, that the works thereof are evil.* Such is

the reason why the world hates now-a-days all honest right-thinking persons, and the ministers of the Gospel who fulfil their duties. A glorious hatred, which ought to be our consolation; but if such is the disposition of the world towards us, wherefore should we seek that world? Wherefore should we still desire to obtain its favours, its love, its esteem? Those whom the world cannot hate are those who, like it, have no faith, or who speak and act as if they had none. It is a great misfortune to be loved by the world, a misfortune so much the greater that far from lamenting it, we rejoice at it, and congratulate ourselves on it, and strive more and more to maintain the possession of that favour which is so dangerous to us.

3. *The conspiracy of the Jews, in order to seize Him and to cause Him to be put to death on the first day of the Feast. Go ye up unto this feast; I go not up yet unto this feast; for My time is not yet full come.* Neither the relations of Jesus, nor the Pharisees had spoken to Him of Jerusalem or of the feast; it seems even as if they had purposely avoided all mention of it; both spoke only to Him of leaving Galilee and going into Judæa. But Jesus, in answer to His relations, speaks to them of the solemnity which they were about to celebrate in Jerusalem, and He speaks to them about it plainly. Wherefore this conduct, if it is not because it was on that feast-day that the hatred they had conceived against Him was to find its vent? But His time to die was not accomplished, His time to leave Galilee and to go to Jerusalem had not come, His mission in Galilee was not yet fulfilled; in a word He will not go to that feast on the first day on which it was solemnized. If there remained any doubt in the minds of the Pharisees as to the plan of conduct which Jesus intended to adopt, it was now made clear to them. If they could still doubt that their plots were known, they saw at least that for this time they were overthrown, and that He against Whom these snares were directed willed not to fall into them. O Jesus! I adore that divine Wisdom

which thus disconcerted Thine enemies, and assures me that when they triumph over Thee, it will not be from want of power that Thou wilt yield to their efforts, but it will-be Thy love for me which will deliver Thee into their hands, and to the cruel death which they have prepared for Thee.

THIRD POINT.

Of the effects which the absence of Jesus from Jerusalem on the first day of the feast produces.

1. *The search of the Jews in order to find Him.* *When He had said these words unto them, He abode still in Galilee. But when His brethren were gone up, then went He also up unto the feast, not openly, but as it were in secret.* Jesus remained as He had said, three days longer in Galilee, and left his relations to set out by themselves; He then departed Himself in order to be at Jerusalem on the day of the Feast which He had beforehand determined on. He arrived there indeed, not with the crowd of those who came from Galilee and Judæa, who had gone thither on the first day of the feast, but only with His Apostles, and perhaps some few of His disciples, and adopting certain precautions, as we shall see hereafter. *Then the Jews sought Him at the feast, and said, Where is He?* Words of despair, when the wicked cannot find the opportunity they seek to destroy the good : words of triumph, when they have compelled the good to keep themselves hidden, and neither to shew themselves, nor to act; words of insult, when looking upon the prudence of the good, as weakness, they speak insultingly of the justice of their cause, and take the opportunity to make an attack upon holiness and religion. What will not the chiefs of the cabal which had been formed against Jesus say on this occasion, when they see their hopes deceived ? By what impious discourses will they not seek to indemnify themselves for the failure of their conspiracy?

2. *The minds of men divided with regard to Jesus.*

And there was much murmuring among the people concerning Him; for some said, He is a good man; others said, Nay; but He deceiveth the people. Jesus was the chief object of their thoughts and conversations, amongst the people, as well as amongst the upper classes. But the people were not generally so prejudiced as those in a higher class. Some said, He is good, He works, He preaches, He teaches, He edifies by His conduct. Others said, Nay, He seduces the people; all His edifying exterior is only an imposture, all the labours which He undertakes, and all the trouble which He gives Himself, only tend to lead the people astray, and to attach them to Himself. It is thus that men spoke of Jesus, and it is thus that His disciples will be spoken of to the end of time. Those who have upright hearts, who are neither blinded by their own passions, nor by those of others, easily discover the truth. Happy if they have the courage and the constancy to remain always firmly attached to it!

3. Difference between those who were against Jesus, and those who were for Him. The former spoke openly and on every occasion against Him, and this is still the habit of those who make an attack upon religion, faith, or holiness of life. *Howbeit, no man spake openly of Him for fear of the Jews.* Here we have the stumbling-block against which so many fall, namely, human respect. Woe be to those who do not dare to acknowledge themselves Christians for fear of others! Woe be to those who from their position ought to be the support of their brethren, yet fear the world so much as to betray the cause of religion.

Prayer. O Jesus! how few there are at this present time who are on Thy side, and dare to own themselves to be Thy disciples. Support them, Lord, against the tyranny of the world; support me also, and grant that the fear of men may never make me forget what I owe to Thee. Amen.

Meditation CLXXI.

THAT WHICH TOOK PLACE IN THE TEMPLE WHEN JESUS APPEARED THERE AT THE FEAST OF TABERNACLES.

1. Jesus there answers the people, who were surprised at His learning; 2. Jesus there reproaches the Jews with the design they had formed to put Him to death; 3. Jesus there justifies the cure of the paralytic man, which He wrought on the Sabbath day. S. John vii. 14—24.

FIRST POINT.

Jesus replies to the people, who were surprised at His learning.

1. **Admiration of the Jews.** *Now about the midst of the feast, Jesus went up into the temple, and taught. And the Jews marvelled, saying, How knoweth this man letters.* Jesus had so ordered His journey, that He arrived in the neighbourhood of Jerusalem on the Friday evening, without any one being aware of His Presence, and paying any attention to it. On the Saturday, in the middle of the octave during which the feast was celebrated, Jesus appeared in the Temple. The Feast had already commenced three or four days, and He was no longer expected; men's minds had had time to grow calm, the measures that had been taken to seize Him at the commencement of this solemn feast were thus disconcerted. As soon as the people saw Jesus, they hastened to Him in crowds: and the Divine Saviour, according to His custom, began to instruct them. In this vast audience, composed of different persons who had collected from all the tribes of Palestine, there must have been a great number, especially from Judæa and even in Jerusalem, who had never heard Jesus. They were exceedingly astonished to hear the grace, the wisdom, the strength, and the depth of His words. From what source then hath He drawn all His doctrine, said they one to

the other, He Who never made it His study? They spoke thus, either because He had not been seen at Jerusalem to frequent the instructions of the doctors of the law, or else because the scribes and Pharisees had taken pains to represent Him to the people as an unlettered and illiterate person, the son of an artizan at Nazareth, who had no claim to be listened to. Such has always been the habit of the enemies of religion, to speak with contempt of those who uphold it. But do not let us suffer ourselves to be led astray by these vain declamations; let us rather mistrust those who speak with contempt of others.

2. Answer of Jesus. Jesus, in order to continue His instruction, profited by the surprise of the people, and took occasion from it to discover to His audience, 1. the source of His doctrine. *Jesus answered them, and said, My doctrine is not Mine, but His that sent Me.* That is to say, that doctrine which I preach to you as Man, I only preach it to you as being sent by another to do so, and it does not come from Myself, but from Him from Whom I have received My Mission. It is not I, as Man, Who have devised it or brought it to perfection; it is not the fruit of study, nor the production of the human mind; I have not learnt it from blind mortals, I have received it from Him Who sent Me to communicate it to the world, I have drawn it from the bosom of My Father, I have kept back nought, I have added nothing to it, I give it you as I have received it. Such is the source of the Christian doctrine, and this it is which gives to it its sublimity and its truth. Let philosophers and wise men, let great geniuses build up their systems, heap objections upon objections, nothing is more vain; the Christian doctrine is not a human system; it has for its Author the Creator of the universe, Who shews Himself in as impenetrable a manner in the work of religion, as in that of Creation. What blessedness for us to know this doctrine, and what gratitude ought we not to feel! 2. The manner in which we may know the Divinity of this doctrine. *If any man*

will do His will, He shall know of the doctrine, whether it be of God, or whether I speak of Myself. It is not in disputing, imagining or reasoning according to a person's own fancy, or by endeavouring to penetrate that which above us, that we can know this Heavenly doctrine. There is a surer and far easier way, namely, to search out our own heart, to quell its passions, and to begin by keeping God's commandments; then the clouds will disperse, and the truth will appear in all its light. It is from the heart, that spring up impiety, irreligion, and unbelief.

3. The conclusions we ought to draw from these words of Christ. *He that speaketh of himself seeketh his own glory; but he that seeketh His glory that sent him, the same is true, and no unrighteousness is in him.* We ought naturally to mistrust him who puffs up his own inventions and his discoveries; the desire which he has to glorify himself by this means, and to gain honour to himself may deceive him, and lead him to deceive others. Following out these principles, it has been necessary, at all times, to beware of these who disseminate heresy or unbelief, and not to listen to them. The faithful minister of Christ has a claim to be heard; he says, I teach you nothing but what the Church teaches, and the doctrine which she sets forth to-day, and of which I am only the organ, she has received from the Apostles, and they have received it from Christ, and Christ from God His Father. There are those who declaim against the ignorance of their times, and seek their own glory and honour, imagining to themselves that they have made fresh discoveries of which they take the glory to themselves. But the vanity which makes them speak thus is the proof of their error, and the sure index of their imposture. What our Lord here says had an invincible force on His lips; for if it was true, as it was in reality, and as the Jews themselves acknowledged, that He had never gained this wonderful knowledge through study, if He at the same time desired to take no glory to Himself for His doctrine, and referred it all to Him

that had sent Him, no one could suspect in Him either falsehood, or imposture, especially when, on the other side, He proved the divinity of His mission by works which could come only from God Himself. Let us strengthen ourselves more and more in the truths which our Christian Faith teaches us.

SECOND POINT.

Jesus reproaches the Jews with the intention they had formed to cause Him to be put to death.

1. Reproach of Jesus Christ. *Did not Moses give you the law, and yet none of you keepeth the law.* That is to say, I am not surprised that you are opposed to Me, Who, in all My actions, in all My undertakings seek only the glory of God, Who sent Me, and Whose doctrine I set forth to you, since you pay no regard even to Moses, whom you make a profession to honour as your law-giver. He has given you a law, but none of you observe it. Far from observing it, you do just the contrary of that which it enjoins upon you ; *Why go ye about to kill Me?* His law commands you to protect the innocent, and instead of protecting them, you oppress them. None of you observe the law as religiously, as exactly as I do, and yet you contrive secretly My Death, as if I was the person who violated it, I am innocent, you have nothing to reproach Me with, and nevertheless you desire to make an attempt upon My life, although the law forbids murder, although it gives you no rights save over the guilty. What have I done to you? what motive animates you against Me? wherefore do you desire to add to your other prevarications of the law, that of an attempt against My life? Alas! to how many does not this reproach of our Saviour apply? does it not apply to ourselves? We have God's commandments; but do we make them the rule of our conduct? Do we not rather make use of them to judge, censure, outrage, and condemn the conduct of others, conduct which is often innocent, whilst our's is

so guilty? Do we not sometimes go still further? Are we not prone to carry our injustice to excess, so as to hate, to wish evil or to rejoice at the evil that happens to our brethren, or to seek all possible occasions to do them harm, as if that had not been forbidden by God's commands.

2. *Answer of the Jews. The people answered and said, Thou hast a devil; who goeth about to kill Thee?* Probably these words, *Thou hast a devil,* did not convey amongst the Jews as atrocious an insult as would appear to us; but still, however we may endeavour to soften their meaning, we cannot deny that such a reply was most outrageous. Who were those amongst all this concourse, who had the hardihood to make this answer? It was doubtless not the Galileans and the other strangers assembled there, for they could not have known what was passing at Jerusalem with regard to Jesus. It could not have been either those Jews who had just expressed their admiration of the teaching of Jesus; could it have been a portion of the people of Jerusalem, who were ignorant of the designs of the Pharisees? But not only was their intention already too public in Jerusalem for them to be ignorant of it, nor was it likely that this people, who would probably have interpreted the words of Jesus as being dictated by fear, should have put into their reply so much bitterness. It is then much more probable that such an answer was only made by those who felt themselves guilty, that it was made by that portion of the people whom the Pharisees had already gained over to their side, and who had been bribed over to take part with those who sought to put Him to death. Is it not often thus that wicked men act, when they are found out and their base and criminal attempts are discovered, that they only defend themselves with more temerity, and even turn the tables upon those who know them the best, recriminate with audacity, and lade them with insults and injuries, and make a crime of their very penetration and of their alarms? By this stratagem, the enemies of Jesus succeeded in time in directing against

Him the hatred of the people, of which they would have been themselves the victims, if the people had not blindly yielded to the hardihood and constancy with which they brought forward their accusations against Jesus. However it may have been, Jesus foreknew this insult; He suffered it in silence, and continued to teach the people. What virtues, what an Example has not Jesus left us here for our imitation!

THIRD POINT.

Jesus justifies the cure of the paralytic man, which He wrought on the Sabbath Day.

1. Authenticity of the miracle. *Jesus answered and said unto them, I have done one work, and ye all marvel.* In other words, I know well that there is no unjust design, no bad intention which people do not seek to excuse. You wish to put Me to death, because I have wrought here in your presence, a work which appeared to you an infraction of the law. I have healed a paralytic man, I have commanded him to walk, to take up his bed, and carry it away with him. I have wrought this miracle on the sabbath day, behold My crime, which makes me hated of you; but I only desire, in order to cure you of your prejudices, and to make you understand that I have done nothing which is not right, that you should hear Me, that you should be My judges, and see if My action is a crime, and if you are not making use of false pretexts to cover and give a colour to your own passions. Doubtless, the immediate cure of a man who had been paralysed for 38 years, which Jesus had effected with a word, which the circumstance of its having taken place on the Sabbath day could not invalidate, ought to have been to the Jews a decisive proof of the truth of the words of Jesus Christ, if there were any thing decisive in the matter of religion against prejudiced minds strengthened by evil passions: but when men are determined to yield nothing, they can always find something to object, or to contest; and

in the minds of credulous people, a single inference, a nothing, which is made much of and distorted by those who seek skilfully to mispresent it, will do away with the most solid reasons, and the best attested facts.

2. *Answer of Jesus to the objection which was grounded upon the circumstance of the miracle having been wrought on the sabbath day.* *Moses therefore gave unto you circumcision; (not because it is of Moses but of the fathers;) and ye on the sabbath day circumcise a man. If a man on the sabbath day receive circumcision, that the law of Moses should not be broken; are ye angry with Me because I have made a man every whit whole on the sabbath day?* That is to say, if, in order to observe the law of circumcision, you do not think yourselves obliged to observe so exactly the day of rest; if even, far from feeling any scruple about it, you look upon it as an act of religion to circumcise without delay one of your children, if the eighth day after his birth happens to fall on the sabbath day, why do you condemn Me as if I had infringed that precept by doing a work of charity? Circumcision doubtless demands an especial respect, because it is more ancient than Moses himself, who enjoined it, not as a simple ceremony of the law, but as an ordinance instituted by God in the time of Abraham, and handed down from that patriarch to Moses; but works of charity are of the law of nature, which is the first, and most indispensable of all laws. The law of mercy, which has led Me to heal this paralytic man, is a law of God which is more ancient than Moses and Abraham. Wherefore then should this cure, wrought by My Word on the sabbath day, be looked upon as a sacrilege, whilst circumcision, which demands preparations beforehand, action whilst it is performed, and cares afterwards, is yet received on the sabbath day, and is not opposed to the injunction of rest? But how could an objection which was so opposed to reason and to the rules of equity, and which our Saviour nullified in so clear a manner, still have any hold on the people? Alas! we are all people:

it needs but that calumny should be boldly and constantly asserted for us to believe in it.

3. Conclusion. A rule whereby to judge aright. *Judge not according to the appearance, but judge righteous judgment.* Is that which is brought forward, is it proved, is it even likely? That is what we do not examine. But we ask instead, Who said it? How was it said? Against whom is it said? Such is the rule which we follow. Rank, titles, renown, wealth, numbers, all that is external imposes upon us. A tone of assurance, circumstantial details, a semblance of wit, or an amusing style carry us away: our prejudices, our jealousies, our dislikes deceive us. Such are the rules we follow in our judgments, rules which are opposed to those laid down for us by our Saviour, and which lead us into numberless breaches, not only of charity, but still more often of faith.

Prayer. Grant, O God, that I may reform my judgments, and may judge henceforth only *righteous judgments,* and *not according to the appearance:* or if I am the victim of the false judgments of men, grant that I may find comfort in the thought that Thou, O my Saviour, hast willed to suffer also from their wrongful judgments, so as to serve me for an example. Grant me to accept, believe and practise the holy doctrines which Thou hast received from Thy Father, and which Thy Church teaches, and which will lead me to Thee. Amen.

Meditation CLXXII.

CONCLUSION OF THAT WHICH TOOK PLACE IN THE TEMPLE WHEN JESUS APPEARED AT THE FEAST OF TABERNACLES.

Consider, 1. the discourse of the inhabitants of Jerusalem; 2. the answer which Jesus made to them; 3. the discourse of the people; 4. the words which Jesus addressed to them; 5. the interpretation which the Jews gave to these words. S. John vii. 25—36.

FIRST POINT.

Of the discourse of the inhabitants of Jerusalem.

1. Remark the admission which they make. *Then said some of them of Jerusalem, Is not this He, Whom they seek to kill?* It was then known in Jerusalem that the chiefs of the synagogue and those of their party sought for Jesus in order to put Him to death. Their animosity was known, and their intention was no longer a secret; nevertheless, when Jesus reproached them with it, and asked them their reason for so doing they denied it boldly, they insulted Him Who desired only to justify Himself, and they accused Him of breaking the law and of *having a devil,* only because He had formed such a suspicion of them. O abyss of malice! thou art not impenetrable to the eyes of unprejudiced and thoughtful men, how shalt thou be so to the eyes of God? O Jesus, it is Thou Whom they seek for, it is Thou Whom they desire to put to death, and yet it is not even permitted to Thee to make a complaint of it? How then can I complain of ought that befalls me?

2. Observe their surprise. *But lo, He speaketh boldly, and they say nothing unto Him. Do the rulers know indeed that this is the very Christ?* Doubtless, this was not the reason of their silence. It was that they dared not come forward in the presence of a disinterested and equitable people, before

Him Who had so often unmasked and confounded them. To spread false reports against Him, to utter calumnies against Him in His absence, to seek for occasions to seize Him in order that they might get Him into their power, such were their manœuvres, and such are still those which the enemies of His Name and of His Church employ. They attack religion on all sides insidiously. Its defenders shew themselves, and are known; but its enemies work in secret.

3. Consider the error into which the inhabitants of Jerusalem fell. That cannot be, they add, *we know this Man whence He is; but when Christ cometh, no man knoweth whence He is.* This idea of the Jews may have been founded on that text of Isaiah, " Who shall declare His generation?" But if Christ, in that He was God, was to have an eternal and ineffable generation, He must also have a generation, in that He was Man, which must be known, since according to the prophets, He must be Son of Abraham, of the tribe of Judah, of the family of David, and be born at Bethlehem. But when everyone arrogates to himself the right of interpretating Holy Scripture, and of deciding on matters of religion without being capable of searching into its depths, they cannot fail to go astray, and their errors will be so much the more deeply rooted, since they spring from presumption and are nourished by pride.

SECOND POINT.

Answer of Jesus.

In His answer, Jesus makes known to us three mysteries.

1. The truth of God His Father. *Then cried Jesus in the temple as He taught, saying, Ye both know Me, and ye know whence I am ; and I am not come of Myself, but He that sent Me is true, Whom ye know not.* God is eternal, essential, and substantial truth ; and it is on this truth of God that the whole building of faith rests. God has promised a Saviour to the world, and

He has sent Him at the time fore-ordained, with all the circumstances foretold by the prophets, and He has confirmed this mission by works which could only come from God, and which consequently can only attest His Truth. Jesus, the Son of God, sent by God the Father, has sent His apostles; He has promised them that He will be with them to the end of the world, and He has told them that the gates of hell shall not prevail against His Church; therefore the faith which she teaches comes through Jesus Christ, and is the truth of God Himself. The Jews who do not acknowledge the mission of Christ, heretics and unbelievers who do not believe the doctrines taught by His Church, may profess to know God, but they do not know Him, this God of truth. As for us who hold the true faith, we know that this God of all truth cannot deceive us, we ought therefore to be assured of our faith, and ready, like our forefathers to die for it: but are these our feelings?

2. Jesus makes known to us His eternal generation. *I know Him; for I am from Him.* Jesus, in that He is God, is the second Person of the Holy Trinity, proceeding from the Father by way of generation; He is His Son, His Word, very God of very God, being with His Father and the Holy Spirit but one and the same God, an ineffable, incomprehensible generation, which Jesus Christ alone knows, because it is He Who is this adorable Son. O what depths, what hopes, what delights, do not pure souls discover in meditating on this mystery, although they do not comprehend it.

3. Jesus makes known to us His temporal mission. *I know Him, and He hath sent Me.* This mission is the Incarnation of the Word with all the effects which result from it. Jesus is the Incarnate Word, true God, and true Man, in one Person, Which is that of the Word. We have everything in Christ and through Christ; and God the Father in sending Him to us, and in giving Him to us, has with Him freely given us all things. What ought then to be our feelings towards Jesus Christ? The sainted forerunner had indeed reason to

say that he was not worthy to unloose the latchet of His Shoes. My Saviour is man; but He is God like His Father. Who could teach us these mysteries but Himself? Therefore He raises His Voice in the Temple in order to teach us them, without being intimidated by the conspiracies of those who sought to kill Him, nor driven back by the unteachableness of those who heard Him. Raise then that Voice again, Oh my God! cause It to be heard by all the nations of the earth, and let all people adore Thee! Make It heard in my heart, already it believes these truths; make it to relish them; grant that it may be penetrated with such feelings of reverence, gratitude and love, as these great mysteries should inspire into it.

THIRD POINT.

Discourse of the people.

1. Of the inaction of the evilly disposed amongst them. *Then they sought to take Him; but no man laid hands on Him, because His hour was not yet come.* It was well known that the princes of the nations, the chiefs of the synagogue, the magistrates, doctors, scribes, and Pharisees were only seeking an opportunity to cause Jesus to be seized, and that it would be an extreme pleasure to them if any one would deliver Him up to them; there did not fail to be many persons amongst the audience who were disposed to execute this measure, and perhaps the Pharisees were in expectation that some one would carry it into execution; but, whether those who were thus evilly disposed feared the people, or whether they were impressed by the words and appearance of Jesus, no one made an attempt to take Him, because His hour was not yet come. All the enemies of Jesus could do nought against Him, except according to His will, and He willed it to be only at the time and in the manner that God His Father had appointed it. Let us unite ourselves to our Head, let us await as He did the times appointed of God our Father, let us submit our-

selves to His Holy Will, and let us fear nothing under the protection of His Almighty Power.

2. *Of the faith of the people.* *And many of the people believed on Him, and said, When Christ cometh, will He do more miracles than these which this Man hath done?* This reasoning of the people was simple and conclusive, and it did away with all difficulties. Those who gave utterance to it had seen several miracles which Jesus wrought, and had heard an account of many others from those who had seen them, and probably from others on whom they had been wrought. Thus, who ever will consider dispassionately the Christian religion, its history, its dogmas, and its morals, the books of the Old and the New Testament, when he beholds this accordance of all times, this testimony borne by all nations, this chain of facts, this divine Wisdom so far above all earthly power and prudence, can he help acknowledging that God alone could be the Author of it?

3. *Of the fury of the Pharisees.* *The Pharisees heard that the people murmured such things concerning Him; and the Pharisees and the chief priests sent officers to take Him.* These words, which were being widely spread amongst the people, came to the ears of the Pharisees, who were alarmed at them; these latter instead of yielding to so plausible a reasoning, or at least coming forward to combat it, hastened to inform the chief priests of it, and all together deliberated how they might cause Jesus to be taken. This divine Saviour, Who could not be ignorant of the proceedings of His enemies, nor of the steps they were taking in order to secure His Person, and the orders they had issued to that effect, profited by this interval of time, in order to let His audience perceive that He knew the attempt which was being meditated on His life at that moment, and in order to escape them, willing neither to anticipate the hour appointed by His Father, nor to use miracles needlessly in order to deliver Himself from the hands of His enemies. What blindness! what fury on the one

side! what goodness! what gentleness! what patience! what humility on the other!

FOURTH POINT.

Words which Jesus addresses to the people.

1. Jesus foretells His approaching death. *Then said Jesus unto them, Yet a little while am I with you, and then I go unto Him that sent Me.* It was a matter of great importance to the Jews, that they should profit by the short time that Jesus would yet remain amongst them. Is it less important for us to make a good use of the short time during which this same Jesus is with us as our Saviour, after which He will become our Judge? Alas! if we only knew how short this time is, we should not lose it uselessly, we should not defer our conversion and our sanctification, we should not regret the objects from which we must soon part, and we should not fear the pain it must cost us.

2. Jesus foretells to the Jews their vain inquiries after Him. *Ye shall seek Me, and shall not find Me.* Since Jesus Christ ascended into heaven, the unbelieving Jews have sought for Him as Man, by using all their efforts to abolish His Name and His Memory, and to destroy His Church; but they have not been able to succeed. They have sought for Him and are still seeking for Him as Messiah, awaiting the promised Deliverer Whom they would not acknowledge when He was with them. They call upon Him, they invoke Him in the long captivity which they are undergoing; and in the excesses of calamities with which they are overwhelmed, but in vain do they seek, or look for any other deliverer than Him Whom they have crucified. Such are the vain efforts of the ungodly man against Jesus, such is the vain hope of the sinner, who seeks to be saved otherwise than by the Cross and by renunciation of his sins, who desires to pass his life in sin, to cherish it until his death, and then to find a propitious Saviour instead of a severe and inexorable Judge. Let us seek Jesus

whilst He may be found, and in the way in which He may be found. Alas! He seeks us Himself and offers Himself to us, let us not drive Him back, otherwise the time will come when we shall seek Him in vain.

3. *Jesus foretells to the Jews their final impenitence. And where I am thither ye cannot come.* Jesus, as God, was in Heaven, in the Bosom of His Father; Jesus, as man, was in the enjoyment even in this life of the Beatific vision, which even His best beloved disciples could not obtain until after their death. Jesus, as man, would, after His Resurrection, ascend to Heaven and sit down there at the Right Hand of God His Father; it was there that His Passion and Death were to bring Him, and it is there that after their death, the faithful servants of Jesus Christ, who have departed this life in His faith and fear, will go, in order there to live and reign with Him eternally; whilst the unbelieving Jews, as also sinners, who die in their sins, will never attain thither. O death, how much to be desired art thou, if thou find us in a state of grace? Must it be, alas, that the greater number of men do nothing in order to obtain the former, and fearlessly do that which leads to the latter?

FIFTH POINT.

Discourse of the Jews.

1. *Remark in their discourses a spirit of levity and dissipation. Then said the Jews among themselves, Whither will He go, that we shall not find Him?* After Jesus had spoken to them, He withdrew from the Temple, and left them to their own reflections; but, instead of making reflections which would have been useful, upon themselves, under their own unteachableness, on their hardness of heart, on the punishment which they deserved, and with which they were threatened; instead of making the best use of the first rays of faith which had begun to dawn upon their eyes, they only occupied themselves with making fruitless comments on that

which Jesus had just spoken to them. Whither will He go, they said amongst themselves? where will He hide Himself, that we cannot find Him? Let us beware of thus commenting on the words of Jesus Christ; let us put away whatever we find that is either obscure or difficult in them, let us set aside all curious or needless questionings; let us only seek in them instruction for ourselves, edification, amendment of life, and growth in holiness.

2. Remark in the discourse of the Jews a spirit of malice and jealousy. *Will He go unto the dispersed among the Gentiles, and teach the Gentiles?* No, blind Jews, He will not go, and you only suppose that He will do so, in order to impute it to Him as a crime, but there will come a day when your unteachableness will compel His apostles to go thither, and soon after, conquered and driven out of your own inheritance, you will be obliged to go amongst the Gentiles yourselves, to teach them the enormity of your crime and the perpetuity of your punishment. We see only too often such evilly-disposed and jealous spirits who neither will to profit themselves by the instructions which are given them, nor suffer that others should profit by them.

3. Remark in the discourse of the Jews a spirit of raillery and contempt. *What manner of saying is this that He saith, ye shall seek Me, and shall not find Me, and where I am, thither ye cannot come.* It seems that it was only in a spirit of mockery, and as a kind of insult, that the Jews repeated the words of the Saviour, and that they asked one another, What does He mean? what are these words which He has just addressed to us? what are we to understand by them? what meaning is there in them? We may look upon this spirit of raillery as the last degree of hardness of heart, which makes a sinner no longer able to understand the things of God, so that he turns into ridicule the highest mysteries, and trifles with the most terrible threats, of which he will himself be one day the eternal victim.

Prayer. Ah Lord, far from ever becoming guilty of

such blasphemies, I will guard myself from listening to them; and if I have the misfortune to break Thy holy law, I will not proceed to this height of impiety, by outraging Thy supreme Majesty, and thereby closing the door of return to Thy mercy. Preserve me, O my God, from that terrible threat, from that judgment pronounced beforehand upon the blinded Jews who obstinately refused to acknowledge Thee. Grant me grace to be faithful to Thy grace, to believe in Thy words, and to keep Thy holy commandments. Amen.

END OF THE SECOND VOLUME.

TABLE OF MEDITATIONS CONTAINED IN THE SECOND VOLUME.

	Page
LXXX. Sermon in the plain.	1
LXXXI. Continuation of the Sermon in the plain.	8
LXXXII. Conclusion of the Sermon in the plain.	14
LXXXIII. Jesus returns to Capernaum, and answers the blasphemies of the scribes.	20
LXXXIV. Healing of the servant of a centurion considered again.	26
LXXXV. Instructions given by Jesus to His Apostles on their first mission.	31
LXXXVI. First continuation of the instructions given by Jesus Christ to His Apostles.	37
LXXXVII. Second continuation of the instructions given by Christ to His Apostles.	45
LXXXVIII. Conclusion of the instructions given by Jesus Christ to His Apostles.	50
LXXXIX. Sending forth of the twelve Apostles.	55
XC. Jesus raises to life the son of a widow of Nain.	59
XCI. S. John Baptist sends two of his disciples to Jesus.	66
XCII. Discourse of Jesus Christ respecting S. John Baptist after the departure of his messengers.	73
XCIII. Continuation of the discourse of Jesus Christ, after the departure of the messengers sent by S. John Baptist.	82

	Page
XCIV. The woman that was a sinner at the house of Simon the Pharisee.	90
XCV. Of the holy women who ministered unto Jesus, whilst He was engaged on His missions.	100
XCVI. A sick man who had an infirmity for thirty-eight years cured by Jesus Christ, on the Sabbath day, by the pool of Bethesda in Jerusalem.	105
XCVII. Discourse of Jesus Christ to the Jews, after the healing of the man who had been ill for thirty-eight years.	113
XCVIII. First continuation of the discourse of Jesus Christ to the Jews, after the healing of the man who had had an infirmity for thirty-eight years.	122
XCIX. Second continuation of the discourse of Jesus Christ to the Jews after the healing of the man who had had an infirmity for thirty-eight years.	126
C. Conclusion of the discourse of Jesus Christ to the Jews after the healing of the man who had had an infirmity for thirty-eight years.	133
CI. The ears of corn plucked on the sabbath day.	137
CII. How we should act under controversies which trouble the peace of the Church.	145
CIII. Jesus withdraws to the shores of the Sea of Galilee.	154
CIV. Of prayer.	161
CV. Jesus heals a man who was possessed with a devil, and was blind and dumb.	169
CVI. Answer of Jesus to the blasphemy of the Pharisees.	173
CVII. The devil returning to his former abode.	181
CVIII. Exclamation of a woman on the blessedness of the mother of our Lord.	188
CIX. Jonas given as a sign of the resurrection of Jesus Christ.	192
CX. Of the mother and brethren of Jesus.	201

	Page
CXI. Jesus dining at the house of a Pharisee reproves the Pharisees and scribes.	210
CXII. Parable of the seed.	215
CXIII. Parable of the field in which seed has been sown.	223
CXIV. Of the parable of the grain of mustard seed.	227
CXV. Parable of the leaven.	230
CXVI. Parable of the tares.	234
CXVII. Parables of the hidden treasure and the precious pearl.	242
CXVIII. Parable of the net.	248
CXIX. Jesus makes a second journey to Nazareth.	253
CXX. Beheading of S. John Baptist.	260
CXXI. The first multiplying of the five loaves.	271
CXXII. Jesus avoids being made king.	278
CXXIII. Jesus walks on the water.	281
CXXIV. Discourse of Jesus in the synagogue at Capernaum.	288
CXXV. First continuation of the discourse of Jesus on the Eucharist.	297
CXXVI. Second continuation of the discourse of Jesus on the Eucharist.	305
CXXVII. Of the results which the discourse of our Lord on the Eucharist had.	314
CXXVIII. Pharasaical superstition.	323
CXXIX. Of the faith of the woman of Canaan.	331
CXXX. Jesus heals a deaf and dumb man, and several other sick and infirm persons.	339
CXXXI. Second multiplying of the loaves of bread.	345
CXXXII. The Pharisees ask for a sign.	351
CXXXIII. Jesus passes from the coasts of Magdala over to Bethsaida.	355
CXXXIV. Healing of a blind man at Bethsaida.	360

	Page
CXXXV. Confession of S. Peter.	366
CXXXVI. Jesus foretells His Passion to His Apostles.	374
CXXXVII. Instruction given by Jesus Christ to the people.	381
CXXXVIII. Continuation of the instruction given by our Lord to the people.	390
CXXXIX. Of the Transfiguration of our Lord.	397
CXL. Conversation of Jesus with the three Apostles, as they came down from Mount Tabor.	406
CXLI. Deliverance of a young man possessed from his infancy by a deaf and dumb spirit.	412
CXLII. Jesus foretells for the second time His Passion to His Apostles.	423
CXLIII. Tribute is demanded of Jesus.	428
CXLIV. Questions of the Apostles on the subject of pre-eminence.	432
CXLV. Of one who drove out devils in the name of Jesus.	438
CXLVI. Of offences.	443
CXLVII. Of hell.	449
CXLVIII. Parable of the salt.	459
CXLIX. Of offences received.	463
CL. Parable of the creditor and debtor.	468
CLI. A city of Samaria refuses admittance to Jesus.	475
CLII. Of the Apostolic calling, and of the Priestly vocation.	480
CLIII. The choice and sending forth of the seventy disciples.	487
CLIV. Return of the seventy disciples.	493
CLV. Jesus questioned by a doctor of the law.	501
CLVI. Parable of the Samaritan.	507
CLVII. Jesus at the house of Martha and Mary.	515
CLVIII. Discourse of Jesus to the people, in which He again enjoins that which He had taught elsewhere.	521

	Page
CLIX. First continuation of the discourse of Jesus to the people.	528
CLX. Second continuation of the discourse of Christ before the people.	536
CLXI Third continuation of the discourse of Christ before the people.	542
CLXII. Fourth continuation of the discourse of Christ before the people.	547
CLXIII. Fifth continuation of the discourse of Christ before the people.	555
CLXIV. Sixth continuation of the discourse of Christ before the people.	562
CLXV. Conclusion of the discourse of Christ before the people.	569
CLXVI. Of the woman who was healed on the Sabbath day.	575
CLXVII. Parables of the grain of mustard seed and the leaven.	581
CLXVIII. Of the small number of those who will be saved.	585
CLXIX. Answer of Jesus to the Pharisees who tried to frighten Him in order to cause Him to depart from Galilee.	590
CLXX. Answer of Jesus to His relations who pressed Him to go to Jerusalem.	597
CLXXI. That which took place in the Temple when Jesus appeared there at the Feast of tabernacles.	604
CLXXII. Conclusion of that which took place in the temple when Jesus appeared there at the Feast of tabernacles.	612

www.ingramcontent.com/pod-product-compliance
Lightning Source LLC
Chambersburg PA
CBHW021225300426
44111CB00007B/433